PRIVATE EQUITY

The *Robert W. Kolb Series in Finance* provides a comprehensive view of the field of finance in all of its variety and complexity. The series is projected to include approximately 65 volumes covering all major topics and specializations in finance, ranging from investments, to corporate finance, to financial institutions. Each volume in the *Kolb Series in Finance* consists of new articles especially written for the volume.

Each *Kolb Series* volume is edited by a specialist in a particular area of finance, who develops the volume outline and commissions articles by the world's experts in that particular field of finance. Each volume includes an editor's introduction and approximately thirty articles to fully describe the current state of financial research and practice in a particular area of finance.

The essays in each volume are intended for practicing finance professionals, graduate students, and advanced undergraduate students. The goal of each volume is to encapsulate the current state of knowledge in a particular area of finance so that the reader can quickly achieve a mastery of that special area of finance.

PRIVATE EQUITY

Fund Types, Risks and Returns, and Regulation

Douglas Cumming

The Robert W. Kolb Series in Finance

John Wiley & Sons, Inc.

Library of Congress Cataloging-in-Publication Data:

Cumming, Douglas.
    Private equity / Douglas Cumming.
        p.   cm.
    Includes bibliographical references and index.
    ISBN 978-0-470-49915-3 (cloth)
    1. Private equity.   I. Title.
    HG4751.C86 2010
    332.6–dc22   2009028343

Contents

CHAPTER 1

Introduction to Private Equity

DOUGLAS CUMMING
Associate Professor and Ontario Research Chair, York University,
Schulich School of Business

INTRODUCTION

Private equity markets experienced a golden age up to the second quarter of 2007 (Shadab 2009). The massive amounts of capital flowing to private equity funds up to this period are highlighted on an absolute and relative basis in Exhibits 1.1 and 1.2, respectively. This rise of the private equity mark has been attributed to the superior governance model of private equity relative to the publicly traded corporation (Jensen 1989), regulatory costs of being a publicly traded company (see more generally, e.g., Bushee and Leuz 2005), the comparatively low price of debt finance up to the second quarter of 2007 (Acharya et al. 2007; Kaplan 2007), the rise of the hedge funds (Acharya et al. 2007; Shadab 2007) and sovereign wealth funds (Fotak et al. 2008; Bortolotti et al. 2009), among other things.

The collapse in private equity since mid-2007 can be explained perhaps most directly by the collapse in credit markets and inability to effectively leverage private equity investments. Further, there are diseconomies of scale in managing private equity funds (Kanniainen and Keuschnigg 2003, 2004; Cumming 2006; Bernile et al. 2007; Cumming and Dai 2008; Cumming and Walz 2009; Lopez de Silances and Philappou 2009). Funds grew too large leading up to 2009, thereby leading to too much money chasing too few quality deals, inefficient due diligence, and too little value-added provided by fund managers. The crisis has brought on increasing calls for regulation of private equity funds (Cumming and Johan 2009), as well as hedge funds (Verret 2007; Cumming and Dai 2007, 2009) and sovereign wealth funds (Epstein and Rose 2009).

In the 1980s and 1990s, there was comparatively little academic work on private equity finance. This gap in the literature was largely attributable to a dearth of systematic private equity data. More recently, however, there has been a growing number of academics who have taken an interest in the topic and have collected systematic data for empirical studies both in the U.S. context and abroad. This empirical work has in turn inspired theoretical analyses of private equity finance. As of 2009 there are a significant number of academics who have contributed greatly to our understanding of private equity markets.

This book provides a comprehensive view of private equity by describing the current state of research to better understand the current state of the private equity market. The chapters herein discuss the structure of private equity funds

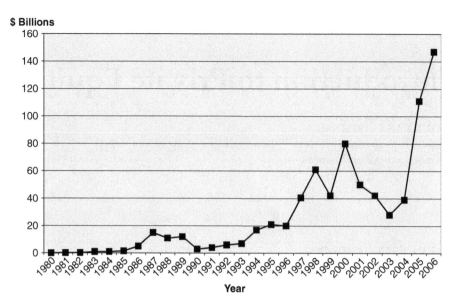

Exhibit 1.1   Commitments to U.S. Private Equity Partnership, 1980–2006
Source: Acharya et al. (2007), Kaplan (2007), Venture Economics database.

and fund-raising, the structure of private equity investments with investees, financial and real returns to private equity, and international perspectives on private equity and the regulation of private equity markets. This book is organized into four parts that collectively cover each of these areas, as explained below. This brief introduction serves as a road map to the range of topic areas covered in this book.

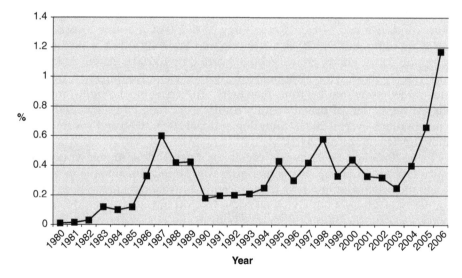

Exhibit 1.2   Commitments to U.S. Private Equity Partnerships as a Fraction of Total Stock Market Capitalization, 1980–2006
Source: Acharya et al. (2007), Kaplan (2007), Venture Economics database.

Part One of this book covers the structure of private equity funds and fundraising. In Chapter 2, Grant Fleming analyzes institutional investment in private equity, including motivations for limited partnership private equity investment, strategies for achieving objectives and evidence on performance. Sridhar Gogineni and William Megginson in Chapter 3 analyze the recent phenomenon of the public listing of private equity funds, with funds like Blackstone selling equity in their fund on stock exchanges. In Chapter 4, Bastian Bergmann, Hans Christophers, Matthias Huss and Heinz Zimmermann provide a further analysis of the overall listed private equity market, with detailed statistical information on structure and performance.

Part Two of this book focuses on the structure of private equity investments with their investee firms. In Chapter 5, Andy Lockett, Miguel Meuleman, and Mike Wright describe the practice of syndication in the private equity industry. In Chapter 6, Gennaro Bernile, Douglas Cumming, and Evgeny Lyandres present theory and evidence on the structure of private equity fund portfolios, and the efficient size of private equity portfolios in terms of the number of investees per fund manager.[1] Alternative forms of private equity investments have emerged in the twenty-first century, particularly a growing importance of PIPE (private investments in public equity) investments, which are examined in Chapter 7 by Na Dai. In Chapter 8, Cécile Carpentier and Jean-Marc Suret empirically analyze private placements in the Canadian market in view of the interesting lessons from the institutional setting in Canada. In Chapter 9 Stefano Gatti and Chiara Battistini explore the convergence of hedge fund and private equity investment activities, and provide an international context of this convergence in practice.

Part Three of this book considers both financial and real returns to private equity. The financial returns to private equity are difficult to measure, as private equity investments are held with the view towards capital gain, and it typically takes at least a few years before an exit event (such as an IPO, acquisition, secondary sale, buy-back or write-off) can come to fruition. Hence, private equity fund returns have a mix of exited and unexited investments at any given point in time. Simulated returns in private equity are studied in Chapter 10 by Axel Buchner, Philipp Krohmer, Daniel Schmidt, and Mark Wahrenburg. Value creation in buyout transactions are discussed in Chapter 11 by John Chapman and Peter Klein. In order to secure additional capital from their investors, private equity fund managers often exaggerate the value of their unexited portfolio. These and related issues in measuring the financial returns to private equity are discussed in Chapter 12 by Ludovic Phalippou.[2] Oliver Gottschalg discusses appropriate things to consider for due diligence when selecting private equity funds in Chapter 13. But returns to private equity are not just about financial rewards; that is, private equity may also significantly influence the value of investee companies in terms of the productivity (as discussed in Chapter 14 by Don Siegel) and employment (as discussed in Chapter 15 by Robert Cressy).

Part Four of this book provides analyses of international differences in private equity markets, many of which are attributable to legal and regulatory factors. In Chapter 16 Douglas Cumming, Andrej Gill, and Uwe Walz describe a need for the role of regulation in curbing overreporting behavior by private equity funds in terms of inflating unexited returns that are reported to institutional investors. Joe McCahery and Eric Vermeulen discuss further reporting standards and other methods to regulate private equity funds. International private equity flows are studies in Chapter 18 by Sophie Manigart, Sofie De Prijcker, and Bivas Bose. Alexander Groh provides empirical evidence on private equity in emerging markets in Chapter 19. Laura Bottazzi considers private equity developments in Europe in Chapter 20. Specific country studies on private equity in Europe are provided by Simona Zambelli for Italy (Chapter 21), Wolfgang Bessler, Julian Holler, and Martin Seim for Germany (Chapter 22), Morten Bennedsen, Kasper Meisner Nielsen, Søren Bo Nielsen, and Steen Thomsen for Denmark (Chapter 23). Finally, Canada's experience with regulation and phasing out inefficient legislation in recent years is empirically examined by Douglas Cumming and Sofia Johan in Chapter 24.

Specific features of earlier stage venture capital deals are not the focus of this volume, but are examined in detail in the *Companion to Venture Capital*, a related volume published by John Wiley & Sons in the Companion to Finance Series. There are various other topics related to private equity and other authors have made important contributions, many of which are highlighted in each of the chapters herein. Areas where further research is needed are likewise highlighted in each chapter. In view of the empirically documented importance of private equity as an efficient governance model, we hope and expect private equity research will help guide the theoretical understanding and practical implementation among students, academics, practitioners, and policymakers alike. The contributions in each of the chapters in the *Companion to Private Equity* likewise provide insights into the current state of the market and how the market is likely to evolve over coming years in terms of fund structures, fund-raising, investment structures, financial and real returns, and regulation.

NOTES

1. For related work see Kanniainen and Keuschnigg (2003, 2004) and Keuschnigg (2004).
2. See also Cumming and Walz (2009), Phalippou and Zullo (2005), and Lopez-de-Silanes and Phalippou (2009).

REFERENCES

Acharya, Viral V., Julian Franks, and Henri Servaes. 2007. Private equity: Boom and bust? *Journal of Applied Corporate Finance* 19:1–10.

Bernile, Gennaro, Douglas J. Cumming, and Evgeny Lyandres. 2007. The size of venture capital and private equity fund portfolios. *Journal of Corporate Finance* 13:564–590.

Bortolotti, Bernardo, Veljko Fotak, and William L. Megginson. 2009. Sovereign wealth fund investment patterns and performance. Available at SSRN: ssrn.com/abstract=1364926.

Bushee, Brian J., and Christian Leuz. 2005. Economic consequences of SEC disclosure regulation: Evidence from the OTC bulletin board. *Journal of Accounting and Economics* 39 (2): 233–264.

Cumming, Douglas J. 2006. The determinants of venture capital portfolio size: Empirical evidence. *Journal of Business* 79:1083–1126.

Cumming, Douglas J., and Na Dai. 2007. A law and finance analysis of hedge funds. Financial Management, forthcoming. Available at SSRN: ssrn.com/abstract=946298.

Cumming, Douglas J., and Na Dai, 2008. Fund size and valuation. Available at SSRN: ssrn.com/abstract=1099465.

Cumming, Douglas J., and Na Dai. 2009. Capital flows and hedge fund regulation. *Journal of Empirical Legal Studies*, forthcoming.

Cumming, Douglas J., and Sofia A. Johan. 2009. *Venture capital and private equity contracting: An international perspective*. Amsterdam: Elsevier Science Academic Press.

Cumming, Douglas J., and Uwe Walz. 2009. Private equity returns and disclosure around the world. *Journal of International Business Studies*, forthcoming (formerly, Center for Financial Studies Working Paper 2004, presented at the European Finance Association Annual Conference 2004.) Available at SSRN: ssrn.com/abstract=1370726.

Epstein, Richard A., and Amanda M. Rose. 2009. The regulation of sovereign wealth funds: The virtues of going slow. *University of Chicago Law Review* 76:111–134.

Fotak, Veljko, Bernardo Bortolotti, and William L. Megginson. 2008. The financial impact of sovereign wealth fund investments in listed companies. Available at SSRN: ssrn.com/abstract=1108585.

Jensen, Michael. 1989. The eclipse of the publicly held corporation. *Harvard Business Review* 67:61–74.

Kanniainen, Vesa, and Christian Keuschnigg. 2003. The optimal portfolio of start-up firms in venture capital finance. *Journal of Corporate Finance* 9:521–534.

Kanniainen, Vesa, and Christian Keuschnigg. 2004. Start-up investment with scarce venture capital support. *Journal of Banking and Finance* 28:1935–1959.

Kaplan, Steven N. 2007. Private equity: Past, present and future. Paper presented at the American Enterprise Institute, Washington D.C., November.

Keuschnigg, Christian. 2004. Taxation of a venture capitalist with a portfolio of firms. *Oxford Economic Papers* 56:285–306.

Lopez-de-Silanes, Florencio, and Ludovic Phalippou. 2009. Private equity investments: Performance and diseconomies of scale. Available at SSRN: ssrn.com/abstract=1344298.

Phalippou, Ludovic, and Mario Zullo. 2005. Performance of private equity funds: Another puzzle? University of Amsterdam and INSEAD Working Paper, presented at the European Finance Association Annual Conference, 2005.

Shadab, Houman B. 2009. Coming together after the crisis: The global convergence of Private Equity and Hedge Funds. *Northwestern Journal of International Law and Business* 29:603–616.

Verret, Jay W. 2007. Dr. Jones and the raiders of lost capital: Hedge fund regulation, Part II, a self-regulation proposal. *Delaware Journal of Corporate Law* 32:799–841.

ABOUT THE EDITOR

Douglas Cumming, B.Com. (Hons.) (McGill), M.A. (Queen's), J.D. (University of Toronto Faculty of Law), Ph.D. (Toronto), CFA, is an Associate Professor of Finance and Entrepreneurship and the Ontario Research Chair at the Schulich School of Business, York University. His research is primarily focused on law and finance, market surveillance, hedge funds, venture capital, private equity, and IPOs. His work has been presented at the American Finance Association, the Western Finance Association, the European Finance Association, the American Law and Economics Association, the European Law and Economics Association, and other leading international conferences. His recent publications have appeared in numerous journals, including the *American Law and Economics Review, Cambridge Journal of Economics, Economic Journal, European Economic Review, Financial Management, Journal of Business, Journal of Business Venturing, Journal of Corporate Finance, Journal of Empirical Legal Studies, Journal of International Business Studies, Oxford Economic Papers*, and *Review of Financial Studies*. He is the coauthor (along with his wife, Sofia

Johan) of the new book *Venture Capital and Private Equity Contracting: An International Perspective* (Elsevier Science Academic Press, 2009, 770 pp.). His work has been reviewed in numerous media outlets, including *Canadian Business*, the *Financial Post*, and *The New Yorker*. He was the recipient of the 2004 Ido Sarnat Award for the best paper published in the *Journal of Banking and Finance* for a paper on full and partial venture capital exits in Canada and the United States. As well, he received the 2008 AIMA Canada-Hillsdale Research Award for his paper on hedge fund regulation and performance, and the 2009 Best Paper Award from the Canadian Institute of Chartered Business Valuators for his paper on private equity valuation and disclosure. He is a research associate with the Paolo Baffi Center for Central Banking and Financial Regulation (Bocconi University), Groupe d'Economie Mondiale at Sciences Po (Paris), Capital Markets CRC (Sydney), Venture Capital Experts (New York), Cambridge University ESRC Center for Business Research, Center for Financial Studies (Frankfurt), Amsterdam Center for Research in International Finance, and the University of Calgary Van Horne Institute. He has also consulted for a variety of governmental and private organizations in Australasia, Europe, and North America, and most recently is working with Wilshire Associates.

PART I

The Structure of Private Equity Funds and Fund-Raising

CHAPTER 2

Institutional Investment in Private Equity

Motivations, Strategies, and Performance

GRANT FLEMING
Managing Director, Wilshire Private Markets and Visiting Fellow, Australian
National University

INTRODUCTION

The supply of capital for private equity comes from a variety of investors. Banks and corporations have for a long time invested in the equity of private companies in order to gain financial and strategic benefits for their businesses. Over the last 20 years endowments, foundations, and pension funds have allocated a proportion of their assets to private equity, primarily through intermediaries (fund managers) managing venture capital, leveraged buyout and distressed asset funds. The historical returns enjoyed by early movers into the asset class has encouraged large inflows of capital, and subsequent growth in the size and depth of the funds management industry specializing in private equity investments.

This chapter examines the motivations, investment structure and strategies, and returns related to institutional investment in private equity. First, the chapter describes the different types of investors and their motivations to supply funding to private companies. Next, alternative implementation models and investment structures are reviewed. Finally, the chapter assesses the empirical evidence on the returns (and risks) institutional investors have received in the asset class.

INSTITUTIONAL INVESTMENT: MOTIVATIONS AND BEHAVIOR

Private capital markets comprise an important part of the financial system, providing intermediation between sources of funds (savings) and private companies seeking risk capital. Private equity is a growing proportion of private capital markets, although its relative size is most noticeable in the developed Western economies of the United States and United Kingdom. The sources of capital for private equity take a variety of forms driven by the motivation and investment behavior of the funding institution. Some institutions seek to invest in private equity in order to improve absolute returns of their investment portfolios. These "return focused" investors tend to be relatively sophisticated, long term, and committed to their investment programs. However, private equity is also sourced from nonfinancial return institutions, which can have broader motivations associated with strategic (banks, corporations) and public policy (government) goals.

Exhibit 2.1 shows the type of investors who invest in private equity in the United States and Europe, taken from recent data on sources of fund-raising. The data shows a moment in time rather than sources of finance since inception, but is nevertheless instructive.

Institutional investors (pension funds, endowment, foundations and fund-of-funds) comprise 71 percent of private equity capital in the United States and 36 percent in Europe. Pension funds comprise the majority of capital in the United States, whereas financial institutions are the largest group in Europe (almost twice the proportion as in the United States). Intermediation also varies across markets, with fund-of-funds three times more important as a source of capital in Europe than the United States. The large proportion of sources categorized as "Others" in Europe is largely due to the use of public capital markets as a funding source.

The key motivations to invest into private equity are shown in Exhibit 2.2 for three types of investors—institutional investors (professionally operated organizations with the mandate to invest capital on behalf of beneficiaries), banks (and other financial institutions) and corporations, and governments. We have also identified for each investor their sources of funding, and the approach they tend to adopt in order to gain access to private companies.

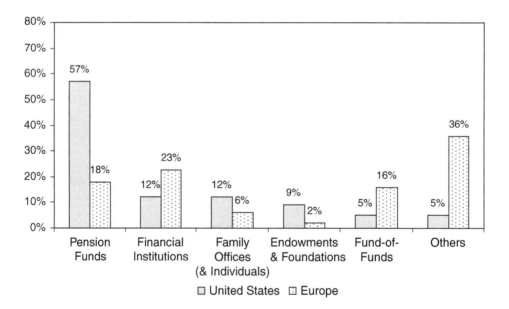

Exhibit 2.1 Types of Private Equity Investors: United States and Europe

Exhibit 2.1 presents the type of investors for the United States and Europe, as determined by the amount of capital the investor committed to private equity. U.S. data is for capital committed to private equity in 2006, and Europe data is for capital committed in 2007. "Others" category includes capital raised from public capital markets and government funding.

Source: U.S. data from Thomson Financial/National Venture Capital Association; Europe data from the European Venture Capital Association.

Exhibit 2.2 Key Features of the Motivation for Investment into Private Equity

Type of Investor	Motivation(s)	Sources of Funding	Approach to Implementing Investment Program	Contracting Features
Institutional investors	Financial returns (return on investment, internal rate of return)	Pension funds, endowments, fund-of-funds, life insurance company balance sheets	Invest indirectly into private companies via independent private equity funds (limited partnership)	Limited life; multiple fund-raisings; contract covenants; limited liability
Banks, other financial institutions and corporations	Strategic goals including access to businesses to cross-sell products; new technologies and/or products; limiting competitive threats; financial returns	Balance sheet funds; business development or R&D budgets	Invest directly into companies through captive division or business unit (or indirectly through third-party private equity funds)	Unlimited life; formal administrative control and informal control through corporate culture
Government (national and regional)	Public-policy goals including development of the local venture capital industry; accelerating economic growth and employment; commercialization of technology	Government finances (and sometimes matching private-sector capital from third-party investors)	Invest indirectly into private companies via government-sponsored fund (various structures)	Limited life; single fund-raising; contract covenants often with geographic, company type, and investment stage restrictions

Source: Adapted from Cumming, Fleming, and Schwienbacher (2007).

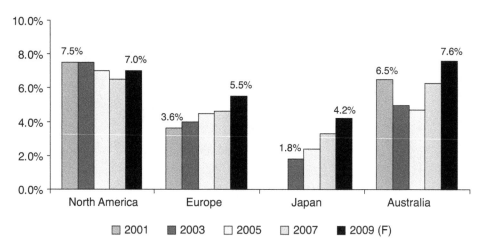

Exhibit 2.3   Institutional Investor Allocations to Private Equity, 2001–2009
Source: Russell Survey on Alternative Investing, 2007–2008.

Institutional investors are motivated to invest into private equity in order to improve the absolute returns to their asset portfolios. These investors are typically pension funds, endowments, life insurance companies, and specialist intermediaries such as fund-of-funds. Institutional investors prefer investing through private equity partnerships with specialist private equity firms, commit capital over a 10- to 12-year period, and tend to build private equity programs over multiple years ("vintage years"). The amount of capital allocated to private equity is determined with reference to asset allocation and portfolio liability modeling. Most asset allocation studies suggest that a 5 to 10 percent allocation of the total asset portfolio to private equity should, assuming historical risk-return characteristics, improve risk-adjusted returns of the portfolio. In practice, institutional investors have been a major source of capital for private equity, although importance varies by country (Jeng and Wells 2000; Mayer, Schoors, and Yafeh 2005; Cumming, Fleming, and Suchard 2005).

Exhibit 2.3 shows allocations to private equity for institutional investors in North America (United States and Canada), Europe, Japan, and Australia.

North American and Australian investors expect to have 7 to 8 percent of their assets committed to private equity in 2009, consistent with asset allocation studies. These allocations have remained at similar levels over the last 10 years in North America, where institutional investors committed early to private equity. There is now empirical evidence that early adopters (e.g., U.S. endowments) have experienced superior performance to more recent entrants (Lerner, Schoar, and Wong 2007), although some endowments are better than others (Lerner, Schoar, and Wang 2008). Allocations to private equity by investors in Europe, Japan, and Australia have increased since 2001.

Banks, nonbank financial institutions (e.g., securities firms), and corporations provide capital to internal "captive" private equity divisions, and sometimes third-party managers, in order to invest into private companies. The motivations for these investors lies in broader strategic goals to cross-sell products, gain insights on new technologies and/or limit competitive threats. Banks supply capital to in-house private equity groups from their balance sheet in order to develop a broader financing relationship with portfolio companies (Hellman, Lindsay, and Puri 2008) or to generate fee income from third-party private equity funds (Lerner, Schoar, and Wong 2007). Banks are also important providers of capital in certain economies, such as Germany and Japan (Mayer, Schoors, and Yafeh 2005; Cumming, Fleming, and Schwienbacher 2008). Financial institutions such as securities firms also invest in private equity in order to access potential customers and cross-sell products. Nonfinancial motivations for private equity can lead these investors to behave differently to institutional investors and expect different outcomes from private equity. For example, banks are more likely to invest domestically than internationally (Mayer, Schoors, and Yafeh 2005) and construct more diversified portfolios than professional fund managers (Yoshikawa, Phan, and Linton 2004; Cumming, Fleming, and Schwienbacher 2008). Securities firms can be faced with clear conflicts of interest between financial returns from investment and ensuring an initial public offering is successful (Hamao, Packer, and Ritter 2000; Li and Masulis 2004).

Corporate private equity investments tend to focus on venture capital in early stage entrepreneurial businesses. Corporate venture capital programs are motivated by access to new technologies and the development of potential new products (Siegel, Siegel, and MacMillan 1988; Winters and Murfin 1988; Hellman and Puri 2000; Hellman 2002; Chesbrough 2002). The evidence on whether corporations achieve their strategic goals in investing in early stage firms is inconclusive (Siegel, Siegel, and MacMillan 1988; Gompers and Lerner 1998; Maula and Murray 2002; Dushnitsky and Lenox 2005; Riyanto and Schwienbacher 2006) and corporate investors are often the first to close down (or sell-off) investments when a market downturn occurs. Corporate programs can also face higher staff turnover as investment professionals working in captive venture capitalist divisions are paid less than professional venture capitalists, and typically have less pay-at-risk (Gompers and Lerner 1999b; Birkinshaw, van Basten Batenburg, and Murray 2002).

The third type of investor in private equity is government entities, at both the national and local/regional levels. Government sponsored private equity investment has been popular around the world in order to promote economic development goals (economic growth; employment) including commercialization of technology (see Cumming, Fleming, and Schwienbacher 2007, 166–168 for a review). Motivation for investment in this case is often due to perceived market failure in the supply of risk capital. These programs are funded through taxation revenue and, in certain circumstances, have been found to operate successfully alongside private sector fund managers (Lerner 1999, 2002; Armour and Cumming 2006; Da Rin, Nicodano, and Sembenilli 2006; Cumming 2007).

Our review of the types of investors and motivations for investment has demonstrated the breadth of private equity capital available to private companies. We turn now to focus on the structural alternatives investors face when implementing a private equity program. In doing so, we restrict our attention to institutional investors, the dominant providers of capital to the private equity industry.

STRUCTURE AND STRATEGIES

Institutional investors manage diverse investment portfolios comprising allocations to public and private assets in debt and equity. Allocations to nonpublicly traded investments (often termed "alternative assets") have increased over the past 20 years as institutional investors seek higher returns than those available in publicly traded assets. This includes investments in private equity (buyout, venture capital, and distressed), natural resources (e.g., timberland), commodities, infrastructure, and real estate. Private equity has been a popular alternative asset, and has been credited with providing superior investment performance for those investors who introduced the asset class early into their investment portfolios (Lerner, Schoar, and Wang 2008).

The structure of the private equity investment process typically involves layers of contracts between the institutional investor and the portfolio of private companies. Thus, private equity is an intermediated process with multiple principal-agent relationships. There is a large body of theoretical and empirical research on the structure of private equity, drawing upon economics, finance, and organizational theory. In sum, the research can be organized with reference to a stylized model of private equity (see Exhibit 2.4).

The institutional investor has three main implementation models.

1. Private equity funds (limited partnerships), which are managed by specialist private equity firms dedicated to identifying, investing, managing, and realizing investments in private companies;
2. Fund-of-funds (and advisors), which select private equity funds for the institutional investor and manage the investment portfolio; and
3. Directly into private companies, sourced either from private equity funds or through the investor's own contacts/network and process.

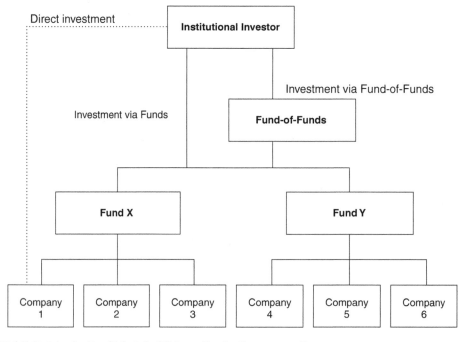

Exhibit 2.4   Stylized Model of Private Equity Investment Structures

Models 1 and 2 involve intermediaries to help maximize the probability of achieving superior risk-adjusted returns from private equity investments. In both cases the investor commits capital which is drawn down (or "called") by the private equity fund when required to complete investments. Therefore, the amount of capital committed to private equity by an investor and the amount invested in private equity backed companies differs, and investors can take many years to achieve their desired level of exposure to private companies (Takahashi and Alexander 2002; Cumming, Fleming, and Suchard 2005). Indeed, the modeling of drawdowns shows that private equity fund investment activities vary according to supply of investible opportunities, competition for deals, and cost of financing (especially for buyouts) (Gompers and Lerner 2000; Ljungqvist and Richardson 2003; Gompers, Kovner, Lerner, and Scharfstein 2008). Similarly, distributions back to investors from private equity firms (following the sale of a portfolio company) are dependent on the state of public finance markets and the economy. Expectations about drawdown and distribution rates influence the investor's capital commitment decisions (see Takahashi and Alexander 2002).

Private equity firms typically use limited partnerships as the legal form for their private equity funds (Cumming and Johan 2009). The structure of the partnership agreement between institutional investors (limited partners) and the fund manager (general partner) includes covenants that describe the "rules of behavior" governing the private equity firm (Sahlman 1990; Gompers and Lerner 1996, 1999a; Schmidt and Wahrenburg 2003). These covenants, terms, and conditions include:

1. Description of the investment mandate, including stage of company development of target investments, industry, and so on;
2. Restrictions on investment decisions, such as the length of the investment period; maximum equity investment; prudential limits of exposure by location;
3. Restrictions on financial activities, such as maximum borrowings; cross-fund investing (between two funds, both managed by the fund manager); reinvestment of capital after it is realized;
4. Investor rights and protections, such as the ability to remove the fund manager; reporting, accounting, and valuations requirements; investor representations (e.g., on an advisory committee); and
5. Description of the economics of the fund. Private equity firms charge a management fee (1 to 3 percent of capital committed to the fund) and a performance fee (20 to 30 percent of the profits after return of capital) that often applies only to a fund that has provided a minimum rate of return (e.g., 8 to 10 percent per annum) (Gompers and Lerner 1999a; Litvak 2004; Metrick and Yasuda 2007).

The use of limited partnerships and covenants has been shown to be an optimal structure through which to mitigate principal-agent conflicts in the private equity investment model. Limited partnerships have finite horizons (usually set at 10 to 12 years), providing a flexible legal structure for fund managers to identify, complete, and realize investments (over a two- to seven-year holding period for each company). Fund managers signal investment quality to institutional investors by the extent to which they remain consistent with investment mandates (or styles) (Gompers and Lerner 1996; Cumming, Fleming, and Schwienbacher

2009a) and have the flexibility to price discriminate (within limits) by changing the balance between management and performance fees (Gompers and Lerner 1999a; Litvak 2004). Performance fees at the fund level also influence the behavior of private equity managers by imposing a "whole-of-portfolio" perspective. Managers trade-off effort involved in managing and adding value to portfolio companies against expected costs in terms of potential lower returns on other investments. This behavior has been studied extensively in work on portfolio size and investment duration (see Keuschnigg 2004; Kanniainen and Keuschnigg 2003; Fulghieri and Sevilir 2004).

The use of fund-of-funds (and advisors) (model 2) has attracted less attention in the research literature to date. Studies of hedge fund-of-funds have shown that a specialist intermediary helping institutional investors select funds can add value over and above selection by the institutional investors themselves (see Ang, Rhodes-Kropf, and Zhao 2005). However, in the private equity industry fund-of-funds (and advisors) have been found to have selected funds that lag the performance of funds selected by endowments and foundations (see Lerner, Schoar, and Wong 2007). More research is required on this topic.

Institutional investment directly into private companies is also relatively unresearched. Lerner, Schoar, and Wong (2007) argue that institutional investors typically lack the networks and due diligence skills required to select and manage a portfolio of private equity investments. While this has traditionally been the case, large institutional investors have recently established "co-investment" or "direct" investment programs as a way to increase exposure to private equity and reduce the overall level of fees of a program. Sovereign wealth funds, in particular, have been at the forefront of this movement. Meisner Nielson (2008) examines the case of Danish institutions that invest directly into private companies. Institutional investors prefer to syndicate investments in order to diversify risk, and introduce new corporate governance mechanisms in order to reduce likelihood of company management opportunism. To this extent, direct private equity investment by institutional investors has similar effects on a firm as active investors (blockholders) in public companies (Holderness and Sheehan 1988; Bethel, Liebeskind, and Opler 1998). We await further research to determine the generality of the Danish results to a wider set of institutional investors.

In summary, institutional investors have predominantly invested into private equity through intermediaries managing private equity funds. This implementation model provides an efficient structure to mitigate agency problems and still achieve exposure to returns available to private company investment. Limited partnerships facilitate a long-term investment approach by fund managers, with a focus on performance. We turn now to examine literature on whether private equity provides excess returns to public equity investments, given the additional illiquidity investors must bear in this sector of the capital market.

PERFORMANCE

Institutional investors commit to private equity in order to generated excess returns to public markets. Does private equity provide the level of excess return expected by investors? How can we measure excess returns and risk in private equity? In this final section we review the research on return and risk of private equity.

Measuring the Returns to Private Equity

Private equity performance studies have focused on the returns to investments at the portfolio company level, or returns to investment at the private equity fund level. In doing so, the literature has typically adopted the internal rate of return (IRR) approach to measure returns. This is due to the fact that time-weighted rates of return, by definition, remove the impact of cash flows on the rate of return calculation. This may be desirable in many areas of asset management, as portfolio managers usually have no control over either the timing or the magnitude of cash flows into and out of their portfolios (Tierney and Bailey 1997). However, this is not appropriate for opportunistic investment strategies such as private equity, where the private equity fund manager has, within broad guidelines, discretion as to the timing of drawdowns into and distributions of cash from the fund.

In order to evaluate private equity manager performance (or performance of an underlying investment), institutional investors use the IRR calculated on cash flows into and out of an investment (or fund). The investment "round trip" determines the performance of the fund and the manager's ability to add value.[1] Recently, investors have been able to compare their own returns with those available from fund cash flows reported by private equity firms to third-party data providers such as Thomson Financial's VentureXpert. These databases are also the primary source of data for academic studies on private equity performance.[2] Finally, investors can compare their returns to aggregate industry performance as measured through an index of fund IRRs (see, for example, Peng 2001; Woodward and Hall 2003; Metrick 2007). Index returns are also commonly used in the asset management industry when seeking an industry benchmark return.

A more recent innovation in the funds management industry is to calculate "market-adjusted" private equity returns. This approach integrates an opportunity-cost benchmark into the measurement of returns, recognizing that the cash flows to private equity are not risk-free, but require adjustment by an "opportunity cost." The most appropriate technique, and the most commonly adopted, is to create an opportunity cost benchmark utilizing alternative public markets asset returns (Bailey, Richards, and Tierney 1988; Nesbitt and Reynolds 1997; Tierney and Bailey 1997; Anson 2001, 2002). Ljungqvist and Richardson (2003) create a profitability index, which (implicitly) assumes risk equivalence for each cash flow to and from the private equity investment—outflows discounted at the risk-free rate, and inflows discounted at the market index rate (e.g., S&P 500) (see also Phalippou and Gottschalg 2009). Kaplan and Schoar's (2005) "public markets equivalent" provides a similar return measurement.

Do investors generate attractive risk-adjusted returns from private equity? The empirical studies on private equity investments for fully realized fund returns (i.e., funds that have largely finished their investment life) suggest that mean (i.e., average) private equity investments at the fund level generate absolute net mean IRRs (i.e., returns after fees) on the order of 15 percent to 20 percent p.a. and are similar to those generated from public equities over long time periods. There are several caveats we should be aware of when interpreting these returns. Please see Exhibit 2.5.

First, there are significant differences in the mean IRR reported across studies and sample periods. Jones and Rhodes-Kropf (2003) use a large sample from

Exhibit 2.5   Private Equity Returns—Empirical Results for Large Sample Studies

| Study | Sample Period | Sample Size | Venture Capital | | Buyout | |
			Mean Equally Weighted	Mean Dollar Weighted	Mean Equally Weighted	Mean Dollar Weighted
Internal Rate of Return (% p.a.)						
Lerner, Schoar, & Wong (2007)	Pre-2002	1,398	—	14.00%	—	0.00%
Jones & Rhodes-Kropf (2003)	1969–2002	1,245	19.25%	19.31%	9.67%	4.57%
Ljungqvist & Richardson (2003)	1981–1993	73	14.08%	—	21.83%	—
Phalippou & Gottschalg (2009)	1980–1993	852	8.45%	13.23%	13.74%	16.79%
Market-Adjusted Return (public market return = 1.00)						
Kaplan & Schoar (2005)	1980–2001	746	0.96	1.21	0.97	0.93
Phalippou & Gottschalg (2009)	1980–1993	852	0.76	0.95	0.97	1.06
Ljungqvist & Richardson (2003)	1981–1993	73	—	1.15	—	1.27

Exhibit 2.5 reports the returns to venture capital and buyout from selected academic studies. A key feature of each study is its focus on private equity funds which are fully, or substantially, divested. The table contains the sample period and size for each study, and return measures. Internal rate of return studies show the mean internal rate of return for venture capital and buyout funds (equally and value weighted). Market-adjusted returns show the rate of return of a one dollar investment in venture capital or buyout, discounted at the market index rate (e.g., S&P 500) (Kaplan & Schoar; Phalippou & Gottschalg), or both the risk-free rate (outflows), and the market index rate (inflows) (Ljungqvist & Richardson).

VentureXpert (1,245 funds) and report a mean value-weighted IRR of 19.31 percent p.a. for venture capital funds, and 4.57 percent p.a. for buyout funds. By contrast, Lerner, Schoar, and Wong (2007) collected data on 1,398 funds from 417 institutions, reporting mean value weighted IRRs of 14.00 percent p.a. for venture capital funds, and 0.00 percent p.a. for buyout funds. Finally, Phalippou and Gottschalg (2009) report higher returns for their buyout sample, as compared to their venture capital sample. In sum, sample composition matters. This implies that not all investors' experiences in private equity will be the same.

Second, market-adjusted return studies show that it is inconclusive whether private equity provides average returns equivalent to, or above, those generated from public equities over long time periods. Phalippou and Gottschalg (2009) find that in most cases private equity does not out-perform public markets; only buyout returns outperform on a dollar-weighted basis. Kaplan and Schoar (2005) report that venture capital has a public markets equivalent of 1.21, indicating that $1.00 invested in private equity discounted at a public markets rate of return would generate $1.21 over its life. However, buyout funds underperformed public markets. Ljungqvist and Richardson (2003) report outperformance for their venture capital and buyout samples, although their sample is substantially smaller than the other studies. The assumption in these studies is that private equity investors do not require risk premia above the public markets.

Third, all researchers report a large variation (standard deviation) in the returns to private equity fund investments (note that the table does not show statistics for variation between the private equity fund returns). Wide variation in the reported performance of private equity funds is a hallmark of the private equity industry, in both venture capital and buyout funds (by contrast, variation in performance between "active" public equities managers is relatively low). For example, Lerner, Schoar, and Wong (2007) report a sample-wide standard deviation of 51.0 percent p.a., with a maximum (minimum) IRR of 512.0 percent p.a. (–94.2 percent p.a.). Ljungqvist and Richardson's (2003) smaller sample has a standard deviation of 22.3 percent p.a., and an interquartile range of 18.7 percent p.a.[3] Furthermore, Phalippou and Gottschalg (2009) show that sample bias and overstated accounting values substantially influence the reported fund returns (even for mature funds). This means that for institutional investors (which measure returns "net/net," i.e., after all management fees), the average private equity fund underperforms public equities. These findings reinforce our first observation: Investors' experience in private equity may vary due to manager selection factors.

Fourth, the historical time period relating to realized returns is still short, comprising a relatively small number of investors and fund managers who began investing in the 1980s. Returns to private equity have historically been clouded by the lack of externally provided, verifiable data and the relative youth of private equity as an asset class. The private nature of private equity partnerships has meant that return series (and external data providers) face sample selection issues, the most important being the potential for positive selection bias from self-reporting. In addition, private equity funds invest capital over 10 to 12 years so that it is only recently that large data sets have become available, comprising private equity funds that have finished (or substantially finished) their investment life. Most studies examine fully realized fund returns, typically defined as a fund (or partnership) that has completed its investment life and has been liquidated. In some cases, researchers have also used cash flows from "mature" funds where the residual value (or remaining market value) is less than 10 percent of the capital paid into the fund) (e.g., Kaplan and Schoar 2005). In most cases, institutional investors are still waiting for the historical returns enjoyed by early movers to appear in their own portfolios.

Finally, there is very little empirical evidence on returns to private equity fund investments outside the United States (an important exception is Cumming and Walz 2008). At present the academic research is U.S.-centric, calling into question whether private equity managers in different markets around the world can generate appropriate (or similar) returns to those observed in the United States. While this gap in the literature provides a fruitful area of research for academics, it does little to reassure institutional investors seeking to invest in private equity globally.

The Measurement of Risk

How do institutional investors measure the risk of their private equity investments? The equity risk embedded in private equity has only recently been a topic of research in academic literature, despite advances in our understanding of asset pricing. Several studies have made important first steps in integrating private equity asset pricing into finance theory, with a focus on utilizing single- and multifactor models to estimate private equity risk. Beta estimates are regularly used in asset allocation modeling to determine the level of risk of private equity for an investor. However, very little, if any, analysis of risk is undertaken by institutional investors when evaluating investment performance.

Single-Factor Models

The single-factor private equity asset pricing model applies the Capital Asset Pricing Model (CAPM) to private equity, stating that the return to private equity is related to market (systematic) risk. Equation (2.1) below shows the single-factor model, where the private equity return over the risk-free rate $(r_{i,t} - r_{f,t})$ is a function of systematic risk β_1. The alpha in equation (2.1) measures the excess return from private equity.

$$r_{i,t} - r_{f,t} = \alpha + \beta_1(r_{m,t} - r_{f,t}) + \varepsilon_{i,t} \qquad (2.1)$$

Estimates of β_1 for venture capital (β_{VC}) and buyouts (β_{BO}) using this model vary depending upon the time period of returns data, and the return measurement adopted. Gompers and Lerner (1997) found a single fund β_{VC} of 1.08, while other studies have provided estimates ranging from 0.60 (Woodward 2004; regressing venture capital returns against the Wilshire 5000 index) to 4.70 (Peng 2001; regressing venture capital returns against the NASDAQ index).

Why do we observe large differences in β_1? First, the single-factor CAPM assumes that contemporaneous returns to private equity are related to the equity premium $(r_{m,t} - r_{f,t})$. However, there is good evidence to suggest that returns to private equity are "stale" and adjust with a lag to valuation changes in the public markets (Emery 2003; Woodward 2004). This "stale" valuation issue is akin to non-synchronous trading (or thin trading) observed in less liquid stocks in the public equity market. Therefore, estimating β_1 in a single-factor model without allowing for serial correlation of returns leads to *underestimation* of risk, and *overestimation* of excess returns (α).

To illustrate the importance of adjusting for serial correlation, we show in Exhibit 2.6 below several estimates of β_{VC} and β_{BO} from single-factor models.

We have separated risk estimates by type of private equity, given the differences in the risk characteristics of venture capital and buyout companies. One of the first studies to examine the importance of lag estimators in single-factor models was Woodward (2004). Using a comprehensive returns index Woodward showed that β_{VC} and β_{BO} were grossly underestimated if lags were not included in the factor model. As indicated in the table, $\beta_{VC} = 0.60$ without adjustment, and $\beta_{VC} = 2.00$ with lag estimators. Cochrane (2005) and Metrick (2007) have found similar results for β_{VC} (see also Reyes 1990; Peng 2001).

Exhibit 2.6 Single-Factor Model β Estimates

	Venture Capital		Buyout	
Study	No Lag Estimators	Lag Estimators	No Lag Estimators	Lag Estimators
Gompers & Lerner (1997)	1.08	—	—	—
Woodward (2004)	0.60	2.00	0.40	0.90
Cochrane (2005)	1.70	2.00	—	—
Metrick (2007)	0.81	1.83	—	—

Exhibit 2.6 reports the results of beta estimations for venture capital and buyout investments from four studies. Betas are typically calculated using a single factor "market model" without and with lagged regressions between private equity returns and the market index. The Cochrane beta estimates are derived from a maximum likelihood model, with his sample corrected for sample selection bias.

While risk estimation can incorporate stale valuations through lag estimators, a more fundamental reason for differences in β_1 relates to its stability over time. Venture capital and buyout investing involves active management of the firm to bring about improvements in earnings and equity value. As a result, it is common for a private equity backed company to undergo changes in revenue and earnings growth rates, business structure and capital structure during the investment hold period. Does equity risk also change?

The empirical evidence suggests that equity risk for venture-capital backed companies and leveraged buyouts is related to investment hold periods. Cochrane (2005) and Woodward (2004) find that β_{VC} are not stable over time, while Phalippou and Zollo (2006) explicitly model changes in β_{BO} for each month of an investment's life to capture risk changes associated with changes to the capital structure. With respect to venture capital, Cochrane argues that β_{VC} declines over the age of an investment, with a positive association between β_{VC} and a firm listing on a public stock market. He reports β_{VC} substantially lower for firms which do not go public. Cochrane's results are consistent with the notion that more established firms are less risky than younger firms. Woodward postulates that β_{VC} estimation changes over time due to the pricing behavior of equity holders, with valuation lags shortening during periods of positive market momentum. We expect similar changes in β_{BO} associated with a leveraged buyout investment, where debt is paid down over time.

Multifactor Models

The single-factor model CAPM has been augmented in recent years through the inclusion of additional factors that have systematic relations with expected returns. Pioneering research by Fama and French (1993) has led to the adoption of a three-factor "Fama-French" model, which relates equity returns to market, company size, and value/growth characteristics. This model has recently been employed in private equity research (see Gompers and Lerner 1997; Jones and Rhodes-Kropf 2003), and is described in equation 2.2 below.

$$r_{i,t} - r_{f,t} = \alpha + \beta_1(r_{m,t} - r_{f,t}) + \beta_2(\text{SIZE}_t) + \beta_3(\text{VALUE}_t) + \varepsilon_{i,t} \qquad (2.2)$$

The Fama-French three-factor model allows equity risk to be estimated as the summation of three betas measuring the relation between returns to a private equity investment and:

1. public equity return premia (the difference in returns between the public equity market and the risk free rate) (β_1);
2. difference in returns across company size (as measured as the difference in returns between a portfolio of small capitalization minus large capitalization stocks) (β_2); and
3. difference in returns between value and growth companies (as measured as the difference between the returns to value stocks (high book-to-market stocks) and growth stocks (low book-to-market stocks) (β_3).

These factors and associated betas (or factor loadings) are now commonly available for public equities and have been the topic of extensive empirical research in public asset pricing.

The estimation of private equity risk using equation (2.2) can be performed with lags to adjust for stale pricing, as in the single-factor model case. Using a three-factor model, Jones and Rhodes-Kropf (2003) find $\beta_{VC} = 1.80$ and $\beta_{BO} = 0.65$ with only some of the factors loadings exhibiting statistical significance (see Exhibit 2.7).

The Fama-French factors have also been used in risk estimation to calculate private equity "portfolio betas." Kaplan and Ruback (1995) developed a new method for estimating β_1 using an unlevered industry beta (using Fama and French industry betas), applying this value to each portfolio company in a portfolio, and "levering up" the capital structure to reflect venture capital or buyouts. In this way private equity risk reflects the riskiness of an industry, as well as characteristics of investment style. Ljungqvist and Richardson (2003) and Phalippou and Zollo (2006) follow this method and report lower betas than in the single-factor lagged

Exhibit 2.7 Multifactor Model β Estimates

Study	Venture Capital	Buyout
Three-Factor Model		
Jones & Rhodes-Kropf (2003)	1.80	0.65
Industry-Adjusted "Portfolio Betas"		
Ljungqvist & Richardson (2003)	1.12	1.08
Phalippou & Zollo (2006)	1.53	1.14
Four-Factor Model		
Metrick (2007)	1.83	—

Exhibit 2.7 reports the results of beta estimations for venture capital and buyout investments from four studies. Betas are calculated using a multi factor models. The industry-adjusted portfolio betas studies report the "average" beta for a portfolio of venture capital (or buyout) investments. The three- and four-factor models report the sum of betas from the three (or four) factors, and have been calculated using lagged variables.

estimator models, perhaps due to the portfolio benefits of diversification (note that lagged estimators are not required using the industry-matching method).

The final refinement to multifactor private equity risk models has been the inclusion of illiquidity as a factor. This is a relatively new area of asset pricing literature, following the work of Pastor and Stambaugh (2003). Metrick (2007) models an illiquidity factor in his four-factor private equity factor model (see equation 2.3 below), with LIQUIDITY defined as the return difference from holding a portfolio of "low liquidity" stocks minus "high liquidity" stocks. Pastor and Stambaugh (2003) found that this factor is related to expected public equity stock returns, even after including traditional Fama-French factors.

$$r_{i,t} - r_{f,t} = \alpha + \beta_1(r_{m,t} - r_{f,t}) + \beta_2(\text{SIZE}_t) + \beta_3(\text{VALUE}_t) + \beta_4(\text{LIQUIDITY}_t) + \varepsilon_{i,t}$$

(2.3)

Metrick estimates equation (2.3) using venture capital returns data. His findings, reported in the exhibit above, show that $\beta_{VC} \sim 1.80$ (the summation of factor loadings), much closer to the lagged estimator single-factor model betas reported earlier. Notably, three-factor loadings were statistically significant: market risk, value/growth risk, and liquidity risk. Metrick (2007) also found that $\alpha = 0$ in the four-factor model, indicating that, on average, there are no excess returns to venture capital. The four-factor model has yet to be incorporated into buyout research.

Additional Factors Related to Fund-Level Returns

Institutional investors have yet to embrace factor models as a method of analysing the equity risk in their private equity portfolio. Other areas of research have made an impact, however. In particular, four variables are often examined when assessing private equity investments: manager experience, fund size, capital flows, and country systematic risk ("legality"). We briefly explain why each of these variables has been important in assessing capital allocation decisions to private equity.

> *Fund size:* The returns to private equity are related to fund size, but not proportionally. Ljungqvist and Richardson (2003) find that excess fund IRRs (i.e., market adjusted returns) increase with fund size, although they decrease with its level. Kaplan and Schoar (2005) find that private equity returns (as measured by the public market equivalent method) are higher for larger funds. However, once they explicitly model for nonlinearities, they find that returns decrease after a certain fund size; that is, the relation is concave. Their results are particularly strong for venture capital funds. We have illustrated the relation between fund size and private equity fund returns in Exhibit 2.8.
>
> The diagram assumes that there is a minimum fund size for a private equity fund, which on average generates a positive return. As fund size increases, fund returns increase up to the "optimal" fund size (the return maximising fund size)—a theoretical construct. Returns then decline as fund size increases. The optimal fund size will vary for venture capital and buyout funds, and most likely will also vary by other factors such as geographic location of underlying companies, company size versus fund size, and investment strategy (e.g., distressed versus control buyout). In

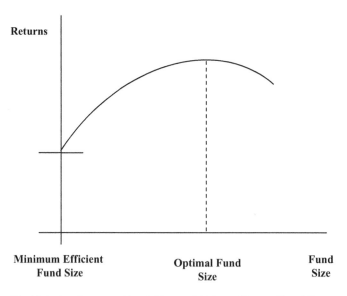

Exhibit 2.8   The Relation between Fund Size and Private Equity Fund Returns

sum, we should expect returns models to control for the fund size, as the capital available to the private equity manager impacts the types of transaction and returns to those transactions.

Manager experience: The returns to private equity investment are higher for more experienced managers (see Gompers and Lerner 1999). In addition, returns exhibit persistence, with more experienced managers performing well over successive funds (Kaplan and Schoar 2005). These findings are often explained by the specialist skills required to be successful in private equity, and the apparent inability of new entrants to compete away returns. While persistence is exhibited in venture capital and buyout firms, it is more prevalent in venture capital where human capital, investment strategies and personal networks are more difficult to replicate.

Capital flows: Early work by Gompers and Lerner (2000) showed that private equity capital inflows are associated with lower returns. The economic rationale is that capital inflows create excess supply of capital, leading to greater competition for transactions, higher acquisition (equity) prices and lower investment returns. As a result, venture capital and buyout funds started in market upswings have lower returns than those started in "downturns." Notably, Kaplan and Schoar (2005) find that more experienced managers are better able to avoid lower performance during periods of increased capital flows (again, experienced venture capital managers do better than buyout managers).

Legality: We have seen that institutional investors can measure risk in private equity through factor models. These models control for the geographic location of the company in estimating equity risk, as in most models the company's equity return is regressed against the local country stock market index (the local country market premia) in order to produce the market risk factor (β_1). This approach captures a country's institutional and finance market idiosyncrasies, which have an impact on the risk of the local company. In the case of private equity backed companies, an additional country factor is required, related to the wider institutional and legal framework (termed the "legality" features of a country). Cumming, Fleming, and Schwienbacher (2006, 2009b) have shown that the efficiency of the judicial system, rule of law, level of corruption, risk of contract repudiation and shareholders' rights ("legality" factors) are related to the equity returns of private equity backed companies (see also Cumming and Walz 2008). The results from Cumming, Fleming, and Schwienbacher (2006, 2009b) are robust to inclusion of traditional country factors such as stock markets. Private equity returns are influenced by whether a country has strong investor protection laws providing investors with the ability to contract with certainty. High-quality legal environments are positively associated with successful exits from private equity backed companies.

CONCLUSION

This chapter examines the types of investor, motivations, investment structures, and returns to private equity. We have seen that motivations to invest in private companies can vary, with nonfinancial returns being as important as cash-on-cash rates of return for many investors. This means that entrepreneurs and management teams do not view all sources of private equity equivalent, and the decision to take private capital can be influenced by factors such as access to future funding (from banks), technological support, or access to distribution channels (from corporations). What impact these self-selection factors have on the supply of opportunities presented to pure financial investors is not known.

The growth of the institutional private equity industry has been facilitated by legal structures (in particular, limited partnerships) that allow asset management contracts to be long-term and sensitive to complexities of agency problems such as opportunism and asymmetric information, and to align financial returns of investors with fund managers. While this has led to a degree of standardization of terms and conditions across the industry (lowering transaction costs), it has also limited the extent to which true price discrimination has been used by fund managers to differentiate themselves in the market.

Returns to private equity, on average, do not compensate investors for the risks they assume in investing in illiquid, small private companies. The research reviewed in this chapter shows that implementation of a private equity program, especially manager selection, is key to attractive risk-adjusted returns. Not all private equity investors have had a good experience with private equity to date, and the decision to continue with a private equity program (once embarked upon) is often made by an investor with little evidence that current investments will ultimately generate the expected returns used in asset allocation models. Academic research has an important role to play in facilitating investors' understanding of how private equity should be evaluated against other investments options, so that institutional capital can be allocated to its most productive use.

NOTES

1. Empirical venture capital studies also use this approach. For example, Woodward and Hall (2003), Woodward (2004), and Cochrane (2005) use data on capital-raising rounds from all private company capital raisings (available through capital filings) to evaluate returns, whereas Fleming (2004) examines private equity managers' investments using proprietary data on investment cash flows.

2. An important exception is Lerner, Schoar, and Wong (2007) data collected from 417 U.S. institutional investors.

3. Individual company returns also show skewed samples. Cochrane (2005), for example, reports mean venture capital returns of 59.0 percent p.a. with a standard deviation of 107.0 percent p.a., even after adjusting for selection bias.

REFERENCES

Ang, Andrew, Matthew Rhodes-Kropf, and Rui Zhao. 2005. Do fund-of-funds deserve their fees-on-fees? Working Paper, Columbia University.

Anson, Mark. 2001. Performance presentation standards: Which rules apply when? *Financial Analysts Journal* (March/April):53–60.

Anson, Mark. 2002. Managed pricing and the rule of conservativism in private equity portfolios. *Journal of Private Equity* (Spring):18–30.

Armour, John, and Douglas Cumming. 2006. The legislative road to Silicon Valley. *Oxford Economic Papers* 58 (4):596–635.

Bailey, Jeffrey, Thomas Richards, and David Tierney. 1988. Benchmark portfolios and the manager/plan sponsor relationship. *Journal of Corporate Finance* Winter.

Bethel, Jennifer, Julia Liebeskind, Tim Opler. 1998. Block share purchases and corporate performance. *Journal of Finance* 53:605–634.

Birkinshaw, Julian, Rob van Basten Batenburg, and Gordon Murray. 2002. Corporate venturing: The state of the art and the prospects for the future. London Business School.

Chesbrough, Henry. 2002. Making sense of corporate venture capital. *Harvard Business Review* 80:90–99.

Cochrane, John. 2005. The risk and return of venture capital. *Journal of Financial Economics* 75:3–52.

Cumming, Douglas. 2006. The determinants of venture capital portfolio size: Empirical evidence. *Journal of Business* 79 (3):1083–1126.

Cumming, Douglas. 2007. Government policy toward entrepreneurial finance: Innovation investment funds. *Journal of Business Venturing* 22:193–235.

Cumming, Douglas, Grant Fleming, and Armin Schwienbacher. 2006. Legality and venture capital exits. *Journal of Corporate Finance* 12:214–245.

Cumming, Douglas, Grant Fleming, and Armin Schwienbacher. 2007. The structure of venture capital funds. In *Handbook of research on venture capital*, ed. Hans Landstrom, 155–176. Cheltenham, UK: Edward Elgar.

Cumming, Douglas, Grant Fleming, and Armin Schwienbacher. 2008. Financial intermediaries, ownership structure and the provision of venture capital to SMEs: Evidence from Japan. *Small Business Economics* 31 (1):59–92.

Cumming, Douglas, Grant Fleming, and Armin Schwienbacher. 2009a. Style drift in private equity. *Journal of Accounting, Banking and Finance*, forthcoming.

Cumming, Douglas, Grant Fleming, and Armin Schwienbacher. 2009b. Corporate relocation in venture finance. In *Entrepreneurship theory and practice*, forthcoming.

Cumming, Douglas, Grant Fleming, and Jo-Ann Suchard. 2005. Venture capitalist value-added activities, fund-raising, and drawdowns. *Journal of Banking and Finance* 29: 295–331.

Cumming, Douglas, and Sofia Johan. 2009. *Venture capital and private equity contracting: An international perspective*. Burlington, MA: Academic Press.

Cumming, Douglas, and Uwe Walz. 2008. Private equity returns and disclosure around the world. *Journal of International Business Studies*, forthcoming.

Da Rin, Marco, Giovanna Nicodano, and Alessandro Sembenilli. 2006. Public policy and the creation of active venture capital markets. *Journal of Public Economics* 90 (8–9): 1699–1723.

Dushnitsky, Gary, and Michael Lenox 2005. When do incumbents learn from entrepreneurial ventures? Corporate venture capital and investing firm innovation rates. *Research Policy* 34:615–639.

Emery, Kenneth. 2003. Private equity risk and reward: Assessing the stale pricing problem. *Journal of Private Equity* (Spring):43–50.

Fama, Eugene, and Kenneth French. 1993. Common risk factors in the returns on stocks and bonds. *Journal of Financial Economics* 33 (1):3–56.

Fleming, Grant. 2004. Venture capital returns in Australia. *Venture Capital* 6 (1):23–45.

Fulghieri, Paolo, and Merih Sevilir. 2004. Size and focus of a venture capitalist's portfolio. University of North Carolina Working Paper.

Gompers, Paul, Anna Kovner, Josh Lerner, and David Scharfstein. 2008. Venture capital investment cycles: The impact of public markets. *Journal of Financial Economics* 87:1–23.

Gompers, Paul, and Josh Lerner. 1996. The use of covenants: An analysis of venture partnership agreements. *Journal of Law and Economics* 39:463–498.

Gompers, Paul, and Josh Lerner. 1997. Risk and reward in private equity investments: The challenge of performance assessment. *Journal of Private Equity* 1:5–12.

Gompers, Paul, and Josh Lerner. 1998. What drives venture fund-raising? NBER Working Paper 6906 (January 1999).

Gompers, Paul, and Josh Lerner. 1999a. An analysis of compensation in the U.S. venture capital partnership. *Journal of Financial Economics* 51:3–44.

Gompers, Paul, and Josh Lerner. 1999b. *The venture capital cycle*. Cambridge: MIT Press.

Gompers, Paul, and Josh Lerner. 2000. Money chasing deals? The impact of fund inflows on private equity valuations. *Journal of Financial Economics* 55:281–325.

Hamao, Yasushi, Frank Packer, Jay Ritter. 2000. Institutional affiliation and the role of venture capital: Evidence from initial public offerings in Japan. *Pacific-Basin Finance Journal* 8:529–558.

Hellmann, Thomas. 2002. A theory of strategic venture investing. *Journal of Financial Economics* 64:285–314.

Hellmann, Thomas, and Manju Puri. 2000. The interaction between product market and financing strategy: The role of venture capital. *Review of Financial Studies* 13:959–984.

Hellmann, Thomas, Laura Lindsay, and Manju Puri. 2008. Building relationships early: Banks in venture capital. *Review of Financial Studies* 21 (2):513–541.

Holderness, Clifford, and Dennis Sheehan. 1988. The role of majority shareholders in publicly held corporations: An exploratory study. *Journal of Financial Economics* 20:317–346.

Jeng, Leslie, and Philippe Wells. 2000. The determinants of venture capital fund-raising: Evidence across countries. *Journal of Corporate Finance* 6:241–89.

Jones, Charles, and Matthew Rhodes-Kropf. 2003. The price of diversifiable risk in venture capital and private equity. Working Paper, Columbia University.

Kanniainen, Vesa, and Christian Keuschnigg. 2003. The optimal portfolio of start-up firms in venture capital finance. *Journal of Corporate Finance* 9:521–534.

Kaplan, Steve, and Richard Ruback. 1995. The valuation of cash-flow forecasts: An empirical analysis. *Journal of Finance* 50 (4):1059–1093.

Kaplan, Steve, and Antoinette Schoar. 2005. Private equity performance: Returns, persistence, and capital flows. *Journal of Finance* 60 (4):1791–1823.

Keuschnigg, Christian. 2004. Taxation of a venture capitalist with a portfolio of firms. *Oxford Economic Papers* 56:285–306.

Lerner, Josh. 1999. The government as a venture capitalist: The long-run effects of the SBIR program. *Journal of Business* 72:285–318.

Lerner, Josh. 2002. When bureaucrats meet entrepreneurs: The design of effective "public venture capital" programmes. *Economic Journal* 112:F73–F84.

Lerner, Josh, Antoinette Schoar, and Jialan Wang. 2008. Secrets of the academy: The drivers of university endowment success. NBER Working Paper W14341, September.

Lerner, Josh, Antoinette Schoar, and Wan Wong. 2007. Smart institutions, foolish choices?: The limited partner performance puzzle. *Journal of Finance* 62 (2):731–764.

Li, Xi, and Ronald Masulis. 2004. Venture capital investments by IPO underwriters: Certification, alignment of interest or moral hazard? Working Paper, Owen Graduate School of Management.

Litvak, Kate. 2004. Venture capital limited partnership agreements: Understanding compensation arrangements. Working Paper, University of Texas Law School.

Ljungqvist, Alexander, and Matthew Richardson. 2003. The cash flow, return and risk characteristics of private equity. NBER Working Paper No. 9454.

Maula, Markku, and Gordon Murray. 2002. Corporate venture capital and the creation of U.S. public companies. In *Creating Value: Winners in the New Business Environment*, eds. Michael Hitt, Raphael Amit, Charles Lucier, and Robert Nixon. 164–187. Oxford, UK: Blackwell.

Mayer, Colin, Koen Schoors, and Yishay Yafeh. 2005. Sources of funds and investment activities of venture capital funds: Evidence from Germany, Israel, Japan, and the United Kingdom. *Journal of Corporate Finance* 11:586–608.

Meisner Nielson, Kasper. 2008. Institutional investors and private equity. *Review of Finance* 12 (1):185–219.

Metrick, Andrew. 2007. *Venture capital and the finance of innovation*. Hoboken, NJ: John Wiley & Sons.

Metrick, Andrew, and Ayako Yasuda 2007. The economics of private equity funds. Working Paper, Wharton School, University of Pennsylvania.

Nesbitt, Steve, and Hal Reynolds. 1997. Benchmarks for private market investments: Public indexes to gauge private investments. *Journal of Portfolio Management* (Summer):85–90.

Pastor, Lubos, and Robert Stambaugh. 2003. Liquidity risk and expected stock returns. *Journal of Political Economy* 111 (2):642–685.

Peng, Liang. 2001. Building a venture capital index. Yale ICF Working Paper 00-51.

Phalippou, Ludovic, and Oliver Gottschalg. 2009. The performance of private equity funds. *Review of Financial Studies*, forthcoming.

Phalippou, Ludovic, and Maurizio Zollo. 2006. What drives private equity fund performance? Manuscript, November.

Reyes, Jesse. 1990. Industry struggling to forge tools for measuring risk. *Venture Capital Journal*, Thomson Financial.

Riyanto, Yohanes, and Armin Schwienbacher. 2006. The strategic use of venture capital financing for securing demand. *Journal of Banking and Finance* 30 (10):2809–2833.

Sahlman, William. 1990. The structure and governance of venture capital organizations. *Journal of Financial Economics* 27:473–521.

Schmidt, Daniel, and Mark Wahrenburg. 2003. Contractual relations between European VC funds and investors: The impact of reputation and bargaining power in contract design. CFS Working Paper 2003/15.

Siegel, Robin, Eric Siegel, and Ian MacMillan. 1988. Corporate venture capitalists: Autonomy, obstacles, and performance. *Journal of Business Venturing* 3:233–247.

Takahashi, Dean, and Seth Alexander. 2002. Illiquid alternative asset fund modeling. *Journal of Portfolio Management* (Winter):90–100.

Tierney, David, and Jeffrey Bailey. 1997. Opportunistic investing: Performance measurement, benchmarking and evaluation. *Journal of Portfolio Management* (Spring):69–78.

Winters, Terry, and Donald Murfin. 1988. Venture capital investing for corporate development objectives. *Journal of Business Venturing* 3:207–222.

Woodward, Susan. 2004. Measuring risk and performance for private equity. Sand Hill Econometrics. www.sandhillecon.com, accessed November, 20, 2008.

Woodward, Susan, and Robert Hall. 2003. Benchmarking the returns to venture. NBER Working Paper No. 10202.

Yoshikawa, Toru, Phillip Phan, and Jonathan Linton. 2004. The relationship between governance structure and risk management approaches in Japanese venture capital firms. *Journal of Business Venturing* 19:831–849.

ABOUT THE AUTHOR

Grant Fleming received his Ph.D. in Economics from the University of Auckland, New Zealand. He is currently a Managing Director at Wilshire Private Markets (WPM), where he is a member of the global investment committee and responsible for origination, due diligence, and monitoring of private equity investments in the Asia-Pacific region. He heads the WPM's applied research group and is a Visiting Fellow at the Australian National University. Prior to joining WPM, Dr. Fleming held faculty (and visiting) positions at the Australian National University, Duke University, and the University of Auckland. He has authored over fifty journal articles and two books with research spanning economics, corporate governance and private equity. He has published in academic journals including *Accounting and Finance, Business History, Economic History Review, Financial Management, International Labor Review, Journal of Corporate Finance, Journal of Banking & Finance, Journal of Monetary Economics, Pacific Basin Finance Journal,* and *Small Business Economics.*

CHAPTER 3

IPOs and Other Nontraditional Fund-Raising Methods of Private Equity Firms

SRIDHAR GOGINENI
Doctoral Candidate, Michael F. Price College of Business, The University of Oklahoma

WILLIAM L. MEGGINSON
Professor and Rainbolt Chair in Finance, Michael F. Price College of Business, The University of Oklahoma

INTRODUCTION

The private equity industry as we know it emerged during the 1980s. While its roots can be traced back over 50 years,[1] it was not until the late 1970s that changes in regulations and tax laws helped in the expansion and institutionalization of the private equity industry. A significant regulatory change was the Labor Department's 1979 adoption of a "Prudent Man Rule" that allowed pension funds to invest in venture capital and private equity. In addition, factors that helped the growth of private equity industry include: (1) increased investment activity in information technology, (2) creation of buyout activity as a recognized subsector distinctly differentiated from merger and acquisition (M&A) activities of publicly traded companies, and (3) a dramatic cut in capital gains tax rate to 20 percent by Congress in 1981. In the wake of these changes, private equity investing took off. Between 1980 and 2007, the U.S. private equity market grew from about $2.5 billion in commitments to more than $200 billion in commitments. In 2006 and 2007 the private equity industry binged, buying companies with an enterprise value of $1.4 trillion. After adjusting for inflation, that is the equivalent of one-third of all the LBOs ever executed.

As the industry developed, private equity funds evolved into two species: venture capital (VC) and buyout (LBO) funds. VC funds provide financing to high growth potential firms that cannot access the public equity markets or secure traditional debt financing. VC investments are typically made, in less mature companies, for the launch, early development, or expansion of a business. LBO funds, on the other hand, occupy a different place in the corporate life cycle. They are created with the goal of acquiring public corporations or divisions thereof and taking them private, and generally fund their acquisitions with borrowed funds.

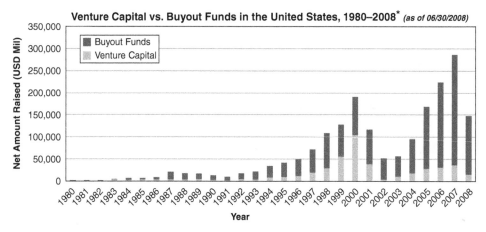

Exhibit 3.1 Fund-Raising Patterns in the United States
Source: Venture Expert database.

Exhibit 3.1 plots the net amounts raised by the private equity industry each year, from 1980 through 2007. While venture capital funds dominated in the earlier years, buyout firms captured the lion's share of capital raised since 2000.

Research over the past few years helped us gain valuable insights about the history, organizational structure, fund-raising methods, exit strategies, and the economic impact of venture capital and buyout funds in the United States.[2] According to a recent study published by the National Venture Capital Association, in 2006, total revenue of venture capital backed companies is 17.6 percent of U.S. GDP and these companies generated 9.1 percent of U.S. private sector employment.[3] With respect to the employment effects of buyout and private equity transactions, research (e.g., Davis, Haltiwanger, Jarmin, Lerner, and Miranda 2008) indicates that private equity groups act as catalysts for "creative destruction." That is, while gross job creation at target firms is similar to that of a group of control firms, gross job destruction is substantially greater at targets. This finding falls in line with the view that private equity firms shrink inefficient, lower value segments of underperforming target firms. Further, Davis et al. note that private equity targets engage in relatively more acquisitions and divestitures and hence, create more "green field" jobs. The tremendous growth and influence of private equity industry is not confined to the United States only. It is estimated that 21 percent (8 percent) of the workforce outside the public sector in the United Kingdom (Australia) is employed by firms that are, or have been, invested in by a private equity firm. Further, it is estimated that during 2001 to 2006, the annual employment growth rate in U.K. private equity–backed companies is around 8 percent, much faster than the 0.4 percent annual growth rate than FTSE 100 companies.[4] However, Cressy, Munari, and Malipiero (2007) note that the employment patterns exhibited by U.K. private equity targets is similar to their U.S. counterparts. That is, Cressy et al. find that target firms' employment falls in the first few years after the buyout and increases in the later years.

The growing importance of this industry can be illustrated by the fact that venture capital and private equity have become a standard curriculum in most graduate and higher-level finance texts. While the recent growth in private equity has been striking, researchers and investors alike agree that the potential for future development is even more impressive. In order to support their astounding growth rates, private equity firms are raising higher levels of debt and are on the lookout for nontraditional sources of financing, such as listing their shares on stock markets. In addition, the recent emergence of sovereign wealth funds (SWF) as powerful players has changed the dynamics of the private equity industry.[5] Sovereign wealth funds are government-controlled entities with roughly $3 trillion under management. The amount of capital that sovereign wealth funds control is expected to rise to between $10 trillion and $12 trillion by 2012.

The objective of this chapter is to initiate a discussion on the new trends in private equity fund-raising practices. More specifically, we focus on the recent trend of private equity IPOs (initial public offerings) and their inclination to attract investments from sovereign wealth funds (SWFs). There have only been a few PE fund IPOs (raising a cumulative $4.7 billion), and a couple of SWF investments in the United States so far. This trend is expected to increase over the next few years and we hope this chapter serves as a good starting point for understanding the fundamentals of these nontraditional fund-raising methods.

RECENT TRENDS IN THE PRIVATE EQUITY INDUSTRY

Since its emergence in the 1980s, private equity has been regarded very much as a niche player in the broader U.S. and global market for corporate control. But the rapid development of this industry over the past 10 years is starting to challenge this view. In the United States the proportion of buyout funds raised has continued to increase in recent years, reaching over 80 percent of total funds raised in 2007 (see Exhibit 3.1 and Exhibit 3.2). In addition, there was an increase in the amount of buyout funds raised, from $51 billion in 1997 to $250 billion in 2007.[6]

On the other hand, capital raised by venture capital firms for early stage investing has decreased after reaching a peak in 2000. This highlights the comparatively difficult position of venture capital managers in recent years, possibly caused by the Internet bubble of the new millennium and the wider downturn in the U.S. and the world economy at that time. This trend is not limited to the United States alone and, according to a recent report published by the European Venture Capital Association (EVCA), venture capital firms in Europe performed at a similar level to their U.S. counterparts during the same period.

Like most industry sectors, the private equity industry is dominated by a few big players and most of these funds were raised by those firms. The top 50 private equity firms sponsored nearly 75 percent of the total deal volume globally since 2002 even though they represent only 27 percent of the number of total deals sponsored. This is not surprising, given the size of some of the deals. For instance, a private equity consortium led by KKR and the Texas Pacific Group completed a $43.8 billion buyout of TXU Corp, a electric utility giant, in February 2007 in the largest completed private equity deal to that date.

While the private equity industry has witnessed impressive growth globally, the U.S. market is still by far the most mature and developed, accounting for

Exhibit 3.2   Fund-Raising Patterns

Year	Venture Capital Funds		Buyout and Mezzanine Funds	
	No. of Funds	Amount Raised	No. of Funds	Amount Raised
1980	52	2,025.60	4	183.50
1981	75	1,486.50	7	350.80
1982	87	1,705.40	14	759.30
1983	143	3,949.20	19	1,546.80
1984	116	2,964.30	24	3,541.90
1985	120	3,974.30	23	3,027.90
1986	103	3,788.40	34	5,083.00
1987	116	4,376.70	51	16,328.00
1988	104	4,435.00	64	13,123.60
1989	104	4,888.40	84	12,167.80
1990	87	3,229.00	75	9,926.80
1991	42	2,002.80	35	7,512.00
1992	80	5,215.30	67	12,476.00
1993	88	3,943.60	90	18,322.80
1994	140	8,913.00	119	25,863.40
1995	172	9,859.60	131	32,634.00
1996	162	11,844.20	135	38,589.40
1997	243	19,686.80	154	51,825.60
1998	287	29,642.00	211	79,827.80
1999	452	56,293.90	195	71,891.80
2000	650	104,640.90	194	86,520.40
2001	321	38,994.40	178	77,736.90
2002	206	3,877.90	171	47,875.40
2003	163	10,722.80	161	46,413.80
2004	217	19,144.80	204	77,289.50
2005	233	28,983.90	249	140,281.10
2006	238	31,751.00	231	192,212.90
2007	250	36,754.20	285	249,712.60
2008*	136	16,345.10	162	131,479.20

Exhibit 3.2 presents the number of funds and net period amount raised (unadjusted, $ millions) by private equity funds in the United States. The time period spans from 1980–2008* *(as of 06/30/2008)*. *Source:* VentureXpert database.

approximately 75 percent of the funds raised during the period 1980 to 2007. It is therefore not surprising to know that nearly 66 percent of the top 50 PE firms are located in the United States (see Exhibits 3.3 and 3.4). In a separate study, McKinsey, a prominent management consulting firm, reckons that 62 percent of American private equity assets in 2006 were in the hands of the top 20 firms.

Outside the United States, private equity industry is largely concentrated in Europe. Historically, funds raised in Europe were largely comprised of local investors. However, over the course of the last decade, there has been an increasing tendency for inflows from the members of European Union and other countries, especially the United States. For instance, European private equity funds were able to raise approximately $140 billion in 2006, of which nearly 28.8 percent originated

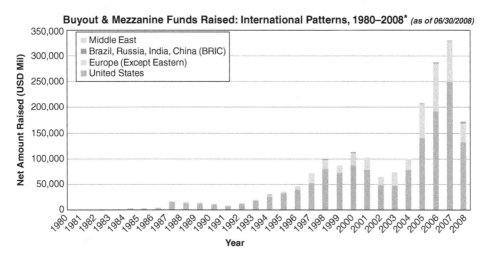

Exhibit 3.3 Fund-Raising Patterns of Buyout Funds: International Comparison
Source: VentureXpert database.

from the United States (see Exhibit 3.5). The United Kingdom is close behind at 21.3 percent, followed by France (7.9 percent) and Sweden (5.1 percent). Further, the United Kingdom seems to be the favorite destination for investments, with nearly 33 percent of investments in U.K. companies, followed by France with 15.2 percent and Germany with 10.2 percent.[7]

A new class of PE funds that specialize in emerging markets evolved over the last few years. These funds invest in the emerging market regions of Asia, Central and Eastern Europe and Russia, Latin America and the Caribbean, the Middle East

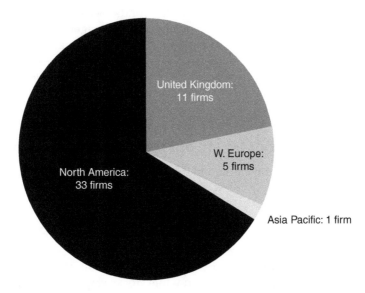

Exhibit 3.4 Geographical Concentration of the Top 50 Private Equity Firms
Source: Private Equity International, May 2007.

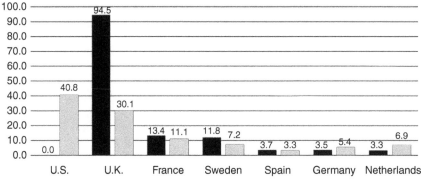

Exhibit 3.5 Fund-Raising Patterns of European Private Equity Firms
Figures in billions of Euros. Average 2006 exchange rate of $1.26 per Euro is used to present dollar estimates.
Source: European Venture Capital Association final performance and activity figures, 2006.

and North Africa, and sub-Saharan Africa, and were able to raise $33.2 billion in capital commitments in 2006.[8] It is estimated that China- and India-focused funds alone account for nearly 21 percent ($7.1 billion) of the total amount raised. It is likely that the potential for superior returns is driving interest in the emerging market funds. According to a survey conducted by the Emerging Markets Private Equity Association, these funds are expected deliver on average a 6.7 premium relative to U.S. buyout funds. At the same time, management fees charged by these funds are not significantly different from the funds focused on North American and Europe (1.95 percent versus 1.8 percent). With management fees on par with other funds and the popular opinion that China and India are poised to be the future economic superpowers withstanding, private equity investors continue to foresee a potential for strong returns in these markets in the long-term.

TRADITIONAL FUND-RAISING METHODS

Factors that Led to the Growth of Private Equity Industry

Two interrelated factors contributed to the enormous growth of the private equity industry over the past decade. First, the availability of cheap credit made it easy for private equity firms to load up with cash and shop for supposedly "undervalued" firms. This opportunity arose in the wake of the tech and telecom bubbles that burst in 2000, causing stock prices to decline by almost 40 percent and threatening to pull the economy into recession. In response, the Federal Reserve pushed interest rates to historic lows to keep the economy growing. As a result, the economy and corporate profits kept chugging along even while stocks stagnated. The combination of low interest rates, depressed stock prices, and rising corporate profits created ideal conditions for private equity firms to flourish. Using a mix of their own cash and cheap debt, they were able to buy publicly traded companies at a bargain. In fact, in 2002, buyout prices averaged just four times cash flow (defined as earnings before interest, taxes, depreciation, and amortization, or EBITDA).

Second, pension funds and other institutional investors learned from their past mistakes of insufficient diversification and started investing heavily in private equity firms. That is, back in the late 1990s, the long bull market created an illusion that share prices could move only upwards, and investors who did not have a big allocation of equities seemed to lag behind in terms of profitability. Consequently, pension funds and institutional investors committed large fractions (in some cases 80 to 90 percent) of their portfolios to equities under the assumption that the high returns in the stock market would continue. The 2000 to 2002 bear market revealed this to have been an unwise bet. To compound the problems for pension funds, their liabilities rose because of the drop in bond yields, even as their assets fell with the stock market, making it much more expensive to find the income needed to pay pensioners. So pension funds (and their advisers) decided to broaden their bets and reduce their risks, and started to invest in alternate investment vehicles that generated (or, at least, promised to generate) attractive returns. According a survey by the Russell Investment Group,[9] up to 7 percent of the allocations of pension funds, foundations, and other endowments over the last decade went to private equity assets. The corresponding figure for Europe is 4.5 percent. Even though this data does not cover the entire spectrum of institutional investors, these numbers are representative of institutional investors' interest in the private equity industry.

Another example of the emergence of private equity industry as an attractive investment vehicle is the evolution of a new class of mutual funds that specializes in private equity investments. Such funds are active in countries such as Canada, Germany, Japan, Sweden, and the United Kingdom. Cumming and MacIntosh (2007) examine the characteristics and performance of one such fund: the Canadian Labor Sponsored Investment Fund (LSIF). Cumming et al. note that that despite underperforming and having a weak governance structure compared to industry benchmarks, these funds continue to attract substantial capital inflows.[10]

What Went Wrong?

During the summer of 2007, the private equity boom was deflated in a matter of weeks. The credit crunch that originated as a consequence of the subprime crisis made raising cheap debt extremely difficult and, as a result, the volume of buyouts shrank dramatically.[11] The sequence of events can be summarized as follows: Between 1997 and 2006, according to the S&P/Case-Shiller national home-price index, American house prices rose by 124 percent (during the same period prices in Britain went up by 194 percent, those in Spain by 180 percent, and those in Ireland by 253 percent). Ironically, this housing boom was partly fueled by the ability of large numbers of subprime borrowers—those with poor credit records—to take out mortgages and buy homes. In fact, by 2006 a fifth of all new mortgages were subprime. Unlike the interest rates on traditional mortgages, the rates on many of the new loans were adjustable, and to make things even dicier, these loans charged low rates for a while before higher, market-based rates kicked in.

For their part, banks were happy to lend money to borrowers with poor credit records, thanks to the recent innovations in financial engineering. As with all financial assets, both subprime and mainstream mortgages were turned into securities that could be bought and sold. Lenders no longer kept loans on their books, but sold bundles of them to other banks and investment funds worldwide. And, like any other security, they could be used as collateral by their buyers when raising new loans. By divorcing lenders from the risk of default, securitization reduced their incentives to look carefully at their borrowers: at times one side or the other, or both, descended to outright fraud. And no one, least of all financial regulators, could be quite sure who in the global financial system was on the hook for which risks.

The trouble began in June 2007, when the U.S. housing market slowed and subprime defaults started to increase. In that same month, Moody's, a rating agency, downgraded the ratings of over 130 securities backed by subprime mortgages and said it was reviewing the ratings of 136 others. More such bad news followed, which made these securities increasingly more difficult to value, borrow against, or sell. Eventually, banks began to feel the heat and in August 2007 raised three-month interbank rates, indicating their reluctance to lend to each other. The spread between those rates and the rate on government bills, a measure of the perceived riskiness of lending to other banks, rose worldwide. Banks were reluctant to lend to external borrowers such as private equity firms because they did not know which counterparties might prove to be bad credit risks.

NONTRADITIONAL FUND-RAISING METHODS
(Ir)rationality behind Private Equity IPOs

With fund-raising from their traditional sources becoming increasingly more difficult, private equity firms started to look for alternate sources. During the first nine months of 2007, two private equity firms went public in the United States. Before turning to an examination of the performance of these IPOs, we present a brief discussion of why IPOs by private equity firms are drawing attention from practitioners and academics alike.

Traditionally, companies mention three main reasons to go public and list their shares on a stock market. First, being listed makes it easier for firms to raise capital, either to expand the business or to allow the founders to monetize their wealth. Second, it helps firms retain staff and provide them with incentives to work hard, by incorporating share options in their compensation schedules. Third, public listing acts as an advertising tool and brings prestige; customers, suppliers, and potential employees may be reassured (and attracted) by the apparent seal of approval given by a public listing.

At the outset, it seems that these rationales do not apply to private equity firms. Private equity firms, at least the large ones, typically generate enough cash to pay employees and are famous enough not to need the extra publicity associated with a publicly traded company. More importantly, the core business of private equity is predicated on the idea that being quoted is a disadvantage. Flotations cut against the rationale of the industry—that companies can be run better in private hands than public ones. In closed corporations, the interests of managers and investors can be more closely aligned as shareholders are typically few in number, knowledgeable about firms' operations, and involved in management. For their part, managers can make decisions without worrying about public scrutiny, the threats of activist investors and short sellers, and the stock market's reaction to every decision they take.

Then Why Are These Companies Going Public?

There appear to be two principal reasons why PE firms are going public. First, private equity firms do not want to depend entirely on traditional funding sources and are eager to diversify their fund-raising practices. From 2002 to 2006 conditions were almost ideal for private equity firms, with low interest rates, plentiful liquidity, and rising asset prices. But recent events have been moving against them. Bond yields have been rising, making takeovers (which replace equity with debt) more expensive. Private equity firms are keen to raise a large pool of capital upfront that they can invest without fear of redemptions. Additionally, for investors such as pension funds, buying a stake in a listed entity may appeal if their internal rules stop them investing directly in private equity or hedge funds.

Second, many existing shareholders want to sell out. Traditionally, investments in private equity flow through private equity funds and limited partnerships and are managed by investment professionals. Investors' stakes in these limited partnerships are highly illiquid and the secondary market for private equity investments is still in its nascent stages. Therefore, an initial public offering is the only way a private equity firm (and more specifically, the founders) can realize value. Listed funds help investors avoid the risks of long lock-up periods.

PRIVATE EQUITY IPOs: PERFORMANCE AND IMPLICATIONS FOR THE FUTURE

We now focus on the going-public process and the performance of two recent private equity IPOs. While Blackstone Group and Fortress Investment Group are the two "pure" private equity firms that are publicly traded, there are a couple of other alternative investment companies that are now public. Examples include hedge funds such as Sears Holdings (NASDQ–SHLD) and Allied Capital Corporation (NYSE-ALD).[12]

We focus on Blackstone Group and Fortress Group, as they are two hedge-fund and private equity managers, and not individual funds that are publicly listed in the United States. Large private equity firms such as Blackstone Group and Fortress Group earn profits by raising and managing several investment, real estate, and hedge funds, in addition to private equity. Each fund is a separate partnership with its own set of managers and contractual structure, and the fund sizes range from $10 million to over $10 billion. These firms earn fees by advising corporate clients. It is crucial to recognize that investors who buy shares of such firms are buying a stake in the company, not their funds. Shareholders will receive a right to share in those fees, which are directly tied to the success of the firm's investments. They will also receive dividend payments, if any. Consequently, the stock price performance of a private equity firm will depend on whether the company can keep its clients satisfied—and thus keep lucrative management fees rolling in. Put differently, stockholders of private equity firms are paying the principals in advance for a cut of the fees they hope to make.

Short-Term Performance

Fortress Group

New York–based Fortress Investment Group manages almost $30 billion in three primary businesses: private equity, hedge funds, and two publicly traded companies managed by Fortress that invest mainly in real estate and real estate debt instruments. Between 2002 and 2007, Fortress raised an aggregate $8.6 billion for its private equity arm. According to the financial filings submitted by Fortress, its performance in the few years before going public has been impressive. Fortress claims it has generated an average annual return of 39 percent on its private equity investments since 1999 and annual returns of about 14 percent on its hedge funds since their inception in 2002.

On February 9, 2007, Fortress Group became the first hedge fund and private equity company to go public in the United States when it sold an approximately 39 percent stake and raised $634 million. Goldman Sachs and Lehman Brothers were the lead underwriters of the offering, along with Bank of America Securities, Citigroup, and Deutsche Bank. Fortress made an impressive market debut and after the first day of trading, its shares were selling at a 68 percent premium, compared to the offer price of $18.50. A positive first-day return is consistent with empirical evidence on IPO underpricing. Prior studies[13] found that between 1981 and 1994, the average first-day return is around 8 percent, whereas every year between 1995 and 2000 (the dot-com boom) saw average first-day returns of at least 13 percent.

Despite an impressive start, Fortress Group's stock started to tumble and the one-month holding period return was −8.2 percent. Exhibit 3.6 compares the one-month, three-month, six-month, and one-year holding period returns of Blackstone stock and the S&P 500 index. It is evident that Fortress grossly underperformed with respect to the market index over all horizons. For instance, an average investor who invested in Fortress would have realized a −45 percent return instead of −0.66 percent had she invested in the market index. Similarly, a one-year holding period return on Fortress is −79 percent compared to −7.5 percent on the S&P 500 index.

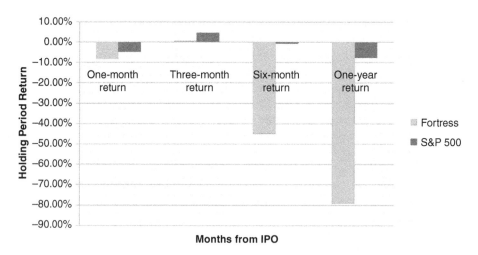

Exhibit 3.6   Stock Performance of Fortress Group
Source: Yahoo! Finance.

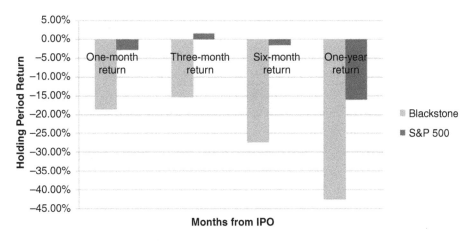

Exhibit 3.7 Stock Performance of Blackstone Group
Source: Yahoo! Finance.

Blackstone Group

Private equity powerhouse Blackstone Group announced in March 2007 that it intends to raise $4 billion by selling nearly 20 percent of the firm in a much-anticipated initial public offering. The offering was underwritten by Morgan Stanley and Citigroup, with smaller roles played by Merrill Lynch, Lehman Brothers, Credit Suisse, and Deutsche Bank. Blackstone Group, like many other large private equity firms, has traditionally been a secretive but a highly profitable investment firm. Blackstone Group's flagship corporate private equity portfolio has returned 30.8 percent annually since 1987 and the real estate portfolio returned 38.2 percent since 1991.

On June 21, 2007, the Blackstone Group priced the initial public offering of 133,333,334 common shares at $31 per share, yielding gross proceeds of over $4.1 billion. This is the largest IPO since 2001 and the seventh-largest in U.S. history. Shares of Blackstone gained 13 percent on the first day and closed at $35.06 by the end of business on June 22, 2007.

After a strong start, Blackstone Group's share price dipped below the offer price on June 26, 2007, on fears of (among other things) an imminent peak in the buyout cycle. Within a month of the offering, Blackstone's shares had fallen by a fifth since the firm's flotation. The stock price has continued to tumble since then. Exhibit 3.7 compares the one-month, three-month, six-month, and one-year holding period returns of Blackstone stock and the S&P 500 index. It is evident that Blackstone also grossly underperformed with respect to the market index over all holding periods. For instance, an average investor who invested in Blackstone stock instead of betting on the market index would have realized a −15 percent return instead of +1.6 percent. Similarly, one-year holding period return on Blackstone has yielded −43 percent compared to −16 percent on the S&P 500 index.

Long-Run Performance and Implications for Future IPOs

Analysis of 3i Stock Performance

While Blackstone Group and Fortress Group stocks underperformed relative to market benchmarks in the first few months of their IPOs, it might be too early

Exhibit 3.8   Financial Ratios of 3i Group

Year Ending	Current Ratio	Interest Cover	Solvency Ratio (%)	Return on Shareholders' Funds (%)	Return on Capital Employed (%)	Return on Total Assets (%)
3/31/1999	5.23	—	67.90	3.79	2.83	2.57
3/31/2000	4.27	—	71.05	2.29	1.78	1.63
3/31/2001	3.35	2.03	66.85	2.41	2.28	1.61
3/31/2002	2.72	1.96	63.31	2.76	2.75	1.75
3/31/2003	2.31	4.02	58.73	5.86	5.84	3.44
3/31/2004	9.33	3.73	62.73	4.09	2.78	2.57
3/31/2005	0.66	3.74	63.80	4.29	4.19	2.74
3/31/2006	3.39	7.20	62.89	21.34	14.89	13.42
3/31/2007	1.59	5.38	62.04	24.92	19.76	15.46
3/31/2008	0.70	4.25	58.04	20.56	14.49	11.93

Source: FAME database provided by Bureau Van Dijk.

to draw inferences about their long-run performance. In the ensuing discussion, we examine this issue at a greater details by analyzing the stock performance of 3i Group, a U.K.-based private equity firm that was publicly listed in 1994.[14] We compare the performance of 3i Group relative to an industry benchmark, a market benchmark, and with the stock performance of Blackstone and Fortress Group.

Exhibit 3.8 presents key indicators of 3i Group's liquidity and performance during the ten-year period from 1999 to 2008. Current ratios during the first five years are on average higher than the second five years. This indicates the initial easy access to and the subsequent tightening of credit. Regardless of the existing economic conditions, it is surprising (and perhaps reassuring) to see that 3i Group has always been in a healthy state as far as meeting short-term and long-term obligations. This is evident from the interest cover ratio and solvency ratios, which averaged 4.04 and 63.73, respectively.[15]

Further, the three profitability ratios presented in the last three columns of Exhibit 3.8 indicate that the management is effective in employing the capital and assets to generate revenues. For example, return on assets, a measure of the effectiveness of management in generating revenues and managing costs, has increased from 2.57 in 1998 to 1999 to 11.93 during 2007 to 2008.

A comparison of 3i Group's performance with its peers warrants special attention as this helps us gain a better understanding of the industry dynamics during this period. Exhibit 3.9 depicts how efficiently 3i Group employed its capital to generate returns compared to a peer group firms belonging to the same industry (the median values of the peer group are used as a benchmark). It is evident that the 3i Group outperformed industry benchmarks during most of the time.[16]

Comparing 3i Stock Performance with S&P 500, Blackstone Group, and Fortress Group Stocks
Having established that 3i is a financially healthy firm and has constantly outperformed its industry benchmark in the United Kingdom, we now compare the stock-price performance of this company with a U.S. market index and stocks of

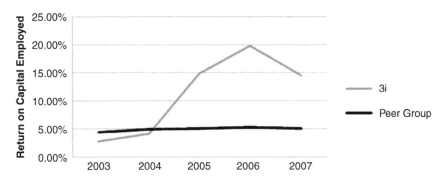

Exhibit 3.9 3i Group versus Industry Benchmark
Source: FAME database provided by Bureau Van Dijk.

the Blackstone and Fortress Groups. While we recognize that market-wide events in the United States may not have the same impact on 3i's stock prices as U.S.-based stocks, we believe that this exercise will provide valuable insights into the long-run prospects of private equity IPOs in the United States.

Exhibit 3.10 compares the stock performance of the 3i Group with that of S&P 500 index. Assuming an investor bought one unit of 3i Group and one unit of S&P 500 index in January 2003, monthly buy-and-hold returns are plotted until December 2008. Exhibit 3.10 indicates that the 3i Group outperformed S&P 500 index from late 2005 to mid 2007 and underperformed the index since then. Exhibit 3.11 repeats a similar analysis, assuming that an investor bought one unit each of S&P 500, 3i Group, Blackstone Group, and Fortress Group in July 2007.[17] It is clear that our hypothetical investor lost money on all her bets, had she held on to her stocks beyond November 2007 (except for the 3i Group, which is in the red starting from August 2007).

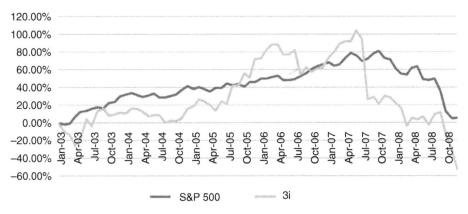

Exhibit 3.10 3i Group versus S&P 500 Index
Source: Yahoo! Finance.

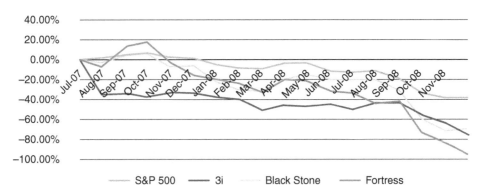

Exhibit 3.11   Stock Performances of 3i Group, Blackstone Group, Fortress Group, and S&P
500 Index
Source: Yahoo! Finance.

Implications for Future IPOs

The simple analysis presented above has important implications for the long-run
outlook of these stocks. It seems that the short-term underperformance of Fortress
Group and Blackstone Group is largely driven by existing market conditions and
is not an accurate indicator of the future prospects of these firms. There are several
possible reasons that explain the sluggish performance of these IPOs. First, this is
not unique to private equity firms. Stock markets worldwide took a hit starting
2007 because of various factors such as the U.S. housing and mortgage crisis, credit
crunch, volatile oil prices, and inflation, which eventually lead the United States
and the world economies into a recession that is almost 13 months old as of January
2008. This is evident from the poor performance of the S&P 500 index during
this period. Also, private equity activity is highly correlated with overall M&A
activity in the economy. It has been well documented that M&A activity occurs
in waves and most economists believe that the latest wave came to an abrupt
end in 2007.

Furthermore, investing in private equity firms is tricky for individual investors
as it is a very long-term business. Individual investors are typically more fickle than
institutions and other sophisticated investors, and panic at the first sign of trouble.
Furthermore, the stock market may fail to appreciate the uneven nature of the firm's
earnings. Private equity gains are realized at irregular intervals, when holdings
are sold. According to Ljungvist and Richardson (2003), who examined the private
equity cash flows of large U.S. institutional investors in private equity, the average
(median) fund in the group invested 80 percent or more of its commitments within
3.69 (4) years. Further, the study finds that it takes almost seven years for the
average PE fund to generate and disburse returns.

To summarize, while the initial evidence on the success of private equity IPOs
in the United States is not encouraging, it is undeniable that general economic
conditions played a crucial role in determining their performance. Coupled with
the evidence on the long-run performance of 3i Group's stock, it is too early to
discount PE shares as a viable investment tool. It seems only a matter of time until
another stream of private-equity IPOs hit the U.S. market.

SOVEREIGN WEALTH FUNDS COMPLEMENTING AND SUBSTITUTING FOR PRIVATE EQUITY INVESTMENTS

Sovereign wealth funds (SWFs) are state-owned investment pools that have an estimated $3 trillion under management and are playing an increasingly muscular—and controversial—role in cross-border investment. While SWFs attracted the attention of popular financial press in recent months, they are definitely not a new phenomenon. The first sovereign wealth fund, then called the Kuwait Investment Office, was created as early as 1953 and many of the largest funds—such as Abu Dhabi Investment Authority (ADIA), the world's largest SWF, and Singapore's Government Investment Corporation (GIC)—have been actively and successfully investing around the world for decades, attracting little attention.

The sheer size of SWFs can be attributed to the source of their funds. In a majority of cases, SWFs are set up by governments with revenue streams that are dependent on the value of one underlying commodity (Exhibit 3.12). These funds are set up in order to diversify their investments and stabilize revenues. Accordingly, they are often termed "stabilization funds," and most SWFs have been established by countries that are rich in natural resources. Oil-related SWFs set up by oil-rich countries in the Persian Gulf, Russia, and Norway are the most common, while a few SWFs from African and South American countries derive their funds from diamond and copper mines and other raw materials.

Another group of SWFs created by countries such as China, Singapore, and other East Asian exporters have been funded with foreign currency holdings accumulated by running persistent current-account surpluses. In the last decade or so, these emerging economics recycled their foreign exchange reserves by purchasing U.S. government bonds. Many countries were keen to amass reserves as they wanted a buffer against an event like the Asian financial crisis of 1997 to 1998. It turned out to be the case that economies like China, South Korea, and Taiwan ended up having more reserves than they need to defend themselves against global and local financial shocks. Understandably, their governments wanted to earn a higher return than U.S. Treasury bonds pay, so they created SWFs to manage their assets.

A majority of SWFs are secretive with respect to their objectives and investment activities. Except for Norway's Government Pension Fund, very few SWFs opt for public information disclosure or provide information about the fund's objectives, precisely how much money it manages, and where it has made its investments. Countries such as Russia and Iran have stabilization funds, to counter the volatility of energy prices. On the other hand, China and South Korea expect higher returns and have easy access to markets, ideas, and technology. For example, China Development Bank views its investment in Barclays Bank as a valuable source of commodities expertise.

Although sovereign wealth funds hold only 2 percent of the world's $165 trillion worth of traded securities, they have more capital than private equity and hedge funds (Exhibit 3.13). Moreover, sovereign wealth is growing fast. It is estimated that SWFs will be worth between $10 trillion and $12 trillion by 2012. But even at that rate of growth, the funds will probably still account for less than 3 percent of global traded securities.

Exhibit 3.12   Major Sovereign Wealth Funds

Country	Fund Name	Size (US$bn)	Launch Date	Origin
Algeria	Revenue Regulation Fund	47.00	2000	Oil
Angola	Reserve Fund for Oil	0.20	2007	Oil
Australia	Australian Future Fund	58.50	2004	Noncommodity
Azerbaijan	State Oil Fund	5.00	1999	Oil
Bahrain	Mumtalakat Holding Company	10.00	2006	Oil
Botswana	Pula Fund	6.90	1966	Diamonds & minerals
Brunei	Brunei Investment Agency	30.00	1983	Oil
Canada	Alberta's Heritage Fund	16.60	1976	Oil
Chile	Social and Economic Stabilization Fund	15.50	1985	Copper
China	SAFE Investment Company	311.60	—	Noncommodity
China	China Investment Corporation	200.00	2007	Noncommodity
China	National Social Security Fund	74.00	2000	Noncommodity
China	China-Africa Development Fund	5.00	2007	Noncommodity
China— Hong Kong	Hong Kong Monetary Authority Investment Portfolio	163.00	1998	Noncommodity
East Timor	Timor-Leste Petroleum Fund	3.00	2005	Oil & gas
Iran	Oil Stabilisation Fund	12.90	1999	Oil
Ireland	National Pensions Reserve Fund	30.80	2001	Noncommodity
Kazakhstan	Kazakhstan National Fund	21.50	2000	Oil
Kiribati	Revenue Equalization Reserve Fund	0.40	1956	Phosphates
Kuwait	Kuwait Investment Authority	250.00	1953	Oil
Libya	Libyan Arab Foreign Investment Company	50.00	1981	Oil
Malaysia	Khazanah Nasional	25.70	1993	Noncommodity
Mauritania	National Fund for Hydrocarbon Reserves	0.30	2006	Oil & gas
New Zealand	New Zealand Superannuation Fund	13.80	2003	Noncommodity
Nigeria	Excess Crude Account	11.00	2004	Oil
Norway	Government Pension Fund— Global	396.50	1990	Oil
Oman	State General Reserve Fund	2.00	1980	Oil & gas
Qatar	Qatar Investment Authority	60.00	2000	Oil
Russia	National Welfare Fund	162.50	2008	Oil
Saudi Arabia	SAMA Foreign Holdings	300.00	n/a	Oil
Saudi Arabia	Public Investment Fund	5.30	2008	Oil
Singapore	Government of Singapore Investment Corp	330.00	1981	Noncommodity
Singapore	Temasek Holdings	159.00	1974	Noncommodity
South Korea	Korea Investment Corporation	30.00	2005	Noncommodity
Taiwan	National Stabilisation Fund	15.00	2000	Noncommodity
Trinidad & Tobago	Heritage and Stabilization Fund	0.50	2000	Oil
U.A.E.—Abu Dhabi	Abu Dhabi Investment Authority	875.00	1976	Oil

Exhibit 3.12 (*Continued*)

Country	Fund Name	Size (US$bn)	Launch Date	Origin
U.A.E.—Abu Dhabi	Mubadala Development Company	10.00	2002	Oil
U.A.E.—Dubai	Investment Corporation of Dubai	—	2006	Oil
U.A.E.—Federal	Emirates Investment Authority	—	2007	Oil
U.A.E.—Ras Al Khaimah	RAK Investment Authority	1.20	2005	Oil
U.S.—Alabama	Alabama Trust Fund	3.10	1986	Gas
U.S.—Alaska	Alaska Permanent Fund	39.80	1976	Oil
U.S.—New Mexico	New Mexico State Investment Office Trust	16.00	1958	Noncommodity
U.S.—Wyoming	Permanent Wyoming Mineral Trust Fund	3.90	1974	Minerals
Venezuela	FIEM	0.80	1998	Oil
Vietnam	State Capital Investment Corporation	2.10	2006	Noncommodity
Total Oil & Gas Related		**2,316.00**		
Total Other		**1,463.00**		
TOTAL		**3,779.00**		

Source: Fotak, Bortolotti, and Megginson, 2008.

Private equity firms started to benefit from the enormous cash reserves held by SWFs. One of the largest sovereign wealth funds, the China Investment Corporation, had already invested $3 billion in Blackstone Group before Blackstone went public in June 2007. Along the same lines, Carlyle Group, another American private equity firm, sold a 7.5 percent stake to an Abu Dhabi fund for $1.35 billion

Assets under Control, US$bn

Exhibit 3.13 Investor Types and Assets under Control
Source: Fotak, Bortolotti, and Megginson, 2008.

in September 2007. Other wealth funds such as China's social security fund are actively considering taking a minority stake in big private equity firms like Kohlberg Kravis Roberts and TPG. SWFs benefit from these investments as stakes in private-equity firms protect them from scrutiny while offering juicy investment opportunities.

For their part, private equity firms are eager to raise funds from SWFs, because they represent an alternative to increasingly expensive credit. Moreover, unlike individual investors who typically invest for the short-term, SWFs are long-term investors. In addition, unlike institutional investors who are sophisticated and are actively involved in the operations and financial decisions of the firms they invest in, SWFs are passive investors. This combination of passive and long-term investments is turning out be irresistible to private equity firms. This is perhaps the reason why Carlyle Group sold its stake to the Abu Dhabi–based SWF at almost a 10 percent discount to its valuation. The long-run outlook of private equity is positive and it seems that the current trend of private equity firms diversifying their traditional fund-raising sources is going to continue.

CONCLUSION

This chapter initiates a discussion on the new trends in private equity fund-raising practices. Private equity industry in the United States has witnessed tremendous growth in recent years, fueled by the availability of cheap credit during the early 2000s. However, a combination of tightening credit conditions and the eagerness of existing investors to sell out led private equity firms to look for alternate sources of funds, such as listing their shares on stock markets and attracting investments from passive investors such as sovereign wealth funds.

We review the short-term performance of IPOs of Blackstone Group and Fortress Group, two leading private equity firms in the United States. While the initial evidence on the success of these IPOs is not encouraging, we argue that the prevailing market conditions played an important role in explaining their underperformance. We substantiate our claim by analyzing the long-term performance of 3i Group, a U.K.-based private equity firm that has been listed on the London Stock Exchange for over 15 years. Even though the financial status of 3i group is healthy, as indicated by several liquidity and profitability ratios, its stock price performance over the past few years reflected the broader market sentiments. This leads us to believe that it is too early to forecast the demise of private equity IPOs.

We briefly discuss the evolution and structure of sovereign wealth funds (SWFs) and their impact on the private equity industry. SWFs are acting as both complements and substitutes to private equity industry, by being a source of funds and at the same time by buying equity interests in individual companies. Private equity firms are eager to attract investments from SWFs, as initial evidence suggests that SWFs are passive, long-term investors, which suits the requirements of PE firms. The long-run outlook of private equity is positive and it seems that the current trend of private equity firms diversifying their traditional fund-raising sources is going to continue.

NOTES

1. It is widely accepted that the private equity industry in the United States started in 1946 with the founding of two venture capital firms: *American Research and Development Corporation* (ARDC) and *J.H. Whitney & Company.*

2. See, for example, Megginson and Weiss (1991), Kaplan and Stromberg (2003), Kaplan and Schoar (2005), and Lerner and Schoar (2005).

3. From *Venture Impact: The Economic Importance of Venture Capital Backed Companies to the U.S. Economy, 4th edition* by GlobalInsight.

4. From *The Economic Impact of Private Equity in the UK 2006/7* and *The Economic Impact of Private Equity and Venture Capital in Australia, 2006* by IE Consulting on behalf of the British Private Equity and Venture Capital Association, PricewaterhouseCoopers.

5. More specifically, sovereign wealth funds, while investing money in private equity firms, also began competing with private equity firms to buy out companies.

6. However, total funds raised by PE firms still pale in comparison to those raised by IPOs and seasoned offerings. According to the *Private Equity International* magazine May 2007 edition, global IPOs and follow-on offers raised nearly $2.3 billion dollars from 2002 to 2007. During the same period, PE firms were able to raise $551 billion. Published by Peimedia (www.peimedia.com).

7. From the European Private Equity and Venture Capital Association final performance and activity figures, 2006. The report contains figures in billions of Euros. The average 2006 exchange rate of $1.26 per Euro is used to present dollar estimates.

8. From EM PE 2006 Fundraising Review by the Emerging Markets Private Equity Association.

9. From *The 2005–2006 Russell Survey on Alternative Investment* by Russell Research of the Russell Investment Group, 2005.

10. Cumming and MacIntosh (2007) note that the underperformance of LSIFs is a result of statutory constraints and that the objectives of these funds are often different from a regular mutual fund.

11. Interested readers should refer to "A Boom in Bust-Ups" published in the September 27, 2007, edition of *The Economist.*

12. In addition, a few other U.S.-based private equity firms started raising public money through private placements and by listing their shares in Europe. For instance, Kohlberg Kravis and Roberts (KKR) and Apollo Group, two prominent U.S. private equity groups, launched publicly traded private equity vehicles—KKR Private Equity Investors and AP Alternative Assets, respectively—in Europe. These investment vehicles in turn issued IPOs in May 2006 and August 2006, raising nearly $5 billion and $2 billion, respectively.

13. Interested readers should refer to Ritter and Welch (2002) for more details.

14. 3i Group is one of the Europe's leading private equity investors and one of the largest investment trusts on London's stock exchange. The group invests in buyouts, growth capital, infrastructure, and quoted private equity (QPE). The company has approximately €12 billion in assets under management.

15. Interest cover is a measure of adequacy of a firm's profits relative to interest payments on its debt. An interest cover of less than 1 is considered risky in terms of generating enough revenue to make interest payments on debt. Solvency ratio is a measure of firm's ability to meet its long-term obligations and is calculated as (net profit after tax + depreciation)/total liabilities. While solvency ratios vary depending on industry, as

a general rule of thumb, a firm with a ratio greater than 20 is considered financially healthy and in a good shape to meet its future debt obligations.

16. Median industry values are available for the period 2003 to 2007 only.

17. Blackstone group went public on June 22, 2007.

REFERENCES

Cressy, Robert, Federico Munari, and Alessandro Malipiero. 2007. Creative destruction? UK evidence that buyouts cut jobs to raise returns. Working paper, available at SSRN: ssrn.com/abstract=1030830.

Cumming, Douglas, and Jeffrey MacIntosh. 2007. Mutual funds that invest in private equity? An analysis of labor-sponsored investment funds. *Cambridge Journal of Economics* 31:445–487.

Davis, Steven, John Haltiwanger, Ron Jarmin, Josh Lerner, and Javier Miranda. 2008. Private equity and employment. U.S. Census Bureau Center for Economic Studies Paper No. CES-WP-08-07. Available at SSRN: ssrn.com/abstract=1107175.

Fotak, Veljko, Bernardo Bortolotti, and William Megginson. 2008. The financial impact of sovereign wealth fund investments in listed companies. Working Paper, available at SSRN: ssrn.com/abstract=1108585.

Kaplan, Steve, and Per Stromberg. 2003. Financial contracting theory meets the real world: An empirical analysis of venture capital contracts. *Review of Economic Studies* 70:281–315.

Kaplan, Steve, and Antoinette Schoar. 2005. Private equity performance: Returns, persistence and capital flows. *Journal of Finance* 61:1791–1823.

Lerner, Josh, and Antoinette Schoar. 2005. Does legal enforcement affect financial transactions? The contractual channel in private equity. *Quarterly Journal of Economics*, 223–246.

Ljungvist, Alexander, and Matthew Richardson. 2003. The cash flow, return and risk characteristics of private equity. NBER Working Paper No. 9454.

Megginson, William, and Kathleen Weiss. 1991. Venture capital certification in initial public offerings. *Journal of Finance* 46:879–903.

Ritter, Jay, and Ivo Welch. 2002. A review of IPO activity, pricing, and allocations. *Journal of Finance* 57:1795–1828.

Sahlman, William A. 1990. The structure and governance of venture capital organizations. *Journal of Financial Economics* 27:473–524.

Various issues of *The Economist, Financial Times,* and *The Wall Street Journal.*

ABOUT THE AUTHORS

Bill Megginson is Professor and Rainbolt Chair in Finance at the University of Oklahoma's Michael F. Price College of Business. He is also Executive Director of the Privatization Barometer. From 2002 to 2007, he was a voting member of the Italian Ministry of Economics and Finance's Global Advisory Committee on Privatization. During spring 2008, he was the Fulbright Tocqueville Distinguished Chair in American Studies and Visiting Professor at the Université-Paris Dauphine. Professor Megginson's research interest has focused in recent years on the privatization of state-owned enterprises, especially those privatizations executed through public share offerings. He has published refereed articles in several top academic journals, including the *Journal of Economic Literature*, the *Journal of Finance*, the

Journal of Financial Economics, the *Journal of Financial and Quantitative Analysis*, and *Foreign Policy*. He is author or coauthor of eight textbooks. He has been a Visiting Professor at Vanderbilt University, the University of Zurich, the University of Amsterdam, Bocconi University, and Université-Paris Dauphine.

Sridhar Gogineni is a Doctoral Candidate at the Michael F. Price College of Business at the University of Oklahoma. Sridhar's research focuses on corporate control, governance issues in private companies, and market microstructure.

CHAPTER 4

Listed Private Equity

BASTIAN BERGMANN
Equity Analyst, LPX Group, Zurich

HANS CHRISTOPHERS
Managing Director, LPX Group, Zurich

MATTHIAS HUSS
Partner, LPX Group, Zurich

HEINZ ZIMMERMANN
Professor, University of Basel

INTRODUCTION

Investments in private equity are often associated with unlisted private equity funds, usually structured as limited partnerships. The large amount of capital that has to be committed to limited partnerships and the long investment horizon contributes to this asset class being primarily the domain of large institutional investors. What has been neglected for some time is the existence of listed private equity—an exposure through a share in a private equity company traded on a stock exchange. It is somehow surprising that both from the academic and investor viewpoints, few have paid attention to this group of companies until the listings of prominent private equity industry participants such as KRR Private Equity Investors, L.P., in 2006 and Blackstone Group, L.P., in 2007.

Basically, a listed private equity company provides shareholders an immediate exposure to a diversified private equity portfolio and occasionally the opportunity to participate in the management fees and carried interest earned by the managers of the company. This article is dedicated to the exploration and description of the listed private equity universe as a part of the whole private equity asset class. A frequently named caveat from an academic perspective is the lack of reliable risk and return data for private equity. There are numerous factors that inhibit disclosure by private equity firms and detailed discussion is beyond the topic of this paper. However, listed private equity companies demonstrate increased efforts to provide more information to current and prospective shareholders, and we show that looking at the listed part of private equity provides an innovative way of applying traditional risk and return measures.

First, we show that the typical private equity features such as investment styles, financing styles, and other important characteristics are shared between the unlisted and the listed private equity universe. Second, we focus on the different organizational structures and characteristics within listed and unlisted private equity. Whereas in the unlisted universe there is only one dominant organizational structure, limited partnerships, the listed universe can be categorized into listed indirect private equity investment companies (funds-of-funds), listed direct private capital investment companies, and listed private equity fund managers. We conclude that although there are different organizational structures, an investment in listed private equity exhibits similar or even equivalent characteristics to an investment in unlisted private equity. We also show that listed private equity possesses additional features, such as a flexible investment horizon and liquidity, which makes it very attractive from an investor's perspective. Finally, we present an empirical overview of the listed private equity market.

LISTED PRIVATE EQUITY: DEFINITIONS AND CATEGORIZATION

The phrase "private equity" became widespread in the late 1980s following major buyout fund activity. *Private equity*, as the term suggests, involves investments of equity capital in private businesses. It provides long-term, committed share capital, to help unquoted companies grow and succeed. The term *private equity* does not require that the investing company itself is private. The fact that a private equity company is listed on a stock exchange does not influence its core business: investing in unquoted companies.

From an investor's perspective there are typically two ways to get exposure to private equity. The first way is via private equity funds. Certain "limited partners," such as banks, insurance companies, pension funds, or high net-worth individuals and families, commit capital to a fund. The fund itself is run by a management team called the general partner. The general partner is compensated by management fees and performance fees (carried interest). The limited partners commit their capital for a fixed time horizon. Over the investment horizon the general partner identifies investment opportunities and "calls" the money from the limited partners to undertake certain investments. If the general partner decides to liquidate an investment, the proceeds are paid back to the limited partners. Calls and liquidations do not follow a fixed time horizon. *Ex-ante*, the limited partner knows nothing about the cash flow stream (for a detailed introduction to the structure of unlisted private equity funds, see Phalippou 2007).

A complement to buying a limited partnership interest is to get exposure to private equity through private equity companies traded on recognized stock exchanges. In contrast to unlisted private equity funds, where the investor base is primarily a limited number of institutional investors, the listed private equity market opens this asset class for everyone. Having an organized market at hand to buy and sell a private equity portfolio makes this asset class highly liquid. Indeed, some institutions who invest in limited partnerships also invest in listed private equity to reach and manage their private equity asset allocation more efficiently, selling their listed private equity investments as their limited partnership "calls" arise and reinvesting in listed private equity when they receive distributions. By nature, similar to secondaries in the traditional private equity market, through listed private equity an investor is able to get a direct exposure to a more or less mature private equity portfolio. Also there is no need to commit capital for a fixed period of time. In this sense, listed private equity can be seen as an evergreen exposure to private equity through the permanent capital character of a listed company.

Seeing these advantages it is somehow surprising that listed private equity has been undiscovered for so long. For example, Electra Private Equity has been listed on the London Stock Exchange in 1976. As of January 2009 the total market capitalization of the global listed private equity market amounted to US$31 billion.

Getting exposure to private equity by purchasing a share on a stock exchange sounds simple. However, it can be challenging to identify the relevant companies within the universe of all listed companies compared to other major industry sectors. For example, an investor seeking an exposure to the automobile sector or the health care sector will face few problems picking the relevant companies given that there are leading data providers sorting stocks into major industry classifications. However, listed private equity can't be found in these classifications, nor are these companies in the public focus, barring such candidates as KKR, Blackstone, or 3i. A pioneer in identifying and researching the global listed private equity universe is Swiss-based LPX Group. Their listed private equity index family has been the first set of benchmarks based on objective market valuations only. Today these indices are accepted as a reliable tool for valuation and representative benchmarks for private equity in both the academic community and industry experts. Their flagship index, the LPX50, comprises the 50 largest liquid private equity stocks on a global scale.

It is the purpose of this article to show that both listed and unlisted private equity provide investors an exposure to private companies. For an investor it is the same to participate in a buyout deal financed with equity or mezzanine capital via an unlisted or a listed private equity company. The major difference between both forms of private equity is in the organizational structure.

TERMS AND DEFINITIONS

For both listed and unlisted private equity vehicles it makes sense to distinguish between three types of investment styles: buyout, venture, and growth capital. There is no fundamental difference whether an unlisted fund or a listed private equity company undertakes one of these investment styles.

Investment Styles

Buyout typically refers to a strategy of making equity investments as part of a transaction in which a company, business unit, or business asset is acquired from the current shareholders typically with the use of financial leverage. The companies involved in these transactions are typically mature and generate operating cash flows. A prominent example is the London Stock Exchange (LSE)–listed HgCapital Trust PLC in the United Kingdom, which specializes in middle-market buyouts.

Venture capital refers to investments made in immature companies, typically start ups, for the launch, early development, or expansion of a business. For example, the Swiss Stock Exchange (SWX) listed HBM BioVentures AG as a major venture capital provider on a global scale.

Growth capital refers to minority investments in mature companies. It is a type of investment suited to a diverse range of growth opportunities, including acquisitions, increasing production capacity, market or product development, turnaround opportunities, shareholder succession, and change of ownership situations (a similar definition of the investment styles can be found in 3i Group PLC Annual Report 2008). Growth capital is much more present in listed private equity, as exits from a growth capital position that do not involve a majority holding can be less predictable. Since an evergreen listed private equity company is not obliged to distribute the money back to the limited partners after a specified period of time, it can be more flexible in setting a variable and therefore suitable investment horizon. This major advantage of listed private equity as permanent capital is evident in the largest listed private equity company in Europe, the LSE listed 3i Group PLC, which has one of the largest growth-capital portfolios in the world.

Financing Styles

As in the unlisted private equity market, deals in the listed market are either financed with equity, mezzanine capital, or debt. Calling "mezzanine" a financing style is often confusing. In contrast to other existing methodologies we define mezzanine capital as any capital between equity and debt, for example, subordinated debt, convertible debt, or loans with equity kickers. We observe that most of the mezzanine capital provided is within a buyout deal. However, a small proportion of mezzanine capital is also provided in venture and growth deals. This leads us to the decision to define "mezzanine capital" as a financing style instead of an investment style.

Categorization of Listed Private Equity

As already pointed out, the defining "economic" characteristics of private equity—investment styles and financing styles—are shared between both listed and unlisted private equity. However, differences are seen in the heterogeneity of organizational structures, which can be regarded as a mainly legal difference. Whereas unlisted private equity is almost always structured as limited partnership, the listed universe is more complex and we propose the following categorization: listed direct private equity investment companies, listed direct private mezzanine capital investment companies, listed indirect private equity investment companies (fund-of-funds), and listed private equity fund managers (J.P. Morgan Cazenove uses a similar categorization). Listed direct private equity investment companies and listed direct private mezzanine capital investment companies exhibit the same organizational structure and these two categories are therefore combined in Exhibit 4.1 into "listed private capital investment companies."

Unlisted Private Equity Fund

Exhibit 4.1a shows the simplified organizational structure of an unlisted private equity fund. An investor commits a certain amount of capital to a fund of typically fixed size and time horizon, that is, he or she buys a limited partnership interest.

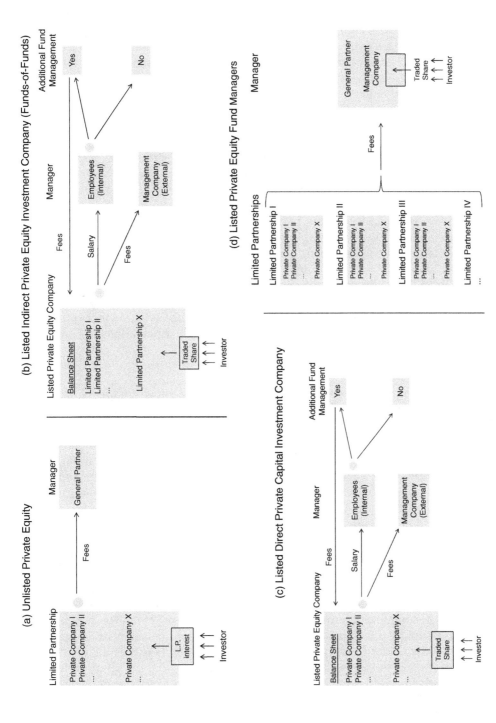

Exhibit 4.1 Different Organizational Structures of Listed and Unlisted Private Equity

This limited partnership is managed by the general partner. Over a specified time horizon (usually 10 years) the general partners can call the money for deals (Private Company I, Private Company II, and so on). The investments are typically done at asset value. In the case of an exit of the investments, the general partner pays the proceeds back to the limited partners after deducting management fees and carried interest. The limited partnership organizational structure is by far the most common structure in the private equity market. Although the first vehicle was a listed company, founded in the 1940s, today limited partnerships are the dominant organizational structure (Hsu and Kenney, 2005).

Listed Indirect Private Equity Investment Companies

Organizational forms of the listed private equity market are depicted in Exhibit 4.1b. Exhibit 4.1b shows the structure of listed indirect private equity investment companies (funds-of-funds). A listed private equity fund of funds is a company that floats on the exchange with the purpose of committing capital to traditional private equity limited partnerships. "Indirect" indicates that the company does not directly invest capital to private equity deals but "indirectly" via investments in limited partnership, so this category could be described as "actively managed traditional private equity." An investor buys a share of the listed company over an exchange and in the end he owns a portfolio of limited partnerships diversified across vintages, regions, and so on. Within the listed private equity universe there are currently 27 companies of this category. A prominent company among these is the U.K.-based Pantheon International Participations PLC, which has been listed on the LSE since 1987.

We observe that listed private equity funds of funds can basically be created in two ways. Either an empty shell is listed on a stock exchange via an initial public offering, or an already existing portfolio of limited partnerships is sold via an initial public offering. In the first case, the majority of the investment portfolio consists of cash until the committed capital is gradually drawn down from the respective limited partnerships. This leads to the so-called "cash drag" in the first month after the listing. Cash drag can also be observed in the case of committing capital to an unlisted private equity fund. In the second case, an investor gets immediate exposure to private equity because the majority of the investment portfolio consists of various limited partnerships diversified across regions and vintages. A fully invested fund of funds bears the advantage over an unlisted fund of providing a diversified and permanent exposure to the private equity asset class. It is permanent in the sense that it has no finite life but reinvests proceeds from older vintage funds in new funds. A fund-of-funds' balance sheet consists to a large extent of the portfolio of limited partnerships. The managers of the fund can either be employees of the fund itself (internal management) or be managed by an external management company. Internal management is infrequent (2 of 27 funds of funds) but enables the fund to earn additional income for fund management. More typically, 25 of 27 funds-of-funds have external management where the fund has to pay management fees so there is a "double fee structure" paying the salary or fees of the listed private equity company and also the fees charged by the general partners of the limited partnerships. Funds of funds say that this reflects the considerable resources they devote to investment screening, due diligence, and negotiation to select and work with private equity managers who can achieve the best results;

often their long-standing relationships with top managers will provide access that investors could not achieve on their own.

Listed Direct Private Capital Companies

The majority of listed private equity companies are organized as listed direct private capital investment companies. There are currently 91 listed direct private capital investment companies. A prominent example is the U.K.-based 3i Group PLC. The term *direct* indicates in this context that the company is invested directly in the underlying companies, and not via limited partnerships. As shown in Exhibit 4.1, the balance sheet of the listed private equity company contains largely the acquired interests in the private companies (Private Company I, Private Company II, and so on). Through the purchase of a share traded on an exchange, the investor gets exposure to a diversified portfolio of private companies directly held by the listed company. In contrast to the category "fund-of-funds" where only a few companies have internal management, about half of the listed direct private capital companies are internally managed. Often the managed limited partnerships co-invest in the same private companies. In the course of a new deal, a part of the transaction volume is financed by the available resources from the balance sheet and the remainder coming from the managed limited partnerships. In contrast to an investment in a traditional limited partnership, this organizational structure offers an investor not only a direct exposure to a diversified portfolio of private companies but also a participation on general partner revenues generated by the additional fund management business.

Listed Private Equity Fund Managers

The last organizational structure is characterized as listed private equity fund managers. This category represents a minority of the listed private equity universe. A prominent example is the New York Stock Exchange–listed Blackstone Group L.P. Typically, listed fund managers have no direct or indirect exposure to private companies. The acquired interest is instead held in managed limited partnerships. Exhibit 4.1d shows the organizational structure of a listed fund manager. Basically, this structure is congruent to the organizational structure depicted in Exhibit 4.1a, with the exception that the investor buys a listed interest in the general partner and not an unlisted limited partnership interest.

To summarize, apart from the different organizational structures, an investor gets an exposure to private equity whether he buys a limited partnership interest or a share of a listed private equity company. In case of the former, the investor faces a high minimum size of committed capital and usually a fixed time horizon, whereas in the listed case the investor faces no minimum size and the time horizon is the investor's own. What has been significant over the last decades is that unlisted funds tend to focus on one investment style, for example, "leveraged buyouts." An investor seeking diversification over investment styles within the unlisted world is forced to invest in a several unlisted funds, which requires an enormous amount of capital. Diversification in the listed universe is simply achieved by buying a stock portfolio of listed private equity companies. Additionally, listed private equity companies are usually more diversified according to deal type and vintage. One significant difference from an investor's perspective is the fact that in the listed case, the investor is often able to buy at a major discount, whereas investments in the unlisted universe are initially invested at net asset value. It is therefore key to trace the historic and current net asset values (NAVs) as well as the market prices of the listed private equity companies.

FURTHER EMPIRICAL INSIGHTS ON LISTED PRIVATE EQUITY

In this section we present some empirical results on the historic evolution, geographical distribution, investment and financing styles, internal and external management of the base universe of listed private equity companies. In addition we provide detailed empirical analysis of the four categories of listed private equity companies. We conclude this section with some remarks on the current underlying portfolio distribution of the base universe and some risk and return figures.

The empirical investigation is based on a major sample of 122 globally listed private equity investment companies called base universe. To be included in the base universe, the majority of the assets of the company consist of either direct or indirect private equity investments. In the case of listed private equity fund managers, at least 50 percent of the assets under management have to be dedicated to private equity. Additionally all companies from the base universe are investible in the sense that they all fulfill predefined liquidity criteria. The liquidity criteria correspond to the Guide to the LPX Equity Indices. The base universe only contains companies currently listed on an exchange. Nonsurviving companies are excluded from the analysis.

Exhibit 4.2 shows the historical evolution of the base universe. In 1980 there were only three listings, by 1995 there were less than 25 companies listed on a stock exchange. In the following years the number has more than doubled, reaching 50

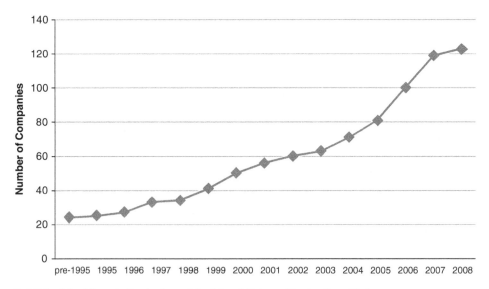

Exhibit 4.2 Historic Evolution of the Listed Private Equity Base Universe

listed private equity companies in 2000. With the beginning of the year 2004 a new wave of initial public offerings emerged, with 38 new listings in the years 2006 and 2007, making listed private equity a serious investment niche for investors seeking exposure to private equity.

Exhibit 4.3 and Exhibit 4.4 show some important characteristics of the base universe. Exhibit 4.3a shows the regional breakdown of the current base universe according to the market capitalization in USD. Total market capitalization of the base universe as of January 2009 amounts to US$31 billion. This is a decline of around 70 percent from its peak of more US$100 billion in June 2007. By market capitalization, 19 percent of the base universe is listed in the United Kingdom and 50 percent listed in other European countries, making Europe, with 69 percent (by number), the major listed private equity market.

Sixteen out of 34 listed companies from the United Kingdom are listed direct private equity investment companies with the remainder being 11 funds-of-funds, six listed direct mezzanine capital investment companies, and one listed private equity fund manager. For Europe (excluding the United Kingdom), the majority of the companies are listed direct private equity companies with a

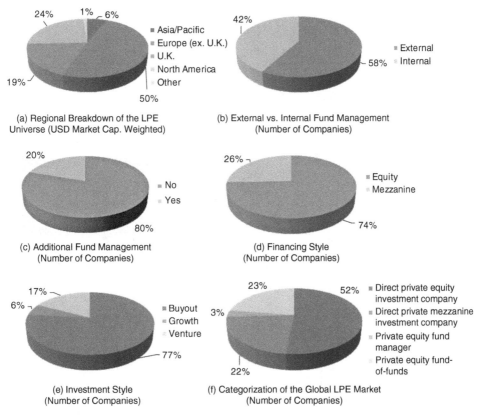

Exhibit 4.3 Characteristics in Pie Chart Form

Exhibit 4.4 Breakdown According to Market Capitalization

Listed Direct Private Equity Inverstment Companies

USD billion

Region	Number	Market Cap	Investment Style	Number	Market Cap
Asia/Pacific	7	1.86	Buyout	3	0.44
			Growth	1	0.16
			Venture	3	1.26
Europe (ex. U.K.)	32	11.16	Buyout	21	10.54
			Growth	5	0.16
			Venture	6	0.45
North America	7	2.76	Buyout	5	2.61
			Growth		
			Venture	2	0.16
U.K.	16	3.56	Buyout	10	2.80
			Growth		
			Venture	6	0.76
Other	1	0.42	Buyout	1	0.42
			Growth		
			Venture		
Total	63	19.77		63	19.77

Listed Direct Mezzanine Capital Investment Companies

USD billion

Region	Number	Market Cap	Investment Style	Number	Market Cap
North America	22	3.93	Buyout	20	3.70
			Growth	2	0.22
			Venture		
U.K.	6	0.73	Buyout	6	0.73
			Growth		
			Venture		
Total	28	4.65		28	4.65

Listed Indirect Private Equity Investment Companies

USD billion

Region	Number	Market Cap	Investment Style	Number	Market Cap
Asia/Pacific	1	0.01	Buyout Growth Venture	1	0.01
Europe (ex. U.K.)	15	2.26	Buyout Growth Venture	13 1 1	1.99 0.20 0.08
U.K.	11	1.55	Buyout Growth Venture	10 1	1.48 0.07
Total	**27**	**3.82**		**27**	**3.82**

Listed Private Equity Fund Manager

USD billion

Region	Number	Market Cap	Investment Style	Number	Market Cap
Europe (ex. U.K.)	2	1.83	Buyout Growth Venture	2	1.83
North America	1	0.78	Buyout Growth Venture	1	0.78
U.K.	1	0.03	Buyout Growth Venture	1	0.03
Total	**4**	**2.64**		**4**	**2.64**

market capitalization of US$11 billion. There are no listed direct mezzanine capital investment companies for Europe (excluding the United Kingdom).

The majority of the listed direct mezzanine capital investment companies are located in North America. Twenty of the 22 direct mezzanine capital investment companies from North America provide mezzanine capital in buyout deals, representing US$3 billion. Total market capitalization of the 31 North America companies amounts to US$7.4 billion. The regulatory background in the United States inhibits the formation of listed funds-of-funds, some of which have chosen to list in Europe instead. The Asia-Pacific region plays a minor role in the global listed private equity market, representing 6 percent of the total market capitalization. It consists largely of listed direct private equity investment companies, well diversified over investment styles. Exhibits 4.3b and 4.3c show the proportion of companies who are externally or internally managed. The majority of the companies (58 percent) are externally managed. Twenty percent of the companies of the base universe derive income from additional fund management. As already indicated above, additional fund management is a major advantage because it gives an investor the opportunity to participate in a steady cash-flow stream. Exhibits 4.3d and 4.3e show the financing and investment styles. Not surprisingly buyout is the dominant investment style representing 77 percent of the base universe. Seventy-four percent of the companies pursue an equity financing style. Only 26 percent follow a mezzanine strategy.

To give an idea of the distribution of assets of the global listed private equity companies, we use a kind of "aggregate balance sheet." Exhibit 4.5 shows a balance sheet of a sample of listed private equity companies. These companies represent about 76 percent of the total market capitalization of the base universe.

The breakdown of assets of fair value basically consists of the direct and indirect private equity portfolios as well as cash and cash equivalents (intended to finance coming deals) and other assets such as investments in listed assets, real

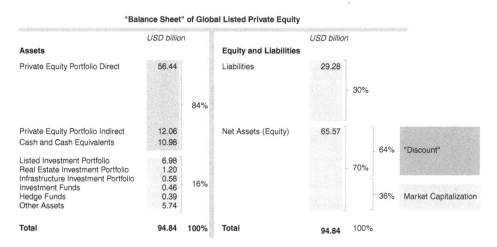

Exhibit 4.5 Distribution of the Sum of the Underlying Portfolios of a Representative Sample of Listed Private Equity Companies as of January 30, 2009

estate, infrastructure, investment funds, hedge funds, and other assets. We derive these numbers directly from the reports and press releases of the companies and by own calculations. Interestingly, US$79.500 billion, or 84 percent of total assets, consist of the aggregated direct and indirect investment portfolio. This means that an investor in this sample gets an immediate high exposure to the private equity asset class, avoiding the cash drag typically associated with an investment in a limited partnership. The total portfolio of US$95 billion is financed with debt of US$29 billion and US$65.6 billion with equity (net asset value). A very important ratio in the private equity industry is the price to net asset value (price to book ratio). In our sample we calculate a surprising price to book ratio of 0.36, implying a "discount" of about 64 percent. Such a price to book ratio is historically low and represents the current status of markets. This fact is one of the most important advantages of listed private equity over unlisted private equity as an investor has the possibility to get an exposure to private equity at a discount. In the LPEQ Preqin Survey "How Do Institutional Investors Regard Listed Private Equity?" (a research survey of 100 European LPs in December 2008), 70 percent of those interviewed agreed that "widening discounts of listed private equity shares create a buying opportunity."[1]

Yet many investors generally believe that private equity has relatively low return volatility, although often producing double-digit rates of return. High expected returns and low volatility would translate into an appealing risk/return profile, while low correlations to traditional asset classes imply attractive portfolio diversification benefits. As mentioned, when measuring risk and return, listed private equity provides a way to overcome the inherent difficulties with traditional private equity. Having a daily market price makes it possible to apply basic concepts that are generally accepted in academic financial research to a market that otherwise needs to rely on specially designed methodologies, leading to empirical results that are hard to compare with other (traditional) asset classes. Thus, looking at the development of the listed private equity market is revealing and provides insights to issues that have been difficult to uncover previously. The first key issue of interest to investors and more broadly is to investigate the "risk and return profile" of private equity investments. Please see Exhibits 4.6 and 4.7.

These derived results might be surprising at a first glance. Private equity has experienced both years with outstanding (excess) returns and also years with poor performance. Volatility has been higher than usually assumed and correlations, though still low compared to traditional asset classes, might be higher that one would have guessed. Please see Exhibit 4.8.

A caveat is that different private equity investment styles develop differently over time. Venture capital behaves dramatically differently to buyout or growth capital. Obviously, the contribution of different investment styles to the overall performance of the private equity market (here proxied by the LPX50) changes over time. Strong returns in Phase 1 result mainly from the rise of valuations in the venture business. As venture capital was often invested in dot-com and high-tech businesses and valuations came down in the years after the burst of the dot-com bubble (Phase 2), venture capital returns were necessarily affected, leading to three years of negative performance in the LPX50 index. In contrast, returns up to 50 percent p.a. in the years 2003 to 2006 were triggered by the buyout boom

Exhibit 4.6 Risk and Return between January 1994 and December 2008 for LPX50 TR, MSCI World, and NASDAQ Composite

	LPX50		MSCI World		Nasdaq Composite	
	Return	Risk	Return	Risk	Return	Risk
Phase 1 January 1994–February 2000 *Index launch until high-tech boom*	31.81%	18.47%	18.84%	15.69%	37.05%	24.70%
Phase 2 March 2000–March 2003 *Burst of the "dot-com bubble"*	−30.29%	24.70%	−19.12%	19.87%	−36.01%	40.51%
Phase 3 April 2004–June 2007 *"Buyout boom"*	34.50%	11.83%	16.39%	9.15%	11.19%	14.57%
Phase 4 July 2007– December 2008 *Credit crunch–financial crisis*	−56.04%	41.66%	−30.68%	17.53%	−30.00%	22.98%

Return is annualized over the relevant period. Risk is calculated as the annualized standard deviation over the relevant period. All figures are calculated on a USD basis.

(Phase 3) that ended in 2007 with the first turmoil in the credit market and led to a sharp decline in prices in 2008 as a result of the global financial crisis (Phase 4).

A possible objection is that these price movements are unique to the listed private equity market and might not necessarily represent the development of traditional private equity investments, where no market prices exist. However,

Exhibit 4.7 Correlation among Selected Asset Classes

Asset Class	Stocks Global	Real Estate Global	Bonds Global	Infrastructure Global	Private Equity Global
Stocks Global					
Real Estate Global	0.423				
Bonds Global	0.371	0.127			
Infrastructure Global	0.686	0.517	0.050		
Private Equity Global	**0.772**	**0.442**	**0.002**	**0.659**	

Asset Class	Underlying Index
Stocks Global	MSCI World TR
Real Estate Global	FTSE European Real Estate
Bonds Global	JPM Global Government Bond
Infrastructure Global	NMX30 TR
Private Equity Global	LPX50 TR

Correlations are calculated on a monthly basis based on historical data from January 1994 to December 2008.

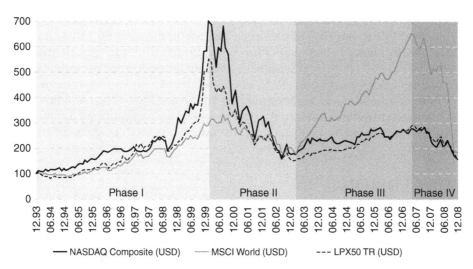

Exhibit 4.8 Performance of LPX50 TR versus MSCI World and NASDAQ Composite

classical return measures for traditional private equity, such as the calculation of IRR, rely on the assumption that interim distributions are reinvested at the same rate of return. Moreover, the fact that it is not possible to calculate meaningful risk measures such as volatility does not mean that volatility is low or does not exist.

From an empirical perspective, discounts in the secondary market for traditional private equity dramatically differ over time. It is appropriate to assume that trading in these markets—and thus making market prices available—would translate into a similar price pattern to that observed in public markets. Seen from an economic perspective and from the background of this chapter, it seems appropriate to assume that both forms of private equity, unlisted and listed, face an equivalent behavior in terms of performance. A study from the University of Basel (Huss/Zimmermann 2005) looks at more than 7,000 cash flows from unlisted private equity funds. The data is drawn from a database compiled by Preqin (Private Equity Intelligence Ltd., London, U.K.). The company has been highly successful in collecting data from over 800 different private equity funds by using a wide spread of sources, such as voluntary disclosures of both general and limited partners, but also utilizing public information.

The drawdowns (or capital calls) from unlisted private equity funds are "virtually" invested in the LPX50, which serves as a public market benchmark. Similarly, distributions are deinvested from the benchmark. This approach, called the Public Market Equivalent (PME), takes the de facto timing of all cash inflows and outflows into account, which is one of the key advantages of the model.

Intuitively, the PME approach can be seen as buying "shares" of a public market index when capital is called by a private equity fund, and selling "shares" when distributions are made. The value of the actual number of "shares" bought (sold) equals the cash flow to (from) the private investment at the time it occurs. So, the cash flow pattern of a private fund is perfectly replicated by an investment in the benchmark. The PME shows, in terms of present value, the amount of money that it is necessary to invest in the public benchmark for every dollar invested in the private equity fund in order to yield equivalent cash flows as they are generated by the fund. Thus, the PME is a sensible and useful measure for LPs as it reflects the return to unlisted private equity funds relative to a public market alternative. If the PME exceeds 1, the private equity investment outperformed the public market alternative. Correspondingly, a PME less than 1 reveals underperformance.

Ending up with PME ratios around 1 and median PME ratios around .8 to .9, depending on the sample, the study concludes there are no significant differences in the behavior of listed and unlisted private equity vehicles during the investigated time span.

CONCLUSION

This chapter introduces an alternative way to look at private equity investments. The listed private equity market, despite its long history, is often overlooked by both participants in the private equity industry and the academic community. While the listed market is small compared to its unlisted counterpart, it benefits from a variety of advantages that make this form of private equity worth further consideration. But is public private equity a contradiction in terms?

From an economic perspective the differences between listed and unlisted traditional private equity are small. The core business and thus the way investment decisions are taken, investments are financed, and the portfolio is managed is little influenced by the legal form of the private equity investment company. It does not matter if a venture capital or buyout deal is pursued via an unlisted fund or a listed company. What makes the difference between the listed and unlisted world of the private equity asset class is the categorization of its organizational structures. In the unlisted world, limited partnerships are the single dominant structure, while the listed world is more heterogeneous.

The universe of listed companies can be categorized in four categories: listed direct private equity investment companies, listed direct private mezzanine investment companies, listed indirect private equity companies (funds-of-funds) and listed private equity fund managers. Listed private equity fund managers give an investor the opportunity to participate in the fees generated by the managers (general partners) of a private equity fund management business. The other categories provide an investor with a diversified direct or indirect portfolio of private equity assets with different investment and financing styles.

Furthermore, listed private equity has some significant advantages for investors. Quotation on a public stock exchange provides the liquidity for listed private equity vehicles that is lacking through a limited partnership investment. Since a fund has to fulfill strict requirements when listing on a stock exchange, the transparency of listed private equity to all shareholders is significantly higher than unlisted funds. The availability of market prices is a further advantage. We present some descriptive facts on the listed private equity market to give an impression on the size, development and geographical location of this market. We further show how assets are invested in this industry. The private equity investment portfolio makes up more than 60 percent of total assets of a "typical" listed private equity company. It is a function of the current market environment that listed private equity companies trade with price to book ratios of less than 0.4 on average.

From an empirical perspective, listed and unlisted private equity funds behave very similarly in their risk and return pattern, when comparing listed results with a representative sample of unlisted private equity funds, covering 20 years of data. Having market prices available makes it easy to apply common statistical concepts to the private equity industry and thus calculate a variety of measures for straight-forward comparison with other asset classes. We show risk and return figures for different phases in the private equity market cycle, along with a correlation table to indicate the magnitude of these key figures in finance.

NOTES

1. LPEQ was established in 2006 to increase awareness and understanding of listed private equity through research and information. They provide information on private equity in general, and the listed sector in particular (www.LPEQ.com).

2. www.LPEQ.com.

REFERENCES

Cochrane, John. 2005. The Risk and Return of Venture Capital. *Journal of Financial Economics* 75 (1):3–52.

Hsu, David H., and Martin Kenney. 2005. Organizing venture capital: The rise and demise of American research and development corporations, 1946–1973. *Industrial and Corporate Change* 14 (4):579–616.

Huss, Matthias, and Heinz Zimmermann. 2005. Performance characteristics of private equity. Working Paper, University of Basel.

JP Morgan Cazenove Limited, European Listed Private Equity Bulletin, December 2008.

Kaplan, Steven N., and Antoinette Schoar. 2005. Private equity performance: Returns, persistence, and capital flows. *Journal of Finance* 60 (4):1791–1823.

Ljungqvist, Alexander, and Matthew Richardson. 2003. The cash flow, return and risk characteristics of private equity. NBER Working Paper 9454.

LPX. 2009. Guide to the LPX Equity Indices, 2009. www.lpx-group.com.

Moskowitz, Tobias J., and Annette Vissing-Jorgensen. 2002. The returns to entrepreneurial investment: A private equity premium puzzle? *American Economic Review* 92 (4):745–778.

Phalippou, Ludovic. 2007. Investing in private equity funds: A survey. Working Paper, University of Amsterdam.

3i Group PLC, Annual Report 2008, www.3igroup.com.

ABOUT THE AUTHORS

Bastian Bergmann holds a Master (Magister Artium) of Economics, Political Science, and Philosophy from the University of Konstanz. He works for LPX Group in the field of equity research.

Hans Christophers holds a Master of Business Administration from the WHU Koblenz. He is a founding partner of LPX Group and is the Head of LPX Research.

Matthias Huss holds a Master of Science in Finance from the University of Basel. He is a partner of LPX Group and works in the field of business development.

Heinz Zimmermann is a professor of finance at the University of Basel. From 1990 to 2001 he served as a professor of economics at the Universität St. Gallen. His research interest is in applied finance, asset pricing, risk management, and derivatives. His professional experience also includes consulting activities and several board memberships in the financial industry.

ACKNOWLEDGMENT

The authors want to thank Andrea Lowe, principal of LPEQ,[2] for her valuable comments on this chapter.

PART II

The Structure of Private Equity Investments

CHAPTER 5

The Syndication
of Private Equity

ANDY LOCKETT
Professor of Strategy and Entrepreneurship, Nottingham University Business School

MIGUEL MEULEMAN
Assistant Professor of Entrepreneurship, Vlerick Leuven Gent Management School and Research Associate, Centre for Management Buy-out Research, Nottingham University Business School

MIKE WRIGHT
Professor of Financial Studies, Centre for Management Buyout Research, Nottingham University Business School

INTRODUCTION

Private equity (PE) comprises equity held in enterprises that are not publicly traded, which includes early-stage "classic" venture capital (VC), expansion stage and later stage investments in management buyouts and buyins (MBO/Is) (Wright and Robbie 1998). PE firms may invest in enterprises either as a solo investor or in a syndicate with other PE firms. Syndicates are a form of interfirm alliance in which two or more PE firms co-invest in an investee firm and share a joint pay-off (Lerner 1994). Much of the literature on the syndication of PE investments has been developed focusing on only early-stage VC. After early contributions in the entrepreneurship literature by Bygrave (1987, 1988) and in the finance literature by Lerner (1994) and Admati and Pfleiderer (1994), there has been a more recent increase in interest in this area (Brander, Amit, and Antweiler 2002; Cumming 2005; De Clercq and Dimov 2007; Filatotchev, Wright, and Arberk 2006; Hochberg, Ljungqvist, and Lu 2007a; Wright and Lockett 2003).[1] Syndication, however, is also prevalent in the later, buyout stage of the PE industry, and arguably is becoming increasingly important in the move toward larger deals (Wright 2007). An overview of syndication in European private equity markets is provided in Exhibit 5.1. The data indicates that syndication is an enduring feature of the private equity markets, both in the United Kingdom and the rest of Europe, and also in the United Kingdom across both early and late-stage deals. Furthermore, the figures for 2007 suggest that the proportion of deals has increased to 42.9 percent for the United Kingdom and 37.7 percent for the rest of Europe across all private equity deals. Yet, to date

Exhibit 5.1   Overview Private Equity Market and Syndication

Year	U.K. Syndicated Private Equity Investments		U.K. Syndicated Buyout Investments		European Syndicated Private Equity Investments	
	% of No. of Private Equity Investments	No.	% of No. of Private Equity Investments	No.	% of No. of Private Equity Investments	No.
1993	46.3	800	36.28	78	48.4	2634
1994	46.6	910	29.94	97	42.3	2404
1995	41.8	716	31.01	111	40.6	2010
1996	34.4	589	32.23	126	39.2	2031
1997	21.1	355	22.05	97	22.5	1410
1998	17.1	345	16.14	66	23.2	1767
1999	27.0	671	27.37	101	32.1	3606
2000	13.1	259	26.80	78	29.5	3863
2001	13.6	281	16.29	43	28.7	3053
2002	26.5	661	15.02	32	27.9	2853
2003	36.7	921	16.13	35	23.2	2407
2004	10.5	577	21.21	56	20.8	2122
2005	12.3	560	19.63	53	25.0	2724
2006	22.5	682	13.33	40	30.1	3237
2007	42.9	705	16.72	54	37.7	3075

This table reports the frequency of syndication in the United Kingdom and Europe. Data for the U.K. syndicated private equity market and the European syndicated private equity market represents the overall private equity market including early stage investments. This data was collected through the yearbooks of the European Venture Capital Association. The percentages shown are calculated as the number of investments syndicated. Data for the extent of syndication in the U.K. syndicated buyout market were provided by the Centre for Management Buy-Out Research. The figures are calculated as the number of private-equity backed buyout investments syndicated.

there is limited analysis of syndication in the PE market as whole and in the buyout stage of the market in particular. Given that there are important differences in early- and late-stage PE investments, investors' syndication behavior may differ according to the stage of investment. For example, the risk and information aspects of early- and late-stage deals are quite distinct with potential different implications for the extent and nature of syndication. Early-stage ventures are generally much riskier and involve greater information asymmetries than later-stage enterprises that have established track records and markets. In addition, the composition of syndicates at the early-stage VC end of the market may change over the different investment rounds that are typical for this type of investment. In contrast, at the buyout end of the PE market, syndicates are more likely to be one off, unless major restructuring is required.

This chapter is a first attempt to redress this imbalance by focusing on syndication in the PE industry as a whole. Our focus on the syndication of PE investments is warranted, given the economic significance of later-stage buyout investments in comparison to early-stage VC investments in many economies. Outside the United States, PE industries are dominated by these buyout stage deals. In Europe, for example, buyout stage deals accounted for €58.3 billion or 79 percent of total amounts invested in 2007 (EVCA, 2008). We review the extant research into the syndication of PE, adopting a broad definition of PE that ranges from early to late-stage deals. We focus our discussion on theory and evidence in relation to the PE industry as a whole. Given the neglect of the later-stage buyout market from the majority of PE syndication studies, we highlight evidence relating to the later buyout stage of the market and compare these findings with those relating to early-stage VC where appropriate.

In the remainder of the chapter we structure our review around four major issues surrounding syndicates: motives for forming syndicates, partner selection, the structure and management of the syndicate and the impact of syndication on performance. Finally we conclude and outline an agenda for further research based on our review of the extant literature and five emerging themes in PE.

MOTIVES FOR SYNDICATION

In this section we examine the question: why do PE firms syndicate investments? As noted earlier, the vast majority of studies of syndication to date have focused on early-stage (or classical VC) investments only. However, we cannot simply assume that syndication behavior in the early- and late-stage segments of the market is the same. Below, we present the different motives for syndication that have been outlined in the PE literature, focusing on: risk sharing, risk reduction, and deal flow (Lockett and Wright 1999, 2001; Manigart, Lockett, Meuleman et al. 2006).

Risk Sharing

The risk associated with an investment portfolio may be reduced, without reducing expected returns, by constructing a well-diversified portfolio. By spreading finance across a greater number of investments that do not covary, syndication has the potential to reduce risk considerably (Markowitz 1952). Hence the variation in returns is reduced without lowering the expected return of the portfolio. A fully diversified portfolio is, however, difficult to obtain for PE firms when compared to institutional investors who invest in listed stock, because of the capital constraints arising from the size of a PE firm or fund (Sahlman 1990; Wright and Robbie 1998). Where the size of the investment is large relative to the size of a PE firm's available capital (i.e., accounts for a substantial proportion of a PE firm's available capital), syndication may be the only available investment strategy if the PE firm is not to unbalance its portfolio. The mean number of investors in buyout deals over a range of deal sizes is presented in Exhibit 5.2 and suggests a positive correlation between deal size and the average number of investors in a deal. Furthermore, syndication gives the PE firm the opportunity to invest in a larger number of portfolio companies than it could do without syndication, thereby increasing diversification and reducing the overall risk of the fund.

A second finance-related motive for syndication concerns the illiquidity of PE investments (Lockett and Wright 2001). Minimum investment periods make equity illiquid in the short to medium term. As a result, private equity cannot be continuously traded, unlike listed stock. Due to *ex-ante* informational asymmetry, the real risk of the investment may only be fully revealed once the investment

Exhibit 5.2   Deal Size and Average Number of Investors in the U.K. PE Market for MBO/MBIs

Size Deal	N	Mean	S. D.	Min.	Max.
<£5 million	1972	1.22	0.52	1	5
£5 million–£10 million	643	1.40	0.79	1	12
£10 million–£25 million	868	1.44	0.85	1	7
£25 million–£100 million	822	1.54	1.08	1	10
>£100 million	426	1.77	1.41	1	12

This table reports the average number of investors for different deal sizes. These data cover the U.K. PE market for MBO/MBIs over the period 1990 to 2007. Data for the average number of investors for the U.K. buyout market were provided by the Centre for Management Buy-Out Research.

has been made. If the risk associated with the investment turns out to be higher than anticipated, it may be difficult to adjust the portfolio by divesting because of the illiquid nature of the PE market. Syndication, therefore, provides a means of sharing risk on a deal-by-deal basis that may help to reduce overall portfolio risk.

Evidence from Manigart et al. (2006) and Lockett and Wright (2001), covering all forms of risk capital including early stage (classic venture capital), expansion, and late-stage (PE) in Europe, indicates that the risk-sharing motive is particularly important for PE firms. In addition, the need for firms to share risk via syndication is particularly acute for firms that are small, and hence are more exposed to the risk associated with individual investments (Manigart et al. 2006). All other things being equal, a smaller firm benefits more from syndication than a larger firm under the finance perspective, as this decreases the level of concentration in its portfolio.

Risk Reduction

Authors have argued that, in addition to risk sharing, syndication may enable PE investors to reduce company-specific risk both *ex ante* and *ex post*. *Ex-ante* decision making relates to the selection of investments, whereas *ex-post* decision making relates to the subsequent management of the investment.

Improved Deal Selection

Syndication may enable firms to make *ex-ante* better investment selection decisions. Given the potential agency problem that exists between the investor and investee, potentially leading to problems of adverse selection, syndication enables firms to work together when evaluating risky investment decisions. This position is supported by Sah and Stiglitz (1986) who contrast decision making in hierarchies and polyarchies: that is, settings in which projects are undertaken only if one of the parties thinks it worthwhile, and where it is necessary for both parties to approve. They show that it may be more efficient to undertake only those projects that are approved by both parties. Interestingly, empirical evidence using questionnaire data from Europe indicates that *ex-ante* risk reduction is not an important motivator for syndication behavior in the PE industry as a whole (Lockett and Wright 2001; Manigart et al. 2006), and may be especially of lower importance in larger deals that are also a proxy for later-stage buyout deals (Lockett and Wright 1999). Chiplin et al. (1997) in their study of syndication in the United Kingdom. PE market as a whole that used archival data found a weak relationship between risk reduction and syndication. Given the variance of this finding with evidence from the early-stage VC industry (Cumming 2006b; Lerner 1994), we suggest that this effect may be due to fundamental differences in the information available to PE investors as compared to VC investors. In the case of later stage deals, investors will be much better able to make an informed decision about the investment given the provision of information arising from the venture's history as compared to their early stage VC counterparts.

Value Added

Syndication may also enhance PE firms' ability to manage better their investments *ex post*. The need for specialist expertise in the *ex-post* management of portfolio companies can be met by the PE firm's own resource base, by outside industry specialists, or by syndicate partners. Consistent with the empirical evidence on the importance of *ex-ante* risk reduction, however, empirical evidence from the United Kingdom and continental Europe, covering the whole of the PE industry that is dominated by later-stage buyout deals, indicates that *ex-post* risk reduction is not an important motivator for PE firms to syndicate their investments (Lockett and Wright 2001; Manigart et al. 2006). As with *ex-ante* deal selection, we suggest these findings reflect the underlying nature of later stage PE investments as compared to VC investments.

Interestingly, the importance of risk reduction as a motivation for syndication is arguably increased in the context of cross-border PE syndicates involving later stage buyouts. In particular, Meuleman and Wright (2008c) argue that cross-border syndication involving PE-backed buyouts, rather than direct investment, will be related to the extent to which a host country lacks formal investor protection in its legal system. They show that, in an international context, PE firms are more likely to engage in cross-border syndicates when they have limited experience in investing overseas and also have limited experience of the country they are investing in. Their findings lend further support to both the *ex-ante* and *ex-post* arguments surrounding the risk reduction of deals. We return to a discussion of cross-border syndicates below.

Access to Deal Flow

Access to quality investment opportunities, via deal flow, is important for all PE firms. By syndicating out deals, a PE firm may create an expectation for recipro-cation in the future. If so, the PE firm may be invited to join other syndicates as a nonlead in the future, and deal flow is increased. The reciprocation of syndicated deals between firms means that deal flow can be maintained even when an indi-vidual firm may not be the originator of the deal (Boviard 1990). Further, empirical analyses demonstrate that the syndication networks in the VC industry diffuse in-formation about investment opportunities and, therefore, expand the geographical and industrial scope of investment opportunities a VC firm has access to. Venture capitalists that build central positions in the industry's syndication network invest more frequently in companies that are outside a firm's current geographical or industrial focus (Sorenson and Stuart 2001).

Multivariate analysis from the United Kingdom and continental Europe in-dicates that deal flow motives are considered more important for early-stage VC firms than for later buyout stage PE firms (Lockett and Wright 2001; Manigart et al. 2006). Arguably this result of reduced importance of deal flow motives for syndication in PE-backed buyouts is driven by the publicly available information about the companies, which makes the source of deals more transparent than in early-stage financing.

The access to deal-flow argument for buyout stage PE investors, however, is arguably more important in contexts where deal flow is less transparent in nature. For example, the privatization of state-owned enterprises and subsequent restruc-turings in many transition economies may offer interesting buyout investment opportunities for many PE firms (Wright, Kissane, and Burrows 2004). The prob-lem facing outside firms, however, is how they can get access to the appropriate networks to source such deals. One strategy for achieving this aim is to syndicate with experienced local firms who are better embedded in the local networks but which lack expertise in monitoring and internationalizing investees. We anticipate that such an approach may be particularly appropriate in a Chinese context (Wright 2007) as well as in Central and Eastern Europe, as enterprise in the more advanced countries in the transition process undergo postprivatization restructuring (Wright et al. 2004).

PARTNER SELECTION

There is a dearth of literature relating to syndicate partner selection in the context of the PE market as a whole and later-stage buyouts in particular. Much of the literature has focused on the early VC stage of the market, although some of the ideas are now being imported into and extended by the later-stage buyout part of the market. Managing a network of partners actively and expanding it by carefully selecting new partners is important for several reasons. First, firms with broader networks have access to a wider range of potential investments (Hochberg et al. 2007a; Sorenson and Wright 2001). Second, firms with more central network positions enjoy better financial returns (Hochberg et al. 2007a). Third, by syndicating deals, PE firms expect their partners to reciprocate the gesture in the future. As such, a broad co-investment network helps to assure access to future deal flow (Manigart et al. 2006). Fourth, as Milanov and Shepherd (2008) show for the U.S. venture capital industry, partner selection decisions in the early life of a venture capital organization have an enduring effect on its future network status because of imprinting. They show that a firm's initial partners' prominence has an enduring impact in shaping the firm's future status.

A first set of studies looking at partner selection decisions have highlighted desirable characteristics of potential partner firms, and there appear to be common-alities across different stages of the PE market. For example, Lerner's (1994) study of early-stage venture-capital firm behavior in the U.S. biotechnology industry showed that in first-round investments, established venture capital firms syndi-cate with one another, and in later rounds they syndicate with less-established organizations. These results are in line with theoretical predictions that experi-enced PE firms should syndicate with experienced venture capitalists (Casamatta and Haritchabalet 2003; Cestone, Lerner, and White 2006). Under certain circumstances, however, PE firms may choose to syndicate with less-experienced partners if the latter accumulate experience through syndication and are willing to pay for this (Tykvova 2007). In a study of the U.K. PE market as a whole, that is, covering early- through late-stage buyout investments, Lockett and Wright (2001) also identified the reputation of a potential partner as an important driver of partner firm selection. In particular, they found the reputation of the firm and individuals for being trustworthy, and positive past interactions with the firm and its personnel were important criteria for the selection of nonlead partners (Lockett and Wright 1999).

These studies have neglected symmetric mechanisms of partner selection, such as trust and social embeddedness, that induce interfirm collaboration. For example, using data on U.S. investment banking firms' syndication in underwriting corporate stock, Chung et al. (2000) show that previous syndicate relationships are one of the most important drivers of syndicate partner selection. In the context of venture capital and private equity, one important source of relationships is the formation of previous syndicates (Bygrave 1987; Hochberg, Ljungqvist, and Lu 2007b; Hochberg et al. 2007a; Meuleman, Manigart, Lockett, and Wright 2006; Sorenson and Stuart 2001). As a result, venture capital and private equity firms are bound by their current and past investments into a web of previous relationships.

In the context of partner selection, Meuleman et al. (2008b) show for the buyout stage of the U.K. private equity market that lead investors are more likely to select partners with complementary knowledge with respect to the industry of the underlying investment. Their results indicate that previous interfirm relationships are one of the most important drivers of partner selection decisions in syndicate arrangements. For example, figures from the buyout stage of the U.K. private equity market in the period 1993 to 2006 indicate that private equity firms had previous relationships with about 32 percent of their syndicate partners.[2] Exhibit 5.3 provides an overview of the number of different partners a private equity had worked with in the five years preceding the reported year. There is a

Exhibit 5.3 Average Number of Syndicate Partners in PE-Backed Buyouts, 1992–2006

Year	N	Mean	S. D.	Min.	Max.
1992	75	6.1	6.8	1	38
1993	75	6.5	7.3	1	40
1994	78	7.1	8.6	1	51
1995	81	7.3	8.7	1	50
1996	81	7.4	9.1	1	51
1997	83	7.2	8.6	1	48
1998	86	7.2	9.0	1	51
1999	87	7.3	9.1	1	52
2000	87	7.6	9.5	1	53
2001	87	7.8	9.7	1	56
2002	88	8.0	10.1	1	58
2003	87	8.2	10.2	1	58
2004	87	8.3	10.3	1	58
2005	86	8.5	10.4	1	59
2006	91	8.2	10.3	1	59

Source: CMBOR/Barclays Private Equity.

slight increase from about six partners in 1992 to eight partners in 2006. The standard deviation indicates that there is quite some heterogeneity among the firms in the sample. Whereas the minimum number of partners equals one, the maximum number of different partners equals fifty-nine.

Relying on previous relationships affects the nature of interaction and expectations between parties in three important ways: increased trust, enhanced information transfer, and joint problem-solving (Uzzi 1997). An important question, however, is when do private equity firms invite new partners in order to expand their network? Combining insights from agency theory and social embeddedness theory, Meuleman et al. (2008) show for the buyout stage of the U.K. private equity market that previous interfirm relationships are less important for partner selection decisions when: (1) potential agency problems at the level of the investee are less severe, and therefore, monitoring becomes less important; (2) when the lead investor has established a reputation for acting as a lead; and (3) when knowledge complementarities exist with potential syndicate partners. These results complement a recent study by Sorenson and Stuart (2008) that investigates the conditions under which early stage U.S. venture capital firms co-invest with partners distant in location and industry specialization. Their results show that lead venture capital firms are more likely to select syndicate partners if they are geographically proximate and if their investment profiles share common industry allocations. They show, however, that the probability that geographically and industry distant ties will form between venture capital firms increases with several attributes of the target-company investment setting: (1) the recent popularity of investing in the target firm's industry and home region, (2) the target company's maturity, (3) the size of the investment syndicate, and (4) the density of relationships among the other members of the syndicate. Creating a geographically and industry diverse system of trusted partners enables venture capitalists to participate in attractive, nonlocal opportunities (Sorenson and Stuart 2001).

Even though later stage PE investors are more likely to select partners with whom they have previous partner experience, previous partner experience is likely to be more important for early stage VC investments for several reasons. First, as early-stage investments involve more informational asymmetries, the role of the lead investor in screening and monitoring the investee will be more important. Further, the initial VC who asks the second opinion of a potential syndicate partner may incur a substantial cost. Disclosing the existence of an investment opportunity to another venture capitalist makes him a potential rival: He could compete with the initial venture capitalist to obtain exclusive financing of the project. From the point of view of the venture capitalist first informed of a new project, revealing the existence of the project creates the conditions for profit-dissipating competition (Casamatta and Haritchablet 2003). As investment opportunities for later stage buyout investments are more transparent, and often are subject to an auction, the role of trust and previous partner experience is likely to be more important in early stage VC investments. Second, whereas later stage buyout investments often involve only one investment round, early-stage VC investments frequently involve different rounds. When there are multiple investment rounds, the incumbent investors may be tempted to provide a false assessment of the project and propose a syndication contract to outside VCs even in case the incumbents have bad news. Hence, outside investors will fear that they are buying an overpriced claim

(Admati and Pfleiderer 1994; Cestone et al., 2006). Relying on a network of trusted partners is one important mechanism in order to resolve these incentive problems.

STRUCTURING AND MANAGING THE SYNDICATE

Traditionally, research has focused on the structure and management of a dyadic relationship between the investor and investee, the case of a classic vertical principal-agent relationship where there are clear and well-defined lines of authority (Mitchell, Reid, and Terry 1995; Wright and Robbie 1998). Agency problems can arise, however, in any situation involving cooperative effort by two or more parties (Jensen and Meckling 1976). In essence, the presence of multiple investors in syndicates creates additional agency problems for the management of investments. PE syndicates are an example of such a situation, where the sharing of formal decision making powers among the syndicate creates agency (or management) costs (Fried and Hisrich 1995). These costs are associated with mitigating the problems of agency (or management) risk. This creates the need to examine the structural and management mechanisms that PE firms use in syndications to mitigate these problems.

Equity Ownership Structure

Syndicates typically involve a lead investor and one or more nonlead investors, and the role of the firm in a syndicate will typically influence the ownership structure within the syndicate. The lead firm has the task of coordinating the syndicate and generally seeks a larger equity stake as a means of obtaining a greater return in recognition of this effort. The larger equity stake may also reflect the role of the lead in identifying the deal, that is, creating deal flow. In addition, the motive for syndicating the deal (see the second section, titled "Motives for Syndication") may be an important influence on the distribution of equity. As highlighted above, evidence from the United Kingdom and mainland Europe encompassing both early- and late-stage PE indicates that the risk reduction arguments are much less important for later stage PE deals (Lockett and Wright 1999, 2001). Furthermore, evidence comparing early- and late-stage firms in the United Kingdom suggests that risk sharing is the dominant motive for syndication. If risk sharing is the main motivation for syndication, the lead may have a larger equity stake, as they are the party bringing the most resources to the syndicate. Where risk reduction is more important, equity stakes may be more even, reflecting the provision of information by the nonlead in the selection/management of the syndicated deal.

The Investment Agreement

Given the distinction between the lead and nonlead roles in a PE syndicate, potential problems associated with access to information may be created. Without a specific agreement, the level and timeliness of information disclosure selected by the syndicate lead is not clear. It is for this reason that the syndicated investment agreement typically specifies the items to be disclosed and their timing. For example, where a syndicate member is not to have formal board representation, because of their small equity stake, rights of access to information will be specified. These rights may include board observer status or some other form of face-to-face investor liaison meeting that provides for access to management (Wright and Lockett 2003).

However, while the syndication agreement specifies the rights of the contracting parties, stipulation of behavior is more difficult. This is because it is not possible to write a complete contract due to the bounded rationality of economic agents (Hart 1995). Also, the drafting and enforcement of such contracts becomes prohibitively expensive (Al-Najjar 1995) and ineffective in getting parties to act in accordance with agreements (Charny 1990). Syndicates may also need to be dynamic should the project not perform to expectations (Gompers 1995). As a result, the syndication contract should be considered as a legal "backdrop" to the relationship between transacting parties (Das and Teng 1998). There is thus a distinction between the residual rights of control that are bestowed through ownership and the specific rights of control detailed in contracts (Grossman and Hart 1986; Hart 1995).

Contractual Enforcement

The problems associated with trying to anticipate future contingencies in drawing up the initial contract are well-documented (Hart 1995; Sahlman 1990). Furthermore, the contractual mechanisms that may be employed to enable contractual enforcement between syndicate partners may be problematic (Cestone et al. 2006). For example, Cumming (2005) has highlighted problems associated with the use of fractional contracts as a means of overcoming the agency problems associated with syndicated investments. Therefore, the problems associated with enforcing contracts through legal measures may mean that nonlegal sanctions are used extensively to get the parties to act in accordance with the terms of the investment agreement. In the case of syndicated PE investments, the transactions are not discrete and the interaction between the firms continues over a considerable period of time covering the life of different funds. Moreover, PE industries are typically close-knit communities, with a high degree of interconnectivity between firms (Chiplin et al. 1997). PE firms that fail to abide by the spirit of agreements risk damaging their reputation in an environment of repeat investing, making it very difficult for them to win competitions to be lead investor in the most attractive companies. Similarly, the role of a PE firm's reputation for acting in a cooperative manner may be very important in terms of partner selection, and hence the operation of syndicates.

Empirical evidence from the U.K. PE market as a whole has highlighted the importance of past interaction, reputation and investment style when a lead PE firm selects its nonlead partners (Lockett and Wright 1999). The threat of damage to firm and personal reputations for noncompliance suggests a greater incentive to conform to syndicated investment agreements than resorting to legal sanctions or the threat of future nonparticipation by other members in syndicating further deals. This is supported by evidence that the PE industry is characterized by a high degree of network connectivity (Chiplin et al. 1997; Meuleman et al. 2008b). Firms, therefore, can select alternative partners in subsequent deals if a partner firm does not act in a reputable manner.

Findings from the buyout stage of the U.K. PE market indicate that investments characterized by a high degree of agency risk are less likely to be syndicated by less reputable and less networked investors (Meuleman et al. 2008b). Given the agency costs associated with a syndicate arrangement, it will be more difficult for investors without a reputation to find potential partners to join a syndicate when *ex-post* monitoring of the investee is more important and hence nonlead investors have to rely more on the lead investor. These findings are consistent with recent evidence from the debt syndication market (Sufi 2006). Firms without an established reputation and without substantial network ties, therefore, may be limited with respect to the range of investments they are able to syndicate. Other investors will only join a syndicate with a lead investor that has not yet established a reputation when the latter's role is less important in overseeing the investee.

Monitoring of Investees

PE firms commonly perform both lead and nonlead roles across different investments, but will only play one role in a specific syndicate. However, the nature of the role performed (i.e., lead or nonlead) in an individual syndicate matters. While the investment agreement may specify rights of access to information, board membership rights, and so on, the type of information received and the nature of interaction with investees may differ according to whether a PE firm is a lead or nonlead.

Rights of access to information may be "specified" in the syndicated investment agreement. Information may be distinguished broadly into (1) accounting-based, (2) major event-based, or (3) management-based information. Accounting-based information includes monthly, half-yearly and annual accounts, forecasting and budgeting, management commentary on performance and debt repayment schedules. Second, major event-based information relates to significant events such as changes in management, acquisitions/disposals, and information relating to breach of covenants. Third, management-based information includes more commercially sensitive information such as order book levels and capital expenditure plans. Common across the range of PE investment stages, Mitchell et al. (1995) note the emphasis on demands for accounting information in the investment agreement and the articles of association of an investee company may typically also include powers for disclosure and approval of major events (Wright and Robbie 1998). This accounting-based and major event-based information tends to be available to all syndicate members (Wright and Lockett 2003).

In contrast to the provision of information, the nature of involvement between the investor and investee is influenced by the role the firm performs (i.e., lead or nonlead). Evidence from the PE market as a whole suggests that lead investors are more likely to be represented on the board, are more likely to have frequent formal and informal contact with the investee than nonlead investors (Wright and Lockett 2003). For example, when acting as a lead, they were on average likely to contact investees by post or telephone more frequently than every fortnight, whereas as nonleads the frequency of this form of contact was likely to be approximately monthly. With respect to formal board meetings, PE firms acting as lead investors were also likely on average to contact investees more frequently, approximately monthly, whereas as nonlead investors the average time was closer to quarterly, with the large standard deviation suggesting that some nonlead investors participated in monthly board meetings whereas for others it might be only six monthly.

Decision Making

Although the syndicate lead may select partners with whom they know they can work, the presence of multiple investors may create complications and delays in decision making. The lower the certainty of cooperation by other syndicate members, the greater the levels of relational (agency) risk and hence the associated agency (management) costs. Citron et al. (1997) show that syndication complicates and slows decision making in the related case of loan covenants between banks and MBOs. The origins of the agency (management) cost imposed by the syndicate may be created by the diverse objectives of members, which may become more apparent with larger numbers of partners. Evidence from the U.K. PE market as a whole indicates that large syndicates became more unusual in the early 1990s (Chiplin et al. 1997), perhaps for this very reason. Furthermore, with larger numbers of syndicate members it may be more difficult and time-consuming to renegotiate both the investment agreement and to take action with respect to problem investees (Wright and Lockett 2003). This problem may be exacerbated where some partners have changed their investment focus since the initial syndicate was formed, either because they face problems in their portfolios as a whole or because their fund is fully invested. Therefore, syndication is likely to increase the management costs associated with a PE investment.

Evidence from the U.K. PE market as a whole suggests that decision making within syndicates, all other things being equal, involves discussion and collective agreement. However, the residual rights of control bestowed by equity ownership are the most important factor in terms of power in timely decision making (Wright et al. 2003). The importance of residual rights over specific rights is highlighted by the fact that a dominant equity holder can force all other syndicate members to comply with their decisions if they own enough equity. Although a contract may stipulate other syndicate members' rights of consultation this does not necessarily mean that they will be able to influence the outcomes of decisions. An example of this is the use of the so-called "come-along letters," which enable a syndicate lead to communicate a decision to other nonlead members. Such letters may be used to force other investors to sell when the lead investor has received an offer for the investee. In a multiperiod world where the PE firm wishes to invest again with its syndicate partner, this approach may need to be used sparingly. Where a syndicate partner is uncomfortable with this arrangement, the right to consultation may be incorporated into the side letter.

SYNDICATION AND PERFORMANCE

Limited work has examined the performance effects of PE syndication. Studies have typically examined the performance of PE-backed firms and incorporated syndication measures as part of the estimation equation. Brander et al. (2002) show for the U.S. early-stage VC market that syndicated investments perform better than sole investments lending support to the value adding perspective. However, some studies that have used the early-stage VC firm as the level of analysis have found a negative impact of the extent of syndication on the overall performance of VC firms. For a sample of U.S.-based VC firms, De Clercq and Dimov (2007) illustrate the potentially detrimental effect of investment syndicates on fund performance resulting from reduced commitment and free riding on others' (i.e., co-investors') efforts. These results are in line with Cumming (2006a), who shows that the optimal portfolio size is smaller for investors who frequently rely on syndication because each VC must monitor other syndicated VC investors, and not just the entrepreneur.

Using deal level data from both early-stage VC and later-stage buyout PE investments in 39 countries, Cumming and Walz (2007) show that syndication significantly enhances returns, consistent with the view that syndication facilitates value-added investments. Cumming and Walz (2007) do not distinguish between early- and late-stage deals. In contrast, Meuleman et al. (2008a), using a sample of 238 private equity-backed divisional, family, and secondary buyouts in the United Kingdom completed between 1993 and 2003, find no effect of syndication on post-buyout efficiency and growth measures. The experience of the PE firm was, however, significantly positively related to investee performance.

Syndicated investments may provide higher returns because investors may collude and, hence, pay lower prices at the time of the investment. The emergence of mega-buyouts in the period 2006–2007 was accompanied by a resurgence in syndicated transactions, following a period when the major PE players funded quite large deals on their own. Although referred to as "club deals," these transactions are essentially the same as syndications. Club deals have increasingly received attention because of their potentially detrimental impact on the extent of competition, especially for larger deals (GAO 2008). Club deals may lead to the depression of acquisition prices by reducing the number of firms bidding for target companies. Conversely, others have argued that club deals may increase the number of potential buyers by enabling firms that could not individually bid for a target company to do so through a club. A recent report by the United States Government Accountability Office (GAO 2008) found no indication that public-to-private club deals in the United States over the period 1998 through 2007 were associated with lower premiums paid for target companies. This is consistent with Boone and Mulherin (2008), who find that public-to-private club deals in the United States over the period 2003 to 2007 are associated with significantly greater levels of takeover competition than other types of bidders. Officer et al. (2008), on the other hand, show, for a sample of U.S. public-to-private club deals, that acquisitions by clubs of PE-backed buyout acquirers are priced significantly lower than sole-sponsor PE transactions and non-PE merger and acquisition transactions, lending support to the collusion argument. The differences are economically large: target shareholders receive on the order of 10 percent less in club deals compared to sole-sponsor buyouts. They also show that high institutional ownership in the target firm mitigates the club deal effect, suggesting that sophisticated institutional investors are able to bargain effectively with clubs. These inconsistent results are potentially driven by different sample frames. For example, Officer et al. (2008) use a narrow sample frame that focuses on the transactions of leading private equity firms and, therefore, this study might not be representative of the entire population of public-to-private club deals.

THE FUTURE OF SYNDICATION RESEARCH

Our review of the literature on the syndication of PE indicates a general paucity of research that compares early- and late-stage syndication and that focuses on the buyout stage in particular. This lack of extant studies suggests several interesting avenues for future research.

There is a quite extensive body of evidence concerning the motives for syndication in general and between the early- and later-stage parts of the PE market, which we reviewed above. Similarly, our review indicates quite extensive research on partner selection for the early-stage VC end of the market. However, partner selection research for the later buyout stage is more limited. Further research needs to consider which partners PE firms select to join a syndicate, particular in respect of new, less familiar partners. Clearly, all other things being equal, there are obvious benefits for PE firms syndicating with firms with which they have established good working relationships in the past, that is, firms with which they are relationally embedded. However, if PE firms syndicated only with firms with which they are embedded, then their syndicate networks would remain static, limiting access to new knowledge. The potential paradox of relational embeddedness is an important area for future research. We suggest that future research should go beyond the current focus on the characteristics of the potential PE partner firm to incorporate consideration of how this decision is influenced by the nature and location of the underlying transaction. For example, under what conditions will firms syndicate with less (or non-) relationally embedded partners? Further detailed work is also needed on the stability of the composition of subsequent investment syndicates over time between PE firms and the factors that influence this stability.

The evidence we reviewed relating to the monitoring of syndicated PE investments has tended to focus on the market as a whole, with little distinction being made between early-stage VC investments and late-buyout stage investments. Given the different informational asymmetries expected between early- and late-stage deals, different monitoring approaches may arise. For example, do nonlead partners play a more important role in early-stage VC deals than in later stage buyout deals? If early-stage VC investors provide more specialist expertise, they may be expected also to become more involved in monitoring. Alternatively, even within the later stage part of the PE market, deals may be heterogeneous in their monitoring demands—for example, insider-driven MBOs may require less restructuring than outsider-driven MBIs, while divisional buyouts may need greater involvement by a syndicate of investors if they are to realize the apparently greater growth opportunities (Meuleman et al. 2008b).

Our review suggests that there is only limited research focusing on the issue of syndication and performance, and in particular, how syndicated deals perform relative to nonsyndicated deals. The evidence we have reviewed provides mixed results, and there is little comparative evidence on the different effects in early- versus late-stage buyout deals. A number of interesting questions remain, including: How is the performance of an investment influenced by the structure, composition, and purpose of an investment syndicate? Further research is needed that goes beyond simple dummy variables relating to whether a deal was syndicated or not to include measures of the expertise provided by the different partners in the syndicate in relation to the type of deal.

Emerging Themes in PE

In addition to the four areas we have reviewed in the main body of this paper, we have identified five important trends relating to the nature of syndicated PE deals at the buyout end of the PE spectrum. The five trends suggest important areas for further research: syndication clubs in large deals, distress cases, the interaction between debt and equity syndicates, cross-border syndication, and secondary buyouts.

Club Deals

Given the expected need for deals acquired in an auction to generate value through both efficiency gains and growth, club deals may bring together the diverse specialist skills required to restructure and regenerate a particular deal, as well as providing for the spreading of risk (Wright and Lockett 2003). For example, a generalist PE firm may link with a second firm with specialist technology skills. Limited partners seeking to diversify their investments in private equity may be concerned when the different funds in which they invest are part of the same syndicate to complete a particular deal. Despite the presence of "drag along" and similar provisions, noted earlier, coordination may be problematical when restructuring of distressed buyouts is required. Where these syndicates involve partners who are highly experienced players in the market, the potential for tensions when egos clash about strategy and restructuring seems clear.

Financial Distress

Empirical evidence relating to the financial distress of syndicates is limited. A notable exception is the work of Citron and Wright (2008) who, based on a sample of 57 U.K. buyouts that had entered the bankruptcy process, find that inefficiencies in syndicated debt results in significantly lower secured creditor recovery rates, but that in such cases the senior secured lender gains at the expense of other secured creditors. Citron and Wright, however, do not examine the role PE investors in this process. We suggest that research is required to examine governance in syndicated private equity transactions, particularly in underperforming and distressed cases. Interesting questions here would relate to how syndication affects the investor recovery process.

Interaction between Debt and Equity

Much of the attention in PE syndication research has focused upon syndication between PE firms. In VC deals, investors are principally VC firms. However, in buyouts, debt providers also play an important role. There are few studies of the links between PE and (subordinated and senior) debt providers in buyouts (Cotter and Peck 2001). Further work is required that analyzes this vertical aspect of syndication, for example, to examine patterns of (repeat) syndication, the influence of reputation effects on the nature and success of different syndications, differences in the financial terms in different syndications and their association with deal outturn, the nature of incentives for private equity and lender executives, and coordination of restructurings in case of distress.

Cross-Border Syndicates

The literature relating to syndication of VC investments has analyzed the nature of syndicates involving combinations of foreign and domestic VC firms. For example, Mäkelä and Maula (2006a) examine the role of local venture capital firms in attracting foreign venture capital investors, while Mäkelä and Maula (2006b) look at the antecedents of venture capitalists' commitment to portfolio firms in cross-border syndicates. Further, Güler and McGahan (2007) examines whether VC syndication varies in its effectiveness based on the institutional context. Their findings indicate that the number of investors in the syndicates for non-U.S. ventures is larger if intellectual property protection in the region of the entrepreneurial venture is relatively strong. Such analysis is absent from the PE literature, which is surprising given that cross-border syndication in the buyout end of the PE market is extensive. For example, during the period 1991 to 2006, almost 50 percent of the international investments by U.K. PE investors were syndicated. Yet, the percentage of deals syndicated by U.K. PE investors varies across European countries (Exhibit 5.4). Further research could also usefully compare the nature of foreign-domestic VC and PE syndicates.

As syndication might be used to reduce the extent of uncertainty when entering a country, one would expect less syndication activity the more experience U.K. PE investors gain with a certain country. Even though increased levels of experience seem to reduce the extent of syndication, cross-border syndication activity remains relatively large (Meuleman et al. 2008c). For example, the extent of syndication in

Exhibit 5.4   Syndication by U.K. PE Firms in Different European Countries, 1991–2006

Country	Sole Investment	Syndication	Total
Austria	5	8	13
	38.46%	61.54%	100
Belgium	18	17	35
	51.43%	48.57%	100
Denmark	8	6	14
	57.14%	42.86%	100
Finland	9	12	21
	42.86%	57.14%	100
France	199	220	419
	47.49%	52.51%	100
Germany	162	86	248
	65.32%	34.68%	100
Ireland	22	18	40
	55%	45%	100
Italy	59	50	109
	54.13%	45.87%	100
Netherlands	31	52	83
	37.35%	62.65%	100
Norway	3	0	3
	100%	0%	100
Portugal	3	2	5
	60%	40%	100
Spain	69	61	130
	53.08%	46.92%	100
Sweden	25	24	49
	51.02%	48.98%	100
Switzerland	26	16	42
	61.9%	38.1%	100
Eastern Europe	7	4	11
	63.64%	36.36%	100

Source: CMBOR/Barclays Private Equity/Deloitte.

the French market is still relatively high. One reason for this might be that France is still considered a challenging destination from a legal and cultural perspective. Contrary to France, in Eastern Europe, which is relatively new for U.K. PE investors, only 36 percent of the deals are syndicated. One potential reason for this finding is that those investors who enter relatively new markets have already gained experience in other countries and, therefore, feel more confident to invest alone. However, an increasing number of U.K. PE firms have local offices in Continental European countries staffed with local partners, which reduces the need to rely on domestic PE players through syndication; moreover, there is relatively little local private equity capacity. These stylized facts about the extent of cross-border PE syndication raise a number of research issues that have yet to be addressed. In particular, while there has been recent theoretical development concerning the resource-related rationales for different foreign entry modes in general (Meyer, Wright, and Pruthi 2008), there is an absence of empirical work that examines the extent to which PE firms seek to exploit or augment their resources when they syndicate with domestic PE firms in a foreign country. The relative importance of resource exploitation or augmentation may vary between different PE firms, different PE markets and different investees but at present systematic understanding is limited.

Cross-border syndication may pose particular issues if deals become distressed. Distress regimes vary across institutional environments (Armour and Cumming 2006). As private equity firms internationalize, different distress regimes may impact both where they undertake deals but also the returns they and the debt providers who invest alongside them earn. Research is thus warranted in an international context that examines distress costs in failed private equity transactions and how these are particularly dealt with in cross-border syndications.

Secondary Buyouts

A further significant development in the buyout end of the PE market concerns secondary buyouts, in which initial PE investors exit either fully or partially, and are replaced by a new set of investors. These transactions, which have accounted for some of the largest transactions in Europe (www.nottingham.ac.uk/business/cmbor), raise a number of interesting issues surrounding syndication. First, there is a need to analyze the extent to which there are exits by only some members of a syndicate who are replaced by new financial and/or strategic investors or whether there is a complete change in the set of investors. Second, there is a need to analyze the rationale for different types of changes. Third, how are new syndicate members selected and how does this differ from the selection process for first time buyouts? Fourth, how do the mechanisms for coordinating syndicates change between the first and second buyout?

NOTES

1. The seminal contribution of Admati and Pfleiderer (1994) has been subject to debate. In particular, Cumming (2005) demonstrates a number of problems associated with Admati and Pfleiderer's (1994) contractual solution to the agency problems of syndication.

2. These figures are calculated from data provided by the Centre for Management Buyout Research at the University of Nottingham. Previous interfirm relationships were measured in the five years preceding the investment.

REFERENCES

Admati, Anat R., and Paul Pfleiderer. 1994. Robust financial contracting and the role of venture capitalists. *Journal of Finance* 49 (2):371–402.

Al-Najjar, Nabli I. 1995. Incomplete contracts and the governance of complex contractual relationships. *American Economic Review: Papers and Proceedings* 85 (2):432–436.

Armour, John, and Douglas J. Cumming. 2006. The legislative road to Silicon Valley. *Oxford Economic Papers* 58:596–635.

Boone, Andra L., and J. Harold Mulherin. 2008. Do private equity consortiums impede takeover competition? AFA 2009 San Francisco Meetings Paper.

Boviard, Chris. 1990. *Introduction to venture capital finance*. London: Pitman.

Brander, James A., Raphael Amit, and Wener Antweiler. 2002. Venture capital syndication: Improved venture selection vs. the value-added hypothesis. *Journal of Economics & Management Strategy* 11 (3):422–451.

Bygrave, William D. 1987. Syndicated investments by venture capital firms: A networking perspective. *Journal of Business Venturing* 2:139.

Bygrave, William D. 1988. The structure of the investment networks of venture capital firms. *Journal of Business Venturing* 3 (2):137–157.

Casamatta, Catherine, and Carole Haritchabalet. 2003. Learning and syndication in venture capital investments. CEPR Discussion Paper, 3867.

Cestone, Giacinta, Joshua Lerner, and Lucy White. 2006. The design of syndicates in venture capital. Working Paper.

Charny, David. 1990. Nonlegal sanctions in commercial relationships. *Harvard Law Review* 104:375–467.

Chiplin, Bran, Ken Robbie, and Mike Wright. 1997. *The syndication of venture capital deals: buyouts and buyins*. Wellesley, MA: Babson College.

Chung, S., Andy, Harbir Singh, and Kyungmook Lee. 2000. Complementarity, status similarity and social capital as drivers of alliance formation. *Strategic Management Journal* 21:1–22.

Citron, David, and Mike Wright. 2008. Credit recovery rates of secured creditors in management buyouts in distress. *Accounting and Business Research*, forthcoming.

Cotter, James F., and Sarah W. Peck. 2001. The structure of debt and active equity investors: The case of the buyout specialist. *Journal of Financial Economics* 59:101–147.

Cumming, Douglas J. 2005. Agency costs, institutions, learning, and taxation in venture capital contracting. *Journal of Business Venturing* 20 (5):573–622.

Cumming, Douglas J. 2006a. The determinants of venture capital portfolio size: Empirical evidence. *Journal of Business* 79 (3):1083–1126.

Cumming, Douglas J. 2006b. Adverse selection and capital structure: Evidence from venture capital. *Entrepreneurship: Theory & Practice* 30 (2):155–183.

Cumming, Douglas J., and Udo Walz. 2007. Private equity returns and disclosure around the world. *Journal of International Business Studies*, forthcoming.

Das, T. K., and Bing-Shen Teng. 1998. Between trust and control: Developing confidence in partner cooperation in alliances. *Academy of Management Review* 23 (3):491.

De Clercq, Dirk, and Dimo P. Dimov. 2007. Internal knowledge development and external knowledge access in venture capital investment performance. *Journal of Management Studies* 45 (3):585–612.

EVCA. 2008. *The EVCA yearbook*. The Hague: VUGA.

Filatotchev, Igor, Mike Wright, and Mufit Arberk. 2006. Venture capitalists, syndication and governance in initial public offerings. *Small Business Economics* 26:337–350.

Fried, Vance H., and Robert D. Hisrich. 1995. The venture capitalist: A relationship investor. *California Management Review* 37 (2):101–113.

GAO. 2008. Private equity: Recent growth in leveraged buyouts exposed risks that warrant continued attention. GAO-08-885.

Gompers, Paul A. 1995. Optimal investment, monitoring and the staging of venture capital. *Journal of Finance* 50 (5):1461–1489.

Grossman, Sanford J., and Oliver Hart. 1986. The costs and benefits of ownership: A theory of vertical and lateral integration. *Journal of Political Economy* 94 (4):691–719.

Güler, Isin, and Anita M. McGahan. 2007. The more the merrier? Institutions and syndication size in international venture capital investments. Working Paper.

Hart, Oliver. 1995. *Firms, contracts, and financial structure*. New York: Oxford University Press.

Hochberg, Yael, Alexander Ljungqvist, and Yang Lu. 2007a. Whom you know matters: Venture capital networks and investment performance. *Journal of Finance* 62 (1):251–301.

Hochberg, Yael., Alexander Ljungqvist, and Yang Lu. 2007b. Networking as a barrier to entry and the competitive supply of venture capital. *SSRN.*

Jensen, Michael C., and William H. Meckling. 1976. Theory of the firm: Managerial behavior, agency costs and ownership structure. *Journal of Financial Economics* 3 (4):305–360.

Lerner, Joshua. 1994. The syndication of venture capital investments. *Financial Management* 23 (3):16–27.

Lockett, Andy, and Mike Wright. 1999. The syndication of private equity: evidence from the U.K. *Venture Capital* 1 (4):303.

Lockett, Andy, and Mike Wright. 2001. The syndication of venture capital investments. *Omega* 29 (5):375–389.

Mäkelä, Markus, and Markku Maula. 2006a. Attracting cross-border venture capital: The role of a local investor. Working Paper.

Mäkelä, Markus, and Markku Maula. 2006b. Interorganizational commitment in syndicated cross-border venture capital investments. *Entrepreneurship: Theory & Practice* 30 (2):273–298.

Manigart, Sophie, Andy Lockett, Miguel Meuleman, Mike Wright, Hans Bruining, Hans Landstrom, H., Philppes Desbrieres, and Ulrich Hommel. 2006. The syndication decision of venture capital investments. *Entrepreneurship: Theory & Practice* 30 (2):131–153.

Markowitz, Harry. 1952. Portfolio selection. *Journal of Finance* 7:77–91.

Meuleman, Miguel, Kevin Amess, Mike Wright, and Louise Scholes. 2008a. Agency, strategic entrepreneurship and the performance of private equity backed buyouts. *Entrepreneurship: Theory & Practice*, forthcoming.

Meuleman, Miguel, Sophie Manigart, Andy Lockett, and Mike Wright. 2006. Working with unfamiliar partners: Relational embeddedness and partner selection in private equity syndicates. Working Paper.

Meuleman, Miguel, and Mike Wright. 2008c. Determinants of cross-border syndication: Cultural barriers, legal context and learning. Working Paper.

Meyer, Klaus, Mike Wright, and Sarika Pruthi. 2008. Managing knowledge in foreign entry strategies: A resource-based analysis. *Strategic Management Journal*, forthcoming.

Milanov, Hana, and Dean Shepherd. 2008. One is known by the company one keeps: Imprinting effects of a firm's network entry on its future status. *Frontiers of Entrepreneurship Research*. This paper is available online at ssrn.com/abstract=1346086.

Mitchell, Falconer, Gavin Reid, and Nicholas Terry. 1995. Post investment demand for accounting information by venture capitalists. *Accounting and Business Research* 25: 186–196.

Officer, Micha S., Oguzhan Ozbas, and Berk Sensoy. 2008. Club deals in leveraged buyouts. Working Paper.

Sah, Raaj Jumar, and Joseph E. Stiglitz. 1986. The architecture of economic systems: Hierarchies and polyarchies. *American Economic Review* 76 (4):716–727.

Sahlman, William A. 1990. The structure and governance of venture-capital organizations. *Journal of Financial Economics* 27 (2):473–521.

Sorenson, Olav, and Toby E. Stuart. 2001. Syndication networks and the spatial distribution of venture capital investments. *American Journal of Sociology* 106 (6):1546–1588.

Sorenson, Olav, and Toby E. Stuart. 2008. Bringing the context back. In Settings and the search for syndicate partners in venture capital investment networks. *Administrative Science Quarterly* 53:266–298.

Sufi, Amir. 2006. Information asymmetry and financing arrangements: Evidence from syndicated loans. *Journal of Finance* 62 (2):629–668.

Tykvova, Tereza. 2007. Who chooses whom? Syndication, skills and reputation. *Review of Financial Economics* 16 (1):5–28.

Uzzi, Brian. 1997. Social structure and competition in interfirm networks: The paradox of embeddedness. *Administrative Science Quarterly* 42 (1):35–67.

Wright, Mike, and Ken Robbie. 1998. Venture capital and private equity: A review and synthesis. *Journal of Business Finance & Accounting* 25 (5-6):521–570.

Wright, Mike, and Andy Lockett. 2003. The structure and management of alliances: Syndication in the venture capital industry. *Journal of Management Studies* 40 (8):2073–2102.

Wright, Mike, Jonathan Kissane, and Andrew Burrows. 2004. Private equity and EU accession by CEE countries. *Journal of Private Equity* 7 (3):32–46.

Wright, Mike. 2007. Venture capital in China: A view from Europe. *Asia Pacific Journal of Management*, forthcoming.

ABOUT THE AUTHORS

Andy Lockett received his Ph.D. from the University of Nottingham, where he now teaches in the Masters and Ph.D. Program as well serving as the Director of the Ph.D. Program. He has published widely on a range of issues in the domains of strategy and entrepreneurship.

Miguel Meuleman received his Ph.D. from Gent University. He is currently teaching in the field of entrepreneurship and is involved in several research projects on venture capital and private equity. He has published in journals such as *Entrepreneurship Theory and Practice* and *Journal of Business, Finance and Accounting*. He is also the author of a book on entrepreneurial finance.

Mike Wright received his Ph.D. from the University of Nottingham and is the recipient of an honorary doctorate from the University of Ghent. He is Director of the Centre for Management Buy-out Research (CMBOR), the first center for the study of private equity and buyouts, which he founded in 1986. He was Research Director of NUBS from 1991 to 2001. He has published widely on academic entrepreneurship, venture capital, private equity, and related topics in journals such as *Academy of Management Review, Academy of Management Journal, Strategic Management Journal, Journal of Corporate Finance, Review of Economics and Statistics, Economic Journal, Journal of Management Studies, Journal of Management, Journal of International Business Studies,* and *Journal of Business Venturing*. He was an editor of *Journal of Management Studies* from 2003 to 2008 and was ranked number one worldwide for publications in academic entrepreneurship during 1981 to 2005. His latest books include *Academic Entrepreneurship in Europe* (2007, with Clarysse, Mustar, and Lockett), *Private Equity and Management Buyouts* (2008, with Bruining) and *Private Equity Demystified* (2008, with Gilligan).

CHAPTER 6

The Structure of Venture Capital and Private Equity Fund Portfolios

GENNARO BERNILE
Assistant Professor, School of Business, University of Miami

DOUGLAS CUMMING
Associate Professor and Entrepreneurship and Ontario Research Chair,
Schulich School of Business, York University

EVGENY LYANDRES
Assistant Professor, School of Management, Boston University

WHY THE STRUCTURE OF VENTURE CAPITALISTS' PORTFOLIOS MATTERS

Venture capital provides an opportunity for young, innovative firms to develop and grow. Unlike most investors, venture capitalists (VCs) are actively involved in the management of their portfolio companies. VCs provide assistance with strategic and operational planning, management recruitment, marketing, and obtaining additional capital.[1] However, the relationship between VCs and entrepreneurs is characterized by a double-sided moral hazard because in most cases the parties' effort levels are unobservable and nonverifiable. This makes writing contracts based on the parties' effort levels difficult, if not impossible.

Alternatively, an optimally designed VC portfolio structure that recognizes the underlying moral hazard problem may align the interests of VCs and entrepreneurs without explicitly governing the parties' effort levels.[2] Two basic features of a VC's portfolio structure are the size of the portfolio (i.e., the number of firms a VC finances and advises) and the profit-sharing rule (i.e., how profits are divided between the VC and entrepreneurs).

Investing in multiple ventures, as opposed to a single project, allows a VC to make the best use of her funds, while reducing the risk of her investment. However, because the VC invests time and effort in advising her portfolio firms, increasing the size of the portfolio dilutes the quantity and quality of her managerial advice to each entrepreneurial venture. For example, Cumming and Walz (2008) find that

93

VC portfolio size, defined as the ratio of the number of firms in a fund to the number of fund's general partners, is negatively related to internal rate of return on fund's investments.

On one hand, because the number of experts is limited, the human capital necessary to fulfill a VC's mission is not easily scalable. Hence, the larger the number of ventures financed and advised by a VC, the lower the amount and/or quality of advice provided to each venture. If entrepreneurs' and a VC's efforts are complementary, reduced VC's advice may also lead to a lower commitment of the entrepreneurs to their ventures. On the other hand, if a VC's wealth is unconstrained, investing in more ventures increases the expected total dollar return of her portfolio. Ultimately, the choice of the optimal portfolio size hinges on the trade-off between the number of projects and each project's expected value net of the cost of the VC's effort devoted to it. Furthermore, given the size of the portfolio, the optimal profit-sharing rule trades off each project's expected value, which is a function of the entrepreneur's effort level among other things, and the VC's share of the project.

The literature on the optimal size and composition of VCs' portfolios is rapidly developing. Kanniainen and Keuschnigg (2003, 2004) provide seminal theoretical analysis of the optimal size of VCs' portfolios, while abstracting from the optimal profit-sharing rule problem. Fulghieri and Sevilir's (2004) model analyzes VCs' incentives to concentrate on a single venture versus investing in two ventures. Cumming (2006) provides an empirical analysis of VCs' portfolio size using a Canadian dataset, whereas Kaplan and Strömberg (2003) and Hege, Palomino, and Schwienbacher (2003) provide evidence on the allocation of cash flows between VCs and entrepreneurs.

In our model, the VC chooses both the number of firms in her portfolio and the shares of the ventures' profits that the entrepreneurs retain. Both the portfolio size and profit-sharing rule affect the optimal effort levels exerted by the VC and the entrepreneurs, which, in turn, determine the expected value of each entrepreneurial venture and, thus, of the portfolio. We show that one should account for the inherent endogeneity of the profit-sharing rule and the portfolio size when empirically examining the relations between portfolio structure and the VC's, entrepreneurs', and projects' characteristics.

To test the predictions of the model we obtained comprehensive data for 42 generalist venture capital and private equity funds based in Europe and North America through a survey and follow-up phone interviews conducted in 2004.[3] While the data do not support every specific detail of the model, the evidence is consistent with the notion that the VC's portfolio size and the profit-sharing rule are determined jointly.

OPTIMAL EFFORT LEVELS

Consider a single venture capitalist who advises multiple risky entrepreneurial ventures and provides them with one round of financing. The likelihood of each venture's success depends on the effort exerted by the entrepreneur, the effort (the amount of advice to the venture) exerted by the VC, the productivity (quality) of the entrepreneur, and that of the VC. Although the VC's and entrepreneur's efforts affect the likelihood of a project's success, they are not verifiable and, thus, not contractible.

Initially, the VC chooses the number of projects to finance, which we denote by n, and the profit share in each venture offered to entrepreneurs, which we denote by x. Then she makes an irreversible investment in each project and makes a take-it-or-leave-it (TIOLI) offer to each entrepreneur, specifying the share of the profits she retains in exchange for her investment and future advice $(1 - x)$.

Assuming that the entrepreneurs' reservation utility is zero, each entrepreneur accepts the TIOLI offer as long as it leaves him with a positive profit share.[4]

After accepting the VC's offer, the entrepreneurs and the VC choose their nonverifiable effort levels. Effort, however, is costly, and we assume that the entrepreneur's private total and marginal costs are increasing in his effort level (i.e., it becomes increasingly costly to exert each additional unit of effort). Moreover, both the total and marginal costs of effort are assumed to be increasing in an entrepreneur's "disutility of effort." Similarly, total and marginal costs of effort of the VC are increasing in the total amount of advice provided to the projects. Moreover, because of "coordination costs," total and marginal costs of the VC's efforts are increasing in the number of firms she invests in. The cost of the VC's effort, the contribution of the marginal unit of effort to the total cost of effort, and the coordination costs are increasing in the VC's disutility of effort. The VC and entrepreneurs maximize the expected values of their respective shares of the projects net of effort costs, given the sharing rule, x, and the size of the VC's portfolio, n.

In what follows, we describe the intuition underlying the subgame perfect equilibrium outcome of the model. In the second stage of the game, n entrepreneurs and the VC maximize their expected values, net of effort costs, with respect to their own effort levels, given the size of the VC's portfolio and the profit-sharing rule. In the first stage, the VC chooses the number of portfolio companies and the profit shares given to the entrepreneurs, while accounting for her own and entrepreneurs' second-stage optimal effort levels choices. Intuitively, the results of the analysis presented below depend on whether entrepreneurs' and the VC's efforts are complementary, that is, whether an increase in one party's effort raises the net marginal benefit of the other party's effort. We start by describing the effects of VC portfolio size on optimal VC's and entrepreneurs' effort levels:

Result 1: *For any given profit-sharing rule, the VC's equilibrium effort devoted to each project is decreasing in the number of firms in her portfolio. If there are no complementarities between entrepreneurs' and VC's efforts, then the equilibrium effort level of each entrepreneur is independent of the number of portfolio firms. If efforts are complementary, then each entrepreneur's equilibrium effort level decreases with portfolio size.*

We illustrate the relation between the optimal effort of the VC and entrepreneurs, and the number of portfolio firms in Exhibit 6.1.

Exhibit 6.1a describes the case of "no complementarities" between entrepreneurs' and VC's efforts, while Exhibit 6.1b presents the case of "complementary efforts." Increasing the number of portfolio firms stretches the VC's effort over more projects. If, as we assumed, the marginal cost of effort is increasing in n, then the optimal level of the VC's advice to each firm decreases as n increases. In

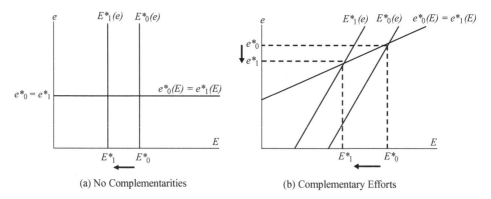

(a) No Complementarities   (b) Complementary Efforts

Exhibit 6.1   The Effects of a Change in Portfolio Size on Equilibrium Effort Levels
This figure presents the best response functions in terms of their optimal effort levels of the VC (entrepreneur) before an increase in n, $E^*_0(e)(e^*_0(E))$ respectively, and after the increase in n, $E^*_1(e)(e^*_1(E))$. $E^*_0(e^*_0)$ and $E^*_1(e^*_1)$ are the resulting VC's (entrepreneur's) equilibrium efforts before and after the change in n.

addition, if the entrepreneurs' and VC's efforts are complementary, reduced advice by the VC induces entrepreneurs to optimally exert less effort. This latter effect, in turn, reinforces the VC's incentive to exert less effort. Therefore, the direct and indirect effects of a change in n on the effort levels of the entrepreneurs and the VC are reinforcing. The indirect effect is zero in the absence of complementarities, in which case the optimal effort of a typical entrepreneur is not affected by n.

The next result describes the relation between the VC's and entrepreneurs' equilibrium effort levels and the profit share offered to the entrepreneurs.

> Result 2:
> 1. *If the VC's and entrepreneurs' efforts are not complementary, then, for any given portfolio size, the equilibrium effort level of each entrepreneur is increasing in the profit share given to entrepreneurs, x, and the equilibrium effort of the VC devoted to each project is decreasing in entrepreneurs' profit share.*
> 2. *If the VC's and entrepreneurs' efforts are complementary, then, for any given portfolio size, the entrepreneurs' and the VC's equilibrium efforts do not vary monotonically with the profit share given to entrepreneurs, x. For high x, both the VC's and entrepreneurs' equilibrium efforts are decreasing in x. For low x, both the VC's and entrepreneurs' efforts are increasing in x.*

Entrepreneurs' profit share has a direct and, in the case of complementarity, an indirect effect on VC's and entrepreneurs' optimal effort levels. The direct effect of an increase in x is the reduced (increased) incentive of the VC (entrepreneurs) to exert effort for any given effort level of the entrepreneurs (VC). If the entrepreneurs' and VC's efforts are complementary, then there is also an indirect effect of increasing x. Increased entrepreneurial effort raises the expected value of each venture, given the VC's level of effort, thus increasing the VC's net marginal benefit of exerting effort. Because the two effects have opposite implications for the equilibrium VC's effort level, the sign of the relation between the VC's optimal effort and x depends on their relative magnitude. The same discussion applies, of course, to entrepreneurs' effort levels, which are affected by x directly and indirectly (through the change in the optimal VC's effort).

We illustrate the two parts of Result 2 in Exhibit 6.2.

Exhibit 6.2a presents the case of "no complementarities," while Exhibits 6.2b and 6.2c describe the case in which efforts are complementary for the cases of high x and low y, respectively. If efforts are complementary and the profit share of a typical entrepreneur is close to one, a further increase in x does not (directly) increase the entrepreneur's effort enough to offset the indirect negative effect of reduced VC's effort. Hence, as x approaches one, the indirect effect more than offsets the direct effect and, thus, the net effect on both VC's and entrepreneurs' effort levels is negative. Conversely, when x is close to zero, the direct negative effect of increasing x on the optimal VC's effort level is more than offset by the indirect positive effect of increased entrepreneur's effort. Hence, as x approaches zero, both the entrepreneurs' and the VC's effort levels are increasing in x.

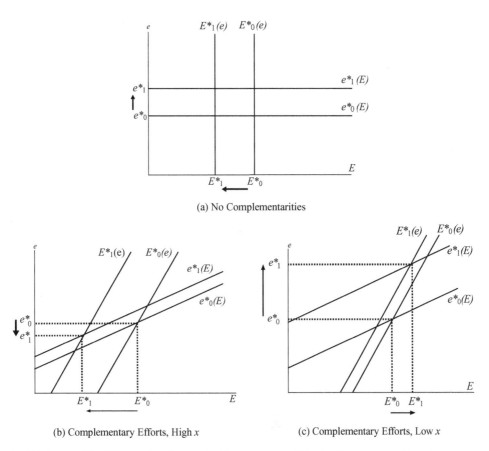

Exhibit 6.2 The Effect of a Change in Entrepreneurs' Profit Share on the Best Response Functions and the Resulting Equilibrium Effort Levels

This figure presents the best response functions in terms of their optimal effort levels of the VC (entrepreneur) before an increase in x, $E^*_0(e)(e^*_1(E))$ respectively, and after the increase in x, $E^*_1(e)(e^*_0(E))$. $E^*_0(e^*_0)$ and $E^*_1(e^*_1)$ are the resulting VC's (entrepreneur's) equilibrium efforts before and after the change in x.

The next result summarizes the effect of changes in the qualities (productivities) of the VC and entrepreneurs, their disutilities of effort, projects' profitability, and the required initial investment in each venture on the optimal level of the entrepreneurs' and VC's efforts.

> Result 3: *For any given VC portfolio structure (portfolio size and profit-sharing rule), the equilibrium effort level of each entrepreneur and the equilibrium effort devoted to each project by the VC are: increasing in each party's own productivity; decreasing in each party's own disutility of effort; increasing in the value of a successful project; and independent of the required investment. Moreover, if the VC's and entrepreneurs' efforts are complementary, then their equilibrium effort levels are increasing in the counterparty's productivity and are decreasing in the counterparty's disutility of effort.*

This result is rather intuitive. The VC's and entrepreneurs' efforts are increasing (decreasing) in the value of a successful project and in their own quality (disutility of effort) because of the trade-off between the marginal costs and benefits of exerting effort. If efforts are complementary, the same logic holds for the VC's and entrepreneurs' counterparty's quality and disutility of effort. In the absence of complementarities, each party's effort level is independent of the counterparty's characteristics. The equilibrium effort levels do not depend on the cost of initial investment because in the effort choice stage this investment is a sunk cost.

OPTIMAL PORTFOLIO SIZE AND PROFIT-SHARING RULE

In what follows, we discuss the first stage of the game, where the size of a VC's portfolio and the profit-sharing rule are determined. First, we analyze how the VC chooses the optimal number of projects to invest in when the profit-sharing rule is predetermined. This allows us to derive the partial effects of the VC's, entrepreneurs', and projects' characteristics on the optimal portfolio size. Then, we perform a similar analysis for the profit-sharing rule—that is, we examine the effect of the VC's, entrepreneurs', and projects' attributes on the optimal profit-sharing rule when the portfolio size is fixed.

> Result 4: *The optimal number of firms in the VC's portfolio does not vary monotonically with the profit share given to entrepreneurs, even x. For low x, the optimal portfolio size is increasing in x. For high x, the optimal portfolio size is decreasing in x. Moreover, holding x constant, the optimal portfolio size is: increasing in the quality of entrepreneurs; independent of the quality of the VC; decreasing in the disutilities of effort of the entrepreneurs and the VC; increasing in the value of a successful project; and decreasing in the required investment in each project.*

The direct effect of increasing entrepreneurs' profit shares on the value of the VC's portfolio is negative. In addition, increasing x reduces the optimal VC's per-project effort level, which further reduces the expected value of each project. However, it also increases the optimal entrepreneurs' efforts, increasing the value of the VC's portfolio. The VC's optimal reaction to the change in x in terms of portfolio size may take two forms. The VC can invest in fewer projects and increase her level of advice to each venture, thus increasing each project's value. Alternatively, the VC can decide to invest in a larger number of ventures, possibly increasing the total value of her portfolio. Which of these two alternatives is optimal depends on the profit shares retained by the entrepreneurs. For large x, the positive (indirect) effect of decreasing n on the VC's expected profits through her increased effort level is larger in magnitude than the negative (direct) effect of the reduced number of projects. However, for low enough x, the reverse is true: the positive direct effect of increasing n dominates the negative indirect effect.

Rather intuitively, optimal portfolio size is positively related to the profitability of each venture. Because higher quality of entrepreneurs, lower disutility of the parties' efforts, higher value of a successful project, and lower required initial investment increase the value of each venture, they also support larger portfolios. The VC's quality does not affect the optimal portfolio size. A higher VC's quality increases the value of each venture, given the VC's per-project effort level. This, in turn, leads the VC to fund a larger number of projects. However, the optimal VC's per-project effort level decreases as the number of firms in her portfolio increases, reducing the value of each venture. Holding everything else constant, this reduces the optimal number of projects to be funded. In our model, the two effects exactly offset each other. Thus, the optimal number of firms chosen by the VC is independent of her productivity.[5]

> Result 5: *The optimal profit share given to entrepreneurs is increasing in the number of portfolio firms*, n. *Moreover, holding* n *constant, the optimal entrepreneurs' profit share is: increasing in entrepreneurs' productivity and VC's disutility of effort; decreasing in VC's productivity and entrepreneurs' disutility of effort; and independent of the value of a successful project and of the required investment in each venture.*

Increasing the number of portfolio firms reduces the equilibrium per-firm effort level of the VC, thus reducing the expected value of each project. In order to mitigate the negative direct effect of reduced VC's per-project effort, the VC optimally increases the profit shares offered to the entrepreneurs. This increases entrepreneurs' optimal effort, which, in turn, raises each projects' expected value.

The relations between the VC's, entrepreneurs', and projects' characteristics and the optimal profit-sharing rule follow from their direct effects on the expected value of the ventures and from the indirect effects through the optimal efforts of the VC and the entrepreneurs. The relations in Result 5 reflect the relative magnitudes of the direct and the indirect effects. Because the parties' equilibrium effort levels are independent of the required initial investment, the latter does not interact with x and, thus, does not affect the equilibrium sharing rule.

EMPIRICAL TESTS

Results 4 and 5 provide the basis for our empirical tests. Specifically, the implied relations among the optimal number of portfolio firms, the entrepreneurs' optimal profit shares, and VC's, entrepreneurs', and projects' characteristics assume that

Exhibit 6.3 Empirical Predictions

	n^*		x^*	
	Structural Relation	Reduced-Form Relation	Structural Relation	Reduced-Form Relation
α	+	?	+	+
β	0	?	−	−
γ	−	?	−	−
δ	−	?	+	0
R	+	+	0	+
I	−	−	0	−
x	+ for small x − for large x			
n			+	

Column 1 summarizes the empirical predictions for the signs of the relations between VC's, entrepreneurs', and projects' characteristics and the equilibrium VC portfolio size. Column 2 summarizes the empirical predictions for the signs of the relations between VC's, entrepreneurs', and projects' characteristics and the equilibrium entrepreneurs' profit shares. "+" indicates a predicted positive relation, "−" indicates a negative relation, and "0" means that the model predicts no relation between an exogenous and an endogenous variable.

one of the two choice variables is held constant. Thus, proper testing of our model's predictions requires estimation of a system of two equations using an instrumental variables approach. In the first equation, the dependent variable is the number of firms in the VC's portfolio and the independent variables are the entrepreneurs', VC's, and projects' characteristics, the profit shares given to entrepreneurs, and control variables. In the second equation, the dependent variable is the profit share given to entrepreneurs, and the independent variables include the aforementioned characteristics, the portfolio size, and controls.

The predictions of our model are summarized in Exhibit 6.3.

The first column presents the signs of the predicted relations between the equilibrium portfolio size, the profit share accruing to entrepreneurs, and the characteristics of the parties and projects. The second column shows how the equilibrium profit share given to entrepreneurs is expected to covary with the portfolio size and with the parties' and projects' characteristics.

Data Source

The data were obtained from a survey of and follow-up phone interviews with venture capital and private equity funds (VC funds hereafter) in Europe and North America. The survey and interviews were conducted during the Spring and Summer of 2004. We were able to obtain reliable, private, and confidential data from 42 limited partnership VC funds from Canada (2), Czech Republic (1), Denmark (1), France (3), Germany (5), Israel (2), Italy (1), the Netherlands (1), Switzerland (1), the United Kingdom (3), and the United States (22).

These 42 funds have financed a total of 668 entrepreneurial firms by June 2004. Two reasons motivated us to obtain data from a diverse set of countries in Europe and North America. First, there does not exist any international evidence on VCs' portfolio structures. Second, by considering a diverse set of countries, we attempt to mitigate the effects of country-specific legal and institutional structures on VCs' portfolio composition. Our data comprise details on each investment from each VC fund, which go beyond those available from VC associations.

The funds in our sample almost invariably have a typical finite horizon of 10 years, with the option 11 to continue for two to three years. The scope of our sample is broadly similar to that of other empirical studies. For example, Lerner and Schoar (2005) examine a dataset consisting of 208 transactions by 23 private equity funds. Kaplan and Strömberg (2003) use a dataset of a similar size.

As discussed in Lerner and Schoar (2005), it is difficult to ascertain the representativeness of proprietary datasets given the lack of a comprehensive source of data for international private equity or venture capital funds. However, it is important to note that the response rate to our survey was arguably low. Specifically, three rounds of surveys were e-mailed to over 8,000 funds, indicating a response rate of about 0.5 percent. Because of the diverse characteristics of respondent funds and because the summary statistics discussed below are generally in line with other empirical VC studies, we cannot conclude that our results are influenced by a self-selection bias. Nonetheless, the low response rate precludes us from generalizing our results to the whole population of VC and private equity funds.

Summary Statistics

We group the variables into three broad categories: (1) entrepreneurs' ownership percentage and VCs' portfolio sizes, (2) proxies for VCs', entrepreneurs', and projects' characteristics, and (3) control variables. Group 1 encompasses the endogenous variables in the model, and groups 2 and 3 contain the explanatory variables. Exhibit 6.4 provides the definitions of the variables and basic summary statistics.

The median number of entrepreneurial firms per VC fund *(NUM_FIRMS)* is 9.5, and the mean is 15.9. The profit share of entrepreneurs *(ENT_SHARE)* typically varies over the life of investment, subject to entrepreneurs' performance (e.g., Kaplan and Strömberg 2003). In gathering the data, we therefore asked VC fund managers to indicate the typical ownership percentage held in their investee companies. The median entrepreneurs' ownership percentage is 80 percent in our sample, and the mean is 70 percent. These numbers are somewhat higher than the typical ownership percentage reported by Kaplan and Strömberg, whose study indicates that U.S. VCs typically hold about 50 percent equity in the investee companies. For U.S. VCs in our sample, the average entrepreneurs' ownership is 68 percent, and the median is 80 percent.

We use the average number of years of post–high school education of entrepreneurs in a VC fund *(ENT_EDU)* as a proxy for entrepreneurs' quality. A proxy for entrepreneurs' disutility of effort is the average age of entrepreneurs *(ENT_AGE)*. We proxy for VC fund managers' quality by the average number of years of managers' post-high school education *(MGR_EDU)*.[6] VCs' disutility (cost) of effort is proxied by the average age of the managers *(MGR_AGE)*. The average required investment in a project is proxied by the average capital invested in a venture *(CAP_INV)* as of June 2004. The expected projects' profitability is proxied

Exhibit 6.4 Summary Statistics

Variable	Model's Parameter	Mean	Median	Min.	Max.	Std. Dev.
Portfolio size and entrepreneurs' ownership percentage						
NUM_FIRMS	n	15.90	9.5	1	85	16.89
ENT_SHARE	x	70.26	80	0	97.5	24.02
Proxies for the model's parameters						
ENT_EDU	α	9.74	8.75	2.5	23	4.44
ENT_AGE	γ	44.08	45	33	50	3.92
MGR_EDU	β	7.02	6	4	12	2.04
MGR_AGE	δ	42.45	43	33	55	4.9
CAP_INV	I	11.79	4.10	0.22	103.80	20.35
IRR_100	R	12.08	12	0	38.10	10.26
Control variables						
FND_MGR		6.64	5	1	17	4.96
CAP_RAISED		264.90	101.50	11	3100	496.60
DUR		5.08	3.46	1	33.94	5.93
CGOVT		5.32	0	0	70	14.78
EARLY		22.26%	20.00%	0.00%	100.00%	26.28%
FINANCE		9.36	12	4	20	3.88
AVG_RISK		5.82	6	2	10	1.76
PERCENT_LEAD		58.36%	58.00%	0.00%	100.00%	28.43%
LEGALITY		20.31	20.85	14	21.91	1.50

by VCs' perception of the proportion of projects with expected internal rate of return above 100 percent *(IRR_100)*.

Our control variables are as follows. First, VCs' portfolio size is expected to be positively related to the number of managers employed by the fund. VC funds employed a median of five fund managers *(FND_MGR)*.[7] Second, we expect the number of firms in a VC fund to be positively related to the total capital raised by the fund *(CAP_RAISED)*. Third, the number of portfolio firms is expected to be increasing in the fund's life as measured from the date of the first investment to June 2004 *(DUR)*. Fourth, we expect it to be affected by the amount of government guarantees for failed investments *(CGOVT)*, both because of a potential negative effect of government guarantees on VCs' effort levels and because of the potentially different maximization function of a fund having government guarantees.[8] We expect the profit-sharing rule to be affected by whether a fund specializes in funding ventures in their early stage *(EARLY)*. About 22 percent of firms in our sample are in the early stage. We also expect entrepreneurs' profit shares to be negatively related to the number of financing rounds *(FINANCE)*. The VC fund managers' assessment of the average risk of their entrepreneurial ventures *(AVE_RISK)*, measured on a scale of 1 to 10, is also expected to affect profit sharing. In addition, we expect the proportion of firms in which a VC is the lead investor *(PERCENT_LEAD)* to be positively (negatively) associated with the VC's (entrepreneurs') profit shares. Finally, because the funds in our sample are located in different countries, we control for countries' institutional environment using a "legality index"

(LEGALITY). The legality index, based on Berkowitz, Pistor, and Richard (2003), reflects the following factors: civil versus common law systems, efficiency of judicial system, rule of law, corruption, risk of expropriation, risk of contract repudiation, and shareholder rights.[9]

Regression Analysis

We estimate the portfolio size equation while instrumenting for entrepreneurs' profit share by its predicted values from first-stage regressions and, similarly, estimate the profit share equation while instrumenting for the VC's portfolio size by its predicted values from first-stage regressions.[10] Exhibit 6.5 presents the results of the second-stage regressions.

The model predicts a nonmonotonic relation between entrepreneurs' profit shares, x, and the optimal number of portfolio firms. Specifically, portfolio size is expected to be increasing in x when the latter is low, whereas it is expected to be decreasing in x when the latter is high. We rely on two specifications to capture the nonmonotonicity predicted by the model.

In the first column of Exhibit 6.5, we model the nonmonotonicity of the relation between equilibrium portfolio size and entrepreneurs' profit share by regressing the number of firms in a VC fund *(NUM_FIRMS)* on the predicted first-stage entrepreneurs' ownership percentage *(INST_ENT_SHARE)* and on the squared predicted entrepreneurs' ownership percentage *(INST_ENT_SHARE²)*. The coefficient on entrepreneurs' ownership percentage is positive and significant. The coefficient on the squared ownership percentage is negative and marginally significant, indicating that is n increasing in x when the latter is low, while it is decreasing in x when x is high enough.

The other predictions of the model are partially supported by the data. Consistent with the model, the number of years of entrepreneurs' education, proxying for their quality, is positively and marginally significantly related to the number of portfolio firms. The coefficient on managers' average age, proxying for their disutility of effort, is negative and significant at the 10 percent level. The average capital investment in a venture is negatively and significantly related to VC portfolio size.

The coefficients on other control variables are mostly insignificant. This is not caused by multicollinearity, because the (unreported) correlations among the independent variables are small and, in most cases, insignificant. However, some of the variables exhibit very small variation. The legality index is a good example: the vast majority of the observations come from countries with developed legal systems, leading to almost no variation in *LEGALITY*. One exception is the amount of capital raised. Consistent with managers having strong incentives to exhaust funds that have been raised, the number of firms in VC's portfolio is positively associated with *CAP_RAISED*.

In the second column, we model the nonmonotonicity of the relation between portfolio size and entrepreneurs' profit shares by constructing a variable that is equal to the absolute deviation of the predicted first-stage value of x from a given threshold, below (above) which the effect of increasing x on n is expected to be positive (negative). We use 80 percent as the threshold value in Panel 2 because the median entrepreneur's profit share in our sample is 80 percent.[11] Consistent with the model's prediction, the coefficient on the absolute deviation from the threshold

Exhibit 6.5   Regressions of Portfolio Sizes and Profit Shares

	Model's Parameter	Dependent Variable		
		NUM_FIRMS	NUM_FIRMS	ENT_SHARE
Intercept		−75.245	−28.349	187.430
		(−1.28)	(−0.87)	(2.54)
INST_NUM_FIRMS	n			0.582
				(1.78)
INST_ENT_SHARE	x	2.042		
		(2.06)		
INST_ENT_SHARE^2	x^2	−0.016		
		(−1.61)		
| INST_ENT_SHARE-80% |	$\|x-80\%\|$		−0.612	
			(−2.15)	
ENT_EDU	α	0.304	0.315	0.345
		(1.92)	(1.94)	(0.66)
ENT_AGE	γ	−0.471	−0.453	−1.266
		(−0.84)	(−0.82)	(−1.34)
MGR_EDU	β	0.288	0.301	−0.201
		(2.32)	(2.33)	(−2.12)
MGR_AGE	δ	−0.650	−0.632	1.671
		(−1.77)	(−1.72)	(1.59)
CAP_INV	I	−0.558	−0.571	0.862
		(−2.95)	(−3.01)	(1.12)
IRR_100	R	0.162	0.169	0.152
		(0.82)	(0.83)	(0.14)
FND_MGR		−0.201	−0.177	
		(−0.22)	(−0.20)	
CAP_RAISED		0.020	0.019	
		(2.55)	(2.45)	
DUR		0.652	0.666	
		(1.57)	(1.60)	
CGOVT		0.014	0.007	
		(0.34)	(0.19)	
EARLY				0.049
				(0.61)
FINANCE				−0.612
				(−0.88)
AVG_RISK				3.214
				(1.24)
PERCENT_LEAD				−23.613
				(−1.73)
LEGALITY		0.970	0.894	−2.691
		(0.65)	(0.59)	(−1.07)
Adjusted R^2		0.528	0.519	0.396

is negative and significant. Thus, when entrepreneurs' ownership percentage is low—below the threshold—an increase in x (i.e., a reduction in the absolute deviation from the threshold) is typically associated with an increase in the number of portfolio firms, whereas the opposite holds when x is large—above the threshold. Increasing the deviation of entrepreneurs' ownership percentage from the threshold by one percentage point reduces the number of portfolio firms by about 0.6 firms. The relation between n and the other variables is generally consistent with the results in the first column.

The third column presents the results of the second-stage regressions of entrepreneurs' profit shares on the predicted first-stage portfolio size. First, and most importantly, entrepreneurs' ownership percentage is positively and marginally significantly associated with the instrument for n (INST_NUM_FIRMS). In addition, consistent with the model, managers quality, as proxied by years of their education, is negatively related to entrepreneurs' profit shares.

Overall, the evidence is consistent with the theory presented earlier. Importantly, we do find substantial support for the nonmonotonic relation between VC portfolio sizes and entrepreneurs' ownership shares. The weakness of some of the other results is possibly due to the size of our sample and, thus, our ability to simultaneously control for numerous factors with a limited number of observations. It is important to emphasize that because of the small sample size we view our empirical results as preliminary and illustrative.

CONCLUSION

This chapter discusses a theoretical model that characterizes a venture capitalist's (VC's) simultaneous choices of the size of her portfolio of entrepreneurial ventures and the profit-sharing rule between her and entrepreneurs. Profit sharing and portfolio size are both central to venture capital finance, as VCs write contracts to mitigate the double-sided moral hazard problem and undertake a limited number of investments to add value to entrepreneurial ventures they invest in. The joint analysis of equity participation and portfolio size illustrates an important nonmonotonic relationship between the optimal number of entrepreneurial ventures a VC finances and the profit shares given to entrepreneurs.

In our model, a VC maximizes her expected portfolio value net of her effort costs, with respect to the number of projects she invests in and to the share of the projects' expected values that she gives to entrepreneurs. The portfolio structure affects unobservable effort levels of the entrepreneurs and the VC, thus influencing the value of the VC's portfolio.

Our analysis generates predictions regarding the partial effects of various characteristics of VCs, entrepreneurs, and projects on optimal VC portfolio size and profit sharing when both are chosen endogenously. Optimal VC portfolio size is predicted to be positively related to the quality of entrepreneurs and to the value of a successful project, and to be negatively related to the disutilities that the VC and entrepreneurs have from exerting effort, and to the required initial investment in the projects. The relation between the optimal portfolio size and the profit-sharing rule is predicted to be nonmonotonic: The optimal number of firms is first increasing and then is decreasing in the share of profits retained by entrepreneurs.

We test the predictions of the model using data collected through a survey of venture capital and private equity funds in Europe and North America. Our sample includes 42 VC funds. The empirical analysis of VC portfolio structure is performed while accounting for the endogeneity of the profit-sharing rule. Using instrumental variables we find that VC portfolio size varies nonmonotonically with the profit share retained by entrepreneurs. Another finding that is consistent with the model is that entrepreneurs' profit shares are increasing in the portfolio size. In addition, the relations among VC portfolio sizes; entrepreneurs' profit shares; and the VC's, entrepreneurs', and projects' characteristics are generally consistent with the theory.

Given the small size of our sample of VC funds, we view the empirical results discussed here as preliminary and believe that further research is warranted. In particular, we think that the most interesting and potentially rewarding area of research is a further empirical examination of the determinants of VC portfolio structures using larger and more representative datasets of VC funds. Such tests can greatly improve our understanding of the choices venture capitalists make.

NOTES

1. See Sahlman (1990) for a discussion of the nature of the relationship between VCs and entrepreneurs, and Gorman and Sahlman (1989) and Wright and Lockett (2003) for some survey evidence of VCs' activities.

2. There is a large literature concerned with the design of financial contracts that mitigate the agency problems between VCs and entrepreneurs. See Bascha and Walz (2001), Bergemann and Hege (1998), Cornelli and Yosha (2003), Garmaise (2001), Houben (2002), Kaplan and Strömberg (2004), Marx (1998), Repullo and Suarez (2004), and Schmidt (2003), among others, for models of optimal structure of contracts between VCs and enterpreneurs. See Gompers (1995) and Gompers and Lerner (1999) for empirical investigations of venture capital contracts.

3. Generalist funds are those investing in a wide array of firms, both in early and late stages.

4. An entrepreneur does not commit to exert any effort by accepting the offer. Therefore, because he does not provide any financing for the venture, the worst he can do is receive zero expected value.

5. This result is an artifact of the specific functional forms in the model, which we choose for analytical tractibility. In a more general setting, the effect of the VC's quality on the optimal number of portfolio firms would likely be positive.

6. We also use an alternative proxy based on the average number of years of managers' work experience and obtain results similar to those reported.

7. Because the number of managers employed by a VC fund can be considered an endogenous variable, we repeat the analysis while excluding this variable from the regressions. Omitting the number of managers does not affect the qualitative results.

8. See, for example, Keuschnigg (2004), Keuschnigg and Nielsen (2003), and Lerner (1999). None of the funds in our sample are "pure" government funds with 100 percent government support; however, eleven funds did receive some capital from government entities, and two of the funds received more than 50 percent of their capital from government sources.

9. We also considered GNP per capita and country dummy variables as alternative controls in our multivariate tests. However, GNP per capita is highly correlated with *LEGALITY* (the correlation coefficient is 0.85), and including country dummy variables does not affect any of the results.

10. The two first-stage regressions include the variables that are expected to affect portfolio size and profit sharing, discussed above. The results of the first-stage regressions are not reported for conciseness.

11. Various thresholds, ranging from 50 to 80 percent, provide results that are qualitatively similar to those reported.

REFERENCES

Bascha, Andreas, and Uwe Walz. 2001. Convertible securities and optimal exit decisions in venture capital finance. *Journal of Corporate Finance* 7:285–306.

Bergemann, Dirk, and Ulrich Hege. 1998. Venture capital financing, moral hazard, and learning. *Journal of Banking and Finance* 22:703–735.

Berkowitz, Daniel, Katharina Pistor, and Jean-Francois Richard. 2003. Economic development, legality, and the transplant effect. *European Economic Review* 47:165–195.

Casamatta, Catherine. 2003. Financing and advising: Optimal financial contracts with venture capitalists. *Journal of Finance* 58:2059–2086.

Casamatta, Catherine, and Carole Haritchabalet. 2004. Learning and syndication in venture capital investments. University of Toulouse Working Paper.

Cassiman, Bruno, and Masako Ueda. 2006. Optimal project rejection and new firm start-ups. *Management Science* 52:262–275.

Cestone, Giacinta, and Lucy White. 2003. Anti-competitive financial contracting: The design of financial claims. *Journal of Finance* 58:2109–2142.

Cornelli, Francesca, and Oved Yosha. 2003. Stage financing and the role of convertible debt. *Review of Economic Studies* 70:1–32.

Cumming, Douglas. 2006. The determinants of venture capital portfolio size: Empirical evidence. *Journal of Business* 79:1083–1126.

Cumming, Douglas, and Uwe Walz. 2008. Private equity returns and disclosure around the world. York University Working Paper.

Fulghieri, Paolo, and Merih Sevilir. 2004. Size and focus of a venture capitalist's portfolio. University of North Carolina Working Paper.

Garmaise, Mark. 2001. "Informed investors and the financing of entrepreneurial projects." University of Chicago Working Paper.

Gompers, Paul. 1995. Optimal investment, monitoring, and the staging of venture capital. *Journal of Finance* 50:1461–1489.

Gompers, Paul, and Josh Lerner. 1999. *The venture capital cycle.* Cambridge, MA: MIT Press.

Gorman, Michael, and William Sahlman. 1989. What do venture capitalists do? *Journal of Business Venturing* 4:231–248.

Hege Ulrich, Frederic Palomino, and Armin Schwienbacher. 2003. Venture capital performance: The disparity between Europe and the United States. HEC School of Management Working Paper.

Houben, Eike. 2002. Venture capital, double-sided adverse selection and double-sided moral hazard. University of Kiel Working Paper.

Kanniainen, Vesa, and Christian Keuschnigg. 2003. The optimal portfolio of start-up firms in venture capital finance. *Journal of Corporate Finance* 9:521–534.

Kanniainen, Vesa, and Christian Keuschnigg. 2004. Start-up investment with scarce venture capital support. *Journal of Banking and Finance* 28:1935–1959.

Kaplan, Steven, and Per Strömberg. 2003. Financial contracting theory meets the real world: An empirical analysis of venture capital contracts. *Review of Economic Studies* 70:281–315.

Kaplan, Steven, and Per Strömberg. 2004. Contracts, characteristics, and actions: Evidence from venture capitalist analysis. *Journal of Finance* 59:2173–2206.

Keuschnigg, Christian. 2004. Taxation of a venture capitalist with a portfolio of firms. *Oxford Economic Papers* 56:285–306.

Keuschnigg, Christian, and Søren Nielsen. 2003. Tax policy, venture capital and entrepreneurship. *Journal of Public Economics* 87:175–203.

Lerner, Josh. 1999. The government as venture capitalist: The long-run effects of the SBIR program. *Journal of Business* 72:285–318.

Lerner, Josh, and Antoinette Schoar. 2005. Does legal enforcement affect financial transactions?: The contractual channel in private equity. *Quarterly Journal of Economics* 120:223–246.

Marx, Leslie. 1998. Efficient venture capital financing combining debt and equity. *Review of Economic Design* 3:371–187.

Repullo, Rafael, and Javier Suarez. 2004. Venture capital finance: A security design approach. *Review of Finance* 8:75–108.

Sahlman, William. 1990. The structure and governance of venture-capital organizations. *Journal of Financial Economics* 27:473–521.

Schmidt, Klaus. 2003. Convertible securities and venture capital finance. *Journal of Finance* 58:1139–1166.

Wright, Mike, and Andy Lockett. 2003. The structure and management of alliances: Syndication in the venture capital industry. *Journal of Management Studies* 40:2073–2104.

ABOUT THE AUTHORS

Gennaro Bernile received a Ph.D. from the University of Rochester. He specializes in empirical corporate finance, in particular, mergers and acquisitions, venture capital, and corporate governance. Professor Bernile has published in the *Journal of Corporate Finance* and the *Journal of Accounting and Economics*. His work was presented at numerous prestigious academic conferences, such as the Western Finance Association Meetings, the American Finance Association Meetings, the European Finance Association Meetings, Utah Winter Finance Conference, and Texas Finance Festival, among many others.

Douglas Cumming, B.Com. (Hons.) (McGill), M.A. (Queen's), J.D. (University of Toronto Faculty of Law), Ph.D. (Toronto), CFA, is an Associate Professor of Finance and Entrepreneurship and the Ontario Research Chair at the Schulich School of Business, York University. His research is primarily focused on law and finance, market surveillance, hedge funds, venture capital, private equity, and IPOs. His work has been presented at the American Finance Association, the Western Finance Association, the European Finance Association, the American Law and Economics Association, the European Law and Economics Association, and other leading international conferences. His recent publications have appeared in numerous journals, including the *American Law and Economics Review, Cambridge Journal of Economics, Economic Journal, European Economic Review, Financial Management, Journal of Business, Journal of Business Venturing, Journal of Corporate Finance, Journal of Empirical Legal Studies, Journal of International Business Studies, Oxford Economic Papers,* and *Review of Financial Studies*. He is the coauthor (along with his wife, Sofia

Johan) of the new book *Venture Capital and Private Equity Contracting: An International Perspective* (Elsevier Science Academic Press, 2009, 770 pp.). His work has been reviewed in numerous media outlets, including *Canadian Business*, the *Financial Post*, and *The New Yorker*. He was the recipient of the 2004 Ido Sarnat Award for the best paper published in the *Journal of Banking and Finance* for a paper on full and partial venture capital exits in Canada and the United States. As well, he received the 2008 AIMA Canada-Hillsdale Research Award for his paper on hedge fund regulation and performance, and the 2009 Best Paper Award from the Canadian Institute of Chartered Business Valuators for his paper on private equity valuation and disclosure. He is a research associate with the Paolo Baffi Center for Central Banking and Financial Regulation (Bocconi University), Groupe d'Economie Mondiale at Sciences Po (Paris), Capital Markets CRC (Sydney), Venture Capital Experts (New York), Cambridge University ESRC Center for Business Research, Center for Financial Studies (Frankfurt), Amsterdam Center for Research in International Finance, and the University of Calgary Van Horne Institute. He has also consulted for a variety of governmental and private organizations in Australasia, Europe, and North America, and most recently is working with Wilshire Associates.

Evgeny Lyandres received a Ph.D. from the University of Rochester. He specializes in theoretical and empirical corporate finance, in particular, mergers and acquisitions, venture capital, real options, and the interaction of financial and real decisions. Professor Lyandres has published in the *Review of Financial Studies, Journal of Business,* and *Journal of Corporate Finance*. His work was presented at numerous prestigious academic conferences, such as the Western Finance Association Meetings, the American Finance Association Meetings, the European Finance Association Meetings, Utah Winter Finance Conference, and Texas Finance Festival, among many others.

ACKNOWLEDGMENT

This paper is based on work in Bernile, Gennaro, Douglas Cumming, and Evgeny Lyandres, 2007, The size of venture capital and private equity fund portfolios, *Journal of Corporate Finance* 13:564–590.

CHAPTER 7

The Rise of the PIPE Market

Assistant Professor, SUNY at Albany, School of Business

INTRODUCTION

The private investment in public equity (PIPE) market has been growing rapidly over the last decade. The number of PIPE deals grew from 306 in 1996 to 1,249 in 2007. The total amount of capital raised via PIPEs has increased from $4 billion dollars in 1996 to $56 billion in 2007. In comparison, in 2007, the number of seasoned equity offerings (SEOs) was 377 and the total amount of capital raised in the SEO market was $75 billion. These numbers suggest that the PIPE market has grown to an important alternative equity selling mechanism for U.S. public companies. Please see Exhibits 7.1 and 7.2.

With the rapid growth of this market segment, the PIPE market has drawn attention from more and more investors, small- and medium-size public corporations that are barred from traditional financing venues such as public debt market and SEOs, and the regulators. Many issues and concerns have emerged. For instance, potential issuers are concerned why and when they should choose PIPEs rather than SEOs, how expensive PIPEs are, how the firm's stock performance will be impacted by the offering; investors have questions such as what is the return and risk profile of PIPE transactions, how to protect investors' benefits using various contract provisions; and regulators are concerned whether and to what extent existing shareholders' benefits will be affected by the PIPE offering, whether there are illegal insider trading and market manipulations by PIPE investors, and how to fix these problems. The research in this field, however, is rare. The purpose of this chapter is to provide a detailed review about the structure and development of this market, the problems associated with this market, and the existing research on PIPEs.

The chapter starts with an introduction of the PIPE market, including the definition of PIPE, security structure, and commonly used contract terms. Next, the chapter reviews the cost of PIPEs to issuers, returns of PIPEs to investors, and the role of placement agents in the offering. Then I discuss the recent SEC enforcement on hedge funds that are involved in some PIPE transactions. Finally, I analyze how the current financial crisis has affected the PIPE market and where this market is going down the road.

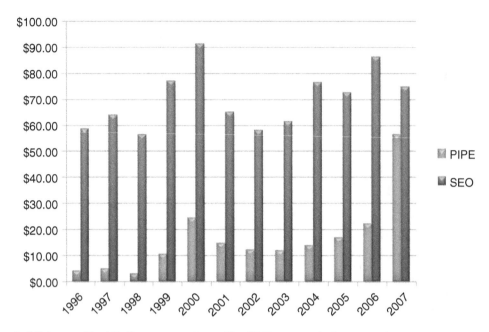

Exhibit 7.1 Total Dollar Amount Raised by PIPEs versus SEOs, 1996–2007

WHAT IS A PIPE?

In the United States, PIPEs are private placements by public companies to accredited investors made in reliance on Section 4 (2) and/or Regulation D. Section 5 of the Securities Act of 1933 requires that a registration statement must be in effect and a prospectus must be delivered prior to sale. Section 4 (2) or Regulation D

Exhibit 7.2 Overview of the PIPE Market, 1996–2007

	PIPE		SEO	
Year	N	Capital Raised ($Billion)	N	Capital Raised ($Billion)
1996	306	$4.1	714	$58.5
1997	456	$4.7	677	$63.8
1998	440	$3.0	542	$56.2
1999	691	$10.3	412	$76.9
2000	1,254	$24.4	373	$91.1
2001	1,036	$14.6	384	$64.9
2002	757	$12.0	377	$58.0
2003	889	$11.7	466	$61.3
2004	1,285	$13.7	533	$76.3
2005	1,317	$16.8	420	$72.6
2006	1,260	$22.0	450	$86.2
2007	1,249	$56.3	377	$74.8
1996–2007	10,940	$193.59	5,725	$840.7

provide exemption to issuers from Section 5 registration requirement when the offering involves the following elements:

- The offer is made to a limited number of financially sophisticated investors or accredited investors.[1]
- The offering does not involve any general advertising or general solicitation;
- Investors are given information relevant to their investments.

Following the closing of a PIPE transaction, the issuer prepares and files with the Securities and Exchange Commission (SEC) a resale registration statement. In contrast to a traditional private placement, the closing does not depend upon the SEC review process. This feature makes PIPE a time-efficient mechanism for issuers to raise capital. However, investors cannot resell or short securities purchased until the SEC declares the effectiveness of the registration statement. To compensate investors for this temporary illiquidity, PIPE issuers often offer the securities at a discount to market price.

The security structure is very complex in the PIPE market. The option generally includes: plain vanilla common stock issuance, common stock reset issuance, common stock shelf sale, company installment convertible issuance, fixed price convertibles, floating price convertibles, convertible reset issuances, and structured equity lines. Typically, plain vanilla common stock issuance and fixed-price convertibles issuance are categorized as "traditional PIPEs" and others are called "structured PIPEs."

As shown in Exhibit 7.3, plain vanilla common stock and fixed convertibles are the top two security types used in the PIPE market, based on the number of transactions and the amount of capital raised. For instance, during the period from 1996 to 2007, plain vanilla common stock PIPEs account for 45 percent (46 percent) of the market, while fixed convertible PIPEs account for 25 percent (31 percent) of the market, based on the number of transactions (amount of capital raised). While there is a fairly large number of floating convertible PIPEs, nevertheless, the amount of capital raised through this security type accounts for only 11 percent of the total market. Furthermore, as shown in Exhibit 7.4, it seems that the number of floating convertible PIPEs has been declining since 2001. In comparison to the peak of 237 floating convertible PIPEs in 1997, there were only 48 such PIPEs in 2001. The number of transactions further declined to 18 in 2003. Hillion and Vermaelen

Exhibit 7.3 Security Structure of PIPE Offerings

Security Type	N	Capital Raised ($Billion)
Common Stock	4,972	$89.75
Common Stock—Reset	98	$0.81
Common Stock—Shelf Sale (Registered Direct)	576	$14.07
Convertible—Company Installment (Self-Amortizing)	318	$2.27
Convertible—Fixed	2,700	$59.27
Convertible—Floating	1,278	$20.66
Convertible—Reset	218	$3.98
Nonconvertible Debt/Preferred Stock	63	$2.56
Structured Equity Line	717	$0.22

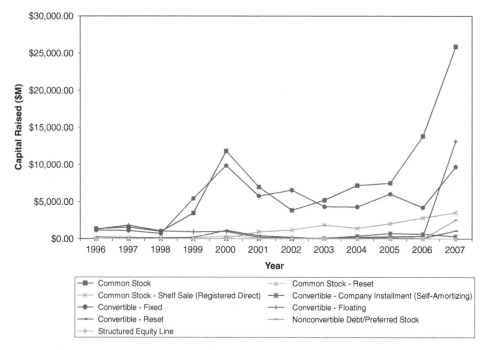

Exhibit 7.4 Amount of Capital Raised by Security Type, 1996–2007

(2004) demonstrate that firms issuing floating convertible bonds tend to perform poorly in the long run. They suggest that such floating convertibles encourage short selling by convertible holders and that the resulting dilution triggers a permanent decline in the share price. One of the reasons for the declining popularity of floating convertible PIPEs is SEC's investigations on potential unlawful behaviors of investors (insider trading, market manipulation, etc.) involved in this category.[2]

PIPEs seem to be most popular in four sectors: healthcare, communications, technology, and industrial. About 72 percent of the PIPE transactions are conducted by firms in these sectors. Please see Exhibits 7.5 and 7.6.

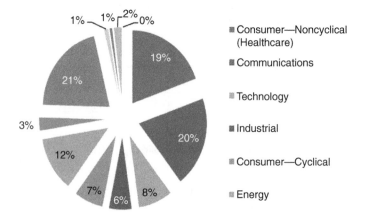

Exhibit 7.5 Distributions of PIPEs by Industries, 1996–2007

Exhibit 7.6 Distribution of PIPEs by Industries

Sector	N	Capital Raised ($Billion)
Consumer—Noncyclical (Healthcare)	2985	$37.60
Communications	2155	$38.78
Technology	1495	$15.87
Industrial	1246	$10.71
Consumer—Cyclical	785	$13.57
Energy	698	$23.75
Consumer—Noncyclical (Nonhealthcare)	552	$5.72
Financial	512	$40.23
Basic Materials	309	$2.19
Diversified	153	$1.31
Utilities	38	$3.80
Other	12	$0.06

PIPEs are also becoming more popular in Canada, Europe, and Asia. The definitions of PIPEs could be slightly different across countries due to the different securities regulation frameworks. For instance, in Canada, before November 2001, the restricted period when PIPE purchasers were prohibited from reselling their PIPE shares to the public market ranged from six to eighteen months, a period that was thereafter reduced to four months.[3] In the United States, the restricted period depends on when the PIPE-issuing firm files the registration statement and how long it takes the SEC to declare it effective. Thus, it varies across deals. On average, it is about 120 days, comparable to the existing length of restricted period in Canada.

CONTRACT TERMS IN PIPE OFFERINGS

In this section, I describe the contracts between the PIPE investors and issuers in great detail. In particular, I focus on contract terms that are designed to protect benefits of both new shareholders (PIPE investors) and the company.

Antidilution Protection

PIPE offerings frequently include antidilution protection that protects the PIPE investors against future financing at a lower valuation than the valuation of the current (protected) offering. In the extreme case, the company is not allowed to issue or sell any equity securities or securities convertible into equity during a certain period after closing, for example, from closing date until 90 trading days following the effectiveness of the Registration Statement, or is not allowed to issue or sell any equity securities or securities convertible into equity at a price below the current offer price or a benchmark price while the security remains outstanding. In other cases, PIPE investors are protected from the above-mentioned events by being able to reduce the current offer price or conversion price to the lowest price paid for such security in future financing, or having the right to receive cash or additional common shares without additional consideration.

Redemption Rights

Investor optional redemption is commonly used to strengthen the liquidation rights of the PIPE investors' investment. This provision gives the PIPE investors the right to demand that the firm redeems the investors' claim upon a change of control, typically at face value or a certain percentage of face value (often higher than 100 percent, occasionally, higher than 200 percent) plus accrued and unpaid interest. In some cases, the interest rate will also increase by some basis points per annum. Many PIPE offerings also have a company optional redemption provision, which gives the company the right to force the PIPE investors to exercise the redemption right after a certain date or upon certain events.

Investor Registration Rights

The key feature of PIPE offerings is that firms can close the offering before filing any registration statements with the SEC, which makes the PIPE offering time-efficient. Nevertheless, PIPE investors assume the risk of illiquidity before the effectiveness of Registration Statement simply because they are not allowed to resell the stocks obtained through PIPEs. Most PIPE contracts specifically request the company to file a Registration Statement covering the resale of common stocks (underlying the issued securities) no later than certain days after the closing and to make it effective within a certain time window. In some cases, investors place a cap on the amount of capital that the company can drawdown before the effectiveness of the Registration Statement.

Investor Board Representation

The board of directors is generally responsible for (1) hiring, evaluating, and firing top management; and (2) advising and ratifying general corporate strategies and decisions. In a relatively small percentage of cases, PIPE investors have the right to nominate a certain number of directors to the company's board after the PIPE (in some cases, investors have to keep a certain percentage of the company's shares or purchased shares in offering to keep this right). Sometimes the designation is contingent upon certain events, for instance, in the event that the company fails to redeem the investors' claim upon a change of control.

Trading/Hedging Restrictions

Many PIPE offerings have provisions restricting investors' trading/hedging behavior during a certain time period. Typically, such provisions ask investors not to engage in any short transactions or hedging of the company's common stock or in excess of the amount of shares owned (an offsetting long position) prior to the effectiveness of the Registration Statement, which otherwise will result in insider trading according to the SEC regulation. Sometimes investors are asked not to short or hedge in a longer period than the SEC's requirement or as long as the purchased security remains outstanding. If the company is planning a public offering shortly subsequent to the PIPE, it will ask investors not to affect any sales to the public of shares of the company for a period of certain days following the effectiveness of the Registration Statement in order to avoid the price pressure from investors' resale of their shares to the public.

An additional provision related to restrictions on investors' trading behaviors is the so-called lock-up period. Basically, with this provision investors may not sell any shares of the company's common stocks purchased or received through the exercise of warrants for the duration of a few months following the closing.

Company-Forced Conversion

Securities in PIPE offerings often include company-forced conversion provisions in which the security held by the PIPE investors will automatically convert or are forced to convert into common stock under certain conditions. These conditions often relate to the stock performance of the company, for instance, the stock price or the weighted average stock price during a period exceeds a certain benchmark or the daily trading volume exceeds a certain level for some consecutive trading days. In some extreme cases, such as the company taking a 10,000-to-1 reverse stock split, the security will also automatically convert into common stocks.

The effect of the company-forced conversion provisions is to require the PIPE investors to give up their superior rights if the company attains a desired level of performance. Upon such performance, the PIPE investors retain only those rights associated with their ownership of common stock. If the company does not deliver that performance, the investors retain their superior rights.

Investor Call Option, Investor Right of First Refusal, and Company Put Option

Investor call option and investor right of first refusal give investors the right to purchase additional shares of the company's security during a certain period in the future, while company put option gives the company the right to request PIPE investors to purchase an additional amount of securities at a specified price in the future. As for Structured Equity Lines, the company has the option to obtain as much as the agreed amount of capital from the PIPE investors over the term of Equity Line by delivery of Draw Down Notice specifying the amount to be drawn. These provisions give investors/companies the rights for future investment/financing opportunities with a lower transaction cost. Please see Exhibit 7.7.

Some of the above-mentioned provisions are widely used in all types of PIPEs. For example, over 95 percent of PIPEs have the investor registration right. Investor right of first refusal is also commonly (on average 39 percent) included in all types of PIPE contracts. On the other hand, some provisions are more often used in certain types of PIPEs, but not in other types of PIPEs. For instance, price floors (hard floor and green floor) are more often to be seen in the term sheets of convertible PIPEs. About 52 percent of convertible PIPEs include antidilution provisions, while less than 5 percent of the common stock PIPEs include this provision. Trading and hedging restrictions are also more likely to be included in convertible PIPEs, but less often in common stock PIPEs. Investor board representation is more commonly seen in plain vanilla common stock PIPEs and fixed-convertible PIPEs but less

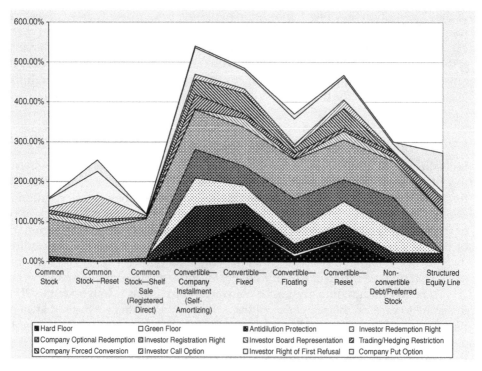

Exhibit 7.7   Contract Terms Included by Security Type

often in floating convertible PIPEs or security equity line or company installment convertible PIPEs.

Chaplinsky and Haushalter (2008) examine when investors are more likely to include price protection terms in the purchase agreements of PIPEs. They find that all else equal, there is a higher probability of price protection the greater the degree of uncertainty regarding the issuer's future performance and the more difficult it is for investors to protect against downside risk, such as high trading costs that make shorting costly.

FIRMS ISSUING PIPEs

Why Firms Choose PIPEs

Most PIPE issuers are small, young, and risky (see Dai [2007], Brophy, Ouimet, and Sialm [2008], and Chaplinsky and Haushalter [2008]). Many of these issuers have difficulty to obtain capital through more traditional means of financing, such as SEOs. Chen, Dai, and Schatzberg (2009) examine how firms choose between traditional SEOs and PIPEs. They find that PIPE firms possess high levels of information asymmetry and poor operating performance. More than 50 percent of the PIPE issuers are not covered by any financial analyst, the stock bid-ask spread of the PIPE issuers are much greater than that of SEO issuers, and majority of the PIPE firms are not profitable at the time of PIPEs. Jointly, these represent characteristics that are unattractive to the traditional SEO process. Chen, Dai, and Schatzberg

(2009) further find that following unsuccessful SEOs (withdrawn SEOs), firms that subsequently switch to the PIPE market have characteristics suggesting greater information asymmetry and worse operating performance than firms that are successful with second-attempt SEOs. Overall, these findings suggest that PIPE issuances may represent the last resort for these firms with high information asymmetry or poor operating performance to obtain additional equity capital. Because most PIPE transactions are highly risky for investors, investors often ask for a large discount as compensation, which is on average five to six times the discount of SEO offerings.[4] Thus, the emergence and rapid growth of the PIPE market fills the capital need of at least some firms that are rejected by the traditional SEO market; and in doing so, this market also compensates investors willing to bear such risks by offering large risk premia in the form of attractive discounts. Hence, the PIPE market may act as a supplement to the traditional SEO market.

In addition to solving the capital needs of firms with high levels of information asymmetry, PIPEs also provide an enhanced market environment for the issued securities. Dai, Jo, and Schatzberg (2009) show that both the information environment and the stock liquidity of issuing firms after the PIPE offering are significantly improved. Issuing firms, in general, are followed by more analysts, have smaller bid-ask spreads, and smaller price volatilities after PIPEs.

Cost of PIPEs

Due to the high-risk nature of PIPE issuers, the cost of PIPE is found higher than that of traditional SEO. Dai and Chen (2008) calculate both the direct cost and the indirect cost of PIPE transactions and compare those with SEOs. The direct cost is measured as agent fees in PIPEs or gross spread in SEOs. Agent fees/gross spreads are the commissions paid to investment bankers when securities are issued, expressed as a percentage of gross proceeds. The indirect cost is measured as discount, which is computed as the percentage change from the offer price to the closing price on the day prior to the offering. Discounts are the money left on the table by issuers. According to Dai and Chen (2008), the mean (median) agent fee of common stock PIPEs is 6.8 percent (6.6 percent), 230 (160) basis points higher than the mean (median) gross spread of SEOs, which is 4.5 percent (5.0 percent). The discounts of PIPE offerings are also much higher than SEO discounts. The mean (median) discounts are 31.5 percent (18.4 percent), more than eight times the SEO discounts, which have a mean of 4.1 percent and a median of 3.0 percent. As mentioned earlier, firms issuing PIPEs are often small, young, and risky. Both investment banks and PIPE investors are taking substantial risk, which could potentially explain both the high agent fees and large discounts. Furthermore, PIPE investors take the risk of illiquidity because they are not allowed to resell the PIPE shares to the public market before the registration statement becomes effective. Dai and Chen (2008) also find that there exist economies of scale in the PIPE market in that agent fees and discounts decline as issue size increases.

Stock Performance at Closing and in the Long Run

The short-run market reaction around the announcement of a PIPE is on average positive (see Dai [2007], Brophy, Ouimet, and Sialm [2008], etc). Nevertheless,

PIPE issuers typically have negative post-issuance long-run performance. It is not yet fully understood why market reacts to the PIPE issuance positively in the short run and negatively in the long run. Scholars have provided several potential explanations for the puzzle.

Dai (2007) examines whether the identity of PIPE investors can explain the short-run market reactions. She finds that VC-led PIPEs on average have a CAR (0, 3) of 5.6 percent, while hedge fund invested PIPEs on average have negative CAR (0, 3). Furthermore, VC-led PIPEs have a significantly positive abnormal alpha, which implies one-year abnormal return of about 39 percent. In contrast, hedge funds invested PIPEs have an alpha not different from 0. Brophy, Ouimet, and Sialm (2008) find similar results. They show that PIPE-invested hedge funds have less positive short-run market reaction but more negative long-run post-PIPE stock performance than PIPEs invested by other investors. They further show security type also matters for the short-run market reaction. For instance, traditional PIPEs have more positive short-run market reaction and less negative long-run stock performance than structured PIPEs.

Dai (2007) further explores why investor identity matters for the market reaction to PIPEs. She examines the changes in ownership structure and board structure before and after PIPE to determine whether PIPE investors are active or passive investors. She finds that VCs often purchase a substantial stake of the firm via PIPEs and request board seats after the PIPE. Furthermore, VCs usually keep their stake for a long period, with 71 percent of VC investors holding their stake for more than one year, and 47 percent holding for more than two years. These findings indicate that VC investors have the control power to affect the management after the PIPE. In contrast, hedge funds rarely sit on the board of the firm and often exit from their investment shortly after the PIPE, even though they also obtain a block stake through the PIPE, suggesting hedge funds are more likely targeting the quick profits from trading and are more likely passive investors. Dai (2007) shows that the difference in ownership stake acquired through PIPEs and the length that investors keep their stake could partially explain the short-run and long-run stock performance of firms issuing PIPEs. Specifically, larger ownership by VCs increases CAR (0, 3) and the length that investors keep their stake after PIPEs increases buy-and-hold abnormal return (BHAR) during one year following the PIPE.

INVESTORS IN THE PIPE MARKET

As we mentioned earlier, Regulation D requires that PIPEs must be offered to accredited investors. Regulation D Rule (501) defines investors from the following categories as accredited investors: banks, broker or dealer, insurance company, registered investment company or business development company, small business investment company, pension funds, director, executive officer, or general partner of the issuer, corporation, limited liability company, trust or partnership with total assets in excess of $5 million not formed for the specific purpose of acquiring the securities offered, any natural person whose individual net worth, or joint net worth with that person's spouse, at the time of the purchase exceeds $1 million, or income or joint income exceeds $200,000 or $300,000, respectively, in each of the

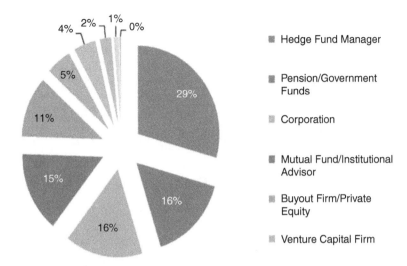

Exhibit 7.8   Market Share by PIPE Investor Type, 1996–2007

two most recent years, and any entity in which all equity owners are accredited investors.

According to the amount of capital invested in the PIPE market, the major investors in the PIPE market are the following: hedge funds, pension/government funds, corporation, mutual fund/institutional advisors, buyout firm/private equity, venture capital firm, broker/dealer, bank, insurance company, charitable/educational/family trust, and various individual investors. Please see Exhibits 7.8 and 7.9.

Several studies have examined how investor identity impacts the funded firms' performance.[5] For example, Brophy, Ouimet, and Sialm (2008) report that hedge funds tend to invest in firms with poor fundamentals and pronounced informational asymmetries. Hedge funds require substantial discounts, repricing rights, and enter short position of the underlying stocks of funded firms. Authors also find that firms obtaining funding from hedge funds substantially underperform

Exhibit 7.9   Primary Investors in the PIPE Market

Investor Type	Amount of Capital Invested
Hedge Fund Manager	$49,239.83
Pension/Government Funds	$26,489.10
Corporation	$26,033.99
Mutual Fund/Institutional Advisor	$24,887.45
Buyout Firm/Private Equity	$18,863.19
Venture Capital Firm	$8,483.09
Broker/Dealer	$7,450.14
Bank	$3,943.72
Insurance	$1,811.63
Charitable/Educational/Family Trust	$497.73

those obtaining funding from other types of PIPE investors during the following two years.

Dai (2007) examines the PIPEs invested by venture capital funds and compares the investment behavior of VCs and hedge funds in the PIPE market. She finds that the stock performance of VC-invested firms is significantly better than hedge-fund invested firms both in the short run and in the long run. She further reports that VCs gain substantial ownership, request board seats, and often keep their stake after the PIPEs. In contrast, hedge funds rarely join the board of directors and typically cash out their positions shortly after the PIPE.

THE ROLE OF PLACEMENT AGENTS

An issuer undertaking a PIPE generally engages the services of an investment bank to serve as its agent. Unlike the straight (traditional) private placement, whereby a lead investor or a group of lead investors dominates and shapes the process, the PIPE process is led by the placement agent. The major obligations of placement agents include assisting with preparation of the private placement memorandum, assisting with preparation of a road show or investor presentation, and introducing the issuer to potential investors. These duties are typically outlined in an engagement letter with the issuer. The engagement letter also sets forth the agency fees and the terms and conditions for payment. A placement agent often negotiates for itself a "tail," affording it the right to receive a fee in respect of future financings, especially other PIPEs during some set period. A placement agent may also negotiate with the issuer a right of first offer or a right of first refusal to participate in future financings or to serve in an advisory capacity. Different from most of the U.S. IPO/SEO underwriting business, the placement agent has no commitment to purchase any of the securities, suggesting the best efforts contract rather than the firm commitment contract. In PIPEs, placement agents conduct their own due diligence and many take the view that they may be regarded as "underwriters" under the securities laws.

While the underwriters of IPO and SEOs supposedly take the third-party "gatekeeping role" between issuers and investors, PIPE placement agents could be exposed to additional risk of alleging violations of both stock registration and investor misrepresentation. Because PIPE investors are aware of the possibility that an issuer's stock can decline after the PIPE announcement, they have a strong incentive to short-sell the number of shares they purchase in the PIPE and cover the sale by purchasing the needed shares in the market following the price drop upon the announcement of the PIPE offering. Both regulators and prosecutors have taken the position that this type of transaction is unlawful insider trading. In addition, because the nature of the relationships between issuers and investors can be difficult to discern in PIPE offerings, PIPE offerings often raise the question whether there was an affirmative misrepresentation regarding investment intent.

According to Dai, Jo, and Schatzberg (2009), some of the placement agents are well-known names in the IPO and SEO underwriting business, such as Citigroup, UBS, Lehman Brothers, and so on. Others, such as Coastline Capital Partners, Halpern Capital, and ThinkEquity Partners, are less well-known and are specialized players in this market. Dai, Jo, and Schatzberg (2009) also relate PIPE agents to the Carter and Manaster (C&M) ranking, which is commonly used to represent the participation and reputation of IPO/SEO underwriters. Among the 215 PIPE placement agents in their sample (1996–2005), a total of 121 agents have C&M ranking with a mean (median) ranking of 5.4 (5.1). A total of 20 placement agents have a C&M ranking of at least 8.1. In very rare cases, PIPE placement agents are the issuers' IPO underwriters or previous SEO underwriters (only 1.5 percent).

Dai, Jo, and Schatzberg (2009) examine how placement agents select PIPE firms and how their reputation impacts the PIPE transactions' discounts, agent fees charged, and information environment of the firm before and after the PIPE offering. They find that there exits a positive assertive matching in the PIPE market, where reputable placement agents are associated with larger offers and firms with less risks. More reputable agents offer higher quality services in that their deals are priced at lower discounts in an improved information environment. Issuers pay a higher dollar fee for these benefits, although more reputable agents charge a lower percentage fee. The evidence suggests that it is the quality of the issuing firm, and the pricing and reputational concern of the placement agent that drives the equilibrium in the PIPE market.

Huang, Shangguan, and Zhang (2008) investigate the networking function of placement agents in the PIPE market. They find that placement agents with stronger networking abilities help issuers attract more investors. Similarly, investors are more likely to participate in an issue if they have an existing relationship with the placement agent.

ISSUES IN THE PIPE MARKET AND SEC REGULATIONS

Some problems emerge while the PIPE market has been picking up its steam over the past few years. Recently, the SEC has filed complaints against several PIPE investors.[6] The common charges include (1) false representation, (2) illegal insider trading, and (3) sale of unregistered securities. During the PIPE offering, the placement agent will distribute nonpublic information about the issuer to the potential PIPE investors and the latter are requested to sign an agreement to keep the information confidential and not to trade or direct others to trade on the issuers' securities. Many PIPE investors "hedge" their investment by selling short the PIPE issuer's securities before the resale registration statement is declared effective or even before the public announcement of the PIPE offering. There is nothing per se illegal about "hedging" a PIPE investment by selling short the issuer's securities. Such short sales do not violate the registration provisions of the Securities Act if, among other things, the investor closes out the short position with shares purchased in the open market. An investor violates Section 5 of the Securities Act, however, when it covers its pre-effective date short position with the actual shares received in the PIPE. This is because shares used to cover a short sale are deemed to have been sold when the short sale was made.

For instance, in the case of Hilary L. Shane in connection with a PIPE offering of stock by CompuDyne Corporation, the SEC alleges that Shane had sold short CompuDyne's stocks before the company publicly announced the PIPE offering using material nonpublic information about the company disclosed by the placement agent to Shane.[7] At the time of her short selling, she did not borrow, or deliver to the purchaser, the shares of CompuDyne that she sold short. She ultimately used the shares that she obtained from the PIPE offering to cover her short position. Thus, Shane breached her duty of trust and confidence because her transactions violated her agreement with the company and placement agent not to trade on the nonpublic information and was engaged in insider trading. Furthermore, when she executed her short sales of CompuDyne securities, there was no resale registration statement in effect for the PIPE shares and no exemption from registration applied to the sales of those shares. By short-selling CompuDyne securities before the effective date of the resale registration statement for the CompuDyne PIPE shares and covering her short sales with the PIPE shares after the resale registration statement became effective, Shane effectively sold the shares prior to their registration, thus violating Section 5 of the Securities Act.

According to the SEC documentations, to avoid detection and regulatory scrutiny, some PIPE investors employed a variety of deceptive trading techniques, including wash sales and matched orders, to make it appear that they were covering their short positions with legal, open-market stock purchase when in fact the covering transactions were not open-market transactions. For example, in the case of Langley Partners in connection with the PIPE offering by the MGI Pharma, Inc., Langley Partners invested $1,100,000 in the offering, receiving 100,000 restricted MGI Pharma shares at $11 per share, which represents a discount of approximately 15 percent from MGI Pharma's then-market price of approximately $13 per share.[8] Langley Partners quickly short-sold all 100,000 of its restricted shares (50,000 at $13.15 and 50,000 at $13.56), garnering proceeds of $1,335,500. Thus, Langley Partners had purchased 100,000 shares in the PIPE and shorted 100,000 shares before the resale registration statement was effective.

Using its Canadian broker-dealer, Langley Partners executed "naked" short sales by, among other things, selling short without either owning unrestricted shares or borrowing unrestricted shares to deliver.[9] In addition to its "naked" Canadian short selling, Langley Partners also engaged in short-selling in the United States through domestic broker-dealers or by executing short-sale orders itself through electronic communications networks. Once Langley Partners had established its short position, it waited until the SEC declared effective the resale registration statement and then began to use its PIPE shares to cover (or "unwind") the short positions.

To close out Canadian short positions, Langley Partners engaged in prearranged matched orders with its Canadian broker-dealer. To execute the matched orders, Langley Partners called the Canadian broker to inform him that Langley Partners intended to sell a certain number of its PIPE shares from its domestic prime brokerage account at a particular time and price using a particular exchange. At the same time, Langley Partners asked the broker to enter a buy order for Langley Partners' Canadian account for the same number of shares at the same time and price and on the same exchange. Thus, the buy and sell orders would meet on the specified exchange, and the Canadian broker-dealer would use the PIPE shares that he had just purchased from Langley Partners' domestic account to close out Langley Partners' short positions.

To close out its short position in its U.S. domestic prime brokerage account, Langley Partners used wash sales. Langley Partners asked broker-dealers to register as market makers in particular PIPE securities to assist Langley Partners in washing its PIPE shares. With the help of these broker-dealers, Langley Partners sold its PIPE shares to the brokers, which then sold the exact same shares back to Langley Partners. Once Langley Partners had received its PIPE shares back from the broker-dealers, Langley Partners used those PIPE shares to close out its short positions.

Through the deceptive methods described above, Langley Partners used the shares obtained from the PIPE offering to close out its short position established before the SEC declares the effectiveness of the security registration statement. Langley Partners' profit was therefore locked in at the moment its short sales were executed: the $1,335,500 short sale proceeds minus the $1,100,000 investment, for a net profit of $235,500. Thus, Langley Partners violated Section 5 of the Securities Act.

In addition to the above-mentioned issues (false representation, insider trading, and sales of unregistered securities), another primary concern of the SEC involves the structured PIPEs where floating convertibles, which are often called "Death Spiral" convertibles or "Toxic" convertibles, are issued.

Any PIPE that involves issuance of a security at a discount from its current market value can expose a company's existing shareholders to the risk of significant dilution. In particular, in a structured PIPE, the amount of securities issuable upon conversion is indeterminate and variable. Typically, to protect the investors, the conversion price or ratio reset downward if the market price of the common stocks decline. As the company is required to issue more stocks upon a lower conversion price, its stock price drops further, thus causing the stock to enter a death spiral. Unless the securities have a cap or floor that limits such adjustments, the extent of potential dilution could be substantial. Hillion and Vermaelen (2004) demonstrate that firms issuing floating convertible bonds tend to perform poorly in the long run. Furthermore, they suggest that such floating convertibles encourage short selling by convertible holders and that the resulting dilution triggers a permanent decline in the share price.

A sample case on the manipulative trading is *SEC vs. Rhino Advisers* in connection to the PIPE offering by Sedona Corporation.[10] Sedona issued convertible debentures to one of Rhino's clients. The debenture granted the investor the right to convert all or any portion of the debenture into Sedona common stock at a price equal to 85 percent of "the volume weighted average price of the Common Stock on the Nasdaq Small Cap Market during the five trading days immediately prior to the Closing Date or Conversion Date." The debenture does include a provision that prohibits investors from selling Sedona's stock short while the issued debentures remain issued and outstanding. Despite this contractual provision, Rhino engaged in extensive short-selling prior to exercising the conversion rights. The extensive short selling substantially depressed Sedona's stock price. As a result, Sedona had to issue more shares when Rhino exercised its conversion rights.

While the SEC has made the above arguments with respect to PIPE investors, as far as we know, the courts have not yet validated the SEC's positions. Despite this unsettled state of the law, various hedge funds and their advisers have agreed to multimillion dollar settlements as well as suspensions or bars when faced with SEC enforcement actions. When asked whether the SEC plans any rulemaking to attack this problem at the 27th SEC Government-Business Forum on Small Business Capital Formation Program, Brian Breheny, the deputy director of the division of corporation finance of the SEC, replied, "I don't know what we'll see in the future. It is something that we're certainly looking about and it is something that we're looking for."

THE PIPE MARKET DOWN THE ROAD

The U.S. PIPE market totaled $121 billion raised through 1,035 transactions in 2008.[11] While 2008 was a record year for total dollars raised in the PIPE market, we wonder given the current equity market turmoil, how the PIPE market has been impacted and where the market is heading for. I analyze the trends from four perspectives, investor profile, issuer profile, placement agents, and the internationalization of this market.[12]

The statistics provided by Sagient Research show that the PIPE investor profile has changed in 2008. For instance, hedge funds used to be the predominant investor in the PIPE market. Investments by hedge funds often account for 40 to 50 percent of the total deals. Nevertheless, in 2008, hedge fund activities in the PIPE market dropped dramatically to about 10 percent of the market. On the other hand, VC/PE investors and corporate investors, who are often regarded as strategic investors, have been picking up the slack. Each group counts for more than 20 percent of the market in 2008. The trend makes economic sense. Given that many public firms' stocks are undervalued and have the high risk of continuing to decline in the near future, it is becoming more difficult for hedge funds, who are typically targeting for the short-term financial profits, to earn quick bucks out of the PIPE deals. As for VC/PE investors and corporate investors, who typically are long-term value investors, it is a great opportunity to invest in companies with solid fundamentals, but that are short of cash due to the market condition, at a more attractive price.

While the revenue sources from IPO/SEO underwriting and M&A advisory services have been drying for investment banks, many investment banks will consider cultivating the business opportunities in the PIPE segment. Potentially, more competition will improve the efficiency of the offering process and make the deal less costly in terms of lower agent fees. The average agent fee rate has decreased to 3.3 percent in 2008 from 6.0 percent in earlier years and could be declining further more.

PIPEs used to be the last-resort type of financing for small- and medium-sized public firms who are barred from more traditional financing approaches. The credit crunch and the miserable stock market have made debt financing and public equity financing highly expensive, or inaccessible even for large firms. PIPE could be an alternative financing technique for those large firms. In 2008, firms with market capitalization exceeding $1 billion have raised about $80 billion from the PIPE market, accounting for more than 70 percent of the total dollar amount raised from this market. We will observe more mega-size PIPE offerings in the future. Furthermore, distressed firms will be less likely to obtain funding from PIPE investors, while fundamentally solid firms with promising growth potential will be more likely to get capital infusion from strategic investors, such as VC/PE and corporate investors.

So far, the United States and Canada have been the most active PIPE markets. This type of financing is still rare in other parts of the world. However, we do see some development of the PIPE market outside the United States and Canada in

2008. For instance, there were 83 PIPE transactions totaling $2.9 billion conducted in Hong Kong, 324 transactions totaling $10.5 billion completed in Australia, 204 transactions totaling $8.9 billion closed in U.K.[13] This trend will continue. We shall see more PIPE transactions in developing economies as well, such as China and India, in the future as investors and investment banks look for alternative investment opportunities.

NOTES

1. Regulation D Rule (501) defines investors from the following categories as accredited investors: banks, broker or dealer, insurance company, registered investment company or business development company, Small Business Investment Company, pension funds, director, executive officer, or general partner of the issuer, corporation, limited liability company, trust or partnership with total assets in excess of $5 million not formed for the specific purpose of acquiring the securities offered, any natural person whose individual net worth, or joint net worth with that person's spouse, at the time of the purchase exceeds $1 million, or income or joint income exceeds $200, 000 or $300,000, respectively, in each of the two most recent years, and any entity in which all equity owners are accredited investors.

2. The SEC has filed complaints against some PIPE investors alleging insider trading and registration violations. Specifically, the allegations involve short-selling prior to both the initial public announcement and to the effective date of the resale registration statement.

3. Maynes and Pandes, 2008.

4. According to Dai, Chen, and Schatzberg (2008) the mean and median discount of PIPEs is 21.1 percent (13.6 percent), with 3.6 percent (2.7 percent) for SEOs during the period of 1996–2003.

5. Also see discussions on how investor identities impact the short-run and long-run stock performance of PIPE firms in Section 3.3.

6. See www.sec.gov.

7. For more details of the case, see www.sec.gov/litigation/complaints/comp19227.pdf.

8. For more details of the case, see www.sec.gov/litigation/complaints/comp19607.pdf.

9. "Naked" short selling was permissible in Canada during the relevant period.

10. For more details on this case, see www.sec.gov/litigation/complaints/comp18003.htm.

11. www.placementracker.com.

12. I would like to thank Brian Overstreet, CEO of the Sagient Research Systems, and Mike Kotecki, also from Sagient Research Systems, for providing data on this matter.

13. Overstreet, 2008.

REFERENCES

Brophy, David J., Paige P. Ouimet, and Clemens Sialm. 2008. "Hedge funds as investors of last resort." *Review of Financial Studies*, forthcoming.

Chaplinsky, Susan, and David Haushalter. 2008. "Financing under extreme uncertainty: Contract terms and returns to private investments in public equity." Working Paper, University of Virginia.

Chen, Hsuan-Chi, Na Dai, and John Schatzberg. 2009. "The choice of equity selling mechanisms: PIPEs versus SEOs." *Journal of Corporate Finance, forthcoming*.

Dai, Na. 2007. "Does investor identity matter? An empirical examination of investments by venture capital funds and hedge funds in PIPEs." *Journal of Corporate Finance* 13:538–563.

Dai, Na, and Hsuan-Chi Chen. 2008. "Seasoned equity selling mechanisms: Costs and innovations." *Journal of Private Equity* 11 (3):16–29.

Dai, Na, Hoje Jo, and John Schatzberg. 2009. The quality and price of investment banks' service: Evidence from the PIPE market. *Financial Management,* forthcoming.

Hillion, Pierre, and Vermaelen, Theo, 2004. "Death spiral convertibles," *Journal of Financial Economics* 71:381–415.

Huang, Rongbing, Zhaoyun Shangguan, and Donghang Zhang. 2008. "The networking function of investment banks: Evidence from private investment in public equity." *Journal of Corporate Finance* 14:738–752.

Maynes, Elizabeth, and Ari Pandes. 2008. Private placements and liquidity. Working Paper, York University.

PIPEs: A guide to private investment in public equity (edited by Steven Dresner and E. Kurt Kim), Princeton, NJ: Bloomberg Press, 2003.

Overstreet, Brian M., 2008. *The PIPE market trends 2008.* San Diego, CA: Sagient Research Systems.

Sjostrom, William K., 2007. PIPEs. *Entrepreneurial Business Law Journal* 2:381–414.

The SEC 27th Government-Business Forum on Small Business Capital Formation Program Record of Proceedings, November 20, 2008. www.sec.gov/info/smallbus/sbforumtrans-112008.pdf.

ABOUT THE AUTHOR

Na Dai obtained her Ph.D. in Finance from the University of Kansas. Dr. Dai is currently an assistant professor of finance at the School of Business at SUNY–Albany. Her primary research interests are private investment in public equities, venture capital, private equities, and hedge funds. Her works have appeared in the *Journal of Corporate Finance, Financial Management,* and the *Journal of Empirical Legal Studies.*

CHAPTER 8

Private Placements by Small Public Entities

Canadian Experience

CÉCILE CARPENTIER
Professor, Laval University, School of Accountancy

JEAN-MARC SURET
Professor, Laval University, School of Accountancy

INTRODUCTION

The specificities of the Canadian securities market render the analysis of private placements particularly insightful in this country. First, Canada applies very lax listing requirements, allowing tiny capitalization companies to list at a prerevenue stage (Carpentier and Suret 2009). Most of the private placements are offered by these companies—in essence, entrepreneurial ventures—for which the asymmetry of information and adverse selection problems are particularly acute. Second, public companies tend to use private placements more frequently than seasoned equity offerings as a financing source, probably owing to the lax regulation of this activity. Private placements seem to be a very important source of equity for these emerging businesses, which allows the analysis of a large number of placements. Third, hedge funds and other institutional investors that are strongly involved in the private equity activity in the United States are only marginally active in Canada, where individual investors are the main buyers of private placements. In contrast with the public offering process, placements of shares are made in the exempt market with accredited or sophisticated investors, and mandatory disclosure is dispensed with because it is assumed that these investors would be knowledgeable enough to protect their own interests. The question of whether such investors can indeed invest wisely in emerging companies should be analyzed. Lastly, in Canada, private placements are mainly composed of ordinary stocks, in contrast with the United States, where structured private investments in public equity (PIPEs) make up a large proportion of private placements. The valuation problems associated with the specificities of structured PIPEs are then largely absent.

This situation provides a unique opportunity to analyze the information and pricing dynamics around private placements, which are quite different from PIPEs in the United States. The aim of this chapter is to analyze the extent to which this financing tool can be considered "fair," that is, if it provides investors with a fair rate of return and if accredited investors are indeed able to price these placements correctly in a context of a large asymmetry of information.

We observe a strong rally before the announcement and a significant negative abnormal return following the placement. This long-run underperformance persists even when the return is adjusted for the discount, providing an estimation of the rate of return of private equity investors. This indicates that, on average, the private investors overpaid for the shares they acquired during private placements. The implicit assumption behind the exempt distribution is that the sophisticated investors are informed and skilled enough to accurately appraise the stocks in which they invest. Our results evidence that this is not the case, particularly for growth and hard-to-value stocks, and that investors do not earn a fair rate of return.

This chapter is organized as follows. In the next section, we present the Canadian securities market and regulation of private placement. We then examine the characteristics of issuers and their operating performance ("Private Placement and the Issuers"), the returns surrounding the private placements ("Returns Surrounding Private Placements"), and the discount ("Discounts"). In each case, we provide evidence taken from the population of private placements we analyzed and we attempt to explain the observed phenomenon in light of previous conceptual work and our knowledge of the specificities of the Canadian market. In the last section, we summarize and discuss our results in terms of policy, regulation, and firm financing.[1]

THE CANADIAN CONTEXT

To understand the characteristics of the private placement market in Canada, two main dimensions should be discussed: the Canadian securities market and the regulation.

The Canadian Stock Market

The stock market in Canada is devoted to small capitalization stocks. There are two important stock exchanges in Canada: Toronto Stock Exchange (TSX) and TSX Venture Exchange (TSXV). The first exchange is the main market, but it can be roughly considered a junior market, according to international criteria. The distribution of market capitalizations is similar to that observed on the Alternative Investment Market in London. The TSXV is considered a public venture capital market. Overall, only 245 companies listed in Canada do not fall in the small or micro-capitalization categories, as defined by the Advisory Committee on Smaller Public Companies to the U.S. Securities and Exchange Commission (SEC). The very low initial listing requirements, the frequency of backdoor listings, and the existence of a public venture capital market that feeds the main stock market with a large number of small firms at a prerevenue or preearning stage explain this particular situation. Carpentier and Suret (2009) illustrate that during the 1986-2006 period, the median preissue shareholders' equity and gross proceeds of Canadian firms newly listed on the TSXV were CAN$260,000 and CAN$650,000 respectively. Moreover, more than 49 percent of issuers report no revenues and 80 percent report negative earnings. The majority of Canadian IPOs can be considered penny-stock IPOs, while in most countries, minimal listing requirements exclude micro-capitalization and start-up companies from the stock exchange, even in so-called junior markets. Their financial needs are generally modest and do not justify a public offering. This can explain the relative frequency of private placements.

A second relevant dimension in the analysis of Canadian private placements is the relative importance of the resources and oil and gas sectors. At the end of 2004, TSX and TSXV mining companies had an aggregate market capitalization of US$140 billion, and represented over 50 percent of the world's listed mining companies, according to data provided by the exchanges. More than 50 percent of the private placements originated from companies involved in the natural resource sector, where the financing tradition differs from those prevailing in other sectors.

Regulation of Private Placements in Canada

Regulation is another explanation for the popularity of private placements. The rules governing the exempt market are generally more lax in Canada than in the United States. Several rounds of regulatory changes have been implemented in Canada, notably in 2001 and in 2006.

The changes introduced in Ontario in 2001 through rule 45-501 and the shortening of lock-up periods implemented concomitantly in all Canadian provinces may have reduced the barriers for issuing private equity. These changes have mainly impacted private corporations.[2] As this chapter is devoted to the private placements of public companies, we simply describe the main elements of the regulation of the types of transactions existing during our period of analysis. Prior to 2001, the legislation in many Canadian provinces, including Ontario, offered two exemptions from the requirement to issue a prospectus and register: the private company exemption and the $150,000 exemption, where people with $150,000 to invest were deemed sophisticated enough to make investment decisions without the need for a prospectus. Following the recommendations of the Ontario Securities Commission (OSC) Task Force on Small Business (Ontario Securities Commission 1996), the Ontario Government implemented significant changes to the securities regulation. In effect, Rule 45-501 replaces several previous exemptions with a closely held business issuer exemption and an accredited investor exemption. The accredited investor exemption permits issuers to raise any amount from any person or company that meets specified qualification criteria. Accredited investors include banks, loan and trust companies, insurance companies, the federal, provincial, and municipal governments and their agencies and international counterparts, mutual funds, and nonredeemable funds that distribute securities under a prospectus or to accredited investors, certain pension funds and charities, individuals (together with their spouses) with a net worth of at least $1,000,000, persons having had in the last two years and expecting in the next year a net income of not less than $200,000 individually or $300,000 as a couple, corporations and other entities having net assets of at least $5,000,000, directors, officers, and promoters of an issuer and the issuer's controlling shareholders. Issuers are not required to provide accredited investors with an offering memorandum or other disclosure document. Further, several securities exchange commissions, including the OSC, have adopted the new Multilateral Instrument 45-102 Resale of Securities (MI 45-102). Essentially, this rule harmonizes certain provincial and territorial resale restrictions applicable to securities distributed under prospectus exemptions. The MI 45-102 also changes the resale restriction periods. Under the previous rule, securities acquired in a private placement are subject to a four-month holding period if the issuer is a qualifying issuer (i.e., if its securities are listed on an exchange). If the issuer is not a qualifying issuer, resale is restricted for 12 months. MI 45-102 reduces the restricted period from 12 to 4 months for the securities of a nonqualifying issuer.

On September 14, 2005, the Canadian Securities Administrator's (CSA) National Instrument 45-106 (NI 45-106) entitled "Prospectus and Registration Exemptions" became effective in most provinces. This rule was an effort to harmonize and consolidate the various prospectus and registration exemptions available across the country. This rule sets the minimum investment exemption uniformly across Canada. Securities can be sold on an exempt basis to any purchaser if the purchaser, acting as principal, acquires securities with an acquisition cost of not less than $150,000, which is paid in cash at closing. According to this regulation, firms can use the accredited investor exemption to raise any amount, at any time, from any person or company that qualifies as an accredited investor. To summarize, in Canada, numerous individuals and institutions can participate in private placements, and the resale restrictions are minimal.

PRIVATE PLACEMENTS AND THE ISSUERS

Data

We collected information on 4,592 private placements from the Financial Post database, and provide similar information for seasoned equity offerings (SEOs) for comparison purposes. Our data span the 1993 to 2003 period. Exhibit 8.1 illustrates that Canadian firms have issued more private placements than public SEOs. During the 1993 to 2003 period, private placements represented 61.60 percent of all Canadian post–initial public offering (IPO) placements. The gross proceeds raised by private placements are generally less than those raised in the public market. The median private placement is CAN$3 million, versus CAN$8.87 million for SEOs. We have probably overlooked a significant number of small size placements because private placements lower than CAN$1.5 million are not referenced in the database. The total proceeds obtained via private placements represent CAN$35.68 billion, that is, 21.66 percent of the total post-IPO offerings.

Exhibit 8.1 shows strong variation in the number of private placements, from a high of 685 in 1996 to a low of 149 in 1999. The number of SEOs fluctuates to a lesser extent, and there is some indication of a switching effect: the year 1999 is a trough for private placements, but a peak for SEOs. To verify this possibility, we present the monthly numbers of both categories of financing in Exhibit 8.2. Apart from during the 1999 to 2000 period of the technology bubble, both categories exhibit a similar pattern. For Canadian public companies, private placements can be seen as a complement, rather than a substitute, to public financing.

Exhibit 8.1 Annual Statistics on Canadian Private Placements and Public Offerings by Issuers Listed on the Canadian Stock Exchanges, 1993–2003

	Private Placements			Public Offerings		
Year	Number of Issues	Median GP, CAN$M	Total GP, CAN$M	Number of issues	Median GP, CAN$M	Total GP, CAN$M
Panel A: Population						
1993	668	1.73	3,372.12	331	7.00	15,334.16
1994	775	1.30	3,589.73	237	4.35	8,485.64
1995	317	3.45	2,403.82	174	5.23	6,618.11
1996	685	4.07	5,909.06	291	11.00	10,649.63
1997	530	4.12	5,021.83	228	25.85	16,367.74
1998	260	4.42	4,217.61	141	23.14	7,729.88
1999	149	3.20	1,394.27	333	8.00	16,360.33
2000	241	2.93	1,499.92	364	7.69	12,351.14
2001	164	2.96	1,394.67	274	5.34	8,274.48
2002	280	3.08	1,781.88	248	8.34	14,691.96
2003	523	4.08	5,096.42	241	15.00	12,209.08
Total	4,592	3.00	35,681.31	2,862	8.87	129,072.15
Panel B: Final Sample						
1993	509	1.58	2,407.12	255	7.20	11,153.43
1994	501	1.50	2,247.03	156	3.71	5,176.60
1995	220	3.50	1,402.85	113	9.10	5,122.21
1996	477	4.00	4,023.10	196	13.25	7,840.73
1997	314	4.55	2,693.72	136	24.83	8,074.39
1998	172	4.00	1,669.54	103	30.80	6,622.31
1999	115	3.00	970.32	241	8.10	13,494.47
2000	182	2.94	1,130.64	262	8.25	10,308.41
2001	138	2.87	911.91	209	7.50	6,902.21
2002	245	3.46	1,777.97	213	10.92	13,776.51
2003	418	4.75	3,454.25	195	19.07	9,713.15
Total	3,291	3.00	22,688.44	2,079	10.04	98,184.42

Panel A reports the population of 4,592 Canadian private placements and 2,862 public offerings that occurred between January 1993 and December 2003. All issues are equity issues reported by the Financial Post database which comprise common stocks and unit (equity and warrant). Panel B reports the final sample restricted to observations, with market data (DataStream) and with accounting data (Thomson's Cancorp financials). Each of the following placements, reported as distinct in the database, is considered as a single issue: two sets of units placed within a few days; two sets of securities, issued within 5 transactions days, with one of them being a flow-through; an SEO sold simultaneously in several countries; and securities placed under the same conditions and at the same price with several investors, within five transaction days. This method reduces the sample by 396 issues. We include in the analysis companies with market data for the 3 months before and after the placement date.

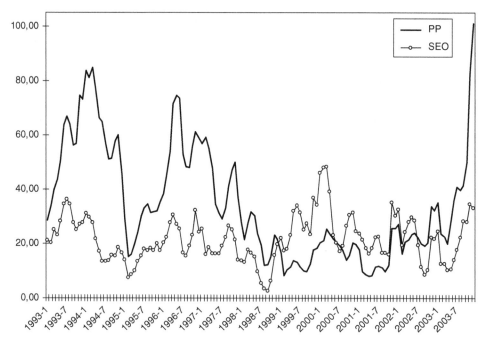

Exhibit 8.2 Monthly Canadian Private Placements (PP) and Seasoned Public Offerings (SEO) in Canada, 1993–2003

Which Firms Issue Private Placements?

Empirical studies report that the U.S. PIPE issuers are generally small capitalization firms with mean market value around US$120 million and median value around US$40 million. Kim (2002) states that more than 86 percent of PIPEs between January 1, 2001, and October 5, 2002, were issued by companies with assets below US$250 million. Brophy, Ouimet, Sialm (2005) report a median book value of assets of US$26 million. The book-to-market ratio is a proxy for the growth opportunities of a firm. This ratio is lower for firms with more growth opportunities and higher for firms with fewer growth options. In the United States, the median book-to-market ratio for companies issuing PIPEs is around 0.34 according to Krishnamurthy, Spindt, Subramaniam et al. (2004, 12). Brophy et al. (2005) and Hertzel, Lemmon, Link et al. (2002) find a mean (median) book-to-market ratio of 0.42 (0.23) and 0.43 (0.26) respectively. Companies issuing PIPEs seem to be growth-oriented.

In Canada, private placements are often raised by small capitalized firms traded on the TSXV. However, during the 1993 to 2003 period, firms listed on the main board issued 1,500 private placements; approximately 70 percent of the TSX listed companies used this type of financing during this period. Accordingly, private placements are not limited to junior stocks and exchanges; they have entered into very widespread use among the vast majority of Canadian listed stocks.

Exhibit 8.3 presents the main characteristics of the Canadian issuers of private placements, and allows a comparison with U.S. studies. This table indicates that the issuers are generally small firms, with a median shareholders' equity of CAN$10.69 million and total assets of CAN$15.17 million. This is in line with the

Exhibit 8.3 Sample Characteristics and Distribution of the Sample of Private Placements According to Industry and Use of Proceeds

Panel A: General Characteristics

	#	Mean	Median	Total
Gross proceeds, $M	3,291	6.89	3.00	22,688.44
Proceeds-to-size	3,234	0.55	0.27	–
BTM >0 at time T_{-1}	2,337	0.49	0.22	–
Total assets T_0, $M	2,352	74.23	15.17	–
Shareholders' equity T_0, $M	2,352	34.53	10.69	–
Debt to assets T_0	2,352	0.39	0.22	–

Panel B: Industrial Distribution

	Resources	Oil & Gas	High-Tech	Other
Gross proceeds	35.49%	24.80%	18.09%	21.62%
Number of issues	41.36%	26.71%	17.32%	14.62%

Panel C: Use of Gross Proceeds

	#	#%	TGP CAN$M	TGP%
Exploration	1,379	52.10%	7,436.01	39.17%
Investment	498	18.81%	5,633.26	29.67%
Corporate	770	29.09%	5,915.70	31.16%
Not available	644	–	3,703.46	–

Panel A reports the sample characteristics. Gross proceeds, total assets and shareholders' equity are expressed in millions of Canadian dollars ($M). Proceeds-to-size is the gross proceeds divided by the pre-money market value of equity. BTM stands for book to market, T_0 for the end of the issuing year, and T_{-1} for the end of the preceding year. Total assets, shareholders' equity and debt ratios are estimated on a post-money basis. Panel B reports the industrial distribution. Resources, Oil & Gas, High Tech and Other is the percentage of the total gross proceeds of private issues respectively by resources, oil and gas, high tech-biotech and other companies. Panel C reports the distribution of issues according to the use of gross proceeds.

characteristics of the Canadian market. Accordingly, the median gross proceeds are limited to CAN$3 million. The mean book-to-market estimated at the end of the year preceding the placements is 0.49. This book-to-market is higher than the one reported by Brophy et al. (2005) in their sample of 3,793 companies (0.42). Canadian private placement issuers seem to be smaller and to have fewer growth opportunities than the American companies issuing PIPEs. This can be traced to the fact that, in the United States, private placements are more concentrated in the technology sector than in Canada.

Industry Clustering

There is evidence of industry clustering among companies issuing private placements. Hertzel et al. (2002) show that in their sample of 619 PIPEs, 55 percent of companies belong to six manufacturing and services industries (chemicals and allied products, electric and electronics equipment, holding and other investment offices, instruments and related products, industrial machinery and equipment and business services). Dresner and Kim (2003) show that PIPEs in the United States are primarily issued by technological and health companies, particularly biotechnological and pharmaceutical firms. Exhibit 8.3 presents the industrial distribution of our sample of Canadian private placements over the 1993 to 2003 period, and shows that 68.07 percent of the private placements (60.29 percent of the total gross proceeds) are issued by natural resources companies. The other important issuing sectors are the technologies and biotechnologies sector, with 17.32 percent of the private placements (18.09 percent of the raised amounts). Canadian private placements are largely concentrated in the primary sector, which differs from the U.S. situation.

Disparate industrial structures in both countries partly explain these differences. Faruqui, Gu, Kaci, Laroche, Maynard et al. (2003) assert that the primary industry accounts for 8.2 percent of nominal output and 7.3 percent of hours worked in Canada, whereas these figures are 3.6 percent and 3.6 percent respectively in the United States. We also calculate that 15.6 percent of public U.S. firms operate in the resources sector, whereas the corresponding proportion is 38 percent in Canada. Accordingly, this difference cannot totally explain the large concentration of private placements in the primary sector in Canada.

In Panel C of Exhibit 8.3, we report the intended use of proceeds, where data were available. In line with the high proportion of issuers involved in activities linked to natural resources, 52.10 percent of private placements are assumed to finance exploration projects. Close to 30 percent of placements are levied to finance working capital (corporate uses) and only 18.81 percent finances investment projects. In Canada, emerging companies thus issue private placements to finance their development or their exploration projects.

Financing Strategies and Clustering of Issuers

Issuers and private placements constitute a very heterogeneous universe in Canada. Alongside a few large placements of half a billion dollars and more, we note hundreds of very small issues, which explain the median size of around CAN$3 million. Moreover, some issuers are occasional users of the private equity market, while others carry out private placements on a regular basis. In Exhibit 8.4, we present a distribution of the issuers (Panel A) and of the placements (Panel B) to paint a better defined picture of this phenomenon.

In Panel A, we observe that the four most active issuers (group 1) collectively attracted more than CAN$4 billion, that is, 11.50 percent of the total amount of the private equity placements issued by public companies in Canada during the studied period. The mean market capitalization of these issuers is CAN$6.97 billion.[3] This group is mainly composed of financials (Fairfax, Great-West Lifeco, and Newcourt Credit Group) and of Falconbridge in the resources sector.

The second group consists of 37 issuers that each issued from CAN$100 million to CAN$500 million, for a total of CAN$5.77 billion. Together, the 41 most important issuers included in groups 1 and 2 levied approximately a quarter of the private equity gross proceeds, and launched four placements, on average, during the

10 years analyzed. Seventeen of these issuers belong to the resource sector, and nine can be considered technology companies.

The 401 firms included in group 3 issued four private placements in 10 years, on average; this type of financing has became commonplace for these firms. Each issuer in this group obtained an average amount of CAN$39 million from private equity investors during this period. These companies account for the bulk (44 percent) of the total gross proceeds, and the largest share of the placements (31.23 percent). The issuers are mid-sized companies (according to Canadian criteria), with a mean (median) market capitalization of CAN$188 ($88) million.

Issuers in group 4 are small-sized, with a mean (median) market capitalization of CAN$47 ($25) million. They raised two placements, on average, for a total amount of CAN$10 million per firm, and a total for this group of CAN$8.06 billion. Lastly, group 5 consists of very small issuers whose median capitalization is about CAN$8 million. Collectively, they obtained CAN$2 billion from private equity issuers, and the average amount per issuer is CAN$2.3 million. The bulk of private placements are launched by medium-sized companies, which use this mode of financing on a regular basis. Smaller issuers are very active, as estimated by the number of placements, but the total proceeds are small. Please see Exhibit 8.4.

Operating Performance

In the United States, PIPEs are often considered as a financing mode for distressed or heavily constrained companies (Chaplinsky and Haushalter 2006; Gombola, Liu,

Exhibit 8.4   Distribution of Private Placement Issuers Based on the Total (Panel A) and Per Placement Gross Proceeds (Panel B)

	Number of		Gross Proceeds		Market Cap. (CAN$M)	
	Issuers	Issues	$M	%	Mean	Median
Panel A: Groups Based on the Total Gross Proceeds of Private Placements, 1993–2003						
Group 1: more than 500	4	15	4,102	11.50	6,974	5,681
Group 2: 100 to 500	37	128	5,770	16.17	849	340
Group 3: 20 to 100	401	1,434	15,696	44.00	188	88
Group 4: 5 to 20	785	1,855	8,056	22.58	47	25
Group 5: less than 5	890	1,160	2,050	5.75	16	8
Total	2,117	4,592	35,673	100.00	96	21
Panel B: Groups Based on Gross Proceeds of Each Placement						
A more than 500	4	4	2,740	7.68	9,597	4
B 100 to 500	24	30	4,707	13.19	1,999	24
C 20 to 100	237	283	9,934	27.85	287	237
D 5 to 20	855	1,267	11,776	33.01	81	855
E less than 5	1,659	3,008	6,516	18.27	26	1,659
Total	2,779	4,592	35,673	100.00	82	2,779

Chou et al. 2006; Anderson and Rose 2007). We analyze the operational characteristics of Canadian issuers, both before and after the announcement. In each case, we collected the main accounting data for the seven years surrounding the private placements, to analyze the evolution of this performance after the financing. Exhibit 8.5 summarizes the results for each year from –3 to +3; the year 0 is the year of the private placement. In Panel A, we report the main statistics related to revenues, Panel B presents statistics on the operating income before depreciation (OIBD), and Panel C describes the raw and adjusted return on assets (ROA), estimated as follows. First, we purged the Canadian universe, by omitting issuing firms for the three years surrounding any equity issue. From this sample, we then estimated the median of the ratio for six size groups (estimated by the book value of equity) and by sector (three digits, or two, if the number of observations is lower than six). The abnormal performance of a firm is estimated by its raw return minus the median ratio of its size and sector matching group.

Preissue Performance

The proportion of firms that report no revenues decreases from 46.94 percent to 39.36 percent at year 0. More than four out of every ten private issuers report no revenues at time -1, but the proportion decreases by the issue time. The issuers that do not report revenues are generally in the resources or technology sectors. Canadian issuers of private placements are indeed in the development stage, or are involved in exploration activities. However, the slight increase in the amount of operating revenues before the placements is consistent with an attempt to time these placements to coincide with a slight improvement in the numbers. However, the increase in revenues does not translate into a significant improvement in profitability. The median OIBD is largely negative before the placement and the proportion of negative OIBD fluctuates around 66 percent. This proportion increases up to year -1, and decreases slightly at the placement time. Reported values illustrate that a large proportion of Canadian issuers are in the early stages of development.

The median raw ROA ratio, estimated after depreciation, is strongly negative. Although negative, the median ROA is high relative to the results reported for PIPEs in the United States. The high proportion of resources and exploration firms explains this situation. They have few operations before the placement, and the net income is only slightly negative. The median ROA at time $t = 0$ for technological firms is -32 percent, a result similar to the values reported by the U.S. studies. This result is in line with the observation of Hertzel et al. (2002) that PIPEs tend to follow periods of relatively poor operating performance. We also provide the industry-adjusted performance ratios, which indicate that while clearly negative, the operating performance of issuers is generally better than that of comparable nonissuer firms. This can partially explain why private investors agree to participate in these placements.

Private Canadian issuers exhibit a negative median ROA, and a large proportion report negative operating income. However, the proportion of firms reporting no revenues decreases before the placement, and the ROA is slightly higher than that of comparable firms. This can explain the relative optimism of private investors, who usually overprice the stocks that are sold during private

Exhibit 8.5 Main Operating Performance Statistics of Private Equity Issuers during Seven Years Surrounding Announcement

Panel A: Revenues

	Median, CAN$M	Proportion with No Revenues	Nb Observations
Year−3	0.02	46.94	1,960
Year−2	0.05	44.68	2,209
Year−1	0.20	42.12	2,393
Year 0	0.69	39.36	2,350
Year 1	0.88	38.82	1,986
Year 2	0.59	40.64	1,693
Year 3	0.34	42.50	1,494

Panel B: OIBD

	Median, CAN$M	Proportion of Negative OIBD	Nb Observations
Year−3	−0.13	66.51	1,493
Year−2	−0.15	67.51	1,868
Year−1	−0.23	67.46	2,219
Year 0	−0.42	65.64	2,232
Year 1	−0.51	66.60	1,901
Year 2	−0.40	66.73	1,632
Year 3	−0.33	66.94	1,446

Panel C: ROA

	Median, (%)	Sector and Size-Adjusted Median	Nb Observations
Year−3	−10.93	0.80	1,949
Year−2	−10.59	1.47	2,199
Year−1	−8.53	2.98	2,386
Year 0	−6.49	3.02	2,350
Year 1	−8.18	0.00	1,984
Year 2	−8.99	−0.36	1,690
Year 3	−9.70	−0.29	1,492

placements, as evidenced by our analysis of the long-run performance following private placements.

The Postplacement Performance

Both sales and OIBD decrease after private placements. The proportion of no sales (negative OIBD) is 38.82 percent (66.60 percent) after the issue, but increases to 42.5 percent (66.94 percent) at the end of the third year following a private placement. The issuers we analyze fail to improve both their operations and their operating income in spite of a significant injection of equity. The median raw ROA decreases sharply after the placement. This effect is more evident when the ratio is adjusted for the sector and size effects. The median adjusted ROA falls from

3.02 percent at the time of the placement to −0.29 percent at the third year. There is a significant decrease in relative performance from the offering year to each of the following years for private placement issuers.

In line with several studies on issues in the United States, we observe a significant decrease in operating performance following private placements. One possible interpretation of this pattern is that managers use windows of opportunity, associated, for example, with a temporary increase in operational performance, to issue new equity.

RETURNS SURROUNDING PRIVATE PLACEMENTS

In this section we present the methodology used to estimate the abnormal return. We then examine the pre- and post-issue return of the individual investors. We conclude by analyzing the differences between the long-run performances, and discuss our results.

The Estimation of Abnormal Returns

The estimation of abnormal returns over the long-run is a difficult task. Event-time models such as cumulative abnormal returns or buy-and-hold returns (BHAR) suffer from numerous problems, especially when the studied events are clustered in time. As depicted in Exhibit 8.2, this is indeed the case with private placements. For this reason, we mainly focus on abnormal returns obtained through the alphas of the Three Factor Pricing Model (TFPM) developed by Fama and French (1993), but we complement the analysis by the estimation of the event-time abnormal returns. We estimate the following regression for each period analyzed (the year preceding the private placement, and one, two, and three years after)

$$R_{p,t} - R_{f,t} = \alpha_p + \beta_p(R_{m,t} - R_{f,t}) + s_p SMB_t + h_p HML_t + e_{p,t} \qquad (8.1)$$

The dependent variable of the regression is the monthly excess return of the portfolios $(R_{p,t} - R_{f,t})$, which corresponds for a given month t to the returns of the portfolio of private issuers $(R_{p,t})$ less the risk-free rate (the monthly rate of 91-day Canadian Government Treasury bills, $R_{f,t}$). The independent variables are the excess market return and two zero-investment portfolios constructed to mimic the risk factors common to all securities. SMB and HML are constructed according to Fama and French (1993). β_p, s_p, and h_p represent the loadings of the portfolio on each risk factor: the market, SMB (size) and HML (book-to-market ratio). The parameter (α) indicates the monthly average abnormal return of our private issuer sample. Market, risk factors and portfolio returns are value-weighted and capped. Following Loughran and Ritter (2000), we scrutinize the performance of private issuer portfolios using purged risk factors, to improve the power of the long-run performance tests.[4] We eliminate returns from issuing firms during the 36-month postissue period in order to reduce benchmark contamination.

We complement the analysis of post-event performance with the study of individual returns, at the issuer level using the BHAR method (namely the investor's experience measure). These returns are estimated against reference portfolios composed of firms of comparable size and book-to-market ratio.[5] To construct the reference portfolios, we extract Canadian firms' book equity from the accounting database and estimate the book-to-market ratios after matching the stock market and accounting databases. To construct the size-control portfolio, all Canadian stocks are ranked each month according to their market capitalization, and three portfolios are formed. Independently, all Canadian stocks are also ranked according to their book-to-market ratios, and three portfolios are formed. The returns of the nine monthly rebalanced portfolios are calculated as the value-weighted average of the individual-firm monthly returns in each of the size/book-to-market intersections. Each issuer is then assigned a control portfolio based on its market capitalization and book-to-market ratio over the performance test period examined. BHARs are based on the calculation of the average abnormal return from a buy-and-hold strategy from the RM month (1) to the month q (36):

$$\overline{BHAR_{1 \text{ to } q}} = \sum_{i=1}^{Nq} w_{i,q} BHAR_{i,1 \text{ to } q}$$

where

$$\text{BHAR}_{i,\ 1 \text{ to } q} = \prod_{s=1}^{q} (1 + R_{i,s}) - \prod_{s=1}^{q} (1 + R_{bi,s}) \qquad (8.2)$$

Thus, BHARs measure the average multiyear returns from a strategy of investing in all firms issuing private placements and selling at the end of a particular holding period, versus a comparable strategy using a benchmark (R_{bi}).

The Preissue Return of the Public Investors

We report, in Exhibit 8.6, the results of the analysis of the preannouncement run-up. The variable of interest is the alpha. This value indicates the monthly abnormal return when size and book-to-market effects are accounted for. To simplify the interpretation of this result, we also report the annual equivalent abnormal return and the total abnormal return. We note a significant value weighted over-performance of 22.82 percent in the year preceding the announcement of the private placement. Our results are consistent with the price run-up observed during the year preceding the issue of U.S. private placements (Hertzel et al. 2002; Marciukaityte, Szewczyk, Varma et al. 2005). We attempt to determine whether the abnormal performance is uniformly distributed over the months preceding the issue, or is concentrated in particular months. In the first case, it can be extrapolated that the market was optimistic about the firm (for reasons to be determined) and that the managers used this optimism to "time" the issue. If the latter situation prevails, and if the rally is concentrated in the few months preceding the announcement, then the timing hypothesis becomes less plausible. We examine four mutually exclusive windows: [−12;−10], [−9;−7], [−6;−4] and [−3;0]. The alpha coefficients corresponding to the [−12;−10] and [−9;−7] windows are not statistically significant, while that for the [−6;−4] window is positive and statistically significant, at 1.39 percent. The alpha coefficient of the [−3; 0] window is highly significant and reaches a monthly 3.29 percent, equivalent to an annual abnormal return of 39.48 percent. This analysis shows that most of the price run-up is concentrated in the

Exhibit 8.6   Abnormal Returns of Canadian Private Issues Using Fama-French
Three-Factor Pricing Model as Benchmark

Holding Period (Month)	Alpha	Beta	s	h	Adj. R2	Annual Abnormal Return	Total Abnormal Return
Panel A: Preplacement Abnormal Return							
−12 to 0	1.76%	1.20	0.56	−0.24	0.65	22.82%	22.82%
	4.43	1.99	9.64	−2.16			
−12 to −10	0.27%	1.18	0.62	0.01	0.56		
	0.45	1.18	6.59	0.06			
−9 to −7	0.82%	1.14	0.45	0.00	0.41		
	1.23	0.73	4.19	−0.03			
−6 to −4	1.39%	0.92	0.37	−0.23	0.38		
	2.13	−0.45	3.71	−1.16			
−3 to 0	3.29%	1.18	0.78	−0.67	0.69		
	5.85	1.24	10.88	−4.06			
Panel B: Post-Placement Abnormal Return							
1 to 12	−0.69%	1.09	0.57	−0.28	0.63	−8.32%	−8.32%
	−1.82	1.03	9.11	−2.43			
1 to 24	−0.66%	1.14	0.60	−0.37	0.68	−7.96%	−15.93%
	−1.88	1.70	10.30	−3.56			
1 to 36	−0.87%	1.17	0.55	−0.25	0.71	−10.47%	−31.42%
	−2.66	2.18	10.44	−2.58			

We estimate abnormal returns for the year preceding the private placements, during four mutually exclusive pre-event windows: [−12;−10], [−9;−7], [−6;−4], and [−3;0] and for the one-, two-, and three-year horizons following a private placement. The sample comprises 3,291 private placements that occurred from January 1993 through December 2003. We examine value-weighted (monthly-rebalanced) calendar-time portfolio returns. We regress the monthly excess returns to the calendar-time portfolios, $R_{p,t} - R_{f,t}$, on the Fama-French (1993) three-factor model:

$$R_{p,t} - R_{f,t} = \alpha_p + \beta_p(R_{m,t} - R_{f,t}) + s_p SMB_t + h_p HML_t + e_{p,t}$$

$(R_{p,t} - R_{f,t})$ corresponds, for a given month t, to the returns of the portfolios of private equity issues $(R_{p,t})$ less the risk-free rate (the monthly rate of 91-day Canadian Government Treasury bills, $R_{f,t}$). β_p, s_p, h_p are the loadings of the portfolios on each risk factor: the market (10% capped index), purged SMB (size) and purged HML (book-to-market ratio). α indicates the monthly average abnormal return of our private equity issue sample. We estimate the weighted least squares (WLS) time series regression in which the weights are proportional to the square root of the number of firms present in each month t. The t-statistics for each parameter are shown below each estimated parameter. H_0 for the β coefficient is β equal to one.

last three months of the preannouncement period. The concentration of the price run-up in the months immediately preceding the issue and the time necessary to decide on and organize an issue constitute challenging evidence against the timing hypothesis.

To add to the evidence related to preissue run-ups, we examine the trading volumes. We observe strong signs of abnormal trading volume before the announcement date: this sharp increase in trading volume coincides precisely with stock price increases. We illustrate the evolution of the median relative trading volume in Exhibit 8.7. The average trading volume across the [−48; −37] period is used as a benchmark. For a given month t, the relative volume is expressed by the observed total trading volume divided by the benchmark. During month −1, before any official announcement of the placement, the median relative trading volume is 2.65 and the average is 8.7. Corresponding median (mean) values for month −3 are 2.11 (7.87). To verify the possibility of simultaneous events, we study the 70 private placements exhibiting the strongest increase in market value before the announcement in 2003. We examine all the official releases around the event date, as available in SEDAR and in article reference systems, but we do not detect any public announcement that could explain the observed excitement over the stocks. For this subsample, we also analyze the level of insider activity, using the trades summarized in SEDI.[6] We note a strong increase in trading by insiders before the announcement. This result is consistent with the findings of Hauser et al. (2003) concerning insider trades before the announcement of placements aimed at limiting the dilution effect. However, insider trading alone is not sufficient to explain the excess trading volume. First, after several months of rising prices, the insider trading activity escalates significantly at month −4. Second, the ratio of sell to buy of insiders is around 3. Insiders appear to use the temporary overvaluation around the announcements to realize significant gains.[7] Our observations are consistent with opportunistic behavior of insiders after an unexpected increase in prices, and with the lack of fundamentals explaining the price increases in the year before the announcement. Our evidence seems in line with the hypothesis that the placement is a cause rather than a consequence of stock price increases.

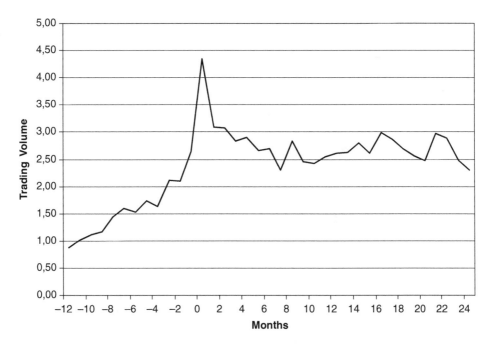

Exhibit 8.7 Evolution of the Median Relative Trading Volume of Private Issuers

The Postissue Return of the Public Investors

Panel B of Exhibit 8.6 shows the monthly underperformance of the private issuers over the three-year period following the issue based on alphas. The monthly abnormal return is −0.87 percent, for an annual return and a three-year equivalent of −10.47 percent and −31.42 percent, respectively. The aftermarket performance of private issuers over a three-year horizon is significantly negative, and the shares lose a third of their value during this period. A comparison with the abnormal returns estimated during shorter periods indicates that the performance decreases with the years. The aftermarket performance of private issuers tends to be worse three years after the issue than it is one or two years after the issue. The one-year post-issue abnormal performance is −8.32 percent versus −10.47 percent per year for the three-year performance. Our results are consistent with the three-year aftermarket performance observed for U.S. private equity placements (Hertzel et al. 2002; Brophy et al. 2005; Marciukaityte et al. 2005). This stock market performance is also consistent with the decrease in operating performance after the placement, which we document in the previous section.

However, the previous results report average effects. We analyze the distribution of abnormal returns at the firm level, using the BHAR method. The results are stated in Exhibit 8.8. The adjusted return is lower than 100 percent in a sizeable proportion of private placements (41.84 percent). Such returns occur, for example, when the stock price falls sharply during a period where the market return is positive. A large proportion of private placements (35.95 percent) exhibits negative adjusted returns between −100 percent and 0. The total proportion of negative adjusted returns is 77.79 percent. On the opposite end of the distribution,

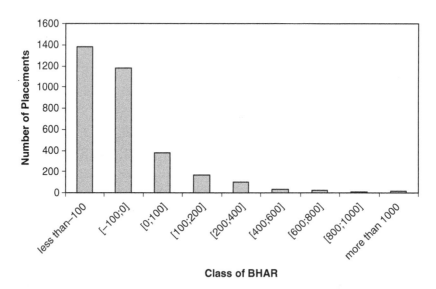

Class of BHAR

Exhibit 8.8 Distribution of Abnormal Returns during the Three Years Following the Private Placement

We estimate the relative monthly trading volume for each of the private and public issuers, for the [0; +36] month windows around the announcement, which is located in the first day of month 0. We use the buy and hold method to estimate these individual returns.

a few private placements generate very large returns over the three years. We estimate that 2.49 percent of private placements are followed by returns in excess of 400 percent, and the proportion of outstanding returns over 1000 percent is 0.5 percent. Such a distribution is very close to the one observed in lotteries, and the stock issued during private placements in Canada can very likely be qualified as lottery stocks. These low-priced stocks exhibit high volatility and a poor expected return on average. They generate very high returns in a very limited number of situations.

Analysis of Differences in Long-Run Performance

In the similar field of SEOs, several studies evidence that the long-run underperformance is essentially limited to small subsamples of the issuer population. Eckbo et al. (2000, 253) argue that the SEO issuers' underperformance is driven primarily by relatively small-sized stocks. Gombola et al. (1999) note that issuers with greater growth opportunities are associated with worse post-SEO long-term performance. Brown et al. (2006) observe that overvalued (undervalued) SEO firms perform worse (better) than their benchmark in the postissue period. Given the large heterogeneity in the private placements and the issuers, we attempt to determine whether patterns can be evidenced in the long-run performance of private placement issuers and if, as for SEOs, the performance is driven by certain subsamples. We do not report the detailed results in tables, but we can summarize the results of this part of the analysis as follows. We investigate whether the glamour/value profile of issuing firms explains cross-sectional differences in long-run performance. We use the book-to-market ratio as a criterion to discriminate between glamour and value firms. We rank private issuers according to this criterion, and divide firms into two groups, using their respective medians as a breakpoint. We estimate the alpha coefficient for each subsample.

The difference in performance between glamour and value issuers is very significant: glamour issuers statistically underperform value issuers. The underperformance of private issuers disappears for value issuers. The underperformance is negative but not significant over the three-year horizon following the issue. By contrast, the underperformance is negative and very significant for glamour issuers: −29.88 percent over three years. The categorization into glamour and value issuing firms helps us to discriminate between a nonsignificant postissue underperformance for value-issuing firms and a very significant underperformance for glamour issuers. The long-run underperformance following private placements mainly concerns the glamour firms, and can be traced to the fact that most of the value of these issuers is composed of growth opportunities, rendering valuation mistakes more probable. This result is consistent with previous evidence obtained from samples of SEOs issuers.

Discussion

The poor market performance following private placements is consistent with the lack of improvement in the operating performance evidenced in the previous section. However, the reasons the shareholders are unduly optimistic at the private placement date are unclear and are generally in line with an irrational pricing of a subsample of private placements. Several authors contend that the return of private equity investors is normal because of the discount they receive when they negotiate the private placement. We analyze this hypothesis in the section devoted to the discount. Barclay et al. (2007) evidence a negative return for their sample of 559 private placements between 1979 and 1997, using an event-time methodology. They show that this negative abnormal performance is mainly driven by passive placements, and argue that managerial entrenchment could account for many private placements: managers would issue private placements with a discount to investors who would not intervene in business management, for which they would be rewarded. Another possible explanation is that the distribution of returns of private equity issuers is highly skewed. In such a case, the preference for skewness can explain the abnormal low performance. Finally, Canadian private equity issuers are strongly financially constrained and, in several cases, in a distress situation. For the shareholders, the announcement of a private placement is equivalent in a sense to an easing of the constraint, a lower probability of failure, certification by outside, and likely knowledgeable, investors of the potential of the firm, or a combination of these elements. Overreaction to these pieces of information can explain long-run underperformance.

DISCOUNTS

As private placements are generally sold at a discount, the long-run return available to private equity investors may differ from the return of investors that are not involved in the placement (i.e., public investors). For example, Krishnamurthy et al. (2005) find that although the shareholders not participating in the placement experience post-issue negative long-term abnormal returns, the participating investors purchase the shares at a discount and earn normal returns. Accordingly, we examine the previous evidence and explanation of the discount, and estimate the returns for both categories of investors in Canadian private placements.

Previous Evidence and Explanations

Private placements are generally issued at a discount, that is, at a price lower than the market price of the equivalent public stock. In the United States, the discount varies between 9 percent and 20 percent. Some placements (approximately 20 percent), however, are carried out at par, or with a premium. The estimated discounts depend partly on the nature of the securities issued. According to Kim (2002), when nonconvertible ordinary stocks are issued without warrant, the discount is 9 percent; it reaches 22 percent when fixed price warrants are issued jointly. Wu (2004) maintains that the discount could be related to the costs incurred to motivate informed investors to reveal positive information. Under tacit contracts, the discount rewards investors that reveal information that would have been in their best interest not to disclose. The effect of a private placement dominated by informed investors is then positive. The discount could also be connected to the assumptions of self-dealing or entrenchment. The effect of a private placement dominated by informed investors would then be negative. Barclay et al. (2007) document a significantly lower discount for PIPEs carried out by active investors (−1.8 percent on average and −7.5 percent in median) compared with those done by passive investors (−20.8 percent and −19.5 percent). They conclude that the price discount rewards investor passivity. The authors also show that, in the medium term, post-issue returns are significantly negative, which confirms the assumption of entrenchment. In the same vein, Dai (2007) shows that venture capitalist and hedge funds differ in their willingness to monitor management. For example, hedge funds do not sit on the board of the company in which they invest, and cash out shortly, whereas VCs sit on the board and usually stay invested longer than one year. Dai finds that the mean discount of venture capital–led PIPEs is significantly lower (3 percent) than the mean discount of hedge fund–led PIPEs (15.4 percent). Krishnamurthy et al. (2004, 18) posit that the discount could also compensate for the lack of liquidity of the private placements, because of the two-year restriction on the resale of nonregistered securities. The discount for stocks subject to such a resale restriction is 34 percent compared with 19.44 percent for other stocks. However, because this discount also exists for stocks not subject to resale restrictions, the authors conclude that the lack of liquidity does not suffice to explain it. In Canada, Maynes and Pandes (2008) associate the discount with the lack of liquidity and information asymmetry. They show that private placements with shortened resale restrictions made by firms with less information asymmetry are offered with smaller price discounts. They affirm the importance of liquidity in the market for private placements. Our objective is not to explain the discounts, but rather to estimate this discount as part of our calculation of the return earned by the private equity investors.

Measure and Stylized Facts

In keeping with common practices, we calculate the discount using the issue price of the private placement and the market price 10 days after the announcement date. First, Exhibit 8.9 presents the main parameters of the distribution of discounts on an annual basis to evidence changes over time. The median of the distribution is 9.09 percent, which is close to the mean (10.54 percent). The discounts observed

Exhibit 8.9 Annual Distributions of Private Placement Discounts in Canada, 1993–2003

| | Gross Proceeds (CAN$M) | | | Discount (%) | | | |
Year	Number	Median GP	Mean GP	Mean	25th Perc.	Median	75th Perc.	% of Premium
1993	495	1.58	5.37	16.41	1.60	13.79	31.03	20.55
1994	499	1.33	5.70	11.25	−1.43	11.28	26.76	27.50
1995	218	3.60	6.68	12.64	0.00	10.34	25.00	21.00
1996	496	4.40	9.45	13.55	1.64	11.94	25.66	19.16
1997	347	4.59	10.76	8.28	−4.17	7.89	21.88	30.91
1998	196	4.68	20.10	5.37	−5.77	5.00	15.34	34.95
1999	130	3.06	8.60	6.92	−6.19	5.55	27.27	36.36
2000	197	2.88	5.99	14.06	−4.65	11.76	33.33	29.57
2001	151	2.85	8.53	1.00	−19.05	0.66	19.43	47.95
2002	270	3.30	6.84	6.61	−8.11	4.76	20.83	39.61
2003	477	4.09	9.69	8.20	−3.51	6.45	19.23	30.70
Total	3,476	3.00	8.45	10.54	−2.04	9.09	25.00	28.37

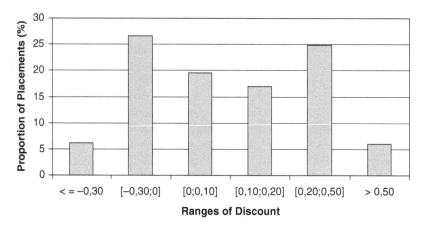

Exhibit 8.10   Distribution of Discount of 3,476 Private Placements, 1993–2003

in Canada are lower than those reported in the United States. However, the cross-sectional and time variations in discounts are very large. Discounts are considerable in 1993 to 1994, and then in 2000, when the median discount reaches 11.76 percent. In 1998, 2001, and 2002, the median discount is less than or equal to 5 percent. In 2001, 47.95 percent of private placements command a premium. The crash of the technologies sector occurs later in Canada than in the United States, and most of the private placements are observed before the decrease in technological values (September). This can explain the low level of discount, as investors were very optimistic during this period. The interquartile range shows that, for each year, the dispersion of discount is also very wide. The 25th percentile is generally negative, indicating a premium, while the 75th percentile reveals that 25 percent of private placements are sold at a discount higher than 25 percent. For the whole period, the proportion of private placements sold at a premium is 28.37 percent. The proportion is higher than the one reported in the United States but is in the same range as the proportion reported in New Zealand by Anderson (2006). Exhibit 8.10 illustrates the very large dispersion of the discount across the placements. The explanation of these differences has been left for further studies.

Discount and Long-Run Performance

In this section we analyze the relation between long-run performance and the discount. We observe a significant negative relation between both measures. The group of issuers that posts positive long-run abnormal performance also exhibits lower discounts. The difference in discount between the two groups based on the long-run performance is 4.5 percent. This is consistent with the fact that private equity investors negotiate the discount as a partial compensation for the paltry performance of the stocks in the future. It is worth exploring whether this discount is large enough to provide a "fair" rate of return. To estimate the return obtained by the private investors, we adjust the buy-and-hold return estimated at the firm level for the discount. If BHAR$_i$ is the abnormal return for the public investor in firm i that sold a private placement at a discount of 20 percent, the abnormal return for the private investor is $BHARA_i = [(1 + BHAR_i) \times (1 + 0.20) - 1]$. We estimate this return for each placement.

After three years, the average abnormal returns of the public investors, according to this method, is −21.80 percent and the median of the individual abnormal returns is −80.48 percent. Corresponding values for the sophisticated investors that participate in the private placement are −15.84 percent and −78.17 percent. This evidences that the private investors are unable to price the placements correctly, and that their long-run return is abnormally low, from both the economic and statistical standpoints. The discount is too low to provide these investors with a fair rate of return. Even for private investors who obtain shares at a reduced price, private placements are not a good investment, on average and for a very large proportion of the population. One possible explanation for this result, which contrasts with the United States situation, is that in Canada most of the private placement investors are individuals. They seem to be unable to correctly appraise the value and risk of these placements.

CONCLUSION

We analyze the various dimensions of private placements by Canadian issuers, which generally concern small and emerging companies, operating mainly in sectors associated with natural resources or technology. These issuers exhibit poor operating performance at the placement time. At the end of the fiscal year preceding the placement, 67.46 percent of Canadian private placement issuers report negative operating income, even before depreciation. Private placements appear to be a very important source of equity for these small and medium-sized businesses, and the number of private offerings largely surpasses the number of public seasoned equity offerings.

The number of firms reporting revenues increases before the event, yet the operating performance, already poor at the placement time, deteriorates after the placement. The return pattern surrounding the private placements is in line with the observation of previous studies in the United States. We observe a strong rally before the announcement and a significant negative abnormal return following the placement. The long-run underperformance subsists even when the return is adjusted for the discount. This indicates that on average, the private investors overpaid for the shares they acquired during private placements. These results raise three important questions. First, did the managers of emerging firms time the market with private placements, as evidenced in several previous studies of public offerings? Second, are exempt investors able to correctly assess the value of private placements, as the exempt system implicitly assumes? Third, why do public and private investors willingly keep or even acquire stocks of private equity issuers if the average adjusted long-run return is abnormally low?

The answer to the first question is mixed. There are signs of a slight revenue increase before the placement, but this increase has no effect at the operating income level. After the placement, all indicators of operating performance decrease sharply. Such a pattern is consistent with the timing proposition, as is the return pattern surrounding the placements. However, the following observations are less consistent with the timing proposition. The increase in operating performance is very slight, and most of the issuers report a loss at the placement time. This situation has nothing in common with the strong performance observed before the announcement of U.S. seasoned equity offerings, for which timing is an explanation often invoked. Second, the issuers generally lack the financial slack required to effectively time the market. Without the placement, most of them would be out of business in the months following the placement and would hardly be able to defer the financing round. Third, the preannouncement rally is observed only during the few months immediately before the announcement, when the placement decision has already been made and the discussions with potential investors already held. The rally, like the increase in trading volume we observe at this time, can probably be explained by the rumour of a private placement that relaxes the financial constraints binding the issuer.

According to Gray and Kitching (2005),[8]

> ... *private placements offer securities to a limited group of investors through an exempt distribution. In a private placement, the company is exempt from certain securities laws, such as the requirement to prepare a prospectus (. . .), that would otherwise apply if the securities were being sold to the general public. The issuer can sell shares only to a limited group of "sophisticated" investors, such as banks, pension funds, and wealthy individuals, or to company insiders (i.e., a director, senior officer, or employee of the issuing company).*

The implicit assumption behind the exempt distribution is that the sophisticated investors are informed and skilled enough to accurately appraise the stocks in which they invest. Our results evidence that this is not the case, particularly for growth and hard-to-value stocks. Sophisticated investors who invest in private placements in Canada realize abnormally low returns during the years following their placement, even when we disregard the lack of liquidity of these investments. Further work could examine which category of exempt investors suffers the most from investing in private placements.

The last, and perhaps most important question to explore is why the former shareholders of the private placement issuer do not sell their shares at the time of the announcement, and why private investors are involved in financing transactions that provide a poor adjusted rate of return in the long-run. One explanation is that stocks issued during private placements are lottery stocks, which can provide huge returns in a very few cases but a total loss in the majority of cases. The return's distribution is highly asymmetric, but several authors demonstrated that individual investors have a preference for skewness and lottery stocks (Kumar 2007; Bali, Cakicy, Whitelaw et al. 2008). This explanation seems to be the most plausible in the Canadian context.

NOTES

1. Some authors introduce a clear distinction between PIPEs and private placements in the United States, even if these placements are done by public companies. PIPE investors receive warrants, price resets and other cash-flow rights that can differentiate their returns from those of shareholders (Chaplinsky and Haushalter 2006). Such a distinction is not required in Canada, where private placements are not identical to PIPEs in the United States. Accordingly, we use the term "private placements" to refer to private placements by public firms in Canada.

2. For an analysis of the impact of this regulatory change, see Carpentier, L'Her, Suret et al. (2008).

3. We estimate the market capitalizations on a premoney basis, before the most recent private placement.

4. The intuition behind the notion of purged factor is that the performance cannot be correctly estimated if the benchmark is affected by the phenomenon analyzed, in this case the abnormal performance following private placements. Our results are materially the same when nonpurged factors are examined.

5. Several authors use the control firm benchmark in lieu of or as a complement to the portfolio benchmark. We opt for portfolios. The characteristics of our sample are very particular, including a high proportion of firms at an early development stage, and with a limited life expectancy. The choice of a control firm could engender random results, in case of delisting and when the returns reach extreme values.

6. SEDI stands for the System for Electronic Disclosure by Insiders, established by the applicable securities regulatory authorities. It has been available only since 2001, and does not allow electronic downloading of data, meaning that data must be collected. Accordingly, the analysis of insider trading around private equity issues has been left for further study, and we do not test for the significance of our estimations.

7. We estimate the gains and losses of each category of insiders between $t - 12$ and $t + 12$, where t is the announcement date. We assume that the acquisition cost of the shares owned at $t - 12$ is the $t - 12$ market price. We also assume that the selling price of the shares owned at $t + 12$ is the market price at this moment. During the 25 months, we account for each transaction at the price recorded in SEDI. Each category of insiders appears as a winner, except for the "new insiders," who become insiders by buying parts of the private placements.

8. See Gray, T., and A. Kitching, 2005, "Reforming Canadian Securities Regulation," September 19, Library of Parliament, at www.parl.gc.ca/information/library/PRBpubs/prb0528-e.htm.

REFERENCES

Anderson, Hamish D. 2006. Discounted private placements in New Zealand: Exploitation or fair compensation? *Review of Pacific Basin Financial Markets and Policies* 9 (4):533–548.

Anderson, Hamish D., and Lawrence C. Rose. 2007. Firm quality and the placement price of private equity. Available at SSRN: ssrn.com/abstract=968249.

Bali, Turan, Nusret Cakicy, and Robert Whitelaw. 2008. Maxing out: Stocks as lotteries and the cross-section of expected returns. Working Paper, Available on SSRN.

Barclay, Michael J., Clifford G. Holderness, and Dennis P. Sheehan. 2007. Private placements and managerial entrenchment. *Journal of Corporate Finance* 13 (4):461–484.

Brophy, David J., Paige P. Ouimet, and Clemens Sialm. 2005. PIPE dreams? The performance of companies issuing equity privately. NBER Working Paper No. W11011. Available at SSRN: ssrn.com/abstract=641065.

Brown, Philip, Gerry Gallery, and Olivia Goei. 2006. Does market misvaluation help explain share market long-run underperformance following a seasoned equity issue? *Accounting and Finance* 46 (2):191–219.

Carpentier, Cécile, Jean-François L'Her, and Jean-Marc Suret. 2008 Stock exchange markets for new ventures. Forthcoming in *Journal of Business Venturing*. Available at SSRN: ssrn.com/abstract=1132285.

Carpentier, Cécile, Jean-François L'Her, and Jean-Marc Suret. 2008. Does securities regulation constrain small business finance? An empirical analysis. *Small Business Economics* 31 (4):363–377.

Carpentier, Cécile, and Jean-Marc Suret. 2009. The Canadian public venture capital market. In *The handbook of venture capital*, ed. D. Cumming. Hoboken, NJ: John Wiley & Sons, forthcoming.

Chaplinsky, Susan J., and David Haushalter. 2006. Financing under extreme uncertainty: Contract terms and returns to private investments in public equity. Working Paper, Virginia University. Available at SSRN: ssrn.com/abstract=907676.

Dai, Na. 2007. Does investor identity matter? An empirical examination of investments by venture capital funds and hedge funds in PIPEs. *Journal of Corporate Finance* 13:538–563.

Dresner, S., and K. Kim. 2003. *PIPEs: A guide to private investment in public equity*. Princeton, NJ: Bloomberg Press.

Eckbo, Espen, Ronald W. Masulis, and Oyvind Norli. 2000. Seasoned public offerings: Resolution of the "new issues puzzle." *Journal of Financial Economics* 56 (2):251–291.

Fama, Eugene F., and Kenneth R. French. 1993. Common risk factors in the returns on stocks and bonds. *Journal of Financial Economics* 33 (1):3–56.

Faruqui, Umar, Wulong Gu, Mustapha Kaci, Mireille Laroche, and Jean-Pierre Maynard. 2003. Differences in productivity growth: Canadian-U.S. business sectors, 1987–2000. *Monthly Labor Review* 126 (4):16–29.

Gombola, M., F. Y. Liu, and D. W. Chou. 2006. *Distress risk and stock returns following private placements of equity*. New Orleans: Eastern Finance Association Working paper.

Gombola, Michael J., Hei Wai Lee, and Feng-Ying Liu. 1999. Further evidence on insider selling prior to seasoned equity offering announcements: The role of growth opportunities. *Journal of Business Finance & Accounting* 26 (5/6):621–650.

Hauser, Shmuel, Elli Kraizberg, and Ruth Dahan. 2003. Price behavior and insider trading around seasoned equity offerings: The case of majority-owned firms. *Journal of Corporate Finance* 9 (2):183–199.

Hertzel, Michael, Michael Lemmon, James S. Link, and Lynn Rees. 2002. Long-run performance following private placements of equity. *Journal of Finance* 57 (6):2595–2617.

Kim, Kurt. 2002. PIPEs marketplaces: A guided tour. www.privateraise.com/downloads/PIPEs%20Marketplace%20-%20A%20Guided%20Tour.pdf.

Krishnamurthy, Srinivasan, Paul Spindt, Venkat Subramaniam, and Tracie Woidtke. 2004. Does investor identity matter in equity issues? Evidence from private placements. *Journal of Financial Intermediation*, in press.

Krishnamurthy, Srinivasan, Paul Spindt, Venkat Subramaniam, and Tracie Woidtke. 2005. Does investor identity matter in equity issues? Evidence from private placements. *Journal of Financial Intermediation* 14 (2):210–238.

Kumar, A. 2007. Who gambles in the stock market? AFA 2006 Boston Meetings Paper. Available at SSRN: ssrn.com/abstract=686022.

Loughran, Tim, and Jay R. Ritter. 2000. Uniformly least powerful tests of market efficiency. *Journal of Financial Economics* 55:361–389.

Marciukaityte, Dalia, Samuel H. Szewczyk, and Raj Varma. 2005. Investor overoptimism and private equity placements. *Journal of Financial Research* 28 (4):591–605.

Maynes, Elizabeth, and Ari Pandes. 2008. Private placements and liquidity. Available at SSRN:ssrn.com/paper=1106668.

Ontario Securities Commission. 1996. Task force on small business financing—Final report. *Corporate Relations Branch*. Toronto: Ontario Securities Commission.

Wu, YiLin. 2004. The choice of equity-selling mechanisms. *Journal of Financial Economics* 74:93–119.

ABOUT THE AUTHORS

Cécile Carpentier received a Ph.D. in finance from the Lille II University (France). She is a Chartered Accountant (France) and a Chartered Financial Analyst (CFA).

She specialized in corporate finance and small-business finance. She has published in several academic journals such as the *Journal of Business Venturing, Small Business Economics, Venture Capital, Canadian Tax Journal,* and *Canadian Public Policy.* She is a CIRANO Fellow.

Jean-Marc Suret received a Ph.D. in finance from Laval University (Canada). He is a Canadian Business Valuator (CBV). He specializes in corporate finance, public policy, and financial accounting. He has published many articles in academic journals such as the *Journal of Business Venturing, Contemporary Accounting Research, Small Business Economics, Journal of International Business Studies,* and *The Financial Review.* He served as Director of the School of Accountancy of Laval University from 1999 to 2006. He is a CIRANO Fellow.

CHAPTER 9

Hedge Funds' Activism

A New Trend of Convergence toward Private Equity in Public Firms?

STEFANO GATTI
Associate Professor of Banking and Finance, Università Commerciale Luigi Bocconi, Department of Finance

CHIARA BATTISTINI
Analyst, Consumer, Healthcare and Retail M&A Advisory Team, J.P. Morgan, London

INTRODUCTION

With almost 2.3 trillion US$ under management at the end of 2007 and with more than 11,000 active funds, the hedge funds industry has become an important player in modern global financial markets. Although put under pressure by the recent financial turmoil, their activity has significantly changed the way financial markets work. On one side, hedge funds have enabled investors to implement a larger set of investment strategies and reach better risk-return combinations. On the other side, however, the aggressive approach that some of them have used in order to achieve higher returns—particularly by using higher leverage and derivatives—have raised questions from regulators about the induced instability in financial markets.

Hedge funds have also contributed to the evolution of corporate governance mechanisms in the United States and, to a lesser extent, in Europe (Brav and Mathews 2008). Evidence shows that hedge funds investment strategies have changed over time from the acquisition of only minor portions of the equity capital of corporations and with a typical short-term horizon to a more aggressive and active approach on a longer holding period. In many cases, hedge funds have engaged in fights with incumbent management questioning managerial choices and forcing for a change of strategy in order to increase stock prices and maximize their return on investment. Although this trend is pretty clear, little is still known about the effects on corporate performance coming from an increased activism by these market agents. The question whether hedge funds activism is beneficial to firms' shareholders or hedge funds do simply try to extract value from firms leaving them with a lower potential after they get rid of shares is even more important today in a period of severe financial crisis where effective corporate governance can make the difference between successful and unsuccessful corporations.

In this chapter, our objective is to review the existing theoretical and empirical literature on activist policies by hedge funds' and to empirically verify—by means of a clinical case study—if hedge funds' activism creates value not only for the activist but for all the shareholders of the firm.

In the next section, after a quick overview of the size of hedge funds and private equity markets, we introduce the evolution of hedge funds' investment strategies in the past few years, pointing out the increased similarities between hedge funds' and private equity investors' approaches to shareholders' activism. The section titled "Hedge Funds Approach to Activism" presents an analysis of hedge funds' approach to activism and highlights the most evident characteristics of the firms that are likely to be targeted by activist hedge funds. The section titled "How Hedge Funds Engage a Fight against Incumbent Management" deals with the strategies that hedge funds implement in order to start a fight against incumbent management and present an in-depth analysis of empty voting and hidden ownership. Finally, "The Clinical Study of Carl Icahn versus Time Warner, Inc.," examines the period going from August 2005 to March 2006. The case, carried out by implementing an event study methodology for various relevant steps of the struggle between the hedge fund and Time Warner's CEO, is particularly interesting because it helps us demonstrate that the market looked favorably at Icahn's activism and instead heavily punished Time Warner stock performance once Icahn gave up the fight. In a sense, it is an indirect confirmation that hedge funds' activism matters in influencing shareholders' value. The "Conclusion" then summarizes pros and cons coming from hedge funds' activism.

HEDGE FUNDS AND PRIVATE EQUITY: MARKET DATA AND TRENDS TOWARD CONVERGENCE

The first time the term *hedge fund* was used was in 1949 when Alfred Winslow Jones, a journalist for *Fortune* magazine, set up, with some of his friends, a fund in order to write an article about forecasting instruments used by investors in the stock market. He raised $100,000 (investing personally $40,000) and instituted the A. W. Jones & Co. as a general partnership in order to avoid the restrictive SEC regulation and to benefit from the maximum flexibility and latitude in portfolio construction. Jones's investment strategy consisted in using two techniques: short selling and leverage. Each of them, if used separately, bears very high risks but, if properly combined together, as Jones's experience shows, they allow investors to achieve a more aggressive management and, at the same time, to bear a lower risk.

Compared to Jones's first hedge fund, which relied on isolating investment skills from market trends by placing a portion of a portfolio within a hedged structure, hedge funds on the market nowadays are very different and, for most of them, the term *hedge* is not even appropriate. This form of investment in these days has become even more popular than it was in the 1980s. Hedge funds are very common in the United States and they are increasing in use in Europe and in Asia as well. They pursue a wide range of strategies and, every day to a greater degree, they look for new ways to obtain higher returns. On the market at the end of December 2007 there were about 11,000 funds with a total asset under management of $2.3 trillion (see Exhibit 9.1), while assets under management in the private equity industry

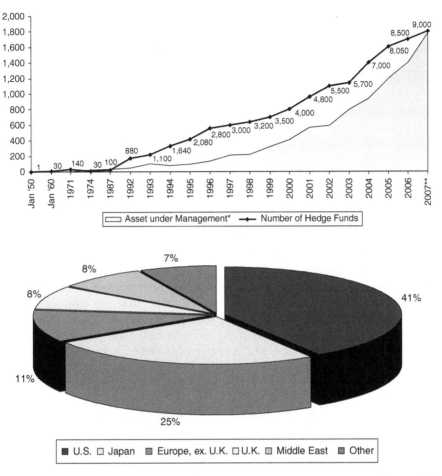

Exhibit 9.1 Trends in Asset under Management, Number of Hedge Funds, and Geographic Location
*$ Billions.
**As of December 31, 2007.
This figure shows the evolution of the number of hedge funds and asset under management between 1950 and 2007. In addition, a breakdown of the geographical location of hedge funds is reported.
Source: International Financial Services, London.

was, at the end of 2007, $4.9 trillion. Even if the private equity market is double the size of the hedge funds', the growth the two industries have been experiencing in the last few years is higher for hedge funds. While private equity asset under management has grown by a compounded annual growth of about 10.5 percent, hedge funds' assets have been growing by more than 27.5 percent since 2000.

Private Equity and Hedge Funds: Competitors or Allies?

Typically, private equity funds have stood out as the best response to Berle and Means' questions about separation of ownership and control and about potential management's conflicts of interest. In fact, in the 1980s financial entrepreneurs started to assemble new pools of capital to buy out entire public companies that were underperforming the market and their peers. In this way, the first private equity funds were set up. These funds were mostly financed by debt and with capital raised through private offerings directed to specific classes of investors. As the takeover industry grew, private equity teams became professional structures and important players in merger and acquisition (M&A) transactions looking for profit opportunities.

Until recently, distinguishing hedge funds from private equity funds was an easy task. Both kinds of funds are managed by a team of skilled investors who solicit financiers directly rather than through a public offering or general advertisement. Furthermore, both hedge funds and private equity funds are treated similarly by federal securities laws.[1] Besides regulation, these two types of funds used to carry out different strategies. Private equity funds usually take the target company private and invest the capital they raised long term from a control position. While the company stays private, the funds often redesign business plans, change inefficient management, and modify the corporate and financial structure. They usually target firms that need development or management over a period of time, typically three to five years, and are not susceptible, on an interim basis, to being marked to market. Typically, they run the company for a fixed period of time and then take it public again gaining a positive return. On the other hand, "hedge funds are traditionally fast-paced environments where trading professionals with a focus on public securities . . . move in and out of investments after short holding periods to generate returns. The nature of the investment is market driven" (Schwartzman and Snyder 2007).[2]

Recently, though, financial markets have witnessed an increasing convergence between private equity firms and hedge funds.[3] And not just because hedge funds are exploring activism, but also because private equity firms are setting up their own hedge funds.[4] Even though private equity funds and activist hedge funds can look very similar, there are key issues that allow investors to distinguish one from the other and decide which investment is more suitable for them.

First of all, the approach the two have toward the targeted company is different. Private equity funds' goal is to run the company with a so-called "hands-on" approach that involves a long-term commitment to work with, or take active control over, the management. On the other hand, hedge funds limit their activity to proposing actions that the target company should undertake. If management does not pay attention to the fund's suggestions, than the fund may decide to engage in a proxy battle against the management and become more active. From this distinguishing feature, another follows. Since private equity funds seek control of the targeted company, they buy a larger stake than the one acquired by hedge funds whose sole goal is to exercise pressure and influence on incumbent management.

Additionally, hedge funds, to be successful in activism, had to introduce lock-up periods and the so-called gates, in order to be free in undertaking more illiquid investments.[5] On the contrary, private equity funds are established for a fixed period of time, usually between five and ten years. Participants receive distributions only after the realization of a stake in the fund's portfolio and cannot redeem their contributions before the expiration date. As a result, investments in private equity funds are way much more illiquid than those in hedge funds. Furthermore hedge funds' shorter duration, especially when combined with a quite large and illiquid position, push them to aggressiveness and impatience. Private equity funds, instead, are focused on the long term and, consequently, carry out their activity with more patience and putting less pressure on management.

Finally, many scholars have argued that, while private equity funds' managers are management experts, hedge funds' are "numbers guys."[6] Evidence shows that hedge funds are quicker in picking the investments and less precise when conducting due diligence.[7] Lately, though, activist hedge funds are hiring former investment bankers and consultants to overcome this limit.

The entry of hedge funds in the activism arena, has given rise to several concerns for private equity. The first is that, since hedge funds seek lower returns than those expected by private equity firms, the first can bid up to higher prices for companies. Second, hedge funds intensify anyhow the competition in M&A transactions and this can cause lower returns to private equity funds. At last, hedge funds pay annually, rather than on an average of six years, their management, and this may attract most of the best skilled managers.[8] Put under pressure, private equity funds are now beginning to play more aggressively to keep up with their rising competitors.

Although at first sight the two kinds of investors seem still to be competitors, changes that are affecting both private equity funds and hedge funds could bring to a more efficient market. The two types of investments are starting to complement each other and in a foreseeable future they may converge, forming a new hybrid form of investment.[9] So far, empirical evidence has shown that many funds of both kinds have teamed up using their own expertise not in competition, rather in cooperation.[10] In addition, hedge funds may represent a source of coinvested equity when a private equity firm intends to lead an acquisition and needs an "ally" willing to share the risk in a multibillion dollar transaction.

In conclusion, activist hedge funds can be considered as an alternative to private equity firms. The evolution of financial markets will show whether the relationship between the two will turn to competition, cooperation, or convergence.

HEDGE FUNDS' APPROACH TO ACTIVISM

As already discussed, recently hedge funds have come up as a new and important player in financial markets. Hedge funds have always engaged in speculative investment strategies but, more recently, they have started to play an increasingly valuable role in corporate governance as well. This impressive growth of hedge funds has been associated with an increase in the number of cases of shareholder activism by them.[11] In fact, as their asset under management has increased, so have their strategies and styles.[12]

At this point, the obvious question is: why has hedge funds' activism emerged now? There are several answers to this issue. Surely, one of the most important reasons is the huge explosion the hedge fund sector has experienced in the last period (see "Hedge Funds and Private Equity"). An increasing competition among old and new hedge funds was eroding the absolute returns this form of investment used to achieve in the past and a new way of investing was needed. Given the high returns private equity funds were gaining, hedge funds believed that to be a good path to achieve their historical returns. Furthermore, the larger amount of capital that hedge funds manage now allows them to buy out larger stakes in their target companies and pursue activism more effectively. In addition, high-profile M&A disasters such as the AOL-Time Warner merger discussed later in this chapter, and the corporate scandals of the 1990s (Enron, WorldCom, Tyco International) have all attracted the attention of investors, of the economic community and legislators over management teams and their ways to conduct companies. As a result, a growing concern about corporate governance issues has emerged and shareholders have started to more closely monitor their directors and managers.[13] Thus, hedge funds, richer and more entitled to question management's activity, looked at activism as a potential alternative strategy from the traditional ones that no longer brought returns as high as they used to be.

Partnoy and Thomas (2006) have suggested that hedge funds' activism can be outlined based on four different strategies.

The first is defined by the economists as the information asymmetry and convergence trends. This approach to activism is very similar to the traditional hedge funds' activity of arbitrage-related trading. What hedge funds do is exploiting information asymmetry between securities sellers and buyers. So, for example, they collect negative information about a firm and than take a short position on its shares gaining a positive return.

The second strategy is related to firms' capital structures. This strategy is not as typical as the first one for hedge funds but, at the same time, it is not a new concept. In fact, already private equity funds engaged in this approach in the late 1970s. Hedge funds that apply this strategy take long positions on the targeted company's shares and then demand changes in the capital structures. They might ask, for example, for share buy-backs, payments of dividends, or increases of debt.[14] Jana Partners, for example, forced Deutsche Borse to pay a special dividend to its shareholders when it attempted to acquire London Stock Exchange. The same hedge fund, in cooperation with Carl Icahn and his fund, pushed Kerr-McGee to implement its share buyback program in the first months of 2005.[15] Scholars have argued that this tactic tends to increase firm's value rather than shareholders'.

Third, hedge funds have traditionally undertaken merger and risk arbitrage by using new financial techniques, such as short-selling and derivatives, betting on the outcome of announced transactions. In these situations, hedge funds may act differently from other shareholders. In fact, if they have short positions on the acquirer and long on the target, they will vote in favor of the transaction even if the deal will bring a reduction of value in the end. Following this approach, hedge funds sometimes engage in antimerger campaigns and take positions that would be successful if the merger failed. They therefore vote against the merger even if such a deal would represent the best opportunity for the companies involved. Hedge funds have in the past obstructed a corporation from going through an acquisition that could destroy value for the acquirer. The most famous examples of these interventions are surely the cases of Deutsche Borse and Mylan Laboratories. In the first case, the German stock exchange wanted to acquire the London Stock Exchange and the hedge funds' efforts caused Deutsche Borse to abandon the deal.[16] In the second example, Carl Icahn blocked Mylan Laboratories to acquire King Pharmaceuticals because he believed the deal would have depressed the aggregate value of the two companies.

Usually, after a deal announcement, the buyer's stock price drops and therefore it appears clear why hedge funds get involved trying to stop value-destroying acquisitions. Less likely, on the other hand, is blocking acquisitions on the target side. The most common reason why hedge funds are active in these cases is a proposed cash-out reckoned too low by minority shareholders.

In other situations, hedge funds facilitate the success of a transaction "on the target side via activism on the acquirer side" (Thompson 2006, 15). Mylan Laboratories/King Pharmaceuticals stands out again as a good example to illustrate this kind of activism. The hedge fund Perry Corporation held a stake in the target of the deal, King Pharmaceuticals. After the announcement, the acquirer's share price fell and Perry bought a stake in Mylan Laboratories to be able to vote in favor of the merger. At the same time, Perry hedged its position in Mylan Laboratories with equity swaps and ended up to have a short position on the acquirer and a long on the target but still, it could vote from both sides in favor of the transaction. It appears clear, now, that the hedge fund's interest was to close the deal with a premium as high as possible in order to gain from both sides (Hu and Black 2007, 349). In this last case, hedge funds did not pursue shareholders' interest, rather the maximization of the value of the fund itself and, in the last resort, the interests of the participants of the fund.[17]

Fourth and last, hedge funds have started to engage in an approach that involves corporate governance and strategy. They take long positions in the targeted company and ask for changes mostly related to corporate governance issues. In order to achieve their objectives, they make large use of innovative financial products, derivatives, and private contracts. This approach is less aggressive and speculative than the other three. It requires a longer investment period and more patience from the investors. This activism is similar to the one carried out by the institutional investors but, as already shown, hedge funds have more incentives and fewer limitations to better engage in such strategy. This kind of activism implies that hedge funds discuss with management, and sometimes fight against the board, to modify corporate governance practices, to execute new business strategies, and to remove underperforming directors and managers. Activists usually pursue board representation to achieve one or more of the specific purposes typically sought. There is a broad evidence of these attempts from activist hedge funds. For example, at Blockbuster, Mr. Icahn gained three seats on the board for himself and for another two dissident shareholders.[18] And more: in Computer Horizon, the fund Crescendo Partners replaced the board with five of its directors; at Cornell, its activist shareholder has been able to nominate seven directors; at Office Max, the hedge fund K Capital could nominate an independent director.[19] While many other examples of hedge funds' intervention in replacing managers can be found, it can also happen that the activists' threats of launching a proxy fight are enough to boost the target's share price and the proxy is dropped by the fund. This is what happened between the hedge fund Loeb Partners and Spartan Store. Sometimes they have even attempted to oust the CEO,[20] but, more often, their attention is focused on directors' replacement.

They may even ask for spin-offs of inefficient or unneeded business units. By unbundling companies, hedge funds expect their target companies to work more efficiently[21] and managers to be better incentivized. Hedge funds, therefore, pick diversified companies and, through spin-offs or direct business units sales, seek positive gains (Bratton 2007, 19). An example will be described further in the later section on the case of Carl Icahn versus Time Warner Inc., in which the rider with his fund attempted to split up the company in four different specialized divisions. Other evidence comes from Blair Corporation, which was pushed to sell a business unit to Alliance Data System,[22] and Wendy's International, which was pressured to sell a business unit and to franchise almost all its restaurants.[23]

FEATURES OF TARGETED COMPANIES

Companies targeted by activist hedge funds present some common characteristics (Citigroup 2005):

- Lower market capitalization in comparison to their peers
- Excessive cash on hand
- Unbalanced capital structures with a too high or low debt/equity ratio
- Depressed valuation multiples
- Low market value compared to apparent asset value

If we compare the average market capitalization of targeted firms with the median market capitalization of the companies in the S&P 500, it appears clear that hedge funds mostly target companies that are undervalued by the stock market.[24] One motivation why hedge funds prefer such companies is that, since they are priced less than their real value, hedge funds can acquire larger stakes and obtain a bigger control of the company. The second reason is that hedge funds believe themselves to be able, through their proposals, to bring those companies to their fair value.

When hedge funds started to venture activist campaigns, they would traditionally focus on small companies in order to get a bigger stake. Now that hedge funds' asset under management has increased and hedge funds are becoming more expert and used to activism, they are targeting larger companies. In the past two years, financial markets have witnessed attacks by hedge funds on the most important and largest American companies. Time Warner, Blockbuster, McDonald's, Wendy's International, Tyco, and The New York Times are some highly visible companies that can be mentioned as examples. Robert Kindler, head of M&A at J.P. Morgan Chase, believes that size is not enough protection in itself and stated that "no company is too large to be immune to attack from these new activists."[25]

Targeted companies tend to hold more cash than their peers. Hedge funds focus their attention on corporations rich in cash[26] because they believe that, absent an opportunity for acquisition, all this financial availability can be used to pay a large dividend to shareholders or to repurchase shares in order to boost the stock price. Some economists have also explained how cash can push management to act in conflicts of interest with shareholders and to use that cash in an inappropriate way, like diversifying investments that may not be needed by the company.

Another characteristic common to most targeted companies is that the latter are not adopting an optimal capital structure. Most times, targets present debt-to-equity ratios lower than their peers and a debt capacity not completely exploited. Hedge funds might push such companies, especially those with stable cash flows, to take on additional debt to finance, for example, leveraged recapitalizations (Citigroup 2005). Brav, Jiang, Partnoy, and Thomas (2008) have found out that most of the targeted corporations have a higher leverage compared to their peers.

Regarding operational performance, targeted corporations have considerably higher average ROA (return on assets) and ROE (return on equity) but lower market-to-book ratios than the companies targeted by passive investors (Boyson and Mooradian 2007, 1).[27] Some scholars have asserted that "the typical target is a cash cow with poor growth prospects, possibly suffering from the agency costs of free cash flow."[28] So, for example, activist hedge funds are different from the so-called vulture funds. While the latter focus their attention on bankrupt companies that need institutions to get over financial crisis, hedge funds target healthy firms whose value is misunderstood by the market.

Other characteristics common to many targeted corporations are the bigger presence of takeover defenses[29] and lower expenditures, especially for R&D, than their peers (Klein and Zur 2009; Brav et al. 2006). Hedge funds do not focus on specific industries but, instead, invest in all.[30]

Just a very brief note about the country where these targeted firms are based is needed. This is not a trend restricted to the United States. In fact, in 2005, one of the biggest activist hedge funds' campaigns—the blocked Deutsche Borse's proposed acquisition of the London Stock Exchange—took place in Europe. Hedge funds have started to focus their attention on Asian companies as well. For example, in 2006, Carl Icahn targeted KT&G, South Korea's largest tobacco and ginseng group, where he has achieved a seat on the board. Hence, the country of origin of the target corporation does not really matter, since hedge funds' activism is becoming a global phenomenon.[31]

In the wake of this new trend of hedge funds' activism, many lawyers and the boards of American public companies are seeking strategies and defensive measures to avoid attacks from this new player. One of the most engaged opponents of this wave of activism from hedge funds is the well-known lawyer Martin Lipton,[32] who has even drawn up for potential targets a list of measures they can take to be prepared for attacks.

So far, old and new takeover defenses and a more proactive attitude on the part of management seem not to be enough to oppose hedge funds.

HOW HEDGE FUNDS ENGAGE A FIGHT AGAINST INCUMBENT MANAGEMENT

The initial engagement of a hedge fund's campaign was once to collect a stake in the targeted company large enough to exercise some form of pressure and to then send a letter to, and typically also call, the management, to disclose their intentions about the targeted firm.

After this first approach, the filing of a Schedule 13D[33] follows. Basically, with the filing, the hedge fund makes public its intentions about the target. Some empirical studies (Clifford 2007; Boyson and Mooradian 2007; Brav et al. 2006; Klein and Zur 2009) have shown that most of the time hedge funds, in their Schedules 13D, declare that the purchase purpose is either an "investment purpose," or to "talk with management or the board," or, finally, seeking for some structural changes such as an "increase in dividends," to "appoint more independent directors" or "fire the CEO." Based on what hedge funds announce when filing their Schedule 13D, their activism can be broken out in three different categories: "communication only," "communication first then aggressive," and "aggressive only" (Boyson and Mooradian 2007).[34] Brav et al. (2006) classify as aggressive those funds that demand corporate changes, threaten to start a proxy fight to obtain seats on the board or to replace the entire board, and, last, those funds that state their willingness to either take full control of the targeted company or to sue the firm. At this point, typically, hedge funds start to attract attention from the media to gain visibility. This is a very important step, as hedge funds often look for some allies among other hedge funds or institutional investors to fight harder and this is one of the best methods to gain other investors' attention. At the same time, hedge funds hope that directors and managers will accede to the fund's requests under the pressure of public scrutiny.

Most times, the hedge fund asks management for a meeting to discuss together the fund's suggestions. If management refuses to meet with the fund, usually the latter will publicly criticize management's behavior and start a media campaign against the incumbent directors. On the other hand, if the board agrees to meet, directors and the hedge fund's managers will talk and try to find points of contact between the two groups. Hedge funds do not seek a fight at any cost but, actually, try to mediate with the target's management.[35]

Usually, though, the target turns down the hedge fund's proposals and the two teams engage in long fights that many times result in proxy battles. Targeted companies do not give in to the fund's threats and keep up the pressure, waiting for concessions from the other side. A study conducted by Bratton (2007) has shown that the largest evidence of proxy contests between hedge funds and targets are contests that have been initiated but did not result in incumbent management replacement.[36] This demonstrates that, given the very high costs of proxy fights, neither one group nor the other is willing to undertake a proxy contest and, at a certain point, they try to agree on some terms of the proposal presented by the fund, while the fund may make some concessions on other terms. However, as it has been stated, "whether the company settles with the fund or the fund wins during a proxy fight, hedge funds are having their demands met."[37]

Let's now analyze how large hedge funds' investment in their targeted company actually is. From the existing literature (Briggs 2007; Bratton 2007; Brav et al. 2006), we find evidence that hedge funds, when pursuing activism, acquire a stake that ranges from 5 percent to 10 percent. Existing evidence indicates that most of the hedge funds tend to acquire at least a 9.5 percent stake in the target company. It is not by chance that hedge funds do not pass 10 percent. The reasons for this choice are many. First of all, Section 16 of the Securities and Exchange Act excludes ownerships above that threshold from short-selling.[38] Then, many companies identify passing such percentage as the trigger event for poison pills and for other antitakeover defenses. Usually, the average stake is larger in aggressive campaigns than in friendly cases (Brav et al. 2006, 16; Becht, Franks, Mayer, and Rossi 2006, 13) and, typically, the larger the target, the smaller the percentage of shares acquired by the fund.[39] Hence, small stakes below the 5 percent threshold do not occur very often and the reason why this happens is clear. With the filing of a Schedule 13D, activist hedge funds gain a lot of attention from similar funds and from financial markets in general. Without a formal filing, teaming up with other funds turns out to be much more difficult and the hedge fund risks being unsuccessful in its battle. In addition, the free-rider problem pushes hedge funds to acquire a larger stake. The bigger the holding is, the more the activism costs are spread out on it. Therefore, the campaigns will turn out to be more efficient and effective with a larger percentage of the outstanding shares. Bratton (2007, 16) has also noted that, most of the time, hedge funds widen their positions from 10 percent to 20 percent during the course of the engagement,[40] showing their intentions to be a more long-term investment than the economic community might believe.

Despite the relatively low stock ownership owned by hedge funds, they still can put enough pressure on management, attract attention from the media and, most times, achieve their goals in getting what they are asking for. To enhance their bargaining power with board's directors and their voting power, they often resort to specific tactics, such as "wolf pack," "empty voting," and "hidden ownership."

Stake Owned, Wolf Packs, Empty Voting, and Hidden Ownership

The 13D filing sends a signal to other funds who are interested in the same target and who did not form a Schedule 13D group. As a result, all these funds team up for the same cause.[41] So far, hedge funds that play the same game at each other's side do not have to register or file any statement with the SEC. As Briggs (2007, 691) has stated: "Decisions such as these have enabled hedge funds to engage in 'wolf pack' tactics against companies, undeterred by a fear of somehow magically becoming a group merely because they hunt together and seek the same prey." Typically, hedge funds support each other's activism at a target, and when an issue comes to shareholder vote, they will generally vote in line with their hedge fund allies. Several hedge funds are now forming "temporary" funds, legal entities able to avoid SEC registration, to work together.[42] This trend can vary a hedge funds' acquisitions and the group can end up with a significant stake in the target.[43]

Hedge funds are also seeking new allies such as Wall Street's investment banks and traditional institutional investors. The latter are investing more every day in activist hedge funds[44] and often stand at their side in activist campaigns against targeted companies' management. Some institutional investors have even admitted that "the activists are able to say and do things we [the institutions] can't."[45]

Activist hedge funds are hiring Wall Street investment banks as well to gain more attention from the public and from targets' management. In June 2005, Blackstone Group LP was recruited to write a professional fairness opinion about a restructuring plan proposed by a hedge fund for Wendy's International, Inc., and after such an intervention, Wendy's stock price jumped 28 percent.[46] This was the first time that banks and advisory firms' intervened in activist campaigns. Since then, many hedge funds' managers resorted to these institutions to obtain more bargaining power and voice within the target and the shareholders base.[47] Investment banks are more willing now than in the past to support hedge funds in their battles. In fact, while "until recently [these institutions] felt that their business interests were best served by loyally supporting incumbent management,"[48] banks now look at activist hedge funds as potential winners of these fights and potential promoters of good recommendations that can increase shareholders' value. Some investment banks, principally UBS,[49] have even dedicated teams of bankers to hedge funds' campaigns.

The second tactic hedge funds use to increase their voting power in activist fights is "empty voting" or "hidden ownership."[50]

In the 1980s economists believed that "it is not possible to separate the voting right from the equity interest. Someone who wants to buy a vote must buy the stock too" (Easterbrook and Fischel 1983, 410).[51] Nowadays, this is no longer true and investors who are solely interested in voting power have many ways to increase their administrative rights without buying the corresponding shares. With an increased financial innovation that brought a growth of derivatives, especially equity swaps, and the development of the lending market for stocks, decoupling economic ownership from voting power has become easier and cheaper. Hedge funds take advantage of the fact that they are not restricted in terms of short selling, leverage, and derivatives to fully exploit the stock lending market and the derivative market (Christoffersen, Geczy, Musto, and Reed 2007; Hu and Black 2006). In addition, institutions, including hedge funds, do not have to disclose transactions that offset the voting rights or economic interest due to their share positions and economic ownership acquired through equity swaps or other over-the-counter instruments.

Decoupling may take place either in the form of empty voting or in the form of hidden ownership. Hu and Black (2006, 1014) define empty voting as the presence of more voting rights than economic rights. Hidden ownership, instead, consists in having "economic ownership that exceeds their formal voting rights, combined with informal access to the corresponding voting rights."

Empty voting can be pursued in many ways. The most common method is the so-called "record date capture." This strategy consists in borrowing shares on the stock lending market[52] on the record date—the date established by the company for the purpose of determining the holders who are entitled to vote in a specific shareholders' meeting—in order to gain the right to vote at the shareholders' meeting. As a matter of fact, the borrower obtains both the shares and the corresponding voting rights. At the same time, the lender has the right to have his shares returned at any time and be paid for an amount equal to any dividends or other distributions on the shares for the borrowing period. It appears clear now that, through the stock loan market, voting rights can be traded. The number of votes that can be borrowed is limited only by the amount of the collateral that must be 102 percent of the value of the shares borrowed (Christoffersen et al. 2007, 7)[53]. Hence, whoever is interested in gaining more voting rights than the ones he owns through his shares can borrow shares on the record date, gain the right to vote at the meeting, and return them afterward.

To date, there isn't agreement about the desirability of the practice of empty voting and the need of regulating it in order to avoid possible manipulations. While Kahan and Rock (2007) have described empty voting as "an example of an old problem—conflicts of interests created by exploiting the separation of legal and beneficial ownership—aggravated by modern financial innovation," Brav and Mathews (2008) argue that sometimes empty voting by hedge funds can help reach higher efficiency in corporate governance. In their model, the presence of hedge funds (strategic traders) and the ability to separate voting rights from economic ownership can increase overall efficiency because hedge funds are more likely to vote for the best solution from a firm value perspective.

Another strategy implies the use of equity swaps.[54] The person with the long equity side of the swap gets the economic ownership without voting rights of the corresponding shares while the short counterpart, in these cases a hedge fund, ends up with voting rights decoupled from their economic rights.

An alternative to the previous tactics can be the zero-cost collar. This strategy involves buying a put option and, at the same time, selling a call option (Bettis, Bizjak, and Lemmon 2001, 348). This technique reduces economic ownership but it is useful to preserve voting rights for the underlying assets. The last two tactics, though, require actually owning the stock while the first allows gaining voting power without buying the corresponding shares. On the other hand, investors can have greater economic ownership than voting rights, but be able to redeem such rights as soon as they necessitate them. So, significant investors can remain hidden until it is needed. Hidden ownership can be obtained through derivatives, especially equity swaps.[55] It is necessary to undertake an opposite position to the one exposed earlier when describing empty voting. Equity swaps also give hedge funds the possibility of getting a hidden toehold to be exploited in a takeover situation. In fact, evidence has shown that, by having a small holding in a target company, a hedge fund is more likely to be successful in an acquisition deal (Betton and Eckbo 2000; Bris 2002).

As shown, in order to maximize voting power it is necessary to have free access to derivatives and short selling without any restrictions. As already discussed, the only player in the American financial markets that does not face legal limitations to these instruments is hedge funds. As a result, they are the most suitable figures to undertake these strategies. It is clear that these tactics to exert more voting power give hedge funds a more effective and quieter opportunity to be even more active in their campaigns.

CLINICAL STUDY OF CARL ICAHN VERSUS TIME WARNER, INC.

This part of the chapter describes what happened when Carl Icahn, one of the most aggressive activists on Wall Street, decided to focus on Time Warner, Inc., the world largest media company.[56] As this fight has been defined, it was "the mother of all proxy battles."[57] In the following section we briefly describe who the players of this contest were. On one side there was Mr. Carl Icahn, already known in the 1980s because of his corporate raids. On the other side of the field there were Time Warner, the media giant, and its CEO, Mr. Parsons. In the section titled "The Target," the reasons why the Icahn group decided to attack Time Warner are shown. The next section depicts what happened during the fight in the time span going from August 2005 to March 2006, explains Icahn's attacks, and describes Parsons' responses. An economic analysis through event studies methodology follows in the last section to examine whether and how much value for all shareholders was created by the actions of both parties.

The Parties Involved

Carl Icahn and the Other Hedge Funds

Carl Icahn started in 1961 to work as a stockbroker at Dreyfus & Co. where he got acquainted with the world of securities arbitrage by taking advantage of price discrepancies among option contracts. It is just in the 1980s that Mr. Icahn began to gain popularity and wealth. He used to buy stakes in companies and ask for changes as a corporate raider. He focused his attention on large and important American public companies such as TWA, Texaco, and Western Union. Hence, he was one of the first to engage in "greenmailing": threatening to take over corporations, for example, Philips Petroleum, and ending up by selling his shares at a premium price when another acquirer emerged or the company itself bought his stocks just to get rid of him, at the expenses of the other shareholders.

In 2004, Mr. Icahn decided to move from being a "financier" to being a corporate activist.[58] Hence, he set up his own fund, Icahn Partners. The fund required a $25 million minimum investment, raising in this way up to $3 billion. Icahn himself invested $300 million in the fund. Fund's managers are compensated through a fixed percentage of the asset under management 2.5 percent, and a success fee equal to 25 percent of the net annual profits.[59] The reason why this 69-year-old investor decided to start a fund on his own was that "in the wake of the Sarbanes-Oxley law and with institutional shareholders becoming more outspoken, more investors are interested in Icahn's method of buying up shares of an underperforming company and agitating for change."[60] In March 2007, Mr. Icahn has collected about $7 billion, of which $1.5 billion of his own money. The core business of the fund is taking minority stakes in public companies and pushing for changes, often threatening a proxy fight. The goal is to obtain a stock buyback, asset spin-offs, and replacement of the incumbent board, to positively shake the stock in the short term and, hopefully, gain lasting results. The difference from his own raider's activity is, as Icahn said, "We do the job the LBO guys do, but for all the shareholders."[61] The last activist campaigns he engaged in had all important targets. Blockbuster, Kerr-McGee, Lear, Time Warner Inc., the Korean tobacco and ginseng company KT&G, and, lately, Motorola, Samsung, and Kraft are just some of the largest companies Mr. Icahn has focused his attention on. In less than three years, "Icahn Partners has posted annualized gains of 40 percent,"[62] outperforming the S&P 500 and the return for all hedge funds calculated by research firm HedgeFund.net.[63]

Other three big investors stood by Carl Icahn in this campaign against Time Warner: Jana Partners, Franklin Mutual Advisers, and SAC Capital Advisors.

Jana Partners is another hedge fund that engages in shareholder activism and already successfully supported Icahn Partners in the Kerr-McGee battle. The fund managed, in August 2005, about $4 billion. The company also succeeded in thwarting Deutsche Borse from acquiring London Stock Exchange, ousting its CEO too, and in nominating one director to the board of Sourcecorp.

Franklin Mutual Advisers and SAC Capital Advisors had together, in August 2005, around $48 billion and both have stood out for their activism activity.

The Target: Time Warner, Inc.

As of August 15, 2005, the date Icahn publicly announced to have entered Time Warner as an activist shareholder, Time Warner, Inc. was the world's largest media and entertainment conglomerate based in New York with a market capitalization of $85 billion. Its main operations are film, television, publishing, Internet services, and telecommunications. Its major businesses encompass a selection of the best known and successful media brands.

Time, Inc. was founded in the 1920s. Warner Communications was established as a spin-off of Kinney National Company of the nonentertainment assets in 1972. The new firm was the parent company of important corporations in the media sector such as Warner Bros. Pictures and Warner Music Group. Both companies grew especially through acquisitions. In 1989 Time merged with Warner Communication forming Time Warner. The new company launched a number of magazines, TV channels, and theme parks. In 1996 Time Warner grew even more by acquiring Turner Broadcasting System which included in its portfolio the broadcasting channel CNN. The next important step Time Warner made in order to differentiate its activities is the merger with the internet company AOL. The transaction was announced in January 2000 and started to be effective one year later. The result of this merger was a new corporation, AOL Time Warner. The shareholders of AOL owned 55 percent of the new company, meaning that the smaller AOL had actually bought out the bigger media group.[64] The merger turned out to be disastrous and the aggregate value of the new company dropped on the stock market.[65] In response to this crisis, in 2002 Richard Parsons was nominated as new CEO, in charge of restructuring the group. Since then, the media company went through many transactions.

In 2004 Time Warner reported consolidated revenues equal to $42,089 million increased by 6 percent from 2003. This growth was due primarily to an increase of subscription, advertising, and content revenues. EBITDA grew in 2004 by 12 percent, but such growth was limited by increased expenses at the corporate level.

Net income, in fiscal year 2004, increased by 27 percent to $3,364 million.[66]

Exhibit 9.2 shows break downs by segments of the Group's revenues, EBITDA, and EBIT are available.

In 2004, the group generated cash flow from operations (CFFO) of $6,618 million (in 2003 the cash provided by operations was slightly lower, equal to $6,601 million) and a free cash flow of $3,280 million (down 1 percent from $3,312 million in 2003). As of February 1, 2005, the company had a total of approximately 84,900 active employees.

At the time of the hedge funds' attack, in August 2005, Time Warner was structured into five divisions:

1. Filmed entertainment
2. Cable
3. Networks
4. Publishing
5. AOL

Filmed Entertainment: One of the world's leading studios, Warner Bros. has diversified sources of revenues with its film and television businesses, combined with an extensive film library and global distribution infrastructure. This diversification has helped Warner Bros. deliver consistent long-term growth and performance. The sale of DVDs has been one of the largest drivers of the segment's profit growth over the last few years. Warner Bros.' library consists of more than

Exhibit 9.2 Breakdown of Time Warner Revenues, EBITDA, and EBIT by Line of Business, 2003–2004

$ Millions	Revenues 2003	Revenues 2004	% Consolidated Revenues 2004	EBITDA 2003	EBITDA 2004	% Consolidated EBITDA	EBIT 2003	EBIT 2004	% Consolidated EBIT
Filmed Entertainment	10,967	11,853	27.2%	1,465	1,474	14.2%	1,173	1,157	16.0%
Cable	7,699	8,484	19.4%	2,992	3,278	31.5%	1,531	1,764	24.3%
Networks	8,434	9,054	20.7%	2,027	2,694	25.9%	1,809	2,461	33.9%
Publishing	5,533	5,565	12.7%	955	1,196	11.5%	664	934	12.9%
AOL	8,598	8,692	19.9%	1,505	1,772	17.0%	663	934	12.9%
Intersegment elimination	−1,668	−1,559		−17	−22		−17	−22	
Corporate				−424	−1,020		−458	−1,063	
Total consolidated	39,563	42,089	100.0%	8,503	9,372	100%	5,365	6,165	100.0%

6,600 theatrical titles and 54,000 live-action and animated television titles. During 2004, Warner Bros. released a total of 22[67] original motion pictures for theatrical exhibition.[68] Warner Bros. distributes feature films to more than 125 international territories. For the 2004 to 2005 television season, Warner Bros. had more current productions on the air than any other studio, with prime-time series on all six broadcast networks.

In 2004 total revenues for this segment were $11,853 million (27.2 percent of the consolidated revenues), up 8 percent from 2003. The growth of revenues was driven especially by an improvement in revenues from television and theatrical products.

Cable: It consists principally of interests in cable systems providing video, high-speed data, and digital phone services. The cable segment is operated by Time Warner Cable Inc. and its subsidiaries. As of January 2005, Time Warner Cable was the second-largest operator of cable systems in the United States, in terms of subscribers served.[69] Among the services offered by TWC, packages of video services (basic, standard, and digital) for a flat monthly fee, on-demand, and pay-per-view services were available. In 2004, Time Warner Cable also operated 24-hour local news channels in the states of New York, North Carolina, and Texas and generated revenues by selling advertising time to a variety of national, regional and local businesses.

In 2004 total revenues for this segment were $8,484 million (19.4 percent of the consolidated revenues) up 10 percent from 2003. The growth of revenues was driven by an increase of both subscriptions and advertising.

Networks: This segment encompasses domestic and international basic cable networks, pay television programming services, and a broadcast television network. The principal component of the company's basic cable networks are owned by Turner Broadcasting System, Inc., while the pay-television programming networks—multichannel HBO and Cinemax—are operated by Home Box Office, Inc.[70] Turner Networks generated their revenues principally from the sale of advertising and from receipt of a monthly subscriber fees paid by cable system operators, satellite distribution service, and other customers. The Home Box Office Services generated revenue principally from fees. Turner Networks operates CNN[71] and Headline News, the 24-hour television news channels, and popular entertainment channels for children, such as Cartoon Network and TNT.[72]

In 2004 total revenues for this segment were $9,054 million (20.7 percent of the consolidated revenues) up 7 percent from 2003. The growth of revenues was driven by an increase of subscribers at both Turner and HBO.

Publishing: The publishing segment's operations are conducted primarily by Time, Inc. and its subsidiaries. In 2004, Time, Inc., published 130 magazines worldwide, comprised of 40 in the United States and 90 in the rest of the world.[73] Time Warner Book Group Inc., a Time Inc.'s subsidiary, through Warner Books, Little, Brown and Company, and Time Warner Book Group UK, carries out most of the book publishing operations. During 2004, the Time Warner Book Group placed 58 books on *The New York Times* bestseller lists.

In 2004 annual report, the segment reported total revenues of $5,565 million (12.7 percent of the consolidated revenues) up just 1 percent from 2003. Such growth was due to a slight cut of SG&A costs and, principally, to the impairment of goodwill born in 2003. The increase of revenues was driven mostly by advertising, but such growth was offset by the fact that, in 2004, Time, Inc., did not decide to publish, as happened in 2003, the magazine *Time Life*.

AOL: This segment provides a network of web brands and, in mid-2005, was the largest Internet access provider in the United States with 27 million subscribers in the United States and in Europe. In June 2005, AOL was organized into four business units: access, audience, digital services, and international. The core and historic business of AOL has always been the offer of an online subscription service that includes a component of telephone dial-up Internet access. Given the maturity of this technology, at the time of the hedge funds' attack, AOL was trying to develop and implement a marketing campaign and new technologies such as the broadband service. At the end of 2004, AOL was struggling with its old-fashion technology and its revenues were driven just by advertising services which kept on growing even if offset by the drop of subscriptions. As a result, AOL reported, for fiscal year 2004, total revenues of $8,692 million (19.9 percent of consolidated revenues), up by 1 percent from 2003.

Why Did the Activists Intervene?

Mr. Icahn and his team decided to focus their attention on Time Warner because they strongly believed the company's share price was undervalued. At the time of the initial engagement, in August 2005, the stock price was around $18 and had been lagging for the previous two years, despite CEO's success in reducing debt, selling noncore assets, and dealing with problems coming from the 2001 merger with AOL.

The analysis of comparable market multiples shows such an undervaluation (see Exhibit 9.3).

Exhibit 9.3   A Break-Up Valuation of TW-AOL, July 2005

$ Millions	Revenues	EBITDA	EBIT	Earnings*
Time Warner (ex. AOL)	$34,956	$8,642	$6,316	$3,028
AOL	$8,692	$1,772	$934	$336
Median Multiples TW (ex. AOL)	2.02X	11.29X	13.51X	23.00X
Median Multiples AOL	10.13X	49.95X	69.35X	102.98X
EV TW (ex. AOL)	$70,700	$97,580	$85,308	
EV AOL	$88,042	$88,505	$64,773	
EV Conglomerate	$158,743	$186,085	$150,081	
Net Financial Position	$12,957	$12,957	$12,957	
Market Cap TW (ex. AOL)				$69,624
Market Cap AOL				$34,642
Market Cap Conglomerate	$145,786	$173,128	$137,124	$104,266
Conglomerate Market Multiples	3.77X	19.86X	24.34X	30.99X
Conglomerate Actual Multiples**	2.12X	9.54X	14.50X	22.72X
Share Price Conglomerate	$31.64	$37.58	$29.76	$22.63

*The amount of earnings for AOL and Time Warner (ex. AOL) is an estimate based on the contribution of the unit to the total Revenues, EBITDA, and EBIT.
**As of July 1, 2005.

We have calculated separate market multiples for the division AOL and for the rest of Time Warner to take under consideration the different lines of business the conglomerate operates in. While for AOL we have considered only pure Internet players such as Google and Yahoo!, for Time Warner ex AOL we have taken into account several companies[74] that have diversified their own businesses by all playing an important role in the cable, entertainment, and media industries. As shown in the chart below, all the market multiples calculated over Time Warner comps are clearly higher than the actual multiples Time Warner was trading at. These differences show that, even if the group was performing well and achieving good operating margins, the market did not perceive such high results. This outcome is confirmed by looking at multiples such as price/earnings (P/E) and book-to-market. As a matter of fact, the P/E ratio is lower than the median of Time Warner's comparables. The book-to-market ratio, equal to 0.82, shows that the market value of equity was considered higher than its actual book value.[75] Therefore, if we consider the market multiples of the period, Time Warner's share should have traded at a price in the range between $23 and $38, while the mean stock price was $17.5.

Besides the unfortunate merger with AOL, there were other reasons why the stock price was depressed. First, Time Warner was concerned about the competitive pressures its cable unit was facing because of telephone companies' intention to enter the TV sector. Second, all the firms operating in the media industry were pressured by the need of adopting new digital standards on advertising and by the value of copyrighted film, TV, and music content, threatened by new technologies.[76]

The sentiment that Time Warner was undervalued was shared by all the players in financial markets, including its CEO. Parsons believed that his company's share was behaving exactly as its competitors' stocks because of the negative trend of the industry and the need of innovation. Carl Icahn, on the other hand, did not think that the only reason of this stagnation of the company's share price was due to a negative period of the sector. He addressed most of the fault to Time Warner's board, especially to its CEO, by stating that Parsons had been too passive.

In addition to the fact that the share price did not reflect the fair value of Time Warner, the media group stood out as a good target for activist hedge funds. As shown previously, these activists seek undervalued companies with good operating margins, rich in cash, and with a debt capacity not completely exploited. At the end of 2004, Time Warner reported consolidated revenues increased by 6.4 percent from 2003 and a consolidated income increased by 27.5 percent from the previous year, with a net profit margin of 8 percent. The ROE and ROA for fiscal year 2004 were, respectively, equal to 5.54 percent and 8 percent, both increased compared to 2003. Cash on hand increased in 2004 by 100 percent and it represented 5 percent of the total assets. Finally, the leverage was quite low, being the group financed by debt just for 21 percent of total sources of financing. The media group, at that time, was paying back its debt and showed a large unutilized debt capacity.[77]

After a deep analysis of the group, the activists came up with a fair value between $26 and $28 per share. This estimated value was referred to the sum of the share price of the group with more leverage and the share price of Time Warner

Cable completely spun off. Apparently, Mr. Icahn believed to know the way to get out of such slackness.

What Happened: The Path Followed

The Theatrical Fray

On August 15, 2005, Carl Icahn announced that he, with other three hedge funds, had bought up a $2.2 billion stake in Time Warner, corresponding to about 2.6 percent of the outstanding shares.[78] At the same time, he stated that "a cable spin-off combined with an immediate $20 billion stock buyback[79] 'would eliminate the discount' between Time Warner's share price and the 'inherent value of its unique assets.'"[80] A $20 billion share repurchase would have represented a stock buyback of 25 percent of the shares outstanding at that moment. A share repurchase so much larger than the one planned by Time Warner's management would have had many upsides. First, historical market reactions to a large stock buyback program have always been very positive. Investors tend to perceive such a decision as a management's belief that the company is undervalued. By buying back the company's shares, then, managers send to the market the signal that the insiders are confident that future cash flows are strong enough to support future investments and debt commitments. For these reasons, the hedge funds believed that, in this way, the stock would have soared. Through a larger share repurchase plan, the Icahn group intended to reduce a too-diluted capital and improve fundamentals for the long period. To complete such a significant stock buyback, Time Warner's debt capacity could be exploited, by increasing the group indebtedness and taking advantage of the leverage.

Different considerations brought Icahn to propose a complete spin-off of the cable unit. A conglomerate like Time Warner appeared to be a too-complicated investment choice for the average investor, who necessarily needed to have a clear view of the prospects for cable, content, and Internet. As a result, it is very much likely that the media conglomerate was trading at a discount because investors could not figure out what individual pieces of the group were worth. By separating the cable unit, instead, Time Warner would have attracted more investors who could choose to own a pure cable company, a content company with a significant online presence, or a portfolio of the two. In addition, the combination of cable and content brought little synergy for the group and, instead, caused greater corporate overhead expense. Furthermore, most of the group debt was attributable to Time Warner Cable, and, as a result of the spin-off, the conglomerate would have been able to take on even more financial leverage. Finally, in mid 2005 the dynamics of the cable sector were changing due to an increase of competition and already many competitors—for example, Viacom[81]—had spun off the cable division to better face these new trends and take advantage from them.

At first, the group of hedge funds led by Carl Icahn tried to mediate with Time Warner's management and its CEO, but, when they noticed they were not getting what they were seeking, or even much attention from the company's directors, they increased pressure and demands. As a result, in October 2005, Icahn wrote a letter to all Time Warner's shareholders[82] restating the need of a $20 billion share repurchase and a complete cable unit spin-off, making public his intentions of mounting a proxy fight for all board seats and charging Parsons and the company with mismanagement and "paralysis of inaction." He explained the reasons why the merger with AOL turned out to be such a disaster, listed many transactions where the company could have bargained better terms if the management had been more active, and harshly complained about the company's overexpenditures.

As a response to such attack, Parsons announced a share buyback increased to $12.5 billion and confirmed the partial spin-off of the cable unit, still denying the full divestiture of the division.[83] Still Icahn was not satisfied and kept on proposing his specific and often-colorful objections, ranging from the historical performance of the stock to the company's well-traveled jet fleet and to the size of the cafeteria in the new Time Warner's building in Columbus Circle in New York, defined, by the activists' leader, as "lavish corporate headquarters." At that point, Icahn had moved far beyond his original proposals and the battle had become more personal, reaching very harsh tones. Icahn even said of Parsons that he was not a sympathetic figure, described him as "I, Claudius, the accidental emperor who was there at the right time," and referred to Time Warner's board as a "not-too-bright class of morons." To Icahn, Parsons was a politician, not a tough-minded businessman, "a nice guy, the kind of guy you would meet for a drink. But I [Icahn] question whether he's the guy to run Time Warner." To Parsons, Icahn was still the greenmail corporate raider of the 1980s, who called himself a shareholder activist even if his game was still the same.

In November 2005, Icahn and his group gained more power as Steve Case, AOL's cofounder, resigned from Time Warner's board and decided to support the activists. Steve Case held, at that time, around $250 million shares and was one of the largest stockholders of the company. He stated in an essay[84] that, even if he had been one of the promoters of the merger between Time Warner and AOL, he had spent the previous year asking for a company breakup but, clearly, he never gained much of a following.[85] Nonetheless, he surely obtained Icahn's appreciation, who after this statement by Case became even more aggressive toward the target company.

In the same period, the group of activists announced they had hired Lazard to identify strategic alternatives and help Icahn in choosing a new slate of directors. The reasons why Icahn decided to rely on such an important name in financial markets are easily understandable. The activists' group was attempting to take over one of the largest companies on the market and needed support from the other shareholders, especially from institutions, to be successful. Icahn himself made this point clear: "I only have 3 percent of the stock and that's why we brought Lazard in . . . you have to have someone with credibility to talk to all the index funds that own this stock."[86] In the meantime, CEO Parsons was playing his game by responding to Icahn's offences and trying, unsuccessfully, to move the share price with new acquisitions and new products and services.[87] And, no matter what the CEO did decide to do, the share price did not move and remained stable between $17 and $18.

On February 7, 2006, Lazard's chairman, Bruce Wasserstein, filed with the SEC a 343-page analysis of Time Warner.[88] It addressed the fault for the stagnation of the company's share price to "a lack of a clearly defined strategy and a short-term

Exhibit 9.4   The Results of the Lazard's Report on
TW-AOL, February 2006

$ Millions	Low	High
AOL	$17,500	$21,000
Content	$54,500	$60,000
Publishing	$12,500	$14,000
Cable	$41,200	$46,400
Aggregate EV	$125,700	$141,400

focus." The analysis suggested that Time Warner would have been worth more if split up in four independent companies—America Online, Time Warner Cable, the Warner Bros. movie studio and cable networks, and its publishing businesses. Through comparables multiples and DCF analysis, the investment bank showed that a break-up of the conglomerate would have resulted in an enterprise value ranging from $125,700 million to $141,400 million, while at the date of the presentation Time Warner's enterprise value was $97,540 million (see Exhibit 9.4).[89]

Additionally, Lazard strongly recommended a severe cost-cutting and a $20 billion share buyback. The report ended by stating that, by following such strategic moves, the stock price could soar to $26.57, almost 50 percent higher than where the share had traded for the previous two years.

Lazard's report did not convince the institutional investors and the rest of the shareholder base. On the other hand, though, it pushed Parsons and Icahn to reach a final settlement. Ten days after the conference held by Lazard, the two announced they had found an agreement. Time Warner agreed to increase its share buyback program to $20 billion, to be concluded by the end of 2007, and to intensify the efforts to cut costs. Parsons pledged as well to appoint two independent directors, accepting advices and suggestions from the activists. On Icahn's side, he gave up the idea of mounting a proxy contest and of proposing his own slate of candidates. He also agreed with Parsons that a full spin-off of the cable unit would have resulted in a huge tax burden, even if he was still sure that the single division would have been worth more as an independent company rather than as a unit of a conglomerate.

Hence, this six-month fight between the world's largest media conglomerate and one of the most ruthless and feared shareholder activists ended up in a settlement. On February 17, 2006, the share closed at $17.78.

Icahn stated that he was willing to put aside his intentions to obtain the majority of the board but, as he said: "I'm sold on this company. I plan to make money in it. And, if Dick Parsons doesn't do anything, I'm still going to be here."[90] It is worth quoting what Bank of America Securities' cable analyst Doug Shapiro said in a research note: "To us the bottom line is that the group's effort will prove beneficial for Time Warner shareholders, because we think they have already lit a fire under management to a degree, persuading it to take several positive actions, and we expect to continue on this course. So the Icahn group may lose the battle, but if the stock goes up, it will have won the war."

Quieter, but Still There

In mid February, when Icahn and Parsons reached a settlement, the activist became quieter but was still watching the CEO's movements. The latter, for his part, knew that he had to make some significant moves in order to shake the stock price and avoid another attack from the activists.

Hence, Time Warner's management began the promised share repurchase program for an amount of $20 billion, expected to be completed by the end of 2007. It also reduced the expenses: in 2006 Parsons cut them by $500 million and the same amount was budgeted for 2007.

In the following months the stock actually moved from its historic range of $17 to $18, but not in the wished way: in fact, it dropped down to $16. One of the most reasonable reasons is that, as Icahn gave up pushing forward his demands, a complete cable spin-off became more unlikely. But, while Time Warner continued to stay on its own path by being a conglomerate, things were changing in its industries. As a matter of fact, all the largest American cable distributors were experiencing very high returns on the stock market. If we consider the period starting in April 2006 to September 2006, Comcast gained 22 percent, Cablevision 26 percent, and Charter Communications a remarkable 42 percent. Hence, as Icahn and the other activists had been asserting for the previous months, a cable spin-off could have actually represented the best way to unlock Time Warner's fair value.

Icahn started to buy up shares[91] and expressing his disappointment in such a bad stock performance. Parsons, afraid of another attack from Icahn and his group, accelerated the timing of the cable IPO. In October[92] Time Warner's CEO announced that a separate stock for the cable TV unit was to be created and a 16 percent stake sold through a public offering.[93] The stock, since the first rumors about the spin-off that started to circulate in September, soared. The buyback turned out to be effective and the market liked the partial spin-off.

By February 2007, when the share was trading around $21.5, Icahn and his team reduced their stake in Time Warner to focus on other ventures. As some observers remarked at the time, "though his attack failed, it barely mattered. The stock rose $4."[94] Eventually, hedge funds got what they were asking for from the beginning: a larger share repurchase, a spin-off of the cable unit, and most of all, a profit for their funds. The stake, bought at an average price of $17.56, was sold at $21.54, with a 22.67 percent return. To all who argue that the activists have lost their fight against Time Warner, Icahn's response is: "The stock is up 30 percent. That helps all shareholders. Our fund made $250 million. It's a nice way to lose."[95]

The Event Study Analysis

During all the activist campaign the stock price bounced back and forth from $17 to $18. The efforts of Mr. Icahn and his team did not seem to cause any increase in the share price and value creation. During the same period, all the media industry experienced stagnation and all the companies operating in such sector tried all the possibilities to exit this slackness. As a matter of fact, Time Warner's competitors suffered and their share prices dropped in the stock market.

To assess whether the activists' engagement program created value for share-holders, we examined whether the funds' strategy objectives gave rise to abnormal stock returns in comparison to the media industry. Hence using event studies methodology, we tried to evaluate the effect of the engagement of the activists on the value of Time Warner's stock. The events we took into account are the most important steps Icahn and Parsons took during the period starting in August 2005 and ending March 2006.

For each event considered in the analysis, we measured abnormal stock price returns using standard event study methodology proposed by Brown and Warner (1985) where equity returns are based on the market model.[96] With this approach the variance of the abnormal return is lower than the one resulting from the use of other methods. As a benchmark, we used the media industry index provided by Datastream. The choice not to use as market return other indexes such as the S&P 500 is due to our will to better reflect the specific features of the media and entertainment sector.

The first event we considered in our analysis is the initial announcement concerning the hedge funds' engagement in this activist campaign. Rumors about Icahn's intention on Time Warner's started to circulate in newspapers a few days before the official statement. The information caused significant movement of cumulative abnormal returns in the first days of August 2005, even if the activist fight was publicly announced just on August 15, 2005. As shown in Exhibit 9.5, the market positively reacted to Icahn's intentions about Time Warner since the first rumors about it and a high cumulate abnormal return was made. This shows that investors believed that such actions had some potential to create value for shareholders and certainly did on the stock in those trading days. In fact on the day of the announcement Time Warner's shareholders had, in an event window [−20,0], a cumulate abnormal return of 4.62 percent towards the media industry, and on the day the first news was published about hedge funds' interest about the media group, August 9, 2005, the cumulate abnormal return was 7.06 percent referred to the event window [−20,−4]. On a 40-day window, the median CAR due to the announcement has been 4.28 percent while on a [−3,+3] window, the median CAR has been −2.18 percent. This shows that important leaks took place in the days before the announcement.

The second event we took into consideration is the announcement by Time Warner's CEO about an increase of the share buyback to $12.5 billion. Parsons decided, at that time, to partially satisfy dissidents' demands hoping to get rid of them. The announcement of the increased stock repurchase took place on November 3, 2005. In Exhibit 9.6, the trend of cumulative abnormal returns after such statement is reported. It appears clear that the market did not appreciate management's decision. As a matter of fact, the cumulate abnormal return on the announcement day has been −3.44 percent and, in the event window [−10,+20], −4.13 percent. Historically, abnormal returns after a share repurchase announcement are positive and as higher as the buyback is larger. Since the market reacted in the opposite way this time, we can argue that investors did not believe that getting rid of the activists was value-creating.

Exhibit 9.5   Event Study on the Hedge Funds' Announcement of Engagement

Date	Period	Raw TW Return	Raw Industry Return	TW Return (hat)	Abnormal TW Return	Cumulative Abnormal Return
8/1/2005	Day −10	0.47%	−0.01%	0.00%	0.47%	1.51%
8/2/2005	Day −9	1.87%	0.57%	0.79%	1.08%	2.60%
8/3/2005	Day −8	−0.86%	0.02%	0.04%	−0.90%	1.69%
8/4/2005	Day −7	1.62%	0.38%	0.53%	1.09%	2.78%*
8/5/2005	Day −6	3.08%	−0.06%	−0.07%	3.15%	5.93%***
8/8/2005	Day −5	−0.66%	−0.22%	−0.28%	−0.38%	5.55%***
8/9/2005	Day −4	3.17%	1.22%	1.66%	1.51%*	7.06%***
8/10/2005	Day −3	−1.62%	−0.20%	−0.25%	−1.37%*	5.69%**
8/11/2005	Day −2	0.93%	0.94%	1.28%	−0.35%**	5.34%**
8/12/2005	Day −1	−0.92%	0.09%	0.14%	−1.06%**	4.28%*
8/15/2005	Day 0	1.43%	0.80%	1.09%	0.33%**	4.62%**
8/16/2005	Day 1	−0.54%	−1.06%	−1.42%	0.88%**	5.50%**
9/9/2005	Day 19	0.99%	0.58%	0.80%	0.19%	6.20%***
9/12/2005	Day 20	−0.71%	−0.05%	−0.05%	−0.66%	5.54%**
Mean						3.50%
Median						4.28%

Date	Period	Raw TW Return	Raw Industry Return	TW Return (hat)	Abnormal TW Return	Cumulative Abnormal Return
8/10/2005	Day −3	−1.62%	−0.20%	−0.25%	−1.37%*	−1.37%*
8/11/2005	Day −2	0.93%	0.94%	1.28%	−0.35%	−1.71%*
8/12/2005	Day −1	−0.92%	0.09%	0.14%	−1.06%	−2.77%*
8/15/2005	Day 0	1.43%	0.80%	1.09%	0.33%*	−2.44%**
8/16/2005	Day 1	−0.54%	−1.06%	−1.42%	0.88%*	−1.56%**
9/9/2005	Day 2	−0.54%	0.14%	0.21%	−0.75%	−2.31%**
9/12/2005	Day 3	−0.55%	−0.50%	−0.67%	0.12%	−2.18%*
Mean						−2.05%
Median						−2.18%

***, **, and * denote statistical significance at 1%, 5%, and 10%, respectively.

Going further, the next event we took into account is the announcement of a final agreement between Icahn and the activists with Time Warner on February 17, 2006. Focusing on the 30-day window [−10,+20], we found a mean and median CAR respectively of −5.15 percent and −6.72 percent. In the event window [−3,+3], the mean CAR is −2.79 percent (see Exhibit 9.7).

Therefore, shareholders did not positively react to the final settlement; on the contrary, the agreement was considered by the market as value-destroying. It can be argued that the final settlement meant a step-back of the activists and a slow-down in changes, especially with the spin-off of the cable unit. Generally speaking, in that period, the market appreciated cable companies and fairly valued them. A more unlikely spin-off of the cable unit and the absence of the reason of

Exhibit 9.6 Event Study on the Announcement about the Increase of the Share
Repurchase Plan

Date	Period	Raw TW Return	Raw Industry Return	TW Return (hat)	Abnormal TW Return	Cumulative Abnormal Return
10/20/05	Day −10	−2.58%	−1.35%	−1.84%	−0.74%	−0.74%
10/21/05	Day −9	−0.86%	−0.38%	−0.47%	−0.39%	−1.13%
10/24/05	Day −8	2.50%	1.73%	2.52%	−0.02%	−1.15%
10/25/05	Day −7	−0.68%	−0.13%	−0.11%	−0.57%	−1.72%
10/26/05	Day −6	−0.34%	−0.28%	−0.32%	−0.02%	−1.73%
10/27/05	Day −5	0.00%	−1.44%	−1.96%	1.96%	0.23%
10/28/05	Day −4	1.54%	0.98%	1.45%	0.09%	0.32%
10/31/05	Day −3	0.45%	0.96%	1.41%	−0.96%**	−0.64%**
11/1/05	Day −2	−1.46%	0.30%	0.49%	−1.94%*	−2.58%**
11/2/05	Day −1	1.88%	1.60%	2.32%	−0.44%*	−3.03%**
11/3/05	Day 0	−1.34%	−0.70%	−0.92%	−0.42%*	−3.44%**
11/4/05	Day 1	−0.28%	−0.21%	−0.23%	−0.05%*	−3.49%**
11/30/05	Day 19	0.62%	−0.57%	−0.74%	1.36%*	−3.43%**
12/1/05	Day 20	1.00%	1.15%	1.69%	−0.69%*	−4.13%**
Mean						−3.06%
Median						−3.51%

Date	Period	Raw TW Return	Raw Industry Return	TW Return (hat)	Abnormal TW Return	Cumulative Abnormal Return
10/31/05	Day −3	0.45%	0.96%	1.41%	−0.96%	−0.96%
11/1/05	Day −2	−1.46%	0.30%	0.49%	−1.94%**	−2.91%**
11/2/05	Day −1	1.88%	1.60%	2.32%	−0.44%*	−3.35%**
11/3/05	Day 0	−1.34%	−0.70%	−0.92%	−0.42%*	−3.77%***
11/4/05	Day 1	−0.28%	−0.21%	−0.23%	−0.05%	−3.81%**
11/30/05	Day 2	0.00%	0.46%	0.72%	−0.72%	−4.53%***
12/1/05	Day 3	0.23%	−0.38%	−0.47%	0.70%	−3.83%**
Mean						−3.31%
Median						3.77%

***, **, and * denote statistical significance at 1%, 5%, and 10%, respectively.

so much agitation in the conglomerate could, therefore, be the answers to such
reaction.

Finally, the last event we analyzed is the announcement of the cable unit
spin-off through an IPO. The announcement was publicly made on October
18, 2006. On the 30-day window [−10,+20], the mean and median CAR was
2.70 percent and 2.85 percent respectively. Tighter to the announcement date,
with an event window [−3,+3], the mean CAR has been 0.82 percent (see
Exhibit 9.8).

Exhibit 9.7 Event Study on the Announcement of the Final Agreement between Time
Warner and Carl Icahn

Date	Period	Raw TW Return	Raw Industry Return	TW Return (hat)	Abnormal TW Return	Cumulative Abnormal Return
2/3/06	Day −10	0.88%	0.05%	0.08%	0.79%	0.79%
2/6/06	Day −9	0.92%	0.10%	0.14%	0.78%	1.58%
2/7/06	Day −8	−1.13%	0.32%	0.41%	−1.54%	0.03%
2/8/06	Day −7	0.98%	1.10%	1.34%	−0.36%	−0.33%
2/9/06	Day −6	−1.02%	−0.23%	−0.26%	−0.77%	−1.10%
2/10/06	Day −5	−0.16%	0.14%	0.19%	−0.35%	−1.45%
2/13/06	Day −4	−0.27%	−0.33%	−0.37%	0.10%	−1.35%
2/14/06	Day −3	−0.55%	0.56%	0.70%	−1.25%	−2.60%
2/15/06	Day −2	−1.10%	0.05%	0.08%	−1.18%*	−3.78%*
2/16/06	Day −1	0.00%	−0.06%	−0.05%	0.05%*	−3.73%*
2/17/06	Day 0	−1.06%	−0.61%	−0.71%	−0.35%*	−4.08%*
2/20/06	Day 1	0.00%	0.00%	0.02%	−0.02%*	−4.10%**
3/16/06	Day 19	−0.47%	−0.34%	−0.39%	−0.08%*	−9.10%**
3/17/06	Day 20	−0.23%	−0.27%	−0.30%	0.06%**	−9.04%**
Mean						−5.15%
Median						−6.72%

Date	Period	Raw TW Return	Raw Industry Return	TW Return (hat)	Abnormal TW Return	Cumulative Abnormal Return
2/14/06	Day −3	−0.55%	0.56%	0.70%	−1.25%*	−1.25%
2/15/06	Day −2	−1.10%	0.05%	0.08%	−1.18%*	−2.43%*
2/16/06	Day −1	0.00%	−0.06%	−0.05%	0.05%*	−2.38%*
2/17/06	Day 0	−1.06%	−0.61%	−0.71%	−0.35%*	−2.72%*
2/20/06	Day 1	0.00%	0.00%	0.02%	−0.02%	−2.75%*
3/16/06	Day 2	−0.79%	−0.35%	−0.39%	−0.39%	−3.14%**
3/17/06	Day 3	−1.19%	0.39%	0.50%	−1.69%**	−4.83%**
Mean						−2.79%
Median						−2.72%

***, **, and * denote statistical significance at 1%, 5%, and 10%, respectively.

Hence, the market reacted positively to the announcement and believed
the spin-off could increase shareholders' value. The cumulate abnormal return is not particularly high and arguably a larger spin-off would have caused
higher abnormal returns. An indirect proof comes from the analysis of CARs
around the announcement of a complete spin off of the activities in cable networks at Viacom Inc. The mean CAR for Viacom's shareholders with an event
window [−3,+3] has been 2.88 percent, while, just on the day of announcement, March 16, 2005, the abnormal return for shareholders has been equal to
7.80 percent.

Exhibit 9.8   Event Study on the Partial Cable Spin-off Announcement

Date	Period	Raw TW Return	Raw Industry Return	TW Return (hat)	Abnormal TW Return	Cumulative Abnormal Return
10/4/06	Day −10	1.25%	0.62%	0.53%	0.73%	0.73%
10/5/06	Day −9	0.22%	0.10%	0.05%	0.17%	0.89%
10/6/06	Day −8	0.91%	0.48%	0.40%	0.52%	1.41%
10/9/06	Day −7	0.43%	0.67%	0.57%	−0.14%	1.27%
10/10/06	Day −6	0.64%	0.28%	0.21%	0.42%	1.69%
10/11/06	Day −5	0.74%	−0.09%	−0.12%	0.86%	2.55%
10/12/06	Day −4	0.63%	1.00%	0.87%	−0.24%	2.31%
10/13/06	Day −3	−0.94%	0.20%	0.15%	−1.08%	1.23%*
10/16/06	Day −2	1.26%	0.14%	0.09%	1.17%	2.40%**
10/17/06	Day −1	0.41%	0.01%	−0.03%	0.45%*	2.85%**
10/18/06	Day 0	1.08%	0.56%	0.47%	0.62%*	3.47%**
10/19/06	Day 1	0.56%	0.32%	0.25%	0.31%	3.78%**
11/14/06	Day 19	−0.55%	0.13%	0.08%	−0.63%*	2.42%*
11/15/06	Day 20	0.50%	0.08%	0.03%	0.47%	2.89%**
Mean						2.70%
Median						2.85%

Date	Period	Raw TW Return	Raw Industry Return	TW Return (hat)	Abnormal TW Return	Cumulative Abnormal Return
10/13/06	Day −3	−0.94%	0.20%	0.15%	−1.08%*	−1.08%
10/16/06	Day −2	1.26%	0.14%	0.09%	1.17%	0.09%
10/17/06	Day −1	0.41%	0.01%	−0.03%	0.45%*	0.54%*
10/18/06	Day 0	1.08%	0.56%	0.47%	0.62%*	1.16%*
10/19/06	Day 1	0.56%	0.32%	0.25%	0.31%	1.47%*
11/14/06	Day 2	0.41%	−0.39%	−0.39%	0.80%	2.27%*
11/15/06	Day 3	−0.40%	0.64%	0.54%	−0.95%*	1.32%*
Mean						0.82%
Median						1.16%

***, **, and * denotes statistical significance at 1%, 5%, and 10%, respectively.

CONCLUSION

From what has been said in this chapter, it can be stated that hedge funds, at certain conditions, are able to create value not just for themselves, but also for the targeted companies and for all their shareholders.

The role of the activist, especially in financial markets of significant size and characterized by the separation of ownership and control, is a key and essential part someone has to play in order to gain more efficiency. Through times, many players have attempted to undertake such role, although none of them seems to perfectly suit this task as well and effectively as the hedge funds that focus their attention on activism and corporate governance. The features of the traditional hedge funds—flexibility, independence, free access to all financial instruments, with specific settings and clauses, like a longer focus on their investments—allow them to pursue this new strategy in the best way they can. Empirical evidence has clearly shown that post hedge funds' intervention firm performance is better than before the activists' action. Positive market reactions are also associated with interventions on CEO compensation and turnover and to subsequent changes in the dividend distribution policy. Overall, this definitely confirms a positive role played by hedge funds in the interest of all the other shareholders of the firm.

Yet, an increased activism from hedge funds is not exempt from flaws. Both scholars and regulators have argued that hedge funds' activity is sometimes detrimental to the achievement of value maximization for all the firm's shareholders. There are at least three main issues here. The first is that sometimes hedge funds' interest as acquiring shareholders is maximized at the expenses of target selling shareholders (Kahan and Rock 2007). There wouldn't be shareholders' value creation but rather a simple value redistribution. The second issue is related to the concerns that regulators express on some practices used by hedge funds (for example, empty voting) and the consequent necessity to guarantee and protect investors' interests (Brav and Mathews 2008). The third issue is that capital gain maximization is sometimes reached by giving up better long term performance. In this case, the disciplinary effect that the activists exert on incumbent management could lead to "management myopia" and to an excessive focus on short-term results rather than increased corporate value in the long run.

At the end, the current state-of-the-art of the theory and empirical evidence about the desirability of an increased hedge funds activism seems still to be mixed and without a clear dominant position.

In this puzzled debate, the Icahn/Time Warner case indicates a positive role of hedge funds' activism in line with the empirical evidence provided by Brav, Partnoy, and Thomas (2008). The case is particularly meaningful because, in that case, a success for the activists was considered more unlikely than ever before. As a matter of fact, the massive capitalization of the target, the absence of dominant shareholders the activists could ally with, and the presence of a management team that, in the past, had always pleased the institutional investors, all made this fight an uphill battle for the hedge funds.

Besides, the activists never got much attraction from other financial players. Analysts accused Icahn of short-termism. Institutional investors did not support him because they believed his proposals were too radical. Other hedge funds did not follow the activists as well, watching with interest but detachment.[97] Time Warner's shareholders had a deep understanding of the media industry and had been in the stock for a long time. These are the reasons why Icahn and his group were forced to drop the proxy contest and could not gain any seat on the board of directors.

But still, the rebukes on management and on decision-making put forward by the hedge funds were so well-grounded, that, when the management started to listen to the activists, the corporate value increased with positive returns for all the parties involved, shareholders included.

What the case shows is that maybe hedge funds cannot win control of a big-cap company such as Time Warner, but still, they surely are able to create momentum for change. Whenever the management team does not pursue the optimization of the firm and shareholders' interest as it is supposed to do, this new kind of activist could be at the door. Their goal is to create value for themselves by being shareholders of the target. Their strategies consist in shaking inefficient directors and agitating the company until they get their demands met, at least at some levels. Hence, at the end, management's and activist hedge funds' roles within the targeted company clash and all end up seeking after value-creation for all stakeholders.

As some have said, they could be "the new masters of the buyout universe."[98]

NOTES

1. Generally speaking, both are not subject to regulation under the Investment Company Act of 1940, the Securities Act of 1933, and the Exchange Act of 1934, enjoying the same exemptions.

2. Judd (2006) describes the differences between the two types of firm by defining hedge funds as the value finders while private equity funds are the value creators.

3. This convergence trend has been recently described in a survey conducted by the Association for Corporate Growth (ACG) and Grant Thornton, available at: www.acg.org/portals/0/pdf/ACG_Grant_Thornton_Hedge_PE_Survey_FINAL.pdf. The study shows that there is now a general consensus that markets are witnessing "a blurring of the line between private equity and hedge funds" and that just a very small percentage of the players in both sectors believe that "there is no significant overlap" between the two.

4. Indeed, some of the largest private equity firms, for example Texas Pacific Group, Bain, Blackstone, and Carlyle, have established their own hedge funds (Schwartzman and Snyder 2007).

5. Recently, following the subprime crisis, hedge funds have started imposing longer lock-up periods that can last up to two years. Gates, instead, are limits on the percentages of fund capital that can be withdrawn once the lock-up period has expired.

6. "Private equity firms charge that these often young, impatient, number guys who run hedge funds and sit for hours in front of computer screens are ill-equipped to run companies." "The New Raiders," *BusinessWeek*, February 28, 2005, p. 33.

7. Hence, if private equity funds look at this new player as a threat, they might take advantage of this issue and engage in longer and more time-consuming transactions.

8. "Hedge Funds Rival Private Equity in Effort to Take Over," *Financial Times*, September 17, 2005.

9. "The New Masters of the Buyout Universe," *New York Law Journal*, November 7, 2005.

10. Especially relatively to financing, hedge funds "are getting creative with their new-found private-equity interest, offering cash-strapped companies convertible securities and PIPE financings" ("The New Barbarians?", *Euromoney*, May 2005, p. 48).

11. Briggs (2007), p. 695, defines hedge funds' activism as "any actual or overtly threatened proxy contest or any other concerted and direct attempt to change the fundamental strategic direction of any solvent United States public corporation other than a mutual fund."

12. As a result, "fund activism, whereby hedge funds become active investors and pressure targeted companies to modify current financial or strategic plans, is becoming an increasingly popular investment approach" (Citigroup 2005, p. 2).

13. Shareholders, after all the corporate scandals, also got enhanced powers at the expense of management teams and corporate boards from many regulatory reforms, such as the Sarbanes-Oxley Act and the Regulation Fair Disclosure.

14. As it will be shown, activist hedge funds usually pick companies rich in cash that can face such demands easily.

15. "Kerr McGee Buys Back $4 Billion in Shares," *The New York Times*, April 15, 2005, p. C3.

16. When Deutsche Borse proposed to buy LSE, two hedge funds that held jointly 8 percent of the German stock exchange publicly opposed the bid. The reason was that they had assumed before the announcement a short position on LSE and the deal would have made LSE's share price boost (Hu and Black 2006. Kahan and Rock 2007). See also "Saved by the Growing Power of Hedge Funds," *The Sunday Times*, March 13, 2005, p. 14.

17. "The economic impact of share price movements on the hedged shareholder would be in direct conflict with that on a pure shareholder, whose interest is to maximise share price ... shareholders who enter into derivative transactions can find their interests opposed to those of pure shareholders" (Anabtawi 2006, 591).

18. "Dissident Icahn Wins Board Seats at Blockbuster; Shareholders, Hedge Funds Back Financier's Challenge in Rebuke to CEO Antioco," *The Wall Street Journal*, May 12, 2005, p. A1.

19. *Hedge Funds and Shareholder Activism, Corporate Governance Advisor*, May 1, 2006, p. 26. "Hedge Funds: The New Corporate Activists; Investment Vehicles Amass Clout in Public Firms, Then Demand Management Boost Share Price," *Wall Street Journal*, May 13, 2005, p. C1.

20. In Deutsche Borse, Jana Parners succeeded in ousting its CEO. Third Point LLC as well tried to replace Star Gas Partners L.P.'s CEO and K Capital changed Office Max's.

21. Financial markets apply a 15 percent discount because of diversification (Berger and Ofek, 1996; Rajan, Servaes, and Zingales 2000).

22. "Alliance Data to Buy Credit Portfolio," *The New York Times*, April 28, 2005, p. C3.

23. "Thin Pickings; The Restaurant Business," *The Economist*, July 16, 2005, p. 62.

24. Klein and Zur (2009), p. 15, show that just 10 companies out of the 155 that constitute the sample are part of the Index. Brav et al. (2008) have shown that "in two-thirds of the cases, the hedge fund explicitly states that it believes the target is undervalued."

25. "Dangerous Waters for Dealmakers. Shareholder Sharks are Using their Clout to Influence Deals, Mergers & Acquisitions," *The Dealmaker's Journal*, March 2006, p. 31.

26. Bratton (2007) has defined as cash rich firms those companies that have ratios of cash and cash equivalents over total assets of 0.15 or greater and ratios of cash and cash equivalents to debt of 0.50 or greater.

27. See also: Clifford (2007); Brav et al. (2008); Klein and Zur (2009).

28. The main features of a target company are perfectly summarized by Eric Heyman, coportfolio manager of the Olstein Strategic Opportunities: "We're looking for under-valued companies with solid balance sheets and free cash flow that may have stumbled." "Quietly, Funds Make a Push for Change," *The Washington Post*, April 22, 2007, p. F3.

29. Brav et al. (2008) have shown that target companies tend to have adopted more takeover defences, such as poison pills and state laws, than corporations targeted by passivists. Pat McGurn, a managing director at the Institutional Shareholder Service, has even stated that "traditional defences are the things that attract them [hedge funds]. The more protective measures a board puts into place, the more they look to be entrenching themselves." In "Dangerous Waters for Dealmakers. Shareholder Sharks are Using their Clout to Influence Deals, Mergers & Acquisitions," *The Dealmaker's Journal*, March 2006, p. 31.

30. Clifford (2007) has demonstrated that activist hedge funds have a propensity for special-ising by industry and may acquire many different stakes in the same sector. The largest evidence of hedge funds' activism, however, has been found in Personal/Business Services, Financial, Pharmaceutical, and Business Equipment.

31. "Runners and Raiders," *Financial Times*, June 10, 2006, p. 31.

32. Martin Lipton, the renowned corporate advisor who invented the poison pill in the early 1980s, described the number-one issue for corporate directors as "Anticipating attacks by activist hedge funds seeking strategy changes by the company to boost the price of the stock." See "The New Crisis: Shareholder Activism," Ashton Insight Report 2005/2006, and "Be Prepared For Attacks by Hedge Funds," Wachtell, Lipton, Rosen, and Katz, December 21, 2005.

33. Even though hedge funds are largely unregulated, they still have to comply with some requirements of the Securities Exchange Act of 1934. Rule 13(d) 1(a) states that "any person who, after acquiring directly or indirectly the beneficial ownership of any equity security of a class which is specified in paragraph (i) in this section, is directly or indirectly the beneficial owner of more than five percent of the class shall, within 10 days after the acquisition, file with the Commission, a statement containing the information required by Schedule 13D." When filing, the shareholder has to declare whether he is a passive investor, filing a Schedule 13G, or active with the intention of affecting the control of the firm or its management, filing a Schedule 13D. The shareholder has to state some relevant information, among which the size of the block, the identity of the blockholder, and the purpose of his purchase of such a stake. Filing a Schedule 13D is required only if the 5 percent threshold is passed. There have been important cases of activism, for example Time Warner, Wendy's International, and McDonald's, where hedge funds were holding less than 5 percent of the equity and did not file with the SEC. Hence, it can be asserted that most of the activism starts with the filing but it is necessary not to forget that, sometimes, funds' actions begin with statements from hedge funds' managers directly to the press.

34. Other economists have classified the engagement into "collaborative, mixed, and confrontational" (Becht et al. 2006, p. 12).

35. As Eric Heyman, coportfolio manager of the Olstein Strategic Opportunities Fund, has stated, "We work with management in a cooperative way to trigger changes that will unlock shareholder value . . . Shareholder activism does not always require investors to resort to proxy fights and other high-profile means" ("Quietly, Funds Make a Push for Change," *The Washington Post*, April 22, 2007, p. F3).

36. Contests initiated but not brought to the end, so-called "intent to solicit," are 60 out of 130 companies that constitute the sample examined. No threat of proxy contest follows with 24 out of 130. The study than shows that in 19 corporations the board was replaced through a proxy fight.

37. "Hedge Funds and Shareholder Activism," *Corporate Governance Advisor*, May–June 2006, p. 22.

38. "It shall be unlawful for any such beneficial owner, director, or officer, directly or indirectly, to sell any equity security of such issuer, if the person selling the security or his principal does not own the security sold" (Securities and Exchange Act, Section 16, Paragraph [4], subparagraph c).

39. Bratton (2007, 15) states that "unsurprisingly, the percentage of shares a fund holds in a given target is negatively correlated (-0.21) with the target's market capitalization." As an example, the case of Carl Icahn versus Time Warner, Inc., can be used. Given the large dimensions of the corporation, the former rider acquired just the 3 percent of the

outstanding shares and still was able to put pressure on management. This is one of the very few situations where hedge funds bought less than 5 percent of the equity. Briggs (2006) found just 5 cases out of 50 campaigns he examined.

40. The author found very little evidence of stakes exceeding 20 percent: in those five situations, the bigger holding was due to control of the target's board or to groups' filings.

41. Charles Nathan, a M&A lawyer at Latham & Nathan LLP in New York, has stated "Hedge funds travel in wolf packs. Once you have a leader who starts the ball rolling, others will ride the coattails of the leader and support the leader's aggressive actions" ("Lawyers See No Poison Pill To Feed Hedge Fund 'Wolf Packs.'" *Corporate Governance*, December 21, 2005, p. 4).

42. "Hedge Funds and Shareholder Activism," *Corporate Governance Advisor*, May–June 2006, p. 22.

43. Some professionals have noticed that the teaming of different hedge funds could be a good loophole to avoid triggering poison pills (Citigroup 2005, p. 11).

44. Pearson and Altman reported that CalPERS, the California Public Employees' Retirement System, in 2006 has increased its fund allocation to hedge funds to $2 billion ("Hedge Funds and Shareholder Activism," *Corporate Governance Advisor*, May–June 2006, p. 22).

45. "Dangerous Waters for Dealmakers. Shareholder Sharks are Using their Clout to Influence Deals, Mergers & Acquisitions," *The Dealmaker's Journal*, March 2006, p. 32.

46. "Attacks of the Hungry Hedge Funds," *BusinessWeek*, February 20, 2006, p. 73.

47. Additional evidence of this trend can be found in the Carl Icahn versus Time Warner Inc. case in a section of this chapter. The former rider hired Lazard to strengthen his arguments about suggestions for Time Warner.

48. "Battling for Corporate America," *The Economist*, March 11, 2006, p. 69.

49. UBS has even established a real division, Alternative Capital Group, dedicated to corporate financing and M&A advisory to hedge funds (UBS to Launch a Hedge Fund Service, Financial Times, July 18, 2005, p. 22). However, not all investment banks are in favor of hedge funds' activism. In fact, Credit Suisse's head of M&A activity for the Americas, Boon Sim, has stated: "I don't believe in working with activists. We don't want to associate with them because these guys tend to just stir the pot, and their goals are incompatible with our clients, who are corporates" ("Activist Hedge Funds Win Fans on Wall Street; Some Deep Pockets Have Caught the Interest of Investment Banks; 'New Way to Generate Revenue,'" *Wall Street Journal*, May 8, 2006, p. C1).

50. The expressions "empty voting" and "hidden ownership" have been coined by Hu and Black in their survey "Empty Voting and Hidden Ownership: Taxonomy, Implications, and Reforms" (2006).

51. Shareholders have economic ownership (economic return on shares) coupled with voting rights (actual rights to vote shares or instruct someone else with formal voting rights on how to vote).

52. This market is principally used by those who wish to engage in short selling, but there is no law that prevents its use to influence the outcome of corporate votes. The increase of shares lending has also brought the problem of overvoting where investors vote even if they do not have the right to do so ("Corporate Voting Culture Has a Malignant Side," *Financial Times*, May 11, 2006, p. 17).

53. "One Borrowed Share, but One Very Real Vote," *The New York Times*, April 16, 2006.

54. "In an equity swap, the insider exchanges the future returns on his stock for the cash flows of another financial instrument such as the S&P 500 index, or the returns tied to some interest rate" (Bettis et al. 2001, 349).

55. The most glaring case of hidden ownership has been experienced in the activist campaign between Perry Corp. and the New Zealander Rubicon Ltd. Perry sold its stake in the target to large investment banks and simultaneously entered in an equity swap that gave it the right to reacquire and vote the shares. So Perry stayed hidden and came out as an important investor just when shareholders had to vote (Hu and Black 2006).

56. The case was prepared by the authors as a basis for class discussion rather than to illustrate more or less accurate valuation methodologies or ineffective handling of an administrative situation. The case may contain "forward-looking statements" as defined in the Private Securities Litigation Reform Act of 1995. These statements involve risks, uncertainties, and other factors that could cause actual results to differ materially from those which are anticipated. In addition, the case has been prepared for didactical purposes only: all forward-looking data, figures, and projections and all forward-looking statements included have to be considered as not representative of any actual situation. All evaluation considerations included in this document have been developed for the sole purpose of providing students with a better understanding of valuation techniques using available public information. Moreover, said considerations are not, by any means, related to any confidential document produced to advise any of the companies mentioned in this document. Neither the results of the analysis nor any other conclusion that one can reach through this document should be considered indicative of any actual market situation. Therefore the authors decline any responsibility for improper use of the data mentioned in this document.

57. "Battle for Board Would Be Costly and Carry Risk," *Financial Times*, December 1, 2005, p. 34.

58. "From Raider to Activist, but Still Icahn," *The New York Times*, February 3, 2007, p. C1.

59. "Joint Venturer: Once a Lone Wolf, Carl Icahn Goes Hedge-Fund Route; Doing So Helps Him Go After Big Fish Time Warner, Pursue Good Governance; One Tactic: Singing 'Oklahoma,'" *Wall Street Journal*, August 12, 2005, p. A1.

60. This is the answer to the question "Why start a hedge fund now?" that can be found on page 11 of the fund's marketing material ("Carl Icahn's New Life as a Hedge Fund Manager," *Fortune*, November 29, 2004, p. 79).

61. "Carl Icahn: Shareholders Love Him, CEOs Loathe Him," *Fortune*, June 6, 2007, p. 63.

62. "Carl Icahn: Shareholders Love Him, CEOs Loathe Him," p. 64.

63. *Fortune* reported that for the same period of time the S&P 500 gained a return of 13 percent while all hedge funds a return of 12 percent ("Carl Icahn: Shareholders Love Him, CEOs Loathe Him," p. 64).

64. AOL paid $164 billion for acquiring Time Warner. Many analysts and economists have wondered the possible reasons for such an agreement. The most likely answer seems to be that "AOL's management recognizes that its market value is unsustainable and is shrewdly buying soldier (more rationally valued) assets at the top of its own peculiar market" ("The AOL-Time Warner Merger: Billboarding the Information Superhighway," *The Daily Commentaries*, January 16, 2000).

65. On October 11, 2005, Carl Icahn, in his letter to Time Warner's shareholders, reported that following the merger there had been a "$87 billion of goodwill write-downs over a two-year period and the loss of over 75 percent of the Company's market value in two years." Right after the merger, the price started to decline from its $84 per share getting even to $10 few days before Parsons' appointment as CEO.

66. The complete annual report for fiscal year 2004 is available at: www.sec.gov/Archives/edgar/data/1105705/000095014405002361/g93505e10vk.htm#017.

67. Of Warner Bros.' total 2004 releases, 6 were wholly financed by Warner Bros and 16 were financed with or by others.

68. Among those 22 there are movies such as *Harry Potter and the Prisoner of Azkaban, The Polar Express, Ocean's Twelve,* and the Academy Award–winning *Million Dollar Baby.*

69. At the end of 2004, Time Warner Cable managed cable systems serving nearly 10.9 million basic cable subscribers, of which approximately 9.3 million were in cable systems owned by consolidated entities. At the same time, cable systems owned or managed by Time Warner Cable passed approximately 19 million homes, provided basic video service to nearly 10.9 million subscribers, over 4.8 million of whom also subscribe to Time Warner Cable digital video service, and provided high-speed data services to 4.1 million residential subscribers and commercial accounts. By year-end 2004, Time Warner Cable had launched Digital Phone service in all 31 of its regional operating divisions.

70. HBO, operated by the wholly owned subsidiary Home Box Office Inc., was, at that time, the nation's most widely distributed pay television service. As a matter of fact, together with Cinemax, HBO had approximately 39.4 million subscribers.

71. CNN network had more than 88.8 million households in the United States as of December 31, 2004 and, together with CNN International, reached more than 200 countries and territories.

72. In addition to cable networks, Turner Networks managed at that time various Internet sites, for example CNNMoney.com and CNN.com, that generated revenues from commercial advertising and consumer subscription fees.

73. Some of the best-known magazines published by Time Inc. are *People, People en Espanol, Sports Illustrated, Time,* and *Fortune.*

74. The comparables considered for this study are Sony Corporation, Walt Disney Company, Tribune Company, Bertelsmann AG, Vivendi, News Corporation, Comcast, and Viacom.

75. It may be useful, though, to remind the reader that Time Warner, as shown in the Q2 2005 earnings release, posted in the shareholders' equity, for prudential reasons, a cumulated provision that depressed both the value of the equity and the ratio at issue. Such provision, called "accumulated deficit," was worth, as of June 30, 2005, $94,991 million and had been constantly decreasing for the previous years. By not considering such an item, or considering just part of it, the book-to-market ratio would be higher than 1, showing, in this way, that the market considered the company less valuable than it was actually worth.

76. "Icahn to Push Time Warner to Sell Assets," *Wall Street Journal,* August 10, 2005, p. B1.

77. Interest coverage ratios, calculated either as EBITDA/interest expenses and EBIT/interest expenses, in 2004, were 6.11 and 4.02, very high if compared, for example, to traditional covenants standards, and both increasing from 2003. Net debt/EBITDA was, at the end of 2004, equal to 1.73, quite low and inappropriate for a mature company with stable cash flows.

78. Icahn held 0.67 percent of the outstanding shares through his onshore and offshore funds, Jana Partners owned 0.62 percent, Franklin Partners had a stake of 0.61 percent and SAC Advisers held 0.63 percent of the outstanding shares. All together, the group owned 120,386,200 shares corresponding to 2.624 percent of the shareholders' equity.

79. CEO Parsons, in the weeks preceding this statement, already had announced his intentions, in order to unlock the fair value of his company, to buyback shares for a total amount of $5 billion and about an eventual spin-off of 16 percent of the cable unit.

80. "Icahn Issues Time Warner Challenge; Financier Confirms Alliance with Other Investors to Seek Changes at The Media Company," *Wall Street Journal*, August 16, 2005, p. A3.

81. On March 15, 2005, Viacom, Inc., announced its intentions of splitting the group into two different public companies, one for radio and broadcast television operations and one to manage its cable networks. The market reacted very positively to the announcement and Viacom's share price jumped 6 percent. On the date of the announcement of this split-up, Time Warner's shares soared as well, with a bounce of 2.8 percent, raising the question of whether the conglomerate's board should consider a move similar to Viacom's.

82. Icahn's Letter to Shareholders is available at: http://money.cnn.com/2005/10/11/news/fortune500/icahn_letter/index.htm.

83. Parsons stated: "Owning less of a larger cable company is probably OK. Anything else would just be structural engineering ("Moving the Market: Time Warner Lifts Size of Stock-Buyback Plan Icahn's Effort Help Boost Program to $12.5 Billion; Earning Skyrocket by 80%; Time Warner Increases Share-Repurchase Plan; Size More than Doubles to $12.5 Billion After Icahn Presses to Lift Stock Price, *Wall Street Journal*, November 3, 2005, p. C3).

84. "It's Time to Take it Apart; My Case for Dividing the Media Giant," *The Washington Post*, December 11, 2005, p. B01.

85. Case wrote: "By early 2004, it was clear that Time Warner had to 'integrate or liberate' . . . This past July, having concluded that integration would never happen, I proposed to the company's board that it was time to 'liberate' and split the conglomerate into four freestanding companies."

86. "Icahn Takes Activism to the Next Level," *Euromoney*, January 2006, p. 36. He also added: "With the increased importance of ISS, if I can convince them and others like them how to vote, I think there's a very good chance we can win this."

87. Bewkes was appointed president and COO; the Warner Bros' broadcast network was merged with CBS's UPN network; the Time Warner Book Group, a small publishing operation, was sold to Hachette, a French firm and one of the world's largest publishing companies.

88. Available at: http://www.sec.gov/Archives/edgar/data/1105705/000104746906001488/a2167198zex3.pdf.

89. By the end of 2005 it was already clear that the single units were worth more than the aggregate. Gabelli & Co. showed that the Network division was worth $44.5 billion, Time Inc. Publishing $11.5, Warner Bros. Films $16.5 billion, Cable TV $44.5 billion and AOL $17 billion with a total breakup value of $134 billion while the enterprise value at that time was $94 billion ("Dick and Carl's Goblet of Fire," *Forbes*, December 26, 2005, p. 84).

90. "The Raid," *New Yorker*, March 20, 2006, p. 143.

91. In August 2006, the group leaded by Icahn held a cumulative stake of 3.6 percent of the outstanding. In addition, a Dubai fund that already had expressed support to the dissidents in the previous January, held about 2.4 percent of Time Warner's shares and options through UBS ("Icahn Purchases Additional Shares of Time Warner," *Wall Street Journal*, August 16, 2006, p. B3).

92. On October 18, 2006, Time Warner filed with the SEC a statement declaring that 16 percent of Time Warner Cable would have been listed. The company stated that the 16 percent stake in the cable unit was worth $5.5 billion and the share was to be sold at $32.25 (156 million shares).

93. The first trading day was March 1, 2007. The stock is listed on the NYSE with the ticker TWC.

94. "Carl Icahn: Shareholders Love Him, CEOs Loathe Him," *Fortune*, June 11, 2007, p. 66.

95. "From Raider to Activist, but still Icahn," *The New York Times*, February 3, 2007, p. C1.

96. For any security i, the market model is: $R_{it} = \alpha_i + \beta_i R_{mt} + \varepsilon_{it}$ where R_{it} and R_{mt} are, respectively, the period-t returns on security i and the market portfolio. Market model parameters were estimated over a period beginning 200 days before and ending 35 days before the announcement. Abnormal returns for each day are obtained by subtracting the return predicted by the market model from the actual return.

97. As a journalist has observed: "He [Icahn] wanted to be the Pied Piper of hedge-fund investors. And this didn't happen. When he played the music . . . the hedge funds didn't follow" ("Hedge-Fund Lessons from the Icahn Affair," *The Wall Street Journal*, February 22, 2006, p. A2).

98. "The New Masters of the Buyout Universe," *New York Law Journal*, November 7, 2005.

REFERENCES

Anabtawi, Iman. 2006. Some skepticism about increasing shareholder power. *UCLA Law Review* 53 (3):561–599.

Becht, Marco, Julian Franks, Colin Mayer, and Stefano Rossi. 2006. Returns to shareholder activism: Evidence from a clinical study of the Hermes U.K. Focus Fund. Finance Working Paper, London Business School.

Berger, Philip G., and Eli Ofek. 1996. Bustup takeovers of value-destroying diversified firms. *Journal of Finance* 51 (4):1175–1200.

Berle, Adolf R., and Gardiner C. Means. 1932. The modern corporation and private property. New York: Macmillan.

Bettis, J. Carr, Michael L. Lemmon, and John M. Bizjak. 2001. Managerial ownership, incentive contracting, and the use of zero-cost collars and equity swaps by corporate insiders. *Journal of Financial and Quantitative Analysis* 36 (3):345–370.

Betton, Sandra, and B. Espen Eckbo. 2000. Toeholds, bid jumps, and expected payoffs in takeovers. *The Review of Financial Studies* 13 (4):841–883.

Boyson, Nicole M., and Robert M. Mooradian, 2007. Hedge funds as shareholder activists from 1994–2005. Working Paper, Northeastern University, Boston.

Bratton, William W. 2007. Hedge funds and governance targets. Working Paper, Georgetown University Law Center and ECGI.

Brav, Alon, W. Wei Jiang, Frank Partnoy, and Randall Thomas. 2008. Hedge fund activism, corporate governance, and firm performance. *Journal of Finance* 63:4.

Brav, Alon, and Richmond D. Mathews. 2008. Empty voting and efficiency. AFA 2009 San Francisco Meetings Paper.

Briggs, Thomas W. 2007. Corporate governance and the new hedge fund activism: An empirical analysis. *Journal of Corporation Law* 32 (4):681–737.

Bris, Arturo. 2002. Toeholds, takeover premium, and the probability of being acquired. *Journal of Corporate Finance* 8 (3):227–253.

Brown, Stephen J., and Jerold B. Warner. 1985. Using daily stock returns: The case of event studies. *Journal of Economics* 14 (1):3–31.

Christoffersen, Susan E. K., Christopher C. Geczy, David K. Musto, and Adam V. Reed. 2007. Vote trading and information aggregation. Working Paper, McGill University, University of Pennsylvania and University of North Carolina at Chapel Hill.

Citigroup. 2005. Hedge Funds at the Gate.

Citigroup. 2006. Hot Corporate Finance Topics in 2006.

Clifford, Christopher. 2007. Value creation or destruction? Hedge funds as shareholder activists. Working Paper. Arizona State University.

Easterbrook, Frank H., and Daniel R. Fischel. 1983. Voting in corporate law. *Journal of Law and Economics* 26 (2):395–427.

Hu, H. T. C, and B. Black. 2006. Empty voting and hidden (morphable) ownership: Taxonomy, implications, and reforms. *The Business Lawyer* 61 (3):1011–1070.

Hu, Henry T. C., and Bernard B. Black. 2007. Hedge funds, insiders, and the decoupling of economic and voting ownership: Empty voting and hidden (morphable) ownership. *Journal of Corporate Finance* 13 (2-3):343–367.

Judd, Mattew. 2006. Hedge funds and private equity converge. *International Financial Law Review, Supplement—The 2006 Guide to Private Equity and Venture Capital.*

Kahan, Marcel, and Edward B. Rock. 2007. Hedge funds in corporate governance and corporate control. *University of Pennsylvania Law Review* 155:5.

Klein, April, and Emanuel Zur. 2009. Entrepreneurial shareholder activism: Hedge funds and other private investors. *Journal of Finance* 64:187–229.

Lipton, Martin. 2007. Shareholder activism and the "eclipse of the public corporation." *Insight* 21 (2):36–40.

Partnoy, Frank, and Randall S. Thomas. 2006. Gap filling, hedge funds, and financial innovation. Working Paper, University of San Diego School of Law and Vanderbilt University School of Law.

Rajan, Raghuram., Henri Servaes, and Luigi Zingales. 2000. The cost of diversity: The diversification discount and inefficient investment. *Journal of Finance* 55 (1):35–80.

Schwartzman, Eric, and Chris Snyder. 2007. Competitive convergence. International Financial Law Review, the 2007 Guide to Private Equity and Venture Capital. Available at: www.iflr.com/?Page=17&ISS=23654&SID=681219.

Thompson, Rex. 2006. The limits of hedge fund activism. Law and Economic Workshop, University of California, Berkeley.

REFERENCE WEB SITES

corp.sina.com.cn/eng/sina_rela_eng.htm.
corporate.disney.go.com/index.html?ppLink=pp_wdig.
investor.google.com.
global.factiva.com.
info.euromoney.com.
ir.cnetnetworks.com/phoenix.zhtml?c=67325&p=irol-irhome.
money.cnn.com/magazines/fortune.
www.acg.org.
www.bertelsmann.com/bertelsmann_corp/wms41/bm/index.php?ci=555&language=2.
www.businessweek.com.
www.cmcsk.com.
www.economist.com.
www.forbes.com.
www.ft.com.
www.ilsole24ore.com.
www.law.com/jsp/nylj/index.jsp.
www.lexisnexis.com.
www.newscorp.com/investor/index.html.
www.newyorker.com.
www.nytimes.com.
www.sec.gov.

www.sec.gov/edgar.shtml.
www.sony.net/SonyInfo/IR/?ref=http%3A//www.sony.com/index.php.
www.ssrn.com.
www.timesonline.co.uk/tol/global.
www.timewarner.com.
www.tribune.com/investors/index.html.
www.viacom.com/INVESTOR%20RELATIONS/default.aspx.
www.vivendi.com/corp/en/home/index.php.
www.washingtonpost.com.
www.wsj.com.
yahoo.client.shareholder.com.

ABOUT THE AUTHORS

Stefano Gatti is Director of the B.Sc. of Economics and Finance at Università Bocconi, where he's also Director of the International Teachers' Programme. He has taught banking, corporate finance, investment banking, and infrastructure finance at Bocconi since 1992. He was visiting fellow at the International Finance Corporation (the World Bank Group) in March 2000.

Professor Gatti's academic and consulting work has always been focused on corporate finance, investment banking, and structured and project finance. He has published essays on corporate restructuring and debt renegotiations, risk management of corporate finance transactions, funding of infrastructure projects in developed and developing countries, private equity, and venture capital. On this topic, Professor Gatti has worked on the analysis of company valuation and on the special characteristics that young innovative firms show compared to more mature ones, and on the consequences that such differences can have in terms of valuation methods used to determine the firm enterprise value.

Professor Gatti's publications include articles included in high-impact academic journals such as *European Financial Management, Journal of Financial Services Research,* and the *Journal of Applied Corporate Finance.* In addition, Professor Gatti has published a variety of texts on banking, private equity, project finance, and has acted as a consultant to several financial and nonfinancial institutions and for the Italian Ministry of the Economy. He has been a member of the Board of Directors of the Pension Fund of Doctors of Medicine, of Same Deutz Fahr Group, and of BCC Private Equity SGR, among others.

Chiara Battistini is an analyst within the Consumer, Healthcare, and Retail M&A Advisory team of JP Morgan. She joined the firm in June after graduating at Università Commerciale L. Bocconi, obtaining a master of science in Law and Business Administration. Her main areas of interest are corporate finance, investment banking, and business law.

PART III

Financial and Real Returns to Private Equity

CHAPTER 10

Projection of Private Equity Fund Performance

A Simulation Approach

AXEL BUCHNER
Center of Private Equity Research (CEPRES) and Technical University of Munich (TUM)

PHILIPP KROHMER
Center of Private Equity Research (CEPRES)

DANIEL SCHMIDT
Center of Private Equity Research (CEPRES)

MARK WAHRENBURG
Chair of Banking and Finance, Goethe-University Frankfurt/Main, House of Finance

INTRODUCTION

Despite the increasing importance of private equity as an asset class, there is only a limited understanding of the economic characteristics of this industry. Especially after the boom period of the late nineties, followed by the aftermath of the dot-com collapse that lead to wide variations in the success of venture capitalists, it requires a better understanding of performance characteristics and risk management. As data has gradually become available, several empirical papers have recently documented the risk and return of venture capital investments, albeit research on this special issue is still scarce compared to the volume of literature on private equity.

The contribution of this paper is to shed light on the following two questions: First, how should the risk and return of venture capital investments be estimated and what determines the performance of individual investments in a venture capitalist's portfolio? Second, how should the risk and return patterns of a venture capital portfolio be projected and reliably communicated to the potential investors? To answer this second question, we present a comprehensive and conceptually clear methodology for venture capital performance projection and risk management.

Our unique performance projection and risk management approach is based on a Monte Carlo simulation of the internal rates of return (IRRs) of individual venture capital investments. Our Monte Carlo methodology can be used for the performance projection of a single transaction and for funds of different size and focus. Monte Carlo methods have been introduced into the finance literature by Boyle (1977) and are now widespread among many areas of finance. The basic idea behind this technique is that the behavior of a random variable, such as the IRR of a venture capital investment in our case, can be assessed by the process of actually drawing lots of samples from the underlying probability distribution and then observing the behavior of the resulting artificial distribution. This technique is especially useful in our case, as the "true" distribution of IRRs of venture capital investments is analytically not tractable. If the true underlying probability distribution is unknown or not tractable, the common strategy is to first create a model of the probability distribution, which should, of course, resemble the true probability distribution as closely as possible. This artificial distribution can then be used as a sampling distribution in the next step.

In order to model the probability distribution of the IRRs of individual venture capital investments, we draw on a comprehensive database provided by the Center of Private Equity Research (CEPRES) to formulate an econometric model of venture capital returns. More specifically, we propose a multifactor model of the individual venture capital investments IRRs that is estimated via a simple OLS Regression. The results from this regression analysis are then used as a data-generating process for our subsequent simulation procedure. Therefore, our performance projection and risk management methodology involves two consecutive steps: first, an *Econometric Analysis and Modeling* of the individual venture capital investment returns, and second, a *Monte Carlo Simulation* of the returns of a venture capital fund, where the regression results from our econometric analysis are interpreted as data-generating processes for the individual investment return IRRs.

For the regression analysis, we build upon the prior literature by investigating the determinants of venture capital investment performance based on a comprehensive venture capital data sample provided by CEPRES. We analyse the investment returns of 201 venture capital funds that are part of 96 investment managers with 2,721 portfolio companies over a period of 33 years (1971–2004). The geography spread covers four continents: North America, South America, Europe, and Asia. As we have information on the exact timing and cash streams between the venture capitalists and the portfolio companies, we can precisely calculate the actual investment IRRs for each portfolio company, rather than having to rely on a return proxy. The dataset enables us to analyse the influence of various factors on the returns on a venture capital investment. In specific, our regression analysis accounts for the influence of the investment managers, the fund and the portfolio company levels, as well as differences in transaction structures. Furthermore, we include several macroeconomic factors in our regression analysis. As venture capital investments are typically investments in young innovative companies, characterized by substantial informational asymmetries and uncertainty, the outcome of an investment is to a high degree "opportunity-driven." The high risk and return potential of venture capital investments is depicted by a high number of write-offs on the one hand, and extraordinary returns of the top performing companies on the other. These positive and negative outliers are more the result of mere chance, that is, they are usually less affected by factors such as the overall macroeconomic conditions. Therefore, leaving these outliers in our regression analysis of the investment performance determinants could substantially bias the regression coefficients. For this reason, we first exclude the total losses with an IRR of –100 percent and out-performers, defined as investments with an IRR above +99 percent, and perform the analyses only with the remaining deals, which we denote in the following as "normal-performer-sample." This also has the advantage that historical returns for the "normal-performer-sample" are in good approximation normally distributed. Overall, we are able to explain via an OLS Regression analysis a high degree (over 20 percent) of the total variation in the IRR for this specific data sample, while most of the papers on this topic have accounted for far fewer of the variations.

In the second step, we draw on the results from the previous econometric analysis to simulate the returns distribution of a venture capital fund. In specific, this is done by using the previous regression results as a data-generating process for a Monte Carlo simulation of the returns of the individual investments in the fund portfolio. For the purpose of our regression analysis, we accounted only for individual normal deal returns, while write-off and out-performer deal returns were systematically excluded from the analysis. For the fund portfolio simulation, write-off and out-performer deal returns are now reintegrated in the portfolio construction by the following approach. For the total losses, the projected IRR will always be set to –100 percent, for the normal performers, the projected IRR of each deal is determined by running the regression analysis with partly simulating the parameters, for the out-performers, a simulation process randomly assigns a return out of the defined range to each of the investments in this group. The weighting for each of these subsets in the fund portfolio is thereby based on the historical ratios of write-offs, normal, and out-performer deals in a venture capital fund portfolio. This calculation process is then repeated for a predetermined number of iterations defined in the simulation settings. The final outcome of this iterative approach is a frequency distribution of the portfolio IRR, showing the likelihood of achieving a prespecified outcome, which has a higher informational content compared to the single value results often proposed in other studies.

The chapter begins with a brief overview of previous studies on private equity and venture capital performance determinants. Next, the chapter presents our unique approach for the performance projection and risk management of venture capital funds. Finally, the dynamics of our model are illustrated with simulation results for two artificial funds.

RELATED LITERATURE

Private equity, and especially venture capital, has been the subject of extensive academic research. Despite the volumes of literature on private equity, there are only a few empirical papers analyzing the performance characteristics of this asset class. Limited availability of return data has been the main obstacle for a long time. As data has gradually become available, several papers have recently documented both the gross performance of private equity investments at the single deal level and the net performance at the fund level. While earlier empirical studies on private equity were based on aggregate data from public databases, there is now a set of recently published working papers that examine the relation between risk and return of private equity investments more closely and with more detailed data.

Important research on private equity performance on the *fund level* has been presented, for example, by Kaplan, Schoar, and Schoar (2005), Ljungquist and Richardson (2003), Gottschalg, Phalippou, and Zollo (2003), and Diller and Kaserer (2005). Kaplan and Schoar (2005) for their analysis employ a data set from Thomson Venture Economics. For 746 funds, they investigate individual fund returns measured by the public market equivalent (PME) and find that performance increases with the fund manager's experience and is persistent. They also show that better performing funds are more likely to raise follow-on funds. Gottschalg et al. (2003) analyze returns of more than 500 private equity funds derived from the records of Venture Economics on the basis of a profitability index. They document that the performance of venture funds is more sensitive to business cycles, while buyout fund performance is more sensitive to the state of the bond and stock market. Diller and Kaserer (2005) analyze the return determinants generated by European private equity funds by using a dataset of 200 mature funds raised over the period 1980 to 2003 provided by Thomson Venture Economics. They show that apart from the importance of fund flows, market sentiment, the general partners' skills as well as the idiosyncratic risk of a fund have a significant impact on its returns.

Ljungquist et al. (2003) stress the inappropriateness of the Venture Economics data for investigating the performance of private equity funds due to limitations of self-reporting and accounting treatment. The cash flow data they use in two papers (2003a, 2003b) was provided by one of the largest institutional investors in U.S. private equity. They show that fund managers time their investment and exit decisions in response to competitive conditions in the private equity market. In particular, they find evidence that competition for deal flow with other private equity funds affects the investment timing. Furthermore, they show that improvements in investment opportunities increase performance.

The dataset used in our paper is, in terms of reliability and accurateness, closest to the one used by Ljungquist et al. (2003). Even though we perform projections of fund performance, our analyses rely on detailed transaction and performance information on a single-deal level.

Important research on private equity performance on the *single-deal level* include, for example, Cochrane (2005), Hege, Palomino, and Schwienbacher (2003), and Cumming and Walz (2004). Cochrane (2005) analyzes the performance of venture capital investments based on a dataset from Venture One, which consists of data from the financing rounds of 7,765 companies, using a maximum likelihood estimate that corrects for selection bias. Hege et al. (2003) based their performance measurement first on a hand-collected questionnaire dataset and second on valuations based on Venture Economics data. For the hand-collected questionnaire dataset, they use a proxy for measuring performance by classifying the exit type and counting IPOs as success. Based on the Venture Economics data, they measure the performance as internal rate of return (IRR) of the project between the first financing round and the last self-reported valuation of the project to quantify the impact of VCs' behavior on the profitability of their project. The IRR figures in their study again lack accuracy and reliability due to the measurements' basis on self-reported valuations.

The IRR-calculations in our study are based on exact monthly cash-streams between the portfolio company and the fund. Thus, we do not have to rely on a return proxy based on the first inflow and last cash outflow or on valuation data. The cash-flows are reported gross of fees and as such, are not biased by any externalities such as management fees and carried interest. Our cash-flow-based IRR calculations are extremely precise. The works closest to that presented in this paper in terms of data and performance measurement are those of Cumming and Walz (2004), Schmidt (2006), and Cumming, Schmidt, and Walz (2008). These studies rely on the same database provided by the Center of Private Equity Research (CEPRES) and also perform precise cash-flow-based IRR calculations. For example, Cumming and Walz (2004) use a wide range of variables to proxy value-added activities that explain returns. Furthermore, they compare reported unrealized returns with predicted unrealized returns based on regression estimates of realized returns, and document significant systematic biases in the reporting of unrealized investments and their determinants.

In our paper, we aim to develop a comprehensive, accurate, and easy-to-implement performance projection and risk management model for private equity and venture capital. The exact performance measurement and determinant analyses, as discussed in the aforementioned studies, serve as the starting point of our approach. Recent academic literature on the modeling of private equity and venture capital funds includes Takahashi and Alexander (2002), Malherbe (2004), Buchner, Kaserer, and Wagner (2006, 2008), and Buchner (2008). However, the general approach of these papers differs from ours as they model cash-flows and not the resulting internal rates of return of a venture capital or private equity investment. The approach closest to ours is that presented by Weidig (2002). Weidig proposes a simple risk management scheme for performance and liquidity forecasting based on the reported interim IRR of an unfinished fund, but his approach does not work to predict the performance of the "future" market of funds, that is, funds that not have started investing yet. Furthermore, in contrast to our model, the approach of Weidig (2002) does not capture diversification effects.

A SIMULATION APPROACH FOR VENTURE CAPITAL PERFORMANCE PROJECTION AND RISK MANAGEMENT

Description of the General Approach

In general, venture capital returns can vary significantly among different investments. Therefore, a merely deterministic forecast of the returns of an individual venture capital investment or fund will only provide an incomplete picture of the "true" return dynamics. In a more appropriate modeling setup, the return of an individual venture capital investment or of a venture capital fund must be a stochastic variable. In the following, let IRR denote the random return of an individual venture capital investment, where returns are measured by the internal rate of return (IRR) of the investment. To model the dynamics of this random variable, we draw upon the existing empirical research on the determinants of venture capital investment performance. As already stated in the literature review above, the returns of venture capital investments are, in general, influenced by various factors such as the fund manager's experience or the overall macroeconomic conditions. Let $X_1, \ldots, X_K$ denote a collection of $k = 1, \ldots, K$ variables that influence the return of a specific venture capital investment. Thereby, any of these K variables can either be stochastic or deterministic, depending only on the nature of the specific factor. Under these assumptions, a model that relates these variables to the *IRR* (internal rate of return) of a venture capital investment can be written as

$$IRR = L(X_1, X_2, \ldots X_K),$$

where $L(\cdot)$ is a function that relates the distribution of the K independent variables to the distribution of *IRR*. If this function and the deterministic values or probability distributions of the K independent variables are explicitly known, then this model specifies the probability distribution of the IRR. However, it would be very difficult to work out this relationship analytically. Therefore, we propose a simple multifactor model of the form

$$IRR = \alpha + \beta_1 X_1 + \beta_2 X_2 + \ldots + \beta_K X_K + U, \tag{10.1}$$

where U is an error term for which $U \sim N(0, \sigma^2)$ is assumed. The constant coefficients $\alpha, \beta_1, \ldots, \beta_K$ of this model can be estimated by a simple OLS regression analysis. In a second step, the results from this regression analysis can be used as a data-generating process for our subsequent simulation procedure of the performance of a venture capital fund portfolio. Therefore, our performance projection and risk management methodology involves two consecutive steps: first, an *Econometric Analysis and Modeling* of the individual venture capital investment returns; second, a *Monte Carlo Simulation* of the returns of a venture capital fund, where the regression results from our econometric analysis are interpreted as data-generating processes for the individual investment return IRRs.

The basic intuition behind our approach is to model the relationship between individual portfolio returns and investment-specific as well as macroeconomic factors by the simple multifactor model given in equation (10.1) that can be estimated by an OLS regression. For our regression analysis, we build upon the prior literature by investigating the determinants of venture capital investment performance based on a comprehensive venture capital data sample provided by CEPRES. We analyze the investment returns of 201 venture capital funds that are part of 96 investment managers with 2,721 portfolio companies over a period of 33 years (1971–2004). The geography spread covers four continents: North America, South America, Europe, and Asia. As we have information on the exact timing and cash streams between the venture capitalists and the portfolio companies, we can precisely calculate the actual investment IRRs for each portfolio company, rather than having to rely on a return proxy. The dataset enables us to analyze the influence of various factors on the returns on a venture capital investment. In specific, our regression analysis accounts for the influence of the investment managers, the fund and the portfolio company characteristics, as well as differences in transaction structures. Furthermore, we include several macroeconomic factors in our regression analysis. As venture capital investments are typically investments in young innovative companies, characterized by substantial informational asymmetries and uncertainty, the outcome of an investment is to a high degree "opportunity-driven." The high risk and return potential of venture capital investments is depicted by a high number of write-offs on the one hand, and extraordinary returns of the top performing companies on the other. These positive and negative outliers are often more the result of mere chance, that is, they are usually less affected by factors such as the overall macroeconomic conditions. Therefore, leaving these outliers in our regression analysis of the investment performance determinants could substantially bias the regression coefficients. For this reason, we exclude total losses with an IRR of −100 percent and outperformers, defined as investments with an IRR above +99 percent, and perform the analysis with only the remaining deals, the so-called "normal-performer-sample." This also has the advantage that historical returns for the "normal-performer-sample" are in good approximation normally distributed, as shown in the following section.

In the second step, we draw on the results from the previous econometric analysis to simulate the returns distribution of a venture capital fund. In specific, this is done by using the previous regression results as a data-generating process for a Monte Carlo simulation of the returns of the individual investments in the fund portfolio. Monte Carlo methods have been introduced into the finance literature by Boyle (1977) and are now widespread among many financial applications. For a comprehensive overview also see the classical textbook of Glasserman (2003). The basic idea behind this technique is that the behavior of a random variable can be assessed by the process of actually drawing lots of samples from the underlying probability distribution and then observing the behavior of the resulting artificial distribution. This is especially useful in our case, as the "true" distribution of the IRR is analytically not tractable. Using the estimated regression coefficients $\hat{\alpha}, \hat{\beta}_1, \ldots, \hat{\beta}_K$ from our multifactor model, the IRR of an individual venture capital investment can be simulated by using the equation

$$IRR_j = \hat{\alpha} + \hat{\beta}_1 X_{1j} + \hat{\beta}_2 X_{2j} + \ldots + \hat{\beta}_K X_{Kj} + U_j, \tag{10.2}$$

where IRR_j denotes the IRR in the jth iteration of our simulation procedure, with $j = 1, \ldots, M$. In each simulation trial j, we must specify the values of the factors $X_{1j}, X_{2j} \ldots X_{Kj}$. This is done by either assigning a constant value to the factor in all simulation trials (*if the factor is deterministic*) or by drawing values from the corresponding specified probability distributions of that factor (*if the factor is stochastic*). The detailed procedure for this is explained in the following section. Furthermore, the values of U_j are drawn from a normal distribution with mean 0 and variance σ^2, where σ^2 is the variance of the residuals from the regression analysis. If the total number of simulation trials M is considerably large, then we get an empirical distribution of the investment IRRs that will converge towards the distribution of the IRR that is specified by the multifactor model in equation (10.1). In order to form a venture capital fund portfolio, the simulation procedure of equation (10.2) can be repeated for different venture capital investments with different characteristics such as different industry backgrounds. However, for the purpose of our regression analysis, we accounted only for individual normal deal returns, while write-off and outperformer deal returns were systematically excluded from the analysis. For the fund portfolio simulation, write-off and outperformer deal returns must now be reintegrated. This can be achieved by the following approach. For the total losses, the projected IRR will always be set to −100 percent, for the normal performers, the projected IRR of each deal is determined by running the simulation according to equation (10.2), for the outperformers, a simulation process randomly assigns a return out of the empirical return distribution of the investments in this group. The weighting for each of these subsets in the fund portfolio is thereby based on the historical ratios of write-offs, normal and outperformer deals in a venture capital fund portfolio. This calculation process is then repeated for a predetermined number of M simulation iterations. The final outcome of this iterative approach is a frequency distribution of the portfolio IRR, showing the likelihood of achieving a prespecified outcome, which is of higher informational content compared to the single value results often proposed in other studies.

In order to illustrate the dynamics of our unique approach, simulation results for two fictitious venture capital funds are presented. At the core of this simulation study is a unique set of detailed cash flow data provided by CEPRES. Before the two consecutive steps of our performance projection and risk management model are illustrated in detail with real data, we start by giving a descriptive analysis of the data sample employed for the subsequent study.

Data Description

The unique dataset we use for this study originates from the database of CEPRES. As of October 2005, the dataset provides detailed information on 171 private equity firms, 427 private equity funds, and their 9,950 investments in 8,063 different companies. These investments include more than 27,000 cash injections spanning over a period of 34 years (1971–2005) and cover 50 countries in North and South America, Europe, and Asia. For reasons of confidentiality, names of firms, funds, and portfolio companies are not disclosed. Although the database is completely anonymous, it provides us with high quality in-depth data.

The dataset is extraordinary with respect to the level of detail provided. The data consists of information on the investment manager, the fund and the portfolio companies. Together with detailed transaction specific data, the dataset also provides us with exact monthly cash-flows between the portfolio company and the fund. The cash flows are reported as gross figures, and thus are not biased by any externalities such as management fees and carried interest. Therefore, our cash-flow-based IRR calculations are extremely precise. The dataset contains information on venture capital, private equity buyout, and mezzanine funds. Although these three types of funds share similar characteristics such as the organizational structure, the underlying investments differ substantially and therefore separate analyses should be performed. In this study, we focus on venture capital and exclude all buyout and mezzanine funds and investments where the development stage was not disclosed by the fund. Furthermore, as we strive to explore the determinants of venture capital returns, it is crucial to include only unbiased returns, that is, the calculation of the returns must be based on objective values. Therefore, we include only partially and fully realized investments and eliminate all unrealized investments. In the case of partially realized investments the IRR is calculated by taking the net asset value (NAV) at the valuation date as the last cash flow paid back to the investor.

The resulting dataset comprises of 2,721 (thereof 2,285 fully realized) investments, including 96 investment managers, 201 funds over a period of 33 years

(1971–2004). The geography spread covers four continents: North America, South America, Europe, and Asia, with 1,637 investments in the United States, 813 in Europe (U.K., 172; France, 200; Germany, 145). The remaining investments were pursued in 34 other countries.[1]

Exhibit 10.1, Panel A, provides detailed summary statistics for the performance dynamics, the IRR for the complete venture capital sample, and several IRR subclusters. Exhibits 10.2 through 10.4 illustrate the IRR distributions graphically. For the entire venture capital dataset (Exhibit 10.2), we see that the curve has an asymmetric and positively skewed distribution of returns. This positive skewness and asymmetric shape is due to the high number of write-offs (failed deals with an IRR = –100 percent) and a small number of extreme outperformers. Taking the natural logarithm of the IRR, a common practice in empirical studies, could certainly smooth this distribution. This log-transformation works well when analyzing whether a variable has a significant influence on performance. However, it is not feasible for our specific performance prediction model because the coefficients from our regression analysis would then be biased, due to the incorrect weighting of the outliers. Therefore, we perform the subsequent regression analysis without the extreme values, where extreme values or outliers are defined as follows. A complete loss is the worst outcome for an investment; we take the write-offs (IRR = –100 percent) as the lower bound to determine the outliers. As an upper bound, we define the outperformers as investments with an IRR > + 99 percent. The majority of the deals occur between these two limits, that is, between –99 percent and +99 percent. We refer to deals in this range as "normal" deals. As Exhibit 10.5 reveals, normal deals account for 60.50 percent, whereas outlier and write-off deals account for 9.80 percent and 29.70 percent of our entire venture capital data sample, respectively. Broad analyses of the return distributions of several subsamples for different types of private equity and single funds out of the entire CEPRES dataset show that these cut-off points lead in most cases to the best approximation of normally distributed returns. As can be inferred from Exhibit 10.1, Panel A, for the resulting normal performing subset, skewness is close to 0 and the median are very close to the mean IRR value. These descriptive statistics and additional tests (Kolmogorov-Smirnov and Q-Q-Plots) indicate that the IRR values for the normal subset are approximately normally distributed. This effect is also illustrated graphically by Exhibit 10.3, which shows the IRR distribution for the normal deals only. Therefore, it is this data sample that will be employed for our subsequent regression analysis.

Exhibit 10.1, Panel A, shows in detail the performance results measured by IRR for the entire VC dataset and the outperformer and normal deal subsets. The mean IRR for the complete VC dataset is 16 percent, for the outliers 480 percent, and for the normal deals –2 percent. The dispersion of returns spans a wide range for all three types of data categories, as expressed by the high standard deviation, reflecting the high risk and return profiles of these investments.

The dataset is broadly diversified over more than 20 different industries. For our analyses, we create five sector classifications—Biotech, Telecom, Computer, Financial, and Industrial.[2] Exhibit 10.1, Panel B, shows the dispersion of the sample across these sectors. Overall, 1,948 (71.6 percent) investments of our venture capital sample are considered active in the high-technology sectors (Biotech, Telecom, and Computer). Out of these, 1,397 (51.5 percent of the total sample)

Exhibit 10.1 IRR Summary Statistics

Panel A: Internal Rate of Return (IRR)

Statistics	All VC Investments	Outperformers (IRR>=100%)	Normal Performers (100%<IRR<+100%)	Percentiles	All VC Investments	Outperformers (IRR>=100%)	Normal Performers (−100%<IRR<+100%)
N	2721	266	1647	1%	−1.00	1.01	−0.99
Mean	0.16	4.80	−0.02	5%	−1.00	1.07	−0.87
Minimum	−1.00	1.00	−0.99	10%	−1.00	1.17	−0.72
Maximum	42.14	42.14	1.00	25%	−1.00	1.45	−0.34
Median	−0.15	2.27	0.03	50%	−0.15	2.27	0.03
Std.	2.56	6.33	0.47	75%	0.29	5.27	0.29
Variance	6.56	40.03	0.22	90%	0.99	10.57	0.56
Skewness	8.64	3.33	−0.21	95%	2.22	16.29	0.74
Kurtosis	102.70	13.17	−0.51	99%	10.49	39.17	0.97

Panel B: Internal Rate of Return (IRR)

	N	% of Total N	Mean	Median	Std. Dev.	Minimum	Maximum
All VC Investments	2721	100.00%	0.16	−0.15	2.56	−1.00	42.14
Outperformers	266	9.80%	4.80	2.27	6.33	1.00	42.14
Normal Performers	1647	60.50%	−0.02	0.03	0.47	−0.99	1.00
Total Losses	808	29.70%	−1.00	−1.00	0.00	−1.00	−1.00
Sector Cluster							
Biotech Sector	469	17.20%	0.24	0.01	2.09	−1.00	29.62
Computer Sector	1111	40.80%	0.13	−0.54	2.82	−1.00	39.96
Telecom Sector	368	13.50%	0.48	−0.44	3.53	−1.00	30.58
Financial Sector	50	1.80%	0.00	0.07	0.69	−1.00	2.25
Industrial Sector	657	24.10%	0.02	0.00	1.86	−1.00	42.14
Transportation Sector	1	0.00%	−0.60	−0.60		−0.60	−0.60
Else/not specified	65	2.40%	−0.22	−0.34	0.97	−1.00	5.50

Stage Cluster							
Early Stage	1760	64.70%	0.06	−0.44	2.60	−1.00	39.96
Later stage	961	35.30%	0.34	0.05	2.48	−1.00	42.14
Exit Type Cluster							
IPO	319	11.70%	1.24	0.46	2.72	−1.00	29.21
Sale/Merger	758	27.90%	0.77	0.12	3.50	−1.00	42.14
Write-Off	807	29.70%	−1.00	−1.00	0.00	−1.00	−1.00
Else/not specified	837	30.80%	0.32	−0.01	2.31	−1.00	39.96
Country Cluster							
U.S. Deal	1637	60.20%	0.14	−0.27	2.45	−1.00	39.96
Non-U.S. Deal	981	36.10%	0.18	−0.04	2.73	−1.00	42.14
Else/not specified	103	3.80%	0.23	−0.50	2.74	−1.00	20.28
IM-Age Cluster							
Young	848	31.30%	0.06	−0.24	2.67	−1.00	39.96
Medium	1238	45.60%	0.19	−0.11	2.31	−1.00	30.58
Old	627	23.10%	0.23	−0.16	2.87	−1.00	42.14
Investment Duration Cluster							
Short	882	32.40%	0.00	−1.00	3.03	−1.00	39.96
Medium	1148	42.20%	0.31	−0.10	2.86	−1.00	42.14
Long	691	25.40%	0.13	0.10	0.68	−1.00	7.96
Fund Size Cluster							
Small	943	34.70%	0.37	−0.07	3.03	−1.00	39.96
Medium	1280	47.00%	0.10	−0.20	2.46	−1.00	42.14
Large	498	18.30%	−0.06	−0.26	1.67	−1.00	16.95

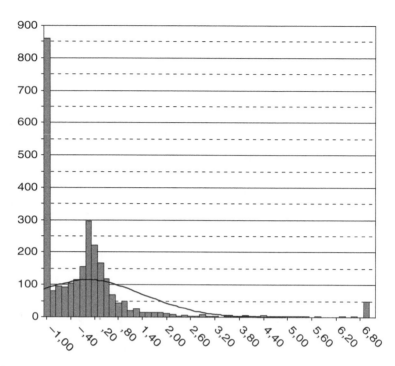

Exhibit 10.2 Frequency Distribution of IRRs (not expressed as percentages) of the Entire VC Sample

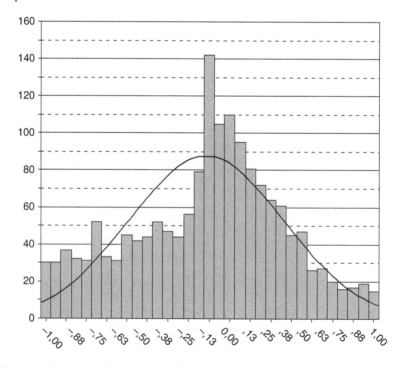

Exhibit 10.3 Frequency Distribution of IRRs (not expressed as percentages) of the Normal Performer Sample

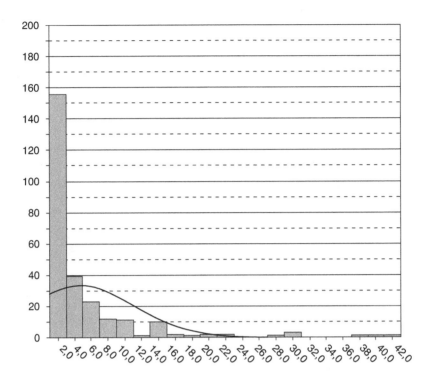

Exhibit 10.4 Frequency Distribution of IRRs (not expressed as percentages) of the Outperformer Sample

investments occurred during an early stage of company development, as depicted in Exhibit 10.5.

We divide the dataset into subclusters to analyze possible trends based on structural differences (i.e., industry sector, stage of company development, exit type, country of origin, investment manager age, investment duration and fund size). The subcluster statistics are presented in Exhibit 10.1, Panel B. We see that in the sector cluster, the highest standard deviations are in the high technology industries of biotech, computer, and telecommunication. Besides for the standard deviation, the high risk and return potential in these sectors is reflected in Exhibit 10.5 by a strong number of write-offs on the one hand, and extraordinary returns of the top performing companies on the other. In terms of mean IRRs, these three sectors clearly outperform the others, but at the same time, the median values are comparatively much lower. Most companies in the high technology sectors struggle to survive in an intensively competitive industry, but those that do succeed perform very well and counterbalance the failures.

The stage cluster of Exhibit 10.1, Panel B shows that the majority of the deals were in the early stage and returned worse performance results in both the mean and median IRR, 6 percent and –44 percent, respectively, compared to later stage investments (34 percent and 5 percent). Companies in the later stage have a greater likelihood to continue to grow and expand, or to undergo a merger/acquisition, whereas an early-stage company either survives the instabilities of birth to enter the growth phase or perishes. This is reflected in Exhibit 10.5 by the high percentage

Exhibit 10.5 Sample Composition and Average IRRs by IRR-Clusters and Sector-Stage-Clusters

Stage	Sector	ALL VC Investments			Total Losses (IRR=−100%)				Outperformers (IRR>=100%)				Normal Performers (−100%<IRR<+100%)			
		N	% of Total N	Mean IRR	N	% of Total N	Mean IRR	% of Total Losses within Subclusters	N	% of Total N	Mean IRR	% of Out-performers within Subcluster	N	Mean IRR	% of Total N	% of Normal Performers within Subclusters
Later Stage	Biotechnology	150	5.50%	0.46	15	0.60%	−1.00	10.00%	17	0.60%	4.18	11.30%	118	0.10	4.30%	78.70%
	Computer	302	11.10%	0.38	82	3.00%	−1.00	27.20%	44	1.60%	4.80	14.60%	176	−0.07	6.50%	58.30%
	Telecom	99	3.60%	0.64	23	0.80%	−1.00	23.20%	16	0.60%	5.34	16.20%	60	0.01	2.20%	60.60%
	Financial	31	1.10%	−0.05	4	0.10%	−1.00	12.90%	2	0.10%	1.29	6.50%	25	−0.01	0.90%	80.60%
	Industrials	368	13.50%	0.23	41	1.50%	−1.00	11.10%	20	0.70%	4.43	5.40%	307	0.12	11.30%	83.40%
	Not Specified	11	0.40%	−0.11	1	0.00%	−1.00	9.10%					10	−0.02	0.40%	90.90%
	Total	961	35.30%	0.34	166	6.10%	−1.00	17.30%	99	3.60%	4.63	10.30%	696	0.05	25.60%	72.40%
Early Stage	Biotechnology	319	11.70%	0.14	78	2.90%	−1.00	24.50%	27	1.00%	4.21	8.50%	214	0.05	7.90%	67.10%
	Computer	809	29.70%	0.04	326	12.00%	−1.00	40.30%	85	3.10%	4.96	10.50%	398	−0.16	14.60%	49.20%
	Telecom	269	9.90%	0.42	109	4.00%	−1.00	40.50%	30	1.10%	7.75	11.20%	130	−0.08	4.80%	48.30%
	Financial	19	0.70%	0.08	2	0.10%	−1.00	10.50%	2	0.10%	2.03	10.50%	15	−0.04	0.60%	78.90%
	Industrials	289	10.60%	−0.23	106	3.90%	−1.00	36.70%	19	0.70%	1.95	6.60%	164	0.01	6.00%	56.70%
	Transportation	1	0.00%	−0.60									1	−0.60	0.00%	100.00%
	Not Specified	54	2.00%	−0.24	21	0.80%	−1.00	38.90%	4	0.10%	2.30	7.40%	29	−0.05	1.10%	53.70%
	Total	1760	64.70%	0.06	642	23.60%	−1.00	36.50%	167	6.10%	4.90	9.50%	951	−0.07	35.00%	54.00%

Total															
Biotechnology	469	17.20%	0.24	93	3.40%	−1.00	19.80%	44	1.60%	4.20	9.40%	332	0.07	12.20%	70.80%
Computer	1111	40.80%	0.13	408	15.00%	−1.00	36.70%	129	4.70%	4.91	11.60%	574	−0.13	21.10%	51.70%
Telecom	368	13.50%	0.48	132	4.90%	−1.00	35.90%	46	1.70%	6.91	12.50%	190	−0.05	7.00%	51.60%
Financial	50	1.80%	0.00	6	0.20%	−1.00	12.00%	4	0.10%	1.66	8.00%	40	−0.02	1.50%	80.00%
Industrials	657	24.10%	0.02	147	5.40%	−1.00	22.40%	39	1.40%	3.22	5.90%	471	0.08	17.30%	71.70%
Transportation	1	0.00%	−0.60									1	−0.60	0.00%	100.00%
Not Specified	65	2.40%	−0.22	22	0.80%	−1.00	33.80%	4	0.10%	2.30	6.20%	39	−0.04	1.40%	60.00%
Total	2721	100.00%	0.16	808	29.70%	−1.00	29.70%	266	9.80%	4.80	9.80%	1647	−0.02	60.50%	60.50%

The table above gives an overview of the sample composition for the entire venture capital sample and the IRR- Subsamples: Total Losses, Outperformers and Normal Performers (see row 1). It shows the mean IRR and the proportion (number and percentage) of observations for several stage- and sector- subclusters (columns 1 and 2).

Sector Cluster: The 26 industry classifications provided by CEPRES were aggregated into the following 6 subclusters according to the FTSE Global Classification System (comprising CEPRES categories in brackets): 1) Industrials (Industrial / Manufacturing, Natural Resources / Energy, others, other Services, Media, Consumer industry / food, Construction, Materials, Waste / Recycling, Traditional Products, Hotel, Leisure, Retail, Textile, Environment); 2) Financials (Financial Services, Fund of Fund Investments); 3) Biotechnology (Health Care / Life Sciences); 4) Computer (IT, Internet, Software, Semiconductor, High Tech); 5) Telecommunications (Telecom); 6) Transportation (Logistics). Due to only a small number of observations, we drop Transportation as a separate industry cluster in our regression analysis. The Computer cluster was taken as the reference class for the sector dummies.

Stage Cluster: The 6 stage classifications for venture capital investments provided by CEPRES were aggregated into 2 subclusters (CEPRES categories in brackets); 1) Early Stage (seed, start up, early) and 2) Later Stage (expansion, acquisition financing, later).

of total losses for early stage investments (36.5 percent), which more than doubles the fraction of write offs for later stage investments (17.3 percent).

In the exit-type cluster of Exhibit 10.1, Panel B, we can observe performance patterns as expected. Companies that achieved IPO status returned the highest mean and median IRR (124 percent, 46 percent), followed by deals that resulted in a sale or merger (77 percent, 12 percent), and lastly, businesses that failed and were written-off (−100 percent, −100 percent).

A comparison of U.S. to non-U.S. investments shows only a slight difference in the mean IRR: 14 percent for U.S. investments versus 18 percent for non-U.S. investments, perhaps a bit of a surprise for some who expect or assume U.S. deals to perform better.

The investment manager age (IM age) is the number of years the investment management firm has been in business at the time of initial investment into the observed portfolio company. We define three categories for IM age: young if it is 5 years old or less, medium between 6 and 19 years, and old if its age is twenty years or more. Considering the age as a proxy for experience, we see that more seasoned IMs achieve considerably higher returns in terms of mean IRR, while young IMs need time to learn the tricks of the trade.

Exhibit 10.1, Panel B, also shows the performance results based on the investment duration cluster. We define investment duration as short if it spans two years or less, medium for durations between 2 and 5 years, and long for investments that last longer than 5 years. We see from the performance numbers that a short duration investment results in a poor median IRR, and this is sensible because it takes time for a company to utilize the investment capital for growth, and it needs even more time before it begins to generate returns for the investors. Staging, the stepwise allocation of capital to the company as a mechanism to control an investment, could provide an alternative explanation. By staging the investment, the investor achieves an option to abandon underperforming companies in time, avoiding throwing good money after the bad. We assume that nonperforming investments will derail some time after the initial investment and will not live as long as successful companies, even if the investor tries to bolster up its lifetime for a while by follow-on financings. Therefore, investments with a short duration might often be total write-offs leading to a median IRR for this group of −100 percent. For the same reason, there will be only a few total losses within the long duration group. However, extraordinarily performing investments show very fast growth and are usually exited earlier, and therefore, will rarely be found in the long duration group. This is reflected by the similar mean and median IRR for this group (13 percent and 10 percent), and the low standard deviation and maximum value.

The last subcluster in the dataset breakdown is the fund size cluster. We use the total amount invested by the fund at the valuation date as a proxy for fund size, if the fund size was not disclosed. The size is expressed in U.S. dollars valued in June 2005. We categorize a fund as small if the investment amount is less than $100 million, medium for amounts between $100 million and $500 million, and large if the investment amount exceeds $500 million. We see in Panel B that deals financed by small funds performed considerably better in terms of mean and median IRR, while deals in medium-sized funds still returned a positive performance of 10 percent mean IRR. However, large funds performed poorly with a

–6 percent mean IRR. A possible explanation for this pattern is that if a fund is too large, then it is unlikely to find enough good investment opportunities and may have to diversify (e.g., invest in new industries) or invest in projects with poor perspectives. Smaller funds, however, can specialize in specific fields (sectors, stages) and develop exceptional expertise, resulting in better performance. Furthermore, for a given level of venture capital fund resources, tighter control and better value-added assistance to all portfolio companies decreases as portfolio size increases.

Our summary statistics in Exhibit 10.1 indicate very distinct risk return profiles for the considered clusters and underline the importance of these variables for further analysis. We examine the dataset in further detail by combining the analysis shown in Exhibit 10.1, Panels A and B. The venture capital data sample is depicted in Exhibit 10.5 according to the three main categories (normal, outlier, write-off), stage and industry sector, relative to the entire dataset. We gain a deeper insight into the structure of the IRR samples by separately comparing the ratio of the outliers and write-offs for each subcluster. The highest failure rate occurs for early stage investments at 36.5 percent and, more specifically, early-stage computer and telecommunication sectors performed the worst considering the number of total losses, with 40.3 percent and 40.5 percent failure rates, respectively. Computer and telecom also have the highest loss rate overall, regardless of stage, at 36.7 percent and 35.9 percent, respectively. These two sectors also show the highest outperformer rates for later stage investments (Computer: 14.6 percent, Telecom: 16.2 percent) and for early stages (Computer: 10.5 percent, Telecom: 11.2 percent). It is evident that the failure or outperformer probabilities strongly depend on the development stage and industry sector of the portfolio company.

Econometric Analysis and Modeling

For the normal performing sample defined above, we determine the factors influencing the outcome of the investment return via an ordinary least square (OLS) regression analysis with the cash flow–based IRR as the *dependant variable*. The regression model we estimate can be stated as

$$IRR_i = \alpha + \beta_1 X_{1i} + \beta_2 X_{2i} + \ldots + \beta_K X_{Ki} + U_i, \tag{10.3}$$

where

IRR_i : Internal Rate of Return of observation (investment) i,
  α : constant factor of the regression function,
  β_k : regression coefficient of explanatory variable $k = 1, \ldots, K$,
  X_{ki} : value of the explanatory variable k in observation i,
  U_i : residual value in observation i,
   $i : i = 1, \ldots, I$ and $I =$ total number of observations in the data sample.

In total, we consider a diverse collection of K explanatory variables on four different levels: (1) the investment manager, (2) the fund characteristics, (3) the portfolio company characteristics, and (4) various market or macroeconomic variables. The variables are chosen with regard to prior academic literature. In addition to the variables presented in detail hereafter, which are the variables kept in the final model, we have tested alternative variables. Overall, more than 50 potential influencing factors have been analyzed.[3] The resulting factors were selected according to their significance level, their contribution to the explanatory power of the model, and multicollinearity restrictions. The final variables of our model variables are as defined in Exhibit 10.6.

Investment Manager: The investment manager is the PE or VC firm that manages the consecutive funds. The experience and reputation of the investment manager generally grows over time, because unsuccessful funds could cause the investment manager to not being able to raise the next fund. Maula and Seppä (2001) provide evidence that reputation strongly affects the IM's ability to select, certify, and add value to investments, and to utilize negotiation power in the new investment's valuation. Therefore, we introduce the investment manager age in years because of its foundation at the initial investment date of the fund into the company in our analyses. Contrary to this idea, Gompers and Lerner (1999) found that reputational concerns induce younger partnerships to work hard to achieve success. A further explanation for a possible negative influence is provided by Schmidt and Wahrenburg (2004). They argue that established fund managers are older and closer to retirement and, therefore, put less weight on the effects of their actions on future business opportunities.

Fund Characteristics: At the fund level, we test for the impact of the fund size on investment return. Several empirical studies have confirmed the importance of the fund size on success, for example Cumming and MacIntosh (2003), Gottschalg et al. (2003), and Diller and Kaserer (2004). Most studies argue that the performance decreases with increasing portfolio size due to less monitoring and value-added assistance.

Portfolio Company Characteristics: At the portfolio company level, we test for five different characteristics: (1) Our dataset includes companies from different nations. We control for the effects of geographic origin of the portfolio company by including a dummy variable, indicating whether the company is based in the United States. Studies reflecting on the relevance of the location, for example, in regard to legal regulations, macroeconomic conditions, or investment patterns include, for example, Bottazzi, Da Rin, and Hellmann (2005), Keuschnigg (2004), Cumming and MacIntosh (2003), Jeng and Wells (2000), and others. (2) Further, we examine the portfolio company industry by introducing several sector-dummies in the analyses. Due to high information asymmetries we observe in Exhibit 10.1, Panel B, the highest IRR standard deviations for the high-tech sectors: biotech, computer, and telecom. This is also reflected by the high numbers of total losses and outperformers for high-tech investments in Exhibit 10.5. These sectors have the highest return dispersions even within the normal subset used for the regression analysis. (3) Analogous to the sector, the degree of information asymmetries, as well as the return on investment, varies strongly depending on the stage of the company development. Therefore, we control for the influence of the stage of the company at the

Exhibit 10.6 Variable Descriptions

Level	Variable Name	Description
Dependent	IRR	The exact IRR based on the investment cashflows
IM	IM Age	The age (years in business) of the Investment Manager at time of initial investment in the portfolio company
Fund	Fundsize	As a proxy for Fundsize, we use the total amount invested by the fund to date of exit or valuation of the portfolio company (in 06/2005 US$)* [for the regression analysis we take logs]
Portfolio Company	US-PC	A dummy variable equal to 1 for portfolio companies from the United States, 0 otherwise
	Biotech-Sector	A dummy variable equal to 1 for companies of the Biotech Sector [The company was classified according to the FTSE Global Classification System]**, 0 otherwise
	Telecom-Sector	A dummy variable equal to 1 for companies of the Telecom Sector [The company was classified according to the FTSE Global Classification System]**, 0 otherwise
	Financial-Sector	A dummy variable equal to 1 for companies of the Financial Sector [The company was classified according to the FTSE Global Classification System]**, 0 otherwise
	Industrial-Sector	A dummy variable equal to 1 for companies of the Industrial Sector [The company was classified according to the FTSE Global Classification System]**, 0 otherwise
	Early Stage	A dummy variable equal to 1 for early stage companies [The company was classified as early stage, when belonging to one of the following CEPRES stage categories: seed, startup, early], 0 otherwise
	Investment Duration	Total Duration between the initial investment and the exit date in years (if not fully realized we consider the valuation date instead of the exit date) [for the regression analysis we take logs]
	No. of Rounds	As a proxy for the number of rounds, we use the total number of cash injections the company received [for the regression analysis we take logs]

Exhibit 10.6   Variable Descriptions (*Continued*)

Level	Variable Name	Description
Macroeconomic	Exit in Bubble (09/98 – 03/00)	A dummy variable equal to 1 for investments exited between September 1998 and March 2000, 0 otherwise (if the investment is not fully realized, we consider date of last valuation as exit date)
	Cold market	A dummy variable equal to 1 for investments with the initial investment date during periods of weak PE-market development (1980–1985 and 1998 to date), 0 otherwise
	Short-term interest rate	The short-term interest rate at investment date (for U.S. investments: The Federal Reserve Bank 1-month treasury bills; for EU investments: the BBA Libor rate)
	Long-term interest rate	The long-term interest rate at investment date (10-year U.S.-Government Securities)
	No. of IPOs	Number of (PE-backed) IPOs at date of exit (if not fully realised at date of valuation)
	GDP	Average variation of Real U.S. Gross Domestic Product p.a. over the entire investment period
	Sector Index	Average variation of the corresponding NASDAQ Sector Index (according to the FTSE Global Classification System)** p.a. over the entire investment period
	Average Fund IRR	Average Fund IRR per vintage year one year before investment date (classified for the following submarkets: U.S. Venture Capital; EU-Venture Capital; U.S.-Buyout; EU Buyout) [for the regression analysis we take logs of the positive IRRs by first adding the lowest market performance to all values and then taking the logs of the sum]

*The inflation adjustment is based on Consumer Price Index (CPI) data for all urban households and all items. Data is derived from the records of the U.S. Department of Labor (www.bis.gov).

**The 26 industry classifications provided by CEPRES were aggregated into the following 6 subclusters according to the FTSE Global Classification System (comprising CEPRES categories in parentheses). (1) Industrials (Industrial-Manufacturing, Natural Resources/Energy, others, other Services, Media, Consumer industry/food, Construction Materials, Waste/Recycling, Traditional Products, Hotel, Leisure, Retail, Textile, Environment); (2) Financials (Financial Services, Fund-of-Fund investments); (3) Biotechnology (Health Care/Life Sciences); (4) Computer (IT, Internet, Software, Semiconductor, High Tech); (5) Telecommunications (Telecom); (6) Transportation (Logistics). Due to only a small number of observations, we drop Transportation as a separate industry cluster in our regression analysis. The Computer Cluster was taken as the reference class for the sector dummies.

fund's initial investment. The last two portfolio company parameters are more related to the investment behavior than to company characteristics. (4) The investment duration is the total time (measured in years) between the initial investment and the exit date. If the deal is not fully realized, then we take the valuation date to be the exit date and determine the investment duration. As described before, the investment duration may be linked to the growth of the investment. We assume that nonperforming investments will derail some time after the initial investment and will not live as long as successful companies. (5) The second variable related to the investment behavior is the total number of rounds, which is represented by a proxy as the total number of cash injections received by the company. The stepwise allocation of capital to a company in several financing rounds, instead of financing the venture upfront, is described as staging. The importance of staging as a mechanism to control an investment and to affect its success has been confirmed uniformly by several authors, for example, Gompers (1995), Neher (1999), and Krohmer, Lauterbach, and Calanog (2009).

Market and Macroeconomic Variables: Furthermore, we control for a variety of market and macroeconomic variables, of which we list eight. (1) First, we want to take into account whether the investment was exited during a period of abnormal market conditions, leading to exaggerated valuations and returns. Therefore, we create a dummy variable which is equal to 1 if the final exit or valuation took place during the "dot-com bubble," that is, between September 1998 and March 2000, and equal to 0 otherwise. (2) Analogous to the exit period, we examine whether the investment was started during periods of poor average vintage year performance on the overall venture capital market. We further account in our model for bank-lending conditions, business cycles, and stock-market fluctuations by considering the (3) short-term and (4) long-term interest rates at investment date, (5) the average variation of the real U.S. GDP growth per annum over the entire investment period, and (6) the average variation of the corresponding NASDAQ Sector Index during the investment period.[4] The short-term interest rate is defined to be The Federal Reserve Bank one-month Treasury bill for U.S. investments and the BBA Libor rate for European investments, and for the long-term interest rate we set it as the 10-year U.S. Government Security.[5] These macroeconomic variables have been recognized as relevant factors in several empirical studies, including, for example, Gottschalg et al. (2003), who can show empirically that PE performance is positively related to public market performance and GDP and negatively related to interest rates. Moreover, to assess venture capital market conditions, we test for two additional variables: (7) the number of PE- or VC-backed IPOs at the date of exit or final valuation (this number is an equivalent for the liquidity conditions on the IPO exit market), and (8) the average fund IRR per vintage year, one year before the investment date, classified for the U.S. and E.U. venture capital submarkets. By including this IRR-market-benchmark in the analyses, we control for possible cyclical effects in the sample.

The last component to consider in the regression analysis formulation is the model residual. We analyze whether the regression model residuals, which assemble the effects not captured by the explanatory variables, are independent and identically distributed or correlated with each other in some way. To do so, we perform a *bootstrap simulation* and estimate the empirical correlations between the residuals. We first create for our entire sample different subgroups of consecutive (two to three) investment years. For each subgroup we create 5,000 independent bootstrap samples of the residual values, each consisting of two data values, and calculate the correlation coefficients. As a result, we get for each subgroup and for the average overall subgroups, a correlation value very close to 0. Hence, our model does not face autocorrelation problems, and therefore, the correlations need not be considered further in our simulation analyses. Additionally, the regression model has been analysed and meets the regression model restrictions like multicollinearity and heteroscedasticity.

The results of the OLS regression analysis are presented in Exhibit 10.7. We can observe that almost all of the included explanatory variables are highly significant and in line with our expectations with regards to the direction of influence. However, two parameters show different signs than expected. First, the "exit in bubble"-dummy, which controls for abnormal market conditions with exaggerated valuations and returns, shows a negative relation with performance. As most of the deals exited in this period fall into the outperformer subsample with extraordinarily high returns, it might be possible, that the remaining deals that are considered in the "normal" regression might be the lemons of this market period, leading to a negative relation with returns. Furthermore, the number of cash injections is negatively related with investment performance. Krohmer et al. (2009) argue that firms in distress receive more frequent rounds of cash injections as investors "gamble for resurrection," perhaps attempting various turnaround efforts in the hope of minimizing losses.

In total, the F-statistic shows a high significance for the overall model at the 1 percent level. The R^2 and the adjusted R^2 values are greater than 0.2 and indicate that our regression model explains more than 20 percent of the variation of the investment performance.

Monte Carlo Simulation

In the second step of our approach, the regression results from the previous section are employed to implement a Monte Carlo simulation of the returns of a venture capital portfolio. Using the estimated regression coefficients $\hat{\alpha}, \hat{\beta}_1, \ldots, \hat{\beta}_K$ from the previous section, the IRR of an individual venture capital investment can be simulated by using the stochastic process

$$IRR_j = \hat{\alpha} + \hat{\beta}_1 X_{1j} + \hat{\beta}_2 X_{2j} + \ldots + \hat{\beta}_K X_{Kj} + U_j, \qquad (10.4)$$

where

IRR_j : Internal Rate of Return of the investment in iteration j,
$\hat{\alpha}$: regression estimate of the constant factor,
$\hat{\beta}_k$: estimated regression coefficient of explanatory variable $k = 1, \ldots, K$,
X_{kj} : value of the explanatory variable k in iteration j,
U_j : random draw in iteration j from a normally distributed variable with mean 0 and variance σ^2,
j : $j = 1, \ldots, M$ and $M =$ total number of simulation trials.

If the total number of simulation trials M is considerably large, then we get an empirical distribution of the individual investment IRRs that will converge

Exhibit 10.7 Regression Results

		Coefficients	Unstandardized Coefficients	Standard Error	Standardized Coefficients	t-statistics
	α	Constant	0,43000*	0.221		1.947
IM	X_1	IM Age	0.00158	0.001	0.032	1.145
Fund	X_2	Fund size	−0,04648**	0.022	−0.057	−2.074
	X_3	US-PC	−0.04072	0.027	−0.043	−1.533
	X_4	Biotech Sector	0,10100***	0.030	0.086	3.347
	X_5	Telecom Sector	0,18000***	0.038	0.122	4.748
	X_6	Financial Sector	−0.02919	0.075	−0.009	−0.388
	X_7	Industrial Sector	0,07294**	0.030	0.070	2.440
	X_8	Early Stage	−0,08520***	0.023	−0.089	−3.646
	X_9	Investment Duration	0,27800***	0.047	0.174	5.876
	X_{10}	No. of Rounds	−0,23400***	0.035	−0.169	−6.651
	X_{11}	Exit in Bubble [09/98–03/00]	−0,10600***	0.038	−0.073	−2.807
	X_{12}	Cold market	−0,12800***	0.027	−0.136	−4.734
	X_{13}	Short-term interest rate	0.00792	0.007	0.040	1.113
	X_{14}	Long-term interest rate	−0,36500**	0.168	−0.085	−2.178
	X_{15}	No. of IPOs	0,00038***	0.000	0.081	2.827
	X_{16}	GDP	4,89500***	1.482	0.105	3.304
	X_{17}	Sector Index	0,22300***	0.038	0.188	5.878
	X_{18}	Average Fund IRR	−0.01421	0.043	−0.009	−0.329
	Model Diagnostics		Number of Observations	R-square	Adjusted R-square	F-Statistic
			1560	0.218	0.209	23,834***

Note: *, **, *** indicate significance at the 10 percent, 5 percent, and 1 percent levels, respectively.

towards the distribution of the IRR that is specified by the multifactor model in equation (10.1). In order to form a venture capital fund portfolio, the simulation procedure of equation (10.4) can be repeated for a prespecified number of different venture capital investments with different characteristics, such as different industry backgrounds. However, for the purpose of our regression analysis, we accounted only for individual normal deal returns, while write-off and outperformer deal returns were systematically excluded from the analysis. For the fund portfolio simulation, write-off and outperformer deal returns must now be reintegrated into the model. This can be achieved by the following approach. For the total losses in the fund portfolio, the projected IRR will always be set to −100 percent; for the normal performers, the projected IRR of each deal is determined by running the simulation procedure according to equation (10.4), for the outperformers in the fund portfolio, the IRR is simulated according to the empirical IRR distribution of our data sample. The weighting for each of these subsets in the fund portfolio is thereby based on the historical ratios of write-offs, normal, and outperformer deals in a venture capital fund portfolio. Therefore, we determine the write-off, outperformer, and normal-performer rates according to the fund structure, based on the historical outlier ratios for the entire venture capital sample presented in Exhibit 10.5. The entire calculation process is then repeated for a predetermined number of M simulation iterations. To obtain the projected portfolio return, we then take the average of all projected deal IRRs.

For the simulation of the normal deals according to equation (10.4), we must specify the values of the K factors $X_{1j}, X_{2j} \ldots X_{Kj}$ in each simulation trial $j = 1, \ldots, M$. This is done by either assigning a constant value to the factor in all simulation trials *(if the factor is deterministic)* or by drawing values from the corresponding specified probability distributions of that factor *(if the factor is stochastic)*. The detailed procedure for all employed variables is explained in the following.

At the *Investment Manager* and *Fund Level*, the two influencing determinants are the investment manager's years in business at initial investment and the total amount invested by the fund to date of exit or valuation, respectively. These values are both deterministic for a given fund and can be extracted from the private placement memorandum and/or other due diligence material of the fund. For our subsequent analysis, we did not determine specific values for these variables; instead we simulated different compositions by randomly selecting the values out of the empirical observations.

For the *Portfolio Company Characteristics* most variables are deterministic and are represented by simple dummy variables, namely the country-dummy, which specifically indicates whether or not the company is located in the United States; the stage dummy, which identifies the deal as an early-stage (categorized in CEPRES as seed, start-up and early) or late-stage investment; and the sector dummies. The industry sector is a collection of five categories, namely biotechnology, telecommunications, financial, industrial, and computer. Computer is the base case, meaning that if we do not declare a specific industry background for the simulation equation, then the investment is by default in the computer sector. These three abovementioned variables are simply dummy variables to indicate true (=1) or false (=0).[6] In contrast, the two remaining portfolio company variables cannot be simply determined with one deterministic value; instead they have to be represented in our model with a probability distribution. For the portfolio company variables, "the total duration of the investment" and "the number of financing rounds," it is difficult to model a probability distribution analytically. Therefore, we account for the stochastic realizations of these variables by drawing values from the empirical distributions of these variables in our data sample. To deal with interaction effects, we further determine the correlation between these variables in our model.

On the *Macroeconomic Level*, there are two further dummy variables that have to be specified. We make the distinction for the exit period, namely, if the deal exited during the dot-com bubble period that we defined as between September 1998 and March 2000. The major purpose of including this variable in the regression analysis is to control for this irrational market period, with the result that the coefficients of the other parameters are not biased by the extreme observations of this time. In the following analyses, we set this dummy to 0. Analogous to the exit period, we indicate whether the investment is started during periods of poor average vintage-year performance on the overall market with a true/false flag in the same way as we described above. We can choose both values, 0 if we have positive expectations for the market development, 1 otherwise. We can even choose the median value 0.5, if we expect a "medium" period of market performance. By running the model for all of the three cases separately, we can perform a scenario analysis for different market development. The analyses presented in the next section were performed with a value of 0.4667 (with 1 for strong and 0 for bad performing overall PE markets), which is the average in our sample over the last 33 years. Besides these dummy variables, we consider several other macroeconomic variables in our simulation approach. The influence of the short-term interest rates, the long-term interest rates, the GDP growth, the NASDAQ Sector Indices, and the number of PE-backed IPOs is accounted for by assuming appropriate theoretical probability distributions for these variables. Another macroeconomic variable we identified in the regression analysis is the average fund IRR per vintage year one year before the investment date, classified for the U.S. and E.U. venture capital and buyout submarkets. Contrary to the other macroeconomic variables, we use the empirical probability distribution of our data sample to model the distribution of this variable for our simulation procedure.

Our approach combines the presented consecutive steps into *one comprehensive simulation procedure*. The final outcome of our iterative approach is then a frequency distribution of the portfolio IRR, showing, for example, the likelihood of achieving a prespecified outcome.

SIMULATION RESULTS FOR TWO FICTITIOUS VENTURE CAPITAL FUNDS

Structure of the Fictitious Venture Capital Funds

In this section, we illustrate the dynamics of our model by simulating two fictitious funds. In order to do so, we first have to determine the *structure of the two fund portfolios*—the number of investments in each portfolio, their geographic origin, industry, and development stage. If the model is applied to project the performance of a real fund, the fund structure can typically be extracted from the information given in the private placement memorandum. Our first fictitious fund should consist of 20 deals, and the second of 100 deals. The structures of both funds are assumed to be equal and correspond to the average fund structure of our entire venture capital sample with respect to geographical regions, sectors, and stages of the investments. Furthermore, the distribution of the investments across the IRR subgroups is also assumed to be equivalent to the average values of our total venture capital sample—30 percent total losses, 10 percent outperformers, and 60 percent normal performing deals. As stated above, we determine the write-off, outperformer and normal-performer rates according to the fund structure, based on the historical outlier rates for the entire venture capital sample presented in Exhibit 10.5. Then, by multiplying the total number of deals in the portfolio by the determined failure, outperformer, and normal rates, we obtain the number of total losses, outperformers, and normal performers in our portfolio. Hence, the 20 (100) deal fund contains six (30) write-offs, two (10) outperformers and twelve (60) normal performers.

Exhibit 10.8   Simulation Results (20-Deal Case): Statistics Forecast Values

Percentiles		Statistics	
0%	−0.4049	Mean	0.2090
10%	−0.1490	Mode	—
20%	−0.0908	Minimum	−0.4049
30%	−0.0395	Maximum	5.5357
40%	0.0152	Range Width	5.9406
50%	0.0756	Median	0.0756
60%	0.1576	Variance	0.1943
70%	0.2619	Std. Dev.	0.4408
80%	0.4246	Mean Std. Error	0.0044
90%	0.7198	Skewness	2.7926
100%	5.5357	Kurtosis	16.8218

Simulation Results

In this section, we present the simulation results for two fictitious funds, where the first contains 20 deals and the second 100 deals. Exhibits 10.8 and 10.9 show the summary statistics for the projected performance of the two funds.

As the funds' geographic-, sector- and stage-focuses are equal and the remaining input variables are exactly the same for both cases, we obviously obtain a very similar mean fund IRR of 20.90 percent for the 20-deal case and 21.08 percent for the 100-deal case.[7] However, we can observe large differences for the median values, the standard deviations, and the percentiles. For the 100-deal fund, the median value is 17.34 percent and more than two times higher than the median of the 20-deal case with a value of 7.56 percent. The standard deviation of the 20-deal case (44.08 percent) exceeds the standard deviation for the 100-deal fund (20.52 percent) by a factor of approximately two. As both funds have exactly the same structure and only differ in the number of deals, we can directly observe the diversification

Exhibit 10.9   Simulation Results (100-Deal Case): Statistics Forecast Values

Percentiles		Statistics	
0%	−0.1854	Mean	0.2108
10%	−0.0086	Mode	—
20%	0.0422	Minimum	−0.1854
30%	0.0868	Maximum	1.6671
40%	0.1292	Range Width	1.8524
50%	0.1734	Median	0.1734
60%	0.2207	Variance	0.0421
70%	0.2785	Std. Dev.	0.2052
80%	0.3548	Mean Std. Error	0.0021
90%	0.4800	Skewness	1.3042
100%	1.6671	Kurtosis	5.9803

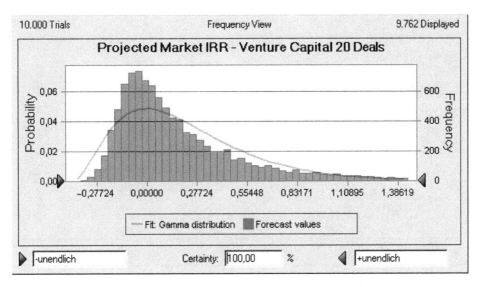

Exhibit 10.10 Projected IRR Probability Distribution (20-Deal Case)

effects of the larger fund. This is also apparent when looking at the percentiles and probability distributions shown in Exhibits 10.10 through 10.13.

The probability of obtaining a positive gross IRR for the 100-deal fund is approximately 90 percent, whereas for the 20-deal fund it is only about 60 percent. When comparing the two funds, which differ only by the number of deals, the

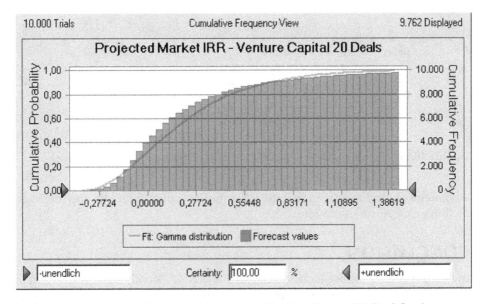

Exhibit 10.11 Projected IRR *Cumulative* Probability Distribution (20-Deal Case)

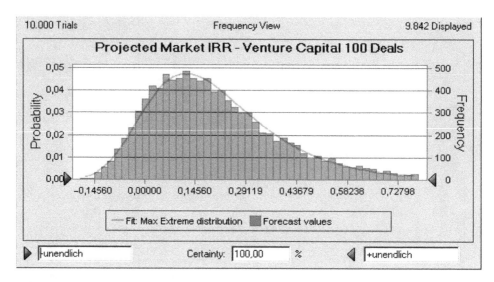

Exhibit 10.12 Projected IRR Probability Distribution (100-Deal Case)

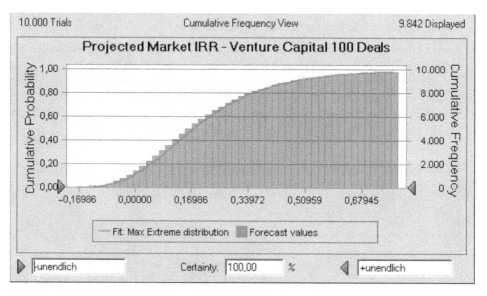

Exhibit 10.13 Projected IRR *Cumulative* Probability Distribution (100-Deal Case)

advantage of producing a probability distribution rather than just one single prediction value becomes obvious.

CONCLUSION

In this paper we propose a comprehensive and conceptually clear simulation approach for performance projection and risk management of venture capital investments. Our unique approach can be used for a single venture capital transaction and for funds of different size and focus. Furthermore, our methodology is also applicable on the fund-of-fund level. At the core of our model is a new method-ology that comprises two consecutive steps: first, an econometric analysis and modeling of individual venture capital investment returns; second, a Monte Carlo simulation of the returns of a venture capital fund, where the results from the econometric analysis are interpreted as data-generating processes for the returns of the individual investments in the fund. For the first step, we draw upon compre-hensive cash flow information from 2,721 venture capital investments taken from the records of CEPRES to develop and estimate a simple multifactor model of the return distribution of individual venture capital investments.

The rich dataset employed for this study enables us to develop and estimate a simple multifactor model of the performance of venture capital investments that accounts for influencing factors on various levels: the investment manager, the fund and the portfolio company characteristics, as well as differences in transac-tion structures. Furthermore, the global nature of the dataset (50 countries) allows us to investigate the potential relevance of geography on the investment return, for example, with regards to legal regulations, macroeconomic conditions, or in-vestment pattern. The data sample comprises investments covering a period of 33 years (1971–2004). Therefore, we are able to avoid a focus on a specific market period, such as boom and bust years with specific investment characteristics. As part of our econometric analysis we are able to explain via an OLS regression a high degree (over 20 percent) of the total variation in the investment IRRs. In a second step, the estimated multifactor model is used as a data-generating process to sim-ulate the returns of the individual investments in a venture capital fund portfolio. This approach also allows us to illustrate the effects of diversification on the return distribution of a venture capital fund portfolio. The final outcome of our iterative approach is then a frequency distribution of the portfolio returns, showing, for example, the likelihood of achieving a prespecified outcome. The dynamics of our model are illustrated by comparing simulation results for two artificial funds with the same structure and focus, which differ only in portfolio size.

To the best of our knowledge, we are the first to propose a comprehensive and easy-to-implement simulation model for the prediction of venture capital future performance based on empirical data. Our approach is usable as a robust risk man-agement tool for fund-of-funds managers, when evaluating potential investment opportunities in the due diligence process and assessing portfolio construction. Several robustness tests (e.g., perfect foresight, back-testing, etc.) show that our model allows us to properly capture the specifics of venture capital portfolios. However, despite the unique breadth of our dataset, we are still limited in con-structing and evaluating the model. A further improvement and better validation will depend on the availability of more comprehensive data for this asset class. As a consequence of limited availability of venture capital return data and our aim to keep the model practicable, there are several limitations of our approach which raise interesting questions for future research. For example, future work should examine additional determinants for the probability of default and outper-forming or address the assessment of probability distributions and correlations of the endogenous factors. Furthermore, with an increasing supply of detailed data, we will be able to perform the analyses for more narrow market segments (e.g., clustered by country) than just venture capital and buyout, which should reveal new idiosyncrasies and enhance the explanation capability of our approach.

NOTES

1. Argentina, Asia, Austria, Belgium, Brazil, Canada, China, Czech Republic, Denmark, Finland, Greece, Hungary, Iceland, India, Indonesia, Ireland, Israel, Italy, Japan, Korea, Luxemburg, Malaysia, Netherlands, Norway, Philippines, Poland, Portugal, Romania, Russia, Singapore, Spain, Sweden, Switzerland, and Taiwan.

2. The 26 industry classifications provided by CEPRES were aggregated into the following five sector clusters according to the FTSE Global Classification System (comprising CEPRES categories in parantheses): (1) Industrials (Industrial/Manufacturing, Natural Resources/Energy, others, other Services, Media, Consumer industry/food, Construction, Materials, Waste/Recycling, Traditional Products, Hotel, Leisure, Retail, Textile, Environment, Transportation), (2) Financials (Financial Services, Fund-of-Funds Investments), (3) Biotechnology (Health Care/Life Sciences), (4) Computer (IT, Internet, Software, Semiconductor, High Tech), and (5) Telecommunications (Telecom).

3. Additionally to alternative measures of the presented variables, time-lagged macroeconomic factors have been analyzed. Furthermore, we test for linearity between dependent and explanatory variable using the "curve estimation" procedure offered in SPSS and include if necessary transformed variables in the analyses. For applied transformations see variable descriptions in Exhibit 10.6.

4. In order to measure the influence of the development of the public equity market on private equity investment performance as precisely as possible, we assign each investment to a sector cluster defined above and consider it relative to the sector-specific public equity return rather than a broad benchmark.

5. For the remaining countries, we apply U.S. interest rates.

6. For example, if a deal is an early-stage biotech company in the United States, then these industry parameters of the regression equation would be: Early stage = 1, Biotech = 1, Financial = 0, Industrial = 0, Telecom = 0, and United States = 1.

7. These numbers will converge to the same value with a growing number of iterations (law of large numbers).

REFERENCES

Bottazzi, Laura, Marco Da Rin, and Thomas Hellmann. 2005. What role of legal systems in financial intermediation? Theory and evidence. American Finance Association Annual Meeting, 2005.

Boyle, Phelim P. 1977. Options: A Monte Carlo approach. *Journal of Financial Economics* 4:323–338.

Buchner, Axel, Christoph Kaserer, and Niklas Wagner. 2006. Stochastic modeling of private equity—An equilibrium-based approach to fund valuation. Working Paper, Technical University Munich (TUM).

Buchner, Axel. 2008. *Stochastische Modellierung von Private Equity-Fonds—Eine theoretische und empirische Analyse.* Lohmar-Koeln: JOSEF EUL Verlag.

Buchner, Axel, Christoph Kaserer, and Niklas Wagner. 2008. A stochastic model for the cash flow dynamics of private equity funds—Theory and empirical evidence. Working Paper, Technical University Munich (TUM).

Cochrane, John H. 2005. The risk and return of venture capital. *Journal of Financial Economics* 75:3–52.

Cumming, Douglas J., and Uwe Walz. 2004. Private equity returns and disclosure around the world. *Journal of International Business Studies*, forthcoming.

Cumming, Douglas J. 2006. The determinants of venture capital portfolio size: Empirical evidence. *Journal of Business* 79:1083–1126.

Cumming, Douglas J., and Jeffrey G. MacIntosh. 2003. A cross-country comparison of full and partial venture capital exits. *Journal of Banking and Finance* 27 (3):511–548.

Cumming, Douglas J., Daniel Schmidt, and Uwe Walz. 2008. Legality and venture governance around the world. *Journal of Business Venturing* (forthcoming).

Diller, Christian, and Christoph Kaserer. 2004. European private equity funds—A cash-flow based performance analysis. Working Paper, Technical University Munich (TUM).

Diller, Christian, and Christoph Kaserer. 2005. What drives cash-flow based European private equity returns?—Fund inflows, skilled GPs and/or risk? Working Paper, Technical University Munich (TUM).

Glasserman, Paul. 2003. *Monte Carlo Methods in financial engineering*. New York: Springer.

Gompers, Paul A. 1995. Optimal investment, monitoring, and the staging of venture capital. *Journal of Finance* 50 (5):1461–1491.

Gompers, Paul A., and Josh Lerner. 1999. *The venture capital cycle*. Cambridge: MIT Press.

Gompers, Paul A., Josh Lerner, Margaret M. Blair, and Thomas Hellmann. 1998. What drives venture capital fund-raising? *Brookings Papers on Economic Activity, Microeconomics*, 149–204.

Gottschalg, Oliver, Ludovic Phalippou, and Maurizio Zollo. 2003. Performance of private equity funds: Another puzzle? Working Paper, INSEAD–Wharton Alliance Center for Global Research and Development.

Hege, Ulrich, Frédéric Palomino, and Armin Schwienbacher. 2003. Determinants of venture capital performance: Europe and the United States. Working Paper, HEC School of Management.

Jeng, Leslie, and Philippe Wells. 2000. The determinants of venture capital funding: Evidence across countries. *Journal of Corporate Finance* 6:241–289.

Kaplan, Steven N., and Antoinette Schoar. 2005. Private equity performance: Returns, persistence, and capital flows. *Journal of Finance* 60 (4):1792–1823.

Keuschnigg, Christian. 2004. Venture capital backed growth. *Journal of Economic Growth* 9 (2):239–261.

Krohmer, Philipp, Rainer Lauterbach, and Victor Calanog. 2009. The bright and dark side of staging—Investment performance and the varying motivations of private equity firms. *Journal of Banking and Finance* 33 (9):1597–1609.

Ljungquist, Alexander, and Matthew Richardson. 2003. The cash flow, return, and risk characteristics of private equity. NBER Working Paper Series.

Malherbe, Etienne. 2004. Modeling private equity funds and private equity collateralized fund obligations. *International Journal of Theoretical and Applied Finance* 7 (3):193–230.

Maula, Markku, and Tuukka T. Seppä. 2001. Investor certification of venture capital investments: Does top-end backing lead to improved value creation? *21st Annual Conference of the Strategic Management Society*, San Francisco.

Neher, Darwin V. 1999. Staged financing: An agency perspective. *Review of Economic Studies* 66, 255–274.

Schmidt, Daniel, and Mark Wahrenburg. 2004. Contractual relations between European VC-funds and investors: The impact of reputation and bargaining power on contractual design. RICAFE—Risk Capital and the Financing of European Innovative Firms, University of Frankfurt.

Schmidt, Daniel. 2006. Private equity vs. stocks: Does the alternative asset class add value to the portfolio? *Journal of Alternative Investments* (Summer)..

Takahashi, Dean, and Seth Alexander. 2002. Illiquid alternative asset fund modeling. *Journal of Portfolio Management* (Winter):90–100.

Weidig, Tom. 2002. Towards a risk model for venture capital funds: Liquidity and performance forecasting. Working Paper, European Investment Fund.

ABOUT THE AUTHORS

Axel Buchner received his Doctorate in Business Administration (Dr. rer. pol.) from the Technical University Munich (TUM, Germany). He is currently a consultant at the CEPRES GmbH Center of Private Equity Research and postdoctoral researcher at the Technical University of Munich (Germany). Dr. Buchner's research interests include private equity, asset pricing, continuous-time finance, and Monte-Carlo methods.

Philipp Krohmer wrote his doctoral thesis at the Goethe-University Frankfurt/Main (Germany) within the Center for Financial Studies research-project "Venture Capital and the New Markets in Europe." His research focuses on empirical finance, in particular risk and return characteristics of private equity. He is currently Director at CEPRES GmbH Center of Private Equity Research, a pioneer in private equity data aggregation and private equity risk management solutions.

Daniel Schmidt is founding partner at CEPRES GmbH Center of Private Equity Research, which was established in the year 2001. Dr. Schmidt wrote his Ph.D. thesis as a member of the pan-European EU-funded "Risk Capital and the Financing of European Innovative Firms" project, which seeks for more professional PE investment processes. He gained his private equity experience also by working as a managing director for groups like Sal. Oppenheim Private Equity Partners or Innovaid Management Partners. Dr. Schmidt published many articles in the *Journal of Business Venturing* and the *Journal of Alternative Investments*, among other publications.

Mark Wahrenburg is head of the Chair of Banking and Finance at the Goethe-University Frankfurt/Main (Germany). He has had both industrial and academic experience. Currently, he also serves as a program director of the venture capital research program of the Center for Financial Studies (CFS). His research interests include bank management and regulation, financial risk management, credit risk pricing, private equity, and education finance.

CHAPTER 11

Value Creation in Middle-Market Buyouts

A Transaction-Level Analysis

JOHN L. CHAPMAN
American Enterprise Institute

PETER G. KLEIN
Associate Professor, Division of Applied Social Sciences, University of Missouri

INTRODUCTION

Since the heyday of leveraged buyouts in the 1980s, researchers, practitioners, and policymakers have sought to understand the role private equity (PE) plays in the economy as a whole.[1] Indeed, the global cataclysm in financial markets that began in 2008 has brought about retrenchment in highly visible segments of the buyout arena. Large firms such as Carlyle Group and Fortress Investments have announced significant staff layoffs, fund-raising is off 90 percent from recent levels, and existing fund holdings have been subject to dramatic write-downs. Private equity, which as recently as 2007 provided 30 percent of all M&A funding globally, will likely provide less than 10 percent worldwide in 2010.[2] Further, the curtailment of bank credit for buyout deals portends a smaller footprint for PE in the next several years. Meanwhile, Blackstone Group's 2007 initial public offering puzzled many observers, including stalwart PE defenders such as Michael Jensen, who called the "publicly traded private equity firm" structure an "oxymoron."[3] Jensen has wondered aloud if PE firms are now subject to the same kinds of agency problems they once resolved so effectively.

Critics argue that the PE sector's recent problems are the logical outcome of Wall Street excesses and faddish investing, ratifying their long-held belief that this sector serves mainly to transfer wealth "from Main Street to Wall Street." However, our knowledge of the nature and effects of private-equity investment is at best fragmentary and incomplete. There is a substantial literature on buyouts, starting with DeAngelo, DeAngelo, and Rice's (1984) study of 42 going-private transactions from the 1970s and now including more than 150 papers in major academic journals. Most of these have dealt with whole-company buyouts, generally of public companies, using data from public sources such as SEC filings and press reports.[4] These sources, while providing valuable background information, lack the transaction-level data needed to perform detailed analyses (and are often incomplete and inconsistent).[5] A few studies have obtained confidential data at the fund level from institutional investors (Bull, 1989; Ljungqvist and Richardson, 2003); one recent study obtained data from private placement memoranda prepared by buyout firms (Groh and Gottschalg, 2008). None of these studies, however, is based on detailed transaction-level data over multiple PE firms and portfolio companies.

In this paper, we report empirical results from a study of 288 exited transactions across 19 NAICS two-digit industries from 13 PE firms. The data were obtained from interviews with the general partners of several leading PE partnerships who provided detailed financial data as well as information on the operating, strategic, and funding decisions the partners made during the investment period. Our sample includes a variety of transaction types: whereas prior studies have focused on going-private buyouts (the deal type that appears most often in publicly available information), our sample includes transactions with minority stakes, syndicate deals, and consolidating roll-up or add-on strategies. We can thus measure performance by PE firm, industry, transaction type, exit strategy, and other characteristics.

Our broader objective is to identify how and why private equity works and to compare it to public equity, particularly as means of corporate governance. What do buyouts do to the target firm's governance, strategy, and execution? What kinds of portfolio companies benefit from being owned by a PE firm? What deals should PE investors pursue: particular industries, deal sizes, transaction types, or other characteristics? Do some investors or investment strategies enjoy persistently superior returns as implied by Kaplan and Schoar (2005), or is there a tendency toward a "normal" rate of return?[6] What drives revenue and profit improvements? How do changes in employment, capital expenditures, or strategy and management vary across PE investments, and how do these compare to similar companies that remain public?

The paper is organized as follows. In the next section we summarize the background and context of the research and review previous findings on PE investment returns, particularly for middle-market buyouts. Next, we describe the mechanics of our small-company buyout research using transaction-level data, and then proceed to describe preliminary empirical results from this sample of U.S. middle-market transactions. Finally, we report regressions of transaction internal rates of return (IRRs) on key variables driving performance in small-company PE investments. Our conclusions and recommendations for future research follow.

BACKGROUND, CONTEXT, AND PRIOR LITERATURE

Our project is motivated by some early, detailed, "behind-the-curtains" looks at buyout deals. Baker and Wruck (1989) presented a detailed description of the organizational and strategic changes following the leveraged buyout (LBO) of O.M. Scott & Sons by Clayton & Dubilier, Inc., explaining how the LBO, as a governance structure, was able to create (unlock) economic value. Changes in ownership, capital structure, strategic direction, and management incentives combined to produce success in this transaction. Later, Baker and Smith (1998) presented a history of KKR upon its 20th anniversary, at which time the firm had done about 75 deals (now more than 150); KKR gave the authors rich inside access to its end-to-end deal execution processes and governance philosophy.[7] The present work is part of a larger project to extend this line of research to a wide swath of the PE sector, to many PE firms instead of just one, and to many hundreds of deals in different industries, of different sizes and types, analyzed at the transaction level.

Our focus is on small and midsized deals. This end of the buyout market features not only the investment goals found in larger public-company buyouts, which include cost elimination via consolidation and exploitation of scale and scope economies, but also a variety of strategies aimed at improved management coordination and control. The range of transaction rationales seen in smaller and middle-market buyouts forces PE investors to take on several roles including banker, operating executive, board member, strategist, headhunter, coach, union negotiator, and occasionally family therapist. There is thus perhaps a "fuller" view available here with respect to the manner by which PE professionals seek to create value in their deal making.

Before turning to the mechanics and results of our analysis we offer a few comments on the controversy surrounding PE investment returns. Exhibit 11.1 highlights 1-year to 20-year returns for various sizes and stages of PE deals using data from Thompson Financial.[8] These data, which include early-stage venture investing along with buyouts, depict pooled IRRs.[9] Beyond highlighting the extreme volatility inherent in PE investing, what is most interesting for our purposes are the long-horizon (20-year) returns. Over this period small-company buyouts, the focus of this paper, exhibited the highest returns.[10]

Exhibit 11.1 Internal Rates of Return for Private and Public Equity

Fund Type	1-Year	3-Year	5-Year	10-Year	20-Year
Early/seed venture capital	2.90%	5.50%	−5.40%	38.30%	20.50%
Balanced venture capital	10.70	12.80	1.80	16.80	14.60
Later-stage venture capital	27.80	10.50	2.70	9.40	13.90
All Venture Capital	**10.80**	**9.40**	**−1.00**	**20.50**	**16.50**
Small buyouts	11.30	9.40	5.00	6.00	25.20
Medium buyouts	37.20	12.30	6.10	10.90	15.30
Large buyouts	23.10	16.40	8.30	8.30	12.40
Mega buyouts	23.40	16.20	10.10	8.90	11.60
All Buyouts	**23.60**	**15.60**	**9.20**	**8.80**	**13.20**
Mezzanine	−8.10	4.70	2.90	5.90	8.40
All Private Equity	**19.00**	**13.20**	**5.90**	**11.20**	**14.00**
NASDAQ	5.50	7.80	8.70	7.10	11.40
S&P 500	9.70	9.90	5.20	7.50	9.70

Note: Buyout fund sizes defined as the following: Small = $0–250 m, Medium = $250–500 m, Large = $500 m to $1 b, and Mega = greater than $1 b.
Source: National Venture Capital Association and Thomson Financial (via VentureXpert).

There is substantial debate among PE researchers and practitioners about categorizing returns. As mentioned, Kaplan and Schoar (2005) challenge the longstanding claim of PE firms that their returns are much higher than standard benchmarks such as the S&P 500. Kaplan and Schoar use fund-level returns (for both early-stage venture capital and buyouts, exactly as shown in Exhibit 11.1) and find that using pooled IRRs, buyout funds performed slightly above the S&P 500 in the long run in gross performance, but underperform the S&P net of fees.[11] They suggest that the results depend critically on the involvement of the general partners (GPs) and that GP capabilities are heterogeneous and difficult to imitate. Moreover, successful funds are better networked and can garner proprietary access to deal flow.

Ljungqvist and Richardson (2003) found different results using data on PE returns from a large, institutional (limited partner, or LP) investor. They concluded that returns to PE investment beat public-market equivalents by over 5 percent per annum over the long term, consistent with the theory that illiquid assets should garner higher returns. Moskowitz and Vissing-Jorgenson (2002) take a broader view of private equity than is commonly used, defining it as any form of nonpublicly traded equity. They focus on entrepreneurial ventures driven from consumer or household finances, and do not find superior returns to PE, despite higher risk. They attribute this to nonpecuniary benefits or entrepreneurial zeal which results in overestimation of a venture's realistic prospects. Phalippou and Gottschalg (2008) investigate returns from a data set of 1,579 mature PE funds using the same source as Kaplan and Schoar (2005) and find, similarly, slight gross-of-fee performance advantages over the S&P 500, and net-of-fees underperformance, based on such issues as inflated values of present holdings.

Our specific aim in this paper is not to compare PE to public-equity returns, but to explain differences in returns among PE investments. Indeed, there is such variety among PE investment types that we doubt the usefulness of treating "private equity" as a homogeneous category. We construct consistent measures of returns among PE investments, for example by adjusting for leverage and other transaction-specific characteristics, to compare the results of different investment strategies.[12] As discussed in the next section, our key dependent variable is transaction IRR, which we take as the best proxy for value creation, broadly speaking, though only a part of the larger story.

Sample and Data

To examine the effect of these characteristics on buyout performance we reviewed 288 exited PE transactions from 1984 to 2006.[13] This sample was constructed through live field interviews with professionals in 13 PE firms in the United States, chosen from discussions with 96 firms in the United States, United Kingdom, and Japan, and based on their willingness to offer detailed transaction data on a confidential basis. We sought specific details of their transactions including not only financials but also governance and execution models, board oversight, strategic and financial advisory services, methods, or strategies by which each firm differentiated its services in adding value, and any other pertinent issues specific to each transaction. After analyzing each firm's portfolio and the varying amounts of information provided, it became clear that the best path for statistical analysis was to include *exited* transactions only. There were 288 of these for the 13 firms.

The 13 firms range from 5 professionals and $25 million under management to 140 professionals and $6.5 billion across 20 years. Appendix 11.A describes the firms in greater detail. Naturally, they are a self-selected group, so we do not claim that our findings necessarily hold for the universe of PE investments. However, the 13 firms in our sample represent a variety of firm types and their 288 transactions vary greatly by industry, deal type, and so on.

Variables

The main dependent variable in this study is transaction IRR.[14] We use both index- and industry-adjusted versions in our regressions. We measure both return on equity and "return on assets," which is really the IRR of the target company's change in market value.[15] In both cases, we ran models based on unadjusted values, S&P 500–adjusted, and Fama-French-adjusted values; results were largely the same, and we report in the following the S&P 500–adjusted results, which is an ultimate economy-wide barometer.

We also collected data on entry and exit dates, industry, type of exit, deal values at entry and exit, percentage of target equity acquired, percent of equity held by management,[16] options to management and fully vested totals, sales revenues at deal entry and exit, *EBITDA* at deal entry and exit, *debt/EBITDA* at deal entry,[17] employment levels at deal entry and exit, and capital expenditures at entry and exit. Additionally we obtained information on the presence of acquisitions or divestitures combined with the deal, whether the buyer is the sole investor or part of a syndicate "club deal" with other PE firms, and, whether there are significant management changes with this deal within six months of entry. In some cases, particularly for target-firm capital expenditures and employment, the PE firms had not tracked (or, for transactions farther back in time, had lost) specific changes during the time of their ownership, but knew the *direction* of a change (e.g., increase or decrease), and we recorded these as binary variables.[18]

The 288 sample transactions were spread among 28 three-digit, 19 two-digit, and 8 one-digit NAICS industries. We collapsed these into five broad industry categories: 8 transactions in agriculture, construction, or utilities; 61 in consumer-goods manufacturing; 80 in capital-goods or equipment manufacturing; 44 in wholesaling, distribution, or retailing; and 95 transactions in professional services, recreation, and entertainment.[19]

To investigate how exit type affects exit valuation and thus investment return we categorized exit types as (1) IPO, (2) sale to industry buyer, (3) sale to another entity (almost always another PE firm), (4) recapitalization, usually involving effective sale or relinquishment of control to management (but occasionally involves a liquidity event or dilutive restructuring), and (5) bankruptcy (in this case, the portfolio firm may well not have entered actual bankruptcy proceedings—though some did—but may hold a *de facto* "fire sale" of assets or go through a similar break-up, which would involve the loss of most or all the PE firm's investment). We attempted to obtain valuations and IRRs for all transactions, including bankruptcies; if not available for bankruptcies, we assumed full loss of equity and coded the IRR as negative 100 percent and assigned an enterprise value of zero, which biases our average IRRs downward. We ended up with 35 bankruptcies out of 288 transactions.

We obtained industry betas for each transaction.[20] Mean beta for the sample is 0.92, which matches the industry distribution of the sample: 140 mostly low-tech manufacturing businesses; 44 distribution or retail deals; 8 in agriculture, construction, or utilities ("outdoor production"); and the remaining 95 in higher-beta services. For entry and exit multiples we use *EBITDA* multiples, as is standard among buyout practitioners.[21]

We also recorded PE firm characteristics (particularly, size and the number of prior transactions, to proxy for experience) and sought a qualitative sense of the firm's general investment strategy for each deal. Most prominently this involved the choice of industry type, but also included size of transaction, deal structure, whether or not a firm preferred healthy businesses or turnarounds (which could be acquired relatively cheaply), and in general, the sources of added value each firm (in theory) brings to their transactions. We were unable to obtain consistent information on portfolio company boards, specific incentive plans offered to portfolio company managers, or the characteristics of individual general partners of the PE companies.[22]

Descriptive Statistics

Exhibit 11.2 provides descriptive statistics for our sample transactions. The unadjusted mean IRR for equity is 40.1 percent, with a median of 30.90 percent.[23] IRR of the firm's assets (or enterprise value) has a mean of 15.1 percent and median of 13.6 percent. By comparison, the pooled IRR for the S&P 500 during the same period is 9.81 percent, with a median 10.1 percent.[24] The S&P 500 index-adjusted IRR for equity is 27.2 percent, with a median-adjusted value of 23.6 percent.[25] Of course, the unadjusted PE IRRs (40 percent) are prior to deal fees; using Swensen's (2000) estimate of 12 percent for fees, our net IRR falls to about 28 percent. As shown in Exhibit 11.1, the 20-year pooled IRR (net of fees) for small buyouts ($< \$250$ million) from 1986 through 2006 is 25.2 percent, close to that in our sample.[26] Moreover, the 20-year IRR of the S&P 500 from 1986 to 2006 is 9.70 percent, close to our unlevered 9.81 percent over about the same period. Mean deal size in our sample is $78.3 million, with a median of $29.2 million. Average leverage is 65.5 percent, and average *debt/EBITDA* ratio is 3.71. The PE firms took an average 55.8 percent stake in these transactions. About 44 percent of the sample transactions involve PE firm syndicates, a surprisingly high number given the small average transaction size.

Turning next to strategic choices, over half of our sample transactions included at least one *add-on* acquisition. Add-ons include both what practitioners call "bolt-on acquisitions" (add-ons to fill out a product line, achieve economies of scope in marketing or distribution, co-opt operating synergies, or expand service offerings) and "consolidating roll-up deals" (fragmented industry deals seeking economies of scale of similar businesses, often former direct competitors). Add-on transactions are perhaps most responsible for PE's impact on overall economic growth. Porter (1980, 191–215) discusses the nature of fragmented industries in terms of industry structure and characteristics, and lists over 100 four-digit manufacturing sectors in which top-four and top-eight market shares were extremely low.[27] He was the first to identify formal strategies for consolidation *given* an industry's

Exhibit 11.2 Descriptive Statistics

	N	Mean	Median	Standard Deviation	Min.	Max.
Returns						
Gross IRR, return on equity	288	40.10%	30.90%	89.30%	−100%	849%
Gross IRR, return on assets	288	15.10%	13.60%	42.70%	−100%	223%
S&P 500—Adjusted return on equity	288	27.20%	23.60%	72.90%	−100%	635%
Value-weighted return on equity	288	43.90%	—	—	—	—
IRR of S&P 500	288	9.81%	10.10%	10.80%	−21%	31%
Leveraged S&P 500 IRR	288	25.90%	21.90%	34.60%	−68%	182%
Value-weighted IRR of S&P 500	288	6.74%	—	—	—	—
Governance						
Leverage	288	65.50%	70%	19.50%	0	94.40%
Debt pay-down (debt/EBITDA)	288	3.71X	3.01X	—	—	—
Management equity	288	19.30%	15%	12.80%	3.21%	80%
PE firm equity	288	55.80%	64.30%	25.20%	2.80%	94.50%
Control Variables						
Transaction size	288	$78.3 m	$29.2 m		$1.4 m	$4.51 b
Holding period	288	4.8 years	4.3 years			
Bankruptcy	288	12.1% of total			0	1
Controlling stake	288	62.8%			0	1
Club deal?	281	44.1%			0	1
Add-on acquisitions?	271	55.7%			0	1
Industry beta	288	0.924				
Performance Variables (Average Annual Increase)						
Revenue growth	254	13.90%				
EBITDA growth	255	11.60%				
EBITDA margin growth	254	−0.33%				
Employment change	59	13.40%				
Capital expenditures	119	8.30%				
Entry multiple	238	7.54X				
Exit multiple	241	7.58X				

underlying economics, and his work helped to usher in the subsequent wave of mass consolidation the U.S. economy has witnessed in the intervening era of massive growth in PE and buyouts. Prior to the leveraged buyout wave of the 1980s, growth via consolidation of an industry sector containing multiple small firms was much harder to accomplish, due to the lack of liquidity in capital markets serving deal makers in the middle market. Private equity has singularly changed and improved accessibility to capital for consolidation (and thereby made easier the unlocking of previously unrealized value in capital assets). Moreover, as we explain below, transactions involving add-on acquisitions performed significantly better than those in which organic growth is the intended strategy.[28]

Management equity averaged 19.3 percent in our sample, ranging from 3.2 percent to 80 percent, while the mean and median holding times were 4.8 and 4.3 years, respectively.[29] Since the 1980s, holding periods have fallen as the PE sector has evolved: more capital in play, more firms, and more speed to the process yield exits and another fund-raising round. Over time PE firms came to learn that operating and strategic changes (as well as those dealing with governance, management, and monitoring and control) were front-loaded in the deal process, and via a *learning effect*, the PE sector has gravitated toward shorter holding times.[30]

As seen in Exhibit 11.2, most transactions brought about increases in revenue, *EBITDA*, employment, and capital expenditures. Slightly less than half reported increases in the *EBITDA* margin (*EBITDA*/revenues). If our sample is representative of small buyouts over time, these figures suggest that in this size range of transaction, at least, the Jensen (1986) agency-mitigation rationale for LBOs is less important than either *growth equity* opportunities, or *coordination-improving* investments in fundamentally sound businesses.

Looking more closely at operating performance yields some surprising results. The 115 transactions in which the *EBITDA* margin increases have a mean return on equity of 75.9 percent, while 139 deals with *EBITDA* margin decreases average only a 14.9 percent equity return. The ratio of *EBITDA* to revenue is thus closely correlated with value creation. Also, the increases in employment and capital expenditures make sense given that over half of our smaller middle-market transactions involve add-on acquisitions; where employment and capital expenditures increased (178 and 139 deals, respectively), mean equity returns were 60.6 percent and 52.8 percent, respectively; where they decreased (72 and 91 deals, respectively), returns were much lower, and negative for employment.[31] For this sample, strong firm performance and returns are associated with growth in employment and capital expenditures. Return on equity is also negatively correlated with both exit year and holding time, suggesting two important long-term trends in PE investing. First, PE "industry maturation" implies elimination of excess returns; indeed, practitioners spoke often to us about the increasing competition for deals and the difficulty in extracting returns. Holding time is also significantly negatively related to equity returns: the correlation in our sample is –0.2907 (statistically significant at the 1 percent level), consistent with the practitioner view that holding times have decreased as deal process and execution have become more efficient over time.[32]

Differences by Subsamples

Exhibit 11.3 shows descriptive statistics by industry groups. Some patterns are predictable; for example, leverage at entry falls from 74 percent to 54 percent as the industry moves from physical asset-intensive manufacturing to high-value-adding human capital-intensive businesses. PE firm equity also falls from 64 percent to

Exhibit 11.3 Descriptive Statistics by Industry Group

Industry	Outdoors Production	Consumer-Goods Manufacturing	Capital-Goods Manufacturing	Retail and Distribution	Professional Services
Industry examples	Agriculture, mining, construction	Food/beverage, furniture, rubber, plastics	Steel, industrial machinery, electronics	Wholesale distributors and retailers	Consulting, administrative services, real estate
Number of observations	8	61	80	44	95
Return on equity	−13%	59%	40.50%	34.10%	36.30%
Transaction size	$29.1 m	$86.4 m	$39.8 m	$74.1 m	$112 m
Leverage	55.50%	74.30%	70.30%	69.80%	54.70%
Debt pay-down	3.69	4.28	8.1	4.35	1.80
Management equity	20%	20.60%	20.20%	17.90%	18.50%
PE firm equity	61%	64.30%	62.10%	55.60%	44.90%
Holding period (days)	1,657	1,820	1,775	1,879	1,638
Bankruptcies	3	5	7	9	11
% Control deals	75% (8)	80.3% (61)	75% (80)	56.8% (44)	43.1% (95)
% Club deals	50% (6)	27.1% (59)	34.1% (79)	44.1% (43)	63% (92)
% Add-on deals	33% (6)	63.1% (57)	57.8% (76)	55% (40)	51% (92)
Industry beta	1.00	0.73	0.99	0.90	0.99
Revenue Δ (#)	−9.4% (5)	9.8% (56)	9.2% (73)	8.8% (40)	25.1% (80)
EBITDA Δ (#)	−5% (5)	6.3% (56)	4.8% (74)	−1.9% (40)	10.2% (80)
EBITDA margin Δ (#)	4.8% (4)	−3.6% (56)	−1.3% (74)	−4.9% (40)	−2.1% (80)
Employment Δ (#)	1% (2)	10.6% (9)	17.1% (13)	1.9% (12)	21.5% (23)
CapEx Δ (#)	−11.3 (3)	9.9% (30)	11% (28)	5.2% (25)	8.6% (33)
Exit multiple	7.17 (4)	6.96 (55)	6.66 (67)	6.71 (40)	9.32 (76)

45 percent as we move along this industry pattern, suggesting that other PE firms or investors assist in equitizing the capital structure of deals in more complex industries that exhibit higher growth (and volatility). The percentage of control-position deals likewise drops sharply from 80 to 43 percent. Meanwhile the percentage of risk-mitigating club deals increases to the same degree, from 27 percent to 63 percent, while add-on acquisitions drop from 63 percent to 51 percent.

These results are consistent with both agency theory and transaction cost economics (Jensen, 1986; Williamson, 1988; Kochhar, 1996). Riskier deals entail lower leverage; at the same time, the greater the likelihood of costly *ex post* bargaining, the greater the equity, and the spread of equity, across multiple owners. Moreover, in dynamic, high-growth industries (e.g., professional services) there is both greater opportunity for organic growth, and added complexity in deal making, so we would expect fewer add-on acquisitions in those industries than in physical asset-intensive businesses, which our data reflect. We also find that revenue and profit (*EBITDA*) increases are greatest in professional services (where overall growth opportunities are highest), though employment and capital expenditures grow in four of the five industry segments. Equity returns are highest in manufacturing segments, which is sensible given the ability to leverage in these businesses as well as the latent growth available via consolidation. The exit multiple is noticeably higher in fast-growing professional services than in the other four mature industries, which again is predictable and based on future prospects.

Next we break down the summary statistics by exit type: IPO, sale to an industry buyer, sale to financial buyer (most often, another PE firm), and recapitalization (usually a sale to incumbent management). These are provided in Exhibit 11.4. The values change in linear fashion as one moves across the columns from IPOs to recaps. Industry buyers by degree have more knowledge about the sector than IPO (ultimately, retail) buyers, and typically in these kinds of industry segments there are several such potential acquirers. PE firms, as buyers, are typically not as aggressive as industry participants, both because they are more discerning and because they do not have *operating* synergies to co-opt.[33] A recapitalization, often involving the firm's incumbent management as new controlling owners, is the least liquid of the four exit types, and by definition involves those who are able to most clearly discern intrinsic firm value (and hence will be the most discerning of buyer types).

IPOs have the highest returns, at 101 percent, followed by trade sales (54.2 percent), sales to PE firms (44.2 percent), and recaps (28.2 percent). IPOs are also the largest transactions, averaging $227 million. IPOs are the least leveraged at 59.8 percent, consistent with the idea that smaller deals for stable, profitable companies are more easily leveraged and more amenable to management having eventual control. Similarly, management equity is highest for IPOs; in our sample management equity and leverage are negatively correlated (statistically significant at the 5 percent level). Meanwhile PE firm equity is strongly positively correlated with leverage (significant at 1 percent); higher PE firm equity usually implies lower management equity. Additionally, the best-performing deals are likely to lead to IPOs, and managers often can maximize their equity bonuses under such a scenario. At the other extreme, recaps might involve businesses that are marginal from the vantage point of the PE investor (though they return a positive IRR for our sample), and at the same time offer incumbent management great equity growth in return for the PE firm's liquidity.

Exhibit 11.4 Descriptive Statistics by Exit Type

Variable	IPO	Trade Sale	PE Firm	Recap	Bankruptcy
Number of observations	37	123	65	28	35
Return on equity	101%	54.20%	44.20%	28.2%	−68.20%
Transaction size	$227 m	$48.8 m	$51.2 m	$115 m	$45.4 m
Leverage	59.80%	65.30%	68.70%	71.10%	61.50%
Debt pay-down	7.37	1.79	4.86	5.06	3.48
Management equity	20.50%	19.80%	19.40%	14.70%	19.80%
PE firm equity	41.40%	59.70%	59.50%	56%	49%
Holding period (days)	1,693	1,733	1,760	2,080	1,604
% Control deals (# deals reporting)	43.2% (37)	71.5% (123)	64.6% (65)	60.7% (28)	51.4% (35)
% Club deals	63.8% (36)	38% (121)	38.4% (65)	51.8% (27)	50% (32)
% Add-on deals	73.5% (34)	52.9% (119)	53.1% (64)	64% (25)	44.8% (29)
Industry beta	0.99	0.90	0.95	0.95	0.86
Revenue Δ (# deals reporting)	32% (34)	17.7% (112)	11.2% (56)	10.4% (24)	−14.7% (28)
EBITDA Δ (#)	45.2% (34)	18.4% (112)	14.9% (56)	2.5% (24)	−56.2% (29)
EBITDA margin Δ (#)	19% (34)	7.2% (112)	2.9% (56)	−9.7% (24)	−36.6% (28)
Employment Δ (#)	49.4% (9)	13.1% (25)	11.9% (17)	−4% (3)	−34.2% (5)
CapEx Δ (#)	8.9% (20)	10% (43)	11.6% (35)	16% (13)	−29.75% (8)
Exit multiple (#)	11.7 (34)	7.62 (110)	7.11 (55)	7.73 (23)	1.11 (19)

Revenue and *EBITDA* growth are highest in IPO deals (32 percent and 45.2 percent per annum, respectively), falling to 10.4 percent and 2.5 percent, respectively, for recaps. Again, the best-performing deals tend to go public, based on strong operating results. *EBITDA* margins are also highest for IPOs and lowest for recaps. Likewise employment growth is highest for IPOs, averaging 49.4 percent for the firms reporting, and linearly decreases to the low for recaps (–4 percent). Rather fascinating are figures for capital expenditure growth: there is a straight-line *increase* from 8.9 percent for IPOs up to 16 percent for recaps. That capital investments increase in exact inversion to investor returns (and employment levels) belies the "conventional wisdom" that PE investors are short-sighted.[34] Exit multiples are highest for IPOs at 11.7, falling to 7.11 to 7.73 for the other exit types.

These data illustrate the variety of middle-market PE transactions. Those leading to IPOs are highly successful, while those exited through other means show more mundane returns. For buyouts in our size range the most common strategy is *buy-and-build*, via add-ons in the same or related markets (73.5 percent of the cases for IPOs), achieving economies across the firm's value chain, and seeing growth in both revenues and cost efficiencies. These in turn allow for increases in employment levels and capital investment. Sales to industry buyers and PE firms are less than 25 percent of the scale of the IPOs ($48 and $51 million, respectively, versus $227 million for IPOs) but exhibit strong returns. Even recaps, more likely to occur for firms with industry or growth challenges, nonetheless exhibit positive returns (28.2 percent mean IRR).

The 35 bankruptcies were, in the aggregate, cases of business plans that did not materialize; mean leverage at deal entry for these was 61.5 percent, and debt pay-down was below the sample mean at 3.48, so they were not overleveraged. However, all operating performance measures are highly negative, and this indicates that growth strategies were unsuccessful. These deals have the shortest holding times, supporting Jensen's thesis that PE is a highly efficient institutional form of restructuring.

We also review the summary statistics by our own measure of dimensions of PE firm strategies—ownership, syndication, or growth. Ownership deals are those in which the PE firm acquires a controlling (as opposed to minority) stake, and syndicate deals (also called "club deals") are those in which the firm partners with other PE firms to make the acquisition, an increasingly common practice.[35] We distinguish growth strategies according to whether the PE firm grows the target organically, or by *add-on* acquisition. Within each dimension, each particular strategy has benefits and costs, and PE firms have advertised opposite choices across all three strategy dimensions in recruiting investors and courting targets.

Exhibit 11.5 shows key summary statistics according to these strategic dimensions. As seen in the table, various strategy pairs yield highly different results. First, it appears that *ownership* and *syndication* strategies are mutually dependent. The

Exhibit 11.5 Descriptive Statistics by Investment Strategy

Variable	Ownership		Syndication		Growth	
	Minority	Control	Solo	Club Deal	Organic	Add-On
Number of observations	107	181	157	124	120	151
Return on equity	25%	48.10%	52%	25.20%	33%	50%
Transaction size	$134 m	45.5 m	43.6 m	125 m	50.7 m	98.3 m
Leverage	57.90%	70.10%	69.70%	59.80%	65.30%	65.40%
Debt pay-down	3.93	3.56	3.57	3.86	5.06	2.72
Management equity	21.70%	18%	21.20%	16.40%	18.80%	19.70%
PE firm equity	27.40%	72.90%	73.10%	33.80%	57%	56%
Holding period	1,828	1,707	1,662	1,849	1,628	1,857
% Control deals	0%	100%	93.60%	22.60%	63.30%	63.60%
% Club deals	90.50%	16%	0%	100%	43.3%	43%
% Add-ons	55%	55.80%	55.80%	55.50%	0%	100%
Industry BETA	0.98	0.89	0.91	0.93	0.87	0.95
Revenue Δ	16.30%	12.45%	11.30%	17.10%	4.10%	21.30%
EBITDA margin Δ	Up	Down	Up	Down	Down	Up
Employment Δ	24.7%	5.1%	4.1%	25.2%	13.4%	13.4%
Employment Δ obs.	(25)	(34)	(33)	(26)	(28)	(31)
CapEx Δ	12.50%	5.80%	5.30%	12.60%	−1.20%	14.30%
Exit multiple	8.46	7.04	6.8	8.51	7.41	7.68
Industry index*	4.04	3.25	3.28	3.92	3.65	3.5

*Note: Industry index is computed by averaging each transaction's assigned industry group, from 1 to 5, moving from left to right in Exhibit 11.3. (i.e., from Agriculture and Mining [1], to Professional Services [5]). Roughly speaking, as the index moves form 1 to 5, the industry type moves from more capital-intensive to less, and the human capital-assets ratio increases.

results for minority ownership deals parallel very closely those of syndicated deals, in almost every respect. Except for *EBITDA* margin change (improves for minority stakes, declines for club deals), the numbers are almost the same, starting with return on equity (25 percent) and transaction size ($125 to $134 million), through leverage, holding time, add-ons, *beta*, revenue growth, exit multiple, and industry index (at 3.92 and 4.04, these deals involve higher risk human-capital-intensive businesses, which are generally faster growth than low-tech manufacturing, but may require more risk sharing and more equity). There is a slight difference only in PE firm and management equity amounts; indeed, 90.5 percent of minority stakes *are* club deals. So, there is a strong propensity for these two choices to be linked.

Likewise, the transactions involving controlling stakes are mirror images of those without syndicates (solo deals); 94 percent of solo deals are controlling stakes deals, and 84 percent of controlling stakes deals are solo deals. Again, in every case but *EBITDA* margin, the results are very similar, starting with equity returns (48 percent and 52 percent). These transactions are smaller in scale at only one-third the size of minority or club deals, and their industry index (3.25 to 3.28) is much lower, which is intuitive—most of these transactions are in low-tech manufacturing, which offers higher leverage opportunities, more fixed assets, often steady cash flows, and slower change. Other things equal, the higher the industry index, the faster growing and more complex the industry dynamics and hence the need for risk sharing; the solo and controlling stake deals occur most frequently in slow-growth businesses.

The slower growth of these industries means that employment increases much more slowly, and as is depicted, is a small fraction of employment growth in more dynamic industry settings (4 to 5 percent versus 24 to 25 percent per annum). Capital expenditures also increase at less than half the rate of the minority-stakes or club deals. Additionally, revenue growth is slower and exit multiples and holding times are lower for these control deals in slow-growth manufacturing, compared to club deals in service or marketing businesses. Interestingly, however, the returns for solo or controlling-stakes deals are double those in club deals and minority stakes (48–52 percent versus 25 percent). Thus, growth in revenues, employment, or capital expenditures—or a higher exit multiple—do not always guarantee the strongest equity return.

Transactions involving add-on acquisitions perform significantly better than organic growth deals (IRRs of 50 percent and 33 percent, respectively). Add-on deals are twice as large ($98 versus $50 million), have half the debt pay-down, and generate higher increases in revenues, profit margins, employment, and capital expenditures. Interestingly, between these two there were no appreciable differences in leverage (65.4 percent), equity splits to either the PE firm or management, the numbers of control/minority deals, numbers of club or solo deals, or exit multiples. These data certainly support the idea that consolidating acquisitions can, when executed properly, create material value for equity holders.

REGRESSION RESULTS

We leave a more comprehensive analysis to future work but report here some preliminary OLS regressions of deal performance on governance and control variables. We start by regressing the S&P 500–adjusted return on equity (IRR) on transaction

Exhibit 11.6 Relationship between Equity IRR and
Governance/Ownership

Leverage	.2951	.3079
	(.2873)	(.2907)
Debt pay-down	−.0004	−.0004
	(.0009)	(.0009)
Management equity	.1248	.1001
	(.4770)	(.4845)
PE firm equity	.2912	.2729
	(.5272)	(.5315)
Controlling stake	−.1027	−.0958
	(.2136)	(.2152)
Club deal	−.0497	−.0616
	(.1905)	(.1946)
Add-ons	.1973**	.1988**
	(.1005)	(.1008)
Log(size)	−.0022	.0057
		(.0542)
PE firm indicator	(.0476)	−.0055
		(.0176)
Constant	−.0618	−.1434
	(.9118)	(.9499)
R-Squared	.0336	.0332

Notes: N = 230. Standard errors in parentheses. ***, **, and * indicate statistical significance at the 1, 5, and 10 percent levels, respectively.

leverage, debt pay-down, management equity, PE firm equity, and dummy variables for the three strategic choice dimensions (controlling versus minority stakes, club deals versus solo, and add-on acquisitions versus organic growth). In a second specification we add indicators for each PE firm. Results are presented in Exhibit 11.6. As seen in the table, the indicator for add-on acquisitions is statistically significant in both specifications. This is consistent with feedback we received from practitioners, who indicate considerable breadth of opportunities in fragmented industry sectors, particularly in basic manufacturing, wholesale distribution, and various business services. A buy-and-build strategy with add-on acquisitions, as followed by several PE firms in our study, has yielded solid returns over time in this industry.[36]

We then repeat these regressions using the IRR of the firm's assets as the dependent variable. PE investing focuses on leveraged returns to equity, and a simple arithmetical exercise can demonstrate that solid returns can be garnered on equity with little or no change in firm value (indeed, our data sample contained such deals). From the vantage point of the broader economy and macro growth, however, we care primarily how PE governance affects firm value.[37] Results are provided in Exhibit 11.7. The dummy for add-on acquisitions is again positive and statistically significant, suggesting that building scale through profitable acquisitions is a good way to increase value. Leverage is also statistically significantly

Exhibit 11.7 Relationship between Total Firm (Assets) IRR and Governance/Ownership

Leverage	−.2779**	−.2533**
	(.1265)	(.1301)
Debt pay-down	−.0000	−.0000
	(.0004)	(.0004)
Management equity	.1563	.0163
	(.1733)	(.2167)
PE firm equity	.1251	−.0784
	(.0960)	(.2378)
Controlling stake		.0393
		(.0962)
Club deal		−.0488
		(.0870)
Add-ons		.1684*
		(.0451)
Log(size)		−.0020
		(.0242)
PE firm indicator		.0016
		(.0078)
Constant	.1603	.2071
	(.0989)	(.4250)
R-Squared	.0275	.0883

Notes: $N = 227$. Standard errors in parentheses. ***, **, and * indicate statistical significance at the 1, 5, and 10 percent levels, respectively.

related to asset IRR, with higher leverage corresponding to lower returns. From Modigliani and Miller (1958) we know that in a frictionless world, capital structure is irrelevant, and hence from the vantage point of all of a firm's assets, value is derived solely from the operating cash flows generated by those assets. Hence leverage, which at high enough levels induces insolvency in a downturn, is negatively related to enterprise IRR (or, the bundle of firm assets in total). In our sample, 59 of 288 transactions (20.4 percent) earned negative asset returns, but the distribution of equity IRRs is highly skewed, with several "home runs." For asset or enterprise IRR, however, leverage has no positive impact.

We turn next to the distinctions among ownership, syndication, and growth strategies, regressing the model above on subsamples split by deal strategy. Exhibit 11.8 shows results when the sample is split into solo and club deals. As noted above, club deals are prevalent in the middle-market buyout arena. However, they have equity returns in our sample of 25.2 percent (from a subsample of 124 deals), strongly underperforming stand-alone deals done by a single-lead PE firm (52 percent equity IRR in a subsample of 157 deals).

For solo deals executed and led by a single PE firm, leverage, management equity, and PE firm equity are statistically significant (at the 10 percent, 5 percent, and 1 percent levels, respectively). This is consistent with what practitioners report: equity splits to management provide incentives, equity to the PE firm ensures

Exhibit 11.8   Equity IRR by Deal Type

	Club Deals	Solo Deals
Number of Observations	89	138
Leverage	.0090	.8673***
	(.3414)	(.4598)
Debt pay-down	−.0002	−.0305
	(.0007)	(.0285)
Management equity	.2342	.3151*
	(.6676)	(.1071)
PE firm equity	−.3975	.3201*
	(.5432)	(.1113)
Controlling stake	.0203	.1592
	(.2245)	(.3766)
Add-ons	.3462*	.1456
	(.1283)	(.1411)
Log(size)	−.0080	.0537
	.0775	(.0535)
Constant	−.8263	−.3218***
	(.9687)	(.1818)
R-Squared	.1266	.0974

Notes: Standard errors in parentheses. ***, **, and * indicate statistical significance at the 1, 5, and 10 percent levels, respectively.

active monitoring and strategic support, and leverage provides both discipline and, where it applies, fuel for expansion (when unlocking firm value and resources via recapitalization). For club deals, only the add-on indicator is statistically significant. Because club deals are pursued primarily to spread risk and combine resources to spur growth, they are a solid vehicle for making scale-building ancillary acquisitions. As we detail below, however, their execution often falls short of expectations because of conflicts of interest among multiple PE investors.

We next split the sample into deals in which the PE firm has a controlling stake and deals in which it has a minority stake. As noted above, transactions in which our PE firm had a majority stake substantially outperformed those in which it took a smaller position (equity IRRs of 48 percent and 25 percent, respectively). Exhibit 11.9 shows the results of the main regressions above run separately for each subsample. The results strongly mirror those in Exhibit 11.8. For transactions with controlling stakes, the four major governance variables are all statistically significant. The management equity and PE firm equity coefficients have the largest magnitudes; the amount of PE firm equity affects IRR negatively for the minority deals and positively for the controlling deals.[38] Leverage is a statistically significant (and positive) determinant of performance for controlling deals, consistent with the Jensen thesis on the value of leverage in mitigating agency problems, at least when performance is measured by equity (not asset) returns.

Exhibit 11.9 Equity IRR by Equity Stake

Number of Observations	Controlling-Stake Deals 149	Minority-Stake Deals 78
Leverage	.9184*	.1415
	(.4707)	(.3476)
Debt pay-down	−.0452*	−.0003
	(.0263)	(.0007)
Management equity	2.771***	.3397
	(1.015)	(.6681)
PE firm equity	3.005*	−.5433
	(1.017)	(.5725)
Club deal	.3632	.2071
	(.2542)	(.3695)
Add-ons	.1537	.2665***
	(.1310)	(.1434)
Log(size)	.0146	.0629
	(.0718)	(.0585)
Constant	−3.218***	−1.209
	(1.692)	(1.224)
R-Squared	.1058	.1124

Notes: Standard errors in parentheses. ***, **, and * indicate statistical significance at the 1, 5, and 10 percent levels, respectively.

CONCLUSION

Focusing on middle-market transactions highlights some interesting characteristics of the PE world that are hidden in studies of larger deals. Most prior work distinguishes between two types of buyouts: restructuring deals designed to mitigate agency costs in mature, low-growth, low-*beta* industries; and growth-equity transactions based on investments in high-growth industries. There is a third category as well, however, an intermediate type we might call *coordination-improving* deals. These typically involve sound businesses that can nonetheless benefit from PE firm ownership bringing access to resources, industry-specific expertise, capital for recombining assets (most often, consolidation in a fragmented industry), or recapitalization and ownership transition. The intended result in these transactions is better *coordination* of deployment of a firm's assets, often in recombination with market-based resources. These kinds of transactions occur often in our sample, and would appear to manifest a major benefit of—and underreported storyline about—private-equity governance.

More generally, our preliminary analysis of this sample of middle-market transactions suggests that, fundamentally, growth is the ultimate driver of wealth creation for smaller companies. Over three-quarters of our sample experienced increases in revenues and operating profits, and, not surprisingly, those transactions with the highest revenue and profit growth rates have the highest rates of return.

The same applies to increases in employment. For these deals, PE was a catalyst for exploiting scale and scope economies and providing operating leverage.

Second, for this sample, return on equity for PE transactions is negatively (and significantly) correlated with exit year, suggesting a secular decline in returns (and, the increasing competitiveness of the PE industry), even for the lower middle-market arena for small-cap transactions. This can be seen as part of the relentless Schumpeterian efficiency wrought from dynamic, innovative, and competitive markets.

Third, insights from agency theory (Jensen 1986, 1988) and transaction cost economics (Williamson 1988, 1996) are substantiated in our sample transactions. The low-tech, slow-growth consumer-goods manufacturers have the highest-return transactions, highest average leverage, highest average levels of management equity and PE firm equity, and most of the controlling-stakes deals. More broadly, the slow-growth manufacturing businesses are more heavily leveraged and exhibit better returns than marketing and services businesses. Marketing and professional services firms have less average leverage, more syndicate club deals, more minority-stakes deals, and exhibit higher revenue and profit growth in absolute dollars (and, more organic growth than those involving add-on acquisitions). IPOs have the highest returns as an exit type, followed in order by exit types characterized by progressively more knowledgeable buyers. These straight-line differences in results across exit types apply as well to leverage, holding time, revenue, profit and employment growth, capital expenditure growth, and management equity.[39]

Fourth, controlling-stakes and solo deals are characterized by twice the return, one-third to one-fourth the size, shorter holding times, much higher leverage, and lower debt pay-down ratios than their counterparts. They are also far more heavily concentrated in slow-growth manufacturing industries. This is not to deny the growing importance of syndication in private equity. However, our data clearly show the long-term performance advantages of control transactions focused on low-beta industries that are amenable to leverage (and, the ability of the majority or sole owner to bring about a new, more focused, strategy).

In our sample, the pursuit of ancillary consolidating acquisitions is the single most important determinant of transaction IRR for equity. This shows the extent of available "slack" in fragmented industries ripe for exploitation by small- and mid-cap PE investors. Additionally, leverage affects equity IRRs positively and asset (or total firm) returns negatively, consistent with received theory. For improvements in operating performance, the presence of an add-on transaction and the amount of leverage are key to explaining revenue growth, and the fastest-growing firms are burdened with the least amount of debt, as Williamson (1988) suggests.

What do these findings imply for future research? Our close-up view of PE practitioners offers several suggestions to guide future work on the process of value creation in PE transactions. Specifically, besides its direct effect on the portfolio companies it owns and manages, the PE sector may be even more influential on the firms that remain public. Manne's (1965) thesis about the disciplinary role of takeovers applies equally well in today's PE world: a liquid and increasingly efficient market for corporate control compels public companies to control costs, to innovate, to build and maintain customer relationships, and to respond more effectively to increasingly global competition. Jensen (1993) decried the failure of internal control systems in the rationalization and restructuring of inefficient industry, but private equity, even as it has provided an *external* impetus to such needed change, has also motivated improvements in internal control as well. What emerges in analyzing these middle-market buyouts at close range is the need for a more fully integrated understanding of all the ways that PE-firm general partners seek to create value in their portfolios.

Hubbard (2005) encourages judgment about the efficacy of financial markets and institutions to be based on how well three related services are provided to market actors: liquidity, information-generating, and risk-bearing. Schumpeter (1911), Mises (1949), Kirzner (1973, 2000), Baumol (2002), and others would add that entrepreneurship, the heart of the market economy, flourishes when economic institutions provide these three services efficiently. Private equity has been particularly important to the U.S. economy, relative to other OECD economies, in the modern era. From viewing these capitalist-entrepreneurs up close, we believe strongly that PE has been good for entrepreneurship, as entrepreneurial activity is fostered not only through the profits accruing to successful ventures, but through the feedback of the trial-and-error process itself, in correcting prior error and redeploying assets quickly to higher-valued uses (Mises 1951; Klein 1999). Private equity can lead to better coordination of assets across firms and markets, as new organizational methods and combinations, structures, and processes are tested and deployed.

Of course, more empirical research is needed to support these conjectures. A critical task moving forward is to build more comprehensive databases of global PE firms for more detailed and rigorous analysis. A particular challenge, of course, is dealing with the potential endogeneity between returns and ownership, governance, and exit characteristics. Obviously, PE firms do not choose their targets, and their strategies for turning them around, at random. The regressions presented above show correlations, not causal relationships. While we control for unobserved PE-firm characteristics, we obviously cannot control for transaction-specific unobservables, and do not have effective instruments for PE firms' strategic choices. These are important issues for future research. Ultimately, such research may help to better quantify and explain the portfolio-firm changes brought by PE ownership or investment, the nature of entrepreneurial initiatives such as buy-and-build strategies (which effectively restructure fragmented industries over time), and the changes in PE contracting itself (in particular, the puzzle of the publicly held private equity firm needs better understanding). These objectives are part of the larger task facing economists, of explaining how changes in ownership, governance, corporate control, and entrepreneurship impact economic growth.

APPENDIX 11.A: SUMMARY OF PE FIRMS

Firm, Number of Deals in Study, Capital Managed, and Summary Comments
*Firm A, 68, $7 billion. Twenty-five years of success based on well-defined industry/situation focus *across six industry sectors*, $200 mm to $1.5 bn range; need *industry dynamics* to be strong, not just company. Increasingly willing to partner in deals. Believes international markets now better for PE investing.
*Firm B, 27, $2 billion. Spin-off of larger investment firm's PE arm. Long tradition of doing club deals successfully though in lead capacity. Has spanned industries and transaction structures in past, but new focus on business services and higher-margin, high-value-add businesses now.

*Firm C, 43, $4 billion. Twenty years of narrow focus (basic manufacturing, > $10 mm EBITDA) and structure type (demand control, seek consolidation). Heavy investments in infrastructure to garner proprietary deal flow.

Firm D, 8, $150 mm. Since 1993 focus on closely held businesses with $2 mm to 15 mm EBITDA, and which have succession/liquidity and/or growth capital needs. Manufacturing, distribution, service businesses.

Firm E, 10, $69 mm. Three small funds, all minority stakes in post-startup growth equity; conservative capital structure. Heavy focus on IT services. One hundred percent minority investor. Had SBIC license but poor showing led to inability to raise follow-on.

Firm F, 14, $275 mm. Focus on $5 mm to 15 mm EBITDA manufacturing companies primarily in industrial Midwest. Usually control position, then consolidate fragmented industries.

*Firm G, 17, $800 mm. Middle market buyouts of companies $35 mm to $300 mm. Extremely well-thought-out value proposition: require strong managers day one, sustainable competitive advantages, diversification in products, customers, markets. Mostly control and manufacturing. Latest fund oversubscribed.

Firm H, 6, $150 mm. Just closed on $120 mm fund; background in control-oriented deals, midsize consumer niche manufacturers up to $100 mm in value.

Firm I, 23, $300 mm. Investment vehicle for two former CEOs. Just raised first formal fund. Heavy focus on services businesses until now; changing strategies. $2 mm to 20 mm EBITDA, California businesses only, avoid auctions.

*Firm J, 16, $1.6 billion. Firm focused on smaller deals (< $100 mm), almost carbon copy of B's strategy. Heavy focus on basic manufacturing, with ability to consolidate product lines or manufacturing facilities.

Firm K, 5, $25 mm. Small buyout firm focused on low-tech manufacturing or easy-to-understand distribution, business services businesses in southeastern United States. $1 mm to 3 mm EBITDA, invest alongside management.

Firm L, 21, $50 mm. Twenty-plus years opportunistic investor does PE as ancillary to real-estate deals. Focused on real-estate-related plays (e.g., small restaurant chain) and services deals in western United States.

Firm M, 30, $2.3 billion. Started in 1984 and for 10 years did earlier-stage tech related. Switched focus to late-stage buyouts; no industry focus, but seek a growth story and "management quality tells all." Increasingly doing club deals.

*Indicates Cambridge Associates (or other) has ranked as top-quartile performer in private equity.

NOTES

1. We follow convention in using the term *private equity* to refer to buyouts or equity investments in mature companies by equity limited partnerships; we exclude early-stage, "venture capital" investing. This chapter is the first installment in an extended research project that seeks to delineate how value is created by private equity via changes in governance, strategy, and operations of existing companies, delivered by investors

possessing specific knowledge of these areas in the respective industries or competitive situations of target investments.

2. From Thomson Financial. Forward estimate cited in *The Wall Street Journal*, February 4, 2009; industry sources confirm the magnitude of current and likely magnitude of the drop-off in activity.

3. Apollo Group, Fortress Investments, and other high-profile PE firms also went public or talked about it before global equity market declines after Fall 2007.

4. Many of these papers appeared during two spikes in research activity by financial economists, one by U.S. researchers from 1988 to 1993 and another, mainly by European researchers, from 2003 to 2007.

5. Anderson and Lee (1997) looked at source data for ownership studies from four databases and found considerable variation in data quality and accuracy. More recently, Kaplan, Sensoy, and Stromberg (2002) examined venture-capital investments in two databases and found serious omissions, leading to "unbiased but noisy" transaction data. We searched Thomson Financial's SDC Platinum database for information on Kohlberg Kravis Roberts & Co (KKR). Its first important deal, an acquisition of Houdaille Industries, was missing, and of more than 150 transactions in which KKR is the named buyer, only 30 appear in SDC Platinum. Meanwhile, in syndicated transactions it is often difficult to distinguish firms coded as "buyer" and firms coded as "investor."

6. Kaplan and Schoar (2005) analyzed several hundred funds from Thomson's SDC Platinum and found average fund returns (net of fees) approximately equal the S&P 500, although there is substantial variety in performance across funds. They also found that returns persist across subsequent funds of a partnership, and that better performing partnerships are more likely to raise follow-on funds and larger funds. These results for PE firms differ dramatically from those for mutual funds, where there is regression to the mean. Beyond the scope of our topic, it is nonetheless interesting to note that Lerner, Schoar, and Wong (2007) found that a similar "persistence effect" is manifested in institutional investor returns in private equity (i.e., the limited partners such as endowment funds who capitalize the private equity partnerships run by general partners such as Blackstone or KKR).

7. See also Baker and Montgomery (1994), an operating and organizational comparison of publicly traded conglomerates and PE firms (known then as "LBO associations"), which in many instances are tantamount to privately held conglomerates. This offers another interesting and useful line of inquiry, more from an industrial organization than a finance perspective.

8. The 20-year period in Exhibit 11.1 is 1986 through 2006, chosen to match as closely as possible with our transaction sample that runs from 1984 to 2006.

9. A pooled IRR is a calculation of an aggregate IRR by summing cash flows from disparate investments together to create a portfolio cash flow. The IRR is subsequently calculated on this portfolio cash flow.

10. This result is perfectly consistent with economic theory, which posits higher returns to the higher risk inherent in less efficient markets. Indeed, small-company buyouts consist almost exclusively of privately held firms in fragmented industries, and are less amenable to standard valuation and auction-pricing as obtained in more organized markets.

11. Kaplan and Schoar (2005) report, however, that they *oversample* first-time funds by 25 percent as compared to the data in the Venture Economics data base; first-time funds underperform follow-on funds in general. Their results differ somewhat from what is

depicted in Exhibit 11.1 (perhaps highlighting the existence of extended controversy about returns).

12. This is the first step toward a broader objective of understanding PE versus public equity from a comparative corporate governance perspective. The focus there is not necessarily returns, given the measurement difficulties mentioned above, but on the more qualitative (and in our view, more important) aspects of governance and performance.

13. Cumming and Walz (2004) discuss an important aspect of the ongoing controversy about PE returns discussed above, and one that has stimulated strong policy debates about PE regulatory oversight in the United States and Europe. They study several hundred PE funds across 39 countries over a 30-year period and find systematic overreporting of *unrealized* IRRs (i.e., the hypothetical "mark-to-market" valuations of nonexited companies still held in a PE fund's portfolio). Such valuations are used mainly for periodic performance reporting to limited partners and for fund-raising. In our interviews with participating PE firms, we found such wide variation in the subjective self-assessed valuation of unrealized investments, we did not use these deals in our analysis. Instead, we utilized only valuations of exited transactions with significant liquidity events. Interestingly, Cumming and Walz report that the degree of misreporting is related to the legal and accounting environment, and to pressures for transparency, in the PE firm's host country.

14. Here we follow Nikoskelainen and Wright (2007).

15. The value of the firm being, of course, the value of the bundle of assets which comprise it; this necessarily includes all claims on assets, not just the equity claims.

16. This proved to be a complex issue, because there are a variety of formulas employed for the vesting of options or related bonus-with-equity pay-for-performance arrangements. We coded this variable in order to capture the full incentive effects of possible payouts and equity awards, so determined what the maximal amount of equity could be at the time of deal entry, assuming there were full vesting based on agreed-upon performance metrics being achieved. In other words, if the ingoing equity split were 90 percent PE firm-owned and 10 percent management (and there were no other investors), but that in three years' time it would be possible, if EBITDA growth targets were hit, for management to own 22 percent of the company, then we coded the deal at 78 percent and 22 percent.

17. We arrive at total debt by subtracting total equity invested from transaction value at entry. This measures the EBITDA multiple of debt owed, and is thus an inverse of a traditional interest coverage ratio. We convert negative EBITDA at entry to the 99th percentile of range of coverage.

18. For example, in the cases of employment and capital expenditures, we received hard numbers for 59 and 126 transactions, respectively, out of the 288 (meaning that we had both deal entry and exit totals and hence could measure percentage changes). But when asked whether employment and capital expenditures went up or down, the responses grew to 250 and 230, respectively. So, we captured these variables both in hard number terms, for their change levels, and in larger subsets, as binary variables.

19. One objective in constructing industry groups from lower- to higher-value-added activities is testing Williamson's (1988) thesis that debt and equity are forms of *governance structure*, each used according to industry and transaction conditions. Specifically, Williamson's thesis argues that debt is suitable for low-beta, slow growth, mature-industry, stable-cash-flow businesses, and hence would concur with Jensen (1986), who argued such businesses would be most suitable for LBOs. Conversely, a business with a high human capital-to-assets ratio (e.g., a biotech, software, or engineering consulting firm) should have a higher *beta* and more equitized capital structure.

20. For each firm, publicly traded matched stocks are found by NAICS industry code. CAPM betas are estimated by regressing the contemporaneous excess monthly stock returns over the market excess returns (excess return being the difference between monthly return and the risk-free rate). Each year for each stock, the slope coefficient *beta* is estimated using an OLS specification for the CAPM equation. Risk-free rates and excess market returns are from Kenneth French's website: mba.tuck.dartmouth.edu/pages/faculty/ken.french/index.html.

21. PE practitioners argue that their strategic oversight, along with negotiation skills and knowledge of industry buyers and market conditions, can optimize firm value at exit, and one measure of this is "uplift" in the value/EBITDA multiple. A modified *DuPont Formula* depicting sources of adding value in a transaction illuminates this:

$$\text{Classic DuPont Formula} = \frac{\text{Net income}}{\text{Sales}} * \frac{\text{Sales}}{\text{Assets}} * \frac{\text{Assets}}{\text{Equity}}$$

where the three ratios signify, respectively, measures of efficiency in operations, marketing, and the finance of the firm, and signify return on equity. The modification for PE is as follows:

$$\text{PE firm value creation} = \frac{\text{EBITDA}}{\text{Sales}} * \frac{\text{Sales}}{\text{Firm value}(n)} * \frac{\text{Firm value}(x)}{\text{EBITDA}}$$

where the product always totals the ratio of exit value to entry value, but can be broken into pieces corresponding to operational efficiency, growth, and added value from PE firm oversight (enclosing the multiplicands in brackets and taking their product to the power of [days held]/365, then subtracting 1, gives the transaction IRR, assuming neutral intermediate cash flows). In actual deals, of course, EBITDA changes; future investigations into the specifics of GP activities will define the degree of their value-add.

22. We also sought information on divestitures, and received responses for 189 transactions. However, there were only 14 which had sold off a part of the business after deal entry, versus 175 who responded in saying that there had been none. Because we inferred that the vast majority of the 99 nonrespondents to this question did *not* make any divestitures, we did not include the *divest* variable in this analysis beyond reporting descriptive statistics for the 14 deals that contained them. Divestiture, in any case, is a strategic tool utilized more appropriately in larger deals.

23. The standard deviation of the sample equity IRR is 89.3 percent, typical for high-variance leveraged investing or venture capital. Skewness was 3.4, and kurtosis 26.7. Discussion of the third and fourth moments is not common in many statistical applications, but they are utilized in the investment world. As the head of one premier firm told us, "We sell skewness," when describing how institutional investors are approached during fund-raising. The Jarque-Bera test confirms this is a nonnormal distribution, which means OLS regression results must be interpreted carefully in terms of broader applicability (however, assuming the residuals are normally distributed in our regression framework, we proceed as usual here and OLS results obtain). High skewness coupled with high kurtosis provide an institutional investor with the opportunity to diversify into alternative assets which offer the potential for superior returns.

24. And, standard deviation, skewness and kurtosis for the S&P 500 for our sample transaction matches are 10.9 percent, −0.15 and −0.40, respectively, so the volatility of our sample is, as expected, high. We also checked the IRRs for Russell-2000 and Fama-French (FF)

smallest 30 percent-, 20 percent-, and 10 percent-of-firms portfolios, and the IRRs range from 7.5 percent to 14 percent, with FF-10 as the highest.

25. Swensen (2000) points out that the best way to analyze PE returns against an index is on a full risk-adjusted basis, accounting for leverage in buyout deals. Investing the same dollar amounts in each of our 288 transactions with equal amounts of leverage in the S&P 500 index triples equity returns, from 9.8 percent to 25.82 percent, with median of 21.93 percent. The other return figure to note here is the value-weighted IRR for equity for our sample; it is 43.90 percent, up nearly four percentage points from the arithmetic mean.

26. Note as well in Exhibit 11.1 that the long-term IRRs for buyouts are higher for smaller deals. As described below, in our sample, as well as those used by Nikoskelainen and Wright (2007) and Loos (2006), IRRs are increasing in deal size. One might expect smaller buyouts to have a higher bankruptcy risk, corresponding to higher long-term returns. On the other hand, there may be a minimum efficient scale for successful deals. We hope to explore this more fully in future research.

27. And Porter's list contained *no* distribution or service industries, arguably more fragmented than most manufacturing sectors.

28. The converse of a strategy based on consolidation via ancillary acquisitions is one of restructuring a firm with an uneconomic mix of assets via divestiture, in an effort to rationalize the core business. We received 189 responses to our request for data about this and 175 had not pursued any divestitures.

29. Nikoskelainen and Wright (2007) report mean and median holding times of 3.5 and 3.3 years, respectively. Our sample goes back in time ten years further than theirs, to the early 1980s, when transactions were held for longer periods. Kaplan (1991) reports mean holding time of 6.82 years for a 1980s deal sample.

30. In his exchange with Jensen (1989), Rappaport (1990) referred to LBO firms almost disparagingly as "transitional," which may have been a *double entendre* referring both to short holding periods and the LBO association itself as a temporary organizational form. Only the first has proven correct so far.

31. We view these results more cautiously than other returns data because there were sizable subsets of deals for both employment and capital expenditures, which were unclear as to the direction of these parameters during the deal's holding time. And in both cases the *unknowns* exhibited strong returns. A larger data sample will shed light on these. It must also be remembered that declines in capital expenditure especially, but also potentially employment, are not inconsistent with a strategy to optimize investment returns and firm performance (and in some cases, survival). This fact often gets lost in discussions about restructuring via private equity.

32. However, this is not a unanimous view in private equity; for a minority of practitioners, especially for those firms organized as open-ended funds (including a few in our sample), their claim is that they offer "patient capital" and can optimize the exit without pressure of a fund's contractual life end. While it is unambiguously true for larger deals that holding times are shorter, here, for growth-oriented investments often involving consolidating roll-ups of smaller firms, holding time to an attractive exit may involve longer periods.

33. The exception to this norm occurred in the recent boom years of record fund-raising; large funds needing to place capital did in several instances outbid "strategic," or industrial, buyers. The advent of club-deals has also increased the bidding power of PE acquirers. Some PE practitioners now question the wisdom of others in the sector who were aggressive bidders in the 2004 to 2007 era of easy money and record fund-raising; vintage returns from this era may suffer. But as a general proposition, the more

knowledgeable the *buyer*, the less "extractable rents" accrue to the *selling* PE firm at exit. Not uncoincidentally, the relationship applies equally well in running from deepest-capitalized buyer class (IPO) to least (recap).

34. Indeed, Exhibit 11.4 depicts a linear relationship between decreasing IRR, increasing capital expenditures, and increasing length of holding time.

35. FTC Commissioner William Kovacic stated in January 2007 that PE firms participating in syndicates would likely come under antitrust scrutiny for anticompetitive (collusive) practices. These are more prevalent today among high-profile deals than the big solo ownership transactions of the 1980s.

36. Nikoskelainen and Wright (2007) find the same for U.K. middle-market buyouts.

37. Additionally, PE investors today increasingly engage in *strip financing*, in which tranches of each layer of the capital structure are doled out to the same investor set (thus, a subordinated debt provider such as Allied Capital Corp. of Washington, D.C., will also hold an equity stake and perhaps preferred stock as well), with the express intent of fostering greater goal congruence among investors and lenders. Looking at IRR on the firm's assets thus provides for a balanced review of the effect of PE firm governance.

38. In related specifications of regression analysis (not reported here) examining minority versus controlling ownership, a derived variable, $MGMTeqty^2$, had negative coefficients as would be predicted, but was not significant. PE practitioners have not spoken to us of any concern about an *entrenchment effect*, but there is great debate about the optimality of the contract with management in terms of the "right" equity splits and type of incentives. In other words, is there a "point of optimality" for the equity split to management, after which managers engage in perquisite consumption? This is a subject for further investigation.

39. The case of management equity (which decreases in linear fashion as one scans the columns from IPOs to recaps, as shown in Exhibit 11.4) goes against some theoretical arguments that highest leverage levels are associated with highest levels of concentrated equity holdings. This theory has support in the "traditional" literature on buyouts, in which public firms are taken private and management acquire substantial equity stakes. In our data sample, which were mostly private-to-private deals, management equity was already held in substantive amounts pretransaction. At *exit*, however, it may become a motivator and driver of performance again (e.g., management recaps looked to vastly increase their holdings). In any case, the differing characteristics that comprised firms based on exit type and/or industry type validate the thesis that the tenets of transaction cost economics lend support to organization theory (see, e.g., Williamson [1996, 219ff.]).

REFERENCES

Anderson, Ronald C., and D. Scott Lee. 1997. Ownership studies: The data source does matter. *Journal of Financial and Quantitative Analysis* 32 (3):311–329.

Baker, George P., and Cynthia Montgomery. 1994. Conglomerates and LBO associations: A comparison of organizational forms. Unpublished manuscript, Harvard Business School.

Baker, George P., and George David Smith. 1998. *The new financial capitalists: Kohlberg Kravis Roberts and the creation of corporate value*. London: Cambridge University Press.

Baker, George P., and Karen H. Wruck. 1989. Organizational changes and value creation in leveraged buyouts: The case of O.M. Scott & Sons Company. *Journal of Financial Economics* 25:163–190.

Baumol, William J. 2002. *The free-market innovation machine: Analyzing the growth miracle of capitalism*. Princeton, NJ: Princeton University Press.

Bull, Ivan. 1989. Financial performance of leveraged buyouts: An empirical analysis. *Journal of Business Venturing* 4 (4):263–279.

Cumming, Douglas J., and Uwe Walz. 2004. Private equity returns and disclosure around the world. *Journal of International Business Studies*, forthcoming. EFA 2004, Maastricht. Available at SSRN: ssrn.com/abstract=514105.

DeAngelo, Harry, Linda DeAngelo, and Edward M. Rice. 1984. Going private: Minority freeze-outs and stockholder wealth. *Journal of Law and Economics* 27 (2):367–401.

Groh, Alexander Peter, and Oliver Gottschalg. 2008. Measuring the risk-adjusted performance of U.S. buyouts. NBER Working Paper No. W14148. Available at SSRN: ssrn.com/abstract=1152689.

Hubbard, R. Glenn. 2005. *Money, the financial system, and the economy*. Boston: Pearson Addison-Wesley.

Jensen, Michael C. 1986. Agency costs of free cash flow, corporate finance, and takeovers. *American Economic Review* 76 (2):323–329.

Jensen, Michael C. 1988. Takeovers: Their causes and consequences. *Journal of Economic Perspectives* 2:21–48.

Jensen, Michael C. 1989. The eclipse of the public corporation. *Harvard Business Review* 67 (5):61–74.

Jensen, Michael C. 1993. The modern industrial revolution, exit, and the failure of internal control systems. *Journal of Finance* 48 (3):831–880.

Kaplan, Steven N. 1991. The staying power of leveraged buyouts. *Journal of Financial Economics* 29:287–314.

Kaplan, Steven N., Berk A. Sensoy, and Per Stromberg. 2002. How well do venture capital data bases reflect actual investments? Available at SSRN: ssrn.com/abstract=939073.

Kaplan, Steven N., and Antoinette Schoar. 2005. Private equity performance: Returns, persistence, and capital flows. *Journal of Finance* 60:1791–1823.

Kirzner, Israel M. 1973. *Competition and entrepreneurship*. Chicago: University of Chicago Press.

Kirzner, Israel M. 2000. *The driving force of the market*. London: Routledge.

Klein, Peter G. 1999. Entrepreneurship and corporate governance. *Quarterly Journal of Austrian Economics* 2 (2):19–42.

Kochhar, Rahul. 1996. Explaining firm capital structure: The role of agency theory vs. transaction cost economics. *Strategic Management Journal* 17:713–728.

Lerner, Josh, Antoinette Schoar, and Wan Wong. 2007. Smart institutions, foolish choices? The limited partner performance puzzle. *Journal of Finance* 62 (2):731–764.

Loos, Nicolaus. 2006. *Value creation in leveraged buyouts: Analysis of factors driving private equity investment performance*. Wiesbaden: Deutscher Universitats Verlag.

Ljungqvist, Alexander, and Matthew Richardson. 2003. The cash flow, return, and risk characteristics of private equity. *NBER Working Paper* 9454, January 2003. Available at: www.nber.org/papers/w9454.

Manne, Henry G. 1965. Mergers and the market for corporate control. *Journal of Political Economy* 73 (2):110–120.

Mises, Ludwig von. 1949. *Human action: A treatise on economics*. New Haven: Yale University Press.

Mises, Ludwig von. 1951. Profit and loss. In *Planning for Freedom*, ed. Ludwig von Mises. South Holland, IL: Libertarian Press, 1952.

Modigliani, Franco, and Merton H. Miller. 1958. The cost of capital, corporation finance, and the theory of investment. *American Economic Review* 48 (3):261–297.

Moskowitz, Tobias J., and Annette Vissing-Jorgenson. 2002. The returns to private equity investment: A private equity premium puzzle? *American Economic Review* 92:4, 745–778.

Nikoskelainen, Erkki, and Mike Wright. 2007. The impact of corporate governance mechanisms on value increase in leveraged buyouts. *Journal of Corporate Finance* 13 (4):511–537.

Phalippou, Ludovic, and Oliver Gottschalg. 2008. The performance of private equity funds. *Review of Financial Studies*, forthcoming. Available at: papers.ssrn.com/sol3/results.cfm.

Porter, Michael E. 1980. *Competitive strategy: Techniques for analyzing industries and competitors.* New York: The Free Press.

Rappaport, Alfred. 1990. The staying power of the public corporation. *Harvard Business Review* 68 (1):96–104.

Schumpeter, Joseph A. 1911. *The theory of economic development: An inquiry into profits, capital, credit, interest, and the business cycle.* Cambridge, Mass.: Harvard University Press, 1934.

Swensen, David F. 2000. *Pioneering portfolio management: An unconventional approach to institutional investment.* New York: The Free Press.

Williamson, Oliver E. 1988. Corporate finance and corporate governance. *Journal of Finance* 43 (3):567–591.

Williamson, Oliver E. 1996. *The mechanisms of governance.* New York: Oxford University Press.

ABOUT THE AUTHORS

John L. Chapman received his Ph.D. in Economics from the University of Georgia. He is an analyst and researcher affiliated with the American Enterprise Institute, where his primary fields of interest are corporate finance, industrial organization, and monetary theory and policy. He is writing a book with Glenn Hubbard on the history and impact of private equity, a retrospective examination of leveraged-equity investing and its effects on corporate governance, mergers and the market for corporate control, entrepreneurship, and economic growth.

Peter G. Klein received his Ph.D. in Economics from the University of California, Berkeley. He specializes in organizational economics, entrepreneurship, strategic management, and corporate governance. His work has appeared in the *Rand Journal of Economics*, the *Journal of Industrial Economics*, the *Strategic Entrepreneurship Journal*, the *Journal of Law, Economics, and Organization*, and other academic and professional outlets. He serves as Associate Director of the Contracting and Organizations Research Institute and is Adjunct Professor at the Norwegian School of Economics and Business Administration. He was formerly a Senior Economist with the Council of Economic Advisers.

ACKNOWLEDGMENTS

The authors thank Glenn Hubbard, Bill Lastrapes, Dwight Lee, Jeff Netter, and Annette Poulsen for helpful comments and conversations about this material, Mario Mondelli for research assistance, and the Contracting and Organizations Research Institute for financial support.

CHAPTER 12

Risk and Return
of Private Equity

An Overview of Data, Methods, and Results

LUDOVIC PHALIPPOU
Associate Professor, University of Amsterdam Business School and Fellow of
Tinbergen Institute

INTRODUCTION

In this chapter, I cover the different methods to measure risk and return of investing into private equity (also called buyout). However, the reader may bear in mind that the challenges and methods are very similar for other assets classes such as venture capital, real estate, or mezzanine. In terms of vocabulary, I call a (portfolio) company the entity receiving the financing from a private equity fund, and private equity firm the organization running private equity funds (e.g., KKR funds, Bain capital funds).

The capital committed to private equity funds increased from $3.5 billion in 1984 to over $300 billion in 2007 and more than $1 trillion of assets are estimated to be in the hands of private equity funds in 2007. This growth has often been attributed to a widespread belief of stellar performance and low risk but no rate of return has even been shown in support of this belief (only some multiples or IRRs) and no risk measure has been computed. Recent academic evidence that I document below is at odds with this belief.

In this chapter, I review studies of risk and return of private equity that I complement with original empirical work. I distinguish between four types of data. Each represents a different level of challenge for measuring risk and return. From the easiest to the most difficult, these are: (1) publicly traded vehicles, (2) round valuation data (the econometrician knows the initial and final value of the investment, but does not know the time series of investment values; there is no intermediary cash flows), (3) investment level (cash flows realized by the fund from an investment), and (4) fund level (cash flows faced by investors for their stake in a fund). In the last two cases, the econometrician does not have a correspondence between each amount distributed and invested. These two cases require the same method, are most challenging, and are the most relevant in practice.

THE DATA

Publicly Traded Vehicles

The first type of private equity investment I cover is that in publicly traded vehicles. These are often closed-end funds. Interestingly, the first investments in venture capital were made right after World War II via closed-end funds. Nowadays, both venture capital and private equity investments made via publicly traded vehicles are relatively marginal but are growing again.[1]

With these data, the challenging part is to establish a list of private equity firms. I use an existing comprehensive database called Capital IQ and request companies whose type is either "Public Investment Firm" or "Public Fund," and that have "Buyout" as one of their stages of interest. A list of 161 firms is returned. Next, I match each firm to the Datastream database and require the firm to be listed as of June 2005 (to ensure at least three years of data) reducing the number of firms to 97. I remove illiquid stocks as they make risk analysis difficult. Specifically, I select the subset with less than 5 percent of the weeks with zero return and with more than 200 consecutive weeks of return data. Next, I remove those that are obviously not private equity firms (Biolin, Prologis, and W. P. Carey) and two venture capital firms (Inspire Investment Limited, and Shrem, Fudim, Kelner Technologies). This brings the number of observations to 19; these firms are listed in Exhibit 12.1.[2]

Some of these firms, however, could be excluded as they have minority stakes in public equity and their private equity activities are a minor part of their business. For example, Eurazeo has $1 billion invested in Danone—a 5 percent stake of a publicly traded company. An alternative data source is the private equity indices. However, they also contain very diverse firms. For example, the S&P private equity index contains Blackstone, which is a claim on the firm fees and not on the underlying investments. This is different from 3i Group and American Capital, which are claims on private equity investments. Making a sample bias-free database of stocks that are mainly claims on private equity investments could be of interest but would be labor intensive. I use this fairly "naïve" list for illustration purposes.

Return data are collected from Datastream: weekly stock return and turnover (volume divided by number of shares outstanding), and weekly return of the local index.[3]

Round Valuation Data

Round valuation data is when the econometrician observes market values at different points in time without cash flows in between. These data are encountered in real estate, art pieces, and venture capital. For venture capital, the most comprehensive data source is Sand Hill Econometrics, which combined data from existing databases (VentureOne and Venture Economics) and added information from proprietary data sources on round valuations. In private equity, this type of data is seldom encountered but the techniques applied on these data are a good starting point for the techniques developed for private equity.

Note that these data give the value of a company at each valuation round until the exit (trade sale, IPO, or bankruptcy). By analyzing these data, one learns about the risk and return of an investment. However, the risk and return faced by an

Exhibit 12.1   Publicly Traded Private Equity Funds

Name	Country	All Years (Max. Last 15 Years)				Last 3 Years	
		% Zeros	Turnover	Alpha	Beta	Alpha	Beta
3i Group Plc	U.K.	0.01	0.87	0.07	1.52	0.03	1.59
American Capital, Ltd.	U.S.	0.02	1.89	0.12	1.25	−0.04	0.51
Colonial First State Private	Australia	0.01	0.12	0.00	1.14	0.07	0.17
Dinamia Capital Privado	Spain	0.04	0.45	0.06	0.68	0.07	0.80
Electra Private Equity	U.K.	0.04	0.35	0.09	1.18	0.09	0.84
Eurazeo	France	0.03	0.82	0.09	0.82	0.04	0.65
GIMV NV	Belgium	0.02	0.09	0.01	0.98	0.06	0.38
Investor AB	Sweden	0.04	0.20	0.05	1.11	0.09	1.01
JAFCO Co., Ltd.	Japan	0.01	0.56	0.20	2.09	−0.07	1.55
KTB Securities Co.	S. Korea	0.02	2.84	0.05	1.86	0.16	2.38
MCG Capital Corporation	U.S.	0.00	1.37	−0.08	1.74	−0.30	1.09
MCI Management	Poland	0.04	1.17	−0.04	2.63	0.45	2.90
MVC Capital Inc.	U.S.	0.03	0.45	0.04	0.87	0.11	0.81
NIF SMBC Ventures Co.	Japan	0.02	0.20	0.01	3.83	0.03	3.66
Onex Corporation	Canada	0.04	0.67	0.13	1.22	0.07	0.76
Safeguard Scientifics	U.S.	0.02	1.92	0.14	2.84	−0.02	2.24
SoPaF SpA	Italy	0.04	0.17	−0.09	1.15	−0.14	0.75
The China Fund, Inc.	U.S.	0.03	1.04	0.10	0.79	0.32	2.24
Wendel	France	0.02	0.39	0.11	1.35	0.01	1.53
Average			**0.82**	**0.06**	**1.53**	**0.05**	**1.36**

This table lists publicly traded private equity with return data as of June 2005; see text for selection details. The table shows the firm country, the fraction of weeks with zero return, the annualized turnover and annualized alpha and beta from a one-factor market model with 10 lags at a weekly frequency (local stock market major index, returns in local currency). Alpha and beta are shown both for the full time period (when data are available) and over the last three years. Data are from July 1993 to June 2008. Averages are equally weighted.

investor will be different. For example, in case of an IPO-exited project, the return observed will be based on the IPO offering price and not on the price at which the investor have sold. An extreme example where this distinction has mattered a lot is the eBay IPO. Benchmark Partners' return in eBay was 20 times the investment at the IPO. However, investors received the eBay stocks six months after the IPO, when the price had increased by more than 3000 percent, making their stake worth 700 times the investment. Of course, the opposite situation happens as well.[4] Results on risk and return from round valuation data should thus be taken with this caveat in mind.

Investment Data

This category corresponds to investments made by a private equity firm. The econometrician observes the cash flows generated by a private equity firm on a portfolio company. For example, KKR invested $30 million to buy company ABC on January 1980, then received a dividend of $40 million on April 1984 and then exited ABC on June 1985 and received $80 million at that time. The econometrician observes cash flows but cannot make a link between each dividend and an investment value. If she could, we would be in the previous case.

The most comprehensive (and ongoing) database of this type I know of is that of CEPRES. As of June 2008, it contains 5,214 mature private equity investments (i.e., made before 2002), of which 3,935 are liquidated. This dataset has been used by Cumming and Walz (2007), among others.

Several researchers have had access to the detailed track record of some investors. They observe the cash-flow amount and date for each portfolio company. An example is the proprietary dataset of Ljungqvist and Richardson (2003), which contains 207 private equity funds.

Finally, the prospectuses that private equity firms send to investors when fund-raising contain multiples and IRRs of all their previous investments. Oliver Gottschalg and I have collected performance information on 6,000 private equity investments from such prospectuses. These data, however, do not give underlying cash flows and are gross of fees. The data are described in Lopez-de-Silanes and Phalippou (2008); two private equity firms show this type of data on the web site. Please see Exhibit 12.2.

Fund Data

The fourth type of data are fund-level data. When investing in private equity, investors typically buy a stake in a private limited partnership. This partnership (a.k.a., fund) lasts for 10 to 13 years. Over this time period, the investor faces a continuous stream of cash flows in and out of its pocket at different times. These cash-flow streams (net of fees) are/were available from two sources.

The first source is Thomson Venture Economics (TVE) cash-flow dataset described in Kaplan and Schoar (2005) and Phalippou and Gottschalg (2008). It contains cash flows and quarterly net asset values (NAVs) of 236 mature private equity funds (at least 10 years old, as of 2003). This dataset is no longer available.

The second source is Prequin. They also provide cash flows and quarterly NAVs. They are currently available for researchers but have little coverage in the 1980s-1990s. They have only 122 mature private equity funds (as of 2007).

Note that online reports of certain institutional investors (e.g., CalPERS) provide net-of-fees IRR and total amounts invested/distributed by private equity funds. Private Equity Intelligence collected all these publicly available data and thereby assembled a large dataset comprising 1,056 mature funds. However, they do not indicate the focus of the funds. Hence, it is thus difficult to isolate private equity funds from venture capital, real estate funds, and others.

Sample Biases

The issue of sample bias is always important when dealing with asset returns. The listed vehicles are probably those for which the issue is least acute. One needs to simply keep track on the delisted stocks. It is not trivial but not unfeasible. For round data, I have never seen them, so I do not know. Bias in Thomson Venture Economics (TVE) cash-flow dataset has been studied and I review it below. Next, I cover the investment-level datasets reviewed above. For both fund level and investment level datasets, documenting sample bias is tricky because we do not know the universe. I provide here a brief mix of my impressions and own analyses.

Exhibit 12.2   Private Equity Investments: Public Information

Panel A: Onex: Substantially Realized and Publicly Traded Investments

Investment	Initial Inv.	Inv.	Realized	Unrealized	Total	Multiple	IRR
Dayton Superior Corporation	Aug-89	14.9	80.4	7.9	88.3	5.9	16.20%
Phoenix Pictures, Inc.	Nov-95	28.3	0.0	0.0	0.0	0.0	NM
Celestica, Inc.	Oct-96	211.0	847.1	248.8	1095.9	5.2	49.60%
Galaxy Entertainment, Inc.	Dec-98	31.7	60.7	35.9	96.6	3.0	24.80%
Loews Cineplex Group	Mar-02	517.4	837.6	145.1	982.7	1.9	29.40%
Canadian Securities Registration Syst.	Apr-04	9.1	28.9	2.5	31.4	3.4	86.60%
ResCare, Inc.	Jun-04	26.9	0.0	42.5	42.5	1.6	19.30%
Emergency Medical Services Co.	Feb-05	99.6	3.9	295.2	299.1	3.0	78.00%
Spirit AeroSystems, Inc.	Jun-05	134.8	419.4	668.0	1087.4	8.1	272.40%
The Town and Country Trust	Mar-06	100.9	100.0	60.1	160.1	1.6	76.60%
Total		**1174.7**	**2378.0**	**1505.9**	**3884.0**	**3.3**	**36.20%**

Panel B: Onex: Realized

Investment	Initial Inv.	Inv.	Realized	Multiple	IRR
Onex Packaging, Inc.	Nov-84	25.6	49.2	1.9	23.50%
Sky Chefs, Inc.	May-86	99.4	1753.9	17.6	30.50%
Purolator Courier, Ltd.	Apr-87	85.5	106.8	1.2	3.20%
Norex Leasing, Inc.	Jul-87	63.7	63.7	1.0	0.00%
Beatrice Foods, Inc.	Nov-87	69.2	145.5	2.1	32.60%
Automotive Industries Holdings, Inc.	Apr-90	22.7	206.0	9.1	61.30%
Dura Automotive Systems, Inc.	Nov-90	7.2	44.2	6.2	27.70%
The Delfield/Whitlenge Companies	May-91	7.8	95.4	12.2	122.80%
Johnstown America Corporation	Oct-91	8.9	74.3	8.3	144.20%
ProSource, Inc.	Jun-92	95.7	155.7	1.6	15.10%
Johnstown Wire Technologies, Inc.	Dec-92	2.2	2.4	1.1	13.40%

(Continued)

Exhibit 12.2 Private Equity Investments: Public Information (*Continued*)

Panel B: Onex: Realized

Investment	Initial Inv.	Inv.	Realized	Multiple	IRR
Tower Automotive, Inc.	Apr-93	11.2	118.4	10.6	103.20%
Alliance Atlantis Communications, Inc.	Oct-94	16.5	29.6	1.8	13.80%
Edwards Baking Company	Oct-95	4.4	7.9	1.8	10.50%
Vencap, Inc.	Jan-96	25.1	164.5	6.5	235.20%
Imperial Parking, Limited	Mar-96	59.3	86.9	1.5	50.00%
BC Sugar Refinery, Limited	Aug-97	74.2	257.6	3.5	211.70%
Commercial Vehicles Group	Oct-97	68.8	166.0	2.4	20.10%
J.L. French Automotive Castings, Inc.	Apr-99	259.0	20.2	0.1	NM
Performance Group	May-99	47.7	13.0	0.3	NM
MAGNATRAX Corporation	May-99	172.5	0.1	0.0	NM
Onex Technology Investments	Sep-99	43.3	30.5	0.7	NM
InsLogic Holding Corporation	Oct-99	51.9	22.4	0.4	NM
Enerflex Systems	Jan-00	4.7	10.8	2.3	25.60%
Armtec, Limited	Aug-01	10.7	26.6	2.5	41.00%
Magellan Health Services, Inc.	Jan-04	30.7	77.9	2.5	84.70%
Futuremed Healthcare Products L.P.	Feb-04	7.9	31.4	4.0	111.90%
Compagnie Générale de Géophysique	Nov-04	24.9	36.2	1.5	235.90%
Total		**1400.7**	**3797.1**	**104.7**	**26.10%**

Panel C: Onex: All Investments from 1984–2000

Investment	Initial Inv.	Inv.	Real.	Unreal.	Mult.	IRR
Onex Packaging, Inc.	Nov-84	26	49	0	1.9	24%
Sky Chefs, Inc.	May-86	99	1754	0	17.6	31%
Purolator Courier, Ltd.	Apr-87	86	107	0	1.2	3%
Norex Leasing, Inc.	Jul-87	64	64	0	1.0	0%
Beatrice Foods, Inc.	Nov-87	69	146	0	2.1	33%
Dayton Superior Corporation	Aug-89	15	80	8	5.9	16%
Automotive Industries Holdings	Apr-90	23	206	0	9.1	61%
Dura Automotive Systems, Inc.	Nov-90	7	44	0	6.2	28%
The Delfield/Whitlenge Companies	May-91	8	95	0	12.2	123%
Johnstown America Corporation	Oct-91	9	74	0	8.3	144%
ProSource, Inc.	Jun-92	96	156	0	1.6	15%
Johnstown Wire Technologies, Inc.	Dec-92	2	2	0	1.1	13%
Tower Automotive, Inc.	Apr-93	11	118	0	10.6	103%
Alliance Atlantis Communications	Oct-94	17	30	0	1.8	14%
Edwards Baking Company	Oct-95	4	8	0	1.8	11%

Exhibit 12.2 *(Continued)*

Panel C: Onex: All Investments from 1984–2000

Investment	Initial Inv.	Inv.	Real.	Unreal.	Mult.	IRR
Phoenix Pictures, Inc.	Nov-95	28	0	0	0.0	NM
Vencap, Inc.	Jan-96	25	165	0	6.5	235%
Imperial Parking, Limited	Mar-96	59	87	0	1.5	50%
Celestica, Inc.	Oct-96	211	847	249	5.2	50%
BC Sugar Refinery, Limited	Aug-97	74	258	0	3.5	212%
Commercial Vehicles Group	Oct-97	69	166	0	2.4	20%
ClientLogic Corporation	Apr-98	292	7	NA	0.0	NA
Cypress P&C Insurance Co.	Nov-98	28	14	NA	0.5	NA
Galaxy Entertainment, Inc.	Dec-98	32	61	36	3.0	25%
J.L. French Automotive Castings	Apr-99	259	20	0	0.1	NM
Performance Group	May-99	48	13	0	0.3	NM
MAGNATRAX Corporation	May-99	173	0	0	0.0	NM
Onex Technology Investments	Sep-99	43	31	0	0.7	NM
InsLogic Holding Corporation	Oct-99	52	22	0	0.4	NM
Enerflex Systems	Jan-00	4.7	10.8	0	2.3	25%
Median					**1.8**	**18%**
Total		**1934**	**4635**	**293**	**2.55**	

Panel D: American Capital: Exited Investments, 1997–2007

Company Name	Initial Date	Exit Date	Inv.	IRR (%)	Duration
Optima Bus Corp.	Mar-98	Sep-06	55.0	0.00	8.51
American Decorative Surfaces, Inc.	Apr-98	Feb-06	42.0	0.49	7.84
The Lion Brewery, Inc.	Jan-99	Mar-05	6.6	0.17	6.17
Caswell-Massey Co., Ltd.	Sep-99	Jul-03	4.2	0.16	3.83
A.H. Harris & Sons, Inc.	Dec-99	Aug-07	10.0	0.16	7.67
Fulton Bellows & Components, Inc.	Mar-00	Aug-04	36.8	−0.26	4.42
Chromas Technologies Corporation	Sep-00	Mar-04	33.7	−0.63	3.50
Iowa Mold Tooling Co., Inc.	Oct-00	Aug-06	34.0	0.25	5.84
Sunvest Industries LLC	Dec-00	Mar-04	16.0	−0.42	3.25
Aeriform Corporation	Jun-01	Sep-06	30.5	0.10	5.25
Weston Solutions	Jun-01	Sep-05	42.8	0.63	4.25
Texstars, Inc.	Jun-01	Dec-04	29.6	0.28	3.50
Logex Corporation	Jul-01	Jun-07	28.0	−0.36	5.92
NMCR, LLC	Jan-02	Jun-02	22.0	0.49	0.41
Automatic Bar Controls, Inc.	Jul-02	Jun-05	35.5	0.26	2.92
Flexi-Mat Corporation	Oct-03	May-07	60.0	−1.00	3.58
KAC Holdings, Inc.	Feb-04	Jul-06	70.0	0.53	2.41
PaR Systems, Inc.	Apr-04	May-06	36.0	0.32	2.08
PaR Nuclear Holding Company	May-04	May-06	36.0	0.32	2.00

(Continued)

Exhibit 12.2   Private Equity Investments: Public Information (*Continued*)

Panel D: American Capital: Exited Investments, 1997–2007

Company Name	Initial Date	Exit Date	Inv.	IRR (%)	Duration
3SI Security Systems	Sep-04	Mar-06	72.0	0.31	1.50
Consolidated Utility Services, Inc.	Oct-04	Mar-07	10.0	0.47	2.41
Weber Nickel Technologies Limited	Oct-04	Aug-06	29.0	−0.97	1.83
The Redwood Companies	Feb-06	Dec-07	79.5	0.20	1.83
ASAlliances Biofuels, LLC	Feb-06	Aug-07	85.0	0.97	1.50
Exstream Software	Jun-07	Mar-08	548.0	0.22	0.75
Median				**0.22**	**3.50**
Average value weighted (deflated)				**0.18**	**2.47**

Panel E: American Capital: All Investments, 1997–2001

Company Name	Initial Date	Exit Date	Inv.	IRR1 (%)	IRR2 (%)
Biddeford Real Estate Holdings	May-97		4.0	−1.00	0.00
JAG Acquisitions, Inc.	Jan-98		4.0	−1.00	0.00
Optima Bus Corp.	Mar-98	Sep-06	55.0	0.00	0.00
American Decorative Surfaces, Inc.	Apr-98	Feb-06	42.0	0.49	0.49
The Lion Brewery, Inc.	Jan-99	Mar-05	6.6	0.17	0.17
Caswell-Massey Co., Ltd.	Sep-99	Jul-03	4.2	0.16	0.16
KIC Holdings, Inc.	Sep-99		0.1	−1.00	0.00
A.H. Harris & Sons, Inc.	Dec-99	Aug-07	10.0	0.16	0.16
Warner Power, LLC	Dec-99		20.0	−1.00	0.00
Fulton Bellows & Components, Inc.	Mar-00	Aug-04	36.8	−0.26	−0.26
Chromas Technologies Corporation	Sep-00	Mar-04	33.7	−0.63	−0.63
Iowa Mold Tooling Co., Inc.	Oct-00	Aug-06	34.0	0.25	0.25
Sunvest Industries LLC	Dec-00	Mar-04	16.0	−0.42	−0.42
Aeriform Corporation	Jun-01	Sep-06	30.5	0.10	0.10
Weston Solutions	Jun-01	Sep-05	42.8	0.63	0.63
Texstars, Inc.	Jun-01	Dec-04	29.6	0.28	0.28
Logex Corporation	Jul-01	Jun-07	28.0	−0.36	−0.36
European Touch Ltd. II	Nov-01		26.0	−1.00	0.00
Median				**−0.13**	**0.00**
Average value weighted (deflated)					

This table lists returns from buyout projects that are available online for Onex and American Capital. Panels A and B show the investments as they are shown on Onex website. In Panel C, we show all mature Onex investments (done before 2001). Panel D and Panel E show respectively the exited investments and the mature investments from American Capital.

Thomson Venture Economics (TVE) Cash-Flow Dataset

TVE obtains data mostly from fund investors and investors that report to TVE might differ from the representative investor. They might be large private equity investors with potentially privileged access to larger and more established funds. Whether the funds held by reporting investors have different performances from the average fund is an empirical issue.

Phalippou and Gottschalg (PG 2008) assess whether investors who report to TVE cash-flow dataset are better than average or not. To do so, they use a separate and widely available "investment dataset" known as VentureXpert. Data include information about 29,739 companies (location, industry description, age), their investment characteristics (time of investment, stage, equity invested, exit date and mode), and funds that invested in them (fund size, investment focus, vintage year, headquarters). The unique feature of the PG dataset is that they have a link between the "investment" dataset and the "cash-flow" dataset. In the "investment" dataset, they can observe the characteristics of funds that are not included in the "cash-flow" dataset. They have 476 funds that are *not* part of TVE cash-flow dataset and find that these funds have fewer investments exited via an IPO or an M&A (45 percent versus 50 percent; *t*-stat is 3.26 for the spread). In the literature, exit success is frequently used as a proxy for fund performance. The widely held belief is that exit success and performance are highly related.

Phalippou and Gottschalg proceed in two steps. First, they verify that exit success is significantly related to true performance and find that it is indeed the case. Second, they extrapolate performance of the "additional" funds and obtain an estimate of the sample selection bias that is about 1 percent per year. This is a smaller bias than in mutual fund and hedge fund datasets but it is conservative as there are still some funds that are not included in the computations. These funds not only do not have cash-flow data, but do not have data about their investments either. Such funds are likely not to have had many successful exits (otherwise TVE would have spotted them).

It is, however, tricky to measure the bias. It is possible that some investors stop reporting what is happening for a given fund if it does not go well. This could not be observed by Phalippou and Gottschalg. Our knowledge of the bias in that dataset is thus still limited and it is problematic because the most widely used PE return benchmarks are derived from these data.

Other Dataset Sample Bias

CEPRES is *a priori* a bit biased towards non-U.S. investments and recent investments, but it has an impressive coverage. The PPM dataset I have is probably biased toward firms that have been successful. Firms that tried a few deals in the 1980s to 1990s and stop fund-raising are not in my database.

The datasets that come from one investor are likely to overrepresent winners. This is because an investor with poor performance is unlikely to share its track record. In addition, investors who show their track records today are "survivors." The investors who had bad performance in private equity are likely to have stopped investing. This remark goes also when using the performance reported by U.S. pension funds like CalPERS. This may not be representative because CalPERS may have a U.S. bias and selection abilities. The Prequin cash-flow dataset is tilted towards recent funds.

Finally, datasets without performance, such as Capital IQ, have a good coverage starting in the late 1990s. Before, say, 1999, these data should be handled with care as they have mostly been backfilled and the coverage is low.

METHODOLOGY

Publicly Traded Vehicles

If the closed-end fund is liquid enough, then standard techniques can be applied to measure geometric and arithmetic average returns, abnormal returns, and risk. If it is illiquid, abnormal returns and risk can be severely biased. However, geometric and arithmetic average returns can be measured as in the liquid case; the error in measurement will decrease with the measurement time horizon.

To correct for illiquidity, the simplest and most common approach is that of Dimson (1979). It consists of adding some lagged factor returns. For example, if one uses a CAPM specification, one adds lagged stock market returns on the right hand side of the equation. A standard time-series OLS regression is run and beta is set to the sum of the coefficients on the contemporaneous and lagged market returns. The abnormal performance (called alpha) is, as usual, the intercept. This technique works well if the data frequency is high (e.g., daily, weekly) because it is based on a log approximation (see Appendix 12.A). At a lower frequency, such as monthly, it works less well unless there is an economic reason to expect the staleness of the return process to have this functional form. For example, Getmansky, Lo, and Makarov (2004) argue that this functional form is appropriate for hedge funds. They also propose other functional form for the staleness of the return process. Once the functional form is assumed, the econometrician may use a standard technique such as Maximum Likelihood to jointly estimate the staleness process and the risk-return parameters.

In this chapter, I implement the simplest technique. I use weekly returns of publicly traded funds and compute their beta as the sum of contemporaneous and 10 lagged of the local market returns expressed in the local currency.

Round Valuation Data

Round valuation data is when the econometrician observes market values at different points in time. This is typical for venture capital data as the portfolio company is valued at each round of financing. These data are not encountered in private equity but it is nonetheless useful for the rest of the discussion to present the methods for these data.

Geometric Returns

A geometric return is trivial to compute. It is simply:

$$\text{Ret}_{geo} = (FV/IV)^\wedge(1/T) \tag{12.1}$$

Where FV is the final value, IV the initial value, and T is time elapsed in between these two valuations.

Unfortunately, these geometric returns are of limited interest. One is typically interested in knowing the return experienced by the "average" investor. For example, what is the return of an individual who would have purchased 1 percent of all the private equity investments, or an individual who would have purchased $1 of all the private equity investments? The average geometric return will not give the answer.

In private equity, there is a large correlation between geometric return and duration (the same is observed in venture capital.) For example, good performance (say 100 percent p.a.) occurs over 2 years on average and bad performance (say −20 percent p.a.) occurs over 10 years on average. If there are as many good as bad performances, the average geometric return is 40 percent, but it is far from what investors will experience in practice.

In terms of solutions, one can weight the observations by duration but this is only a rough correction. Another solution is to first aggregate all the investments and then compute a return. In this case, however, we face intermediary cash flows and we fall in the situation described below for investment level and fund level data.

Abnormal Performance and Risk Measurement

Abnormal performance (alpha) and systematic risk are the statistics of interest and can be found using well-known tools such as Generalized Method of Moments (GMM) or a Maximum Likelihood. The econometrician observes the investment amount (or initial valuation) IV and the next valuation amount (or liquidation value) FV for project j. Furthermore and as always, the econometrician assumes an asset pricing model. For instance, she can assume a CAPM model (more specifically a one-market factor model) and thus write:

$$IV_j * (1 + Rf_1 + \alpha + \beta \cdot (Rm_1 - Rf_1) + \varepsilon_{j,1}) \cdots (1 + Rf_T + \alpha + \beta \cdot (Rm_T - Rf_T)$$
$$+ \varepsilon_{j,T}) = FV_j \tag{12.2}$$

for each pair of $(IV,FV)_j$. Or, equivalently, taking the log on each side, gives:

$$\ln(1 + Rf_1 + \alpha + \beta \cdot (Rm_1 - Rf_1) + \varepsilon_{j,1}) + \cdots + \ln(1 + Rf_T + \alpha + \beta \cdot (Rm_T - Rf_T)$$
$$+ \varepsilon_{j,T}) = \ln(\text{multiple}_j) \tag{12.3}$$

With $\text{multiple}_j := FV_j / IV_j$

Alternatively, the econometrician may assume a log-CAPM (e.g., Cochrane, 2005) and write:

$$T \cdot g + d \cdot (\ln((Rm_1 - Rf_1) + \cdots + (Rm_T - Rf_T)) + Rf_1 + \cdots + Rf_T + u_j$$
$$= \ln(\text{multiple}_j) \tag{12.4}$$

The correspondence between the pair (α, β) and the pair (d, g) is provided by Cochrane (2005, 20, fn 5).

At this stage, the econometrician has several options. One option consists in assuming a distribution for the idiosyncratic shocks $\varepsilon_{j,t}$ (or u_j) and using a

Maximum Likelihood method. That would be along the lines of Cochrane (2005). Another option is to apply GMM. A third and somewhat simpler option is to take a first order Taylor expansion of the above equation. This gives:

$$\alpha + A(Rf_t) + \beta \cdot A(Rm_t - Rf_t) + A(\varepsilon_t) = \ln(\text{multiple}^{1/\text{duration}}) \tag{12.5}$$

where $A(\cdot)$ is defined as the time-series average operator.

This equation can be readily estimated by simply running a cross-sectional OLS regression of $\ln(\text{multiple}^{1/\text{duration}})$ as dependent variable and the average excess market return during the life of the investment as independent variable. Keep in mind that we are on the subset of investments that have no intermediary distributions. If it is not the case, this regression will not provide the correct beta even if the Taylor approximation is precise.

Tackling the Data Issues

There are two types of issues with these data. First is the fact that some round valuations are missing. For example, one observes the valuation of Google at round 1, 4, and 6. This is a problem because money is added at each round. If a round is missing, the econometrician observes an invested amount that is too low and will mechanically overestimate return. The second data issue is that an investment that performs poorly is unlikely to have a new round or an exit. Hence returns cannot be computed for poorly performing investments. This is a classical case of sample selection bias. Ignoring it would again lead to exaggerated returns.

The methods above were described without taking into account these two data issues. Two significant efforts have been made to do so. First, Cochrane (2005) integrates the two data corrections into his maximum likelihood estimation. That is, he estimates the probability that a data point is an error, or is missing, and so forth, and the corresponding market values in each case. In addition, he models the exit process. He assumes that an investment is exited if it reaches a certain threshold value, which is a parameter also estimated by Maximum Likelihood. Second, Korteweg and Sorensen (2008) propose a Bayesian approach for the sample selection bias correction, based on Gibbs sampling. Observations with missing round valuations are discarded. Again, both methods are applied to venture capital and cannot be directly used for private equity because of the intermediate cash flows.

Time-Series Approach: Building an Index

The most common and probably most intuitive approach is to build an index and use traditional time-series techniques to estimate risk and abnormal return. The most significant effort in this vein is that of Woodward and Hall (2003). They interpolate the missing market values at a monthly frequency for every company every month from inception to exit (or present). The interpolation exercise is done via a statistical model using observed market values. This method is similar to the repeated sales approach that is widely used in real estate. All the market values are then aggregated, which constitute the index. This index is then used to refine the interpolations and this iterative procedure is repeated until convergence. This approach is new and the statistical properties of the so-obtained index (e.g., consistency, small sample properties) are yet unknown. A priori, it also tackles the data issues mentioned above by replacing any missing valuation (both intermediaries and final). Finally, note that Woodward and Hall (2003) mention that given the large size skew in venture capital, 100 portfolio companies contribute about a third of the index.

Once the index is constructed, arithmetic returns are simply the times-series average of monthly returns, abnormal returns, and risk exposures and are obtained simply by time-series OLS. Note that given that the index is based on market values, there is no *a priori* justification for using lagged risk factors to obtain risk exposures. In other words, if the model for market values is correctly specified, lagged risk factors should have no explanatory power.

Investment and Fund Data

Econometrically, the situation is the same for investment level and fund level data; hence, the same approaches can be used. Average geometric returns can be computed using IRR or Modified IRR (see Phalippou 2008 for a discussion). The same issues as those mentioned above are present.

To compute abnormal performance and risk, the econometrician observes a series of cash flows without knowing the investment amount that corresponds to each distribution. This is the most commonly encountered situation, and probably the most relevant (as it is what investors face) and most challenging.

Just as with the round valuation data above, the econometrician needs to assume some cross-sectional restrictions for risk. To keep exposition simple, I make the same assumptions as above and thus start with equation (2).[5] Now, however, the correspondence between each investment and its final value is unknown. The econometrician thus faces a pool of investments and needs to bring all the underlying investments to a common date. To see this, multiply each side of equation (2) by

$$(1 + Rf_{1+T} + \alpha + \beta \cdot (Rm_{1+T} - Rf_{1+T}) + \varepsilon_{j,1+T}) \cdots (1 + Rf_E + \alpha + \beta \cdot (Rm_E - Rf_E)$$
$$+ \varepsilon_{j,E}) \tag{12.6}$$

where E is the date at which the fund (i.e., the pool of investments) is liquidated.

It means that the econometrician compounds all the dividends until date E. Next, she adds the left-hand side and right-hand side of the equation. This aggregation can be at the fund level or at a portfolio of funds level. At that stage, it does not matter anymore to know which dividend came from which cash flow. After the aggregation, it is observationally equivalent. The econometrician now faces a cross section of equations that can serve as an input to either a Maximum Likelihood estimator or a Generalized Method of Moments (GMM) estimator.

Driessen, Lin, and Phalippou (DLP 2008) explore the latter. This has the advantage of avoiding distributional assumptions on the returns but brings some new issues. To minimize these issues, they show by simulations that it is best to make the above aggregation at the vintage-year level. That is, all funds raised in the same vintage year are pooled together. If one works at the investment level, one could group all the investments made in the same year. In addition, they find that it is better to take the logarithm on both sides of the equation (after aggregation). Next, one simply minimizes the sum of the squared difference between the left-hand side and right-hand side of each equation with respect to the abnormal performance and risk parameters. This can be done with any numerical method and software, including Excel. Finally, inference is tricky due to a lack of time-series. DLP use a bootstrapping technique on the assumption that errors are not cross-sectionally correlated. They show a diagnostic test that indicates that it is a reasonable assumption in their sample, but it may not always be true.

RESULTS

Publicly Traded Vehicles

Bilo, Christophers, Degosciu, and Zimmermann (2005) is the only comprehensive study I know of that estimates the risk profile of listed vehicles and their work is behind the creation of a private equity index called LPX. They report 287 vehicles in their article, but their inclusion criterion is not specified.[6] They form an index with all the selected vehicles and report a CAPM beta of 1.2 and a negative alpha (−1.2 percent a year).

Exhibit 12.1 shows the alpha and beta in my sample of publicly traded firms. These are obtained in a traditional fashion by regressing the weekly returns of each firm on the local stock market index. Returns start in June 1993, hence a maximum of 15 years of data is used. Alpha ranges from −10 percent annually (SoPaf) to 20 percent (Jafco). Over the last three years, however, Jafco has one of the lowest alphas.

Beta range from 0.2 to 3.8. The average alpha is 6 percent per annum and average beta is 1.5. Restricting the analysis to the last three years—which minimizes sample selection issues—reduces alpha to 5 percent per annum and beta to 1.4.

Hence, at least for liquid publicly traded funds, past performance seems good and the risk relatively low. However, it is difficult to draw strong conclusions from this sample. First, these returns are achievable only to an investor who could predict that these funds would have high liquidity and that they will survive until 2005. Nonetheless, there have not been major bankruptcies of private equity listed funds that I know of. In addition, liquidity seems to be relatively stable and thus relatively easy to predict. It is also the case that the less liquid funds also seem to have positive alpha, although their illiquidity negatively affect the precision of this estimate. Finally, a first look at publicly traded venture capital funds gives a different picture. Although this is besides the scope of this chapter, many venture capital funds got bankrupt and average performance appears low in venture capital even among survivors.

Round Data

As mentioned above, the results here are for venture capital but may still be of interest. Cochrane finds an arithmetic return of 59 percent p.a., but argues that it is lower than small growth stock performance over the same period (62 percent). The beta for venture capital reported by Korteweg and Sorensen (2008) is around 2.6 to 3 (as in et al. 2008) while Cochrane's estimate is 1.9. Cochrane (2005b) and Korteweg and Sorensen (2008) report large positive before-fee alphas for simple returns (30 percent and over 150 percent annual, respectively). With the same data, Woodward and Hall (2003) find a much lower rate of return (4.6 percent per quarter) from 1990 to 2003. That would turn into a negative alpha given betas of 2 and more, which would be consistent with Driessen, Lin, and Phalippou's (2008) findings.

Investment Data

In Exhibit 12.3, I provide a sense of the distribution of multiples and IRRs based on the Phalippou-Gottschalg proprietary dataset for private equity investments made between 1973 and 2003 (most are from 1984 to 2003). Performance is gross of fees and as reported on fund-raising prospectuses. Investments done less than two years before the prospectus date are excluded to minimize the impact of investments held at cost. The median investment as a (gross-of-fees) multiple of 1.80 (all) and 2.25 (liquidated) and an IRR of 20 percent (all) and 31 percent (liquidated).[7] One can see how the sample of liquidated investments is more skewed, with 20 percent of the investments with an IRR above 84 percent and a multiple above 4.76. Another interesting aspect is the relatively small number of bankrupted investments (less than 20 percent). Lopez-de-Silanes and Phalippou (2008) show more detailed statistics on the distribution of performance.

It is, however, important to bear in mind that knowing the average or median IRR/multiple is of little use to assess the performance of an asset class. This because they cannot be benchmarked and, even as a measure of absolute performance, they are of limited interest. IRR cannot be averaged (since it is a geometric average and investments have different durations), but even if it could be averaged, its implicit reinvestment assumption means that the average IRR can be far away from the overall performance experienced by investors. Multiple is equally worthless since without knowing the exact duration, multiple is of little use. The only exception is with extreme multiples. If multiple is below 0.5, we know that performance is bad

Exhibit 12.3 Private Equity Investments: Proprietary Sample

	Liquidated (N_obs = 2,637)		All (N_obs = 4,139)	
	Multiple	IRR	Multiple	IRR
10th percentile	0.00	−1.00	0.04	−1.00
20th percentile	0.41	−0.22	0.53	−0.16
30th percentile	1.33	0.10	1.00	0.00
40th percentile	1.80	0.21	1.35	0.10
50th percentile	2.25	0.31	1.80	0.20
60th percentile	2.76	0.42	2.27	0.30
70th percentile	3.50	0.57	2.88	0.43
80th percentile	4.76	0.84	3.95	0.65
90th percentile	8.20	1.52	6.50	1.20

no matter the duration and if multiple is above 4, we know it is good no matter the duration. The statistics presented in Lopez-de-Silanes and Phalippou (2008) should thus mainly be used to learn about the distribution of performance and treated with caution when looking at averages.

This remark holds for any investment performance data. However, if one has the exact cash-flows for each investment (e.g., CEPRES dataset, Ljungqvist-Richardson dataset), one could apply the above technique and find the true abnormal performance and risk of the asset class.

Fund Data

Using cash flow data from TVE until December 2003, Phalippou and Gottschalg (PG 2008) report that overall private equity funds performance is slightly below that of the S&P 500. Driessen et al. (DLP 2008) find beta around 0.5. In this case, private equity funds have a positive but not statistically significant alpha. Hence if beta is indeed in the range of 0.5, the performance of private equity funds is "normal." However, DLP have relatively large standard errors for their subsample of private equity funds (unlike with the subsample of venture capital funds). So, further work is necessary to assess the risk of private equity investments.

In Exhibit 12.4, I show publicly available performance statistics from TVE as of December 2007. I do not have access to the underlying cash flows, hence cannot say anything precise about risk and return. Panel A shows that performance of the 291 U.S. private equity funds raised from 1980 to 1997 is poor and a substantial amount is unrealized value. The realized multiple is 1.3, which means that irrespective of the duration of the funds, it is likely to be less than public markets. The final NAV is 30 percent of the amount invested, which seems quite large given that these funds are 10 years or older. The 163 EU private equity funds raised over the same period seems to have done better (the answer depends on their duration). Panel C shows that funds covered by PG (funds raised between 1980 to 1993) had better performance. Hence more recent data seem to accentuate the low performance result of PG.

One of the polemical aspects of the PG study was the choice of writing-off the NAVs of the mature and inactive funds. They justified this choice by the fact that for most of these mature funds the same NAV was repeated for many quarters/years without any cash-flow activity. Hence, they thought that it means that the fund is effectively liquidated and has no valuable investments. It is thus interesting to see what has happened with these written-off NAVs four years later. Panel C shows the 12 billion NAV reported as of the end of 2003 that was written off by PG. Four years later, this NAV amount has hardly changed and hardly any cash has been paid in the meantime. These 14-years-old and more funds still report an NAV equal to almost 20 percent of their investments. This means that it was probably more accurate to write-off the NAVs of old and inactive funds rather than treating them as market values.

CalPERSs performance is shown in Exhibit 12.5 for their 1991–1997 private equity funds. It has a multiple (net-of-fees) of 1.7. This number is the same as the TVE number in Panel A and what PG report. Hence, based on this rough estimate of performance, CalPERs appears to be an average performer and TVE statistics may not be too far off reality.

Exhibit 12.4 Private Equity Funds: VentureXpert Summary Cash-Flow Data

Panel A: Private Equity Funds Raised, 1980–1997, U.S. as Primary Market

Year	N	Cash In	Cash Out	Stock Out	NAV	Total
. . .						
2003	291	933	8,116	350	58,822	n.m.
. . .						
2007	291	27	2,703	103	36,974	n.m.
Total		126,245	165,527	12,685	36,974	215,186
Multiples			1.31			1.70

Panel B: Private Equity Funds Raised, 1980–1997, EU as Primary Market

Year	N	Cash In	Cash Out	Stock Out	NAV	Total
. . .						
2003	162	156	1,801	0	11,246	n.m.
. . .						
2007	163	57	1,127	0	4,624	n.m.
Total		22,449	37,400	1,259	4,624	43,283
Multiples			1.67			1.93

Panel C: Private Equity Funds Raised, 1980–1993, U.S. as Primary Market

Year	N	Cash In	Cash Out	Stock Out	NAV	Total
. . .						
2003	158	21	787	63	11,980	n.m.
. . .						
2007	158	0	127	47	9,291	n.m.
Total		52,746	92,447	8,307	9,291	110,045
Multiples			1.75			2.08

Panel D: Private Equity Funds Raised, 1980–1993, EU as Primary Market

Year	N	Cash In	Cash Out	Stock Out	NAV	Total
. . .						
2003	88	1	99	0	1,472	n.m.
. . .						
2007	88	0	49	0	1,174	n.m.
Total		7,701	11,203	1,151	1,174	13,528
Multiples			1,45			1.76

Panel E: Private Equity Funds Raised, 1991–1997, U.S. as Primary Market

Year	N	Cash In	Cash Out	Stock Out	NAV	Total
. . .						
2003	176	933	7,815	350	52,791	n.m.
. . .						
2007	176	27	2,703	103	32,008	n.m.
Total		89,175	96,655	7,766	32,008	136,429
Multiples			1.08			1.53

This table shows private equity fund cash-flow statistics from VentureXpert in the years 2003 and 2007. Performance is as of December 2007. The total amount invested (cash in), distributed in cash or in stock (cash out, stock out) and net asset value at the end of the year are all in million of U.S. dollars. The total is taken over all the years (1980–2007). Multiple is the total value distributed divided by amount invested. All figures are net of fees.

Exhibit 12.5   Private Equity Funds—CalPERS Report

Name	Vintage	Cash In	Out	Total	Multiple	IRR
Permira Europe I	1997	84	217	224	2.70	0.75
Doughty Hanson Fund II	1995	44	85	91	2.10	0.46
Blackstone Capital Partners II	1994	84	175	181	2.10	0.37
WLR Recovery Fund I	1997	50	169	176	3.50	0.35
Hellman & Friedman C.P. III	1995	120	275	275	2.30	0.35
Permira U.K. Venture III	1991	13	37	37	2.80	0.31
Madison Dearborn C.P. I	1993	97	300	331	3.40	0.28
First Reserve Fund VI	1992	35	99	99	2.80	0.26
GTCR (Golder et al.) IV	1994	25	53	53	2.10	0.25
Carlyle Partners II	1996	86	187	195	2.30	0.25
CVC European Equity Partners I	1996	53	125	143	2.70	0.24
Madison Dearborn C.P. II	1997	60	136	146	2.40	0.23
Hellman & Friedman C.P. II	1991	87	239	239	2.70	0.23
Hicks, Muse, Tate & Furst Eq. II	1994	110	220	221	2.00	0.19
WCAS (Welsh et al.) VII	1995	150	314	330	2.20	0.18
FS Equity Partners III	1994	75	164	165	2.20	0.16
TCW Special Credits V—pp	1994	35	61	61	1.70	0.15
Permira U.K. Venture IV	1996	26	43	44	1.70	0.15
Green Equity Investors II	1994	74	153	155	2.10	0.14
Blackstone Capital Partners III	1997	216	316	373	1.70	0.14
WCAS (Welsh et al.) VI	1993	50	97	101	2.00	0.13
Ethos Private Equity Fund III	1996	26	42	43	1.60	0.13
Levine Leichtman C.P. I	1994	108	121	124	1.20	0.12
1818 Fund II	1993	75	117	125	1.70	0.11
GTCR (Golder et al.) V	1997	40	70	74	1.80	0.11
Bachow Investment Partners III	1994	38	39	43	1.10	0.11
Apollo Investment Fund III	1995	137	207	212	1.50	0.11
OCM Opportunities Fund I	1996	20	32	32	1.60	0.10
Aurora Equity Partners I	1994	27	34	42	1.60	0.10
McCown De Leeuw & Co. III	1995	51	67	68	1.30	0.10
Generation Capital Partners	1996	53	52	66	1.20	0.07
Lombard/Pacific Partners	1995	355	467	470	1.30	0.06
Fenway Partners Capital Fund I	1996	99	99	100	1.00	0.00
Stonington Capital Appr '94 Fd	1994	101	42	96	1.00	−0.01
PENMAN PE & Mezzanine Fd	1994	13	11	11	0.90	−0.03
Doyle & Boissiere Fund I	1997	74	33	58	0.80	−0.04
McCown De Leeuw & Co. IV	1997	88	52	66	0.70	−0.05
Beacon Group Energy Inv Fd	1994	132	94	95	0.70	−0.08
TSG Capital Fund II	1995	49	31	32	0.70	−0.09
Beacon Group III, Focus Value	1996	63	11	15	0.20	−0.23
Median					1.70	0.14
Average (value-weighted)					1.72	0.14
Total		**3123**	**5086**	**5412**	**1.73**	**n.a.**

This table shows all the private equity funds in which CalPERS invested until 1997. Performance is as of December 2007. The total amount invested (cash in), distributed (out) and total value (net asset value plus total distributed) are all in millions of U.S. dollars. Multiple is the total value distributed divided by amount invested. All figures are net of fees.

ADDITIONAL DISCUSSION

Examples of the Challenge Facing Performance Evaluation

Onex

Onex is perceived by many investors as one of the best buyout firms in the world. In the summer of 2006 they raised a $3 billion fund. Their track record at that moment is shown in Exhibit 12.2 (displayed on their web site). The objective here is not to criticise or praise Onex but to simply illustrate the challenges of performance measurement in this asset class.

Investments that are substantially realized and those publicly traded are shown first and separately (Panel A of Exhibit 12.2). Overall IRR and multiple are respectively 36 percent and 3.3. Realized investments are displayed next (Panel B of Exhibit 12.2). Overall IRR and multiple are respectively 26 percent and 2.7. Next, nonexited investments are shown without performance. Note that, as discussed in Phalippou (2008), negative IRRs are not reported.

This way of showing performance is typical in this asset class and the potential investor can be only impressed at first sight with such figures. Properly assessing past performance, however, is quite difficult and one should quickly realize that nothing can be said from the previously mentioned numbers.

It is clear that some large dividends have been paid in the mid-1980s. By pooling all these investments together, it is assumed that these early large dividends have been reinvested at a rate of return of 26 percent (or 36 percent) per year for as long as 20 years. These reinvested dividends are so large (after 20 years of earning 26 percent to 36 percent returns!) that irrespective of what recent performance has been, the IRR would indicate high performance (see also Phalippou, 2008, for a discussion). But this is not what investors will have experienced.

The multiple is not useful either because we do not know how long the investments were held for. If a multiple of three is obtained over eight years, it is far less than the performance of stock markets. If it is obtained over four years, then it is far above the performance of stock markets.[8]

Next, and importantly, the separation of exited and unrealized investments creates a sample selection bias. In Panel C of Exhibit 12.2, I group all the investments made between 1984 and 2000. This way there is no sample selection bias because all investments that are more than six years old are selected. Two investments are not valued. If their IRR is below 18 percent (and their multiple below 1.8), then the median IRR of all investments done by Onex is 18 percent and the median multiple is 1.8. This is much less impressive than the initially displayed numbers.

American Capital

Panel D of Exhibit 12.2 shows the exited buyout investments of American Capital. They report only IRR and entry/exit dates. The median duration is 3.5 years and the median IRR is 22 percent. As discussed in Phalippou and Gottschalg (2008) and in this chapter, a striking characteristic of private equity performance data is the negative relation between duration and IRR. It can be seen here. The worse performing investments (in the bottom half in terms of performance) have an average duration of 4.6 years while the investments in the top half have an average duration of 2.9 years. This is important because it says that the unexited and old investments are likely to have lower performance, with all else equal, making the sample bias discussed above worse. It also means that the average IRR will be biased upward. American Capital does not provide a performance for their unexited investments, but some of them are old (four are more than eight years old). Panel E shows all the buyout investments that are more than six years old. If the unexited investments are worthless (worst-case-scenario IRR1) then the median IRR is −13 percent. If the missing IRRs are 10 percent (IRR2) then the median IRR is also 10 percent. In both cases, after this basic sample selection bias correction, the performance is much lower than it seemed at first sight.

CalPERS

Three extra remarks are worth making based on CalPERS performance report. First, the top IRR is 75 percent and the bottom one −23 percent. However, investors have not experience a 75 percent rate of return unless all the dividends were reinvested at that rate all the way to December 2007, which seems implausible. Similarly, investors have not reinvested dividends at a −23 percent rate of return. Hence these IRRs are not informative and their average is even less so.

Second, the wide dispersion in IRR is not mirrored by multiples. Multiples vary between 0.2 and 3.5. For a four-year investment, that would correspond to a rate of return between −33 percent and 37 percent. This illustrates the point in Phalippou (2008) that IRRs exaggerate the perceived dispersion in performance. Third, even though these funds have all reached the normal liquidation age, they still report an NAV of more than 10 percent the value invested. Fourth, the ranking of performance differs if one uses IRR or multiple. The two highest multiple funds are only ranked fourth and seventh with IRR.

Additional Corrections

Performance and risk estimates should also take into account three aspects of private equity funds. To my knowledge, none of them have been addressed in the literature yet.

First is the fact that capital is committed at the beginning of the fund's life and is called at random times. This credit line granted by investors affects the return and risk profile of private equity funds. For example, if an investor does not make a payment, then she may pay a penalty (or be excluded). Also, investors may face larger capital calls when the markets are illiquid, thereby putting an extra cost. Another channel is that the speed at which capital is called may be a function of stock market returns, thereby affecting risk.[9] If investors put their committed capital in an S&P 500 index fund, they prefer it if less capital is called after the market went down because they have to put less capital on the index fund for a given amount of committed capital. If funds are more likely to call after stock markets went down, then investors need to put aside more capital to face the call, which increases their cost.[10]

A second aspect to take into account is that investor's stakes in a given fund are not readily transferable, that is, it is illiquid. This fact affects both risk and return because if the investor is hit by a bad shock, she has to sell the private equity stake at a substantial discount or may not be able to sell it at all. If the investor has zero probability to sell a private equity stake then the illiquidity is not an issue. However, if the probability is nonzero, the cost may be high. Investors in general ask for large compensations for holding illiquid assets (e.g., see Aragon [2007] for hedge funds and Dimson and Hanke [2004] for bonds, among others).[11] In private equity, some "fire sales" have also been witnessed, mainly by banks. For example, in 2001 most banks decided to reduce their exposures to private equity and could not readily do so. Famous examples include that of JP Morgan and Deutsche Bank. In 2000, JPMorgan sold $1 billion on the secondary market with a large discount and sold an extra $0.5 billion via securitization in 2001 to 2002.[12]

Third is the fact that distributions are sometimes made in shares and not in cash. However, as can be seen from Exhibit 12.4, it seems a minor issue for private equity. For venture capital funds, the issue is of first order.

Other Approaches to Estimate Risk and Abnormal Return

Using Intermediate NAVs

Unlike hedge funds or mutual funds, private equity funds do not provide liquidity at the reported NAV. Hence private equity funds do not have strong incentives to mark to market the value of their ongoing investments. The NAVs are thus typically the cost of the investments, especially in private equity (it is less so in venture capital). If one nonetheless assumes that NAVs are unbiased estimates of real fund market value but are stale, then a common approach is to apply to private equity the so-called Dimson (1979) approach (e.g., Jones and Rhodes-Kropf 2004).

I apply this approach using TVE cash flows dataset. Specifically, I calculate the quarterly return series of each private equity fund using their NAV. Betas are then estimated via a time-series OLS regression of returns on contemporaneous and lagged risk factors (market excess return):

$$R_t^{PE} - Rf_t = \alpha + \beta_0(Rm_t - Rf_t) + \cdots + \beta_K(Rm_{t-K} - Rf_{t-K}) + \varepsilon_t \qquad (12.7)$$

where K is the number of lags.

Results are shown in Exhibit 12.6. I find low market beta and high alpha. This method contains a severe bias in the private equity context and does not lead to consistent estimates. The main sign of such inconsistency in the empirical results is that the coefficients on lagged market returns do not decrease regularly. For example, the market returns three quarters ago are significantly related to fund returns, but the market returns one and two quarters ago are typically unrelated to fund returns. The loadings on Fama-French factors show similar irregularities and switch signs at different lags (not tabulated).

Furthermore, results are sensitive to the choice of the starting date. The main reason is that NAVs equal capital invested at the beginning of fund's life and no dividend is paid yet, hence returns are close to zero at the beginning of the time series. Then little by little, as dividends start to be paid, returns become more volatile. It is not clear whether one should skip the initial quarters and if so, how

Exhibit 12.6   NAV-Based Regression Approach for Private Equity Funds

	Default Sample					Jones and Rhodes-Kropf Sample				
	Spec 1	Spec 2	Spec 3	Spec 4	Spec 5	Spec 1	Spec 2	Spec 3	Spec 4	Spec 5
Alpha	0.07	0.06	0.05	0.05	0.05	0.08	0.08	0.06	0.06	0.05
	2.95	*2.64*	*1.94*	*1.68*	*1.38*	*3.46*	*3.07*	*2.28*	*1.69*	*1.57*
Beta (t)	0.13	0.13	0.15	0.16	0.28	0.16	0.16	0.15	0.14	0.19
	1.84	*1.94*	*2.54*	*2.19*	*4.02*	*2.13*	*2.16*	*2.48*	*1.70*	*2.07*
Beta ($t-1$)		0.09	0.09	0.07	0.17		0.05	0.05	0.06	0.11
		1.79	*1.72*	*0.94*	*2.06*		*0.71*	*0.85*	*0.80*	*1.50*
Beta ($t-2$)			0.02	0.02	−0.02			0.07	0.03	0.06
			0.25	*0.15*	*−0.18*			*1.00*	*0.28*	*0.68*
Beta ($t-3$)			0.17	0.17	0.16			0.17	0.18	0.21
			3.23	*2.33*	*2.10*			*2.75*	*1.86*	*2.07*
Beta ($t-4$)			−0.03	−0.03	−0.08			0.03	0.07	0.06
			−0.27	*−0.25*	*−0.55*			*0.33*	*0.45*	*0.39*
β_{SMB} (t)				−0.07	−0.03				−0.03	0.02
				−0.69	*−0.28*				*−0.35*	*0.24*
β_{HML} (t)				0.02	0.05				−0.04	−0.03
				0.21	*0.50*				*−0.46*	*−0.35*
Lagged β_{SMB}, β_{HML}	no	no	no	yes	yes	no	no	no	yes	yes
$\sum$ Beta	0.13	0.23	0.40	0.39	0.51	0.16	0.21	0.48	0.47	0.64
$\sum \beta_{SMB}$				−0.21	0.06				−0.16	0.11
$\sum \beta_{HML}$				0.02	0.08				0.01	0.07
Adj. R^2	0.04	0.05	0.11	0.08	0.14	0.06	0.05	0.11	0.07	0.09
N_obs	80.00	80.00	80.00	80.00	64.00	85.00	85.00	85.00	85.00	77.00

This table shows results from NAV-based time-series regressions. The dependent variable is the quarterly excess return computed as ($\sum$ NAV$_t$ + $\sum$ Dividends$_{(t-1\,to\,t)}$ − $\sum$ Capital_Invested$_{(t-1\,to\,t)}$) / $\sum$ NAV$_{t-1}$ − 1 − Rf), where the sum is taken across all funds. Independent variables are contemporaneous and lagged quarterly excess S&P 500 returns, contemporaneous and lagged SMB returns and HML returns. In specification 5, the first two years of data are skipped. Robust t-statistics are reported in italics. Alpha is annualized and the sum of betas (contemporaneous plus lagged betas) is shown under each specification. The default sample consist of returns from 1985 to 2003 of funds raised between 1984 and 1993. Jones and Rhodes-Kropf sample consists of returns from 1981 to June 2002 of funds raised between 1980 and 1999.

many. In specification 5, I skip the first two years and the market beta increases by 20 percent. When the sample time period changes slightly (from my default sample to that of Jones and Rhodes-Kropf sample), beta decreases by one third.

Using Publicly Traded Stocks

Finance textbooks typical advice for computing the risk of a nontraded asset is to find a matching asset in the public arena. Hence, one may match each private equity portfolio company to estimate the publicly traded stock of a company in the same industry and similar size. For buyout, an extra adjustment is made to risk due to leverage. This procedure is used by Groh and Gottschalg (2008), Ljungqvist and Richardson (2003), and Phalippou and Gottschalg (2008). This typically generates high betas as the match has typically a beta around 1 and leverage brings the beta in the range of 1.5 to 2. The limitation of this approach is that one makes a strong assumption when assuming that the beta of a publicly traded company in the same industry is the same.

One may also use post-IPO risk profiles of ex private equity companies. Cao and Lerner (2009) report post IPO market beta of 1.3. However, risk during the private equity phase may differ from the post private equity phase. In addition, companies that go public may have different risk profiles from those the representative private equity portfolio company.

CONCLUSION

After reviewing the academic literature on risk and return of private equity and adding original data analysis, the picture that emerges contrasts with that of the general public. It may then be interesting to turn to the investor side and see what private equity investors think. A clear statement made by an investor who is perceived as the most knowledgeable on this asset class is that of David Swensen, Yale's CIO, in his investment book: "While the value added by operationally oriented buyout partnerships may, in certain instances, overcome the burden imposed by the typical buyout fund's generous fee structure, in aggregate, buyout investments fail to match public alternatives. ... In the absence of truly superior fund selection skills (or extraordinary luck), investors should stay far, far away from private equity investments. ... Some part of the failure of buyout managers to produce risk-adjusted returns stems from the inappropriate fee structure. ... Because the incentive compensation fails to consider the investor's cost of capital, buyout partnerships capture 20 percent of the returns generated by favorable wind at the long-term equity investor's back. ... The large majority of buyout funds fail to add sufficient value to overcome a grossly unreasonable fee structure" (Swensen 2005, 133–135). I believe this statement is consistent with the above analysis.

APPENDIX 12.A: DISCUSSION ON STALENESS CORRECTION

Applying the Dimson approach to private equity data is theoretically problematic. The reason is that the staleness is clearly in NAVs and not on the returns. Staleness in NAVs can be captured by assuming that NAV_t is equal to the true fund market value at time t with probability θ and to the true fund market value at time $t - 1$ with probability $1 - \theta$. Hence the expected change in the log of NAV writes:

$$E(d \cdot \ln(NAV_t)) = \theta\, d \cdot \ln(P_t) + (1 - \theta)d \cdot \ln(P_{t-1})$$

Where d is the time-series difference operator.

When the delta of log prices is close enough to the return and assuming the CAPM, we obtain:

$$NAV_t/NAV_{t-1} = 1 + Rf + \theta * B * (Rm_t - Rf) + (1 - \theta) * B * (Rm_{t-1} - Rf)$$

The usual result follows that if one adds the coefficients on lagged market returns, then the right beta is estimated. But for private equity funds, the returns are observed quarterly and are highly volatile, hence the delta of log prices can be very far from the rate of return. This means that the usual approach sketched above and based on Dimson (1979) for daily stock returns in *inconsistent* in a statistical sense. That is, estimates of risk are systematically biased.

However, one can still reach consistency by making a distributional assumption such as log-normality. The question will then be whether this is an appropriate distributional assumption. Another possibility is to assume that $E(NAV_t / NAV_{t-1}) = \theta R(t) + (1 - \theta) R(t - i)$ as Getmansky, Lo, and Makarov (2004) do for hedge funds. In private equity, it does not seem a natural assumption.

NOTES

1. In the United Kingdom, these vehicles are important in private equity, mainly due to some special tax alleviation provisions.

2. If I set the limit to 20 percent of the weeks with zero return, the number of observations increases to 56.

3. Local indices provided by Datastream are: S&P 500 composite for the United States, the SBF 120 for France, FTSE All Shares for the United Kingdom, Dax 30 for Germany. . . . All returns are in local currency.

4. A second difference between the round valuation returns and those experienced by investors comes from fees. As fees vary across funds, over time, and are nonlinear in performance, they affect estimates of both risk and abnormal return. Finally, a third difference stems from the fact that the stake of fund managers in a company changes over the project's life. If the stake of a fund manager is higher when the expected return is higher, then the investor's performance will be superior to that of the project. The project and investor risk/return measures may very well be close to one another, but there has not been any evidence on this yet.

5. Relaxing this assumption is trivial (see Driessen et al. 2008).

6. However, using Capital IQ and including venture capital as a stage of interest, I obtain a similar number.

7. Cumming and Walz (2007) report similar descriptive statistics for their subset of private equity investments.

8. We would thus need a cash-flow-weighted duration. Note that knowing entry and exit dates would not be enough. Funds sometimes invest more than once in a company. The entry date is typically that of the first investment. Similarly, when reported, the exit date is often that of the first partial exit. Hence, even if entry/exit dates are reported, duration is still unknown and the multiple is still not informative.

9. Ljungqvist, Richardson, and Wolfenson (2008) find that after controlling for a number of variables, the market returns do not affect the speed of investment. But they do not show a specification with only the market return; hence, we do not know yet the systematic risk of capital calls.

10. In addition, most management fees are paid on capital committed. If the capital is uncalled, then investor pay fees on this capital to have it invested (e.g., fees on their stock or bond holding). Uncalled capital is therefore costly. Uncertainty about the rate of the calls also affects the total fee bill, hence performance.

11. The reader may refer to Lerner and Schoar (2004) for a theory on the illiquidity of private equity funds.

12. Note that a market for private equity stakes is developing, so the compensation for illiquidity may decrease over time.

REFERENCES

Aragon, George. 2007. Share restrictions and asset pricing: Evidence from the hedge fund industry." *Journal of Financial Economics* 83 (1):33–58.

Bilo, Stephanie, Hans Christophers, Michel Degosciu, and Heinz Zimmermann. 2005. Risk, returns, and biases of listed private equity portfolio. Working Paper, University of Basel.

Cao, J., and L. Lerner. 2009. The performance of reverse leveraged buyouts. *Journal of Financial Economics* 91:139–157.

Cochrane, John. 2005. The risk and return of venture capital. *Journal of Financial Economics* 75:3–52.

Cumming, Douglas, and Uve Walz. 2007. Private equity returns and disclosure around the world. *Journal of International Business Studies*, forthcoming.

Dimson, Elroy. 1979. Risk measurement when shares are subject to infrequent trading. *Journal of Financial Economics* 7 (2):197–226.

Dimson, Elroy, Bernd Hanke. 2004. The expected illiquidity premium: Evidence from Equity Index–linked bonds. *Review of Finance* 8 (1):19–47.

Driessen, Joost, Lin Tse-Chun, and Ludovic Phalippou. 2008. A new method to estimate risk and return of non-traded assets from cash flows: The case of private equity funds. NBER Working Paper 14144.

Getmansky, Mila, Andrew Lo, and Igor Makarov, 2004. An econometric model of serial correlation and illiquidity in hedge fund returns. *Journal of Financial Economics* 74:529–610.

Groh, Alexander, and Oliver Gottschalg. 2008. Measuring the risk-adjusted performance of U.S. buyouts. NBER Working Paper 14148.

Jones, Charles, and Matthew Rhodes-Kropf. 2004. The price of diversifiable risk in venture capital and private equity. Working Paper, Columbia University.

Kaplan, Steve, and Antoinette Schoar. 2005. Private equity performance: Returns, persistence, and capital flows. *Journal of Finance* 60:1791–1823.

Korteweg, Arthur, and Morten Sorensen. 2008. Risk and return of infrequently traded assets: A Bayesian selection model of venture capital. Noncirculating Working Paper.

Lerner, Josh, and Antoinette Schoar, 2004. The illiquidity puzzle: Theory and evidence from private equity. *Journal of Financial Economics* 72 (1):3–40.

Lopez-de-Silanes, Florencio, and Ludovic Phalippou. 2008. Private equity investments: Performance and diseconomies of scale. *Working Paper*.

Ljungqvist, Alexander, and Matthew Richardson. 2003. The cash flow, return, and risk characteristics of private equity. NBER Working Paper 9454.

Ljungqvist, Alexander, and Matthew Richardson, and Daniel Wolfenson. 2007. The investment behavior of private equity fund managers. NBER Working Paper 14180.

Metrick, Andrew, and Ayako Yasuda. 2007. Economics of private equity funds. Working Paper, Wharton Business School.

Phalippou, Ludovic. 2007. *Investing in private equity funds: A survey*. CFA Institute Literature Survey Series.

Phalippou, Ludovic. 2008. The hazards of using IRR to measure performance: The case of private equity. *Journal of Performance Measurement* 12 (4):55–66.

Phalippou, Ludovic, and Oliver Gottschalg. 2008. The performance of private equity funds. *Review of Financial Studies*, forthcoming.

Swensen David. 2005. *Unconventional success: A fundamental approach to personal investment*. New York: Free Press.

Woodward, Susan E., and Robert E. Hall. 2003. Benchmarking the returns to venture. NBER Working Paper 10,202.

ABOUT THE AUTHOR

Ludovic Phalippou holds degrees from INSEAD (Ph.D. in Finance), the University of Southern California (master's in both Mathematical Finance and Economics), and Toulouse University (B.Sc. in Economics). Ludovic's research has received considerable attention from the investment professional community and the academic community alike. Several major newspapers echoed his findings: *The New York Times, Pensions and Investments, The Wall Street Journal, Euromoney, Le Monde,* the *Financial Times* and *The Economist*. He has received five best-paper awards and six research grants. His research has been presented at the very best academic conferences in both the United States and Europe (AFA, WFA, and EFA), and at seminars in prestigious universities such as University of California-Berkeley, University of Texas-Austin, and Yale University. Finally, his research has been published in top academic journals—*Review of Financial Studies, Journal of Economic Perspectives, Harvard Business Review* and *Review of Finance*—and top practitioner journals—*Financial Analyst Journal* and *Journal of Performance Measurement*. Most of Ludovic's current research efforts are focused on the risk and return of investing in private equity funds.

ACKNOWLEDGMENTS

This manuscript is prepared as a chapter to John Wiley & Sons/Blackwell's *Private Equity*, edited by Douglas Cumming. I am indebted to my coauthors who worked with me on this topic: Joost Driessen, Oliver Gottschalg, Tse-Chun Lin, and Florencio Lopez-de-Silanes. I am also thankful to the many research assistants who have worked long hours with me fighting with the data over the last five years, and in particular to Mariana Popa for her significant input. I am also grateful to Douglas Cumming, Andrea Lowe, and Morten Sorensen for their comments on this draft.

CHAPTER 13

Private Equity Fund Selection

How to Find True Top-Quartile Performers

OLIVER F. GOTTSCHALG
Associate Professor, HEC School of Management

INTRODUCTION[1]

Recent research (e.g., Phalippou and Gottschalg, 2009) reports that the historic performance of private equity (PE) fund investments has been rather disappointing. The average net past performance of these funds remains below the returns to the S&P 500 index by about 3 percent per annum. At the same time, the variance in performance across PE funds is substantial. The performance persistence of private equity fund managers across different generations of funds first found by Kaplan and Schoar (2005) suggests that private equity is an attractive asset class if (and only if) investors are able to identify and invest in those funds managed by the top-performing fund managers.

The observation that entire categories of institutional investors fail to generate attractive returns with their private equity portfolios (Lerner, Shoar, and Wong 2007) suggests that this ability is scarce and difficult to imitate. Data paucity, limited benchmarking possibilities, and the long time lag between commitment decisions and performance outcomes makes private equity fund due diligence still look more like an art than a science and create a situation in which information asymmetries and adverse selection issues (Cumming 2006) create substantial challenges for private equity investors.

This chapter takes a closer look at the phenomenon of performance persistence, adopting the perspective of a potential investor in a newly raised fund. In doing so, and unlike Kaplan and Schoar (2005), it does not correlate end-of-life performance of a sequence of funds managed by the same fund manager, but links the information about past performance available to a potential investor in a new fund to the ultimate performance of this new fund. Typically, an investor observes only two to five years of the performance of the previous fund when commitment decisions need to be taken, rather than the performance of a fund at the end of its ten-year life.

Based on this approach, a variety of absolute and relative performance measures, as well as a number of strategic variables, are analyzed with respect to their link with subsequent performance. In doing so, both the statistical significance and the economic relevance of this link are considered. Motivated by the relatively low economic relevance of simple performance measures as selection criteria, the discussion proceeds to consider alternative benchmarking techniques and to construct an efficient selection model based on the joint consideration of multiple factors.

The chapter begins with a brief synopsis of the relevant literature to develop key hypotheses regarding possible predictors of the future performance of a newly raised fund. It then describes the data sources and research design and reports the link between these factors and future performance, first in terms of statistical significance. In the next step, a novel measure of the economic selection efficiency of different criteria is developed and applied to assess the economic relevance of these factors. The discussion proceeds to consider alternative performance benchmarking techniques and then presents a multifactor fund selection model that greatly improves selection efficiency above that of any single measure. The last section concludes with implications for research and practice.

HYPOTHESIS DEVELOPMENT

A small but growing literature is focused on the performance drivers of private equity fund investments. These studies point to a number of characteristics of a given fund manager that can be expected to be linked to the performance of the fund manager's next fund.

First and foremost, private equity has been identified as one of the very few asset classes in which performance of a given fund manager seems to persist over time (Kaplan and Schoar, 2005). This points to the relevance of past performance as a possible predictor of future performance. Accordingly we propose that:

1. *The performance of a newly raised fund will be positively related to the past performance of the fund manager.*
   Private equity investments are discrete investment opportunities and information asymmetries and arbitrage opportunities have been identified as important determinants of investment success (e.g., Jensen 1989; Long and Ravenscraft 1993). Accordingly, a second element to consider is the ability of fund managers to see and screen a sufficiently large number of investments to chose from, in other words, a strong and stable deal flow.
2. *The performance of a newly raised fund will be positively related to the stability in the past deal flow of the fund manager.*
   Consistent with the notion that making successful private equity investments requires specific and tacit skills, prior research has found that investment performance increases with the experience of private equity fund managers (e.g., Kaplan and Schoar, 2005). Accordingly, one would expect the performance of a given fund to increase in the prior experience of the responsible fund managers.
3. *The performance of a newly raised fund will be positively related to the past experience of the fund manager.*
   Finally, it is important to realize that fund managers are limited in their ability to scale their activity. Investing increasing amounts of money over the same time period forces them to either make more deals or to increase the size of their typical target company. In the first case, performance is likely to suffer as the pool of attractive investment opportunities for a given investor is limited, and hence fund managers will start investing in (at least

relatively) less attractive companies. The second option is likely to change the required skills as the turnaround of larger companies creates novel challenges. Accordingly we propose that:

4. *The performance of a newly raised fund will be negatively related to the increase in fund size between the prior and the focal fund.*

THE RESEARCH APPROACH

The dataset used for this study contains detailed (anonymous) information on a large sample of North American and European private equity funds: (1) historical cash inflows and outflows (including fees); (2) historical net asset values of unrealized investments; (3) vintage year, committed capital, and geographic focus of the fund; and (4) the size (equity value), stage, and industry of the underlying investments made by these funds.

From this data 615 historic fund-raising situations have been replicated as follows. First, 615 "focal funds" raised in 1999 or before were selected. For these funds, actual performance as of today can already be measured with a sufficient degree of accuracy. For each of the 615 focal funds, data has been composed to reflect the characteristics of the fund manager (or general partner [GP]) at the moment of the fund-raising, similar to the information that would have been available to a potential investor in the fund at that time.

MEASUREMENT AND OPERATIONALIZATION

The 615 simulated due diligence assessments were based on the following information: (1) data on the "latest mature" fund, i.e., the last fund the focal GP has raised prior to the focal fund, which is at least four years old (again to make sure performance information on this fund was reliable at the moment of the hypothetical due diligence); (2) data on the entire track record of the GP, including the past performance of all prior funds of the same GP; (3) GP-level variables, such as GP experience or deal flow; and finally (4) data on how the focal fund differs from its most recent predecessor fund. Exhibit 13.1 illustrates how data for the hypothetical

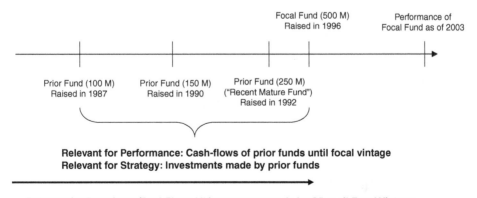

Exhibit 13.1   Example: Composing Data for Hypothetical Fund-Raising Events

historic fund-raising situations has been composed. Based on this data, a number of distinct measures were constructed.

Performance Track Record

As the most widely used—and presumably most important—due-diligence criterion, we put heavy emphasis on the analysis of the GP's performance track record. It is important to keep in mind that all performance data from prior funds is measured as of the beginning of the vintage year of the focal fund, as this snapshot would have been relevant for focal fund due diligence purposes. The final performance of these funds when they reached their liquidation age may differ from this intermediate performance snapshot. We calculate standard performance measures, such as IRR and Performance Quartiles, as well as the "Delta IRR," i.e., the difference between actual IRR and the average IRR of a fund's same-vintage and same-stage peers. We considered either the "latest mature" fund or the average of all prior funds.

Deal Flow

Another important aspect to look at is the ability of a GP to generate an appropriate and stable flow of investments. This ability can be assessed using two complementary measures. First, we take the Percent of Fund Size Invested (measured as of year four after vintage) for the "latest mature" fund. This variable captures if the GP was able to find enough investment opportunities to invest the capital raised in the most recent mature fund. Second, the Variance in Number of Deals per year of the GP prior to focal-fund vintage, which measures whether investments occurred regularly or in waves, where the latter could be interpreted as a possible indication of lower deal flow generation ability.

GP Experience

Experience is measured through two alternative variables: (1) the number of prior funds raised by the GP, and (2) the count of the number of prior investments made by the GP prior to the focal fund's vintage (including multiple investment rounds).

Differences between the Focal and Prior Funds

The relevance of past performance as an indicator of future fund performance is expected to decrease if focal fund characteristics differ from those of previous funds. Particularly relevant in this context are changes in fund size. We capture this effect by including the Percentage Change in Fund Size between focal fund and latest mature predecessor fund in the analysis.

WHICH FACTORS CORRELATE WITH FUTURE PERFORMANCE?

A bivariate correlation analysis shown in Exhibit 13.2 documents which of the different GP characteristics are significantly correlated with the ultimate performance

Exhibit 13.2 Correlation with Focal Fund IRR

	Correlation Coefficient
Latest Mature IRR	0,111(**)
Latest Mature Delta IRR	0,180(**)
Latest Fund % Inv. Year 4	−0,045
Overall Weighted IRR	−0,008
Overall Weighted Delta IRR	0,103(*)
Overall Weighted Performance Quartile	0,126(**)
Change in Fund Size since Latest Mature Funds	−0,066
Number of Prior Funds	0,137(**)
Number of Prior Deals	0,160(**)
Variance in Deals per Year	−0,020

**Correlation is significant at the 0.01 level (2-tailed).
*Correlation is significant at the 0.05 level (2-tailed).

(IRR) of the focal fund. Several observations are in order. First of all, we find support for the Hypothesis 1 in that measures of past performance of a GP's funds (as of the vintage year of the focal fund) are strongly correlated with the subsequent performance of the next fund raised by this GP. Interestingly, measures of relative performance (Latest Mature Delta IRR, Overall Weighted Delta IRR, Overall Weighted Quartile) show stronger correlations than comparable measures of absolute performance (Latest Mature IRR, Overall Weighted IRR).

This suggests that performance persistence is driven by a GP's ability to repeatedly generate returns that are higher than those of a peer group of comparable funds, rather than to always generate returns of the same magnitude. In other words, even high-performing GPs are influenced by exogenous factors that create particularly attractive or difficult investment conditions in a given period and segment of the market. At the same time, the bivariate analysis also shows support for the importance of GP experience as a determinant of future returns of the focal funds: funds raised by GPs with either a larger number of prior funds or a larger number of prior deals perform better ceteris paribus (which supports Hypothesis 3). No support is found for Hypotheses 3 and 4.

RANDOM CHOICE VERSUS THE CRYSTAL BALL: AN APPROACH TO MEASURING PE FUND SELECTION EFFICIENCY

The preceding statistical analysis shows which GP characteristics are significant determinants (in statistical terms) of focal fund performance. The economic relevance of these potential fund selection criteria is a related, yet different question. In other words, we still need to assess the suitability of different GP characteristics to select a portfolio of PE funds that performs better than a random fund choice.

To this end, we first determine the upper and lower "benchmark performance" values for alternative fund selection rules. We calculate the average return of all 615 focal private equity funds in our sample. This lower bound benchmark corresponds to the return an LP would have enjoyed, had she invested proportionally in all private equity funds offered, or in a random subset of those. We find a benchmark performance of 17,13 percent simple average IRR or 13.26 percent weighted average IRR for an investor investing in all 615 proposed funds, with a total portfolio size of US$212 billion. Any efficient fund selection rule should be able to lead to an average performance above this value.

To assess how efficient different criteria are, it is further important to assess the distribution of returns in the fund population. In other words we need to know the aggregate performance of the best 10 percent, 11 percent, and 12 percent of funds in the population and so forth. We determine these values by ranking all focal funds in the population by their end-of-life performance and plot the cumulative average performance of the best 10 percent, 11 percent, 12 percent, and so forth, of these funds relative to the 17.13 percent average as the dashed line in Exhibit 13.3.

The corresponding line can be interpreted as the result of a "crystal ball" fund-selection device through which an investor would have perfectly foreseen the future performance of each focal fund at its vintage and invested accordingly. This selection device is obviously impossible to realize, as the exact future performance of proposed funds is unknown ex ante. However it constitutes a good upper benchmark in terms of selection efficiency that alternative selection schemes can be compared to. For example, an LP with the "crystal ball" could have directly selected the best-performing 22 percent of funds with an average performance improvement of 56 percent. Similarly, the best-performing 57 percent of funds had an average performance improvement of 20 percent over the average performance of 17.13 percent.

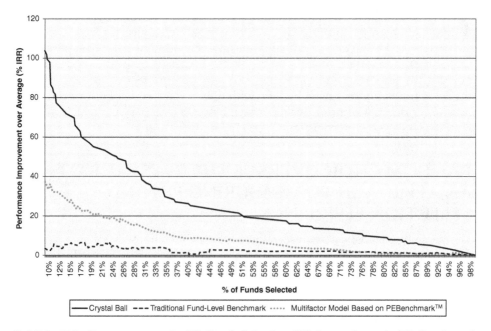

Exhibit 13.3 Improvements in PE Fund Selection Efficiency through PE Benchmark Fund Rating

THE PERACS PRIVATE EQUITY SELECTION EFFICIENCY MEASURE™

We can use these previously developed upper and lower benchmarks to assess and compare the selection efficiency of different fund selection rules in the following way. If we take a given criterion (for example past performance) and apply it to the historic data to select, for example 20 percent of the overall population we can compare the average performance of this choice to the true top 20 percent of the entire population. Based on this intuition, the Peracs Private Equity Selection Efficiency Measure™ (PESEM™) allows us to comprehensively quantify and compare the selection efficiency of different fund selection methods. PESEM™ is defined as the ratio of (1) the integral of the difference between the average performance of all PE funds offered to investors and the average performance of the best x percent of the PE funds as predicted by the selection method, over (2) integral of the difference between the average performance of all PE funds offered to investors and the crystal-ball line, that is, the average performance of the actual best x percent (ex-post) of the PE funds offered to investors. PESEM™ takes values close to 100 percent if the efficiency that the assessed method gets approaches the performance of the crystal ball portfolio and tends towards 0 for methods that offer only average performance. Should a selection method point to below-average funds, PESEM™ turns negative.

The PESEM can be interpreted as follows: a PESEM of 50 percent enables investors (on average) to reach a level of performance improvement over the average portfolio equivalent to half the improvement that a true crystal-ball device would have generated. In the following, we illustrate the use of this method based on popular fund selection criteria.

THE SELECTION EFFICIENCY OF PERFORMANCE-BASED FUND SELECTION RULES

The arguably most "generic" fund selection rule corresponds to the common-wisdom of "backing only top-quartile GPs." Had an LP selected only funds of GP's whose most recent mature fund ranks in the top quartile of their relevant peer group, she would have invested US$99 billion in a portfolio of 216 funds with a weighted average IRR of 16.41 percent. Had she chosen to also include funds with mature predecessor funds in the second performance quartile, she would have invested US$158 in a portfolio of 216 funds with a weighted average IRR of 13,66 percent. It is striking that the rule of selecting funds from the "upper two quartiles" of their respective peer group improves weighted portfolio performance (then 13.66 percent IRR) relative to the benchmark of random investment (13,26 percent IRR) by only 40 basis points.

A slightly more sophisticated version of a past-performance-based selection scheme ranks all focal funds by the weighted average IRR of all their predecessor funds and invests into the top x percent of funds according to this ranking. We assess the performance of the best 10 percent, 11 percent, 12 percent, and so forth, of funds according to this list, and plot the results as the solid line in Exhibit 13.4. We note that, surprisingly, selection schemes based only on past GP performance were historically not very efficient at identifying a high-performing portfolio. In line with what has been indicated already in the analysis of quartile rules as selection criteria, we have to conclude that selection schemes that are based on past GP performance only do not make it possible to improve the average portfolio performance much above the lower benchmark of average portfolio performance. It is also interesting to note that this particular selection scheme does not generate a monotonous relationship between the supposedly best x percent selected and the performance of this selection, as can be seen from the peak of the graph in the area of about 30 percent of funds selected. At best, this past-performance-based selection rule makes it possible to generate average portfolio returns of 26.4 percent IRR for a portfolio size of 28 percent of the proposed funds. This optimum point for the past-performance-based selection rule looks like a substantial improvement over the average portfolio performance (17.3 percent simple average IRR), but remains substantially below the crystal ball upper benchmark of over 63 percent average IRR for the same number of funds.

The efficiency of the past-performance-based selection rule can now be illustrated in Exhibit 13.3. The PESEM for past-performance-based selection is the ratio between the area below the solid line and the area below the crystal ball line in Exhibit 13.3, which corresponds to a value of 2 percent. Hence investors using this rule reach a level of performance improvement over the average portfolio that corresponds to 2 percent of the power of a crystal-ball device.

SHORTCOMINGS OF THE TRADITIONAL BENCHMARKING APPROACH

The traditional approach to assess the quality of a GP based on its performance track record makes intuitive sense: fund by fund, past performance is compared to the established performance benchmarks published by Thomson Venture Economics and/or national industry associations. The judgment is then made depending on whether or how often the GP's prior funds fall within the top- or second-best performance quartiles according to these benchmark statistics. Without a doubt, such a comparison is of value, as it allows assessing the performance of a given fund relative to the population of all funds of the same stage and geographic focus that were raised in the same vintage year as the focal front.

At the same time, this funds-level benchmarking by vintage years has important limitations. First of all, benchmarks are based on groups of funds that can be highly heterogeneous. Consider, for example, the benchmarking group of U.S. buyout funds raised in 2000. The 55 funds in this group range from \$25 M to over \$5 B in terms of their fund size and include everything from focused single-industry specialists to highly diversified generalists. In this group, we find deeply involved operational GPs as well as hands-off investors and observe funds that consistently generate solid returns on almost all of their investments, as well as single-home-run players with one extraordinary success but mediocre performance otherwise. Consequently, comparing the performance of one specific fund to the performance of this diverse population is not really comparing apples to apples, but seems more like an effort to identify some kind of pattern in ratatouille.

An additional set of problems stems from the classification of funds by their vintage year. First, there can be some ambiguity as to whether a given fund falls into one vintage year or another, depending on the "closing date" that is considered relevant for this exercise. Is it the "first close" or the "final close"? And what happens if for some reason a fund opens up again after the "final close" to let in additional capital? If these dates fall into different calendar years, it is not straightforward to identify the appropriate vintage year of the corresponding fund. This partly explains the legend repeated among LPs in which GPs always manage to find some kind of benchmark according to which their performance looks "top quartile."

But even if the vintage year of a given fund could be precisely identified, one may wonder how accurate funds-level benchmarks by vintage year can be. After all, our analysis of thousands of funds reveals that funds from two consecutive vintage years overlap on average to over 50 percent in their respective investment and divestment periods. This raises the question of why a 2000 vintage U.S. mid-cap fund should be compared to a benchmark that includes 2000 vintage U.S. megafunds but that excludes U.S. mid-cap funds from vintages 1999 and 2001. A comparison to funds with a more similar investment focus from adjacent vintage years may be much more meaningful, as this is the relevant peer group of funds that competes for both LP money and suitable deals.

One possibility to partially solve this problem is to conduct a hand-selected fund-level comparison. Taking, for example, the type of data provided by Private Equity Intelligence, it becomes possible to identify a relevant group of funds that are raised, say, in the same three-year period and with a sufficiently similar investment focus. This allows us to come closer to compare apples with apples. At the same time, it introduces a higher level of subjectivity in the benchmarking exercise and sometimes significantly limits the size of the relevant peer group.

More reliable and insightful results are possible, however, if one combines the traditional vintage-year comparison with more innovative benchmarking techniques against public markets and other private equity investments.

USING AND INTERPRETING THE RIGHT PUBLIC MARKET BENCHMARKS

One important way to assess the performance of a private equity investment is to ask the intuitive question "what returns would have been available in public securities instead?" In this context, it is important to point out that such a simple comparison can be highly misleading. For example, the 20-year performance (pooled IRR) of all private equity funds covered by Thomson Venture Economics as of 12/2006 is 14 percent p.a. The S&P 500 increased by about 9.3 percent p.a. over the same time period. However, the comparison of these two numbers is not an accurate assessment of the relative performance of private equity. The 9.3 percent on the S&P 500 are based on a simple buy-and-hold strategy, whereas cash flows in and out of private equity funds occurred almost constantly throughout the 20-year period.

A meaningful comparison between a private equity investment and a broad market index will therefore have to consider the cash flow pattern of private equity. Practically speaking, private equity performance has to be compared to the returns from an investment into and out of a broad index fund that follows the rhythm of takedowns and distributions of the private equity fund. Such a cash flow–matched public-market benchmark provides LPs with two important pieces of information: First it shows the focal fund's performance relative to putting money in a simple investment strategy in public equity. Second, it shows whether and to what extent the GP was able to time the fund's investments in a way that takes advantage of general market trends to enhance the fund's performance.

Such a broad public market benchmark ignores, however, the characteristics of the underlying investments of a focal private equity fund, in particular with respect to their industry sector. This problem can be addressed by calculating a benchmark based on so-called "public peers." For each of the underlying investments of the private equity fund, we calculate the returns to an investment into a peer group of publicly traded firms that are active in the same industry sector. In other words, for an automotive buyout made in 1996 and exited in 1999, we derive the returns to an investment in publicly traded automotive firms from 1996 and 1999 and so forth for all other investments made by a given fund.

Then, we aggregate the performance of all these deal-level "public peer benchmarks" to the fund-level based on the size and the duration of each of the deals. The result is a "public peer benchmark" at the fund level that reflects the performance of public market investments that are similar in timing and industry mix to the focal fund. A comparison between this figure and the "public market benchmark" further indicates to what extent the GP was able to identify attractive industry sectors for the fund's investments.

One final element of precision can be added by considering the differences in leverage between the private equity investments and the public market investments in the comparison. To this end, we can lever up each of the previously calculated deal-level "public peer" returns to the point where the corresponding investments become identical to the respective focal buyouts in terms of their debt-equity ratio. Aggregating these leveraged returns to the fund level gives us the "leveraged peer benchmark." This benchmark closely matches the risk profile of the focal private equity investments and constitutes the most precise way to benchmark a private equity fund against public market investments. See Exhibit 13.4 and Exhibit 13.5 for a comparison of different deal-level benchmarks.

Exhibit 13.4 Alternative Benchmarking Techniques

Benchmark Matches the Investment Characteristics of the Focal PE Fund in Terms of . . .

	Timing of Cash Flows	Industry Mix	Financial Leverage	Governance Structure
Annualized buy-and-hold public market returns	No	No	No	No
Public market benchmark	Yes	No	No	No
Public peers benchmark	Yes	Yes	No	No
Leveraged peers benchmark	Yes	Yes	Yes	No
Vintage-year benchmark	No	No	No	Yes
PEBenchmark™	Yes	Yes	Yes	Yes

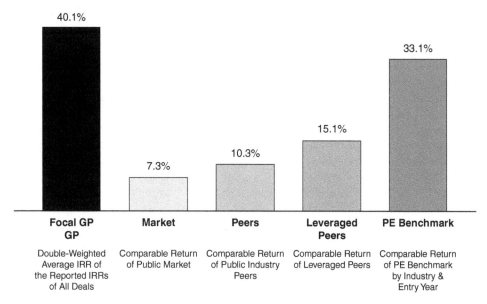

Exhibit 13.5 Focal Fund Performance Relative to Alternative Public Market and PE Benchmarks

ADVANCED PRIVATE EQUITY BENCHMARKING BASED ON DEAL-LEVEL BENCHMARKS

No matter how sophisticated we get in constructing public market benchmarks that imitate the risk and return characteristics of private equity, they will always suffer from the shortcoming that they are unable to correct for differences in corporate governance between the two asset classes. There are many reasons to believe that the fundamental differences between the public corporation and the private equity form of governance make it impossible to exactly replicate private equity based on public securities.

Consequently, the best way to benchmark the performance of a given private equity fund is to compare it to a population of truly similar other private equity investments. As discussed initially, the traditional fund-level performance benchmark by vintage year is generally unable to provide a sufficiently similar basis for such a comparison.

One innovative possibility to derive much more accurate private equity benchmarks is founded on a deal-level comparison with similar private equity transactions. This method considers all underlying investments of a given private equity fund individually and assigns them a deal-level private equity benchmark. Coming back to the previous example of a fund that includes an automotive buyout made in 1996, this particular buyout would be compared to the relevant value for other automotive buyouts made in 1996. In the next step, the deal-level private equity benchmarks of all these investments are aggregated to the funds-level based on the size and the duration of each of the deals. This way we obtain the described benchmark at fund-level reflecting the average performance of private equity investments that are similar in timing (based on the matched timing of the actual investments and not on the year of a fund's closing) and industry to those made by the focal fund.

This provides detailed insights into the value generation ability of a given GP: First, a comparison between the actual performance of a focal fund and its deal-level benchmark tells us whether and to what extent the GP has been able to outperform the other GPs making similar investments. Second, a comparison between a fund's deal-level benchmark and the average performance of its vintage-year peers illustrates whether and to what extent the GP has been able to identify attractive industries for its investments and to time its investments in a way that outperforms its vintage year peers. To some extent, the first comparison speaks to a GP's ability to create more value than its peers, holding investment characteristics constant, while the second comparison speaks to a GP's ability to make investments with attractive characteristics.

For a long time, such an analysis has been impossible, as sufficient data on deal-level private equity performance has been unavailable. Thanks to a joint research project between HEC Paris and the due diligence advisory firm PERACS, the necessary deal-level performance benchmark data and the relevant analysis is now available as PEBenchmark™ from Peracs through its PE Due Diligence Analytics™ tool. Researchers from HEC and PERACS were able to develop a proprietary methodology that combines information on thousands of private equity funds and their underlying investments to derive reliable proxies for deal-level private equity performance by year and industry sector. For further information, please visit www.peracs.com.

QUANTITATIVE DUE DILIGENCE CASE STUDY: ADVANCED PRIVATE EQUITY BENCHMARKING

To illustrate the methodology and the relevance of the previously presented benchmarking techniques, consider the following example of a hypothetical U.S. buyout fund raised in 1995. This imaginary fund has made eight investments with an aggregate IRR of 40.1 percent (see Exhibit 13.6). According to the Thomson Venture Economics performance statistics, some 23 U.S. buyout funds from the 1995 vintage year had an average performance of 11.5 percent. Our focal fund would fall into the top performance quarter of this vintage year.

Let's see how additional public market and private equity benchmarks can help us gain additional insights into the attractiveness of this fund and its corresponding GP. First, we perform a simple public markets benchmarking exercise and determine for each of our eight focal buyouts the return that would have been obtained by an investment in the S&P 500 Index during their respective holding. The corresponding data can be found in the column "Market Return Benchmark IRR" in Exhibit 13.6. We observe that for many deals the focal IRR and the public market benchmark seem to be positively correlated, while there are some cases in which the two seem to move in opposite directions (e.g., Deal PCs 3, 5, or 11). Once aggregated to the fund level, we observe a public market benchmark performance of 7.3 percent, compared to 40.1 percent of the focal fund. Considering that the returns to a simple buy-and-hold investment in the S&P 500 Index from the focal fund's first investments to its last realization would have been 5.9 percent, we

Exhibit 13.6 Deal-Level and Fund-Level Performance Benchmarks

Focal Deal	Entry Year	Exit Year	Focal IRR	Equity Invested	Holding Period (days)	Industry Sector	Market Return Benchmark IRR	Public Peer Benchmark IRR	Leveraged Peer Benchmark IRR	PEBenchmark™ IRR
PC1	1995	1996	66.4%	11.328	335	Consumer Services	25.1%	25.8%	61.3%	16.8%
PC3	1996	2001	6.0%	30.96	1879	Financial Services	14.0%	17.6%	32.2%	24.5%
PC5	1998	2004	162.0%	8.4	2401	Energy and Mining	−2.8%	5.2%	1.4%	31.3%
PC7	1998	1999	12.1%	2.79	365	Product Manufacturing	17.7%	6.2%	3.0%	50.5%
PC8	1999	2000	22.0%	13.35	335	Industrial Products & Services	6.7%	−19.7%	−54.1%	40.5%
PC9	1999	2000	6.6%	7.44	335	Media and Entertainment	10.8%	24.3%	45.5%	33.7%
PC11	2000	2002	11.4%	3.75	849	Healthcare	−19.0%	6.2%	5.2%	50.9%
PC12	2000	2004	13.4%	6.6	1675	Computer Software	−9.2%	−14.0%	−40.5	77.1%
Fund-Level IRR			**40.1%**				**7.3%**	**10.3%**	**15.1%**	**33.1%**

conclude that the GP gained a small advantage from its ability to invest more during periods of general market upswing.

In a second step, we refine the benchmarking exercise by considering the performance of the publicly traded peers of each focal buyout, rather than an investment in the S&P 500 Index. Looking at the consumer services buyout "Deal PC 1," for example, we find the performance of publicly traded peer companies from the consumer services sector over the holding period of this buyout to be 25.8 percent. The corresponding data for all deals can be found in the column "Public Peer Benchmark IRR" in Exhibit 13.6. The aggregate public peer benchmark performance at fund level is 10.3 percent IRR. The fact that our GP was able to identify industry segments for the focal fund's investments that performed better (by 3 percent annually) than the public market benchmark suggests a fair degree of public market sector picking ability. To put it differently: had this GP not been in the business of making private equity investments but managing public market investments instead, its fund would have beaten the S&P 500's 5.9 percent by 440 basis points over the life of the focal fund.

As the last element of the public markets benchmarking, we add buyout-equivalent leverage to each of the public-peer benchmarks, which results in the data shown in the column "Leveraged Peer Benchmark IRR" in Exhibit 13.6. At the fund-level, the aggregate leveraged peer performance benchmark comes to 15.1 percent. Thus we conclude that the actual performance of this fund (40.1 percent) is substantially above the performance that could have been generated by public-market investments of the same timing and risk profile in terms of operating and financial risk.

Shifting our attention to the question of how the performance of our focal funds compares to similar private equity investments, we need to determine the deal-level PEBenchmark^{TM} values for each of its underlying investments. The column "PEBenchmark IRR" in Exhibit 13.6 contains the corresponding information, i.e., the average returns to private equity investments made in the same industry sector and at the same time as each of the focal investments. Collectively, the PEBenchmarkTM performance of all eight investments comes to 33.1 percent. This implies that our GP-made investments with characteristics in terms of timing and industry mix that are relatively more attractive than those of the average fund raised in that year: the focal fund's PEBenchmark^{TM} is almost three times as high as the fund's vintage year performance benchmark of 11.5 percent. In addition, our GP was able to generate returns with the focal fund of 40.1 percent, which is 7 percent above the fund's PEBenchmark^{TM} value and points to a value generation ability of this GP beyond what the average GP would have been able to achieve with similar investments.

THE FUND SELECTION EFFICIENCY OF ADVANCED PRIVATE EQUITY BENCHMARKING TECHNIQUES

The most powerful way to assess to what extent the presented advanced benchmarking techniques for private equity funds increase the efficiency of an LP's fund selection process is to "backtest" them based on historical data. To this end, 531 historic fund-raising situations have been replicated as follows. First, 531 "focal funds" raised in 1999 or before were selected. For these funds, actual performance as of today can already be measured with a sufficient degree of accuracy. For each of the 531 focal funds, detailed data on the performance and investment character-istics of all previous funds managed by the same GP have been gathered, similar to the performance-track-record information that would have been available to a potential investor in the fund at that time. Using this data, we can compare the power of different selection criteria to identify focal funds with superior perfor-mance. In other words, we turn back the clock and simulate the choices made by a hypothetical LP who is being presented with 531 fund-raising documents during the 1980s and 1990s. We then turn the clock forward again and observe the actual performance of the selected portfolio of funds. In doing so, we can assess and compare the efficiency of different decision rules.

In a first analysis, we compare the ability of different benchmarks to statistically explain the actual future performance of the 531 focal funds. In doing so, we find the statistical explanatory power of the standard fund-level vintage year bench-marks to be rather limited. In our regression analysis, past performance relative to the vintage-year benchmark explains little over 4 percent of the variance in future fund performance. If, instead, we combine several of the discussed advanced per-formance benchmarks in a multivariate statistical model, this model is more than twice as powerful in explaining variation in actual future fund performance.

The economic relevance of alternative performance benchmarks as fund se-lection criteria is a related, yet different question. To this end, we calculate the PESEM^{TM} measure for different alternatives. Evaluating the 531 performance track records based on the traditional fund-level vintage year benchmark leads to only small improvements over a random capital allocation process, as is illustrated through the corresponding PESEM^{TM} of 3 percent for the traditional performance benchmark. In other words, investors relying only on fund-level vintage year benchmarks in their fund selection are able to reach only a level of performance improvement over the average portfolio that corresponds to no more than 3 percent of the power of a crystal-ball device.

If, on the other hand, we combine several advanced performance bench-marks in a multifactor fund-rating model and use this model to identify future high-performing funds in our due diligence simulation, we obtain a PESEM^{TM} of 36 percent. Thus, the combination of multiple advanced performance benchmarks to assess a given performance track record enables investors to reach a level of performance improvement over the average portfolio equivalent to 36 percent of the improvement that a crystal-ball choice would have generated (see Exhibit 13.3). This clearly illustrates that the presented advanced benchmarking techniques are not only statistically more powerful in predicting future performance, but that based on our analysis of actual historical data they are also of greatest practical relevance in helping LPs to identify future high-performing funds.

CONCLUSION

This chapter identified several commonly used criteria to select PE fund managers and assesses their fund selection efficiency of based on historic data. Drawing on a comprehensive analysis of 615 historical due diligence situations, it documents the relationship between GP characteristics (measured at the time a new fund is raised) and the subsequent performance of that focal fund, looking at various measures of past GP performance, but also at other aspects, such as deal flow or experience and assess to what extent these are statistically significant determinants of focal-fund performance. In a second step, the selection efficiency of different criteria, i.e., the degree to which their use for fund selection purposes would have historically led to above-average portfolio performance, has been assessed along with a discussion of the advantages and limitations of existing performance benchmarking approaches for fund selection purposes. Our results point to the limited efficiency of "generic" selection rules, such as the "top quartile" rule, especially compared to more comprehensive fund-rating approaches that simultaneously consider multiple complementary selection criteria.

These results confirm the difficulty for investors without a particular expertise to achieve attractive returns in this asset class. This may in part explain why over decades the average returns to private equity have been disappointing (Phalippou and Gottschalg 2009) and why most categories of investors have been unable (on average) to construct high-performing private equity portfolios (Lerner et al. 2007).

The results also have important practical implications. First, investors without substantial experience in private equity may be better off investing in other asset classes or relying on outside expertise or PE fund-of-funds for the composition of their PE portfolio. Second, measures should be considered to improve the ability of investors to reliably select those fund managers who are indeed able to generate attractive returns, for example by making more precise benchmarks available and providing investors with sufficiently detailed information about investment opportunities to accurately evaluate them. While this may erode the ability of some investors to outperform, it will increase the average performance of this asset class and direct money to those fund managers who know best how to profitable invest it.

NOTE

1. This chapter is based in part on the articles "Quantitative Private Equity Fund Due Diligence: Possible Selection Criteria and Their Efficiency," *Private Equity International*, May 2007, and "Picking Winners: Efficient Techniques for PE Fund Selection," *Private Equity International*, March 2008.

REFERENCES

Cumming, D. 2006. Adverse selection and capital structure: Evidence from venture capital. *Entrepreneurship Theory and Practice* 30:155–184.

Jensen, M. C. 1989. Active investors, LBOs, and the privatization of bankruptcy. *Journal of Applied Corporate Finance* 2 (1):35–44.

Kaplan, S. N., and A. Schoar. 2005. Private equity performance: Returns, persistence, and capital flows. *Journal of Finance* 60:1791–1823.

Lerner, J., A. Schoar, and W. Wong. 2007. Smart institutions, foolish choices: The limited partner performance puzzle. *Journal of Finance* 62 (2):731–764.

Long, W. F., and D. J. Ravenscraft. 1993. LBOs, debate, and R&D intensity. *Strategic Management Journal* 14 (4):119–135.

Phalippou, L., and O. Gottschalg. 2009. The performance of private equity funds. *Review of Financial Studies* 22 (4):1747–1776.

ABOUT THE AUTHOR

Oliver F. Gottschalg is a member of the Strategy Department at HEC School of Management, Paris. He serves as Director of the Entrepreneurship Track in the HEC MBA program, directs the HEC Buyout Research Group, and teaches courses on strategy, entrepreneurship, business-plan design, and management buyouts. He holds a Wirtschaftsingenieur Diploma from the University of Karlsruhe, an MBA from Georgia State University, and a M.Sc. and Ph.D. degree from INSEAD. His current research focuses on the strategic logic and the performance determinants of private equity investments. His work has been published in leading academic journals and in various publications for practitioners and has been widely featured in the business press. He regularly presents his research at academic conferences and private equity symposia and serves as an advisor to leading investors in the private equity industry. He is Head of Research at Peracs Ltd., a specialized advisory firm providing advanced private equity fund due-diligence and benchmarking services. Most recently, he served as an advisor to the European Parliament in the context of the current debate about a possible need for regulation of the private equity industry.

CHAPTER 14

Real Effects of Private Equity

Empirical Evidence and a Research Agenda

DONALD S. SIEGEL
Dean and Professor, School of Business, University at Albany

INTRODUCTION

The recent rise in private equity deals has created renewed interest in assessing whether these transactions improve economic performance. There is also growing concern regarding how such ownership changes affect workers, because any productivity gains may be due to measures undertaken by the new owners or managers to reduce wages, lay off workers, and reduce investment in physical capital and R&D.

A standard empirical approach to assessing the performance effects of private equity deals has been to analyze the impact of these transactions on stock prices and accounting profits. These include examining effects on short-run share prices ("event studies"), long-run share prices, returns to investors, or accounting profits of publicly traded firms. Such approaches focus on firm-level, financial "returns" to private equity.

Although it is useful to assess financial effects, it is even more important to evaluate the societal impact of private equity. Regulatory decisions relating to this activity should be determined based on its impact on economic efficiency ("real" effects), not on its financial effects.

In this chapter, I review recent global evidence on the real effects of private equity. I also outline a research agenda on this topic.

EVIDENCE OF THE REAL EFFECTS OF PRIVATE EQUITY

A focus on the financial performance of firms involved in buyouts and private equity deals suffers from several limitations. One drawback, as noted in Harris, Siegel, and Wright (2005), is that the firm is not the appropriate unit of analysis, because many private equity transactions occur below the firm level. That is, the majority of private equity transactions do not involve a transfer of ownership of an entire publicly traded firm. Instead, most private equity deal or buyouts are divestments of a unit of a large firm, or a transaction that affects only a few establishments. The end result is that full-firm transactions involving publicly traded companies constitute only a very small percentage of aggregate private equity activity. This is a key issue, because we have little systematic data on transactions occurring below the firm level.

Another concern relates to the metric used to evaluate performance impacts. Many scholars use the event study methodology to assess private returns, which focuses on analyzing how the stock market reacts to announcements of private equity–related events. A maintained assumption of this method is that markets are efficient.

Unfortunately, some researchers have become increasingly skeptical about the "efficient markets" hypothesis, which asserts that changes in share prices following announcements of an event (e.g., a buyout) reflect changes in future real performance or economic efficiency. This is a critical issue, because market efficiency is a maintained assumption for use of this method. Alternative measures of firm financial performance based on accounting data are also problematic. It is well known that accounting profits are subject to managerial manipulation. Furthermore, even when such indicators of *financial* performance are perfectly measured, accounting profits are not perfectly correlated with *real* performance.

These stylized facts underscore the difficulties of gathering and interpreting pre- and post-buyout performance data. Two concerns are that there are few publicly available data on divisions and individual plants. Note also that many of the entities involved in private equity transactions are privately held firms. It is interesting to note that it is easier to collect information on the characteristics of privately held firms in the United Kingdom, as opposed to the United States, due to the existence of the FAME and ONESOURCE UK Private+ databases. Both files contain similar firm-level data from corporate financial statements, as do COMPUSTAT and the British equivalent of COMPUSTAT, known as DATASTREAM.

Amess (2002, 2003) presents U.K. evidence on the effects of full-firm management buyouts on productivity, based on ONESOURCE company-level data. Unfortunately, it is inappropriate to estimate productivity using *firm-level* data for two reasons. First, the construction of total factor productivity (henceforth, TFP) measures requires reliable and comprehensive information on capital and intermediate materials. These variables are typically not reported in financial statements and thus, are not contained in COMPUSTAT, DATASTREAM, or ONESOURCE files. Second, the accuracy of productivity measures also depends on the accuracy of input and output price deflators, since inputs and output should be computed in constant dollars. The problem is that many large firms have plants in diverse industries, where there may be substantial variation in price changes. However, in files such as COMPUSTAT, these organizations must be classified, at the corporate level, into a single four-digit SIC industry. As shown in Lichtenberg and Siegel (1991), the use of a single set of output and input deflators can introduce substantial measurement error into the calculation of TFP measures. And finally, as mentioned previously, much private equity activity occurs below the firm level.

To overcome these limitations, some authors have conjectured that it is more desirable to assess the productivity of establishments or plants before and after buyouts. Plants are physical units of firms that report data on physical output and inputs, or resources consumed in production, such as labor, physical capital, and intermediate goods and materials. Such data can be used to construct indicators of productivity, which measure the efficiency of resource utilization. Exhibit 14.1 presents the salient characteristics of studies of the real effects of buyouts.

The first study to estimate the impact of LBOs and MBOs on productivity was Lichtenberg and Siegel (1990). The authors analyzed data from the U.S. Census Bureau's Longitudinal Research Database (LRD), which contained data on more than 19,000 mostly large U.S. manufacturing plants for the years 1972 to 1988. In this paper, the authors employed a two-stage approach to assess the impact of MBOs on TFP. In the first stage, they computed residuals from within-industry (four-digit SIC) OLS regressions of Cobb-Douglas production functions of the following form (with error terms suppressed):

$$\ln Q_i = \sum_{k=1}^{K} \beta_k \ln X_{ki} \tag{14.1}$$

where Q denotes output, X represents a vector of k inputs, and i refers to a plant. The second stage equation was:

$$\text{RELEFF}_{i,\,t+m} = f(\text{LBO}_{it}) \tag{14.2}$$

where RELEFF is the productivity residual of plant i in year $t + m$; LBO is a dummy variable that equals 1 if the plant was involved in a leveraged or management buyout in year t; 0 otherwise.

They found that buyout plants had higher total factor productivity (TFP) than representative establishments in the same industry before they changed owners. However, they also reported that buyout plants experienced significant improvements in TFP after the buyout. More importantly, the authors also found that this enhancement in economic performance could not be attributed to reductions in R&D, wages, capital investment, or layoffs of blue-collar personnel.

Harris et al. (2005), analyzing longitudinal data for approximately 36,000 U.K. manufacturing establishments, extended the Lichtenberg and Siegel (1990) study in three important ways. First, the authors analyzed a considerably larger sample of buyout, basically the entire population of U.K.-manufacturing MBOs. Their final sample consisted of 979 MBOs and 4,877 plants, as opposed to 48 MBOs and 399 plants in the Lichtenberg and Siegel study. This allowed them to assess the "returns" to MBOs by industry. Second, they employed more sophisticated econometric techniques (Generalized Methods of Moments estimation) and estimated a one-stage model.

Specifically, the authors employed GMM estimation of within industry (two-digit SIC), one-stage augmented Cobb-Douglas production functions. A one-stage estimation procedure provides more efficient econometric estimates of the conventional arguments of the production function and other determinants of productivity (e.g., a set of MBO dummy variables) than the two-stage approach used by Lichtenberg and Siegel (1990). The authors also included more explanatory variables than in Lichtenberg and Siegel (1990) (in terms of explaining changes in productivity). Finally, they had more recent data, for the authors found that MBO establishments were less productive than comparable plants before the transfer of ownership. They also reported that MBO plants experienced a substantial increase

Exhibit 14.1 Studies of the Real Effects of Leveraged and Management Buyouts and Private Equity

Authors	Country	Unit of Analysis	Nature of Transactions	Findings
Lichtenberg and Siegel (1990a)	U.S.	Plant	Divisional and full-firm LBOs and MBOs of public and private companies	Plants involved in LBOs and MBOs are more productive than comparable plants before the buyout; LBOs and especially MBO plants experience a substantial increase in productivity after a buyout; employment and wages of nonproduction workers at plants (but not production workers) declines after an LBO or MBO; no decline in R&D investment
Wright, Thompson, and Robbie (1992)	U.K.	Firm	Divisional, and full-firm MBOs of private companies	MBOs enhance new product development
Long and Ravenscraft (1993)	U.S.	Division	LBOs and MBOs	LBOs result in a reduction in R&D expenditure
Zahra (1995)	U.S.	Firm	MBOs	MBOs result in more effective use of R&D expenditure and new product development
Bruining and Wright (2002)	Holland	Firm	Divisional MBOs	MBOs result in more entrepreneurial activities such as new product & market development
Amess (2002)	U.K.	Firm	MBOs	MBOs enhance productivity
Amess (2003)	U.K.	Firm	MBOs	MBOs enhance productivity
Bruining, Boselie, Wright, and Bacon (2005)	U.K and Holland	Firm	MBOs	MBOs lead to increases in levels of employment, training, employee empowerment, and wages: These effects were stronger in the U.K. than in the Netherlands
Harris et al. (2005)	U.K.	Plant	Divisional and full-firm LBOs and MBOs of public and private companies	Plants involved in MBOs are less productive than comparable plants before the buyout; they experience a substantial increase in productivity after a buyout; plants involved in an MBO experience a substantial reduction in employment

Exhibit 14.1 *(Continued)*

Authors	Country	Unit of Analysis	Nature of Transactions	Findings
Amess and Wright (2007)	U.K.	Firm	MBOs and MBIs	Employment grows in MBOs but falls in MBIs after buyout
Amess, Brown, and Thompson (2007)	U.K.	Firm	MBOs	Employees in MBO firms have more discretion over their work practices
Cressy, Malipiero, and Munari (2007)	U.K.	Firm	Private equity–backed firms	Employment at buyout firms falls initially and then rises
Davis, Haltiwanger, Lerner, Miranda, and Jarmin (2008)	U.S.	Firm and Plant	Private equity–backed firms and plants	Employment growth is lower among private equity–backed firms and plants in the aftermath of such transactions; job growth at such firms and establishments starts to improve four years after the deal
Amess, Girma, and Wright (2008)	U.K.	Firm	Private equity–backed LBOs	Employment is unchanged and wages lower in the aftermath of private equity-backed LBOs
Bacon, Wright, Demina, Bruining, and Boselie (1998)	U.K.	Firm	Private equity–backed MBOs	Employees at "insider" buyouts demonstrate higher levels of commitment than comparable workers at nonbuyout firms
Lerner, Strömberg, and Sørensen (2008)	Worldwide	Firm	Private equity–backed LBOs	Patent citations increase in the aftermath of buyouts, but the quantity of patenting is unchanged; patent portfolios appear to be become more focused after private equity investment.

Note: Real effects comprise changes in factor productivity, changes in employment and employee relations conditions, new product development, and R&D expenditure.

in productivity after a buyout (+70.5 percent and +90.3 percent more efficient in the short and long run, respectively) and that these post-buyout productivity gains are pervasive across industries (the average manufacturing plant experienced a substantial increase in TFP in 14 out of 18 industries). The results imply that the improvement in economic performance may be due to measures undertaken by new owners or managers to reduce the labor intensity of production, through the outsourcing of intermediate goods and materials. This evidence suggests that MBOs may be a useful mechanism for reducing agency costs and enhancing economic efficiency.

Perhaps the most comprehensive analysis of the employment effects of private-equity backed deals was recently conducted by Davis, Haltiwanger et al. (2008). These authors linked data on millions of establishments and firms from the U.S. Census Bureau's Longitudinal Business Database (LBD) to a file from Capital IQ, which contains detailed information on most private equity transactions. The LBD is richer than the LRD (analyzed in several studies by Lichtenberg and Siegel) because it contains data on nonmanufacturing establishments, consisting of the entire nonfarm private sector (not just the manufacturing sector). These comprehensive data enable the authors to construct robust control groups for their econometric analysis. Specifically, they were able to match private equity–backed establishments with comparable non–private equity–backed plants. The authors report that employment growth is lower among private equity–backed firms and plants in the aftermath of such transactions. However, job growth at such firms and establishments starts to improve (on average) four years after the deal.

It is also important to note that there is little evidence on organizational changes associated with MBOs and other types of mergers and acquisitions. We know a lot about how MBOs affect financial and economic performance, but virtually nothing about the impact of such transactions on work life. To fill this gap, some U.K. and European authors have amassed an extremely rich dataset to assess the effects of management buyouts on employee "empowerment" and other aspects of the work environment.

Bruining et al. (2005) find that MBOs result in the United Kingdom and the Netherlands an improvement in human resource management practices. Specifically, they found that there were higher levels of employment, employee empowerment, and wages. These effects were found to be stronger in the United Kingdom than in Holland and emphasize the importance of understanding different institutional contexts even within Europe.

Amess et al. (2007) also conducted an extensive analysis of the relationship between empowerment and supervision and MBOs. In general, they report that employees in MBO firms have more discretion over their work practices than comparable workers at non-MBO firms. Skilled employees, in particular, were found to have very low levels of supervision at MBO firms. Amess and Wright (2006) show in a panel of 1,350 U.K. LBOs observed over the period 1999 to 2004, indicate that when LBOs are disaggregated, employment growth is 0.51 of a percentage point higher for insider-driven MBOs after the change in ownership and 0.81 of a percentage point lower for outsider-driven MBIs. These findings are consistent with the notion that MBOs lead to the exploitation of growth opportunities, resulting in higher employment growth. The same patterns do not emerge from MBIs, typically because the latter transactions involve enterprises that require considerable restructuring.

The end result is there is a general consensus that across different methodologies, measures, and time periods, regarding a key stylized fact: LBOs and especially, MBOs enhance performance and have a salient effect on work practices. More generally, the findings of the productivity studies are consistent with recent theoretical and empirical evidence (Jovanovic and Rousseau 2002) suggesting that corporate takeovers result in the reallocation of a firm's resources to more efficient uses and to better managers.

RESEARCH AGENDA

Analysis of the real effects of private equity and buyouts is still relatively embryonic. First, it would be useful to examine the productivity impact of different types of private equity deals and buyouts. For instance, we might expect that private firms have lower agency costs than publicly traded firms. That is because privately held companies are usually owned and managed by a small, concentrated group of shareholders, typically consisting of a founder and his family. Thus, we might want to compare the productivity performance of public-to-private and private-to-private MBOs. It would also be interesting to assess whether there are differences in the effects of domestic and foreign MBOs on economic efficiency.

Another type of MBOs that warrants further attention is the management buyin (MBI). In theory, MBIs occur when incumbent managers do not possess the requisite skills to manage the firm (or unit of the firm) effectively, so an external management group is brought in to take the firm private. Thus, it is conceivable that the impact of an MBI on productivity may be greater than the impact of an MBO on economic performance. The occurrence of an MBI, rather than an MBO, may be indicative of shortcomings in the quality of management. The introduction of new, external equity-owning managers with more talent and experience could have a positive impact on the quest for higher TFP. Indeed, there is some evidence that managers involved in MBIs are more entrepreneurial than managers in MBOs (see, e.g., Wright, Wilson, and Robbie 1996).

There is also the phenomenon of the "reverse" buyout (Degeorge and Zeckhauser 1993), which occurs when a buyout goes public again. While we have evidence that private-to-public buyouts yield improvements in financial and accounting performance, these improvements appear to decline over time (Holthausen and Larcker 1996). Studies also reveal that IPOs of MBOs backed by more reputable private equity firms perform better than those backed by less prestigious private equity firms (Jelic, Saadouni, and Wright 2005). We also need more evidence on the impact of private equity transactions on human capital. Some scholars (e.g., Wright, Wilson, and Robbie 1996) have suggested that the skill-sets of managers must change in the aftermath of such transactions. Specifically, there appears to be a need to broaden beyond traditional financial skills to acquire marketing and operations expertise. It would also be useful to assess the effects of such deals on the propensity of companies to train workers. Addressing these types of research question would require additional microdata.

Such research will have to be based on novel data sets. For instance, the unit of analysis in many private equity and buyout research has been the firm. Additional empirical studies should also be based on data at the plant/establishment level, or even at the individual employee level. A new class of data sets has emerged (Siegel, Simons, and Lindstrom 2009) that link establishment data (from the economic census) to voluminous information on workers at these establishments (from the decennial census). These linked, longitudinal employer-employee data could be used to assess the relationship between buyout activity and additional real variables, such as workforce diversity and relative compensation (Siegel, Simons, and Marsh 2007). Such data could also provide important insights into the impacts of different types of private equity firms on real returns that would complement evidence of their effects on financial returns. Currently, most private equity and buyout research involves hand-collecting data sets. Thus, there is ample room for improving the breadth and depth of the available data, especially if information on these financial transactions can be linked to these rich longitudinal employer-employee datasets.

Other dimensions of economic welfare require more analysis. From an industrial organization and public policy perspective, a key concern is whether these transactions result in changes in product prices or output. That is, it would be useful to assess whether such events lead to an increase in "market power." To the best of my knowledge, Chevalier (1995) is the only paper that assessed changes in product prices following buyouts. It is important to note, however, that this study was focused on a single industry: supermarkets. Although there have been other papers on the interactions between capital markets and product markets (e.g., Maksimovic and Phillips 2001, 2002), these studies have not focused on private equity transactions. Finally, there have been no studies of the impact of such deals on product or service quality.

REFERENCES

Amess, Kevin. 2002. Management buyouts and firm-level productivity: Evidence from a panel of U.K. manufacturing firms. *Scottish Journal of Political Economy* 49:304–317.

Amess, Kevin. 2003. The effects of management buyouts and on firm-level technical efficiency: Evidence from a panel of U.K. machinery and equipment manufacturers. *Journal of Industrial Economics* 51:35–44.

Amess, Kevin, Stephen Brown, and Stephen Thompson. 2007. Management buyouts, supervision, and employee discretion. *Scottish Journal of Political Economy* 54:447–474.

Amess, Kevin, and Mike Wright. 2007. The wage and employment effects of leveraged buyouts in the U.K. *International Journal of Economics and Business* 14:179–195.

Amess, Kevin, Sourafel Girma, and Mike Wright. 2008. What are the wage and employment consequences of leveraged buyouts, private equity and acquisitions in the UK? Centre for Management Buy-out Research Occasional Paper.

Arellano, Manuel, Stephen R. Bond. 1998. Dynamic panel data estimation using DPD98 for GAUSS. Mimeo.

Bacon, Nicholas, Mike Wright, Natalia Demina, Hans Bruining, and Paul Boselie. 2008. HRM, buyouts and private equity in the U.K. and the Netherlands. *Human Relations*, forthcoming.

Bruining, Hans, and Mike Wright. 2002. Entrepreneurial orientation in management buyouts and the contribution of venture capital. *Venture capital: An international journal of entrepreneurial finance* 4:147–168.

Bruining, Hans, Paul Boselie, Mike Wright, and Nicholas Bacon. 2005. The impact of business ownership change on employee relations: Buyouts in the U.K. and the Netherlands. *International Journal of Human Resource Management* 16:345–365.

Chevalier, Judith A. 1995. Do LBO supermarkets charge more? An empirical analysis of the effects of LBOs on supermarket pricing. *Journal of Finance* 50:1095–1112.

Cressy, Robert, Alessandro Malipiero, and Frederico Munari. 2007. Playing to their strengths? Evidence that specialization in the private equity industry confers competitive advantage. *Journal of Corporate Finance* 13:647–669.

Davis, Steven, Joshua Lerner, J. Haltiwanger, Javier Miranda, and Ron Jarmin. 2008. Private equity and employment. In *The global impact of private equity report 2008: Globalization of alternative investments*, eds. J. Lerner and A. Gurung, pp. 43–64. Working Papers, Volume 1, World Economic Forum.

Degeorge, Francis, and Richard Zeckhauser. 1993. The reverse LBO decision and firm performance: Theory and evidence. *Journal of Finance* 48:1323–1348.

Harris, Richard, Donal S. Siegel, and Mike Wright. 2005. Assessing the impact of management buyouts on economic efficiency: Plant-level evidence from the United Kingdom. *The Review of Economics and Statistics* 87:148–153.

Holthausen, Robert W., and David F. Larcker. 1996. The financial performance of reverse leverage buyouts. *Journal of Financial Economics* 42:293–332.

Jelic, Ranko, Brahim Saadouni, and Mike Wright. 2005. Performance of private-to-public MBOs: The role of venture capital. *Journal of Business Finance and Accounting* 32:643–682.

Jovanovic, Boyan, and Peter Rousseau. 2002. Mergers as reallocation. Working Paper no. 9279, National Bureau of Economic Research.

Lerner, Joshua, Per Strömberg, and Morten Sørensen. 2008. Private equity and long-run investment: The case of innovation. *The global impact of private equity report 2008: Globalization of alternative investments*, eds. J. Lerner and A. Gurung, pp. 27–42A. Working Papers, Volume 1, World Economic Forum.

Lichtenberg, Frank R., and Donald S. Siegel. 1990. The effect of leveraged buyouts on productivity and related aspects of firm behavior. *Journal of Financial Economics* 27:165–194.

Lichtenberg, Frank R., and Donald S. Siegel. 1991. The impact of R&D investment on productivity—New evidence using linked R&D-LRD data. *Economic Inquiry* 29:203–229.

Long, William F., and David J. Ravenscraft. 1993. LBOs, debt and R&D intensity. *Strategic Management Journal* (Summer Special Issue) 14:119–135.

Maksimovic, Vojislav, and Gordon Phillips. 2001. The market for corporate assets: Who engages in mergers and asset sales and are there efficiency gains? *Journal of Finance* 56:2019–2065.

Maksimovic, Vojislav, and Gordon Phillips. 2002. Do conglomerate firms allocate resources inefficiently across industries? Theory and evidence. *Journal of Finance* 57:721–767.

Siegel, Donald S., Kenneth Simons, and Tomas Lindstrom. 2009. Ownership change, productivity, and human capital: New evidence from matched employer-employee data in Swedish manufacturing. In *Producer dynamics: New evidence from micro data*, eds. Mark Roberts, Tim Dunne, and Brad Jensen, pp. 650–736. Chicago: University of Chicago Press (NBER/CRIW Conference Volume for the University of Chicago Press).

Siegel, Donald S., Kenneth Simons, and John Marsh. 2007. Assessing the effects of mergers and acquisitions on women and minority employees: New evidence from matched employer-employee data. *International Journal of the Economics of Business* 14:161–179.

Wright, Mike, Natalia Wilson, and Ken Robbie. 1996. The longer term effects of management-led buyouts. *Journal of Entrepreneurial and Small Business Finance* 5:213–234.

Wright, Mike, Stephen Thompson, and Ken Robbie. 1992. Venture capital and management-led leveraged buyouts: A European perspective. *Journal of Business Venturing* 7:47–71.

Wright, Mike, and Andy Lockett. 2003. The structure and management of alliances: Syndication in venture capital investments. *Journal of Management Studies* 40:2073–2104.

Zahra, Shaker. 1995. Corporate entrepreneurship and financial performance: The case of management leveraged buyouts. *Journal of Business Venturing* 10 (3):225–247.

ABOUT THE AUTHOR

Donald Siegel received his bachelor's degree in economics and master's and doctoral degrees in business economics from Columbia University. He is editor of the

Journal of Technology Transfer and an associate editor of *Journal of Business Venturing, Journal of Productivity Analysis,* and *Academy of Management Learning & Education.* His research interests include productivity analysis, corporate governance and social responsibility, and university technology transfer. He has published in such top journals as *American Economic Review, Economic Journal, The Review of Economics and Statistics, Journal of Law and Economics, Journal of Financial Economics, Brookings Papers on Economic Activity, Academy of Management Review, Academy of Management Journal, Strategic Management Journal, Journal of Business Venturing, Journal of International Business Studies,* and *Journal of Management.* His most recent books are *Innovation, Entrepreneurship, and Technological Change* and the *Handbook of Corporate Social Responsibility,* both published by Oxford University Press.

ACKNOWLEDGMENT

This paper is based on work in Cumming, Douglas, Donald Siegel, and Mike Wright, 2007, Private equity, leveraged buyouts, and governance, *Journal of Corporate Finance* 13:439–460.

CHAPTER 15

Employment, Wage, and Productivity Effects of Private Equity Transactions

ROBERT CRESSY
Professor, University of Birmingham

THE UNIVERSE OF PRIVATE EQUITY TRANSACTIONS

In this chapter we study the employment and productivity effects of private equity (PE) activity. This requires a definition of the four component terms. *Employment* we define as the number of full-time equivalent employees of a company. Wages are defined as the total wage bill per employee.[1] *Productivity* is defined as labor productivity or output per person employed.[2] *Private equity activity* in this chapter is defined as the buying of shares of a *public* company that is then taken private, usually with a view to restructuring and later refloatation.[3]

In this chapter we focus on specific subset of private equity activity, namely leveraged buyouts or LBOs. A *buyout* in this chapter then consists of the purchase of the shares of a company by an external private equity organization and the subsequent delisting of the company so that it becomes (for a while) privately held. We shall follow Amess and Wright (2007) in defining two subsets of LBOs, namely management buyouts (MBOs), which are done with the agreement of the directors, and management buyins which are not—indeed may involve partial or complete replacement of incumbent managers. Financial engineering in the form of leverage has historically been an important source of profits to private equity firms (PEFs), and has traditionally been deployed in virtually all such transactions—hence the focus on LBOs. Also, despite the fact that there are many buyouts of privately held companies, we shall focus in the chapter only on those of *publicly* quoted companies, since they are the subject of study for almost all academic research in this area.

TASK OF THE CHAPTER

In surveying the literature on the employment, wage and productivity effects of private equity activity,[4] we shall be interested in the evidence for whether an LBO transaction increases or decreases employment in the company concerned over the subsequent years and whether this is associated with changes in wages and productivity in the target organization. Are any changes in wages and employment after a buyout driven by employment change or productivity improvements?[5] Moreover, are any such changes due to the LBO or would they have happened anyway? What role does PEF target-selection play in interpreting what we observe? Finally, are there differences in employment, wage, and productivity between buyouts and buyins? (The latter involve a more radical change of management than the former and may be expected to have a more dramatic influence on key variables.[6])

Doing all this is more difficult than it sounds. We now illustrate some of the problems encountered in assessing studies of the employment, wage, and productivity contributions of PE activity.

Pitfalls for the Unwary

We begin by listing a set of criteria to which a truly scientific analysis of the employment effects of buyouts should conform. Each study in the survey will then be compared with these criteria when assessing its contribution to the literature.

First, to determine the employment and productivity effects of buyouts requires a suitable control sample of firms against which they can be benchmarked. This is essential because LBOs are a very small proportion of the population of quoted companies; a random sample would not pick up enough LBO firms to study.[7] How this matched sample is chosen is of some considerable importance. For example, if matching is done by size and industry as is commonly the case, it is important to control for other variables in a subsequent regression to explain performance (here measured by employment or productivity change).[8] We generally also need to deal with the routine problem of missing (employment) data for some firms for some years. This problem is typically addressed by use of Heckman selection methods.[9] Failing to do so will be likely to result in biased regression coefficients.

Second, the sample period should cover both boom and recession. This way the robustness of the results to changes in the macro environment can be evaluated. Because LBOs by their nature rely on high leverage for enhanced financial performance, their failure rate should be higher in recessionary than in boom periods when credit is tighter.[10] Failure will likely be associated with employment effects.

Third, the specification of the econometric model for the analysis of employment effects involves a number of choices by the researcher. In the employment equation, there is a choice between levels and growth rates of employment as dependent variables; if the latter is chosen it does not directly lead to a comparison of levels of employment and wages. More importantly the specification involves choices among regressors, for example, whether to include financial variables (leverage, etc.) along with real variables (e.g., firm turnover). Management incentives and hence the way labor is used for maximum effect will be likely to change with the degree of leverage.[11]

Fourth, and as hinted at earlier, there is the question of *simultaneity*: for example, should one model employment and wage growth as interactions, or can they be considered independent? Employment effects of buyouts must be separated from other effects such as from wage reductions in the post-buyout period (see Palepu 1990). This is because one of the possible motives of an LBO might be to transfer wealth from employees to pre-buyout shareholders. One obvious way of doing this is by layoffs of workers but another is by imposing wage reductions on existing staff.

Fifth, econometric modeling must also address the potentially important question of endogeneity of the dummy variables (LBO, MBO, MBI)[12] representing the various organizational types in buyouts. This issue is relevant as the role of buyout firms in performance is two-fold: PEFs are responsible for the *selection* of which firms to restructure in addition to the restructuring of the company after the transaction. It is therefore possible that superior *measured* ex post performance (e.g., labor productivity) of bought-out firms may be due to either better selection (endogeneity of LBO dummy) or to superior management of costs after the buyout has taken place. Failing to incorporate this distinction in the modeling may thus lead to erroneous empirical conclusions and mistaken policy advice.

Finally, we must distinguish the time dimension of the study. Improvements in short-term performance may persist into the long term or they may be ephemeral. Thus, an ideal data set should allow longer-term analysis of performance against a control sample. Without this knowledge it is impossible to assess the true impact of private equity on the economy. Because not all of the incentive effects of buyouts persist into the long run whether any benefits from productivity enhancement persist is a moot point.

The above may seem to be a quite formidable set of criteria for the accurate assessment of the employment impact of private equity. Needless to say, we shall find that most studies fall short of these standards along one or more dimensions. However, the criteria remain central to a proper assessment of performance and will provide benchmarks against which actual studies can be assessed. Private equity industry claims about performance suggest in fact a uniformly star-studded contribution of buyouts to profits and employment. However, these issues have only recently begun to be scientifically addressed in a literature which one may describe as still in its infancy. We shall therefore attempt to summarize the emergent findings from this relatively small universe of academic contributions, and in doing so tick off the relevant boxes discussed previously.

EMPLOYMENT AND PRODUCTIVITY IDENTITIES

Employment and productivity are two sides of the same coin, linked by the output of the firm, and cannot be considered independently. A simple model of the firm can be used to elucidate this relationship.

If demand equals supply for the firm's product and there is only labor to consider as a productive input, the growth in total employment of a firm can plausibly be considered proportional to the difference in demand and productivity *levels*, plus a random factor. Expected employment growth is thus proportional to this difference.

To see this, note that total output Q for a firm may be written using the identity

$$Q = qn \tag{15.1}$$

where q is output per man and n is employment. Taking logs we get

$$Q^* = q^* + n^* \tag{15.2}$$

where $Q^* = \log(Q), q^* = \log(q), n^* = \log(n)$. Taking time derivatives we get

$$\frac{dQ^*}{dt} = \frac{dq^*}{dt} + \frac{dn^*}{dt} \tag{15.3}$$

Or,

$$\frac{1}{Q}\frac{dQ}{dt} = \frac{1}{q}\frac{dq}{dt} + \frac{1}{n}\frac{dn}{dt} \tag{15.4}$$

Thus, the percentage change in total output equals the percentage change in labor productivity, plus the percentage change in employment. Now, compressing the notation and rearranging we get:

$$\dot{n} = \dot{Q} - \dot{q} \tag{15.5}$$

where $\dot{x} = \frac{1}{x}\frac{dx}{dt}$. It is immediately obvious from equation 15.5 that

$\dot{Q} < 0,\ \dot{q} = 0 \Rightarrow \dot{n} < 0$: Declining output with constant productivity

reduces employment. (15.6)

$\dot{Q} > 0,\ \dot{q} = 0 \Rightarrow \dot{n} > 0$: Constant productivity with increasing demand

increases employment. (15.7)

$\dot{Q} > 0,\ \dot{q} > 0 \Rightarrow \dot{n} \gtreqless 0\ as\ \dot{Q} \gtreqless \dot{q}$: Increasing productivity with increasing

demand will increase, leave constant or decrease employment as the growth of

demand exceeds, equals or is exceeded by the growth of productivity. (15.8)

These elementary propositions will assist our interpretation of the empirical results later in the chapter. For example, equation 15.6 is consistent with the hypothesis that buyouts have no effect on productivity but instead create monopoly power, which over time raises prices (by reducing output) and enriches shareholders at the expense of consumers. As a result employment in the target falls. Equation 15.7 is consistent with the hypothesis that buyouts have no effects on productivity but that demand is increasing (e.g., as a result of industry growth) and thus employment expands. Equation 15.8 is consistent with the hypothesis that buyouts start by raising productivity, which is later passed on to consumers in price reductions, which in turn stimulate demand, finally resulting in increased employment in the firm.

Now, it is worth noting that the traditional empirical model of the firm (see, e.g., Hart and Prais 1956; Cressy 2006) writes the log of employment $n(t)$ as a stochastic process in discrete time with a systematic component, γ, as follows:

$$n_t - n_{t-1} = \gamma n_{t-1} + \varepsilon_t \tag{15.9}$$

where $\varepsilon_t \approx N(0, \sigma^2)$.[13] Letting the time interval go to zero this can be written as

$$\dot{n}_t = \gamma n_t + \varepsilon_t \tag{15.10}$$

where the dot now indicates the simple time derivative, $\dot{n} \frac{dn}{dt}$. Systematic factors that have been widely identified in the empirical literature include size and age of the firm: larger and older firms tend to grow more slowly. However, the random (unexplained) component of growth in these regressions is large. This may possibly be attributable to a model misspecification in the form of missing variables.[14] We shall see in fact in what follows that the systematic component of growth may be related to a number of factors flowing from the activities of private equity firms (PEFs). Some studies control for size and age of the buyout in the analysis, but not all.

EMPLOYMENT, WAGE, AND PRODUCTIVITY EFFECTS

There are both theoretical arguments and empirical evidence that PE backed firms (LBOs) have superior performance to comparable non-PE backed firms. Jensen (1989), in what one may describe as a manifesto for private equity, hailed what was then a new form of economic organization as the savior of the capitalist system. At the time, the U.S. economy was dominated by large firms whose progress was, according to Jensen, stymied by conflicts of interest between owners and managers. The alleged superior governance structure of private equity-backed firms was seen as the solution to the problem of the divorce of ownership and control in the public corporation.[15] For Jensen this new corporate form was the harbinger of a revolution in the way companies would be managed. The disciplining mechanism of debt involved in an LBO for example, provided one important means, whereby managers' appetite for unprofitable projects that nonetheless enhanced their salaries and prestige, could be curbed. The monitoring of such management by professional outside investors and the significant fraction of equity shares they were offered in the buyout also ensured the alignment of the interests of shareholders and managers that under the traditional form of governance had diverged so seriously. Subsequent empirical studies in both the United States and the United Kingdom suggested that (at least in the short run) performance of bought-out companies does indeed improve as a result of the change in organizational form. We shall call this claim the *Jensen hypothesis*.

We divide the literature review that follows geographically, by country. Only U.K./U.S. studies seem to be available. Exhibit 15.1 compares each study against the criteria listed here.

Exhibit 15.1   Comparison of the Studies

	Amess (2003)	Amess and Wright (2007)	Conyon, Girma, Thompson, and Wright (2002)	Cressy, Munari, and Malipiero (2007)	Davis et al. (2008)	Harris, Siegel, and Wright (2005)	Kaplan (1989)	Lichtenberg and Siegel (1990)	Muscarella and Vetsuypens (1990)
Unit of Analysis	Firm	Firm	Firm	Firm	Plant and firm	Plant	Firm	Plant	Firm and Division
Time Period Studied	1986–1997	1999–2004	1983–1996	1995–2000	1980–2005	1994–1998	1980–1986	1972–1988	1976–1987
Country	U.K.	U.K.	U.K.	U.K.	U.S.	U.K.	U.S.	U.S.	U.S.
Industry	Manufacturing	Unrestricted	Unrestricted	Unrestricted	Plants: 5,000? Firms: 1,300	Manufacturing	Unrestricted	Manufacturing	
No. Buyouts	78	1350	240 (takeovers)	54	Yes	979 (MBOs) 4877 (plants)	76 MBOs; 46 with financial data	48 (MBOs) 399 (plants)	
Control Sample?	No	Yes	Yes	Yes	Yes	Yes	No	Yes	72
Macro Cycle?	Yes	Yes	Yes	Yes	Time period, plant age, plant size, sector, LBO type	No	No	Yes	Yes
Regression Variables	??	Fixed assets, Profits, wages, turnover, employment	Employment, wages, labor productivity, output	Operating profits, total assets, turnover, gearing, bubble dummy, gdp growth, aggregate PE activity, MBO/MBI	No	DV: Output IVs: capital stock, total employment, Materials, Pre-MBO, Post-MBO dummies, age of plant, etc.	No regressions performed	DV: Output Ivs: Labor and capital	Yes

316

Test for Survivorship Bias?	No	No	Yes	No	No; but use an unbalanced panel allowing entry and exit	No	No
Eqns for Wages *and* Employment?	No	Yes	No	NA	No; just output	NA	No regressions performed
Endogeneity Test for Restructuring Dummies?	No	Yes	No	No	No	No	No
Test accounts data selection bias?	No	No	Yes	No	No	No	No
Lower PBO employment levels?	NA	?	Yes: 7.5% fall in levels in both friendly and hostile takeovers Absolute *falls* in hostile takeovers alone.	Overall: No differences. Sector diffs: Retail 9.6 lower Services 9.7% lower	Yes	Absolute levels: 1% higher overall; 5% higher for nondivestors. Industry adjusted levels: 12% lower overall; 6% lower for nondivestors	Yes (14% cases)
Lower PBO employment growth?	NA	LBOs: No MBOs: 0.51% higher MBIs: 0.81% lower	NA	NA	NA	NA	NA
Higher production efficiency?	2 yrs prior: Yes 3 yrs post: Yes 5 yrs post: No	NA	NA	NA	NA	NA	Yes (22% cases costs reduced)

(Continued)

Exhibit 15.1 Comparison of the Studies (*Continued*)

	Amess (2003)	Amess and Wright (2007)	Conyon, Girma, Thompson, and Wright (2002)	Cressy, Munari, and Malipiero (2007)	Davis et al. (2008)	Harris, Siegel, and Wright (2005)	Kaplan (1989)	Lichtenberg and Siegel (1990)	Muscarella and Vetsuypens (1990)
Higher labor productivity?	NA	NA	Yes	NA	NA	NA	NA	NA	Yes (10% cases)
Higher total productivity?	NA	NA	NA	NA	Yes	Yes	NA	Yes, 8.3% above for 3 PBO years	NA
Lower wage levels?	NA	NA	NA	NA	NA	NA	NA	Yes, but for white-collar workers only	NA
Lower wage growth?	NA	LBOs: Yes MBOs: 0.31% less MBIs: 0.97% less	NA	NA	NA	NA	NA		
Years prior BO	2	?	1	2	0	?	2	3	0
Years post BO	3	?	3	5	2	?	3	3	3 (average)
Panel data?	Yes	Yes	Yes	No	Yes Unbalanced	Yes Unbalanced	No	No	No
If so, poolability test?	No	No	No	NA	No	No	NA	NA	NA
Separate MBO and MBI analyses?	No	Yes	Yes (friendly and hostile takeovers)	No	MBIs only	MBOs only	No	No	No

U.S. Empirical Studies

Kaplan (1989) examined 76 large MBOs of U.S. public companies completed between 1980 and 1986. In the three post-BO years the companies showed increases in operating income, decreases in capital expenditures and increases in net cash flow. The market value of the companies also increased over the period, consonant with these internal changes. Kaplan also found that the median decrease in employment for buyout companies was about 1 percent per annum after allowing for layoffs via divestitures.[16] Divestitures seem to have a major influence on employment change in the United States in this period because the subsample of buyouts *not* involving divestitures had a median *increase* in employment of 4.9 percent, over five times that of the divesting group. These findings seem to be consistent with buyouts increasing employment in the target companies, at least in the short run.[17]

Lichtenberg and Siegel (1990) (henceforth LS) examined total factor productivity (TFP) effects of buyouts using, in distinction to Kaplan, *plant*-level data from 12,000 U.S. plants whose companies were engaged in LBOs during the period 1983 to 1986. Their analysis controlled for industry effects by examining industry-relative productivity changes.[18] Compared with first three pre-buyout years they found that TFP at plant-level increased from 2 percent above the industry average to 8.3 percent above it for the three post-buyout years. However, these effects seemed to be confined to a specific time period: buyouts accomplished in the period 1981 to 1982 showed no productivity enhancements at all. Differences emerged also between the employment and wage effects on different categories of worker: in the period 1983 to 1986 white-collar worker wages and employment declined in the post-LBO years, while those of blue-collar workers remained constant. As we have seen,[19] increasing *labor* productivity suggests the shedding of jobs, at least in the short run, before any cost reductions are passed on to the consumer resulting in demand expansion. LS conclude that productivity enhancements in the period 1983–1986 could not be attributed to reductions in wages or layoffs of blue-collar workers (or for that matter reductions in R&D and capital investment), leaving the reductions in white collar workers' wages and employment to explain their results.

Muscarella and Vetusypens (1990) (henceforth MV) in a study of the efficiency of so-called *reverse* LBOs (henceforth RMBOs), examined the population of U.S. LBOs that eventually returned to quoted status by 1987. Their analysis sample consisted of 72 U.S. firms with about one-quarter of these experiencing full (whole-company) RMBOs and the remaining three-quarters divisional RMBOs.[20] An important component of efficiency examined was the role of managerial incentives to performance. They found that such incentives were widespread amongst the bought-out entities with virtually all firms having at least one managerial incentive compenzation plan in place in the period of study. The vast majority of these plans were also found to be based on the stock price. The threat of removal or replacement of managers is often thought of as an important incentive to their performance. However, MV found that top managers' jobs were not substantially changed by the buyout with a constant turnover of about one-fifth before and after the event.

This statistic may be interpreted in one of two ways, implying either (1) that the executives chosen for LBO transactions weren't replaced because they were in fact efficient at their jobs, or (2) that these executives were *inefficient,* but this inefficiency was due to demotivation and this could be eliminated by the superior remuneration schemes (stock options, etc.) offered by the new PEF owners. Focusing on the second explanation, MV note that officers' and directors' ownership of company stock was much higher post-buyout than that of comparable Fortune 500 companies,[21] providing buyout management with stronger incentives to boost share price performance before exit.

Restructuring of the target company was also commonplace among the sample MV studied. For example, 75 percent of firms disclosed at least one restructuring activity undertaken since LBO.[22] Most notable was the large number of companies that divested (sold) assets, had reorganized their production facilities (43 percent), or had made acquisitions since the LBO (25 percent). They note two obvious motives for divestitures. On the one hand divestitures are a way of quickly raising cash to pay off the substantially increased indebtedness incurred at LBO.[23] On the other hand, they are a means of reallocating resources to more productive uses, for example, by selling of less profitable parts of the business.[24]

However, MV also found that many (25 percent) of RMBOs involved acquisitions, which by their nature do not raise cash. This is consistent with the hypothesis that RMBOs often aim at restructuring firms (and industries) rather than simply using financial engineering to turn a quick profit.[25] Whether this simply enhances monopoly power of the target firm or raises productivity is a moot point. It is clear however from the MV data that cost savings are a significant part of the buyout activity. Almost a third of firms reported cost savings of some sort including savings in production costs (22 percent) or inventory control and better accounts receivables management (7 percent). Only one in seven reported a reduction in personnel. So this fact suggests that the primary motivation of the buyouts in this sample was to enhance productivity and efficiency rather than to create monopoly power, which would simply involve a reduction in output and a rise in price.

In summary, the MV study is a seminal contribution with an analysis of a wide range of factors associated with the performance of reverse LBOs. Its main deficiency is the smallness of the sample size and the shortness of the sample period.

Davis et al. (2008) carry out an analysis of the employment effects of buyouts on a large sample of U.S. buyouts and matching controls over the 26-year period 1980 to 2005, performing both plant- and firm-level analyses. The data for the "treatment" or buyout sample is taken from the Capital IQ database and other sources. These events/companies are then matched with data from the U.S. Longitudinal Business Database (LBD) by size and industry. The treatment sample initially includes therefore all U.S. LBOs in this period. However, the authors deleted observations with no financial sponsor (MBOs) leaving (see Exhibit 15.1) *only MBIs.* Their final sample seems to be of the order of 1,300 company events, involving around 5,000 plants with the majority occurring in the 1990s.[26] A high proportion (65 percent to 70 percent)[27] of both samples were in manufacturing, retail, and services. The use of establishment data rather than firm data enables them to examine the effects of MBIs on productivity more accurately than some other buyout analyses since divestments can be tracked through time. Importantly, therefore, they examine Greenfield entry[28] by establishment.

Moving to the methodology, employment at 5,000 target establishments (plants) was tracked by Davis for five years both before and after the going-private transaction[29] and the employment trajectories for MBIs compared with those of the control sample. Moving to the firm level analyses, the sample size and tracking period diminishes sharply, to 1,300 target firms and two years post-buy-in respectively.

The central conclusions of the study are that, relative to controls, targeted establishments exhibited (1) net employment contraction, (2) higher job destruction, and (3) higher rates of establishment exit. However they also found that buyouts exhibited (4) greater Greenfield entry of establishments and (5) more acquisition and divestiture than the controls.

Davis et al. tried to examine the factors driving the employment "performance outcomes" for MBI targets over a shorter two-year period, post-buyin.[30] They found that although controls as well as targets created jobs in Greenfield sites, private equity–backed companies created over 50 percent more jobs (15 percent versus 9 percent). This component of job creation compensates to some degree for the job losses from restructuring of existing firms. Finally, firm- (rather than plant-) level analysis by the authors reveals that private equity targets engage both in more acquisitions and more divestitures than control firms. In the two years post-buyout the acquisition rate is 7.3 percent for MBO firms and 4.7 percent for controls. Comparable divestiture rates are 5.7 percent and 2.9 percent respectively.[31]

In terms of explanation, Davis et al. unfortunately have a very limited range of variables to apply. These consist of dummies for time periods (1980s, 1990–1994, after 1995), industrial sector (Manufacturing, Retail and Services are analysed), LBO type (Public to Private, Independent Private/No Seller versus the rest), Divisional/Nonfinancial corporate seller versus the rest and Secondary/Financial firm seller versus the rest). Few of these regressions on subsets produce memorable findings other than the last, which suggests that in the first year after the MBI a Secondary/Financial firm seller will shed 30 percent *more* jobs than a similar non-MBI firm.

To conclude, this is a significant firm- and plant-level study with a remarkably large data set, whose conclusions cannot be ignored. Despite this, the modeling process and the *interpretation* of results are very limited. Firstly, the authors do not specify a sophisticated econometric equation to explain their empirical findings; these are simply reported without comment.[32] Secondly, restructuring dummies may be endogenous but no exogeneity tests are provided by Davis et al. The study, in a word, is long on observations, but short on variables and explanation.[33]

U.K. Empirical Studies

Wright, Thompson, and Robbie (1992) surveyed 182 U.K. LBOs and found that the buyout event was accompanied by an initial decline in employment of 6.3 percent that was followed by a 1.9 percent increase over a five-year period. This short-term decrease in employment was in their view likely to be explained by restructuring of the firm onto a stronger financial footing.

In a useful comparative study to MBIs Conyon et al. (2002) examined the employment effects of both friendly and hostile takeovers on labor demand in the United Kingdom in the period 1983 to 1996. Changes were modeled over the period from one year before to three years after the event. As discussed above, friendly takeovers are similar to MBOs and hostile takeovers to MBIs, the latter being motivated by outsiders while the former is undertaken by incumbent management.[34] The Conyon study is therefore instructive to obtain insight into the employment effects of buyouts and buyout types. Conyon found that friendly and hostile takeovers showed little difference in labor demand, with both demonstrating a negative effect, that is, demand for labor was reduced in the postevent period by about 7.5 percent of the premerger level. However, moving from relative (percentage) effects, hostile takeovers showed a substantial fall in the absolute number of employees by contrast with friendly takeovers. This paralleled the fall in output in such companies in the post-buyout period. He attributed this result to the high level of postmerger divestment (selling off of assets) by the managers of hostile takeovers. This study is particularly interesting because of the parallels with MBOs and MBIs discussed above and because of its analysis of the *longer-term* effects of hostile takeovers.

Conyon, Girma, Thomson, and Wright (2002) used a simultaneous equation approach to examining the productivity and wage effects of 331 domestic and 129 foreign acquisitions in the United Kingdom over the period 1987 to 1996. Foreign firms turn out to pay equivalent employees 3.4 percent more than domestic firms due to their higher productivity. Firms acquired by foreign companies were found to increase their wages and labor productivity by 13 percent and 20 percent respectively. One may be inclined to explain this finding in terms of foreign acquirers sacking low-productivity workers and thus raising the average productivity of those who remain. However, Conyon et al. refute this argument because postacquisition employment levels do not significantly differ from preacquisition values. Thus, it seems that productivity improvements were brought about by more efficient use of labor rather than downsizing of the workforce.

Amess (2003) analyzed the longer-term effect of MBOs on firm-level technical efficiency using a panel data set of U.K. machinery and equipment manufacturers and a stochastic production frontier approach. He found that in the period 1986 to 1997, firms with an MBO governance structure had higher efficiency in the two years before the transaction and in the four years post-buyout of 4 percent to 7.5 percent per annum. This superior efficiency, however, disappeared from year five onward. He argued that this was consistent with MBOs creating managerial incentives that enhance short-run firm-level performance, because those incentives tend to be substantially reduced beyond the five-year span. (Most U.K. buyouts firms are involved in a going-public transaction within five years post-buyout.) This suggests, then, that the incentives and the corresponding performance enhancement are rather short term in nature, as might be predicted.[35]

Harris et al. (2005) estimated the total factor productivity (TFP) of a much larger and broader sample of U.K. manufacturing plants in the period 1994 to 1998 involved in MBOs both before and after the buyout event. They found in an unbalanced[36] panel of 979 buyouts involving 4,877 plants ("establishments") that MBO plants were less productive than comparable plants before the buyout transaction (a selection effect[37]) but showed a considerable increase in productivity in the post-buyout period. This was attributed mainly to the new owners taking measures to reduce labor-intensity of production, in particular the outsourcing of intermediate goods and materials to other plants rather than to acquisitions or divestitures.

Amess and Wright (2007) (henceforth AW) used a simultaneous equations approach to model both wage and employment growth pre- and post-buyout on a sample of 1,350 U.K. LBOs, with separate analyses of MBOs (1,014) and MBIs (336). The total sample constituted an unbalanced panel of 5,369 firms over the period 1999 to 2004. They estimate the following two equations:

$$\Delta n_{it} = \gamma_1 \Delta w_{it} + \gamma_2 \Delta S_{it} + \gamma_2 lbo_i + f_i + v_{it} \qquad (15.11)$$

$$\Delta w_{it} = \beta_1 \Delta \omega'_{it} + \beta_2 \Delta k_{it} + \beta_3 \Delta \pi_{it} + \beta_4 lbo_i + \varepsilon_{it} \qquad (15.12)$$

where

n_{it} = employment in firm i at time t
w_{it} = wage in firm i at time t
S_{it} = output (turnover) of firm i at time t
f_i = firm i specific fixed effect
k_{it} = size (fixed assets) of firm i at time t
π_{it} = profits of firm i at time t
ω'_{it} = industry average wage for firm i at time t
lbo_i = organizational form dummy equal to 1 for buyout; equal to 0 else

Finally, v_{it} and ε_{it} are white-noise error terms.[38]

Using a dummy variable approach in first differences and employing a modeling procedure echoing Conyon et al. (2002), they found that post-buyout, LBOs in general (versus non-LBOs) had an insignificant effect on employment growth, though offered *lower* wage growth than their non-LBO control companies. Within the LBO group, they were able to distinguish between MBOs and MBIs and the results for these subsets were rather different, echoing Conyon et al. (2002). In particular they found that employment growth was half a percentage point *higher* for MBOs and almost 1 percent *lower* for MBIs as compared with the controls. The interdependence of the wage and employment growth equations was also established and, as might be expected, wage growth for MBOs was found to be one-third of a percent lower and for MBIs almost 1 percent lower than that of the controls. Finally, they find that larger firms wages grow more slowly (perhaps because of greater bargaining power of the larger organization) and firms (at any size) whose profits per employee grow faster experience faster wage growth (suggesting rent-sharing behavior).

The study is innovative for a number of reasons. First, in addition to the simultaneous equation approach to modeling wages and employment growth, AW show that the restructuring dummies (LBO, MBO, MBI) are in fact *endogenous*. In other words, not only does (for example) MBI status imply a reduction in employment growth; employment growth also explains MBI status. Intuitively, this means that MBI companies may be *selected* by private equity firms *precisely because* they have slower employment growth. This is the first exact answer to the point on our opening agenda[39] and AW is the first paper to address this important issue. The only remaining question one would like to know the answer to from this study is whether there are differences in the *levels* of employment and wages between the various buyout groups and between the LBOs and non-LBOs. Unfortunately their estimation procedure does not permit us to answer these questions directly.

Building on previous work (Cressy et al. 2007) showing that buyouts have higher operating profitability in the post-Buyout period than matched companies, Cressy et al. (2008) examine contradictory popular claims that private equity (PE)–backed LBOs generate or destroy jobs as a result of the process of "rationalization." Using a sample of 54 U.K. buyouts accomplished in the period 1995 to 2000, and a set of matched controls, they run loglinear employment regressions of the form

$$lemp_{it} = \beta_0 + \beta_1 lemp_{i0} + \sum_{i=2}^{I} \beta_j lx_{ij0} + \beta_3 PE_i + \varepsilon_{it}, t = -2, -1, 0, 1, \ldots 5 \quad (15.13)$$

where

$lemp_{it} =$ natural log of employment in firm i at time t ($t = 0$ is the buyout year)
$lx_{ij0} =$ natural log of characteristic X_j of firm i in the buyout/Control sample in year 0
$PE_i =$ organizational form dummy for firm i equal to 1 for buyouts and 0 for controls
$\varepsilon_{it} =$ white-noise error term

The PE dummy thus represents companies that have PE-backing, while other variables x control for initial employment, gearing, investee size, and profitability, along with industry and macro effects. They find that there is no PEF "choice" effect present in the data: in the buyout year there are no significant differences between buyout companies and controls in terms of job generation/destruction, indicating that buyout firms in this sample are not selected because of their employment trends. However, by contrast, in the post-buyout regressions they find the MBO dummy to be highly significant, negative and quantitatively important. Thus, buyout events involve job losses. More specifically, over the first post-buyout year they estimate that buyout companies' employment falls relative to controls by 7 percent. This figure rises monotonically to 23 percent over the first four years. In the last year of the study (year +5) however, employment increases. LBOs thus seem to bring about quick and substantial reductions in employment in target companies during the period of "rationalization." However, both initial profitability, three-year average post-buyout profitability and three-year sales growth have positive elasticities with respect to future employment. Buyouts generating higher operating profits from job cuts are thus associated with compensating job creation as profitability increases and sales expand, thereby helping to offset job losses arising from initial rationalization of the business.[40]

Their modeling process, unlike the productivity studies discussed above, controls for a range of financial as well as real factors that might affect the conclusions. This approach helps one to answer an important question: If one were to take two samples of otherwise *identical* firms except that one was historically subject to a buyout while the other was not, what would be the employment impact of this change in organizational form (the "treatment" effect)?[41] One contribution of the paper, then, is to construct such a benchmark for comparison. The paper differs from Amess and Wright (2007) in that it operates in levels rather than growth rates as well as addressing the issue of incentives explicitly via the vector of financial explanatory variables. However, unlike Amess and Wright, it is unable, due to the sample size, to analyze the subsets of MBOs versus MBIs nor, due to lack of data, are they able to examine the interdependencies of wage and employment effects.

Going back to the model of growth we presented at the beginning of this chapter, we can explain the Cressy et al. result as follows. In the early post-buyout years restructuring is associated with a fall in demand for labor as reorganization and layoffs occur; demand for the product is in this period relatively low. However, as restructuring increases efficiency, the firm is able to reduce price and/or increase the quality of its products. This has a countervailing effect on the demand for labor and causes it to rise. By year five this effect dominates and eventually (year six and onwards) total employment starts to rise again. This interpretation is consistent with equation 15.22 above. See Exhibit 15.2.[42]

Although as we have seen there is a relative dearth of scientific research on the effects of buyouts on employment, wages, and productivity, extensive studies have been conducted by private sector companies and industry bodies to answer this question. The British venture capital association (BVCA 2005) found that over the previous five years, the number of people employed worldwide by U.K. private equity–backed companies increased by an average of 9 percent per annum,

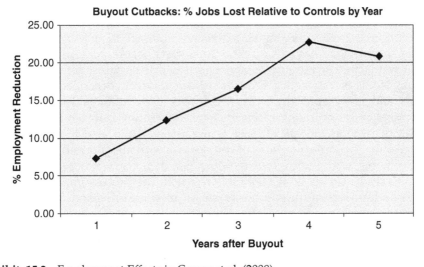

Exhibit 15.2   Employment Effects in Cressy et al. (2008)

compared to only 1 percent in FTSE 100 companies, and 2 percent p.a. of FTSE mid-250 companies.[43] *The Financial Times* (Bryant and Taylor 2007) conducted a survey of the 30 largest PE buyouts in the United Kingdom between 2003 and 2004 and found 36,500 extra jobs had been created in these companies—an increase of 25 percent relative to base levels. A similar report from *The Work Foundation* (Work Foundation 2007) found that although MBOs increased employment levels for up to six years after buyout, MBIs reduced employment by 18.25 percent over a similar period.[44] Using an international data set, the F.A.Z.-Institut in Germany analyzed buyouts occurring in Gemany in the period 1997 to 1999 with respect to growth in sales and jobs. They found buyout companies created jobs at a rate of 4.5 percent per annum compared to 2.2 percent of the benchmark group. Similar results were found by the EVCA (EVCA/CEFS 2007) who apparently "revealed" in a sample of 99 buyout firms that between 2000 and 2004, 420,000 jobs were created.

Needless to say, most papers of this nature suffer from selection bias, because there are no reporting standards for the industry and thus obligation for PEFs to provide accurate statistics on employment and performance. This naturally secretive industry also tends to report only success stories rather than failures.

CONCLUSION

In this chapter we have reviewed a number of papers and reports that attempt to assess the employment effects of buyouts, defined as LBOs (MBOs and MBIs) of publicly quoted companies. These papers covered research in the two largest stock market economies in the world and accounting jointly for the majority of global buyout activity. We found that the studies were subject to a set of limitations (frequently not self-imposed) that impugned robust generalization. However, they seemed to demonstrate collectively that by and large buyouts involve restructuring of companies and in the short run (at least) involve job losses. These losses were more marked for MBIs than MBOs due probably to the fact that outsiders are more able to look at the company in the bright light of day and to act accordingly to close loss-making divisions and sack their workers. They were largely short-run studies covering the three years post-buyout. In the longer run the proverbial jury on the employment effects of private equity activity is therefore still out. While private equity firms have been variously described as barbarians, locusts, and, less graphically, as asset strippers, these findings do not necessarily raise moral issues: economic efficiency may well require that resources (labor and capital) released as a result of these transactions be allocated to maximize society's wealth. The same questions of course arise with mergers and acquisitions of the traditional kind. Future research may also demonstrate that (as indicated in one U.K. study, Cressy et al. 2007) this restructuring process improves the company's performance sufficiently to create an increased demand for its products that in the longer run increases its demand for labor. On the other hand, it may conclude that things return to "business as usual" as the effects of temporary incentives wane.

A final point worth noting is in the interpretation of the results we have discussed. Emerging from the U.K. literature, at least, is the fact that there is a potentially important role for PEF *selection* in the job losses observed: private equity firms may well *choose* to buy out/in firms in employment decline. In other words, their role in the *selection* rather than the restructuring process may account for some of the short-run job losses we observe. Future research may shed further light on this issue.

NOTES

1. This is not an ideal measure because it does not control for hours worked. However, it is the measure often used in the literature and has the advantage of feasibility.

2. Some studies we shall refer to use total factor rather than just labor productivity.

3. Once more, this is not the only possible definition of a buyout, because many buyouts are of privately held companies. However, the choice is data-determined.

4. A good early survey of the area is provided by Palepu (1990).

5. One reason why, for example, productivity and along with it wages may rise in the post-buyout phase is that low productivity workers may be laid off and the remaining high productivity workers paid their (higher) marginal revenue product.

6. More formally, we want to know if (1) an LBO transaction in year t results in more or less employment in years $t + 1, t + 2$ etc. relative to, for example, the base year $t = 0$ (or the prior year $t - 1$), than a *comparable non-LBO company* in those years; and (2) whether an MBI in year t results in more or less employment than an MBO in $t + 1, t + 2$, etc. relative to each other (with one used as control) and relative to non-LBOs.

7. An alternative approach, of course, is to create a stratified sample with LBOs sampled disproportionately. Because the sample is then nonrandom, we then require some weighting system to be applied to the results.

8. A superior but infrequently used method is matching by propensity scores.

9. Essentially, Heckman's procedure is to treat missing data as a missing variable problem where the missing variable is a measure of the hazard (conditional probability) of missing data. See Maddala (1983) for details.

10. At the time of writing the "global credit crunch," as it has come to be known, has resulted in a dramatic decline in LBOs because of the unwillingness of banks to lend, particularly in the face of a major global downturn in aggregate demand.

11. This may not seem obvious at first sight, but the Jensen hypothesis (see further on) suggests that management investment decisions will be influenced by the amount of debt in the capital structure. This in turn should affect the level and productivity of the workforce.

12. For the uninitiated, endogeneity in this context means that at least one independent variable in the regression may depend on the regressand (dependent variable), contrary to the assumptions of OLS. In symbols this means that two relationships need to be considered:

$$e_{t+s} = f(LBO_t, \ldots), \quad s = 1, 2 \ldots$$

$$LBO_t = g(\ldots e_{t-2}, e_{t-1})$$

where t is the date of the buyout. Thus we may find that (1) not merely may LBOs initiate reductions in labor after the buyout event (the first equation), but also (2) that LBOs may take place in firms that were *already* showing signs of labor force decline (labor reduction pre-buyout, for example, in response to falling sales and profits).

13. Special cases of this model include the Random Walk, corresponding to $\gamma = 0$.

14. This can be thought of as restating γ as a function of various explanatory variables.

15. The debate goes back to the seminal work of Berle and Means (1932).

16. A divestiture consists in the sale of a divisions or subsidiary of the company bought out.

17. It is worth noting here that divestitures do not necessarily imply any change in employment in the economy; they may merely involve a change in the distribution between firms with the divesting firm's employment going down by the same amount as the divested firm's goes up.

18. Industry relatives have the advantage that they measure performance relative to an industry benchmark, thus controlling for industry effects. On the other hand, they do not immediately tell us about the quantitative effects on a given firm.

19. Equation 8 above.

20. A divisional MBO involves the buyout of a division of a company only.

21. In fact, this group owned collectively a median 63 percent of the equity before the LBO, falling to 45 percent afterwards.

22. There is no control sample used in this study, so it is difficult to be sure that this restructuring would not have taken place if there had been no LBO. See the discussion of ideal research criteria above.

23. A classic recent U.K. case of this was the buyout of Debenhams department stores, in which the considerable property assets of the company were sold and leased back by the organizers of the buyout to pay off debt.

24. MV also find (not surprisingly) that the extent of divestiture differed amongst LBO types with one-half of full LBOs engaging in divestitures and only 20 percent of divisional LBOs experiencing this.

25. This is certainly consistent with some of the British experience. For example, Vinni Murria of Elderstreet Partners, a senior partner in that organization argued in the early 2000s that a primary strategic aim of theirs was to consolidate fragmented industries via a sequence of acquisitions by a key player in the sector.

26. Number estimated graphically from their Figure 1.

27. Estimated graphically from their Figure 4, panel A.

28. Although the term is not defined in Davis et al., Greenfield establishments appear to be establishments operating under different names from the parents so that they would not be easily identified in the empirical analysis.

29. The length of the periods for the event studies is justified by the authors on the grounds that most going-private transactions have gone public again within five years.

30. This focus reduces the sample size substantially.

31. Percentages measure the change in total employment in establishments as a result of acquisitions and divestitures.

32. One outcome of a U.K. study, for example—see Amess and Wright, 2007, further on—found that the wage and employment growth equations were interdependent,

thus requiring a simultaneous equations approach. This point is ignored by Davis et al.

33. The paper is also rather badly written, making extraction of the key pieces of information laborious.

34. The comparison may stop here, as the instruments for management motivation provided by PEFs are by and large not implemented in a hostile takeover.

35. This is clearly the case with U.S. companies performing RMBOs, because they will typically return to public ownership within three years, according to the U.S. study (MV) reported above.

36. A *balanced* panel is one with a constant time period for each firm. An *unbalanced* panel, by contrast, is one where the time period for each firm may vary, for example, as a result of entry and exit to the sample by birth and death of companies.

37. See point 3 in the Pitfalls listed previously.

38. Thus, the modeling procedure implies that employment depends on the wage but not vice versa.

39. See the introduction to this chapter.

40. See equation 15.8 above.

41. This is a critical policy issue because a test of the Jensen hypothesis demands that we know whether a change in organizational form brings about job cutbacks (a prima facie "bad") to improve performance (a prima facie "good").

42. In Cressy et al. (2007) we note, however, that by year five employment has not *risen* yet; the rate of *job losses* has merely declined.

43. They also calculated that companies that had received PE funding employed 2.8 million people in the United Kingdom, roughly one in five workers.

44. The report uses data from the University of Nottingham's Centre for Management Buy-out Research (CMBO) on 1,350 buyouts in the United Kingdom between 1999 and 2004 discussed above. See Wright et al. (2005).

REFERENCES

Amess, Kevin. 2003. The effect of management buyouts on firm-level technical inefficiency: Evidence from a panel of U.K. machinery and equipment manufacturers. *Journal of Industrial Economics* LI (1) (March).

Amess, Kevin, and Mike Wright. 2007. The wage and employment effects of leveraged buyouts in the U.K. *International Journal of the Economics of Business* 14 (2) (July).

Amess, Kevin, and Mike Wright. 2007. *Barbarians at the gate? Leveraged buyouts, private equity, and jobs.* Centre for Management Buy-out Research, University of Nottingham, U.K.

Berle, Adolf A., and Gardner C. Means. 1932. *The modern corporation and private property.* New York: Commerce Cleaning House.

Bryant, Christopher, and Alan Taylor. 2007. Private equity deals that cement business growth. *Financial Times* (April 2).

BVCA. 2005. The economic impact of private equity in the U.K., 2005. British Venture Capital Association Report, London.

Conyon, Martin J., Sourafel Girma, Steve Thompson, and Peter W. Wright. 2002. The impact of mergers and acquisitions on company employment in the United Kingdom. *European Economic Review* 46 (1):31–49.

Cressy, Robert C. 2006. Determinants of small firm survival and growth. In the Oxford handbook of entrepreneurship, eds. Mark Casson, Bernard Yeung, Anuradha Basu, and Nigel Wadeson, 161–193. Oxford: Oxford University Press.

Cressy, Robert C., Federico Munari, and Alessandro Malipiero. 2008. Playing to their strengths? Evidence that specialization by private equity firms confers competitive advantage. *Journal of Corporate Finance* 13 (Special Issue on Private Equity, Leveraged Buyouts, and Corporate Governance):647–669.

Cressy, Robert C., Federico Munari, and Alessandro Malipiero. 2007. Creative destruction? U.K. evidence that Buyouts cut jobs to raise returns. Entrepreneurship and Innovation Centre, Working Paper, Birmingham University Business School, February.

Davis, Steven J., John Haltiwanger, Ron Jarmin, Josh Lerner, and Javier Miranda. 2008. Private equity and employment. Discussion Paper CES 08-07, Center for Economic Studies, Bureau of the Census, Washington D.C.

Hart, Peter E., and Sigbert J. Prais. 1956. The analysis of concentration: A statistical approach. *Journal of the Royal Statistical Society, Series A (General)* 119 (2):150–191.

EVCA. 2005. *Pan-European survey on performance*. Brussels, October.

EVCA/CEFS. 2007. *Employment contribution of private equity and venture capital in Europe*. December.

Harris Richard, Donald S. Siegel, and Mike Wright. 2005. Assessing the impact of management Buyouts on economic efficiency: Plant-level evidence from the United Kingdom. *The Review of Economics and Statistics* 87 (1):148–153.

Jensen, M. 1989. The eclipse of the public corporation. *Harvard Business Review* 5:61–74.

Kaplan, S. N. 1989. The effects of management buyouts on operating performance and value. *Journal of Financial Economics* 24 (2):217–254.

Lichtenberg, F., and D. Siegel, 1990. The effects of leveraged buyouts on productivity and related aspects of firm behavior. *Journal of Financial Economics* 27 (1):165–194.

Muscarella, Chris J., and Michael R. Vetsuypens. 1990. Efficiency and organizational structure: A study of reverse LBOs. *Journal of Finance* 45 (5):1389–1413.

Maddala, G. S. 1983. *Limited dependent and qualitative variables in econometrics*. Cambridge, U.K.: Cambridge University Press.

Palepu, Krishna G. 1990. Consequences of leveraged buyouts. *Journal of Financial Economics* 27 (1):247–262.

The Work Foundation. 2007. *Inside the dark box: Shedding light on private equity*. London: The Work Foundation.

Wright, Mike, Steve Thompson, and Ken Robbie. 1992. Venture capital and management-led leveraged buyouts: European evidence. *Journal of Business Venturing* 7 (1):47–71.

ABOUT THE AUTHOR

Robert Cressy is Professor of Entrepreneurship and Innovation at The Birmingham Business School and Director of the Entrepreneurship and Innovation Centre (EIC). His early academic research in entrepreneurial finance emphasized the role of human capital in determining both capitalization of the business and its survival: finance flows towards business talent and ideas. His most celebrated paper, "Are Business Startups Debt-Rationed?," published in *The Economic Journal*, 1996, therefore argued that the basic constraint on businesses was not financial but human capital. His recent work has focused on private equity performance and his most important recent finding in this area is that buyouts raise returns to investee companies but at the same time effect short-run job losses. This emerges from two recent papers: "Playing to Their Strengths? Evidence that Specialization in Private Equity Confers Competitive Advantage," published in the *Journal of Corporate Finance* in 2007, and "Creative Destruction? Evidence That Buyouts Shed Jobs in Raising Returns," an EIC Working Paper, 2008.

PART IV

International Perspectives on Private Equity and Regulation

CHAPTER 16

Valuation and (Financial) Disclosure in the Private Equity Industry

Institutional Set-Up, Incentives, and Empirical Analysis

DOUGLAS CUMMING
Associate Professor and Ontario Research Chair, York University,
Schulich School of Business

ANDREJ GILL
Ph.D. Candidate, Goethe University, Frankfurt

UWE WALZ
Professor, Goethe University, Frankfurt

INTRODUCTION

Private equity (PE) firms are financial intermediaries standing between the portfolio firms and their investors. They are typically organized as closed-end funds aiming to overcome informational asymmetries and to exploit specialization gains in selecting and overseeing portfolio firms (see, e.g., Sahlman 1990). However, their existence as financial intermediaries, while reducing but not eliminating the informational asymmetries with respect to the firm, creates new informational asymmetries (with respect to the investors in the PE funds). One of the main instruments used to mitigate informational asymmetries is the disclosure of performance from the portfolio firm to the PE firm and from the PE firm to the investor. Disclosure of performance to the investor is burdened by two main difficulties. On one hand, valuation requires sufficient information on the performance of the firm, whereas on the other hand, even if sufficient information is available, PE firms may choose to disclose information strategically. The main aim of this chapter is to discuss these two issues in detail.

Disclosure takes place against the background of some decisive features of the industry. The business of private equity and most notably that of venture capital funds is based on investments in highly uncertain ventures.[1] These investments are illiquid, so selling and buying takes place on a rather irregular basis. Furthermore, there is little regulation in the PE industry (in contrast to public equity markets; see, e.g., Hand 2005).

The relative importance of the valuation and disclosure topic, especially between the PE fund (the general partner [GP]) and the investors (the limited partners [LPs]) follows the developments in the industry in a countercyclical manner. This was especially pertinent during the market slides in the aftermath of the dot-com boom in 2000 and the financial crisis of 2008. In such phases investors are more sensitive to the valuation of the assets held by private equity firms and are seeking more information with respect to any possible write-downs.

Given the illiquidity of the investment, current investors want to be informed of the value of their investment. One reason for this is that the investors, being either pension funds or other institutional investors, often face disclosure requests as well. This conflict of interest between the PE funds' desire for opaqueness and the investor's request for more transparency and disclosure of information relating to performance became most obvious in the course of the lawsuit against the Californian pension fund CalPERS. In this lawsuit, CalPERS was forced by its stakeholders and the outside public to disclose performance information on its investments in various private equity funds. Subsequently, a number of private equity funds turned down CalPERS when it was willing to invest in said funds.

The valuation of investments is crucial not only for LPs currently engaged in the private equity fund but also for potential future investors considering an investment in the private equity firm's follow-up funds. Hence, in a nutshell, the decisive questions are: What are the incentives for individual PE funds to truthfully report to their investors? And to what extent are existing industry guidelines helpful? Is regulatory intervention necessary and potentially helpful? Can we observe (strategic) misreporting, and if so, in which circumstances is it more likely?

This chapter is to address these questions and provide an overview of linkages between the valuation and disclosure issue in the private equity industry (i.e., from the portfolio firm to the fund as well as between the PE fund and the investors). Our main focus will, however, be on the valuation of unrealized investments and disclosure of this information from GPs to LPs. We will analyze this against the background of theoretical arguments for or against truthful disclosure as well as recent empirical evidence. Furthermore, we provide an overview on the institutional setup as well as topical developments in the countries with the large private equity markets. Last but not least we relate the accuracy of financial reporting of nonlisted portfolio firms to the valuation and disclosure of performance information from the private equity fund to investor. Throughout our entire discussion we focus only on disclosure of performance-related information and forego discussing other investment-related issues such as corporate governance issues, strategic job creation or destruction, and the like (see, e.g., Walker 2007).

In order to stress the main issues even more clearly, it is helpful to compare private equity funds with two mutual funds and hedge funds. Mutual funds and hedge funds invest in highly liquid assets. While mutual funds pool the capital of small investors, hedge funds attract a very limited number of wealthy investors. While there is a need to protect small investors in mutual funds via regulation with hedge funds, investor protection is not regarded as an argument. In contrast, private equity funds pool the money of their limited partners (typically a small number of wealthy investors) and invest it in highly illiquid assets. Hence, there is definitively less need to protect small investors in the private equity than in the mutual funds industry, but there might be a reason to increase transparency.

This chapter is structured as follows. First, in the following section, we provide an overview on the institutional setup and recently developed guidelines and standards in the private equity industry. In the section titled "Main Problems and Conflicts of Interest" we will discuss the main conflicts of interests standing against a voluntary and truthful disclosure of financial information. We discuss circumstances under which we should expect that the valuation and disclosure issue can be more properly approached by voluntary disclosure in the sections titled "Incentives for Voluntary Disclosure versus Mandatory Disclosure." Furthermore, we discuss the costs and benefits of industry standards and regulation in this section. In the following section, "Disclosure and Reporting Patterns of Venture-Backed Portfolio Firms," we briefly look into recent empirical evidence on financial reporting and disclosure for nonlisted companies. Thereby, we ask how private equity and venture capital involvement affects the disclosure behavior of management in these firms. In a final step, we discuss empirical evidence on the degree of potential misreporting of PE firms towards their current investors. A last section summarizes the main points, concludes with the main implications of our analysis, and points to potential avenues of future research.

INSTITUTIONAL SETUP

Valuation and Disclosure Rules for Privately Held (Portfolio) Firms

Private equity funds are financial intermediaries channeling capital from their investors to portfolio firms (see Exhibit 16.1 for a detailed illustration). Hence, an important channel that may affect the disclosure of information of PE funds toward their limited partners is the degree of information disclosed by their portfolio firms to them. The disclosure of financial information of the portfolio firms to their investor (i.e., the private equity fund) clearly forms an important starting point for proper valuation of the PE's investments. Portfolio firms of PE firms are typically not listed[2] and do have limited liability status. While publicly traded firms face rather rigid financial reporting standards across the world with respect to their

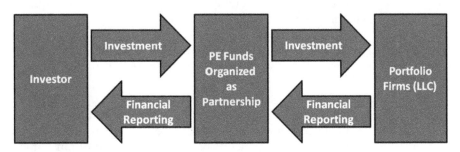

Exhibit 16.1   Information/Investment Flows in a PE Environment

valuation and disclosure policies, these matters are at least in parts significantly different for privately held portfolio firms.

In order to evaluate the degree of financial reporting and disclosure of the portfolio firms of PE funds, we will provide a brief overview of the financial reporting and disclosure rules applicable for privately held firms in the United States and the European Union (EU).

In the United States there are no mandatory financial reporting or disclosure rules imposed on privately held firms (McCahery and Vermeulen 2008). While firms are therefore free to choose how and to what extent they want to provide financial reporting, most of the firms provide financial statements that adhere to some extent to the guiding principles of U.S. generally accepted accounting principles (GAAP). This degree of voluntary disclosure is mainly due to two factors.

The first underlying reason is the often-stressed effect of voluntary disclosure on the cost and availability of capital, especially debt (for an empirical analysis on this effect for publicly traded firms, see, e.g., Welker 1995 and Healy, Hutton, and Palepu 1999). Firms need to create reports because their outside creditors demand financial statements. To receive new credit, firms need to make sure they can repay the loans. Most creditors demand a financial statement that is audited through a certified public accountant (CPA). The CPA therefore attests that the firm created a GAAP conform statement (see McCahery and Vermeulen 2008). A related matter is the desire to attract new financiers. In order to do so, even privately held firms which do not directly rely on the public markets need to convince potential future investors of their financial situation and soundness. Second, firms that are willing to go public in the near future (thereby gaining access to public equity) are required to hold financial statements that are U.S.-GAAP-consistent at least for the last five years (see Hand 2005). As a huge number of PE deals are exited via an IPO this may, especially in PE-backed firms, be a crucial aspect of providing sound financial statements. In a nutshell, this implies that a significant number of privately held firms in the United States provide financial statements whereby they adhere to the standards of U.S. GAAP. Furthermore, given the strong position of PE investors, we should expect that PE firms are able and willing to force their portfolio firms to provide such financial statements, thereby supplying valuable financial information to the general partner of the respective PE fund(s). This, however, is supported by the Delaware Corporation law, which entitles members of close corporations to substantial information (see McCahery and Vermeulen 2008).

In the European Union, matters are somewhat different. The Fourth Council Directive (see Fourth Council Directive 78/660/EEC of 25 July 1978 of the EU) of the European Union sets the minimum standard of reporting for nonlisted companies with limited liability in the European Union as follows:

> ... the annual accounts shall comprise the balance sheet, the profit and loss account and the notes on the accounts. These documents shall constitute a composite whole.

This differentiates the reporting requirements from their counterparts in the United States, as they are based on a binding legal requirement and not on voluntary disclosure, or an agreement between company and investors/funds. In contrast, however, to U.S. GAAP, which is based on the notion of fair value and going concern, the European legal standards rely on the notion of debtor protection.

On top of that, EU-based firms also need to disclose their financial statements to the general public (see Directive 2006/46/EC of the European Parliament and of the Council of 14 June 2006), although state laws may provide exceptions to this:

> *The laws of a member state may, however, permit the annual report not to be published as stipulated above. In that case, it shall be made available to the public at the company's registered office in the Member State concerned. It must be possible to obtain a copy of all or part of any such report free of charge upon request.*

This does not practically differentiate the European way from the United States method. In the United States the pressure to reveal the earnings is simply applied from private organizations/companies instead of through legal requirements.

Overall, this short comparison clearly reveals three matters. The first is that private equity managers should indeed have access to the proper financial reports of the portfolio firms as a starting point for their own valuations. Second, financial reports of portfolio firms limit the discretionary powers of portfolio managers when it comes to valuations, and third, we should expect that the stringency of reporting standards (with respect to reflecting fair value) should be reflected in the valuation of private equity firms vis-à-vis their limited partners.

Valuation and Disclosure Guidelines for Private Equity Funds

Obviously, valuations in the PE industry have always been a difficult task, and this is especially so for venture capital. Disclosure of (financial) information and the valuations of (un-) realized investments in the PE industry, whose companies are typically organized as partnerships, have not been formally regulated around the world, despite some recent discussions about doing so.[3] However, a number of industry guidelines have been proposed by various committees and bodies in the recent past in order to diminish the public perception of opacity within the industry and to avoid regulatory moves.

The first self-regulatory effort can be traced back to the National Venture Capital Association's (NVCA) attempt in 1990 to propose guidelines for consistent valuations in the industry (Hardymon, Lerner, and Leamon 2007). The British Venture Capital Association (BVCA) as well as the European Venture Capital Association (EVCA) followed suit in the early 1990s, proposing guidelines for valuations and their disclosure from the limited to the general partners of private equity funds. The basic notion in all these guidelines was that the general partner is better informed and is therefore in charge of valuing portfolio companies. Furthermore, the early valuation principle strongly relied on the idea of valuation at the price of the most recent investment. This could either imply a valuation at the cost of investment or, in cases in which further investment rounds by other informed outside investors (other PE investors) had taken place, using the price being paid in the last investment round.

In the aftermath of these first attempts towards the establishment of (formally nonbinding) industry guidelines, further versions of these guidelines were published in order to develop matters. These new versions, especially the ones of the BVCA and the EVCA, moved in the direction of "Fair Value" reporting. They were therefore mainly concerned with the problem that, in a downward market, valuation at costs prevents the need to write down the valuations in the PE's portfolio.

After many previously published guidelines in 1991, 1993, and 2001, the International Private Equity and Venture Capital Valuation Guidelines (IPEV guidelines), which form the joint guidelines of many regional industry groups (except the NVCA), have been published in their current version as of October 2006. The goal was to ensure that the needs for greater comparability across the industry are covered and the alignment of reporting standards between U.S. GAAP and IFRS is fulfilled. Throughout these recommended guidelines, the reporting quality seems to have been increased (Mathonet and Monjanel 2006). In addition, their official acceptance in the industry increased: In their study the European Investment Fund (EIF) asked the funds in its portfolio if they comply with the new IPEV guidelines. Nearly 80 percent responded that they will adopt the new guidelines (Mathonet and Monjanel 2006). The authors also tested for the degree of compliance and the impact of the new guidelines on valuations of PE funds. Their findings suggest a positive relationship between following the guidelines and the reported IRR. However, this needs to be handled with caution due to sample selection biases and time effects, which are not taken into account.

Thus, there are currently two types of relevant valuation guidelines in the PE industry that follow the same principles (see Exhibit 16.2 for a comparison). These valuation guidelines are complemented by overall reporting and disclosure standards (e.g., EVCA 2006). It therefore suffices to discuss in more detail the "International Private Equity and Venture Capital Guidelines" proposed by a large number of regional industry associations (IPEV 2007). The key principle behind these guidelines is to apply methods that aim to determine fair value. In order to do so, a number of different applicable valuation methods are proposed. Valuation can rely on six different methods: (1) price of recent investment, (2) earnings multiple, (3) net assets, (4) discounted cash flows or earnings (of underlying business), (5) discounted cash flows (from the investment), and (6) industry valuation benchmarks. To select the appropriate methodology, "the valuer should exercise his or her judgment to select the valuation methodology that is most appropriate. . . ." (IPEV 2007). Over time, "methodologies should be applied consistently from period to period, except where a change would result in better estimates of Fair Value." For all different methodologies, detailed rules are developed on how to use and/or adopt the different methods. This gives significant leeway to the general partner.

A brief discussion of the main methods and their inherent difficulties illustrates the following.[4] First, when using the price of the recent investment, the fact that different rights are attached to the new and existing investments matters for determining the price. Assessing the economic value of these rights is associated with significant uncertainties and opens up room for subjective judgment. With earnings multiples it is suggested that "comparable" multiples be used while taking into account that earnings multiples are adjusted for differences between the comparator and the company valued (e.g., for risk and growth prospects). It is therefore not only the choice of the "comparable" company but also the way adjustments are undertaken that leaves substantial room for interpretation. With method 3, namely that of valuing net assets, one has to take into account that a substantial degree of the assets of portfolio firms consists of nontangible assets that easily distort this valuation principle. Using discounted cash flow methods is without doubt theoretically sound (Lerner, Hardymon, and Leamon 2009). However, choosing the proper input data is inherently difficult, especially for the portfolio

Exhibit 16.2 Comparison of NVCA and IPEV Guidelines

	NVCA	IPEV
General Objective	Fair Value	Fair Value
General Disclosure	Yes	Yes
Frequency of Reporting	Quarterly basis	Periodic
Methods	• Cost/Latest Round of Financing • Performance Multiple • DCF (only in limited situations) • Net assets valuation • Industry-specific benchmarks	• Price of recent Investment • Earnings Multiple • Net assets • DCF • Industry valuation benchmarks
Consistency over Time	Be consistent until a new methodology provides a better approximation of the investment's current Fair Value.	Methodologies should be applied consistently from period to period, except where a change would result in better estimates of Fair Value.
Type of Information	Valuation	Valuation

companies under consideration. Given the high degree of uncertainty in the environment under discussion, this method is very sensitive to discount and terminal growth assumptions. Using the industry benchmark principles would mean that the same difficulties apply as with comparable multiples. Thus, there is obviously the danger that all the methods could, under the given circumstances, give rise to any specific desired valuation.

Exhibit 16.2 provides a short comparison of the main differences, as well as common features of the IPEV and the NVCA valuation guidelines.

A Brief Evaluation of Valuation Guidelines

Valuation of PE investments is inherently based on forward-looking estimates and decisions with respect to market conditions and the underlying business itself. The problem is that a public market, which is a crucial help in translating information into proper valuations, might either exist only rudimentarily or not at all. The question therefore is: to what extent do the industry guidelines help to provide truthful reporting of private equity funds toward their investors? Two matters are worth noting. First, the reporting guidelines, by stressing the need to stick with consistent methods applied over time, improve the comparability of data provided intertemporally. Any deviation from a given method has to be explained and justified. In addition, by providing guidelines to the entire industry they increase the level of transparency by allowing comparisons across PE funds. If, for example, most PE funds use multiples of five in a given industry, it becomes significantly more difficult for a PE fund to permanently justify a multiple of eight in the very same industry. Secondly, despite the entire set of principles and guidelines (and even if properly applied), there is significant room for maneuvering for the PE managers. This is especially true of venture capital investments and their high degree of uncertainty. Therefore plenty of room remains for private equity funds to willingly misinform their limited partners.

Two questions remain. First, is sticking to valuation at cost rather than at fair value an alternative that may overcome the potential problems associated with fair value reporting? Valuation at cost certainly does not overcome one of the most often observed sources of overreporting (see the next section): the lack of write-downs in market downturns. Further, the potential clearly remains for providing less than adequate information to the investor. Given that the limited partners receive information about cash flowing into the company, they may use this as an indicator of cost valuations on their own. The second question, namely whether there are any other possibilities to mitigate this problem, is left to our final discussion.

MAIN PROBLEMS AND CONFLICTS OF INTEREST

In the second half of 2002, several public institutional investors in the United States came under legal pressure to disclose the performance of private equity and venture capital funds they had invested in (EVCA 2003). For instance, the California pension fund CalPERS lost its case and published IRR data for its investments in the PE industry on its web site. In the aftermath, a number of PE funds decided to restrict the access to funds for certain publicly accountable investors.

This incidence clearly highlights potential conflicts of interest arising between investors (LPs) and private equity funds (GPs). Whereas investors, especially if publicly accountable, are interested in more transparent disclosure rules and policies, private equity firms consider this as a threat to their business model, which is focused on illiquid investments and discontinuous trading (and hence valuation).

However, there is not only a conflict of interest between investors and private equity firms as to whether performance data should be disclosed, but also how firms and investment should be valued. Obviously, with exited investments the measurement of performance is relatively straightforward (if one overlooks all the issues associated with the IRR measure; see Phalippou in this volume). With unexited investments, valuation is far less straightforward and hinges to a large extent on the discretionary power of the PE manager (see, e.g., Kut, Bengt, and Smolarski 2007; Wright, Pruthi, and Lockett 2005). Many private equity firms have valued their companies at the higher of cost (as given by the most recent investment) or market value as determined by the most recent outsider-led financing round (Hardymon et al. 2007). With rising valuation during the time of investment, this valuation policy leads to positive surprises at the time of exit. With falling firm values, the degree and speed of write-downs becomes crucial. Besides reflecting overoptimistic portfolio values (with the associated signaling effect on potential investors, as discussed later), this might also have an effect on the compensation scheme of private equity managers and thus, in turn, might affect their incentives to undertake write-downs or delay them into the future. The two major sources of the GPs' income are the performance-independent management fee and the carried-interest, which allows the GPs to participate in superior performance. However, if unexited investments are overvalued (i.e., kept at costs while their true value would have required a write-down below costs), realizations of superior performance with exited investments may potentially lead to excess distributions. The GPs then receive a larger share of total accumulated excess returns than they should have received, based on the true value of the portfolio. So-called claw-back distributions, by which the GP is required to pay back excess distribution, do compensate for this. But in order for this to be effective, claw-back requires that the money is still available and not spent for private purpose. In the latter case, claw-back provisions become ineffective. Hence, this creates potential conflicts of interest between the private equity managers and their investors.

Overreporting is also not in the interest of institutional investors such as CalPERS, which are themselves forced to report to their investors because this may lead to sudden changes in portfolio value that are difficult to "sell" to third parties.

Further conflicts of interest arise due to interorganizational structure in the PE firms that are clearly not homogenous entities (Hardymon et al. 2007). For instance, they might stem from internal promotion schemes in the private equity organization as well as from long-term involvement of particular managers with the firm ("my baby" arguments), which clearly reduce the incentives to truthfully report a reduction in the value of particular portfolio firms.

But even if drops in firm value are overlooked, there are significant problems associated with valuations at cost or market value. If in new financing rounds new outside investors join the investment syndicate, it is highly unlikely that this will come as a plain investment that demands cash flow rights in return to capital infusions only. Rather, new investors typically demand new or additional control and decision rights (Kaplan and Stromberg 2003; Bienz and Walz 2007). It therefore becomes quite difficult to compare different series of equities (with different decision and control rights) and to monetize the inherent value of the decision and control rights. As indicated earlier, such issues are reflected in industry guidelines as well.

A further main source of conflicts of interests arises between private equity funds and potential future investors (LPs). The main asset of private equity managers is their track record. First-time PE managers in particular cannot rely on the past performance of successful PE funds. Instead, they have to rely on the performance of their current fund. Negative performance of the current fund is obviously a negative signal, which clearly makes the closing of future funds more difficult. These mechanisms increase incentives for first-time private equity managers in particular to overreport the valuations of unexited investments. This is especially true for PE managers who are under pressure to fund a follow-on fund and who lack the track record of completely dissolved funds; the conflict of interest with respect to a reporting of a "fair and true" value of the unexited portfolio firms is obviously most pronounced in this case (see also our discussion in the following section).

INCENTIVES FOR VOLUNTARY DISCLOSURE VERSUS MANDATORY DISCLOSURE

If there are sufficient incentives that induce proper, voluntary disclosure of performance measures and valuations, the problems discussed earlier could be resolved via the marketplace without any interference through either standard/guideline setting or regulation (see a general discussion of this in Leuz and Wysocki 2008). In order to shed light on whether and potentially when this is actually the case in the private equity market and the private equity industry, we discuss the following incentives and potential mechanisms, implying that potential benefits exceed the voluntary costs of disclosure.

We proceed in three steps. First, we address the factors that affect the degree and quality of disclosure from the firm to the private equity fund. In order to be able to disclose and report proper valuation to the investors, private equity managers need to be accurately informed as to the economic value of their portfolio firms. Private equity firms are by no means uninformed outside investors in their portfolio firms. This view contrasts—at least to some extent—with comments of private equity representatives:

> Valuation of private, venture backed company's stock is a process which at best is costly, complex and inexact. Absent new rounds of financing, venture capitalists rarely have information upon which to base changes of the set stock price because the stock is not tradable. . . . (Heesen, 2004).

The question therefore arises as to whether this is true in general for nonlisted stocks in private equity portfolio or only for rather early stages of investment (a question that we will also address from an empirical point of view in the next section).

In any case, the degree of disclosure of the portfolio firm's management may lead to an enhancement of the private equity firm's level of information. Additionally, and even more importantly, it allows third parties (potential private equity investors into the portfolio firm, auditors, and LPs) to reduce informational asymmetries.

Second, we look into the potential benefits and costs of private equity investors, which affect their willingness to properly disclose performance information to their investors. The main question in both steps is under which circumstances there are sufficient incentives for proper voluntary disclosure.

Third, we look into the implications as well as the costs and benefits of (binding) industry guidelines and regulation for the disclosure of financial figures from the portfolio firms to the private equity firm as well as of private equity firms to their investors.

Disclosure of Firm-Specific Information

From a theoretical perspective, it has been often argued that there are strong incentives to voluntarily disclose information in order to avoid negative signals conveyed to outsiders if voluntary disclosures are not made (Grossman and Hart 1980; Milgrom 1981). The most notable benefit for firms seeking private equity (or having already private equity investors on board) is the positive effect of corporate disclosure on the cost of capital. Firms then have an incentive to voluntarily report and disclose value relevant information truthfully. For instance, Merton (1987) makes the point that disclosure by lesser-known firms can make investors aware of this firm and thereby enlarge the firm's investor base. In the context of private equity, better quality reporting may reduce the screening costs of private equity firms and thus make the respective portfolio firm more attractive for investments. Increased disclosure is not, however, without cost: it requires higher levels of financial expertise and knowledge, higher preparation costs, and can also have (indirect) costs, as information made public and provided to investors can also be used by other parties, for example, competitors. This reduces the firm's disclosure incentives (Verrecchia 1983; Gal-Or 1985). But the existence of multiple audiences might also induce acceleration of announcing bad news, for example, in order to deter competition (Darrough and Stoughton 1990; Wagenhofer 1990).

It is not fully clear whether the fact that private equity funds are insiders in their portfolio firms after they have invested leads to more or less incentives to disclose information publicly. On the one hand, there may be less need because the main investor is better informed. Revealing less information may imply for the firm's management that it receives less valuable advice; revealing more information may, however, imply more stringent monitoring. Thus, it depends overall on how "management friendly" the monitoring private equity investor is perceived to be. The friendlier the private equity firm is perceived to be towards management (Adams and Ferreira 2007) the more willing the firm's management should be to disclose information. On the other hand, more disclosure may attract more new investors, which is in the interest of the private equity firm seeking either new investor for future financing rounds or a way to exit.[5]

Determinants of Potential Reporting Biases of Private Equity Funds

Even if private equity managers are sufficiently informed of the value of their portfolio firms, this does not necessarily imply that they will report in an unbiased fashion to their own investors. The private equity manager faces a basic trade-off: on the one hand, intentionally reporting excessively high valuations (e.g., by intentionally delaying write-downs) may increase the probability of raising a follow-on fund successfully. On the other hand, reporting excessively high valuations may lead to a potential loss in reputation, often considered the main asset of the private equity firm vis-à-vis its own investors.

In a nutshell, this basic trade-off can be considered to be a repeated game between investors (both current and potential) and the private equity firm. Due to an uncertain endpoint it can be considered as an infinitely repeated game. The private equity firm faces the problem of either playing cooperatively (i.e., reporting truthfully) or cheating (i.e., reporting intentionally too high valuations). Whereas in the former case it will keep its reputation and can also earn the cooperative payoffs in the future, it will lose in the latter case, if detected, its reputation, and earn strictly lower profits in the future. The likelihood of detection depends on whether investors can distinguish between external factors leading to a reduction in value and overreporting. The loss (or, more precisely, the discounted value of this) has to be compared with the one-time benefit of cheating that increases the probability of receiving funding for the follow-on fund. In more formal terms, cheating (i.e., intentionally overreporting) is optimal if benefits exceed costs.

The decision to intentionally overreport is therefore driven by factors which determine this basic trade-off. Reputational concerns are most affected by the track record of the private equity fund and manager. More experienced fund managers have more to lose and relatively less to gain (because they can use their proven track record rather than overvaluations) in order to convince investors to put up capital for a follow-up fund. In contrast, inexperienced private equity managers have an incentive to grandstand and overreport. A similar phenomenon can be observed in the case of IPOs (see Gompers 1996). In addition, the likelihood of detection is, given our above framework, clearly related to the age of the firm as well as to the age of the private equity fund. Regarding early-stage investments, there are many other sources of uncertainty that external investors cannot easily oversee and are therefore very difficult to disentangle ex-post from overreporting. Similarly, investments early in the lifetime of the funds give private equity managers more time until exits have to be realized. Hence, both factors give rise to more pronounced incentives to overreport (or to delay write-downs).

Further factors affecting the above trade-off are market factors in the PE industry as well as accounting standards. The PE industry is characterized by cyclical movements (Gompers and Lerner 1999), throughout which money inflows differ significantly across time. With more money pouring into the industry, funding of follow-on funds is facilitated, reducing the incentives to overstate nonexited investments in the portfolios of existing funds. The link to accounting and reporting standards is more indirect. Since PE funds are organized as partnership in most cases, they are basically not regulated in any country, implying that financial reporting standards do not apply (see above) directly. Accounting and reporting standards may, however, affect the reporting and disclosure behavior of PE funds indirectly, via the reporting standards being in place for the portfolio firms only. More stringent reporting standards make it more difficult for PE funds to avoid write-downs and report potential losses associated with their portfolio firms.

Financial Standards, Disclosure, and Regulation

Insufficient incentives for voluntary disclosure are a necessary but by no means sufficient condition for mandatory disclosure or some degree of regulation in this area. The first step toward a justification of mandatory (regulated) disclosure is that a market failure exists. If that is the case, it needs to be shown that mandatory valuation standards and disclosure achieve better outcomes.

There are two objectives behind potential regulatory intervention in this regard. The first objective is to inform the current investor properly about the true value of the current portfolio and his share therein. The second objective to be addressed is the avoidance of misallocation of capital flowing into the private equity industry and thus into individual funds due to grossly overstated returns.

There are two sources of market failure that cannot be easily covered with private contracts: First, the existence of externalities imposed on other players in the industry by misreporting funds. Second (and related) is the lack of any credible direct sanctions being imposed in the case of fraud and misinformation. A third argument in favor of regulation is that mandatory principles of disclosure of performance information are a cheaper solution compared to market solutions. Given the high degree of uncertainty and complexity associated with valuing venture capital investments in particular it seems, however, to be rather unlikely that state bureaucrats are better equipped than industry professionals to set up sensible rules and guidelines for the reporting of fair values of portfolio companies to investors. Redirecting the reporting standards towards the mandatory reporting of liquidation values may lead to a simpler valuation process and may therefore save resources, but clearly does not fulfill the overall objective of informing current as well as future investors of the underlying true value of the private equity investment.

The first argument for mandatory reporting and disclosure standards expresses the view that, in the absence of regulation, information production by the private sector may lead to misreporting and hence to negative externalities on other players in the industry, most notably other private equity funds (for which it becomes more difficult to raise funds) and potential investors (which may channel too much capital into the industry and thus to the "wrong" funds). While there is little doubt that such externalities exist, it is, given the difficulties with setting up a consistent and binding fair value reporting scheme in the PE industry (see also the earlier arguments), highly questionable whether mandatory regulatory approaches are superior relative to private sector efforts to tackle this problem (see Mahoney [1995] on a similar argument with respect to listed companies). There is a definitive need for transparency in order to reduce transaction costs. But since potential investors in private equity are typically either well informed or capable of gathering proper information (e.g., through gatekeepers and other specialized intermediaries), there is no necessity to protect these investors excessively. It should be noted that this is obviously a clear reason for limiting the direct access of small investors to private equity funds, but not a convincing one for mandatory disclosure and regulation overall. The second argument for regulatory intervention, namely that mandatory reporting and disclosure is a credible commitment with respect to sanctions, is not very convincing either. There are market mechanisms (such as loss of reputation, signaling effect stemming from deviating from industry guidelines, etc.) that may help to overcome this problem. In contrast, given the problem of detecting fraud and misreporting, it is not really clear why a mandatory regime may provide a more efficient solution to this.

Overall, this implies that there are obviously a number of significant problems associated with reporting and disclosure based on industry standards that give a lot of leeway to the fund manager who is applying them. But, despite this, given the limited justification and effectiveness of the mandatory disclosure rule, there seems to be little ground for public intervention regarding financial reporting and disclosure of financial performance (this no means embraces other measures, such as the ones directed towards achieving more transparency in corporate governance and in financial structures in the portfolio firms).

DISCLOSURE AND REPORTING PATTERNS OF VENTURE-BACKED PORTFOLIO FIRMS

Given the incentives to voluntarily disclose information, and given the existence of reporting standards, it is important to understand whether the financial reporting of portfolio firms reflects to some degree the underlying value of the firm. Or to put it more succinctly: are private equity managers really fishing in murky waters without additional information, or can they infer value-relevant information even from the financial reporting of the portfolio firm?

The empirical answer to this question is somewhat ambiguous. Using a panel of U.S. biotech firms, Hand (2005) explores the value-relevance of private firms. He shows that, with the exception of firms at the beginning of their lifetimes, financial statements are value-relevant in the venture capital market. He finds the value-relevance of financial statements of private venture-backed firms as nearly of the same magnitude as in public equity market. Firms' financial statements are value-irrelevant for the initial stock series but become progressively more value-relevant as firms mature. This suggests that private equity investors can indeed extract information from financial statements, except for early-stage and seed investments. Armstrong, Davila, and Foster (2006) confirm and extend this view. They analyze a broader set of venture-backed early-stage companies in different industries and find a significant role of financial statements, not only on the level but also on the change of valuations. Changes in financial statement variables are contemporaneously associated with changes in private equity valuations. The result is that items in financial statements of successful firms such as cash outlays provide a reliable predictor of future success (and hence the implied value of the firm).

All this clearly indicates that even for early-stage investments, private equity firms can infer information concerning firm valuation from financial statements for successful firms (which are finally exited via an IPO). There is, however, one important caveat: major problems with respect to valuation arise for the unsuccessful venture-backed firms that call for potential write-downs. The above studies focus only on successful firms that are exited via IPOs. We are not aware of any study investigating the relationship between financial disclosure and valuation for unsuccessful firms.

A related question is whether the actual or potential involvement of private equity investors has an impact on the quality of the disclosure of firm. Beuselinck, Deloof, and Manigart (2008) address this question by using a sample of Belgian PE–financed companies. They show that firms do not reveal more information before receiving PE investments compared to their non-PE counterparts. However, after having received PE financing these (unlisted) firms voluntarily disclose more information. This is consistent with viewing PE firms as being management friendly as well as with the notion that PE investments leads to a professionalization of the firm. They also find a positive relationship between PE ownership and the degree of disclosure, but only for very high PE ownership levels.[6] Overall, this implies that ownership structure has an impact on the degree of financial disclosure in the sense that closer-held firms seem to disclose more financial information than others.

Reporting Biases of Private Equity Funds Valuation

In a final step, we aim to shed some light into the empirics of financial reporting and disclosure in the private equity industry. We thereby focus on the main aspect of the entire discussion: the reporting of values of unrealized investments. This is difficult for at least two reasons. First, there is a shortage of useful applicable data. Looking at valuation at the fund level is clearly a first step (see Phalippou, in this volume) that, however, only gives indirect hints as to whether private equity funds (and under which circumstances) do indeed overstate the values of their unrealized investments. An important further step is to look into returns and valuations at the level of the individual portfolio company. This second step provides some first indications about the differences in reported returns between realized and unrealized investments.

We make use of data provided to us by the Center of Private Equity Research (CEPRES). The CEPRES data set consists of a very large proprietary private equity data set that provides detailed information about returns realized and reported at the level of the individual portfolio firm. CEPRES was jointly founded by one of the largest European fund-in-fund investors and Goethe-University Frankfurt/Main. Its main purpose is to collect data with the help of the worldwide operations of the fund-in-fund investor who is engaged in venture capital as well as in private equity investments. The data are from venture capital and private equity funds our fund-in-fund investor was in contact with, and include funds in which actual investments were undertaken but also those where this was not the case. The data summarized in Exhibit 16.3 comprise the total current CEPRES database and consist of data from 322 venture capital funds, 102 venture capital firms, 9,907 observations for entrepreneurial firms, 38 years (1971 to 2008), and 61 countries from North and South America, Europe, and Asia. The data is completely anonymous. For reasons of confidentiality, names of funds, firms, and so forth are not disclosed.[7]

With hindsight, comparing the average and median IRRs of unrealized (average: 19.14 percent; median: 0.02 percent) versus realized (average: 29.91 percent; median: 13.53 percent) investments does not initially seem to indicate that private equity funds overstate the valuation of their unrealized investments. Exhibit 16.3, however, reveals that the return data are highly skewed and that most but definitively not all unrealized investments are kept in the books at the cost of the investment (only 8 percent of all unrealized investments in our sample are valued at below the costs of investment implying a negative IRR).

Furthermore, taking a closer look at the breakdowns of the data reveals a number of interesting patterns. Most notably, there is a strong discrepancy between the IRRs of realized and unrealized investments in the case of early-stage investments which account for roughly 20 percent of all observations in our data set. There, median IRRs of unrealized and realized investments are statistically significantly different. While the median realized IRR is −45.3 percent, the median unrealized return is 0 percent. This clearly contrasts not only with the difference in average returns (18.68 percent for realized and 6.83 percent for unrealized returns) but also differs from the overall sample for which the difference in median returns just points in the opposite direction. This clearly suggests that venture capital manager are, to put it cautiously, more optimistic for their current ventures than they should be. The same type of pattern can be observed for start-up companies (and to a lesser extent for seed investments), where the differences in median returns are even more pronounced. There too, venture capital firms seem to be quite reluctant to report write-downs: whereas the median IRR of realized investments is a negative 60.75 percent, the reported IRR on unrealized investments is at 0 percent. Two potential factors may play a role in this observed pattern. On one hand, the negative number with associated realized investments in the start-up sector reflects to some extent the downturn in the high-tech sector in the early years of 2000. On the other hand, unrealized investments are younger in the sense that they are in the portfolio for only a short period of time, implying that write-downs cannot yet be foreseen. But even when taking these factors into account (and the second factor does not

Exhibit 16.3 Overview of Reported versus Realized IRR of Portfolio Firms

| | | Unrealized/Partially Realized | | | Fully Realized | | | Difference Tests (t-Values) | |
| | | Portfolio Firm Investments | | | Portfolio Firm Investments | | | | |
		# Firms	Average IRR (in %)	Median IRR (in %)	# Firms	Average IRR (in %)	Median IRR (in %)	Means	Medians
Part A	**All Funds**								
	All Funds in the Data	9907	19,14	0,02	12216	29,91	13,53	-4,18	-5,25
Part B	**Fund Characteristics**								
	Age of Specific PE Firm >= 10	5425	21,01	0,00	5188	27,37	8,97	-1,70	-2,40
	Age of Specific PE Firm <10	4482	16,88	2,01	7028	31,79	15,16	-4,15	-3,66
	Age of Specific PE Fund >= 5	1299	22,84	8,21	1809	30,30	18,74	-1,41	-1,99
	Age of Specific PE Fund < 5	8595	18,57	0,00	10407	29,84	12,40	-3,93	-4,32
Part C	**Portfolio Firm Characteristics**								
	Early	1606	6,83	0,00	1641	18,68	-45,30	-1,35	5,15
	Expansion	1003	15,21	0,00	1166	15,84	6,98	-0,12	-1,29
	Growth	528	18,26	6,13	963	33,31	18,41	-1,89	-1,54
	Later	504	27,38	0,00	476	65,48	12,89	-2,09	-0,71
	LBO	613	17,19	14,20	451	29,67	24,37	-2,91	-2,38
	MBO/MBI	1729	30,37	10,88	2495	44,34	27,51	-2,77	-3,30
	Mezzanine	6	-24,42	-37,32	11	26,04	31,94	-2,73	-3,74
	Seed	333	4,63	0,00	393	-1,83	-57,55	0,47	4,21
	Special Situations	0			1	22,65	22,65		
	Spin Off	11	6,25	0,00	7	-9,99	-89,17	0,38	2,06
	Start Up	484	-2,21	0,00	509	2,70	-60,75	-0,44	5,39
	Turnaround	32	70,83	49,69	51	63,14	34,86	0,20	0,38

Part D

Countries								
Canada	104	66,73	16,54	125	49,97	18,32	0,36	−0,04
China	312	42,18	0,00	149	−4,21	−11,43	2,78	0,69
Denmark	54	22,35	0,00	45	41,99	22,42	−1,06	−1,21
Finland	89	10,64	3,11	143	41,02	16,96	−1,85	−0,84
France	577	14,83	6,93	721	19,17	14,39	−0,62	−1,07
Germany	453	29,11	1,04	476	45,00	5,99	−0,98	−0,31
India	189	40,39	5,50	116	22,42	17,03	1,15	−0,73
Ireland	45	−0,72	0,00	29	6,67	10,82	−0,72	−1,05
Israel	161	−10,22	0,00	147	20,14	−20,39	−1,54	1,03
Italy	144	48,99	0,37	197	22,28	23,13	0,97	−0,83
Netherlands	102	21,85	9,52	120	20,00	22,21	0,22	−1,48
Spain	104	12,99	6,29	125	32,69	22,42	−1,59	−1,30
Sweden	176	12,62	5,74	233	44,47	20,30	−1,96	−0,89
Switzerland	73	8,77	0,77	62	137,03	26,60	−2,18	−0,44
Taiwan	43	9,54	0,00	51	16,82	9,99	−0,38	−0,53
United Kingdom	937	21,14	4,16	1592	27,63	22,54	−1,10	−3,12
United States	5555	16,51	0,00	6866	29,42	10,41	−3,66	−2,95

even indicate that valuations are correct predictors), the data clearly suggests that the valuations in the venture capital segment are grossly overstated.

While Exhibit 16.3 does not reveal any clear-cut patterns with respect to fund characteristics, there are some significant differences and interesting observations that can be made for different countries. Most notably in China (and to a lesser extent in Israel) reported IRRs for unexited investments are higher than the ones of exited investments. In the case of China this is true for average as well as the median IRRs. In many countries the median return is at 0 percent, clearly reflecting the fact that many valuations are at costs of investment.

These comparisons obviously suffer from differences among realized and unrealized investments as well as from a potential selection bias. Unrealized firms may exhibit endogenous differences compared to realized investments. Cumming and Walz (2007) aim to overcome this endogeneity problem by developing a two-stage approach. They rely on the CEPRES data set as well, mainly the one for the 1990 to 2003 periods.

Their two-step procedure is derived first from a benchmark model based on realized rates of returns with which they derive regression coefficients. These coefficients can then be used in order to compute predicted returns. In a final step, the difference between actual returns (based on the PEs reported valuations) and predicted returns are regressed on a number of exogenous factors.

They find systematic biases in the reporting of valuations of unrealized investments relative to the forecasted IRRs. It turns out that these reporting biases can be traced back to institutional factors as well as firm and fund characteristics. Reporting biases can be explained by cross-country differences in accounting standards as well as legality. This implies that the accounting standards have, via their effects on the stringency of reporting on portfolio firms, an effect on the degree of overreporting: the more stringent the underlying accounting standards are, the less pronounced is the degree of overreporting. Pretty much the same is true for the legal environment: better laws (as measured by the La Porta, Lopes-de-Silanes, Shleifer, and Vishny [1997] legality indices) lead to a reduction in the incentives to overstate by allowing for better contract enforcement.

With respect to firm characteristics, their analysis confirms our first conjecture: there is more overvaluation among early-stage firms than at later stages of the firm's life cycle. Furthermore, it turns out that there is more overreporting for small firms and firms in high-growth industries. Altogether this indicates that, given the more pronounced difficulties in disentangling exogenous uncertainties and overvaluation, PE managers have more pronounced incentives to overstate the value of firms (or delay write-downs) for which the valuations are surrounded by a high degree of uncertainty.

Finally, they also find that fund characteristics matter: the younger the PE fund, the more likely it is to observe values that are—using the difference to predicted returns—overstated. This provides empirical support for the grandstanding hypothesis discussed above.

CONCLUSION

By standing in between the investor and the portfolio firms, private equity funds serve to overcome or at least mitigate agency and control problems. In order to overcome the danger that this process of financial intermediation leads to an increase rather a decrease of agency problems and informational asymmetries, a number of incentive, control, and disclosure devices have to be put in place (for a general discussion, see Gompers and Lerner [1999] and for an analysis of control right allocations see Kaplan and Stromberg [2003]). We have focused in this chapter on the latter, namely the reporting and disclosure process through which private equity funds aim to keep their current as well as future investors informed. Furthermore, we have noted that financial reporting also may affect, via the compensation structure of the PE manager, the distribution of potential gains among the limited and general partners.

While reporting and disclosing cash outflows and cash inflows due to realization of investments is rather straightforward and can be addressed rather easily, the big challenge is the valuation of unrealized investment and their reporting to limited partners. Given that private equity firms typically invest in nonlisted firms, making these assets illiquid and nontradable, valuing and thereby forecasting the future cash flows resulting from these investments is not only surrounded by high degree of uncertainty and complexity, but also by a high degree of subjective assessment. In addition, we show that there are pronounced conflicts of interest that make truthful revelation and objective judgment highly unlikely.

Our empirical discussion clearly reveals that there are indeed reporting biases that are especially pronounced in early stage, venture capital investment. They can be traced back to fund, firm, and country characteristics in a way that is consistent with theoretical reasoning.

What are the implications of all this? We think there are five main implications. First, it has to be noted that valuing nonlisted firms is highly complex and more of an art than a science, especially in an early-stage environment. Second, this does not explain observed reporting biases that systematically tend to be in the direction of overstating (e.g., due to a delay in appropriate write-downs) rather than understating values. Third, in the last decade or so we have seen a larger number of industry guidelines aimed at providing (nonmandatory) standards for the valuation and disclosure of PE investments. These guidelines are pointing in the same direction worldwide, by setting up rules to report the "fair values" of the unrealized investments. But, while creating significantly more transparency and consistency over time, there is still sufficient leeway for PE managers to strategically overreport, at least for a certain period of time. Fourth, we have discussed and rejected the idea of stringent mandatory disclosure rules and reporting standards for the industry for two reasons: there is little room for really pinning down the valuation as there is no discretionary power for the PE managers involved and, in addition, there is little reason to believe that mandatory standards can do any better than private incentives (and contracts) to collect information and disclose financial reports. Limited partners are (and should be) large investors with a pronounced capability of collecting and processing information. And, last but not least: investors should not put too much weight on the valuation of unrealized investment and should definitely avoid compensation contracts that base remuneration on these valuations rather than finally on realized cash flows.

We would like to conclude with a brief outlook on potential avenues for future research. One of the main building blocks of our argumentation has been that overreporting may occur in order to facilitate future fund-raising. While this argument is obvious it would be very interesting to see how and to what extent this actually can be observed. In order to do so, one would have to link the data on unrealized investments with the one of fund-raising in the aftermath of the reporting. A related issue is whether more disclosure in general leads to more inflows of money in the industry and subsequently to more investments in the industry in aggregate. Cumming and Johan (2007) provide some evidence for this, but further research could look at the disaggregate implications of this, that is, to get a better understanding of which funds benefit most from these inflows (e.g., young or old funds) and how this affects reporting incentives in turn. A third potentially interesting future research question relates to the fact that different types of VCs have not only different objectives but also different kinds of corporate governance mechanism setup in their funds (Hirsch and Walz 2008). Therefore, it would be interesting to see, not the least against the background of tighter regulation of PE funds, to what extent strategic overreporting is related to the VC type. Another link that so far remains unexplored is the one between the contracts chosen and the degree of information flows and disclosure policy of PE funds to their limited partners. While the implications of compensation schemes on effort provision by the PE managers have attracted interest among researchers, there is no study we are aware of that investigates the repercussions of potential contractual mechanisms (such as clawbacks and compensation schemes) on the degree and accuracy of PE's disclosure policy. Last but not least, we would like to stress that our discussion did leave the entire topic of transparency and disclosure of information beyond performance-related issues (such as corporate governance issues and financial structure in the portfolio firms) apart. Given the increasing role of PE funds in private equity and given the intensity of public debate, more academic research is clearly required in this field as well.

NOTES

1. In the following we use the term private equity in its broad definition, embracing seed, early-stage, and expansion financing (to which we refer as venture capital), as well as late-stage investments (buyouts). Thereby, we follow the definition of, for example, the European Venture Capital Association (EVCA).

2. Exceptions to this are in cases in which the PE fund has either invested in the course of a buyout in publicly listed firms and in cases in which the PE fund does not sell all of its shares in the course of an IPO.

3. This discussion is most advanced in the United Kingdom, where, however, the discussion is focusing on disclosure rules in general and is also very much centered around tax issues and less so on increasing the informational content of performance disclosure (Walker 2007).

4. Lerner et al. (2009) provide a more extensive discussion of some of these methods, most notably of methods 1, 4, and 6.

5. There are a number of further benefits and costs of disclosure (Leuz and Wysocki 2008) which, however, do not actually apply to firms being engaged in the private equity markets.

6. Beuselinck and Manigart (2007), however, find evidence that increasing PE ownership stakes are to some extent substitutes rather than complements for corporate disclosure.

7. We should note that the return data displayed suffers from the typical shortcoming of return data based on internal rates of returns. Nevertheless, we think that they are very valuable for our illustrative purposes and do not distort matters structurally.

REFERENCES

Adams, Renée B., and Daniel Ferreira. 2007. A theory of friendly boards. *Journal of Finance* 62 (1):217–250.

Armstrong, Chris, Antonio Davila, and George Foster. 2006. Venture-backed private equity valuation and financial statement information. *Review of Accounting Studies* 11 (36):119–154.

Beuselinck, Christof, and Sophie Manigart. 2007. Financial reporting quality in private equity backed companies: The impact of ownership concentration. *Small Business Economics* 29 (3):261–274.

Beuselinck, Christof, Marc Deloof, and Sophie Manigart. 2008. Private equity investments and disclosure policy. *European Accounting Review*, forthcoming.

Bienz, Carsten, and Uwe Walz. 2007. Venture capital exit rights. LSE Working Paper.

Cumming, Douglas, and Sofia Johan. 2007. Regulatory harmonization and the development of private equity markets. *Journal of Banking & Finance* 31:3218–3250.

Cumming, Douglas, and Uwe Walz. 2007. Private equity returns and disclosure around the world. *Journal of International Business Studies*, forthcoming.

Darrough, Masako N., and Neal M. Stoughton. 1990. Financial disclosure policy in an entry game. *Journal of Accounting and Economics* 35:61–82.

EVCA. 2003. EVCA barometer May.

EVCA. 2006. Corporate governance and professional standards for the private equity and venture capital industry.

Gal-Or, Esther. 1985. Information sharing in oligopoly. *Econometrica* 329–343.

Gompers, Paul A. 1996. Grandstanding in the venture capital industry. *Journal of Financial Economics* 43:133–156.

Gompers, Paul A., and Josh Lerner. 1999. *The venture capital cycle.* Cambridge, MA: MIT Press.

Grossmann, Sanford, and Oliver Hart. 1980. Disclosure laws and takeover bids. *Journal of Finance* 35:323–334.

Hand, John R. M. 2005. The value relevance of financial statements in the venture capital market. *The Accounting Review* 80 (2):613–648.

Hardymon, Felda, Josh Lerner, and Ann Leamon. 2007. Between a rock and a hard place: Valuation and distribution in private equity. HBS Case #9-803-161.

Healy, Paul, Amy Hutton, and Krishna Palepu. 1999. Stock performance and intermediation changes surrounding increases in disclosure. *Contemporary Accounting Research* 485–520.

Heesen, Mark. 2004. Independence of the financial accounting standards board. Congressional testimony federal document clearing house. Congressional Information Service, Inc., April 20.

Hirsch, Julia, and Uwe Walz. 2008. Do different VCs choose different contracts. CFS Working Paper.

IPEV. 2007. International private equity and venture capital valuation guidelines. http://www.privateequityvaluations.com.

Kaplan, Steven N., and Per Stromberg. 2003. Financial contracting theory meets the real world: An empirical analysis of venture capital contracts. *Review of Economic Studies* 70 (2):281–315.

Kut, Can, Pramborg, Bengt, and Jan Smolarski. 2007. Managing financial risk and uncertainty: The case of venture capital and buy-out funds. *Global Business and Organizational Excellence* 26:53–64.

La Porta, Rafael, Florencio Lopes-de-Silanes, Andrei Shleifer, and Robert Vishny. 1997. Legal determinants of external finance. *Journal of Finance* 52:1131–1150.

Lerner, Josh, Felda Hardymon, and Ann Leamon. 2009. Venture capital and private equity: A casebook. 4th ed. Hoboken, NJ: John Wiley & Sons.

Leuz, Christian, and Peter Wysocki. 2008. Economic consequences of financial reporting and disclosure regulation: A review and suggestions for future research. SSRN Working Paper, available at: ssrn.com/abstract=1105398.

Mathonet, Pierre-Yves, and Gauthier Monjanel. 2006. Valuation guidelines for private equity and venture capital funds: A survey. *Journal of Alternative Investments* (Fall):59–70.

McCahery, Joseph A., and Eric P. M. Vermeulen. 2008. Corporate governance of nonlisted companies. Oxford: Oxford University Press.

Mahoney, Paul G. 1995. Mandatory disclosure as a solution to agency problems. *University of Chicago Law Review* 62 (3):1047–1112.

Merton, Robert C. 1987. A simple model of capital market equilibrium with incomplete information. *Journal of Finance* 42:483–510.

Milgrom, Paul. 1981. Good news and bad news: Representation theorems and applications. *Bell Journal of Economics* 12:380–391.

Sahlman, William A. 1990. The structure and governance of venture capital organizations. *Journal of Financial Economics* 27:473–521.

Verrecchia, Robert E. 1983. Discretionary disclosure. *Journal of Accounting and Economics* 5:179–194.

Wagenhofer, Alfred. 1990. Voluntary disclosure with a strategic opponent. *Journal of Accounting and Economics* 12:341–363.

Walker, David. 2007. Disclosure and transparency in private equity. Consultation Document 2007.

Welker, Michael. 1995. Disclosure policy, information asymmetry, and liquidity in equity markets. *Contemporary Accounting Research* 801–827.

Wright, Mike, Sarika Pruthi, and Andy Lockett. 2005. International venture capital research: From cross-country comparisons to crossing borders. *International Journal of Management Reviews* 7:135–165.

ABOUT THE AUTHORS

Douglas Cumming, B.Com. (Hons.) (McGill), M.A. (Queen's), J.D. (University of Toronto Faculty of Law), Ph.D. (Toronto), CFA, is an Associate Professor of Finance and Entrepreneurship and the Ontario Research Chair at the Schulich School of Business, York University. His research is primarily focused on law and finance, market surveillance, hedge funds, venture capital, private equity, and IPOs. His work has been presented at the American Finance Association, the Western Finance Association, the European Finance Association, the American Law and Economics Association, the European Law and Economics Association, and other leading international conferences. His recent articles have appeared in numerous journals including the *American Law and Economics Review, Cambridge Journal of Economics, Economic Journal, European Economic Review, Financial Management, Journal of Business, Journal of Business Venturing, Journal of Corporate Finance, Journal of International Business Studies, Oxford Economic Papers,* and *Review of Financial Studies.* He is the coauthor (along with his wife, Sofia Johan) of the new book *Venture Capital and Private Equity Contracting: An International Perspective* (Elsevier Science Academic Press, 2009, 770 pp.). His work has been reviewed in numerous media outlets, including *Canadian Business,* the *Financial Post,* and *The New Yorker.* He was the recipient of the 2004 Ido Sarnat Award for the best paper published in the *Journal of Banking and Finance* for a paper on full and partial venture capital exits in Canada and the United States. As well, he received the 2008 AIMA Canada-Hillsdale Research Award for his paper on hedge fund regulation and performance, and the

2009 Best Paper Award from the Canadian Institute of Chartered Business Valuators for his paper on private equity valuation and disclosure. He is a research associate with the Paolo Baffi Center for Central Banking and Financial Regulation (Bocconi University), Groupe d'Economie Mondiale at Sciences Po (Paris), Capital Markets CRC (Sydney), Venture Capital Experts (New York), Cambridge University ESRC Center for Business Research, Center for Financial Studies (Frankfurt), Amsterdam Center for Research in International Finance, and the University of Calgary Van Horne Institute. He has also consulted for a variety of governmental and private organizations in Australasia, Europe, and North America, and most recently is working with Wilshire Associates.

Andrej Gill is currently working on his Ph.D. at the Goethe University-Frankfurt. His main research is on private equity and corporate governance.

Uwe Walz received his Ph.D. in economics from the University of Tübingen/ Germany in 1991. Prior to joining the faculty of Goethe University in October 2002, Dr. Walz was a Research Fellow at the London School of Economcs and at the University of California-Berkeley as well as Professor of Economics at the Universities of Bochum (1995–1997) and Tübingen (1997–2002). His main current research focuses on private equity, entrepreneurial finance and contract theory. He has published in academic journals including *Journal of Financial Intermediation, Review of Finance, Journal of Corporate Finance, Journal of International Economics* and *Journal of Business Venturing*. Currently, he is director of the research program "Entrepreneurial Finance" at the Center for Financial Studies (CFS).

ACKNOWLEDGMENT

This paper is based on work in Cumming, Douglas, Andrej Gill, and Uwe Walz, 2009, International private equity valuation and disclosure, *Northwestern Journal of International Law & Business* 29:617–642.

CHAPTER 17

Private Equity Regulation

A Comparative Analysis

JOSEPH A. McCAHERY
Professor of Corporate Governance and Innovation, University of Amsterdam Faculty of Economics and Business

ERIK P. M. VERMEULEN
Professor of Financial Market Regulation at the Tilburg Law and Economics Center (TILEC) and Professor of Law and Management, Tilburg University Faculty of Law

INTRODUCTION

The alternative asset sector successfully avoided the scrutiny of regulators and lawmakers, which arguably contributed to its success in attracting investors. Yet, with concerns arising from the increased risk due to overleveraged transactions and the potential costs to investors from insider trading and price fixing arising from "club deals" by mega funds capturing the largest amount of net capital flows, the trend has moved in the direction of increasing regulation of private equity funds and their managers. In this context, there is a division of opinion regarding whether private equity funds and their investments should be subject to regulation designed to protect workers and to discourage asset-stripping tendencies. Proponents of special regulation point to the negative image of private equity arising from decisions to cut jobs at companies—such as the AA, the U.K. motor repair services group, and Gröhe, the German bathroom-fittings maker. They characterize private equity funds as "locusts" interested only in their own enrichment at the expense of other interests within the firm. Conversely, the extant evidence seems to decry regulatory interference by suggesting a positive correlation between private equity investments and firm performance. Economic studies show that private equity investment routinely surpasses the Standard & Poor's (S&P) index, enhances new product and market development, and increases the levels of employment and R&D expenditure.

However, the global turbulence in the credit markets, triggered by the turmoil in the subprime mortgage market in the United States in 2007, has arguably ended the private equity bonanza as well as the laissez-faire era in the alternative asset sector. In fact, the credit squeeze has already slowed down the level of private equity activity and, more importantly for this paper, resulted in increased scrutiny from regulators, policymakers and the judiciary. We can see, moreover, that a wide range of regulatory options, from industry self-regulation to governmental intervention, are being considered in order to lower the level of risk and to redress the balance between investors and private equity firms. Despite the absence of collapses in the buyout market, regulators were, even before the downturn, considering a number of governmental measures designed to reduce the incidence of buyouts, including caps on leverage limits or limits on the levels of interest payments that are tax deductible. There may, however, be other motivations that can better explain the demand for regulatory intervention other than to protect investors from manipulation and to promote certain regulatory responsibilities. That said, what strategy is ultimately implemented could be the result of a pent-up demand, for example, of enhanced regulation that is very difficult to differentiate from what is required to ensure that investors and other stakeholders have an acceptable level of security in dealing with private equity funds and their advisers.

In the main, private equity funds are regulated by contract. These funds, which are predominantly formed as limited partnerships, limited liability partnerships, or limited liability companies, are able consequently to take advantage of various exemptions and exclusions explicitly provided within the regulatory framework. These business forms are, for example, treated as transparent entities for tax purposes, allowing funds to avoid taxation at fund level and to "pass-through" tax liabilities to the fund investors. More important, the contractual flexibility of the limited partnership, limited liability partnership, and limited liability company allows the managers and investors to enter into covenants and schemes that align their incentives and reduce agency costs. To give an example, the investors are usually permitted to vote on important issues, such as amendments of the contractual provisions, dissolution issues, removal of managers, and sometimes even the valuation of the portfolio. At the same time, the "private placement" business arrangement is oriented and structured for large and sophisticated investors, making it possible to be exempted from the securities regulation framework. In the United States, for instance, these funds rely on the exemptions from treatment under the Securities Act of 1933, the Investment Company Act of 1940, and the Investment Advisers Act of 1940.[1]

Still, there are important issues that confront the world of private equity. The private equity industry must face the dilemma of identifying well-suited techniques to increase transparency and reduce the level of risk without substantially damaging the flexibility and the benefits of the business models that have prospered on limited interventions within contractual relations. In a period when private equity flourished, the mere contractual basis for the funds is usually adequate to address the agency problems among the players in this sector. However, when the economy gets weaker and the performance of buyouts is jeopardized because of overaggressive capital structures, lawmakers are more likely to intervene without analyzing the contractual structure of the funds. In this respect, much attention has been directed recently to the reliability of private equity funds in justifying their contribution in the strategic performance delivered. In addition to these concerns, a related set of criticisms that have arisen related to market abuse, conflicts of interest and market opacity that are likely to pose questions whether the current regulatory regime is best suited to address the concerns.

Naturally, the level of regulatory risk will increase substantially should a high-profile buyout fail, for example, leaving selling shareholders and employees in distress. Hence, as the risk becomes more critical for companies and their employees, we would, then, expect more direct government intervention at the expense of the system of private ordering employed by the funds and their investors. Financial considerations, however, invariably prevent lawmakers from simply introducing new legislation that could alter the balance of benefits and gains for the sector. Besides, mandating legal rules that are inflexible in nature may have perverse and uncertain consequences on the industry and some firms preventing them from making well-considered decisions and timely changes in response to innovations underway in the economy. To see this, we should recall that although private equity funds have become an essential part of the global financial system, there is only partial and insufficient information about their governance, impact and strategies.

In assessing whether a regulatory response is required, it is important to be clear about which mode is appropriate, and whether the existing regulatory framework is adequate to address the concerns associated with private equity fund investment. There are a number of considerations that are relevant. First, is the current structure sufficient to support private equity led innovation and development. Second, to what extent are the problems connected with private equity funds familiar, and are the current set of measures appropriate for dealing with the increased risk generated by private equity funds and buyouts. To the extent that a problem does not raise any new problems for existing regulation, it can be presumed that no fundamental changes or new measures are required. Third, if the consequence of private equity fund activity raises a new risk or outpaces the current system of regulation, a question as to which type of response is required arises. In this context, there is a choice between self regulation and other regulatory strategies.

As we will see, traditional solutions, such as self-regulation, industry coregulation and or event the resort to regulation, could play an important role in protecting the stakeholders of the funds as well as the portfolio companies. Self-regulatory strategies are not new to financial regulation. The potential benefits are well established, evidenced by high levels of firm compliance and significant reductions in risk and other factors. Moreover, these strategies, if pragmatic and well designed, are attractive because they are less burdensome, easily updated and permit firms to achieve their regulatory goals with maximum discretion. Self-regulatory strategies are likely to be more effective than direct regulation because they are generated by persons directly involved in the industry. In this context of implementing such measures, we can expect private equity firms will have high powered incentives to adopt the standards and controls in a timely and efficient manner. Moreover, to the extent that large institutional investors are effective monitors, they can act as a counterweight by exerting pressure on funds that either under comply or fail to implement the measures in a timely fashion. The self-regulation approach works best where the company has wide discretion and authority over the implementation of the negotiated industry standard.

It may be tempting to conclude that self-regulation is always the optimal strategy. Concerns about the negative impact of special regulation on the financial industry abound. Self-regulation can involve complex conflicts of interests, which may have a detrimental effect on the confidence that investors have in the industry standards. Moreover, the noncompliance with and enforcement of these regulations is yet another concern. To be sure, the effectiveness of self-regulation is connected closely to the incentives of the firms that are providing the measures and the quality of their efforts to monitor compliance. We are not indifferent to the possibility of ineffective or misdirected policies, but rather assume that the private equity industry has a stake in establishing a good reputation for compliance with industry standards. Second, when private equity funds' interests diverge from investors' interests, existing regulation and market responses should be sufficient for dealing with these problems. At the same time, it might be that current regulation is not sufficient to deal with all the risks of private equity funds or illegal conduct, and consequently a response may be needed.

In this chapter, we evaluate whether the existing contractual arrangements and industry standards are sufficient for dealing with the problems generated by private equity and buyout funds. We consider the rapid growth of private equity and the stresses that have arisen as a result. The range of governance problems and risks are discussed in terms of whether regulatory intervention is warranted. We discuss the effectiveness of different regulatory modes and examine the existing regulatory structure in Canada, Germany, the Netherlands, and the United Kingdom. The survey of the diverse regulatory environments reveals the types of measures that have been considered by regulators, and the reforms that have been implemented.

The chapter is divided into five sections. "The Growth of Private Equity" sets out background facts and figures that are relevant to understand the role of regulation and how it influences the players in this industry. We will make no attempt to provide an in-depth analysis of the economic impact of private equity, but will focus on the structure, investment objectives, and investment strategies of private equity funds. These facts and figures offer important insights and observations about the trends and challenges in this alternative asset sector. Next, "Dealing with Agency Problems: Contractual Arrangements" describes the terms and conditions of fund formation and operation, management fees and expenses, profit-sharing and distributions, and corporate governance. The contractual features show that parties are in principle capable of structuring their particular ownership and investment instruments according to their own preferences without being bound to regulatory requisites. In this section, we also focus on hedge funds. Typically, these funds use similar business forms, but, in contrast to private equity funds (which primarily invest in unregistered securities), they are structured by a team of skilled professional advisers, experts in company analysis and portfolio management, offering investors a wide range of investment styles. Hedge-fund managers employ multiple strategies as well as traditional techniques and use an array of trading instruments such as debt, equity, options, futures, and foreign currencies. Since hedge funds are characterized by the pursuit of absolute returns and the use of leverage to enhance their return on investment, the hedge-fund industry also encounters increased scrutiny from regulators and lawmakers. The question then is if, and under what conditions, special regulations should come to the fore. Now that both the buyout branch of the private equity industry and hedge funds face sharp criticism from lawmakers, labor unions and shareholders in publicly held companies, the industry—convinced of the value-increasing effect of their investments and the benefits for employment, innovation, and research and development—increasingly respond by introducing self-regulatory measures to improve the transparency and accountability of private equity funds and hedge funds across the board, the section titled "Regulation of Private Equity Funds" will explain the function of soft-law principles, guidelines, and recommendations, specifically tailored to the activities of private equity funds. We will assess if self-regulation will come to be seen as a pragmatic and workable approach despite its purported disadvantages, such as the lack of public confidence or the possible inertia on the side of the self-regulatory body. This section also addresses the role of regulators and lawmakers in a number of major jurisdictions, outlining the existing industry codes and legal tools that can be used to address the problems that arise in relation to private equity and buyout fund activity. The last section concludes the chapter.

THE GROWTH OF PRIVATE EQUITY

The private equity industry has seen tremendous growth over the last decade, going from less than $10 billion raised worldwide in 1991 to over $180 billion in 2000 (Kaplan and Schoar 2005). Today, almost a decade later, private equity shows no signs of slowing down. In fact, industry private raised a record $406 billion in 2006. Exhibit 17.1 shows a summary of the leading private equity funds and buyout firms in terms of total value of funds raised over the last decade.

Exhibit 17.1 Top Private Equity Funds

All Funds Firm	Funds Raised in the Past 10 Years
Goldman Sachs	$66.4 bn
Blackstone	$58.4 bn
Carlyle	$52.5 bn
Credit Suisse	$32.4 bn
TPG	$32.0 bn
KKR	$31.7 bn
Warburg Pincus	$31.7 bn
Apax	$30.9 bn
Bain	$30.8 bn
Permira	$29.0 bn

Buyout Funds	Funds Raised in the Past 10 Years
Goldman Sachs	$36.5 bn
Blackstone	$33.7 bn
KKR	$31.7 bn
TPG	$29.7 bn
Carlyle	$29.2 bn
Permira	$29.2 bn
Bain	$26.1 bn
CVC	$25.1 bn
Silver Lake	$21.8 bn
Providence	$20.2 bn

Source: Private Equity Intelligence.

The Performance of Private Equity

This section looks at the performance of private equity firms, particularly the returns of buyout funds. In the case of buyouts, the private equity firms that sponsor and structure the deal will arrange significant debt financing in order to takeover the company. Typically, debt financing for buyout is raised from the syndicated debt market in Europe and the United States (McCahery and Schwienbacher 2008). Private equity firms look for target firms in which there is fundamental inequality between market capitalization and firm value. Buyout firms have high-powered incentives to enhance the value of the target. Value enhancements that are agency-driven extract performance improvements through installing new management, active monitoring, and fundamental changes in the firm's business plan. It is noteworthy that high debt obligations may induce a firm to undertake fundamental governance reforms that can lead to performance improvements. Correspondingly, the high debt levels imply that the tax deductibility of interest is increased. Notice that performance improvements are also the result of financially driven arbitrage opportunities that arise as a consequence of differences in the company valuations.

Whatever the source of gain, the value of the equity investment will increase as a result of high leverage. Questions arise about whether the recent buyout boom was agency- or financially driven. To be sure, even though both elements have contributed, few observers would place primary emphasis on the agency side. As noted, readily available credit at low rates is probably a better explanation. Consider that the risk premium on junk bonds over Treasuries reached a historic low of 2.63 percent, compared to the 20-year average of 5.42 percent. Recall that while buyouts returned to 1990s levels, the leverage in the capital structures was less than in the earlier period. The average ratio of cash-flow to interest cost was 3.4 in deals closing in 2004, 2.6 in 2006, and 1.7 in 2007. At the same time, many of the loans are also "covenant-lite," omitting debt covenants and ratio tests. In terms of measuring the use of covenant-lite debt, the volume reached $48 billion in the first quarter of 2007, compared with $24 billion in 2006.

Shifting now to the returns earned by private equity, we discuss the performance of funds as measured by investors. Even though private equity funds disclose information to investors about returns, it is often difficult to obtain accurate information because funds are under no legal obligation to disclose. Most financial economists rely on databases that comprise voluntary reports of private equity funds, which includes information on returns. In terms of measuring fund-manager performance, there are two leading measures used, namely, the internal rate of return (IRR) and total value to paid-in (TVPI), which supplies an estimate of the size of profits to investors, relative to their initial investment in the fund (Jenkinson 2007). A recent study by Kaplan and Schoar (2005) on U.S. private equity returns analyzed the returns of 169 buyout funds that were close to fully liquidated in the period of 1980 to 2001. They break the results into time periods to show that the IRRs were better for funds raised in the early 1980s and poorer for funds raised in the early 1990s. Moreover, they find that the average returns earned by investors in funds started by 1995 are about the equivalent of the amount that would have been earned on the S&P 500. A related study by Phalippou and Gottschlag (2009), which revised and extended Kaplan and Schoar' data, indicates that the net returns by private equity funds lagged public equity markets by as much as 3.3 percent per year.

The Supply-and-Demand Side of Private Equity

Private equity can be defined as the investment of equity in nonlisted companies. On the supply side of private equity, we find the private equity fund, which is a vehicle formed to pool the capital of different investors, such as pension funds, insurance companies, university endowments, and other wealthy individuals. They pool their money with others so that the fund can help to spread the risk of the investment. Professional fund managers invest the capital across a wide range of different holdings. The value of the investments can go up and down depending on the returns of the different investments. Investments of pooled investment vehicles are characterized by high expected returns and high risks. There are a number of reasons to invest in pooled investment vehicles, which include: (1) to spread the risks and (2) investors have access to markets where the money has the potential for capital growth.

On the demand side, the pooled capital can be made available at several stages in a company's life. Private equity can take the form of venture capital. Venture capital funds have become the main funding source for high-growth businesses in the start-up and the expansion phase. Buyout funds form another subset of private equity. These funds can decide to buy a business from a vendor (an institutional buyout). If the target company's assets are used as collateral to raise additional debt to finance the acquisition, this is called a leveraged buyout. It is also possible that private equity funds assist the existing (management buyout) or new managers (management buyin) in taking over a nonlisted firm. Finally, private equity funds may decide to buy and acquire the shares of a publicly traded company. This is a so-called public-to-private buyout. Thus, there are two types of private equity funds: venture capital funds and buyout funds.

Venture capital funds come in three variations in the United States: small business investment companies (SBICs),[2] traditional venture capital funds, and corporate venture capital funds. In the United States, private equity is often associated with financing and developing companies that are unable to attract sufficient debt financing to support and finance their high-growth and often high-tech businesses. Not-yet-revealed and unproven technologies, the lack of liquid assets, and the importance of human capital all make bank financing unsuitable for these companies. Because future revenue streams are highly indefinable, access to debt financing through, for instance, asset-backed securitization transactions remains a major obstacle for these firms. In the venture capital segment, fund managers make investments in businesses in which they play an important role in monitoring and participating in the day-to-day activities of management. In the first quarter of 2007, venture capitalists invested $7.1 billion in 778 deals in the United States only, which is highest amount invested since the boom period of 2001 to 2002 (United States Venture Capital Association 2007). Recent success stories include YouTube, Web 2.0, and Google. The post-boom resurgence has seen a noticeable shift in the venture capital industry, with data revealing the increasing role of corporate venture capital (United States Venture Capital Association 2006). The surge in corporate venture capital is attributable to a new level of risk-taking by large companies that are looking to profit from investment in new technology and other innovations. With larger companies—such as Cisco, Intel, IBM, Kodak, Microsoft, and Siemens—expanding the scope of their operations to invest in start-ups, entrepreneurs tend to exploit the opportunity to obtain not only financial, but also technical and managerial assistance.

There may be several reasons why alliances between a start-up and a multinational may bear fruit for the venture. First, the start-up may very well offer strategic value of synergy to the multinational's core businesses. Second, even though a high rate of return is usually not the investor's main objective (thereby giving more stability to the venture), having a well-performing high-growth company in the portfolio may prove to be very lucrative. Third, it is generally accepted that these alliances often increase the credibility and reputation of the start-up firm. But there are also a number of disadvantages associated with the involvement of corporate venture capital funds. In particular the complexity of the transaction and the time-consuming decision-making procedures within large firms make traditional venture capital funds a more accessible source of private equity capital financing for high-tech start-ups. Alliances with corporate investors require the negotiation and drafting of a multitude of ancillary agreements relating to the promoting, selling, licensing, and developing of technology and knowledge. More important, corporate investors are more inclined to carefully reconsider the investment and pull the plug in the event of a major downturn.

That is not to say that starting a business with capital from traditional venture capital pools is an easy task to accomplish. Venture capitalists tend to monitor and protect their investments through active participation, namely by due diligence, establishing a relationship with the start-up businesses' managers, and by sitting on their board of directors. As soon as venture capitalists are hooked and involved, entrepreneurs and other key employees should be ready to abdicate control over their company. To be sure, venture capitalists will not typically depose an entrepreneur by acquiring a majority of the corporation's common shares. This is usually counterproductive, as discrepancies between them and the entrepreneur would imply an increase in agency costs. Allocating a substantial equity stake in the firm to the entrepreneur and other employees, which is akin to the stock option compensation system, fortifies the incentive to conduct the business diligently and discourages shirking and opportunism. Instead of seeking a majority of the corporation's equity, venture capitalists usually obtain control by utilizing complicated contractual mechanisms in their relationship with the entrepreneurial team and other investors. These contractual mechanisms protect the venture capitalists extensively from adverse selection and moral hazard problems. For instance, the use of staged financing and convertible preferred stock form an optimal combination which gives motivated entrepreneurs an incentive to take significant risks in order to increase firm performance while securing downside protection for venture capitalists.

It is submitted that the success of a venture capital market is mainly attributed to a private ordering regime in which contractual mechanisms are preferably employed to mitigate agency costs and to support the efficient structuring of staged financing and the sustained level of new entrepreneurs with high capacity to achieve their commercial aims. Governmental interference and oversight appears to be counterproductive. Recent research seems to suggest that government initiatives could crowd out the supply of venture capital. Suppose, for instance, that a tax incentive to encourage individual investors to pour money into special venture capital funds turns out, in fact, to reduce the supply of other, relatively more informed venture capital investments by institutional investors (Gilson 2003).

By way of comparison, we look to buyout funds that invest mainly in mature companies. The legal structure that makes the buyout market so effective also begins with the private equity fund, by which providers of capital convey money to the fund managers who are running the business and actively making the investments in portfolio companies. Like venture capital funds, the relationship is governed merely by contractual provisions that allow the fund managers enough time and space to take firms private and restructure them. Note, however, that there are significant differences in the organizational structure of venture capital and buyout funds. For example, buyout funds typically invest in mature companies with fairly predictable cash flows, which causes investors to give less leeway to the managers and to demand a minimum rate of return before profits are shared with the managers.

Until recently, buyouts accounted for less than 10 percent of the total number of investments. By mid-April 2006, however, there were 205 buyout funds that had raised about $200 billion (*Financial Times*, April 24, 2007). The statistical evidence shows the buyout business continues to boom (*The Economist*, February 10, 2007), increasing in recent years to 20 percent in 2005 (EVCA data 2000–2005). For Europe, the total amount of private equity deals in Europe was €178 billion, 41 percent higher than 2005 (*Financial Times*, January 29, 2007). Remarkably, the European market is dominated by U.S.-based buyout firms. Overall, more than half of the funds raised in the private equity sector are invested in MBO/MBIs.

A clear pattern emerges from the many empirical studies that describe the LBO booms. It is worth noting that the 1980s LBOs boom was largely a U.S. phenomenon during the 1980s. Conversely, with the current LBO wave, the center of gravity has shifted from the United States to Europe and the United Kingdom. This should come as no surprise because the European economy has performed much better than in the 1980s. What are the causes for the current expansive round in LBOs? The now-standard explanation for the highly favorable circumstances to complete deals is the easy credit terms and low interest rates that have prevailed until recently. A second explanation looks to the pressures on fund managers that prompted them to increase the allocation levels for this particular class of assets. A third explanation points to the self-interested behavior of the managements of public companies that have responded to shareholder pressure to obtain higher prices from private equity bidders. Another key feature of the boom has been the increase in corporate governance pressures. As a result, the cost of D&O insurance has increased substantially in the wake of Sarbanes-Oxley, due to the move of making executives personally liable for the accounting practices of their companies. In addition, we have also seen more shareholder scrutiny on executive pay. Given this, talented managers usually receive more generous compensation packages when switching to a firm controlled by a private equity company. Finally, many laws, regulations, and other measures are probably also responsible for the infrastructure to complete deals. One obvious message is that a favorable infrastructure is seen as crucial for the acceleration of the private equity process.

Conversely, the case for leverage may have negative implications. It is note-worthy that the buyout market, which peaked in the middle of 2007, collapsed rapidly in the last half of 2007 with the contraction in the credit market. During the most recent boom period, the leverage in private equity buyouts averaged about two-thirds. In Europe, buyout funds relied almost exclusively on banks and the syndicated loan market to fund their investments. The economic impact of private equity on the loan market has been significant given the amount of equity raised for highly leveraged buyouts over the past decade (Jenkinson 2007).

However, with the credit crunch making it harder to place buyout debt, the average size of buyouts this year has fallen to $120 million (Thompson Financial, 2008, vx.thomsonib.com/NASApp/VxComponent/VXMain.jsp). In the current environment, there are few incentives for private equity funds to make investments and draw-down their clients' capital. This suggests that much of the new capital raised by private equity funds remains uninvested. Thus, to the extent that the current collapse parallels the 1989 decline in the buyout market, there will be a challenge for agency theory. While agency theorists identified faults in regulation for the earlier collapse, there is no easily identifiable regulation that can be held to account for the transformation in the market. As the recent wave has shown, buyouts take place only when the capital structure of target firms can be leveraged up with debt. Since credit market conditions are cyclical, the buyout market can only take off when transactions can be conducted on favorable credit terms. So, even if fund managers have incentives to improve the performance of target firms through agency-driven improvements, it is unlikely that performance improvements alone could suffice for triggering a buyout wave.[3]

DEALING WITH AGENCY PROBLEMS: CONTRACTUAL ARRANGEMENTS

In this section, we begin by reviewing the similarities between private equity and hedge funds. We then discuss the extent to which the two fund types differ. At first glance, one noticeable incidence of convergence is the growth of hedge funds and private equity managers pursuing similar assets and investment strategies to secure superior market returns. When hedge fund advisers are dissatisfied with traditional strategies and unable to obtain their rates of return, they have moved quickly to adopt those strategies usually employed by private equity funds, such as corporate restructuring and buyouts, to achieve better value on their investments. This is partly due to the overcrowding of the hedge fund market place. This has led to clashes with traditional private equity funds. A noteworthy example is the bidding war between one of the largest private equity firms, Kohlberg Kravis Roberts & Company, and Cerberus Capital Management for the acquisition of Toys 'R Us.

Thus, the recent emergence of hedge funds competing with private equity firms for target companies to take private is further confirmation that funds are becoming more similar and harder to distinguish. There are a number of factors that account for this trend. First, the increased number of funds and new capital flowing into private-equity and hedge-funds makes it harder for advisers to produce premium returns. Second, debt continues to be relatively abundant worldwide and at relatively attractive rates. Third, hedge funds and buyout funds are increasingly seeking the same cost savings and synergies that strategic buyers have always achieved to justify their higher multiples. Effectively, these trends have blurred the differences between the two fund types.

The increased convergence caused hedge funds to incorporate private-equity-type features in their fund structures, reducing investor flexibility through side pockets (investments in illiquid stakes, which are accounted for in terms of administrative fees and incentive fees, separately from the fund), gates (caps on the amount of annual withdrawals from the fund by investor to manage the liquidity risk), and lock-ups (investors cannot withdraw from the fund within a certain period). Of course, one can cast doubt on whether these strategies can generate solutions for all the problems associated with hedge funds that provide their investors with diverse investment opportunities. As long as management and performance fees are based on striking a net asset value of the fund, hedge-fund investors are willing to pay the fees. However, investors are more likely to challenge performance payments to an adviser that has invested in illiquid securities that may not have an easily ascertainable market value. Private equity funds have addressed this concern through distributions based solely on realized events or the use of claw-back provisions that mandate funds to return performance fees if the fund subsequently goes into a loss position. These strategies to manage valuation risk have been resisted so far by the hedge fund industry.

Despite these similarities, private equity and hedge funds differ in a number of important ways. For instance, private equity can be distinguished from hedge funds in terms of their investment strategies, lock-up periods, and the liquidity of their portfolios. Moreover, private equity fund managers have incentives to take large illiquid positions in the nonlisted securities of private companies. Investments made by private equity funds take place during the first three to five years of the fund, which is followed by a holding period that averages between five to seven years, in which few new investments are made. Unlike private equity, the shorter lock-in period of hedge funds and their more flexible structure explains the dominance of highly liquid, short-term investments that allow investors easier access to the withdrawal of their investment funds. In the next section, we turn to examine the typical structures pooled investment vehicles, namely private equity and hedge funds. We focus on the three parties: (1) the general partner, (2) the investment adviser, and (3) the limited partners. We consider the extent to which hedge funds and private equity employ similar legal forms and contractual provisions between the GP and LPs. We note that despite some overlap in fund structure and organization, private equity and hedge funds typically employ different trading strategies, compensation and governance arrangements which are reflected in the main contract between the GP and the investors.

The Relationship between Investors and Fund Managers: The Limited Partnership Structure

A fund of a private equity firm, hedge fund or venture capital firm is a pooled investment. The fund can be seen as a vehicle formed to pool the capital of different investors. Contributors of these funds are institutional investors, pension funds, university endowments, and other wealthy individuals. They pool their money with others so that the fund can help to spread the risk of the investment. Professional fund managers invest the capital across a wide range of different holdings. The value of the investments can go up and down depending on the returns of the different investments. Investments in pooled investment vehicles are characterized by high expected returns and high risks. There are a number of reasons to invest in pooled investment vehicles, which include: (1) risks are spread out among investors, and (2) investors have access to markets where the money has the potential for capital growth.

In the United States and elsewhere, the limited partnership form is the dominant legal vehicle used in hedge fund and private equity structuring. Both fund types are usually organized as a LP, with a GP and management company, both structured as separate legal entities, and the limited partners (see Exhibit 17.2).

As we have seen, the popularity of this form is due to its contractual nature, which allows the internal and external participants to reduce opportunism and agency costs. Indeed, the limited partnership structure permits fund managers to achieve extensive control over the operation of their funds subject to few intrusive legal obligations. Other features—such as tax benefits, the flexibility surrounding its structure and terms, and its fixed life—contribute to its continuing viability as the business form of choice for collective investment vehicles. The LP has other important advantages as well. First, it is familiar to most investors and intermediaries, which accounts for its enduring popularity. Second, there is a risk that LLCs, operating outside the United States, could be treated as a nontransparent foreign entity and taxed as a corporate body. As a consequence, some sponsors are reluctant to switch to the LLC.[4] Typically, the sponsor will invest between 1 percent to 3 percent of the fund's total commitments. In order to obtain fees, the sponsor will create two entities: an LP and a management company, which is organized either

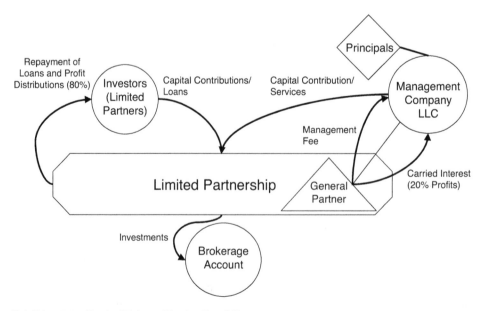

Exhibit 17.2 Typical Private Equity Fund Structure

as an LLC or corporation. Moreover, the management company is either a separate entity from the GP or affiliated with one of the GPs, or is a subsidiary of a bank or insurance company and, accordingly, will exercise effective control over the GP and fund manager. With a management company, the day-to-day management is separated from the fund, which may assist in resolving some tax issues while limiting doing business and other concerns.

The relationship between the limited partners and the general partners mainly relies on explicit contractual measures. Exhibit 17.3 shows the most common contractual measures that have been developed for dealing with the investment activities of GPs, and the relationship between GPs and LPs inside private equity funds.

A key contractual technique, for example, is the compensation arrangement between the fund manager and the investors. Compensation derives from the two main sources. First, fund managers typically receive 20 percent of the profits generated by each of the funds. The second source of compensation is the management fee. Historically, a significant majority of funds assess management fees as a constant percentage of committed capital. It is noteworthy that there has been a decrease in the management fees in recent years due to a number of economic factors. In particular, some funds are more likely to have a fixed fee of 2 percent of the funds assets, which is paid annually for five years and then decreases by 25 basis points for the next five-year period. Other fund managers will allow reductions of the fixed fee based on a change from committed capital in years one to five to net invested capital in years six to ten. Given these changes, a substantial proportion of buyout firms' median take off-the-top of committed capital has been reduced to 12 percent (Metrick and Yashida 2008).

To be sure, investors attempt to ensure fund managers performance by insisting on hurdle rates that climb upwards, anywhere from 15 percent to 20 percent, which means that profits can only be distributed after a certain threshold has been

Exhibit 17.3 Limited Partnership Agreement: Negotiating the Terms

General Partners	Limited Partners
Carry calculations	Carry calculations
Management fees	Claw-back provisions
Claw-back provisions	General partner conflict issues, including limitations of opportunities
General partner capital commitment	Key-man provisions
Limitations of liability	Management fees
Indemnification by general and limited partners	General partner capital commitment
Investment strategy, limitations, and guidelines	Side letters
Fund-raising period, investment period, and terms	Investment strategy, limitations, and guidelines
Permitted activities of general partners	Permitted activities of general partners
Limited partner approval rights	Portfolio company fee offsets

Source: Adapted from Center for Private Equity and Entrepreneurship, Tuck School of Business at Dartmouth.

reached. Thus, from the perspective of private equity, the contractual flexibility of the limited partnership plays a central role in aligning the interests of management and investors. For instance, in order to protect the 80/20 deal, a claw-back provision will be included in the agreement that provides that an overdistribution to a GP will be clawed back to the fund and then distributed to the LPs. What triggers a claw-back provision?

In practice, claw-backs can be triggered when the preferred return or hurdle is not reached and the GP obtained carried interest or if the GP has received more carried interest than the agreed 20 percent of cumulative net profits. Here we can use an example to show how the claw-back is intended to function. If we assume that a fund has six investments: A to F with each was purchased for $100. Also assume that five of these investments were sold each year for $200. As a result, the GP receives a carried interest of 20 percent and the LP receives 80 percent of the cumulative profits of the investments and of course the contributed capital. But, the 6th project defaults to $0. Thus, the total net profits of the fund are $400 − (500–100 loss) or 67 percent for the LPs. Yet, it was agreed that the GP would receive 20 percent of the net profits: $80. But the GP received $100, which accordingly triggers the claw-back provision.

It is noteworthy that there also number of approaches for structuring the claw-back obligation, including the "pay it back now" approach or the segregated reserves approach. Under the first approach, the GP will immediately provide a claw-back to the LPs. This method is remarkably straightforward and requires a potentially large cash contribution by a group of individual managers who may not have the financial ability to make the required contribution. In contrast, the reserve account approach places costly constraints on managers by requiring that the cash deposited in the reserve account is invested in a safe, cash-equivalent instrument in order to satisfy eventually the claw-back obligation. At the same time, there is also a limited partner claw-back that is intended to protect the GP against future claims, should the GP become the subject of a lawsuit. For the most part, the clause will include limitations in the timing or amount of the judgement.

Finally, as it happens, many LP contracts will include a preferred return provision. This is a minimum return rate which ranges most of the times from 5 percent to 10 percent. The idea of preferred return is that it affects the timing of the carried interest. Such a targeted return must be met before the fund manager can share in the fund profits. Preferred returns are normally required by LP's who make commitments to new funds or funds involved in buy outs. Most priority returns have a catch-up provision, which permits a reallocation of the profits to the GP after the priority return has been distributed to the LPs.[5] Please see Exhibit 17.4.

Exhibit 17.4 A Claw-Back Example

	GP	LP
Profits	$5 \times 0.20 \times 100 = \$100$	$5 \times 0,8 \times 100 = \$400$
Contributed Capital		$5 \times 100 = \$500$
Initial Investment		$6 \times 100 = \$600\ -$
Investment Return		$(5 \times 200 - [6 \times 100])/600 = 67$ percent

Overall, the contractual mechanisms for determining GP's compensation include both a profit-sharing arrangement that balances investors' concerns for pay-for-performance, and a distribution scheme to investors that is more likely to limit overall fund risk-taking. Moreover, there are a variety of factors that affect fund-manager compensation. First, fund managers are expected to have higher fixed fees and carried interest percentages in jurisdictions with a high quality legal rules-and-enforcement environment. Second, fund focus and characteristics can result in quite different outcomes for fund managers. For example, funds focusing on venture capital investment are more likely to require professional staff and expertise, which leads to lower yields and higher performance fees to align interests. Conversely, larger funds, such as buyout funds, are more likely to have lower fixed compensation because they require fewer staff than funds focusing on venture capital. Finally, the type of institutional investor and their level of risk may influence the fixed- and variable-fee structures of fund managers.

The Relationship between Investors and Fund Managers: Restrictive Covenants

In the previous section, we examined how the flexibility of the limited partnership form allows the internal and external participants to enter into contractual arrangements that align the incentives of fund managers with those of outside investors. If structured well, the limited partnership agreement can effectively reduce agency costs. In this section we turn to consider how limited partners are usually permitted, despite restrictions on their managerial rights, to vote on important issues such as amendments of the partnership agreement, dissolution of the partnership agreement, extension of the fund's life, removal of a general partner, and the valuation of the portfolio. In addition, we examine how limited partners employ several contractual restrictions when structuring the partnership agreement depending on the asymmetry of information and market for investment opportunities.

In recent years, a number of law and finance scholars have studied the role and frequency of covenants in the agreements between institutional investors and professional fund managers. An early study by Gompers and Lerner (1996) focuses on restrictive covenants imposed by institutional investors on fund managers in respect of the operation of the fund. They grouped the venture capital fund restrictive covenants into three categories: (1) restrictions on management of the fund; (2) restrictions on the activities of the GP; and (3) restrictions on the types of investment (Axelson, Strömberg, and Weisbach 2009).[6]

In terms of the first category of covenants, the first restriction in this class involves limits on the size of investment in any one firm that discourages the GP (the incentives induced by carried interest) from allocating a large portion of fund in a single investment. This is similar to the restrictions on the type of behavior that would increase the leverage of the fund and thereby amplify the risk for institutional investors. A restriction on co-investment is designed to limit the opportunism of fund managers so as to avoid one fund artificially improving the performance of another. A second category of covenants is designed to limit the investment activities of the GP. The restriction on co-investment by fund managers is designed to limit the agency problem that might arise from selective attention to certain portfolio firms at the expense of the performance of the entire fund. The covenant that is designed to limit the sale of fund interest by fund managers ensures that their commitment to the fund is not compromised. Further, the key person provisions and restrictions on additional partners is intended to ensure that management does not opportunistically hire new personnel to manage the fund in breach of their commitments made to the LPs. The third category of covenants is related to restrictions on types of investment that GPs can make. These covenants reduce or eliminate the potential for management to opportunistically alter the focus of the fund for their own concerns at the expense of investors. Restrictions include limitations on investments in venture capital, public securities, LBOs, foreign securities, and other asset classes.

In the context of determining the frequency of the covenants for such funds, Gompers and Lerner found that number and type of covenant correspond to the uncertainty, information asymmetry, and agency costs in the portfolio company. Exhibit 17.5 shows the distribution of covenants for VC funds.

They demonstrated, moreover, that there is a positive relationship between the use of restrictions and the propensity of the fund managers to behave opportunistically. As Exhibit 17.5 shows, there are a number of distinct covenants that address problems relating to the management of the fund, conflict of interests, and restrictions on the type of investment the fund can make. Gompers and Lerner demonstrate, furthermore, that the number and type of covenants correspond to the uncertainty, information asymmetry, and agency costs in the portfolio company. Other factors affecting the use of restrictions are the fund's size, the compensation

Exhibit 17.5   Distribution of Covenants in Venture Capital Funds

Description	% of Covenants
Covenants Relating to the Management of the Fund	
Restrictions on the size of investment in any one firm	77.8
Restrictions on use of debt by partnership	95.6
Restrictions on co-investment by organization's earlier or later funds	62.2
Restrictions on reinvestment of partnership's capital gains	35.6
Covenants Relating to the Activities of the General Partners	
Restrictions on co-investment by general partners	77.8
Restrictions on sale of partnership interests by general partners	51.1
Restrictions on fund-raising by general partners	84.4
Restrictions on other actions by general partners	13.3
Restrictions on addition of general partners	26.7
Covenants Relating to the Type of Investment	
Restrictions on investments in other venture funds	62.2
Restrictions on investments in public securities	66.7
Restrictions on investments in leveraged buyouts	60.0
Restrictions on investments in foreign securities	44.4
Restrictions on investments in other asset classes	31.1
Total Number of Partnership Agreements in Sample	**45**
Average Number of Covenant Classes	**7.9**
Average Number of Covenant Classes (weighted by fund size)	**8.4**

Source: Gompers and Lerner (1996).

system of the managers, and their reputation. In contrast, hedge funds rely less on covenants due to the shorter lock-up periods and the fund's liquidity. Finally, the public nature of the activities of hedge funds, particularly in the market for corporate control, tends to limit the principal-agent problems that might otherwise emerge.

It is noteworthy that the average frequency of use of covenants in non–U.S. VC partnerships is unrelated to the supply and demand of venture capital. Schmidt and Wahrenburg (2003) show that established European funds are more severely restricted by the use of three sub-categories of covenants within VC-partnership agreements. An international comparison of contractual covenants among private investment funds across countries also indicates a significant difference in probability of use of covenants (Cumming and Johan 2006). Exhibit 17.6 shows the distribution of use of covenants of international VC-partnership agreements.

In this context, Cumming and Johan (2006) have offered a "quality of law" explanation for the frequency of use of investment covenants imposed by institutional investors pertaining to GP's activities relating to investment decisions, investment powers, types of investment, fund operations, and limitations on liability. According to Cumming and Johan (2007), the presence of legal counsel who review covenants would increase the probability of covenants. They find evidence, moreover, that the quality of the rule of law and other institutional and legal practice factors is positively correlated with the number of covenants relating to fund operations. In their view, the better the legal system, as measured in the increase in the Legality Index (a weighed average of the legal index variables introduced by La Porta et al. [1997, 1998] as defined by Berkowitz et al. [2002]), that is, from 20 to 21

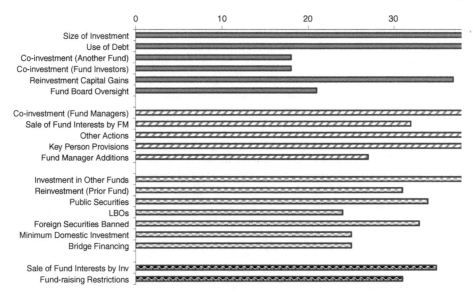

Type 1: Investment Decisions; Type 2: Investmenters;
Type 3: Types of Investment; Type 4: Fund Operation;
Type 5: Limitation of Liability

Exhibit 17.6   Frequency of Use of Each Covenant
Source: Cumming and Johan (2006).

(normal improvement rate for developed country), the higher the probability of an additional covenant relating to fund operation by about 1 percent; but an increase in the Legal Index from 10 to 11 (normal improvement rate for developing country) increases the probability of the presence of an extra fund-operation covenant by about 2 percent.

The above studies emphasize how important it is to recognize the critical role of management influence in determining the management and structural characteristics of a fund, the agency problems and control issues that emerge in the investment process, and the conflicts of interest that occur in times of market upheaval. LPs have high-powered incentives that greatly improve their ability to focus on addressing these problems through negotiating and implementing covenants to protect LPs and ensure the GP's incentives to serve investors' interests. Further improvements in the training of legal counsel who review covenants is likely to positively influence the frequency of some covenants. A more complete solution would require increases to the quality of legal systems generally in developing and civil law jurisdictions.

The Relationship between the Fund and Its Portfolio Companies

In exchange for their investments, private equity funds usually demand control rights in addition to their shareholdings. In practice, it appears that private equity investors often avail themselves of the features of convertible preferred stock (Dent 1992). Initially, finance scholars argued that convertible preferred stock was an optimal instrument to control the substantial double-sided, moral-hazard agency problems related to the investment process.[7] It is argued that convertible preferred stock is predominantly used by venture capitalists seeking to protect themselves against the downside risk of their investment by providing seniority or priority rights over the straight equity.

Convertible preferred stock allows for significant *ex post* flexibility in the determination of control rights and the conditions upon which venture capitalists are allowed to exit their investments. Convertible preferred stock is considered optimal, on one hand, because it secures downside protection for venture capitalists, and on the other hand because it gives entrepreneurs incentives to take significant risks in order to obtain a higher final firm value in the event of success. In fact, convertible preferred stock limits opportunistic behavior by allocating exit control to the venture capitalist. More recent models show that convertibles are an optimal form of finance when entrepreneurs and venture capitalists are required to introduce value into the firm sequentially. The use of convertible preferred stock is crucial for venture capitalists, because, having become active investors, they must obtain a secure means of exit from their investment.[8] The precise scope of the features is established by the terms of the stock purchase contract. Although we speak of a contract, the rights must traditionally be defined in the corporation's articles of incorporation for the purpose of certainty of information.

The following terms can usually be distinguished: preference on dividends and liquidation, voting rights, conversion rights, and antidilution provisions, redemption of the preferred shares, preemptive rights, go-along rights, and information rights. All of these rights must be defined in detail. To be sure, directors' fiduciary duties offer some protection for preferred stockholders.[9]

Venture capitalists can acquire preferred shares with *a cumulative dividend right*. This right means that if a preferred dividend is not paid in any year, it accumulates; the accumulated arrears must be paid in full before any dividends are paid on common stock. Preferred shares can also be noncumulative, so that the portfolio firm has no further obligation for unpaid dividends. In between those two are partially cumulative preferred shares. Furthermore, venture capitalists sometimes use participating preferred shares. In such a case, in addition to the dividend preference, they may participate with the common stock in any dividends declared on that stock. In practice, because most innovative start-ups scarcely yield any profits at the time of the venture capital financing, the parties often agree that the corporation pays no dividends at all.

Preferred stock usually grants the venture capitalists a *liquidation preference*, which provides that on liquidation a designated amount—typically, the price at which the preferred shares were issued—should be paid to the preferred share-holder before any distributions are made with respect to common stock. In the worst-case scenario, this right gives the venture capitalists a senior claim to cash flow and distributions in liquidation, through which they could retrieve at least some of their investment. It shifts the risk from the venture capitalists to the entrepreneur.

Preferred shares are normally nonvoting shares. However, venture capitalists often procure convertible preferred stock that confers a *right to vote*. The voting rights typically correspond to the number of shares they would have after conversion. They are entitled to vote as a separate voting group on amendments that are burdensome to them as a single class and are beneficial to other classes.[10] If the venture capitalists do not actually control the majority of the votes, this "class voting" mechanism protects them against troublesome resolutions. In addition, the class of preferred shares is typically entitled to elect half or more of the members of the board of directors.[11] This implies that venture capitalists may participate directly in management by serving on the board themselves. In so doing, they have substantial control over the board. It also gives them the opportunity to replace the entrepreneur as chief executive officer (CEO) if the business is in danger of failing.

Venture capitalists have a strong willingness to take *convertible* preferred stock. If the business is successful and an IPO is feasible, the venture capitalists may, at their option, convert their preferred shares into marketable common shares and sell them profitably as soon as the corporation goes public.[12] The articles of incorporation must contain the conversion ratio at which the conversion is to take place.[13] A favorable ratio to venture capitalists may mitigate window-dressing by the entrepreneur, because manipulating short-term signals may persuade the venture capitalists to exercise the conversion option and so dilute the ownership of the entrepreneurial team. The ratio may also depend on the performance of the business, that is, "if the company does well, the conversion price might be higher." A contingent conversion ratio will increase the short-term incentive to the entrepreneurial team, as a high price due to good (short-term) results may prevent the venture capitalists from converting. In such a case, "window dressing" would decrease the chance of dilution of the common stock held by the entrepreneur and his key employees.

In addition, the articles of incorporation normally provide for *antidilution* provisions to take into account changes that have occurred in the number of outstanding common stocks since the preferred stock was issued. They ensure that the venture capitalists retain a relatively steady level of ownership.

Preferred stock is often made redeemable at the option of the venture capitalist (often called a "mandatory redemption," a "put," or a "buyout"). This right supplies an exit mechanism in the event that the business "is financially viable but too small to go public." The redemption price is typically the original purchase price increased by a reasonable rate of interest. In a few isolated instances, the entrepreneurial team has the power to redeem the preferred shares from the venture capitalists on behalf of the corporation.

The venture capitalists are usually entitled to purchase new shares proposed to be issued in a *pro rata* portion of their common-stock-equivalent holdings. A *preemptive right* averts the dilution of the proportional interest of the venture capitalists in the corporation.

In the event of the entrepreneur and the key employees receiving an offer to sell their stock, most preferred shareholder contracts provide that the venture capitalists can sell their shares after conversion at the same time and on the same terms. A *go-along right* protects the venture capitalists from the unwanted influence of a third party over the business. While they cannot prevent the third party from buying the shares, they can demand that the third party buy them out on the same terms as the entrepreneur and the key employees. This right prohibits the entrepreneurial team from selling their stock unless venture capitalists are offered the same terms.

Finally, the articles of incorporation often specify that the firm must maintain and provide specific records, including financial statements and budgets. They also provide that the venture capitalists can inspect the business's financial accounts at will. The right to information is essential, as (1) preferred stockholders do not have the broad protection of fiduciary duties, (2) information is necessary for venture capitalists to use preference rights intelligently, (3) it restrains the entrepreneurial team from engaging in reckless conduct, and (4) in most states, corporation statutes by default restrict the right to inspect the books and records either to certain documents or to certain events.

It becomes even more pressing in the era where hedge funds play an increasingly important role in corporate governance and corporate control. The rapid transformation of activism by hedge funds, which has become so prevalent, is heralded by some as the next corporate governance revolution. This activism is, as we have seen, characterized typically by mergers and corporate restructurings, increased leverage, dividend recapitalizations, and the replacement of management and board members. The result has been that if a firm is mismanaged, these funds use their capital in a focused and leveraged way so as to take over control and initiate different, more beneficial, and effective business strategies. Yet even though they have the potential to impose immense discipline on boards and managers of firms, these funds are shrouded in nebulous mystery, obscurity, and complexity. Moreover, hedge funds are being accused of neglecting long-term goals and pursuing short-term payoff. The risk involved in investing huge amounts of capital calls for corporate governance measures for investment funds. By focusing on regulation, we seek to contribute a better understanding of the advantages and limitations of investor-owned firms.

REGULATION OF PRIVATE EQUITY FUNDS

Policymakers and the media have drawn attention to the confusion that private equity funds are currently causing in the world of finance and corporate governance. The recent wave of private-equity-based buyouts of publicly listed companies has prompted questions and political controversy about whether private equity can perhaps be beneficial. For example, the purchase of VNU, a global information and media company, by a consortium of private equity firms triggered concerns that the advantages of taking the firm private, including cost reduction and increased operational efficiency, may not offset the costs involved when the delisting of companies entails a significant reduction in liquidity of equity markets. Moreover, the sophisticated use of financial engineering techniques, in particular the funding of acquisitions with large amounts of debt, which are subsequently loaded on the acquired businesses, raises suspicion.

At the same time, the mixed picture about the costs and benefits of private equity suggests that questions remain about whether more detailed regulation and supervision of funds are required. Given the contractual mechanisms that prevail in the governance of both private equity and hedge funds, an initial hands-off approach might be warranted. What is more, private equity is evolving into more transparent investment vehicles. First, institutional investors, demanding better risk management, encouraged equity funds to adopt better valuation techniques and controls. Secondly, buyout groups attempt to improve their reputation and image by joining respectable industry bodies, like the British Venture Capital Association, or initiating the establishment of such a group in their respective countries, such as the Private Equity Council in the United States. The purpose of these groups is to conduct research and, more important, to provide information about the industry to policymakers, investors, and other interested parties. Last, in search for more stable capital, private equity funds increasingly raise or are planning to raise money by listing funds on public markets. By floating shares or units of a fund, advisors voluntarily subject themselves to regulatory supervision. The contractual nature of private equity funds in combination with the trend towards self-regulation by industry groups suggests that the sophisticated players in the private equity are themselves capable of disciplining opportunistic behavior by fund managers and advisors. This strategy, which ensures that possible rules and regulations are in line with both best practices and standards applied in the world of private equity, is examined in the next section.

Self-Regulation

This section will explain the function of soft-law principles and industry standards specifically tailored to private equity funds in assisting general partners and investors in overcoming bargaining problems and uncertainties connected with the operation of private equity funds. The following questions will be addressed: Is there a credible role for best-practice guidelines in improving the contractual governance arrangements of private equity funds? Does each industry segment require the introduction of governance guidelines specific to the segment and its business model? Which institutions or groups are best placed to develop the right set of principles? Do governmental committees or industry-based associations ensure the creation of optimal guidelines? Having seen that the procedures involved for the creation of best-practice guidelines enhance integrity and awareness for the business practices and stakeholders, the question is whether what matters most is the substantive variation in guidelines across the industry sector or the standardization achieved by a general code.

Answers to most of these questions can be found in practice, which already shows the emergence of distinctive guidelines for private equity firms. A soft-law example is the launch of the European Venture Capital Association (EVCA) Corporate Governance Guidelines for the Management of Privately Held Companies in 2005 (European Venture Capital Association, 2005, www.evca.com). Designed in consultation with industry experts, the EVCA guidelines provide a set of optional measures that focus on the staged investment decisions of venture capital and private equity funds and the contractual circumstances surrounding these investments. In this regard, provisions that enunciate the duties and responsibilities in relation to the design and execution of corporate strategy are a core feature of the recommendations.

These corporate governance recommendations supplement other standards and guidelines in order to provide greater transparency about the venture capital industry. For instance, the development of a timely system of reporting regime is called for with respect to annual reports and financial statements appearing on a company web site within six months of the year-end. Indeed, to the extent that investors need to be informed about the operation of the fund, the guidelines call for a financial review that refers to the risk management objectives and policies in light of the risks and uncertainties facing the company, and the impact of increased leverage and the other fund risks. Likewise, investors of such funds invariably expect timely disclosures and therefore the EVCA guidelines specify that management should issue an interim statement not more than three months after the mid-year. In addition to these guidelines on financial disclosure and governance, there are specific reporting requirements for General Partners pertaining to fund management team composition, including senior members of the general partner team and supervisory committee, experience and responsibility for management of the fund, as well as fund factors such as stage and industry focus, holding periods, and fund history. Also pertinent is the compensation and categorization of the limited partners, as well as the investors' countries of origin and their institutional characteristics.

Industry-based guidelines have also appeared at the national level. For example, a separate code for private equity funds was introduced by the Dutch Private Equity and Venture Capital Association in 2007. Experts immediately praised the code for encouraging more transparency of fund practices and for the educative value to firms. While there had been some doubts about the willingness of firms to even consider adopting these practices in their dealings with investors and third parties, the code will become mandatory for all member of the Association at the end of the one-year trial period. With the introduction of the Code, the Association aims at professionalizing private equity firms by encouraging the adoption of standardized practices such as fund managers providing clients with clarity regarding their plans, investment decisions, and to enhance accountability by taking into account the considerations of other interested parties when making investments in the Netherlands.

The governance principles work in tandem with other core features of the code in order to provide better transparency for investors in private equity firms. This is important, because there are restrictions on the ability of investors to obtain superior information on fund operation and the management of their investments. The principles include, first, that the fund manager take into account the specific information needs of investors based on the specific contractual conditions between the parties. Second, pertaining to the management of the portfolio company, private equity firms—including other shareholders and fund management—must make disclosures about their investment objectives, financial structure, investor participation period, and the responsibilities of the supervising party.

In the case of buyouts, the code obliges the fund to disclose a plan within six months of the transaction. In addition, buyout funds are required to comply with traditional corporate governance measures regarding the international organization of the company, which are designed to improve the relations between the parties, limit potential agency problems, and enhance firm performance. Third, with respect to other shareholders of the portfolio company, the code requires that shareholders must make disclosures about their decision-making powers, the frequency and content of disclosures, management of the portfolio company, confidentiality agreements, and loan agreements. In terms of the monitoring and supervision of portfolio companies, private equity funds have an incentive to achieve high standards of management supervision in order to maximize performance and manage the activities of the fund in the interests of the parties involved. To this end, the code recommends the fund's supervisory board may serve to limit the conflicts of interests between fund manager and fund investors by appointing qualified, knowledgeable members who can act independently. To be sure, the code recognizes that the conflicts will be easier to manage when the supervisory board has full information regarding the investor and management agreements. Finally, fund managers should have incentives to engage with other stakeholders, such as creditors, about management and investor agreements.

It is noteworthy that a similar set of guidelines was produced in November 2007 by Sir David Walker's working group for the British Venture Capital Association (BVCA) on disclosure and transparency in the U.K. private equity industry. The guidelines, which are a voluntary set of rules to be implemented on a "comply or explain" basis, require greater disclosure by private equity firms and their portfolio companies. While the purposes of the guidelines are similar to the Dutch code, it is notable that there are differences in both the scope and details of the guidelines. It is conjectured that the differences in the codes may indicate the growth of some transactional structures (e.g., growth capital transactions) in the United Kingdom that play a smaller role in the Netherlands. Focused primarily on buyout activities of private equity firms, the Walker Guidelines covers firms that advise or manage investment funds or that own or control one or more U.K. portfolio companies. The scope of the guidelines covers portfolio companies that generate more than 50 percent of their revenues in the United Kingdom, employ more than 1,000 employees, and that exceed £300 million pounds of market capitalization plus market premium, or £500 million pounds in enterprise value.

There are three main areas covered by these "comply or explain" measures. The guidelines provide transparency requirements for private equity firms, which include the filing of an annual report and financial statements on a company web site within four months of the end of year as against the current nine months. Like the Dutch code, portfolio firms should also file a short interim statement not more than two months after the mid-year. At the same time, general partners are required to publish an annual review, accessible on their web site, which should serve as an effective channel to communicate their business orientation and the governance structure of their portfolio companies. Finally, there is an expectation that the private equity firms will provide to the BVCA, on confidential basis, data for the previous year involving the amounts of capital raised, acquisitions and disposals by transaction value, fee payments made to advisers and other services related to the establishment and management of their funds, and for exits. In net, the Walker Group did not envisage the need for new regulatory or legislative provisions on disclosure in the United Kingdom. Consistent with this view, the Walker Group expects that the soft-law framework, reinforced by the active monitoring and review role played by the BVCA (along with the likelihood that institutional investors will also strive to monitor the disclosure and governance activities of the portfolio companies in important respects) will provide sufficient incentives for private equity firms to comply with the guidelines.

It goes without saying that a specific set of guidelines induces private equity funds to pay increasing attention to the importance of professional governance structures. Besides enhancing the effect on the adoption of good governance practices, optional industry guidelines can serve another important goal. Accordingly, they can function as a self-regulatory mechanism in response to increased political pressures for greater disclosure and transparency of fund capital structures and management practices. Although voluntary by nature, guidelines could be used by the industry as a "sword of Damocles" in the event of noncompliance. If non-compliers were expelled from the industry's association, the voluntary guidelines would arguably have a mandatory effect, as with the Dutch code. The advantage of this approach over legislative measures is the flexibility and adaptability of the regulations. The next section considers the circumstances in which a combination of industry measures and government involvement in monitoring the activities of portfolio companies may prove beneficial to both investors and the industry.

Coregulation

In view of the factors discussed above, the challenge is to locate the right mix of soft-law and government measures that encourage funds to effectively disclose and inform their investors and the market about their performance, investment strategy, and valuation of their investments, fees, and debt levels. In the spirit of locating the right mix, it is very important to consider coregulation strategies that rely on industry standards that are ultimately reinforced by independent monitoring committees.

Coregulation, which is a combination of governmental and nongovernmental regulatory actions, holds out the advantages of the predictability and legal certainty of legislation along with the flexibility and acceptance of self-regulation. Several reasons suggest that it is an effective means to coordinate public and private resources to manage regulatory risk. First, coregulation holds out the possibility of resolving conflicts through cooperative engagement involving firms choosing from a variety of mechanisms to manage a specific problem. This model's success depends not only on the flexibility of the techniques deployed by parties, but also on the alignment of the regulatory benefits and the incentives of the parties engaged in the regulatory process. In theory, financial benefits themselves provide sufficient incentives, given the removal of regulatory barriers. In practice, however, coregulation is pursued by political entrepreneurs, the agents of private equity funds, who appear to be pursuing reputational gain. Second, while coregulation models concentrate on identifying the basis for cooperative relational advantage, the process largely involves public and private parties in developing ex ante an appropriate set of standards that can be assessed on objective criteria to determine which provisions should be implemented.

As noted above, a number of recent factors have led to questions about whether governments should step up their monitoring and regulation of private equity funds. Regulators have suggested that economic studies show that the respective benefits and costs of private equity funds are inconclusive producing little sympathy for new legislation in the area. In continental Europe, a virtual torrid of press reports on the negative sentiment resulting from buyouts has stimulated interest in self-regulatory and industry actors producing codes of conduct for both private equity funds and private-equity-backed companies (McCahery and Vermeulen 2008).[14] However, coregulation has worked well in the case of best practice codes of corporate governance. In this regard, periodic review of the company compliance is conducted by government-sponsored monitoring committees that publish the industry-wide compliance level yearly. There are implications for companies that undercomply or engage in avoidance strategies. In fact, there is economic evidence, from a number of jurisdictions, that shows a correlation between a company's compliance rate and their share price performance.

In the autumn of 2007, the U.K. Treasury Select Committee recommended that the Walker Guidelines be implemented, and that there is room for extending the guidelines to facilitate portfolio management standards (communication of governance approach to stakeholders and mode of investment of portfolio company), disclosure by general partners (disclosure of performance results and value creation methods), and transparency regarding the structure and level of debt (Treasury Select Committee 10th Report Session 2006–2007, July 24 2007). More importantly, the Select Committee endorsed the view of requiring additional independent monitoring of the industry's code of conduct. Subsequently, the Walker Guidelines were implemented in the fall of 2007.

This is likely to result in greater consistency in disclosure across funds that would not only benefit institutional investors, pension funds, and insurance funds in meeting their fiduciary duties to their clients, but will inevitably facilitate funds in their capital-raising efforts with investors. Second, we suspect that there are a number of practices by private equity firms that will also be effectively curtailed by an independent monitoring committee. Consider conflicts of interests. Investors are greatly concerned about the evidence pointing to large-scale material conflicts of interests between private equity funds and their managers in relation to the allocation of their investments. While many of these allocation problems have been largely addressed by the industry standards, there is concern that abuses may arise in other contexts, such as between proprietary and advisory activities, or when a manager plays more than one role in a single transaction. It is worth stressing that the most effective way of identifying and communicating these conflicts is through the industry-wide compliance system that is reinforced by an independent monitor. Although it is inevitable that some fund managers will not be persuaded to comply fully with the industry guidelines, it can be expected that additional independent monitoring will be supplied by a mixture of institutional investor, trade union, and pressure-group associations.

Moreover, there is at least a suspicion that self-regulation measures and industry coregulation are likely to be more effective, given the complexity and range of activities pursued by private equity funds, than direct regulatory intervention. It is crucial to recall that the challenge here is to comprehend the amount of work required by government regulators to simply understand the impact of their intervention, the scale of their target, and its ultimate effectiveness on firms. At the same time, concerns arise over the decision-making procedures for consultation with funds and their advisers and the standards of review for evaluating their compliance. For coregulation to succeed, consideration must be given to increasing the level of incentives for parties to abide by the industry-wide standards because a positive approach, as the evidence suggests, will be more beneficial in the long run.[15] To the extent incentives are insufficient to induce individual fund-level cooperation, we would expect that some level of harmonization might be needed, given the dispersion of PE funds internationally, to obtain these regulatory goals (Cumming and Johan 2007).

The Regulatory Response

In this section we consider the circumstances where direct government regulation could usefully supplement the industry mix of contractual and self-regulatory strategies. In assessing the need for a regulatory response, we have seen that there are various mechanisms and contractual arrangements available to regulate private equity participants and their transactions. As we have seen, industry-wide standards are intended to illustrate how the industry operates, incorporating schemes for the valuation of investments, the governance of the investment vehicles, the resolution of conflicts of interest, and the transparency of collective investment vehicles. This development is, however, limited across jurisdictions because private equity standards developed by industry bodies have only emerged in the leading countries where private equity funds have a significance presence. Presumptively, the payoff for ensuring the widest diffusion of the new industry wide standards is significant. To date, no empirical analyses have been performed using the EVCA guidelines to measure compliance across the many separate funds and time periods. Consequently, it may be too early to assess whether these measures have reasonably high chances for dealing with the problems that have been identified above.

In the United States the increasing attention to private equity has led to questions as to whether funds and their advisers should be subject to registration and more rigorous information disclosure. More recently, lawmakers have focused on capital gains taxation, considering whether a change in the tax code on carried interest is consistent with the goals of fostering innovation and entrepreneurship.

Arguably, while the debate in the United Kingdom has much in common with U.S. concerns, such as the parliamentary investigations into taxation of carried interest, the U.K. response has managed to diverge slightly with its focus on whether the regulator is capable through its different risk-based regulation to meet its statutory objectives. In this section we document the response by regulators to the rise of the private equity sector within Europe.[16] To this end, we look at the U.K.'s Financial Service Authority's (FSA) recent analysis of the risks posed by private equity buyouts.

With a clear focus on the risks identified, the FSA sought explicitly in a 2006 discussion paper to classify the risks in private equity (Financial Services Authority 2006). A most obvious concern is the risk identified above, namely excessive leverage. The data cited above refer to increasing multiples, transaction structures being extended, and more and more "covenant-lite" loan deals. The concern is that with a serious contraction in the credit market, as we've seen recently, there could be a large number of corporate defaults that might significantly impact the debt and credit markets respectively. The significance of this is that banks and other intermediaries might be exposed to excessively leveraged transactions that could have a detrimental effect on the balance sheet of a number of large banks.

A second and related concern involves the unclear ownership of economic risk. At present, private equity and hedge funds rely on increasingly complex financial transactions, such as credit derivatives, and other risk transfer practices that involve use of off-balance-sheet transactions that arguably could exacerbate existing structural weaknesses and lead to unclear ownership of economic risk. Furthermore, it is worth noting that the different (and sometimes competing) bankruptcy regimes could give rise to different claims creating costly barriers for lenders to negotiate settlements. The evidence suggests, according the to the FSA, that excessive leverage and obscure ownership of economic risk do not bode well for the U.K. economy and are categorized as medium to high significant risks.

Third, private equity funds may, given the shroud of secrecy under which they operate, face charges related to alleged conflicts of interest between interested fund mangers and fund investors. To the extent, for example, that fund managers are allowed to participate in transactions in which a private equity fund participates, there are concerns that managers will capture the greatest source of gains from themselves at the expense of other investors. To be sure, some fund mangers may still be accused of conflicts of interest to the extent that they act as a director of a company owned by the fund. Other potential conflict situations arise where the fund is both a source of finance for a buyout of a target firm, which is also a fund client, or as a result of supplying finance to competing bidders on a deal. Also, there may be other residual conflicts that funds have incentives to resolve in their favor. On the whole, therefore, the FSA indicated that the conflict of interests were of high risk.

Fourth, the other notable concern is the risk of market abuse that could occur in the context of a buyout transactions and proprietary trading. Much attention is given to the possibility that material inside information could be disclosed which could have a detrimental effect on investors. Market abuse is rated as a high risk by the FSA. Finally, there are other risks, such as market access constraints, market opacity, and the reduction of overall capital market efficiency, that the FSA considers as low to medium risks. In assessing the risks, it is noteworthy that the market participants are differentially affected (see Exhibit 17.7).

Exhibit 17.7   Risk Assessment and Private Equity Participants

Participants	Risk			
	High	Medium	Medium-Low	Low
PE Firms	Market abuse & conflicts of interest	Excessive leverage		
Lenders	Market abuse			
Investors		Market access	Market opacity	Reduction in market efficiency
PE-Owned Firms		Excessive leverage		

Source: MacNeil (2008).

It is worth noting that the FSA's review of the regulatory risks supports the view that private equity funds are typically subject to relatively light regulatory oversight. A number of considerations support this view. First, private equity is classified as an alternative investment in which the funds are governed by the same company law, tax, and governance requirements that apply to all partnerships and publicly listed companies involved in the bidding process or other buyout arrangements. Second, it is worth noting that because private equity funds are not typically involved in issuing debt or securities in public markets, they are largely free of regulatory oversight in most jurisdictions. Third, most fund managers contract with clients who are sophisticated institutional investors or individuals who structure their investment activity through partnerships and contractual arrangements that provide for adequate information and investor protections. As a result, private equity firms are largely outside the scope of existing regulatory regime in most jurisdictions. In the next section, we discuss the three broad areas in which the regulation of the private equity market can be considered.

Legal Tools

In this section, we briefly describe four legal tools that are commonly used to deal with the problems involving participants and transactions in the private equity market. The four legal tools considered are (1) reporting and disclosure requirements of private equity funds and general partners, (2) enhancing market access, (3) governance and investor protection measures, and (4) taxation.

Enhancing Disclosure and Fund Reporting

Given the structure of private equity funds, disclosure of financial and operational information, including the valuation of their investments in their annual accounts, provides significant benefits to investors and can be an effective tool in limiting abusive actions by fund managers. Second, well-designed measures on disclosure of performance results may prove more effective than market (fund) competition in supplying the incentives to avoid exaggerating valuations of investment returns and unexited investments. Third, the imposition on the private equity firm to disclose their management fees and carried interest and the independent oversight body will allow investors to make a more informed investment decisions.

Enhancing Market Access

Empirical research on venture capital and private equity shows that the quality of the legal environment is an important determinant in raising the supply of investment funds (McCahery and Renneboog 2004). Since exiting is crucial for buyout funds, the creation of a deep and vibrant securities market is considered crucial for the development of a deep and liquid market for initial public offerings. It again follows that a hospitable IPO market may require liberalizing the stock exchange listing rules on board independence and control, thereby allowing private equity funds to list investment vehicles. Moreover, given that some markets are characterized by a small number of dominant firms that limit or restrict access, largely to the detriment of retail investors, there are good reasons for regulators to address this problem by facilitating more competition.

Governance and Investor Protection

Looking at the circumstances through which the market suffers from harmful conduct has led regulators to simply place a ban on insider trading and market manipulation. Not only does the market suffer, but investors may encounter significant losses, which undermines the confidence in public markets. When it comes to dealing with market manipulation and related misconduct, the existing mix of securities regulations are the most effective tool to prevent specific forms of abusive harms and to undertake investigations. The benefit of this type of intervention is two-fold. First, given the complexity of these transactions and the number of parties involved, the expenditure of resources to investigate these transactions tends to favor centralized oversight. Second, there is evidence that regulatory strategies that favor stiff sanctions will have a strong deterrence effect that offers support for more enforcement actions by securities regulators (Karpoff, Lee, and Martin 2009).

Taxation

Another type of regulatory intervention that affects the private equity market and fund managers is the taxation of capital gains on the sale of entity interest, withholding taxes, the deductibility of interest on debt, and the taxation of carried interest earned by general partners in private equity firms. It is important to note that a favorable taxation regime is an important determinant to the development of a favorable private equity environment. Moreover, the supply of efficient tax vehicles for such investments is considered a necessary mechanism in terms of the structuring and executing private equity transactions. Therefore, fiscal measure that are unattractive for both investors and fund managers, such as the proposed increase in tax on carried interest in the United Kingdom and United States, will inevitably place serious stress on the vitality of a private equity market.

The discussion that follows highlights the efforts of lawmakers to enact private equity reforms that fall under the four categories discussed above.

Regulatory Responses to Hedge Fund and Private Equity in Canada, the European Union, Germany, the Netherlands, and the United Kingdom

The rapid growth in the private equity market in recent years has prompted calls for the introduction of new regulatory measures to control for conflicts that are likely to arise between private equity funds and their investors as well as the problems related to buyouts. We review a few of the measures that have emerged in response to private equity and activist hedge fund engagements with target companies.

Canada

In Canada, the corporate law system, which operates at both the federal and provincial level, has long played a central role in regulating many central transactions, including amalgamations and the sale of all or substantially all assets of a company. The corporate statutes allocates power to shareholders to approve such transactions, the rights to dissent, and a fair value remedy. Canadian securities regulation also operates under a two-tier system and regulates such activities as annual and continuous disclosure, insider trading, public offers, and tender offers. In the case of going private transactions, the Ontario Securities Commission regulation provides a system for a formal valuation that must be prepared for the shares held by minority shareholders, approval by minority shareholders (depending on the transaction), and the recommendation that a special committee of directors negotiate with the controlling shareholder or related parties and ensure that all shareholders receive fair disclosure and the right, where necessary, to approve the transaction. Tax reforms have been undertaken recently in Canada to stimulate investment in private equity and venture capital. In particular, Canada and the United States signed in September 2007 a new protocol to the Canada–U.S. income tax treaty which provides for U.S. resident members of an limited liability company to claim benefits under the treaty. U.S. LLCs, which are fiscally transparent for U.S. federal income tax purposes, are not recognized by the Canada Revenue Agency under the treaty. Thus, the effect of the protocol is to allow gains realized by certain LLCs on the sale of shares of a Canadian corporation and which will apply to dividends received by an LLC with U.S. resident members, and the reduced branch tax rate of 5 percent applies to repatriated earnings of a Canadian branch of an LLC with U.S. resident members that are companies.

Germany

Recently, Germany introduced legislation to curb cooperation between shareholders on share votes, which would be deemed "acting in concert." More specifically, the German Federal Cabinet adopted a draft bill for the Act on Limitations of Risks Relating to Financial Investments or Risikobegrenzungsgesetz (Risks Limitation Act),[17] which was passed on June 27, 2008, by the Deutsche Bundestag and was approved by the Bundestag on July 4, 2008, and came into force on August 19, 2008. While the draft bill would clearly have deterred private equity and hedge fund activism, the legislation actually adopted is unlikely to damper legitimate communication between large and small shareholders.

Under the new act, concerted action will apply not only to cooperation in the voting right behavior, but also to the coordination of other shareholders' interests outside the shareholders' meeting. Second, the act has also provided a basis for determining when acting in concert would be extended to coordinated conduct of shareholders. Examples would includes cases where shareholders agreed to coordinate their voting behavior or if they agreed to cooperate based on a long-term strategy to influence or alter the target firm's business goals. Naturally, agreements that are designed to affect the composition of the supervisory board and the appointment of its chairman would not fall within the ambit of the reform unless the replaced board members or chairman used their power to introduce a new business strategy for the firm. The legislation may serve to deter some potentially damaging actions by activist hedge funds and buyout funds and consequently insulate boards and directors so that they can focus on the long-term interests of the company. However, the reform is likely to have an effect not only on activist shareholders motivated by short-term incentives, but also on institutional investors that might be perceived to be cooperating with other investors when exercising their right to vote or when using their power to call an extraordinary meeting or when undertaking other actions to protect the interests of shareholders.

Netherlands

In the Netherlands, a number of reforms have been prompted by a recent wave of high-profile buyouts of Dutch listed companies. Unsurprisingly, the Dutch Minister of Finance has proposed, based on a recommendation from the Monitoring Committee Corporate Governance, lowering the notification threshold for shareholdings in listed companies, under the Transparency Directive, from 5 percent to 3 percent. Furthermore, the Minister recommended a change in the disclosure rules mandating a higher threshold (from 1 percent to 3 percent) to gain the right to include agenda items at the shareholders' annual general meeting. Finally, the EU Takeover Directive has been implemented that requires a shareholder that owns more than 30 percent in a listed company to make an unconditional offer for the outstanding shares of the target company.

United Kingdom

In the United Kingdom, the Treasury Select Committee Report recommended that the Walker Guidelines, as previously discussed, be implemented, and proposed an independent monitoring committee to ensure industry's compliance with the code. Also, the Pre-Budget Report of the Chancellor addressed the issue of carried interest, declaring that, from April 6, 2008, capital gains tax will be charged at a rate of 18 percent and both taper relief and indexation will be withdrawn. The change will involve an 80 percent increase in the marginal tax rate applicable on investments held for less than two years. However, there has been little done with respect to carried interest being classified as income.

CONCLUSION

This paper analyzed the regulatory alternatives for the private equity and hedge fund industry. We examined the structure of fund formation and operation, and the system of fixed and performance fees that are designed to align investor and fund manager's interests. In particular, we argued that while contractual mechanisms allow parties to structure their particular ownership and investment instruments according to their own preferences, legal and institutional differences may explain the differences in fees and fund performances across jurisdictions. We noted that the industry's contractual system of regulation is being usefully supplemented by self-regulatory measures designed to improve the transparency and accountability of private equity funds and hedge funds. We then examined the costs and benefits of industry-based measures, arguing that the strength of the industry self-regulation outweighs its weaknesses.

Having explored the benefits of both contractual and self-regulatory techniques, we considered whether, under certain conditions, coregulation is an attractive measure to support industry body monitoring and compliance measures. As we made clear, a system of coregulation can induce, if properly designed, effective compliance by providing an effective threat in those hard cases when self-regulation fails. We turned to review the regulatory measures currently in place and designed to provide important checks to limit market abuses by some fund managers and to facilitate growth and innovation. In this context, we showed that there is a well-developed framework of corporate and securities law that is appropriate for dealing with private equity transactions and parties to these transactions. In particular, we indicated that European policymakers have focused on implementing laws recently on the regulation of takeovers, disclosure, and the prohibition of market abuse and insider trading that will improve the procedures for takeovers and buyouts while protecting the interests of investors and promoting confidence in the market. Finally, we examined some of the recent changes in fiscal measures in Canada and the United Kingdom, and the governance and investor protection measures that have been promulgated in the Netherlands and Germany in response to institutional investor activism.

NOTES

1. The Securities Act regulates the issuance and offering of securities to the public. If funds decide to offer their services and products to the public, the Investment Company Act of 1940 and the Investment Advisers Act of 1940 apply. The former governs the operation of the fund itself. The Investment Advisers Act governs the firms that manage the actual funds. Even if there is currently no requirement that private equity advisers register under the act, numerous advisers have, in light of an SEC action against unregistered adviser, opted to create and maintain oversight and independent review in line with SEC expectations of fund behavior.

2. Under the Small Business Administration Act of 1958, the Small Business Administration (SBA) is authorized to license SBICs to make equity and loan investments in smaller entrepreneurial firms in the United States.

3. Equally, we would expect fund manager to look to alternative sources of capital, such as sovereign wealth funds that have estimated combined resources of $2,000 billion to $3,000 billion, to step into the place of banks by funding leveraged buyouts. While it is easy to see why buyout firms are moving towards sovereign wealth funds, we have to acknowledge that a majority of these funds are unlikely to supply debt for buyouts for private equity firms. Reasons for the hesitancy of large sovereign wealth funds to be a

new source of capital for these deals may include the acknowledgment that they do not currently have the institutional capacity to manage more risky investments. Also, many mutual and sovereign wealth funds may be unwilling to lend in the circumstances where the sweetened terms are not sufficiently high to meet the investment objectives of the fund managers. We conjecture that sovereign wealth funds do not have the investment objectives, time, or specialized skills in which to efficiently monitor and add value to investments in private equity and buyout funds. It is possible that private equity will continue to innovate and find new sources of funding, but it is more likely that the new sources funds will not be sufficient to support the level of debt required by these firms. Until confidence returns in the credit markets, the level of debt involved in private equity and buyouts will be considerably smaller than before.

4. Nevertheless, some sponsors are now beginning to structure their funds as a Delaware LLC since it has the same organizational flexibility and tax efficiency as the LP.

5. Interestingly, while the literature has spent much time analyzing the optimal compensation structure for GPs, recent empirical work has found that legal and institutional factors explain the differences in fund manager payment terms, the timing of the distributions to investors, and the probability of claw-backs (Cumming and Johan 2006).

6. The frequency of standard covenants in limited partnership agreements, suggested by Gompers and Lerner's evidence, is related to funds having to seek third-party investment for all investments above a specified fraction of the fund's level (20 percent) or for taking on leverage at the fund level.

7. More recent research has looked at the contractual relationship between institutional investors and fund managers, suggesting that there is a positive correlation between the quality of a country's laws and the use of contractual provisions regulating private equity investment. The implication is that there are significant benefits to encouraging stronger legal conditions that could benefit fund manager compensation, fund returns, and the development of venture capital markets (Lerner and Schoar 2005; Cumming and Walz 2004).

8. It is widely acknowledged that convertible preferred stock is the dominant form of security used by venture capitalists in the United States. This may be due to the standardization of purchase agreements (see Gilson and Schizer 2003). Commentators argue that there are a number of reasons for the significantly higher usage of convertibles in the United States compared to Europe, Canada, and elsewhere (Cumming and Johan 2008). First, it is assumed that U.S. venture capitalists are more sophisticated and better established than the venture capitalists elsewhere, which accounts for the significantly lower use of these instruments by non–U.S. venture capitalists. Second, the size of the European debt market and the preference on the part of venture capitalists in Europe for straight debt may account for a lower rate of use of convertible preferred stock. Third, Gilson and Schizer (2003) have argued that U.S. venture capitalists are attracted to the tax advantages associated with convertible preferred stock, which allows them to make a lower valuation for the entrepreneur's common shares. Implicit in this argument is the view that the tax incentives connected to the reduced initial valuation of common stock for venture capitalists are the reason for the significantly higher use of convertible preferred stock, rather than the agency cost-reducing qualities of the instrument identified by models created by finance scholars.

9. Note that under Delaware law preferred stockholders are protected by the core fiduciary duties of care, loyalty, and good faith. Any special rights attached to preferred stock are interpreted like any other contractual rights. See, for example, *Benchmark Capital v Vague*, 2002 WL 1732423 at 6; *Sanders v Devine* 1997 WL 599539 at 5.

10. The Model Business Corporation Act (1984) §10.04 lists nine types of proposed amendments that trigger the right of a class of shares to vote as a separate voting group on an amendment.

11. See the Model Business Corporation Act (1984) §8.04, which provides that directors may be elected by certain classes of shareholders. As for the removal of directors, §8.08(b) provides that if a director is elected by a voting group of shareholders, only the shareholders of that voting group may participate in the vote to remove him.

12. Agreements usually confer on the venture capitalists the right to register their shares with the Securities and Exchange Commission (SEC) for public sale. "Piggyback" rights entitle the investor to include his stock in the firm's public offerings. "Demand rights" go further by allowing an investor to compel the firm to register the investor's stock with the SEC.

13. The ratio determines how many shares of common stock a preferred shareholder receives upon the exercise of the conversion.

14. An example is the launch of the European Venture Capital Association (EVCA) Corporate Governance Guidelines. Designed in consultation with industry experts, the EVCA guidelines provide a set of optional measures that address the contractual circumstances surrounding venture capital and private equity investments.

15. This argument has been reinforced recently by EC Commissioner Charles McCreavy in a speech to the British Venture Capital Association wherein he stated that "when we look at the numbers, we can quickly see that there is a distance to travel. The number of BVCA firms that have signed up to the Walker Guidelines is a case in point. According to certain reports only 32 out of a possible 200 members would be currently signatories. The limited reach of the Walker Guidelines is also apparent when we look at the number of portfolio companies covered by the guidelines. On 56, out of about 1,300 portfolio companies in the United Kingdom that are targeted by private equity investments, are reported to comply with the disclosure and transparency rules." See Charlie McCreevy, European Commissioner for Internal Market, "Private Equity: Progress on Disclosure and Transparency (Walker Guidelines)," EC/SPEECH/08/701.

16. Italian lawmakers introduced a new Corporate Law Reform (Legislative Decree 6/2003, applicable as of 1 January 2004) that set forth the basis of regulating leveraged buyout transactions. For the implications on buyouts in Italy, see Cumming and Zambelli (2007).

REFERENCES

Axelson, U., P. Strömberg, and M. S. Weisbach 2009. Why are buyouts levered: The financial structure of private equity funds. *Journal of Finance*, forthcoming.

Bratton, W. W. 2007. Hedge funds and governance targets. *Georgetown Law Journal* 95:1375–1433.

Berkowitz, D., K. Pistor, and J-F. Richard. 2002. Economic development, legality, and the transplant effect. *European Economic Review* 32:221–239.

Brav, A., W. Jiang, F. Partnoy, and R. Thomas. 2008. Hedge fund activism, corporate governance, and firm performance. *Journal of Finance* 63:1729–1775.

Cumming, D. J., and S. A. Johan. 2006. Is it the law or the lawyers? Investment fund covenants across countries. *European Financial Management* 12:535–574.

Cumming, D. J., and S. A. Johan. 2007. Regulatory harmonization and the development of private equity markets. *Journal of Banking and Finance* 31:3218–3250.

Cumming, D. J., and S. Johan. 2008. Preplanned exit strategies in venture capital. *European Economic Review* 52:1209–1241.

Cumming, D. J., and U. Walz. 2004. Private equity returns and disclosure around the world. *Journal of International Business Studies*, forthcoming.

Cumming, D. J., and S. Zambelli. 2007. Illegal buyouts. *Journal of Banking and Finance*, forthcoming.

Dent, G. W. 1992. Venture capital and the future of corporate finance. *Washington University Law Quarterly* 70:1029–1085.

Financial Services Authority. 2006. Private equity: A discussion paper on risk and regulatory engagement (DP 06/6, November 2006).

Gilson, R. 2003. Globalizing corporate governance: Convergence of form or function. *American Journal of Comparative Law* 49:329–358.

Gilson, R. J., and D. Schizer, 2003. Understanding venture capital structure: A tax explanation for convertible preferred stock. *Harvard Law Review* 116:874–916.

Gompers, P. A. and J. Lerner. 1996. The use of covenants: An empirical analysis of venture capital partnership agreements. *Journal of Law and Economics* 39:463–498.

Jenkinson, T. J. 2007. The development and performance of European private equity. In *Financial markets and institutions: A European perspective*, eds. X. Freixas, P. Hartmann, and C. Mayer. Oxford: Oxford University Press.

Kaplan, S. N., and A. Schoar. 2005. Private equity performance: Returns, persistence, and capital flows. *Journal of Finance* 60:1791–1823.

Karpoff, J., D. S. Lee, and G. Martin. 2009. The consequence to managers for cooking the books. *Journal of Financial Economics*, forthcoming.

La Porta, R., F. Lopez-de-Silanes, A. Shleifer, and R. W. Vishny. 1997. Legal determinants of external finance. *Journal of Finance* 52:1131–1150.

La Porta, R., F. Lopez-de-Silanes, A. Shleifer, and R. W. Vishny. 1998. Law and finance. *Journal of Political Economy* 106:1113–1221.

Lerner, J., and A. Schoar. 2005. Does legal enforcement affect financial transactions? The contractual channel in private equity. *Quarterly Journal of Economics* 120:223–246.

McCahery, J. A., and L. Renneboog. 2004. *Venture capital contracting and the valuation of high-tech firms*. Oxford: Oxford University Press.

McCahery, J. A., and A. Schwienbacher. 2008. Lead arranger certification in the private debt market. In *Rationality in company law: Essays in honour of D. D. Prentice*, eds. J. Armour and J. Payne. Oxford: Hart Publishing.

McCahery, J. A., and E. P. M. Vermeulen. 2008. *Corporate governance of non-listed companies*. Oxford: Oxford University Press.

Metrick, A., and A. Yashida. 2008. The economics of private equity funds. *Review of Financial Studies*, forthcoming.

Schmidt, D., and M. Wahrenburg. 2003. Contractual relations between European VC funds and investors: The impact of bargaining power and reputation on contractual design. *CFS Working Paper* No. 2003/15, 2003.

United States Venture Capital Association. 2006. Statistical Data.

United States Venture Capital Association. 2007. Statistical Data.

ABOUT THE AUTHORS

Joseph A. McCahery is the Professor of Corporate Governance and Innovation at the University of Amsterdam, Faculty of Economics and Business.

Erik P. M. Vermeulen is the Professor of Financial Market Regulation at the Tilburg Law and Economics Center (TILEC) and Professor of Law and Management at Tilburg University, Faculty of Law.

CHAPTER 18

International Private Equity Flows

SOPHIE MANIGART
Full Professor, Ghent University, Vlerick Leuven Gent Management School

SOFIE DE PRIJCKER
Ph.D. student, Ghent University

BIVAS BOSE
Ph.D. student, Ghent University

INTRODUCTION

Private equity (PE) emerged in the 1970s and 1980s in the United States and United Kingdom; its success spurred the rise of private equity in regions in the geographic or legal proximity of these two regions (Ooghe, Manigart, and Fassin 1991; Megginson 2004). PE investors are currently found on most continents, and the international flows of capital are increasing rapidly. For example, 34 percent of the amount raised by European venture capital (VC) and PE firms in the period 2003 to 2007 is dedicated to nondomestic investments (EVCA statistics). During the same period, U.S. PE firms accounted for 32 percent of all international buyout investments (Zephyr statistics), where a buyout is defined as international when the headquarter of the PE firm and of the target firm are located in different countries. The Australasian market has developed as a third important private equity market with strongly developed markets in Japan, Australia, Singapore, Hong Kong, South Korea, and Taiwan, and emerging markets in China and India (Lockett and Wright 2002). It is estimated that 35 percent of all Asian funds were invested internationally in 2004, with 17 percent of these funds invested outside Asia (Wright, Pruthi, and Lockett 2005).

The international PE market is also increasing in terms of funds raised. However, international fund-raising patterns differ markedly from international investment patterns. While only 10 percent of U.S. PE funds are raised from foreign sources, European and Asian PE funds are much more international in terms of funds raised, as 50 percent of their funds comes from nondomestic partners (Wright et al. 2005). Asian cross-border funds have a more geographically spread fund-raising pattern than European funds. While 37 percent of the Asian PE funds were raised in non-Asian countries in 2004, European PE funds raised only 29 percent of their funds outside the continent (Wright et al. 2005).

Despite the increasing geographical spread, raising funds in nondomestic markets or investing in nondomestic portfolio companies has far-reaching implications for all parties involved. Institutional barriers, consisting of legal, regulatory, cultural, and language differences increase adverse selection risks, transaction costs, and agency risks related to both working with international limited partners and international portfolio companies (Bruton, Fried, and Manigart 2005; Cumming, Fleming, and Schwienbacher 2009; Tykvová and Schertler 2006). The legitimacy of resources may also become problematic in a cross-border context, especially for intangible resources (Guler and Guillén 2007). For example, the reputation of a PE fund may be confined to its home market, making it more difficult to raise sufficient debt at attractive conditions to finance buyouts in nondomestic markets (Demiroglu and James 2007). In order to overcome those barriers, early-stage VC research suggests that it is important to cooperate with at least one local investor (Mäkelä and Maula 2008). We do not know to which extent this is transferable to the later-stage PE market.

The goal of this chapter is to present evidence and academic research on international flows of capital in PE markets and their effects on target companies. While international early-stage financing has recently received much attention from academic researchers, there is a surprising lack of academic research on international private equity. However, especially in Europe, the buyout industry is much larger than the early-stage financing industry. In addition, international PE flows are increasingly important for buyout firms (Meuleman and Wright 2009; Tykvová and Schertler 2006), as there is increasing evidence that later-stage investors are more likely to be international than early-stage investors (Hall and Tu 2003). Moreover, the methods of deal evaluation and involvement differ substantially between international early-stage and international later-stage investors. Monitoring of later-stage investments is less time-consuming (Hall and Tu 2003) and later-stage investors do not necessarily have similar involvement strategies (Manigart, Lockett, Meuleman et al. 2006). These differences increase the need for more knowledge on the behavior of later-stage investors in nondomestic markets.

In this chapter, we will first give an outline of the international development in terms of funds raised. Given the unavailability of reliable large-scale data on the flow of funds from institutional investors to PE funds or to fund-of-funds (FoFs), we will review existing literature on this phenomenon. The central part of this chapter will focus on international investments of PE firms, more specifically those investments in developed PE markets, that is, Western Europe, North America, and Oceania. We show that investing in nondomestic companies is an increasingly important phenomenon in the PE industry, but also highlight some barriers for increasing globalization. We discuss the characteristics of international deals and international investors, including the importance of regional clustering of international funds and syndication in nondomestic investments. Later, we discuss the internationalization of PE investors towards emerging markets. The chapter ends with unanswered questions and avenues for further research within this area.

A BRIEF OVERVIEW OF INTERNATIONAL FUND-RAISING

Compared to investing in traditional investment vehicles, investing in PE entails high risk and high illiquidity in a largely unregulated market (Cumming and

Johan 2007). The rise of the PE industry as a separate asset class has therefore led to the establishment of a new type of intermediaries: fund-of-funds (FoF). FoFs raise money from institutional investors and invest their funds in PE funds. Their value lies in their market knowledge and contacts with a broad range of potentially interesting PE funds, thereby decreasing search, transaction and governance costs for their investors. They also offer diversification possibilities to their investors, whose limited resources allocated to PE might not allow investing in a reasonable number of PE funds. It is clear that the emergence of FoFs has positively impacted the internationalization of fund-raising in the PE industry, as search and transaction costs are relatively lower for FoFs, thanks to their economies of scale and scope.

While the fund-raising market is more internationalized than the investment market, there is little systematic evidence on international fund-raising flows (Cumming and Walz 2004). The limited evidence highlights some important findings with respect to the main origins and destinations of fund providers. First, international funds largely come from the U.S. market. In the developed regions, such as the United Kingdom and Continental Europe, the United States is the largest international fund provider. In 2007, it was even the largest overall fund provider for the European market (EVCA 2008). The development of some emerging markets is also largely driven by the funds provided by U.S. investors (Leeds and Sunderland 2003). For example, the development of PE in India and China is to a large extent caused by U.S. flows of capital (Deloitte 2005; Wright, Lockett, and Pruthi 2002).

Second, European fund providers that invest internationally focus mostly on the same continent (Cumming and Johan 2007; ECVA 2008). As a result, 21 percent of all European funds raised during the period 2003 to 2007 came from nondomestic but European investors (EVCA 2008). Our understanding of their investment behavior outside Europe is limited. Evidence based on the Dutch market, however, indicates that institutional investors dedicate somewhat less than 40 percent of their international funds to the non-European market. They largely prefer the U.S. market (32 percent of their nondomestic investments) over Asia and other emerging markets, which only counted for 5 percent of their nondomestic investments in 2005. In addition, these investors indicated that they were likely to keep these levels of commitment within the next five years (Cumming and Johan 2007). There is limited knowledge on the investment behavior of U.K. fund providers, one of the most important European fund provider countries. While we know that the United Kingdom is an important recipient country, especially for funds providers from outside Europe (EVCA 2008), we have limited understanding of the destination of funds originating from the United Kingdom. They are acknowledged as a very important fund provider for Continental Europe (ECVA 2008), but little is known how important these regions are compared to U.S. or Asian-Pacific countries.

One of the main drivers of equity flows are the interesting risk-return characteristics of PE firms compared to other asset classes and compared to venture capital (Cumming et al. 2009; Megginson 2004). This has attracted the attention of institutional investors and high-net-worth individuals worldwide. These investors seek to invest in top–PE funds, which they may not always find in their home country due to a limited market size, poor economic conditions, or less-favorable legal protection or fiscal environment (Megginson 2004). The tendency of fund investors to target the FoFs of the top PE firms has increased significantly over the past years (Cornelius, Langelaar, and Rossum 2007). Hence, institutional investors focus on a small number of PE firms that are mainly located in the United States and the United Kingdom. This is one of the reasons why there is increasing industry concentration in the developed PE regions. More specifically, in Europe 35 percent of the total PE market is in the hands of only four firms. The four most important investors in the United States own as much as 75 percent of the total U.S. market (Cornelius et al. 2007).

The tendency of large institutional investors to focus on the international PE market is driven by regulatory institutions. First, decreasing governmental constraints to act as a limited partner in a PE firm has an important effect. In addition, regulations that decrease the information asymmetry between PE firms and their investors play a positive role (Cumming and Johan 2007): the international (and potentially intercontinental flow) of PE funds depends on harmonization of risk management standards such as the Basel II norms (Cumming and Johan 2007). In light of the increasing regulation that will arise as a consequence of the current international financial crisis, we speculate that this may probably benefit the flow of international PE funds in the future. As long as comparable standards of risk management and disclosure are introduced worldwide, institutional investors can easily screen and monitor PE funds in different world regions.

There is a lack of knowledge concerning the type of investors in nondomestic funds. It seems that they are more likely to originate from large institutional investors such as pension funds, while bank-based funds have a lower tendency to be international (Mayer, Schoors, and Yafeh 2005). Interestingly, however, Dutch institutional investors seem to have a slightly different international investment pattern in which especially the bank-based funds target the international market (Cumming and Johan 2007). Understanding the link between the investors in a PE firm and its international strategy is, however, important. Different categories of investors have a different investment strategy and risk-return preference. Therefore, this is a very important area for further research, both for academia and for practitioners.

INTERNATIONAL INVESTMENTS OF PRIVATE EQUITY FUNDS IN WESTERN EUROPE, NORTH AMERICA, AND AUSTRALIA

There is a growing tendency of international PE funds to invest in economically developed countries. This investment behavior is largely fueled by the overall growth and maturity of the industry (Wright et al. 2005). We start with documenting the recent investment activity between PE funds and their nondomestic portfolio companies located in North America, the United Kingdom, continental Europe, and Oceania. Our statistics presented hereafter are based on international buyout deals backed by PE funds in 20 internationally developed private equity markets during 2003 to 2007.[1] The findings are based on deals reported in Zephyr, a database commercialized by Bureau Van Dijk.[2] Exhibit 18.1 gives an overview of all cross-border PE deals between these regions within the period 2003 to 2007. Over these five years, 1,133 buyouts were financed by nondomestic PE investors. Due to missing data, the analysis of the value of deals is restricted to 632 deals only.

The number of cross-border deals almost tripled from 119 deals in 2003 to almost 300 deals in 2007. The median value of cross-border deals also increased,

Exhibit 18.1 Cross-Border Buyouts between Western European, North American, and Australian markets

Year	Total Number of Cross-Border Deals	Median Value of Deals (million €)	Average Value of Deals (million €)
2003	119	133,44	208,68
2004	198	187,19	303,63
2005	239	168,00	320,00
2006	280	170,74	425,60
2007	297	204,60	514,98

Source: Zephyr.

from 133 million Euros to 205 million Euros. The average deal value increased even more, from almost 300 million Euros to almost 600 million Euros. Our findings are in line with previous research that reports that nondomestic investments tend to be the larger deals (Raade and Dantas Machado 2008). This increase in international investment activity is in the first place caused by an increase of funds, and more specifically by the interest of fund providers in a small group of very large international and highly reputable investors (Cornelius et al. 2007). The increasing focus to finance very large PE firms makes investing in mega deals feasible, while still keeping sufficient portfolio diversification. In what follows, we will first analyze the most active investor countries, followed by the most important recipient countries of international PE.

Most Important International Investor Countries

Exhibit 18.2 shows the yearly number of international private equity deals per country of investor. The dominance of United States and the United Kingdom is reflected in the large number of international deals that are financed by PE investors from these two countries. Almost one third of all deals that attracted international capital from 2003 to 2007 found that money in the United States (423 deals in total) and another 28 percent found their investors in the United Kingdom (371 deals). The dominance of U.S. investors over the United Kingdom and other European PE firms is especially apparent in the segment of mega deals: while U.S. mega targets can find financing from domestic investors, European mega targets are increasingly forced to search for finance in the United States (Cornelius et al. 2007). We furthermore observed that U.S. PE investors invested in far fewer non-U.S. deals in 2007 (88 deals) than in 2006 (112 deals). As U.K. investors further increased their international investment activities in 2007 (93 non-U.K. deals compared to 78 in 2006), they became the most important international PE investment country in 2007.

Australia, France, and Germany complete the top five of investor countries, but are largely behind in terms of the number of deals: these three countries account each for approximately 5 percent of the international deals within the population (between 65 and 70 deals). Investors from other countries invest each in less than 60 nondomestic deals from 2003 to 2007. Sweden (with 5 percent of the deals), the Netherlands (4 percent), and Canada (3 percent) complete the top eight investor countries. The countries with the highest PE "export activity" are all countries with well-developed and mature domestic PE industries. This is consistent with the patterns observed in the venture capital industry (Megginson 2004).

Exhibit 18.2	Most Active International Investor Countries within Western Europe, North America, and Australia

Foreign Investments Made by	2003	2004	2005	2006	2007	Total	%
United States	53	82	88	112	88	423	32,49%
United Kingdom	43	79	78	78	93	371	28,49%
Australia	1	6	19	21	22	69	5,30%
France	3	6	16	18	24	67	5,15%
Germany	8	9	13	18	18	66	5,07%
Sweden	6	10	18	16	9	59	4,53%
Netherlands	9	9	13	7	13	51	3,92%
Canada	2	5	15	11	16	49	3,76%
Luxembourg	11	7	8	12	8	46	3,53%
Switzerland	3	2	3	8	7	23	1,77%
Belgium		1	6	4	7	18	1,38%
Finland	2	3	3		3	11	0,84%
Italy	4		2	4	1	11	0,84%
Denmark			5	3	2	10	0,77%
Ireland				4	5	9	0,69%
Austria		1		3	4	8	0,61%
Spain		2			4	6	0,46%
Norway				1	2	3	0,23%
Portugal				2		2	0,15%

Source: Zephyr.

Exhibit 18.2 shows that Australian and Continental European PE investors are increasingly active in cross-border deals. There is a striking increase of international investments financed by Australian firms, which invested in only one cross-border deal in 2003 and in more than 20 in 2006 and 2007. The relatively large number of Australian cross-border investments is to a large extent due to the activities of the Macquarie Bank, which accounts for 17 deals (or almost 25 percent of the Australian international deals). Macquarie Bank is the seventh most internationally active PE investor worldwide (see Exhibit 18.3 hereafter). Canada and France are two other countries within the top 10 of international investor countries that faced a substantial increase in the number of international deals in recent years. From almost no involvement in international deals in 2003, their activity has steadily risen to 24 deals (France) and 16 deals (Canada) in 2007.

The top 10 of countries of origin for cross-border PE deals is completed by Luxembourg and Switzerland. These two countries have a prosperous legal environment for companies and financial institutions, but lagged behind in both domestic and international private equity activity. In order to stimulate PE activity in Luxembourg, a new type of legal investment vehicle for risk capital was introduced in 2004. Since then, the country became an interesting location for PE firms (EVCA 2006). It is important to note that the Luxembourg PE firms are often set up by nondomestic organizations, originating for example from the United States, France, or Germany, who appraise the favorable legal environment (PWC 2006). As a result, many Luxembourg PE funds have an explicit international investment strategy. In 2007, only 10 percent of the money invested was dedicated to the domestic market, 61 percent was earmarked for investments in other European countries and the other 29 percent was dedicated to non-European countries (EVCA 2008).

The Swiss market is different from the Luxembourg market. The existence of many financial institutions and know-how of asset management is reflected in a large number of Swiss funds of funds that invest in other PE firms. Direct cross-border investments by Swiss PE firms are less important due to the legal regime which is less attractive for direct investments than it is for indirect ones (Seca 2007). Legal reforms were introduced during the years 2005–2007, but even now PE associations complain that the development of the PE industry, including its international development, would benefit from a more favorable legislation (Seca 2007).

Exhibit 18.2 hence clearly shows that for firms searching for nondomestic PE financing, the United States or the United Kingdom were the only options until 2003, while there is now a broader variety of countries with very internationally active PE firms. Clearly, a PE industry only develops internationally if its domestic industry is mature (Megginson 2004), with the notable exceptions of Luxembourg and Switzerland. Exhibit 18.2 gives also some examples of countries with less developed domestic PE markets that are relatively unimportant as international investors. In Northern Europe, for example, the Swedish PE industry is well-established and quite international, but the Finnish and Danish PE funds invest much less in other countries, and Norwegian PE investors are almost absent on the international market. Further, the international activity of Austrian, Irish, and Southern European PE firms is low, consistent with their PE markets being less developed. These phenomena suggest important research questions. It would be interesting to further understand the drivers and inhibitors of cross-border investment activity in different countries, next to the overall maturity of the PE industry.

While Exhibit 18.2 highlights the countries where the PE firms are most active internationally in absolute figures (number of deals), this does not imply that the PE firms in these countries are *on average* more internationally oriented. Having a large number of PE firms that invest internationally could be a natural feature of countries with mature PE industries and with a large number of PE investors. Research suggests that the proportion of internationally active PE investors may vary widely between countries, however. Survey evidence suggests that Swedish PE firms are, for example, on average more internationally active than U.K. PE firms (Manigart, Maeseneire, Wright 2008). As the Swedish market is smaller than the U.K. market, however, Sweden ranks behind the United Kingdom in Exhibit 18.2. On the other hand, while the German PE market has grown during the last decade, most of the German PE firms still have a domestic focus (Manigart et al. 2008).

Exhibit 18.3 lists the top 10 PE investors with the greatest number of international deals, and their country of origin. The top 10 investors account for 16 percent of all international deals. Five investors in the top 10 come from the United Kingdom, again acknowledging the importance of U.K. PE on the international scene. Three U.S. PE firms, one Australian PE firm, and one Dutch[3] PE firm complete the list of the top-10 most international investors.

Exhibit 18.3   Top 10 of the Investors with the Most International Deals

Top PE Firms	Country of Origin
3i Group plc	United Kingdom
Apax Partners	United Kingdom
Advent International Corporation	United States
CVC Capital Partners Ltd	United Kingdom
Carlyle Group, The	United States
Goldman Sachs	United States
Macquarie Bank Ltd	Australia
Bridgepoint Capital Ltd	United Kingdom
Barclays Private Equity Ltd	United Kingdom
AAC Capital Holdings BV[1]	The Netherlands

[1]Former ABN AMRO Private Equity.
Source: Zephyr.

Most Important International Target Countries

Exhibit 18.4 lists the countries with the largest number of PE deals in which non-domestic firms invested. Exhibit 18.5 further gives the median and average values of all deals within those target countries between 2003 and 2007. Our results are broadly consistent with the findings of Tykvová and Schertler (2006) that mature PE markets attract most of the international flows of PE.

Exhibit 18.4   Target Countries for International Investments (Number of Deals)

Foreign Investments Attracted by	2003	2004	2005	2006	2007	Total	% of total n°
Germany	25	30	53	67	23	198	17.48
France	17	23	31	31	35	137	12.09
United States	7	26	29	22	38	122	10.77
United Kingdom	11	23	21	22	37	114	10.06
Netherlands	9	9	17	16	27	78	6.88
Canada	6	17	12	12	25	72	6.35
Italy	10	11	12	18	13	64	5.65
Spain	6	9	11	18	18	62	5.47
Sweden	4	10	9	12	11	46	4.06
Belgium	6	10	5	10	12	43	3.8
Switzerland	4	7	7	9	13	40	3.53
Denmark	4	5	12	2	8	31	2.74
Finland	2	6	6	7	6	27	2.38
New Zealand	0	1	3	10	9	23	2.03
Austria	3	3	2	6	8	22	1.94
Norway	3	5	1	4	1	14	1.24
Ireland	0	1	2	5	5	13	1.15
Luxembourg	1	2	2	5	3	13	1.15
Australia	0	0	4	3	3	10	0.88
Portugal	1	0	0	1	2	4	0.35

Source: Zephyr.

Exhibit 18.5   Annual Trend of Median and Average Values of Nondomestic Investments

	Total n° of deals	2003		2004		2005		2006		2007	
		M.V	A.V	M.V	A.V	M.V	A.V	M.V	A.V	M.V	A.V
Germany	198	417.5	688.05	484.58	796.07	260	420.1	227.26	868.69	268.61	639.41
France	137	185.5	280.87	171.5	269.02	90	269.83	139.5	507.63	260	631.25
United States	122	97.18	104.48	195.33	221.85	374.8	417.66	124.21	510.76	218.95	913.77
United Kingdom	114	188	291.98	162.27	252.94	147.35	278.39	152.96	540.12	191.51	328.91
Netherlands	78	208.86	310.74	378	706.52	1011	1396.1	520	1322	200.14	648.36
Canada	75	74.46	109.36	103.12	190.17	73.44	143.65	433.92	708.12	492.06	735.55
Italy	64	36.25	148.91	55	264.21	60	389.57	200	286.72	136.5	490.39
Spain	61	30	53.22	72.5	191.85	110	276	300	385	204.6	786.25
Sweden	46	118	202.67	132.49	212.44	190	355.67	134.03	359.61	209.06	701.77
Belgium	43	75.2	205.25	127.5	187.41	118	118	233.9	196.11	200	412.93
Switzerland	40	298.41	298.41	306.51	363.2	27	179.67	60	60	280	509.59
Denmark	29	90	81.07	47.9	80.06	654.79	480.79	13.42	13.42	699.36	658.26
Finland	27			236.5	260.75	359	447.75	90	249.33	35	154.48
New Zealand	23			25.93	25.93	130.81	130.81	95.27	98.14	74.67	232.84
Austria	22	6	6	280	280	3.63	3.63	234	234	1400	1540
Norway	14	9.66	17.89	120.46	120.46	103.73	103.73	234	234	293.12	293.12
Ireland	13			630	630	15	15	173.41	155.22	63.2	71.02
Luxembourg	13	490	490	412.5	412.5	550	550	1024	1024	315	315
Australia	10					103.69	103.69	296.61	558.85	122.35	165.7
Portugal	4	50	50					8.5	8.5	71	71
Total	1133	133.44	208.68	187.19	303.63	168.00	320.00	170.74	425.60	204.60	514.98

Exhibit 18.5 presents Annual median (M.V) and average values (A.V) (in million Euros) of cross-border investments are presented per target country.
Source: Zephyr.

403

The most important target country is Germany with 198 investments (19 percent of all international deals), followed by France with 137 investments (12 percent). While the number of international investments has increased steadily in these countries (except in 2007), it is remarkable that the median deal value did not show a similar pattern. The median value of cross-border deals within Germany even declined, especially in 2005 and 2006. The increase in the average values of cross-border deals, however, indicates that there was a growing number of mega deals that received financing from international sources. The surge in terms of the number of deals and average deal value indicate that there are interesting opportunities for further international development in Germany and France. The availability of international fund investors might also affect further development of entrepreneurial activities in both countries. More research is needed to gain a detailed view on the possible influence of overall economic development.

The dominance of France and Germany as recipient countries is not surprising, as these are attractive investment regions (Wright et al. 2004). They have an important supply of buyout investment opportunities, consisting of both family firms and restructuring groups, in addition to an increasing number of managers who are willing to participate in a buyout. Moreover, the legal framework and the taxation regime are favorable for buyouts in these two countries (Wright et al. 2004). Large buyouts in these countries need to rely on international flows of capital, however. Despite the maturity of the PE market in these countries, their domestic PE market is still not large enough to finance many mega-deals. An unfavorable factor for the further development of the buyout market in these countries is the relative illiquidity of the stock market. Less attractive trade sales and secondary buyouts are therefore the main exit routes. This might lead investors to push their German and French portfolio companies towards the foreign market. The early-stage international financing literature highlights this practice. Relocation of portfolio firms and exits in nondomestic markets is a way to increase return (Cumming et al. 2009; Jääskeläinen and Maula 2008), thereby reducing the positive spill-over effects from investments in the country in which the firm was first established (Cumming et al. 2009; Gompers et al. 2005). Further research is, however, necessary to know whether similar practices are also apparent in the later stage PE market.

The United States and the United Kingdom are the third and fourth most important countries, attracting nondomestic investors in 122 and 114 deals, respectively (see Exhibit 18.4). Exhibit 18.5 however, indicates that international deals with U.S. and U.K. targets are not very large in terms of deal value, except in 2007. Both countries offer a large number of opportunities, liquid stock markets, and a large number of PE investors potentially interested in secondary buyouts (Wright et al. 2004). The relatively low importance of international buyouts in these countries is mainly due to the financial strength of their domestic PE markets, which are able to finance most of the domestic large and mega deals.

The four most important target countries (Germany, France, the United States, and the United Kingdom) account for 50 percent of all international investments within the countries of our study. The top 10 is completed by the Netherlands, Canada, Italy, Spain, Sweden, and Belgium. The top 10 covers 83 percent of the international market. The Netherlands and Canada have combined the gradual increase in terms of number of investments with an even larger increase in deal value, with median deal values ranging between €200 million and €520 million in 2006 and 2007. Italy and Spain lag somewhat behind those two countries, both in terms of the number of deals and of average deal value. The steep increase of median deal values, however, indicates that these countries are attracting the attention of PE firms for a broad range of deals, instead of for a limited number of mega deals only. This can provide interesting opportunities for further international development in both countries, especially because their domestic PE industry is not yet fully mature. Sweden and Belgium are number nine and ten in the list, with Sweden having larger deals.

When comparing the relative of importance of the PE markets, either as investor or as target countries, some important differences are noteworthy. First, on the investor side, only the United States and the United Kingdom dominate the international market, with a market share of 61 percent. The target side of international buyouts is characterized by a much larger spread of countries. This mirrors the development of the PE markets, with the U.S. and the U.K. markets still being by far the most mature ones (Megginson 2004). There is an important surplus of PE funds in these two markets, making these countries net exporters of PE to countries with a lot of interesting investment opportunities, but with lower availability of domestic PE. Italy, Spain, and New Zealand, for example, attract relatively more foreign PE, while their PE firms seldom invest internationally. This trend is positive for owners and managers who have valuable investment opportunities within countries with relatively unimportant PE markets. They increasingly benefit from the internationalization of the PE industry, enabling larger and more buyouts in these countries, where the domestic PE industry is less developed.

As a result of the spread of capital, there are large differences between country ratios of incoming versus outgoing deals. Australia and Luxembourg are two notable examples of countries that are net exporters of PE. They have large PE firms with an international focus, but are not important as recipient countries. Germany, Italy, and Spain are net importers of PE, either driven by the existence of many attractive opportunities (Germany) or the underdevelopment of the domestic PE industry (Spain and Italy).

In general, our findings are in contrast with the international flows of money of the early-stage investments where high-tech regions with a well-developed VC industry attract a lot of international VC funding as well. The high-tech regions around San Francisco (U.S.) and in Bayern (Germany) are two notable examples of this phenomenon (Mason 2007). This is in line with the findings of Tykvová and Schertler (2006), who stressed the maturity of the PE market as very important for being a recipient country. Our findings however show that the international flows of capital in later-stage investments are especially important for countries with interesting opportunities and *less* developed PE industries. These countries are able to attract relatively larger inflows of PE, both in terms of the number of deals and their value. International PE firms active in more mature PE regions face more competition with domestic investors who are also able to finance the mega deals. The reasons why international investors target a specific country is, however, quite similar for early (Guler and Guillén 2005) and later-stage investors (Wright et al. 2004). Both types of investors target regions with numerous entrepreneurial opportunities and a conducive institutional environment (e.g., legal protection, political stability) (Guler and Guillén 2005; Wright et al. 2004). Hence, countries that would seek to attract stronger inflows of PE money should work on both conditions. This will, moreover, have a positive effect for both the PE and the VC industry.

Regional Clustering of the International PE Investment Market

In the previous sections, we analyzed the international flows of PE without linking in- and outgoing flows. In Exhibit 18.6, we explicitly link the distributions of international investments between the different countries. This table clearly shows that U.S. and U.K. PE investors are active worldwide, except for the fact that U.K. PE investors have not been active in Australia. Interestingly, Australian PE investors have been very active in the United Kingdom. Investors in other countries have a much more restricted geographical scope.

Exhibit 18.6 indicates that the international PE market is largely characterized by regional clusters, especially within continental Europe (Manigart et al. 2008). The most notable example of regional clustering is Scandinavia, which attracts

Exhibit 18.6 Distribution of Cross-Border Investments by Number of Deals (2003–2007)

Countries Investing Cross-Border	*Countries Attracting Cross-Border Investments*																				
	U.K.	**Ireland**	**France**	**Germany**	**Netherlands**	**Belgium**	**Luxembourg**	**Switzerland**	**Austria**	**Italy**	**Spain**	**Portugal**	**Sweden**	**Finland**	**Denmark**	**Norway**	**Canada**	**U.S.**	**Australia**	**New Zealand**	**Total invested**
U.K.		11	66	74	35	12	4	8	5	28	38	1	21	8	5	2	4	45		4	**371**
Ireland	6			1							1							1			**9**
France	4			15	9	8	2	9		5	1		2		1			11			**67**
Germany	8	1	9		6	1	2	19	10	2		1						7			**66**
Netherlands	4		4	14		14	1	1	2	1	3		1	2		1		1	2		**51**
Belgium			4	1	4			1		4								1	3		**18**
Luxembourg	3		15	8	5	2				6		1	1		2			3			**46**
Switzerland			3	7					1	2	3				1		1	4	1		**23**
Austria				7				1													**8**
Italy	1	1	1				3	1			2						2				**11**
Spain	1		1	1				1				2									**6**
Portugal	1										1										**2**
Sweden	1		5	8	4	1			1	1				13	13	10		2			**59**
Finland						1							7		2	3					**11**
Denmark			1	3		2		1					3								**10**
Norway													3								**3**
Canada			3		2						1							43			**49**
U.S.	72	3	42	105	29	6	2	9	5	24	14		7	5	11	3	76		7	3	**423**
Australia	21		1	2				1		1	1		1	1			2	21		17	**69**
New Zealand																					**0**
Total attracted	**122**	**16**	**155**	**246**	**94**	**47**	**14**	**52**	**24**	**74**	**65**	**5**	**46**	**29**	**35**	**17**	**85**	**139**	**13**	**24**	

Source: Zephyr.

two-thirds of all international investments of Swedish private equity firms. French and Dutch PE investors invest about half of their international investments in their neighboring countries; Luxembourg and German PE investors about one-third.

Regional clustering is also apparent in North America. U.S. investors are involved in 89 percent of Canadian international buyouts and Canadian PE firms invest in turn 88 percent of their international deals in the United States. Due to the large number of investment opportunities, the United States cannot rely solely on Canada as the main investor of their international buyout deals, but Canadian PE firms are albeit responsible for 31 percent of all international investments in the United States. Canada is therefore almost as important for the United States as the United Kingdom, which, with 32 percent, is the main international investor in the United States. Australian firms complete the top 3 of international investors in the United States, with 15 percent of all international deals. These figures also indicate that U.S. buyouts mainly involve PE firms with similar Anglo-Saxon roots.

The buyout market within the United Kingdom is also dominated by Anglo-Saxon firms. This is one of the few countries where geographical proximity between the headquarters of the international PE firms and their target companies is not apparent. Ninety-three of the 125 international deals in the United Kingdom are financed by United States or Australian PE firms. This is probably due to the financial strength of these PE firms, in addition to the regulatory and cultural proximity between the United Kingdom, United States, and Australia. Many international PE firms have furthermore established branch offices in the United Kingdom, which helps to bridge the geographical distance between the home and target country.

Exhibit 18.6 further shows that international deals in France and Germany are mainly financed by U.S. and U.K. PE investors, but there is a notable difference between those two countries. U.K. PE firms invest more or less to the same extent in France as in Germany, while U.S. PE firms invest twice as often in Germany as in France. In addition, U.S. firms invest relatively more in very large international German deals. The average deal value of investments in Germany is 56 percent higher for U.S. firms than for U.K. firms. In France, the average deal value is only 8 percent higher for U.S. than for U.K. investors. Further research is needed to understand the reasons behind these differing market preferences.

In general, the results clearly show that the very large PE firms originating from the United States and the United Kingdom are not constrained by geographical or institutional distance between their home country and other developed PE regions. Their financial strength, the search for portfolio diversification, and the saturation of the home market explain why they target companies in a broad range of countries (Wright et al. 2005). For PE firms originating from other developed PE markets, regional clusters are more apparent. Due to their more limited fund size and resources, they have to focus on a limited number of target regions, and therefore chose to invest in nearby regions with more familiar institutions. This is consistent with many other studies in early-stage finance. The underlying reasons for this investment strategy are related to investment risk and transaction costs (Bruton et al. 2005; Tykvová and Schertler 2006). Studies in the early-stage market show a preference for geographically close targets, as it eases the selection process of interesting deals and decreases the costs of value-adding (Sorenson and Stuart 2001). Exhibit 18.6 shows a similar trend with respect to later-stage investments originating from PE firms located in France, Germany, Luxembourg, Switzerland, and Sweden. As a result, our findings are consistent with Tykvová and Schertler (2006) who stated that geographic proximity determines both early- and later-stage investment strategies.

We also find indications in Exhibit 18.6 that institutional proximity (especially regulatory and cultural similarities) determines investment behavior. Regulatory and cultural similarities decrease information uncertainty, as familiarity with regulations and culture makes PE firms feel more confident in pre- and postinvestment processes (Alhorr, Moore, and Payne, 2008). Institutional similarities, rather than geographical proximity, seem to be especially important for Anglo-Saxon firms. Based on our findings, it is not possible to distinguish between cultural and regulatory differences or indicate whether other institutional factors play a role. While Tykvová and Schertler (2006) stress the importance of cultural distance (including language similarity), Meuleman and Wright (2009) find that regulatory differences are more important. In addition, the majority of studies have focused on the importance of legal traditions and regulatory harmonizations on international PE flows in very dissimilar markets (e.g., Alhorr et al. 2008; Guler and Guillén 2007; Megginson 2004), which makes it difficult to distinguish the importance of both.

International Syndication of Buyouts

Syndication is often regarded as a way to decrease locational constraints (Mason 2007; Sorenson and Stuart 2001; Tykvová and Schertler 2006). The local, hands-on investor has closer contacts and is expected to have a better understanding of local market conditions (Mäkelä and Maula 2008), useful for postinvestment monitoring and value adding activities. However, PE firms have to manage the relationship with the other equity partner in an investment syndicate, creating additional problems (Lockett and Wright 2001).

Exhibit 18.7 shows the number of international PE investments that are syndicated, either with a local or with another international investor. First, syndication within the buyout market is not as prevalent as in the early-stage market, as only 32 percent of all buyouts are syndicated. Syndication rates vary greatly among countries as well, consistent with Tykvová and Schertler (2006). The rates are the highest in Italy and Portugal, where more than half of the international investments in 2003 to 2007 were syndicated. This is in contrast to low-syndication activity in Ireland, Norway, Sweden, Luxembourg, Germany, and the Netherlands.

Second, when there is syndication, it is in 57 percent of the cases with another international partner. This is again in contrast with the VC market, where most international syndicates involve a domestic investor. However, even a local partner is not always necessary for a nondomestic early-stage investor, despite the need for closer monitoring (Mäkelä and Maula 2008). The reasoning behind is that there is a low need for cooperation with a domestic partner if the entrepreneurial experience of management is high and if the local market is of little importance for the portfolio company.

Several reasons may explain the differences between VC and PE syndication behavior (Manigart et al. 2006). Management in a PE deal is often stronger than in a VC deal. Often, the management team in a VC deal is incomplete or inexperienced. Buyout targets, on the contrary, have often a strong and long established

Exhibit 18.7 Syndication of Foreign Investments by PE Firms (Number of Deals)

	Total Number of Foreign Investments by PE Firms	Sole Investments	Syndication with a Domestic Partner	Syndication with an International Partner
United States	423	280	46	97
United Kingdom	371	254	58	59
Australia	69	44	12	13
France	67	46	7	14
Germany	66	51	6	9
Sweden	59	46	3	10
Netherlands	51	39	10	2
Canada	49	27	18	4
Luxembourg	46	35	3	8
Switzerland	23	15	5	3
Belgium	18	10	3	5
Italy	11	5	3	3
Finland	11	7	2	2
Denmark	10	7	1	2
Ireland	9	9		
Austria	8	5		3
Spain	6	4	1	1
Norway	3	3		
Portugal	2		1	1

Source: Zephyr.

management team. Hence PE investors can rely more strongly on the capabilities of existing management and there is less need to add value to the company post-investment. An active, hands-on approach is therefore often not necessary, reducing the need for a local partner. In addition, it is often important to have PE firms with a large international network of debt financiers to finance the debt side of the buyout. Finally, many large international investors have a local office—the so-called glocal approach (Leeds and Sunderland 2003). These offices combine the skills of a highly reputed PE firm with the advantages of the local approach, thanks to local managers in these branches.

There are two conditions that induce PE firms to syndicate with a local partner. First, the less international experience a PE firm has and the lower its experience in the target country, the more a PE firm is inclined to cooperate with a domestic partner (Meuleman and Wright 2009). Second, the development of the target region, including the maturity of the PE industry (Tykvová and Schertler 2006) and a supportive institutional environment (Meuleman and Wright 2009), drive the propensity to syndicate with a local partner. More specifically, if a PE industry is immature, there is a low possibility of syndication with a domestic partner, as local partners are often inexperienced and hence of little value to the international PE firm (Tykvová and Schertler 2006). In addition, a less-supportive institutional environment makes it more difficult to invest in that country due to increasing information asymmetries, the need for PE investors to align their behavior with this environment, and the need to adjust their style of working (Bruton et al. 2005; Meuleman and Wright 2009).

We found, however, that mega deals have a higher probability of being syndicated. Nonetheless, almost half of the 50 largest international deals in 2003 to 2007 are backed by a single investor. Our findings confirm the trend to syndicate mega deals because they require a very high amount of funding provided by partners to assure sufficient portfolio diversification for the PE firms involved (Manigart et al. 2006). However, there is again a low prevalence of syndication with a domestic partner, that is, in only 15 of the 50 largest deals.

These findings clearly indicate that the competences of large international PE firms, combined with the knowledge of their local offices, reduce the need for syndicating with a local investor. Syndication in the international buyout market is mainly driven by a desire to increase portfolio diversification and hence decrease portfolio risk, at least in developed PE markets. The value adding and local knowledge motive seems to be less important.

PRIVATE EQUITY IN EMERGING MARKETS

PE in emerging markets (eastern Europe, Latin America, and the Asia-Pacific region) is still in its infancy compared to the more-developed regions. However, the interesting growth prospects increasingly attract international investors—mainly from the United States (Cornelius et al. 2007)—in combination with a growing number of local PE firms (Raade and Dantas Machado 2008). The majority of PE opportunities in China, eastern Europe, and Latin America are related to restructuring of mature companies (Wright et al. 2004; Bruton and Ahlstrom 2003).

PE investors are especially welcome in the emerging markets where severe capital shortages keep valuations low. There are, however, a large number of interesting investment opportunities, either related to former government companies or large mature firms that need money for sustained development and exportation (LAVCA 2005). In addition, many governments are highly receptive towards foreign investors (Leeds and Sunderland 2003). As a result, these regions became gradually more important since the 1990s. For example, the Chinese PE industry is now of a size comparable to the French market (Raade and Dantas Machado 2008). Other emerging markets follow this trend, with lower rates of investment though. Despite this growing trend, there are also signals that many PE firms fail to reap the benefits of their opportunities. Especially the investments made during the 1990s provided disappointing returns (Leeds and Sunderland 2003). Four main reasons account for this. First, many firms still have low standards of corporate governance, such as opaque bookkeeping and disclosure, in some cases compounded with a legal system that fails to protect shareholders (Leeds and Sunderland 2003). Hence, estimations of company value differ largely between markets. More specifically, although the valuation techniques may be fungible towards emerging markets, the underlying information needs specific adjustment towards local conditions and institutional differences (Lockett, Wright, and Pruthi, 2002). International PE firms should therefore spend considerably more time on due diligence (e.g., six more months in China) (Bruton and Ahlstrom 2003). Second, cultural differences affect the behavior of managers (Bruton et al. 2005). Investment managers active in emerging markets should therefore find a way to bridge the differences in management styles between their headquarters and their portfolio companies (Wright et al. 2002).

Third, even if regulations have been installed to protect PE firms from the moral hazard behavior of their managers or co-investors, there are often significant issues in the enforceability of the laws or of contractual rights. As locals are more experienced with the legal system, international PE investors are at a disadvantage in cases of disputes (Leeds and Sunderland 2003).

Finally, equity markets, even in the most advanced emerging countries, often fail to provide significant returns. Public markets are often unpopular where only the very large stocks are liquid. This is apparent in Latin America, where 58 percent of the average daily trading volume comes from the 10 largest companies (Leeds and Sunderland 2003). For this reason, returns in the Latin American market were considerably low. The Asian markets performed somewhat better, despite the illiquidity of their capital markets. As a result, different exit options need to be searched for small and middle-sized firms. Hence, PE firms should work towards trade sale and secondary buyouts to exit their firms at a higher price (Farag, Hommel, and Wright, 2004; Wright et al. 2004).

Due to these difficulties, it appears that international PE investors have a long way to go when it comes to investing in emerging markets. Many disappointing returns are, however, at least partly caused by unadjusted entry strategies. Too many PE investors copied fund structures and investment approaches, standards of postinvestment behavior of their U.S.- or European-based headquarters, regardless of their appropriateness. In order to be successful, PE firms should adopt a more local approach (Bruton and Ahlstrom 2003; Bruton et al. 2005). This local approach goes well beyond educating local investment managers in corporate headquarters. Imperfect market information, regulatory differences, different cultures of doing business (Bruton et al. 2005), and the rapid changes in the market require local connections and, in most cases, an office presence very close to the portfolio firm (Leeds and Sunderland 2003). If PE firms' local office managers gradually gain experience and a deeper understanding of how to deal with institutional differences, they will realize that these differences do not solely have a constraining effect on success (Bruton and Ahlstrom 2003). More specifically, they can gain the most advantage from the opportunities within these markets if they make better use of the cognitive institutions and networks. For example, when PE investors investigate entrepreneurs' backgrounds, they should also examine their local network connections. Social networks are important in the Asian market, especially in China, where the local interconnections, or "Guanxi," determine strongly how to do business (Batjargal and Liu 2004). Consequently, PE firms can decrease their investment risk significantly if they can assure that the firm has links with local officials and other reputable firms and managers.

CONCLUSION AND AVENUES FOR RESEARCH

We have shown that the cross-border PE industry has become important. This is especially valid in terms of the international flows of funds. U.S.-based fund investors are very active in all world regions. In addition, for many emerging regions, internationalization in terms of funds raised is much more important than direct PE investments. We have also highlighted the influence of regulatory harmonization of international flows of capital raised (Cumming and Johan 2007) and stressed the tendency of investors in PE funds to target a small number of highly reputable investors, which makes these PE firms very international (Cornelius et al. 2007).

The developed PE markets (North America, the United Kingdom, Continental Europe, and Australia) are also the regions that are most involved in direct cross-border investments. In this chapter, a detailed overview of the countries' international investments, both as an investor or as a recipient country, is provided. Especially the United States and the United Kingdom are very internationally active as investor country. The most interesting targets for international investors are found in Continental Europe, with France and Germany as the most popular destination countries. These countries have already a relative mature domestic buyout industry, but are also very attractive for international PE investors (Tykvová and Schertler 2006). For other countries, such as Italy and Spain, attracting international PE investments is a means to compensate for the underdeveloped domestic buyout market. The development of the PE markets as a recipient industry is largely affected by the entrepreneurial opportunities and the regulatory environment within the country.

Despite the growing internationalization, there are still regional clusters. PE funds have a tendency to invest in either regionally close markets or markets with similar institutions. This indicates that the markets remain segmented to some extent, and this is likely to remain so in the near future (Megginson 2004). However, we do see that PE firms gradually adopt a "glocal" approach where they combine their international competence with adaptations toward the local market. This explains why the international buyout industry has a low need to syndicate with local partners. The reasons for syndication seem more related to financial portfolio diversification motives than to the resources and the value-adding capabilities of investors.

PE is also emerging in the less-developed markets, such as Asia and Latin America, where U.S. investors in particular have been active. However, the large geographical distance and institutional differences require an adapted pre- and postinvestment strategy, which can be challenging for the PE firms entering these markets.

Hereafter, we present some avenues for future research on international private equity investment activity. In our suggestions, we will point at the need for more research on several research topics, such as the drivers of international investment behavior for both PE investors and their fund providers, the entry strategies of these firms, including the adjustments made towards the local market, the effects of cross-border PE for portfolio companies, and the overall economy and the influence of institutional changes on the further development of the international PE market.

1. There is little knowledge on the resources needed for international PE investors. We know that the largest investors are most likely to flourish internationally, but which specific resources do they need to put in place to succeed internationally? Which human and social capital characteristics increase cross-border activity and success? Which role does reputation have in the international buyout market? Are international PE firms equally able to raise debt (Demiroglu and James 2007), a feature that is especially important in buyout markets? How do international investors cope with similar challenges when they structure deals and support portfolio companies? Are other PE firms than the mega funds at a disadvantage when they target international markets?

2. Which types of fund providers are more inclined to target the international market? To which extent do the PE fund providers drive the international strategy of the PE firms they back?

3. There is no knowledge on the industry preference of international investors. For example, it might be that distant investors prefer to invest in familiar industries in order not to compound the risk of investing in an unknown country with the risk of investing in an unknown industry. In addition, more research is needed on which industries are more likely to be a target and why these industries are more attractive to international investors.

4. What are the preferred entry modes of international PE funds? How important are investments at arm's length versus physical presences, which role does syndication have on the need for a local branch? Syndication has received much attention in the early-stage international investment literature. More research is required on syndication in the international later-stage PE market. For example, what determines the choice between a domestic versus an international syndication partner? It is also important to know to which extent international investment strategies are determined by the institutional differences between the domestic and the target region.

5. Are investment contracts adapted to local market conditions, or are domestic contract designs used? Initial analyses (Cumming 2005) suggest that PE investors adapt their security design largely to local market conditions, taxes and agency risk, hence adapting themselves to the new institutional environment (Bruton et al. 2005). This makes international investing more challenging, as long-proven domestic routines may not work in an international environment.

6. How important is international PE ownership for exit options and exit timing? There is increasing evidence that international ownership within the VC market is an important driver for an international exit (Jääskeläinen and Maula 2008). Exits of buyouts in general, and of international buyouts in particular, is under researched but important.

7. More research on the financial performance of international buyouts and private equity is required. Cross-country research comparing the performance of international buyouts in different countries will also help us in understanding the effects of different legal and institutional frameworks and public policy towards PE markets.

8. Finally, the buyout industry is now going through a challenging time. This is already visible in the decrease of international investments by U.S. providers in 2007. U.S. investors were the first to face the storms in financial markets, but this has gradually become a global problem (EVCA 2008). Mega deals were the first to face the downturn, but this has spilled over toward all segments in the industry.[4] To which extent will policy makers change the rules of the game for PE investors and investment funds, as a reaction to the crisis? What are the effects of the upcoming regulations for financial institutions, and more specifically the new transparency rules considered by the European Commission, on (international flows of) private equity? Both Cumming and Johan (2007) and the EVCA (EVCA 2008) report that if regulations are introduced with care, and if the policy makers take the view of all investors—not of only their home investors—into account, they can create the conditions in which private equity can flourish even more than before.

NOTES

1. In detail, North America comprises the United States and Canada. We consider the United Kingdom as a separate region due to its high volume of deals. The continental European sample consists of Ireland, France, Germany, the Netherlands, Belgium, Luxembourg, Switzerland, Austria, Italy, Spain, Portugal, Sweden, Finland, Denmark, and Norway. With respect to Oceania, we include New Zealand in addition to Australia in most of our analyses.

2. Zephyr contains information on private equity transactions worldwide from 1997. Deal records contain various information related to announcement, rumors, completion or expected completed date, general information (deal value, equity value), financing of the deal, textual comments, and information on financial advisors. There is no minimum deal value, so it benefits researchers to analyze deals, irrespective of the transaction size.

3. Remark that the Dutch PE investor, AAC Capital Partners, originates from ABN Amro Capital Holding. After the takeover of ABN AMRO in 2007 by the Royal Bank of Scotland, Santander (Spain), and Fortis (at that time, Belgium/the Netherlands), it was decided that the former ABN AMRO PE group would not be sold to one of the partners involved in the acquisition. Hence, the former private equity transactions were divested and acquired by existing management of the PE holding.

4. This chapter was written February 2009, in full financial and economic crisis. During that time, the U.S. government, the European Commission, and most of the European member states were brainstorming about how to create new regulations for financial institutions.

REFERENCES

Alhorr, Hady S., Curt. B. Moore, and G. Tyge Payne. 2008. The impact of economic integration on cross-border venture capital investments: Evidence from the European Union. *Entrepreneurship Theory and Practice* 32 (5):897–917.

Batjargal, Bat, and Mannie Liu. 2004. Entrepreneurs' access to private equity in China: The role of social capital. *Organization Science* 15 (2):159–172.

Bruton, Garry D., and David Ahlstrom. 2003. An institutional view of China's venture capital industry—Explaining the differences between China and the West. *Journal of Business Venturing* 18 (2):233–259.

Bruton, Garry D., Vance H. Fried, and Sophie Manigart. 2005. Institutional influences on the worldwide expansion of venture capital. *Entrepreneurship Theory and Practice* 29 (6):73-7-60.

Cornelius, Peter, Broes Langelaar, and Maarten van Rossum. 2007. Big is better: Growth and market structure in global buyouts. *Journal of Applied Corporate Finance* 19 (3):109–116.

Cumming, Douglas. 2005. Agency costs, institutions, learning and taxation in venture capital contracting. *Journal of Business Venturing* 20:573–622.

Cumming, Douglas, Grant Fleming, and Armin Schwienbacher. 2009. Corporate relocation in venture capital finance. *Entrepreneurship Theory and Practice*, forthcoming.

Cumming, Douglas, and Sofia Johan. 2007. Regulatory harmonization and the development of private equity markets. *Journal of Banking & Finance* 31 (10):3218–3250.

Cumming, Douglas, and Uwe Walz. 2004. Private equity returns and disclosure around the world. *Journal of International Business Studies*, forthcoming. EFA 2004 Maastricht. papers.ssrn.com/sol3/papers.cfm?abstract_id=514105

Deloitte. 2005. Venture capital goes global: Key findings from the 2005 Global Venture Capital Survey.

Demiroglu, Cem, and Christopher James. 2007. Lender control and the role of private equity group reputation in buyout financing. Working paper, papers.ssrn.com/sol3/papers.cfm?abstract_id=1032781

EVCA. 2006. *EVCA yearbook 2006: Annual survey of pan-European private equity & venture capital activity*. Zaventem, Belgium: EVCA.

EVCA. 2008. *EVCA 2008: Pan-European private equity & venture capital activity report*. Zaventem, Belgium: EVCA.

Farag, Hady, Ulrich Hommel, and Mike Wright. 2004. Contracting, monitoring, and exiting venture capital investments in transitioning economies: A comparative analysis of Eastern European and German markets. *Venture Capital* 6 (4):257–282.

Gompers, Paul, Josh Lerner, and David Scharfstein. 2005. Entrepreneurial spawning: Public corporations and the genesis of new ventures, 1986 to 1999. *Journal of Finance* 60 (2):577–614.

Guler, Isin, and Mauro F. Guillén. 2005. Knowledge, institutions, and the internationalization of U.S. venture capital firms. Working Paper, Wharton School Penn University.

Guler, Isin, and Mauro F. Guillén. 2007. Home-country networks, intangible assets, and foreign expansion. Working Paper, Boston University.

Hall, Graham, and Ciwen Tu. 2003. Venture capitalists and the decison to invest overseas. *Venture Capital* 5 (2):181–190.

Jääskeläinen, Mikko, and Markku V. J. Maula. 2008. The effects of direct and indirect foreign venture capital ties on exit market selection and exit modes. Working Paper.

LAVCA. 2005. Latin American Venture Capital Association: Executive briefing on private equity in Latin America. Presentation by Richard H. Frank, Okinawa, Japan.

Leeds, Roger, and Julie Sunderland. 2003. Private equity investing in emerging markets. *Journal of Applied Corporate Finance* 15 (4):111–119.

Lockett, Andy, and Mike Wright. 2001. The syndication of venture capital investments. *Omega-International Journal of Management Science* 29 (5):375–390.

Lockett, Andy, and Mike Wright. 2002. Venture capital in Asia and the Pacific Rim. *Venture Capital: An International Journal of Entrepreneurial Finance* 4 (3):183–195.

Lockett, Andy, Mike Wright, and Sarika Pruthi. 2002. Venture capital investors, valuation, and information: A comparative study of the U.S., Hong Kong, India, and Singapore. *Venture Capital: An International Journal of Entrepreneurial Finance* 4 (3):237–252.

Mäkelä, Markus M., and Markku V. J. Maula. 2008. Attracting cross-border venture capital: The role of a local investor. *Entrepreneurship and Regional Development* 20 (3):237–257.

Manigart, Sophie, Wouter De Maeseneire, Mike Wright, Sarika Pruthi, Andy Lockett, Hans Bruining, Ulrich Hommel, and Hans Landström. 2008. How international are European venture capital firms? In *A theory of internationalization for European entrepreneurship*, eds. Léo-Paul Dana, Mary Han, Vanessa Ratten, and Isabell Welple, pp. 17–28. Cheltenham, UK/ Northampton, MA: Edward Elgar.

Manigart, Sophie, Andy Lockett, Miguel Meuleman, Mike Wright, Hans Landstrom, Hans Bruining, Philippe Desbrieres, and Ulrich Hommel. 2006. Venture capitalists' decision to syndicate. *Entrepreneurship Theory and Practice* 30 (2):131–153.

Mason, Colin. 2007. Venture capital: A geographical perspective. In *Handbook of Research on Venture Capital*, ed. Hans Landström, pp. 86–112. Cheltenham, UK/ Northampton, MA: Edward Elgar.

Mayer, Colin, Koen Schoors, and Yisheh Yafeh. 2005. Sources of funds and investment activities of venture capital funds: Evidence from Germany, Israel, Japan, and the United Kingdom. *Journal of Corporate Finance* 11 (3):586–608.

Megginson, William L. 2004. Toward a global model of venture capital. *Journal of Applied Corporate Finance* 16 (1):89–107.

Meuleman, Miguel, and Mike Wright. 2009. Cross-border private equity syndication: Institutions and learning. *Journal of Business Venturing*, forthcoming

Ooghe, Hubert, Sophie Manigart, and Yves Fassin. 1991. Growth-patterns of the European venture capital industry. *Journal of Business Venturing* 6 (6):381–404.

PWC. 2006. Private equity in Luxembourg. www.pwc.com/lu/eng/ins-sol/publ/pwc_privateequity.pdf.

Raade, Kristiina, and Catharina Dantas Machado. 2008. Recent developments in the European private equity markets. Economic paper n° 319 of the European Commision. papers.ssrn.com/sol3/papers.cfm?abstract_id=1123988.

Seca. 2007. Swiss Private Equity and Corporate Finance Association Yearbook 2007. www.seca.ch/sec/files/newsletter/pdf-news135/SECA_YBK_2007_withoutMembership Reporting.pdf.

Sorenson, Olav, and Toby E. Stuart. 2001. Syndication networks and the spatial distribution of venture capital investments. *American Journal of Sociology* 106 (6):1546–1588.

Tykvová, Tereza, and Andrea Schertler. 2006. Rivals or partners? Evidence from Europe's International Private Equity Deals. ZEW Centre for European Economic Research Discussion Paper No. 06-091. papers.ssrn.com/sol3/papers.cfm?abstract_id=955776.

Wright, Mike, Jonathan Kissane, and Andrew Burrows. 2004. Private equity in EU—accession countries of Central and Eastern Europe. *The Journal of Private Equity* 7: 32–46.

Wright, Mike, Andy Lockett, and Sarika Pruthi. 2002. Internationalization of Western venture capitalists into emerging markets: Risk assessment and information in India. *Small Business Economics* 19 (1):13–29.

Wright, Mike, Sarika Pruthi, and Andy Lockett. 2005. International venture capital research: From cross-country comparisons to crossing borders. *International Journal of Management Reviews* 7 (3):135–165.

ABOUT THE AUTHORS

Sophie Manigart received her Ph.D. from Ghent University in 1993. While doing her Ph.D., she was a research fellow at the Snider C. Entrepreneurial Center, Wharton School, University of Pennsylvania. Her research interests are entrepreneurial finance, including the supply side (venture capital, business angels, stock markets) as well as the demand side (entrepreneurial companies). Her research has been published in international journals such as (a.o.) *Journal of Business Venturing, European Financial Management, Journal of Business Finance and Accounting, Entrepreneurship Theory and Practice, Small Business Economics* and *Venture Capital*, and in numerous book chapters. She is actively involved in managerial initiatives in the area of entrepreneurial finance. For example, she was founder and director of the first Belgian business angels network, Vlerick BAN, and is still director of BAN Vlaanderen. She is member of the investment committee of Baekeland-fund, the risk capital fund for spin-offs of the Ghent University, of the BEL-20 committee, and of the PEREP Academic Council of the European Venture Capital and Private Equity Association (EVCA).

Sofie De Prijcker obtained her Master's degree in Business Economics from Ghent University. She is currently a Ph.D. student at the same University. Her research interests are in the field of entrepreneurial corporate finance. Her Ph.D. research focuses on the internationalization of private equity firms. She has published in *Management Decision* and in practitioner-oriented books and journals.

Bivas Bose is a doctoral student at Ghent University. His research is directed towards Mergers & Acquisitions (M&A). Specifically, he studies whether the capital markets incorporate the information contained in M&A announcements into the stock prices of rivals (nonmerging firms). He earned his Master's degree in Finance from the University of Strathclyde (Strathclyde Graduate School of Business, U.K.), and his Master's degree in Accounting from the University of Calcutta (India).

ACKNOWLEDGMENTS

We are grateful for the financial contribution of the Special Research Fund (BOF), Ghent University (Sofie De Prijcker), and of the Policy Center for Entrepreneurship and International Business (STOIO—Bivas Bose). Data have been made available via the Hercules fund.

CHAPTER 19

Private Equity in Emerging Markets

ALEXANDER PETER GROH
GSCM, Montpellier Business School, CIIF, International Center for Financial Research,
IESE Business School

INTRODUCTION

Hellmann and Puri (2000), and Kortum and Lerner (2000) show that private equity (PE)–backed companies are more efficient innovators. Belke, Fehn, and Foster (2003) and Fehn and Fuchs (2003) prove that PE firms create more employment and growth than their peers. Levine (1997) documents well the role of PE funds in fostering innovative and competitive firms, and indeed, there now exists a broad consensus that a strong PE market is a cornerstone for commercialization and innovation in modern economies. What is valid for industrial countries should be even more important for emerging markets. The urgent need for capital, especially for financing all kinds of infrastructure and communication in emerging regions, is evident. The growth potential is enormous and deserves capital to be exploited. This capital can be provided by financial institutions that specialize in risk-capital investments in small to medium-size or young firms. Hence, policymakers should focus on the creation of an adequate setting for a prospering PE market to support investments, growth, competitiveness, and entrepreneurial activities, especially in emerging countries. However, the risk capital supply is rather small in emerging countries, even if institutional investors are increasingly looking internationally for new investment opportunities. One would expect emerging regions to attract PE investors due to the assumed economic growth rates, and the proportionate need for financing, especially for nonquoted corporations.

So why is there such a strong market for private equity in the United States, or the United Kingdom, and why is activity zero or close to zero in many emerging countries? Spatial variations in PE activity result from numerous factors. Partly, they can be explained by built-in bias mechanisms. The whole investment process from institutional investors (the Limited Partners or LPs) to the finally backed corporations is geographically biased: the largest, most prominent, and most active institutional investors in the PE asset class are located in the United States. This certainly contributes to the dominant role of the U.S. private equity market. However, and not only in the United States, institutional investors allocate their capital via chains of agents and networks in certain regions, and among countries. These allocations follow, in principle, a simple rationale: First, there is a professional community required to support transactions and to establish the capital supply side. Second, there must be expectation for demand of the committed capital.

The last elements along the chain of agents are the private equity funds (the general partners or GPs). They prefer spatial proximity in their investments to facilitate the transaction processes, monitoring and active involvement. It is popular for GPs to focus on a particular region, or just on one single country when searching for deal opportunities. Hence, the geographical source of PE is generally not very distant from the demand. This built-in bias mechanism is intensified by the institutional investors' international allocation approaches. Diversification needs urge the LPs to commit capital to funds that cover a particular country or region. Therefore, LPs make a geographical selection of promising spots. The selection follows in principle their expectation of the demand for PE, and their evaluation of the host country's professional finance community. However, both the expected demand for PE and the state of a host country's professional environment depend likewise on many individual criteria, which will be discussed later.

First I will give a brief overview over the worldwide PE activity, focusing on the emerging regions. Then I discuss literature on the determinants of spatial differences in PE markets. Next, I will present a survey among institutional investors that deals with their concerns when investing in emerging PE markets. This survey allows the subsequent comparison of emerging regions regarding their attractiveness for PE investments. Finally, I will comment on the most important allocation criteria, and conclude with some recommendations for emerging countries to attract more risk capital.

INTERNATIONAL COMPARISON

Exhibit 19.1 presents the volume of investments in the year 2007 for all countries of the world with some private equity activity. The data is provided by Thomson Financial. The left abscissa represents the amount in US$ invested by private equity funds in the particular countries. The axis is logarithmic scaled to allow for presentation of the different levels of investment activity. For example, the activity in the United States was about $116.5 billion, while it was only $1.88 million in Egypt. On the right axis, the activity is related to the size of the economies measured by their GDP.

Exhibit 19.1 shows the dominant role of the United States and the United Kingdom in the worldwide PE market. However, it also reveals that, related to the economic size of the countries, there are some other PE "hot spots," namely the United Arab Emirates, Singapore, Hong Kong, and Israel. Additionally, the exhibit highlights that major economies, such as Germany and Japan, have rather low PE activity levels. Additionally, some emerging markets such as India, China, South Africa, Malaysia, Vietnam, and Croatia, among others, have more activity in relation to their economic power than Japan, and some of them also have more than Germany.

This comparison raises the question for the determinants of the different levels of activity. The question is comprehensively discussed in literature on the requirements of vibrant private equity markets, and this is presented next.

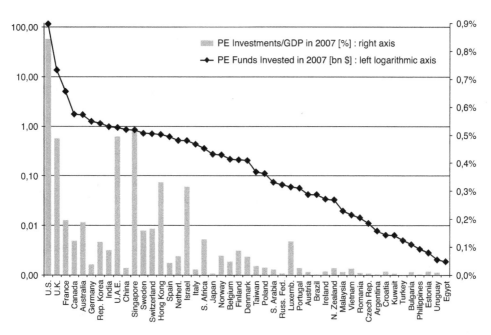

Exhibit 19.1 Worldwide Comparison of Private Equity Activity
Source: Thomson Financial.

WHAT DETERMINES EMERGING MARKET PE ACTIVITY?

A large body of research explores the determinants of private equity markets in particular economies. Some of the papers focus on emerging regions, and some of them report on already established markets. Black and Gilson (1998), and Michelacci and Suarez (2004) highlight the important role of the stock market for the asset class. Kaplan and Schoar (2005) confirm the strong relation between PE activity and stock market waves. Jeng and Wells (2000) explore the determinants of risk capital funding for 21 countries and expand the work of Black and Gilson (1998). They show that IPOs are the strongest driving force of PE investing. Surprisingly, GDP growth and market capitalization are not significant. Gompers and Lerner (2000) emphasize that risk capital flourishes in countries with deep and liquid stock markets.

The availability of debt financing is a key factor for start-ups entering the market, as emphasized by Greene (1998), and hence a determinant for a vibrant, local PE market. Additionally, the maturity of the PE market itself might attract investors. The maturity of a local PE market is reflected by the number of players and supporting institutions, such as law firms, investment banks, M&A boutiques, auditors, and consultants. The supporting institutions are important for creating deal flow and exit transactions. Balboa and Martí (2003) find that annual fund-raising volume is dependent on the previous year's market liquidity. If investors have confidence in the efficiency of a local PE market with an established track record, they continue investing in follow-on funds. Sapienza, Manigart, and Vermeir (1996) claim that investor confidence is determined by whether or not the PE market is accepted within a society, and the historical development of that market. Chemla (2005) argues that the management of PE funds is costly. Particular regions become attractive to investors only if the deal flow is large enough, and if transaction volumes and expected payoffs exceed a certain amount that allows the management fees to be covered. Hence, there is a simple relationship between the size of an economy and PE activity. If an economy is too small, it is simply not on the scope of internationally acting institutional investors and, hence, the sources of PE.

Gompers and Lerner (1998) examine the forces that affected independent PE fund-raising in the United States. They conclude that regulatory changes regarding pension funds, overall economic growth, and fund-specific performance and reputation affect fund-raising. They point out that there are more attractive opportunities for entrepreneurs if the economy is large and growing. Wilken (1979) argues that economic development facilitates entrepreneurship, as it provides a greater accumulation of capital for investments. Romain and van Pottelsberghe de la Potterie (2004) find that PE activity is related to GDP growth.

La Porta, Lopez-de-Silanes, Shleifer et al. (1997, 1998) prove that the legal environment strongly determines the size and extent of a country's capital market and local firm's abilities to receive outside funding. Glaeser, Johnson, and Shleifer (2001), and Djankov, La Porta, Lopez-de-Silanes (118 and 2005) suggest that parties in common-law countries have greater ease in enforcing their rights from commercial contracts. Cumming and Johan (2007) highlight that the perceived importance of regulatory harmonization increases institutional investors' allocations to the asset class. Desai, Gompers, and Lerner (2006) investigate the influence of institutional settings in 33 European countries, in particular the issues of fairness and the protection of property rights, on the entry of enterprises into the markets. The number of new enterprises is a proxy for the demand for PE. Cumming et al. (2006) find that the quality of a country's legal system is much more directly connected to facilitating PE backed exits than the size of a country's stock market. Cumming, Schmidt, and Walz (2008) extend this, and show that cross-country differences in legality, including legal origin and accounting standards, have a significant impact on the governance of investments in the PE industry. Better laws facilitate deal screening and deal origination. They also facilitate investors' board representations and the use of desired types of securities. Lerner and Schoar (2004) analyze PE transaction structures in developing countries and find that the choice of securities is driven by the legal and economic circumstances of the nation and of the investing PE group. La Porta, Lopez-de-Silanes, Shleifer (2002) find a lower cost of capital for companies in countries with better investor protection. Lerner and Schoar (2005) confirm these findings. Johnson, McMillian, and Woodruff (1999) show that weak property rights limit the reinvestment of profits in start-up firms. Even so, Knack and Keefer (1995), Mauro (1995), and Svensson (1998) demonstrate that property rights significantly affect investments and economic growth.

Da Rin, Nicodano, and Sembelli (2005) argue that policymakers should consider a wide set of policies to improve emerging PE markets, rather than simply channeling funds into the segment. Armour and Cumming (2006) confirm this rationale and show that government programs often hinder rather than help the development of PE markets.

Gompers and Lerner (1998) stress that the capital gains tax rate influences PE activity. Bruce (2000 and 2002), and Cullen and Gordon (2002) show that taxes affect the entry and exit of businesses. It can be concluded that this should be mirrored in PE activity.

Rigid labor market policies might negatively affect the attractiveness of a PE market. Institutional investors could hesitate before investing in countries with exaggerated labor market protection and immobility. Lazear (1990), and Blanchard (1997) discuss how protection of workers can reduce employment and growth. Black and Gilson (1998) show that variations in labor-market restrictions correlate with PE activity.

Access to viable investments is probably another important factor for the attractiveness of a regional PE market. Megginson (2004) argues that R&D culture, especially in universities or national laboratories, plays an important role in fostering a growing risk-capital industry. Gompers and Lerner (1998) show that both industrial and academic R&D expenditure is significantly correlated with PE activity. Schertler (2003) emphasizes that the number of employees in the R&D field and the number of patents, as an approximation of the human capital endowment, have a positive and highly significant influence on PE activity. Furthermore, Romain and van Pottelsberghe de la Potterie (2004) find that the level of entrepreneurship interacts with the R&D capital stock, technological opportunities, and the number of patents. Lee and Peterson (2000), and Baughn and Neupert (2003) argue that national cultures shape both individual orientation and environmental conditions, which lead to different levels of entrepreneurial activity in particular countries, and which should affect the level of acceptance of a risk capital culture. The acceptance of a risk capital culture in a society should be reflected in the funding activities of institutional investors.

Several papers analyze the evolvement of PE, especially in transition countries. Farag, Hommel, Witt (2004) focus on the VC/PE markets in Hungary, the Czech Republic, and Poland, and compare them with the German market. From a survey among 68 GPs in the transition countries, they find several factors that hinder the emerging markets in catching up and reaching the chosen benchmark. They conclude that one clear major obstacle is a lack of talented people to manage the PE-backed enterprises, as the quality of management ranks highly as a reason for investment failure. This finding is also consistent with Bliss (1999), Karsai, Wright, Dudzinski et al. (1998), and Chu and Hisrich (2001). Furthermore, debt financing remains limited, thus making it difficult to gain the desired returns by leveraging transactions. The authors suggest that legal and institutional improvements to protect lenders effectively can, therefore, lead to growth in the supply of risk capital. Johnson et al. (1999) emphasize the importance of the protection of property rights in emerging regions, while they also find that access to bank financing does not present a problem. These findings are in line with Klonowski (2005), who defines 26 decision criteria for individual transactions in emerging economies, and identifies the most important ones through a survey among 200 GPs.

This literature overview presents the numerous papers and their results. However, the literature does not provide a clear conclusion on which of the particular criteria is the most important, nor does it provide any ranking of the criteria. One of the major obstacles is that each paper focuses on a small selection of the named criteria only, and none of them includes a larger selection or all of them. The problem is that data are not available when analyzing these parameters on a cross-national comparison. Hence, it is impossible to assess the competitive position of countries regarding the reception of risk-capital funding, and this opens the discussion about the ranking of relevance of the mentioned determinants for institutional investors in their international allocation decision processes. Therefore, Groh and Liechtenstein (2009a) perform a survey among institutional investors to find out about the relevance of the discussed issues when allocating PE in emerging markets. Their findings are summarized in the subsequent section.

SURVEY AMONG INSTITUTIONAL INVESTORS ON THE IMPORTANCE OF EMERGING MARKETS' ALLOCATION CRITERIA

In their paper, Groh and Liechtenstein (2009a) describe a survey they conducted among internationally acting institutional investors in PE limited partnerships (LPs). They directly address the suppliers of PE, and not the managing GPs, and simply ask about the relevance of different allocation criteria when investing in emerging PE markets. This distinguishes their study from others, because other papers perform surveys among local GPs in a certain host country or determine relevant parameters indirectly via regressions. The survey comprehensively deals with socioeconomic criteria that the respondent considers important for allocation decisions. The survey was addressed to 1,079 limited partners worldwide. The geographic distribution of the addressees is as follows: 77 percent United States and Canada, 17 percent Europe, 5 percent Asia, and 1 percent others. The email addresses of the LPs are collected from three commercial databases. Unfortunately, it is not known what the entire population of LPs is, in terms of numbers and funds under management. A reliable or official list of institutional investors that qualify for PE partnerships does not exist. Each of the three databases claims to cover the whole population of LPs, but matching them leads to a larger number of players because some investors are missing from one or other database. Hence, Groh and Liechtenstein (2009a) gain a unique worldwide compendium of LPs. Furthermore, they check several references and actively search for important and well-known LPs manually in their repository. They deliberately attempt to cover as many LPs as possible. Nevertheless, matching the databases and the cross-checks might not secure a valid collection of LPs that, at least, represents the entire population. Regarding the geographical distribution of investors, for example, they have the following concern: Even though the United States, as an economic region and as the best-developed financial market, probably embodies the biggest (in terms of fund volumes), most sophisticated, and the largest number of LPs, other regions, notably Asia, might be underrepresented. However, in terms of funds under management, their data collection reliably represents the population. None of the larger LPs should be missing from their repository, be it in the United States, Europe, or Asia, and the larger institutions are the more important ones because of their market weight. Groh and Liechtenstein (2009a) believe that an overrepresentation of the number of U.S. LPs in their repository of addresses will not harm the conclusions unless they respond in a different manner. However, they address this issue and investigate their sample with respect to differences in the allocation processes of subgroups of the investors.

Exhibit 19.2 Types and Origins of Investors Who Responded to the Groh and Liechtenstein (2009a) Survey

Type of Investor	Occurrence	Origin of Investor	Occurrence
Corporate Investors	4	U.S. and Canada	34
Government Agency	1	Europe	38
Banks	3	Rest of the World	3
Pension Funds	8		
Insurance Companies	1		
Funds of Funds	29		
Endowments	2		
Others	26		
Not Available	1		

They received valuable responses from 75 investors—a response rate of 7 percent and quite satisfying when compared to some other studies that collect primary data about investors' behavior by means of a questionnaire. For instance, Lerner and Schoar (2005) collect data from 28 private equity funds, and Köke (1999) considers a sample of only 21 responses.

The responding LPs are segmented into the following groups: corporate investors, government agencies, banks, pension funds, insurance companies, funds of funds, endowments, and others. A geographic distinction is made according to the origin of the investors: United States and Canada, Europe, and the rest of the world. The segments are presented in Exhibit 19.2.

Unfortunately, the response rate from LPs that qualify themselves as "others" is relatively large and, therefore, only the "funds-of-funds" group can be distinguished as homogeneous. Furthermore, Groh and Liechtenstein (2009a) received more answers from European LPs (49.3 percent of all the answers), as compared to their occurrence in our depository of 17 percent. This might bias the results of our study. Regardless, the geographical distribution might not be the only cause of a selection bias—investors' types, fund sizes, or other criteria might also not be sufficiently representative. Unfortunately, as mentioned above, since no comparable comprehensive repository of investor data exists that provides the necessary information to correct for a potential bias, they are unable to address this issue. However, they separately assess the responses of subgroups of investors, for example, Europeans and non-Europeans, or small and large funds, and find out by mean comparison tests that there are no meaningful differences in their international capital allocation approaches. This leads them to conclude that, even if their sample does not perfectly represent the worldwide population of (potential) Limited Partners, the findings are not biased. The criteria are homogenous among the investors and, hence, their results are representative.

In their questionnaire, they consider the issues discussed in the literature overview, and group them into six main drivers for PE funding: Economic Activity, Capital Market, Taxation, Investor Protection & Corporate Governance, Human & Social Environment, and Entrepreneurial Opportunities. The respondents are asked to evaluate the importance of the individual criteria for their emerging market PE allocation decisions on a seven-point Likert scale, ranging from "not at all important" (1), to "very important" (7). To ensure that they do not miss any relevant determinant, they ask the respondents in parallel to determine their three most important allocation criteria using keywords. The analysis of these keywords reveals that no major topic is left out of their questionnaire. Exhibit 19.3 presents the six major categories, all individual criteria they asked for, the number of valid responses, their mean values, and the +/– range of one standard deviation around the means.[1]

Exhibit 19.3 reveals that, on average, corporate governance principles and the protection of investors' rights is named as the most important criterion for LPs' investment decisions in emerging markets, and that the availability of public subsidies is named as the least important of all of them. The figure allows several comments and many interpretations that are beyond of the scope of this chapter. However, it should be highlighted that public activity via subsidies or privileged credit conditions are obviously not adequate to increase PE funding from institutional investors. Private money does not follow public money; institutional investors are not impressed by government programs intended to spur investment in risk-capital markets. This finding is of particular importance for many (not only emerging) countries that attempt to increase local PE activity, and likewise confirms the findings of Da Rin et al. (2005) and Armour and Cumming (2006). Exhibit 19.3 also presents that the relevance nominations are quite close to each other and have large standard deviations. Hence, it is still not clear which of the criteria has to be considered "the most important." Therefore, in a next step, Groh and Liechtenstein (2009a) focus on the first five criteria—the protection of property and investor's rights (with a mean nomination of 6.55 points), the presence of qualified GPs (6.35), the expected entrepreneurial management quality and skills (6.35), the expected deal flow (6.17), and bribing and corruption (5.91)—and try to determine a clear ranking of their relevance. Wilkoxon Signed Rank tests are adequate to determine this ranking. The nonparametric test considers the mean nominations and their standard deviations, and detects if the difference in the mean nominations of two paired criteria is statistically significant. The resulting rankings are presented in Exhibit 19.4.

The table reveals that the definition of absolute ranks is impossible on a 0.05 significance level. However, the protection of investors can either rank at the first or at the second position. It is not clear if it is ranked prior to the presence of qualified GPs, but it is certainly ranked ahead of the third criterion, the expected entrepreneurial management quality and skills. The investors' claims in the PE funds and, additionally, the claims of the PE funds in the target companies have to be secured. If institutional investors are not confident with that issue, they are reluctant to invest. As a result, issues relating to investor protection are the major obstacles for the development of emerging PE markets. This confirms the cited numerous literature contributions, and highlights the importance of the legal environment and the law enforcement possibilities in emerging host countries. The finding will be discussed further later on in this chapter.

Nevertheless, the presence of qualified GPs also has a very high importance (possibly at rank 1, 2, 3, or 4). This criterion is immediately followed by the expected entrepreneurial management quality and skills (which can rank at positions 2, 3,

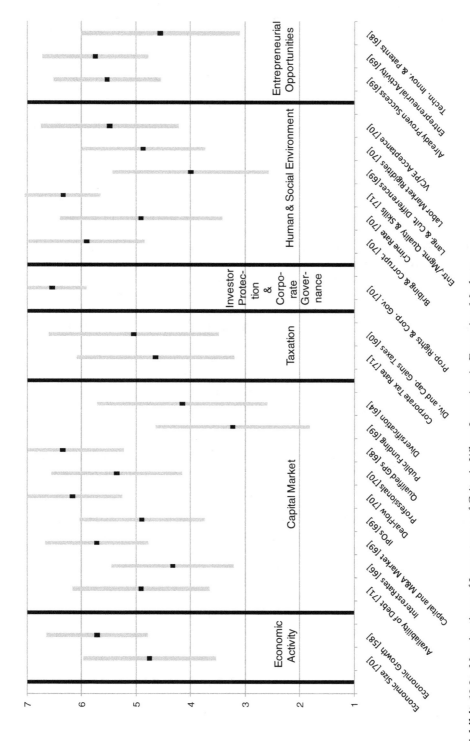

Exhibit 19.3 Nominations of Importance of Criteria When Investing in Emerging Markets
Source: Groh and Liechtenstein (2009b), Figure 1.

Exhibit 19.4   The Five Most Important Criteria for LPs' International PE Allocation
Decisions in Emerging Markets

Criteria	Possible Ranks
Protection of property and investor's rights	1 or 2
Presence of qualified GPs	1 or 2 or 3 or 4
Expected entrepreneurial management quality and skills	2 or 3 or 4
Expected deal-flow	2 or 3 or 4 or 5
Bribing and corruption	4 or 5

Source: Groh and Liechtenstein (2009a), Table 8.

or 4, but not ahead of investor protection). Both criteria emphasize the role of
talented people for the asset class, on the level of the managing PE fund as well
as on the level of the backed corporations. Institutional investors have to rely
on their agents. If they doubt their managerial capabilities, their loyalty, or their
entrepreneurial culture and attitude, in short, if investors do not feel comfortable
relying on people as the driving forces for PE business, they will not commit capital.

Following on, from the role of people, the expected deal flow materializes
(possibly ranked at positions 2, 3, 4, or 5). This criterion is rather comprehensible,
given that the asset class is return driven: Without having the expectation for good
deal opportunities, any allocation is absurd. However, the characteristic of this
criterion in a particular country depends on many different issues. On one hand,
deal opportunities exist due to economic and entrepreneurial activity. Regarding
emerging markets, that means in the first place that the local economy has to initiate deal flow. This requires a certain economic size which might not (yet) be present
in many of the emerging countries. New corporations have to be founded, others
have to be restructured, spun off, streamlined, or positioned for growth. Without
a body of already existing corporations, and without entrepreneurial culture and
activity, these opportunities will not arise. On the other hand, the deal flow has
to be "handled." This means that a supporting financial community has already
been established in the emerging country. There have to be deal-supporting institutions, such as M&A boutiques, banks, lawyers, consultants, accountants, and
others. If they are not present, professional deal making is impossible. At the same
time, one can imagine that all these determinants are interrelated. The supporting
financial community will be established if there is proportionate economic activity. The degree of economic activity depends on the entrepreneurial culture and,
likewise, on the protection of property rights. The legal protection results from the
political and societal will for protection, and might be affected by education and
the historical development of a country. Black and Gilson (1998) call it a chicken-
and-egg problem: A market for risk capital requires legal protection and a financial
community. The financial community requires entrepreneurs who deserve financial backing, sound economic conditions, and legal protection. This relates to, and
strongly confirms the findings on the importance of property rights protection and
law enforcement structures, such as La Porta et al. (1997 and 1998), Johnson et al.
(1999), Glaeser et al. (2001), Djankov et al. (118 and 2005), Lerner and Schoar (2004
and 2005), Desai et al. (2006), Cumming et al. (2006a and 2006b), and Cumming

and Johan (2007). Roe (2003) contributes to that discussion, and comprehensively analyzes the legal systems of different countries, their historical and political development, and their impact on the national financial markets, the corporations and their ownership structure, and governance culture. He emphasizes the advantages in common law systems, but legal systems are historically determined and hardly changeable. However, regardless of their legal system, emerging countries should take into account the benefits provided by common law, and consider important aspects of property rights protection and corporate governance culture within their legislation.

Finally, institutional investors rank the importance of bribing and corruption as high (either at rank 4 or 5). This coincides with their desire for protection: Investors fear bribery and corruption as these directly interfere with the enforcement of their claims. As a result, investor protection, law enforcement possibilities and, hence, the quality of a legal system and its administrational efficiency, all affect investors' allocation decisions regarding many different aspects. Unfortunately, bribery and corruption remain a frequent problem (not only) in emerging regions.

This relates to the question of how institutional investors assess that and the other discussed criteria in emerging markets. The following section deals with this issue.

Perceptions of Particular Allocation Criteria in Emerging Markets

Additional to the determination of the relevance of the PE allocation criteria, Groh and Liechtenstein (2009a) collect data on LPs' concerns when investing in emerging markets. The institutional investors named their appreciation of the criteria from Exhibit 19.3 in emerging regions. The criteria are grouped into the six main drivers: Economic Environment, Capital Market, Social Environment, Investor Protection, Taxation, and Entrepreneurial Opportunities. The respondents rank the characteristics of the criteria in emerging markets on a seven-point Likert scale from "not at all attractive" (1) to "very attractive" (7). The results of the nominations and the number of responses are presented in Exhibit 19.5.

Exhibit 19.5 shows the mean nominations and the $\pm\sigma$-percentiles regarding investors' appreciation of the six key driving factors. Again, as no clear ranking across these factors is possible, Groh and Liechtenstein (2009a) repeat the Wilcoxon Signed Rank tests and receive the ranking result as shown in Exhibit 19.6.

Exhibits 19.1 and 19.6 have to be interpreted with caution. It is clear that no emerging region is easily comparable to the others. Challenges for African countries are certainly different from challenges for Latin American or South East Asian emerging countries, not only with respect to economic development. However, the institutional investors' appreciations regarding emerging regions unfortunately reveal the opposite of what they consider important: The most important allocation criterion, namely, the protection of property rights, is ranked poorly for emerging regions. Hence, missing investor protection and law enforcement capacities are obviously the strongest obstacles for PE investments in emerging markets. This is similar to the criteria ranked second and third in the order of importance: the presence of qualified GPs and the expected entrepreneurial management quality.

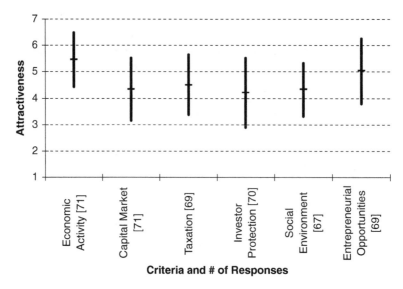

Exhibit 19.5 Appreciation of Allocation Criteria in Emerging Markets (Fluctuating Numbers of Responses)
Source: Groh and Liechtenstein (2009a), Figure 10.

Both criteria are affected by the social environment in emerging countries, and by their capital markets. The social environment and the capital markets receive low rankings in investors' appreciations of emerging regions. This is in line with the findings from Farag et al. (2004), Bliss (1999), Karsai et al. (1998), and Chu and Hisrich (2001) who stress the lack of talented and experienced people in emerging countries as forestalling the development of a vibrant risk-capital community. The lack of talented and experienced people refers to the management level of local GPs, the supporting institutions, and to the level of the PE-backed corporations. It further refers to the management abilities and experiences according to market-oriented and worldwide competitive standards.

On the other hand, investors appreciate the economic growth perspectives, and the resulting entrepreneurial opportunities in emerging regions. However, growth

Exhibit 19.6 Appreciation of Key Driving Allocation Criteria in Emerging Markets

Criteria	Rank(s)
Economic activity	1
Entrepreneurial opportunities	2
Taxation	3 / 4 / 5
Capital market	3 / 4 / 5 / 6
Social environment	4 / 5 / 6
Investor protection	4 / 5 / 6

Source: Groh and Liechtenstein (2009a), Table 6.

opportunities are not enough to attract the institutional capital; it is mandatory to meet the other requirements. Institutional investors refrain from investing if they miss a satisfying level of investor protection, entrepreneurial management skills, and capital market activity.

Investors' Preferences Regarding Different Emerging Regions

Emerging regions are in competition to attract funding from institutional investors. LPs might prefer certain regions due to the characteristics of the previously-discussed allocation criteria. Within their survey, Groh and Liechtenstein (2009a) analyze the institutional investors' preferences regarding the different emerging regions in the world, differentiating between Africa, Central Eastern Europe (CEE), China, the Commonwealth of Independent States (CIS, the former Soviet Union), India, Latin America, and South East Asia. The respondents specify their percep-tions on a range from "not at all attractive" (1) to "very attractive" (7) on the seven-point Likert scale. The mean nominations, the $\pm\sigma$-percentile, and the num-ber of responses for the different emerging regions are presented in Exhibit 19.7.

Exhibit 19.7 shows that India, Central Eastern Europe, and China are ranked top, followed by South East Asia, the Commonwealth of Independent States, and Latin America. Africa is ranked lowest. However, once again, the standard devia-tions of the nominations do not allow a clear order of preferences for the individual regions. Therefore, Groh and Liechtenstein (2009a) again perform Wilcoxon Signed Rank tests to obtain a clearer picture about the institutional investors' apprecia-tions of the emerging economies. Unfortunately, the test results fail to provide a

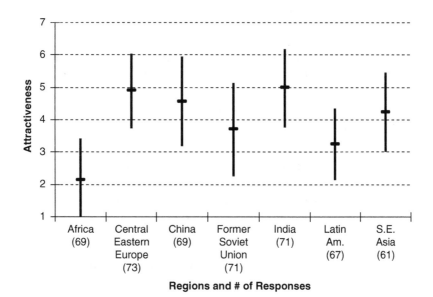

Exhibit 19.7 Attractiveness of Different Emerging Regions (Fluctuating Numbers of Responses)
Source: Groh and Liechtenstein (2009a), Figure 3.

Exhibit 19.8   Ranks of Attractiveness of Different
Emerging Regions

Region	Rank(s)
India	1 / 2
Central Eastern Europe	1 / 2 / 3
China	2 / 3 / 4
Southeast Asia	3 / 4
Former Soviet Union	5
Latin America	6
Africa	7

Source: Groh and Liechtenstein (2009a), Table 4.

final ranking of the individual regions on a 0.05 significance level, as some ranks are tied. Exhibit 19.8 presents the possible ranks.

According to Exhibit 19.8, three tier groups can be identified: The first tier group consists of India (that can rank either at 1 or 2), the Central Eastern European countries (at rank 1, 2, or 3), and China, while China might also form the second tier group (at rank 2, 3, or 4, but not ahead of India), together with South East Asia (at rank 3 or 4, but not ahead of CEE). The Commonwealth of Independent States, Latin America, and Africa belong to the third tier group in the mentioned order of preference.

These investors' expectations are hardly reflected in the pattern of PE activity in 2007, as presented in Exhibit 19.1. India leads the ranking of emerging market investment activity, closely followed by China. Adding up the investment volumes of all individual Central Eastern European countries yields a much lower activity than in China and, therefore, does not correspond to the ranking in Exhibit 19.8. However, the other emerging regions follow with their PE activity according to the preferences in Exhibit 19.8. Latin America and, notably, Africa are little appreciated by LPs, and show very little PE activity. Investments in Africa hardly exceeded $360 million in 2007.

CONCLUSION

Emerging markets should be very attractive for risk capital investors. The urgent need for capital, especially for all kinds of infrastructure and communication financing, is evident, and the large expected growth opportunities over several years deserve capital to be exploited, preferably by small and medium-sized nonquoted corporations. However, expected growth is not all that matters for investors in the PE asset class. There is a large variety of criteria that affect PE funding. Numerous contributions in literature deal with the success factors for vibrant risk-capital markets. Investor protection and corporate governance are the dominant criteria named in literature, but many others are also considered important. Groh and Liechtenstein (2009a) run a survey among institutional investors in the asset class and find that the protection of property rights and corporate governance are indeed perceived as most important for international PE allocation decisions. The criterion is followed by the assessment of the management quality of local GPs and entrepreneurs according to Western management standards, by the expected deal flow, and by bribery and corruption. The availability of public funding and subsidiaries plays no role in allocation decisions. Institutional investors in PE are not impressed by government programs to spur local risk-capital markets: public money will not attract private money.

The ranking of decision criteria reveals the investors' dependency on the subsequent chain of agents. Investors rely on the quality of the GPs they invest in. The GPs themselves rely on the managers of the corporations they finally back. If investors' claims are poorly protected, if they doubt the quality of their investees, or if they doubt integrity in a host country in general, then they refrain from investment.

Unfortunately, institutional investors poorly rank these exact characteristics in emerging regions. They are attracted by expected growth and the corresponding entrepreneurial opportunities. However, they are not satisfied with the protection of their claims, with the required resources and conditions to establish deal flow, and with the management experience of locals. Regarding different emerging regions, investors favor India, Central Eastern Europe, and China. They are less attracted by South East Asia, the Commonwealth of Independent States, Latin America, and Africa.

What needs to be done to improve the emerging regions' ability to attract risk capital investors? If corporate governance and the protection of property rights are the most important criteria in the LPs' allocation process, host country politicians should take into account these concerns of institutional investors. Glaeser et al. (2001), and Djankov et al. (118 and 2005) discuss the impact of law on finance, and La Porta et al. (1997 and 1998) confirm that the legal environment strongly determines the size and liquidity of a country's capital market. Roe (2003) expands this line of research and comments on the historical development of corporate governance rules for major economies. He points to the importance of shareholder protection for the establishment of a vibrant capital market. Cumming et al. (2008) show that differences in legality have significant impact on the governance of investees by PE funds. Cumming et al. (2006) comment on the quality of a legal system to facilitate PE-backed exits. Similarly, Black and Gilson (1998) emphasize the role of the professional infrastructure that accompanies stock market–centered capital markets to divest PE-backed corporations by IPOs. However, they also name it a "chicken-and-egg problem": a risk capital market requires a stock market with its finance professional community, but a stock market requires entrepreneurs and IPOs, which in turn, require a PE market. But instead of creating multiple new institutions, they recommend piggybacking on the institutional setting of another country. If this is successful, it will bring a potential for the development of local institutions. For example, corporations in emerging markets could piggyback on the already well-established financial communities and stock markets in the United States, Europe, or Asia. Additionally, foreign PE funds might find it profitable to hire and train locals in emerging countries to help them find good investment opportunities. Once trained, some of them will found their own companies locally, compete with their former employers, and, hence, establish a competitive risk-capital market.

However, the discussion reflects the capital supply side only. One should also take into account that many emerging countries lack several other criteria to develop a vibrant PE market. Without sufficient entrepreneurial culture and entrepreneurial opportunities, with bureaucratic or societal burdens, or with bribery and corruption, there will be no demand for risk capital. If there is no demand, there is also no need to piggyback on any other country's institutions.

NOTE

1. The ordinate is truncated at level 7 and, therefore, this limits the representation of the standard deviation in some cases.

REFERENCES

Armour, John, and Douglas Cumming. 2006. The legislative road to Silicon Valley. *Oxford Economic Papers* 58:596–635.

Balboa, Marina, and José Martí. 2003. An integrative approach to the determinants of private equity fundraising. SSRN Working Paper 493344.

Baughn, C. Christopher, and Kent E. Neupert. 2003. Culture and national conditions facilitating entrepreneurial start-ups. *Journal of International Entrepreneurship* 1:313–330.

Belke, Ansgar, Rainer Fehn, and Neil Foster. 2003. Does venture capital investment spur employment growth? CESIFO Working Paper 930.

Black, Bernard S., and Ronald J. Gilson. 1998. Venture capital and the structure of capital markets: Banks versus stock markets. *Journal of Financial Economics* 47:243–277.

Blanchard, Oliver J. 1997. The medium run. Brookings Papers on Economic Activity, 89–158.

Bliss, Richard T. 1999. A venture capital model for transitioning economies: The case of Poland. *Venture Capital* 1:241–257.

Bruce, Donald. 2000. Effects of the United States' tax system on transition into self-employment. *Labor Economics* 7:545–574.

Bruce, Donald. 2002. Taxes and entrepreneurial endurance: Evidence from the self-employed. *National Tax Journal* 55:5–24.

Chemla, Gilles. 2005. The determinants of investment in private equity and venture capital: Evidence from American and Canadian pension funds. SSRN Working Paper 556421

Chu, Priscilla, and Robert D. Hisrich. 2001. Venture capital in an economy in transition. *Venture Capital* 3:169–182.

Cullen, Julie Berry, and Roger H. Gordon. 2002. Taxes and entrepreneurial activity: Theory and evidence for the U.S. NBER Working Paper 9015.

Cumming, Douglas, Grant Flemming, and Armin Schwienbacher. 2006. Legality and venture capital exits. *Journal of Corporate Finance* 12:214–245.

Cumming, Douglas, and Sofia Johan. 2007. Regulatory harmonization and the development of private equity markets. *Journal of Banking and Finance* 31:3218–3250.

Cumming, Douglas, Daniel Schmidt, and Uwe Walz. 2008. Legality and venture governance around the world. *Journal of Business Venturing*, forthcoming.

Da Rin, Marco, Giovanna Nicodano, and Alessandro Sembelli. 2005. Public policy and the creation of active venture capital markets. European Central Bank Working Paper 430.

Desai, Mihir, Paul Gompers, and Josh Lerner. 2006. Institutions and entrepreneurial firm dynamics: Evidence from Europe. Harvard NOM Research Paper 03-59.

Djankov, Simeon, Rafael La Porta, Florencio Lopez-de-Silanes, and Andrei Shleifer. 2003. Courts. *Quarterly Journal of Economics* 118; 453–517.

Djankov, Simeon, Rafael La Porta, Florencio Lopez-de-Silanes, and Andrei Shleifer. 2005. The law and economics of self-dealing. NBER Working Paper 11883.

Farag, Hady, Ulrich Hommel, Peter Witt, and Mike Wright. 2004. Contracting, monitoring, and exiting venture investments in transitioning economies: A comparative analysis of Eastern European and German markets. *Venture Capital* 6 (4):257–282.

Fehn, Rainer, and Thomas Fuchs. 2003. Capital market institutions and venture capital: Do they affect unemployment and labour demand? CESIFO Working Paper 898.

Glaeser, Edward L., Simon Johnson, and Andrei Shleifer. 2001. Coase vs. the Coasians. *Quarterly Journal of Economics* 116:853–899.

Gompers, Paul, and Josh Lerner. 1998. What drives venture fundraising? Brooking Papers on Economic Activity, Microeconomics, 149–192.

Gompers, Paul, and Josh Lerner. 2000. Money chasing deals? The impact of funds inflows on the valuation of private equity investments. *Journal of Financial Economics* 55:281–325.

Greene, Patricia G. 1998. Dimensions of perceived entrepreneurial obstacles. In *Frontiers of entrepreneurship research*, ed. P. Reynolds, pp. 48–49. Babson College, Wellesley, MA.

Groh, Alexander P., and Heinrich Liechtenstein. 2009a. International allocation determinants of institutional investments in venture capital and private equity limited partnerships. IESE Business School Working Paper 726.

Groh, Alexander P., and Heinrich Liechtenstein. 2009b. How attractive is Central Eastern Europe for risk capital investors? *Journal of International Money and Finance*, 28 (4):625–647.

Hellmann, Thomas, and Manju Puri. 2000. The interaction between product market and financing strategy: The role of venture capital. *Review of Financial Studies* 13 (4):959–984.

Jeng, Leslie A., and Philippe C. Wells. 2000. The deteminants of venture capital funding: Evidence across countries. *Journal of Corporate Finance* 6:241–289.

Johnson, Simon, John McMillan, and Cristopher M. Woodruff. 1999. Property rights, finance and entrepreneurship. SSRN Working Paper 198409.

Kaplan, Steven N., and Antoinette Schoar. 2005. Private Equity Performance: Returns, Persistence, and Capital Flows." *Journal of Finance* 60, 1791–1823.

Karsai, Judit, Mike Wright, Zbigniew Dudzinski, and Jan. Morovic. 1998. Screening and valuing venture capital investments: Evidence from Hungary, Poland, and Slovakia. *Entrepreneurship & Regional Development* 10:203–224.

Klonowski, Darek. 2005. How do venture capitalists make investment decisions in Central and Eastern Europe? Brandon University Working Paper.

Knack, Stephen, and Philip Keefer. 1995. Institutions and economic performance: Cross-country tests using alternative institutional measures. *Economics and Politics* 7:207–228.

Köke, Jens. 1999. Institutional investment in Central and Eastern Europe: Investment criteria of Western portfolio managers. ZEW Discussion Paper 99-37.

Kortum, Samuel S., and Josh Lerner. 2000. Assessing the contribution of venture capital to innovation." *Rand Journal Economics* 31 (4):674–692.

La Porta, Rafael, Florencio Lopez-de-Silanes, Andrei Shleifer, and Robert W. Vishny. 1997. Legal determinants of external finance. *Journal of Finance* 52:1131–1150.

La Porta, Rafael, Florencio Lopez-de-Silanes, Andrei Shleifer, and Robert W. Vishny. 1998. Law and finance. *Journal of Political Economy* 106:1113–1155.

La Porta, Rafael, Florencio Lopez-de-Silanes, Andrei Shleifer, and Robert W. Vishny. 2002. Investor protection and corporate valuation. *Journal of Finance* 57:1147–1170.

Lazear, Edward P. 1990. Job security provisions and employment. *Quarterly Journal of Economics* 105:699–726.

Lee, Sang M., and Suzanne J. Peterson. 2000. Culture, entrepreneurial orientation, and global competitiveness. *Journal of World Business* 35:401–416.

Lerner, Josh, and Antoinette Schoar. 2004. The illiquidity puzzle: Theory and evidence from private equity. *Journal of Financial Economics* 72:3–40.

Lerner, Josh, and Antoinette Schoar. 2005. Does legal enforcement affect financial transactions? The contractual channel in private equity. *Quarterly Journal of Economics* 120:223–246.

Levine, Ross. 1997. Financial development and economic growth: Views and agenda. *Journal of Economic Literature* 35:688–726.

Mauro, Paolo. 1995. Corruption and growth. *Quarterly Journal of Economics* 110:681–712.

Megginson, William. 2004. Toward a global model of venture capital? *Journal of Applied Corporate Finance* 16:89–107.

Michelacci, Claudio, and Javier Suarez. 2004. Business creation and the stock market. *Review of Economic Studies* 71:459–481.

Roe, Mark J. 2003. *Political determinants of corporate governance.* Oxford: Oxford University Press.

Romain, Astrid, and Bruno van Pottelsberghe de la Potterie. 2004. The determinants of venture capital: A panel analysis of 16 OECD countries. Université Libre de Bruxelles Working Paper WP-CEB 04/015.

Sapienza, Harry J., Sophie Manigart, and Wim Vermeir. 1996. Venture capitalist governance and value added in four countries. *Journal of Business Venturing* 11:439–469.

Schertler, Andrea 2003. Driving forces of venture capital investments in Europe: A dynamic panel data analysis. European integration, financial systems, and corporate performance. United Nations University (EIFC) Working Paper 03-27.

Svensson, Jakob. 1998. Investment, property rights and political instability: Theory and evidence. *European Economic Review* 42:1317–1341.

Wilken, Paul H. 1979. *Entrepreneurship: A comparative and historical study.* Norwood, NJ: Ablex Publishing.

ABOUT THE AUTHOR

Alexander Peter Groh received his Ph.D. in Finance from Darmstadt University of Technology, Germany. He is Associate Professor of Finance at GSCM–Montpellier Business School, France, Adjunct Professor of the Free University of Bolzano, Italy, and Research Affiliate of the International Center for Financial Research (CIIF) at IESE Business School, Barcelona, Spain. Prior to that, he held visiting positions at INSEAD, Fontainebleau, France, and IESE Business School, Barcelona, Spain. His research is focused on Venture Capital and Private Equity and some of his papers are published in the *Journal of Corporate Finance, Journal of Alternative Investments, Journal of International Money and Finance* and the *Quarterly Journal of Finance and Accounting*. In parallel to his academic career, he works for the Frankfurt-based buyout fund Quadriga Capital.

CHAPTER 20

Private Equity in Europe

LAURA BOTTAZZI
Bologna University, IGIER-Bocconi University, RCEA

INTRODUCTION

Private equity, as an asset class, is probably one of the less well understood segments of today's financial markets: it is medium to long-term finance provided in return for an equity stake in potentially high growth unquoted companies.

In Europe the terms *private equity*, *venture capital*, and *risk capital* are used interchangeably. In the United States *venture capital* refers only to investments in early-stage and expanding companies. To avoid confusion, the term *private equity* is used here as a generic term that encompasses all the subsets of financing stages. These include venture capital, later-stage expansion capital, and management buyouts and buyins: Each market segment corresponds to specific companies' profiles and uses different financial structures.

Venture capital is focused on young, entrepreneurial companies: it provides finance for start-ups, which have high growth and earnings potential, at their foundation or shortly after their first technical or commercial developments. Much of this segment is technology-related. Investments are often in individual minority shareholdings with a number of venture capital funds investing in successive rounds of financing. The investors are closely involved in determining the investee company's strategy, hiring key employees, organizing the search for further financial resources and negotiating partnerships with larger corporations.[1]

In later stage expansion (or growth) capital finance is provided to purchase holdings, by subscribing new capital, in profitable companies that necessitate the consolidation of their financial structures to develop new products or services or make an acquisition or increase their capacity.

Buyouts are typically majority investments made in companies together with existing management (management buyout, or "MBO") or with a new management team (management buy-in, or "MBI"). These normally use sophisticated financial techniques that involve financing from a bank or from specialized financial investment companies (e.g., Wright, Thompson, and Robbie 1992; Wright and Robbie 1998; Kaplan and Stein 1993). Buyouts firms typically manage their portfolio companies completely independent from one another (Baker and Montgomery 1994), because the intention is to increase the value of the takeover target as a stand-alone business.

This chapter begins by examining the history and the evolution of private equity in Europe. Next, we briefly explain the key structural feature of private equity funds and review some of the evidence on investment and performance in Europe.

HISTORY

Private equity (PE) has existed since the earliest days of commercial activity: In Europe, the Spanish monarchy and the Italian investors who financed the expeditions of Christopher Columbus were, in a sense, private equity investors. Since the industrial revolution, investors have been acquiring businesses or making minority investments in privately held companies. Merchant bankers in London and Paris financed industries in the 1850s: Credit Mobilier, in 1854, together with New York–based Jay Cooke, financed the United States Transcontinental Railroad. Andrew Carnegie sold his steel company to J.P. Morgan in 1901 in what was possibly the first true modern buyout.

Only in the second half of the twentieth century did private equity financing became a professional, large-scale industry. The seeds of PE were planted in the United States after World War II, with the founding of two venture capital firms: American Research and Development Corporation (ARDC) and J.H. Whitney & Company in the United States; in Europe with the creation of Charterhouse Development Capital (1934), and 3i (1945) in the United Kingdom.[2]

The maturation of private equity was not smooth, though (Gompers 1994). Until the 1980s, private equity firms were in large part publicly funded small business investment companies (SBICs). While SBICs trained many venture capitalists and helped the industry reach a critical mass by channeling large sums to start-ups, their ability to perform was limited by bureaucratic constraints, lack of professional expertise, a faulty design of capital structure and incentives (Lerner 1994a) and, in Europe, the poor exit alternatives offered by the stock markets.

As a consequence, funds developed mainly from banks and financial institutions, funded on their own limited resources. Their investment record was in fact mixed, and spurred a fall in investor confidence and in committed funds around the late 1980s. Also, many private equity firms, including ARDC, were organized as closed-end funds, but this attracted retail investors with short-term horizons, whose needs clashed with the long-term returns of private equity. Only in the late 1980s were SBICs and closed-end funds superseded by the limited partnership as the dominant organizational form of American private equity firms.[3]

Another major contribution to the adoption of a more efficient organizational form was the clarification, in 1979, of the Employment Retirement Income Stabilization Act, which allowed pension funds to invest in venture capital. This resulted in a staggering increase of funds invested, and in a faster professionalization of the industry.

The decision by institutional investors to invest in private equity is based on the investor's desire to optimise its investment returns within the context of its own portfolio risk approach, and for the many institutions managing long term savings or pension's assets, their asset-liability matching requirements within consistent long term returns. The long-term business model horizon of private equity fits, in the long term, the objectives of many retirement money managers.

Generally speaking the large institutional sources of capital, because of their particular mandate to provide for future savings and income, are by nature conservative. Because of the developed professionalism and institutionalised characteristics of the private equity industry and of its managers, these conservative investors have started to allocate increasingly large percentages of their funds to the private equity asset class.

However, until the early 1990s, private equity, and in particular venture capital, remained essentially an American phenomenon. Its success in supporting dynamic companies, which create jobs and wealth, brought many governments to look for ways to nurture a national venture capital industry. At the same time, the high returns enjoyed by U.S. venture capital firms induced venture capitalists to become active also in other countries. Venture capital is by now a sizeable industry also in Europe and Asia.

The development of private equity has experienced periods of boom and bust because it is a highly procyclical activity. In the second part of the 1980s, many of the major banking players of the day—including Morgan Stanley, Goldman Sachs, Salomon Brothers, and Merrill Lynch—were actively involved in advising and financing the parties. By the end of the 1980s, the excesses of the buyout market were beginning to show, with the bankruptcy of several large buyouts. Then came recession, and corporations started to restructure and focus on core activities: Recent investors suffered from their venture in an activity they did not understand. In France, two of the most illuminating experiences were that of the investment arm of Crédit Lyonnais, and that of the SDRs (Société de Développement Régional). In both cases, the state had to intervene to save what could be saved.

As a result, the few surviving funds were able to choose among the best projects and pave the way for what would become their record performance in years to follow. In 1998 United States and then Europe woke up to the Internet, and U.S. VCs started looking also at Europe, opening up London offices or establishing joint ventures. The cycle began to sour in 2000. Many funds had been raised, which were invested at the peak of the dot-com boom, and quite a few were managed by self-assured people new to VC. After the dot-com bubble burst, funds stopped making new investments in order to concentrate on their existing portfolios, reduce headcounts, and reevaluate their investments.

THE STRUCTURE OF PRIVATE EQUITY FUNDS

It was in the 1960s that the common form of private equity fund, still in use today, emerged: Private equity firms organize limited partnerships to finance their activity by raising "funds" from institutional investors, such as pension funds, insurance companies, or endowments that are passive *limited partners* (LPs). Typically, these funds raise equity at the time they are formed, and raise additional capital when investments are made. This additional capital usually takes the form of debt when the investment is collateralizable, such as in buyouts, or it may be equity from syndication partners, as in a start-up. Gaining a reputation for having produced good returns is a key determinant of future successful fund-raising.

Each "fund" is invested by professionals, private equity fund managers, who serve as general partners (GPs), in a number of firms with a five- to ten-year horizon. As long as the basic covenants of the fund agreement are followed, LPs do not intervene in the GPs' investment decisions. Common covenants include restrictions on how much fund capital can be invested in a single company, the types of securities a fund can invest in, and restrictions on debt at the fund level (as opposed to borrowing at the portfolio company level, which is unrestricted). Once a "fund" is ended, by sale to another company, IPO, or recapitalization, its cash proceeds are distributed to investors together with any remaining equity holdings.

Some private equity funds are publicly quoted.[4] In this case they do not return capital to investors after realization but they pay dividends, as any other public companies. In the United Kingdom (Jenkinson 2008) there are currently over 100 *venture capital trusts* (VCTs), which are quoted investment vehicles focusing on smaller companies, whose development was encouraged by government providing generous tax-relief to individual investors.

The compensation structure of PE implies limited partners paying an annual management fee of 1 to 3 percent and a carried interest typically representing up to 20 percent of the profits of the partnership. Generally, only capital gains above a certain annual percentage return, the so-called *hurdle rate*, are considered for the carried interest calculation.

Aside from these, some general partners charge deal fees and monitoring fees to the companies in which they invest. Both of these fees are common features for buyout (BO) funds, and are rare for VC funds. When a BO fund buys or sells a company, it effectively charges a transaction fee to that company that is between 1 and 2 percent of transaction value, similar to the M&A advisory fees charged by investment banks. It is not clear exactly what these transaction fees are paying for, because GPs should already be receiving their fixed costs from management fees. As with transaction fees, monitoring fees have the purpose to compensate the funds for time and effort spent in working with their portfolio companies. Annual monitoring fees typically vary between 1 and 5 percent of EBITDA and, in most cases, these fees are shared with LPs receiving 80 percent and GPs receiving 20 percent.

Metrick and Yasuda (2008) describe the structure of fees in great detail and provide empirical evidence on those fees. Their impacts on the net returns earned by limited partners is much higher than those observed on mutual funds that invest in public equity: Expected private equity returns must consequently be significantly higher.

The aim of these instruments is to provide incentives for the GP to make and manage the fund's investments in the best possible way—in other words, to maximize the return to the LPs while the management fee and carry are fundamental determinants of the cost of a given buyout fund.

We have only scant theory explaining why this financial structure is so prevalent. Sahlman (1990), Gompers and Lerner (1997), Jones and Rhodes-Kropf (2003), and Lerner and Schoar (2004) discuss the economic rationale for these fund structures and recognize that this feature is a part of the contract aimed at reducing the ability of the GP to hold up the LPs once the latter have committed to invest. Kandel, Leshchinskii, and Yuklea (2006) argue that fund structures can lead GPs to inefficient decisions during the intermediate investment stages.

Axelson, Strömberg, and Weisbach (ASW) (2007) develop a model trying endogenously to demonstrate the optimality of this financial structure: they consider regimes where the GP raises capital on a deal-by-deal basis (ex post financing) and raises a fund that can completely finance a number of future projects (ex ante financing). In their model, in good times, where the average project has positive NPV, there is overinvestment, and in bad times there is underinvestment.

Ex ante financing, by tying the compensation of the GP to the collective performance of a fund, supplies the GP with less of an incentive to invest in bad deals, since bad deals contaminate his stake in the good deals. Thus, a fund structure often dominates deal-by-deal capital raising. The downside of pure ex ante capital raising is that it leaves the GP with substantial freedom. Once the fund is raised he does not have to go back to the capital markets, and so can fund deals even in bad times. If the GP has not encountered enough good projects and is approaching the end of the investment horizon, or if economic conditions shift so that not many good deals are expected to arrive in the future, a GP with untapped funds has the incentive to "go for broke" and take bad deals.

It is, therefore, typically optimal to use a mix of ex ante and ex post capital if the intention is to maximizes the value of the fund, while alleviating the agency problems that arise because managers have better information about deal quality than potential investors. As a result the optimal contract implies giving investors a debt claim plus a levered equity stake, while leaving the GP with a "carry" at the fund level that resembles contracts observed in practice.

Groh and Gottschalg (2008) conducted a detailed analysis of over 1,000 PE funds raised during the 2001 to 2005 period. Their data confirms the rule that most funds still follow the pattern of 2 percent management fee, 20 percent carry, and 8 percent hurdle rate. When they dig deeper into the different fee elements, they further observe that on average the fixed-income component (management fee based) has historically been more important than the performance-based remuneration for PE funds (carry based). The dominance of the fixed income component (management fee based) increases with the size of the fund, which raises questions about the suitability of this incentive structure to push fund managers into generating the highest possible returns for their investors.

PRIVATE EQUITY INVESTMENT

The first step in assessing the relevance of European private equity requires a quantitative look at the state and structure of the European private equity industry, and at its evolution over time.

We base our analysis on the aggregate statistics published by the European Venture Capital Association (EVCA). These data come from extensive surveys of private equity firms: EVCA distributes each year a survey to PE firms, irrespective of their EVCA membership status, in cooperation with PricewaterhouseCoopers.

Over the years, EVCA has become the prime source, although not the only one, for information about the private equity industry in Europe. In association with Thomson Venture Economics (TVE), EVCA has been collecting information, resulting in comprehensive data going back to 1984. Exhibit 20.1 gives an idea about the total number of funds covered by the EVCA survey and shows how the sample has expanded over time.

This dataset is not unbiased, however, as it is discussed in the following paragraph. For the period 1987 to 1999 the survey covers 51 percent of the total

Exhibit 20.1   Investment Benchmarks Database

Year	Number of Funds in the Sample	Committed €bn
1998	438	51.4
1999	511	68.8
2000	573	87.6
2001	665	108.8
2002	774	135.4
2003	881	149.5
2004	956	159.6
2005	1,069	205.2
2006	1,141	237.9
2007	1,215	300.3

Source: EVCA Activity Survey 2007.

population of funds and 77 percent by capital under management. In contrast, the most recent surveys reached a response rate close to 90 percent.

The exhibits here report the aggregate data for the period 1996 to 2007. There is much that one can learn from these data. Exhibit 20.2 shows the amount of funds raised by private equity firms. The explosion in private equity activity during the period 1996 and 2001 is apparent, but it is not an easy task to understand all the factors that has determined it, first of all, because fund-raising and investments tend to follow separate patterns, given the heterogeneity between structures and stages of development of private equity in different countries. Second, the list of factors that might explain the increase of private equity and that have been studied in economic literature is vast: initial public offerings (IPOs), returns to investors, capital gain taxation, regulation of pension funds, the growth of capital market

Exhibit 20.2   Evolution Activity Flows (€ billion)

Year	Funds Raised	Investments	Divestments
1996	8.0	6.8	3.6
1997	20.0	9.7	5.8
1998	20.3	14.5	7.0
1999	25.4	25.1	8.6
2000	48.0	35.0	9.1
2001	40.0	24.3	12.5
2002	27.5	27.6	10.7
2003	27.0	29.1	13.6
2004	27.5	36.9	19.6
2005	71.8	47.1	29.8
2006	112.3	71.2	33.1
2007	79.0	74.4	27.0
2008***	29.0	81.0	48.0

*** Until Q3 of 2008.
Source: EVCA Yearbook 2007 and Quarterly Activity Indicator report Q3-2008.

Exhibit 20.3   Investment (%)

	1996	1997	1998	1999	2000	2001	2002	2003	2004	2005	2006	2007
Buyout	52.9	57.8	58.6	57.4	43.7	49.9	64.6	71.1	66.7	70.5	89.7	52.9
V.C.	47.1	42.2	41.4	42.6	56.3	50.1	35.4	28.9	33.2	29.5	10.3	47.1

Source: EVCA Yearbook 2007 & PEREP_Analytics for 2007 figures.

capitalization, and others. IPOs have been mentioned as one of the most important factors that positively influence the raising of venture capital funds. And in effect the level of funding in Europe increased mostly after the opening of Euro.nm in 1997, which paved the way for the listing of high-tech start-ups. Whether this coincidence conceals a causal link or reflects broader changes cannot be discerned, based on simple inspection of these figures.

Balboa and Marti (2001), using panel techniques, have found evidence that lagged investments are important in explaining the flow of new funds raised: this indicates that the market considers the fund manager's ability to invest, before supplying new funds.

The above exhibit measures the equity components of the deals and hence understates the total value of transaction by PE funds. The years 2005 and 2006 witnessed a massive flow of funds raised and invested. The difference between the funds raised and the investment figures reflects the lag between the commitment of capital and its deployment. However, in some cases, in particular for funds raised in the boom years of 2000 and 2001, some funds do not invest all the funds that have been committed. In the same years the size of private equity buyouts has been growing, as Exhibit 20.3 shows.

The proportion of buyout funds has continued to increase in recent years, reaching over 89 percent of total funds invested in 2006. This highlights the comparatively difficult position of venture capital managers after the "bubble" of 2000, and the wider downturn in the EU economy at that time. Since the bubble, venture capital managers in Europe, in particular Europe's smaller markets, have found it more difficult to raise funds, as a result of historic underperformance.

Together with the overall quantity, the distribution between different stages of investment is an important consideration, to which Exhibit 20.4 refers for the years

Exhibit 20.4   Stage Distribution of Investments (%)

	Seed	Start-Up	Expansion	Replacement Capital	Buyout
Amount Invested					
2005	0,20	5,00	21,80	4,80	68,20
2006	0,30	8,00	16,00	5,00	70,70
Number of Investments					
2005	3,80	29,10	41,80	3,60	21,70
2006	4,40	25,80	43,10	3,60	23,10

Source: EVCA Activity Survey 2006.

2005 and 2006. As in the previous exhibit, we again find that buyouts dominate the European Private Equity market, with early-stage investments still representing only 5.2 to 8.3 percent of the funds raised. However, in terms of the number of portfolio company investments, early-stage, seed, and start-up ventures represent a much larger share. These transactions are for relatively smaller amounts than buyouts, where a single equity investment can be several hundred million Euros.

Exhibit 20.5 uncovers a convergence in the structure of private equity funding across the Atlantic. It is well known that institutional investors (mainly pension funds) have been, by far, the largest contributor in the United States, accounting for nearly two-thirds of all funds, as compared to less than one-third in Europe in the 1990s. The stability of the share of institutional investing in the United States is a sign of the maturity of that market. Private equity in Europe was, instead, dominated by funding from financial institutions (mainly banks) and only recently has their importance been reduced as a source of funding. Funds controlled by a financial or corporate entity ("captive" funds) have been more common in Europe,

Exhibit 20.5   European Fund-Raising, 1996–2007 (%)

	1997	1998	1999	2000	2001	2002	2003	2004	2005	2006	2007
Others/Not Available	7,70	7,80	6,70	3,80	3,60	4,00	16,20	7,90	8,20	3,90	22,80
Realized Capital Gains	6,90	8,80	7,30	8,40	4,50	5,40	6,30	14,40	5,70	4,00	0,00
Corporate Investors	11,30	9,80	9,50	10,00	5,50	6,90	4,50	6,00	4,80	3,60	2,50
Private Individuals	4,00	7,60	6,20	6,80	6,30	5,70	3,00	6,50	5,70	8,50	4,70
Government Agencies	2,20	5,10	4,70	5,10	5,70	10,50	6,40	5,30	9,30	8,40	5,40
Banks	25,80	27,80	29,10	19,90	23,00	24,90	20,10	18,50	16,60	13,80	11,80
Pension Funds	25,00	24,00	18,70	22,20	25,60	15,40	18,20	16,50	23,40	26,00	18,00
Insurance Companies	16,40	8,90	13,20	11,80	11,70	13,00	8,20	10,20	10,50	9,70	8,30
Fund-of-Funds	—	—	4,00	10,40	11,60	12,40	15,40	11,50	12,30	17,40	11,20
Academic Institutions	0,70	0,10	0,40	0,40	2,10	1,60	1,40	1,30	2,40	3,40	0,30
Capital Markets	—	0,20	0,20	1,20	0,50	0,10	0,30	1,80	1,20	1,20	7,60
Endowments and Foundations	—	—	—	—	—	—	—	—	—	—	1,60
Family Offices	—	—	—	—	—	—	—	—	—	—	1,40
Other Asset Managers	—	—	—	—	—	—	—	—	—	—	4,50
Total Fund-raising	100	100	100	100	100	100	100	100	100	100	100

Source: EVCA Yearbook 2007 and Quarterly Activity Indicator report Q3-2008; PEREP_Analytics for 2007 figures.

where the share of corporate investment has doubled in the second half of the 1990s. On the contrary, government funding is virtually nonexistent in both geographical areas.

These profound differences in funding patterns largely reflect the different structure of capital markets in the two economies. Europe has long been dominated by banks (and still is), which control a large part of the mutual funds industry. The National Science Board (2000) reports that from 1995 to 1999, around one-half of all U.S. venture capital was derived from pension funds. Furthermore, few European endowments—such as academic institutions—have invested in private equity on anything like the scale observed in their U.S. counterparts (Swensen 2000).

Exhibit 20.6 shows the sectors that have attracted the highest percentage of amount invested: they are consumer goods, communications, and computer-related goods and services. The percentage of funds invested in the high-tech sector has instead declined, recently, with respect to the 1999 to 2000 period, the period of the tech bubble. However, as in 2006 and 2007, the sectors with the largest number of investments (not reported) were computer related and electronics.

This trend in investment is reflected in the distribution by sector of divestments: in the period 2006 and 2007 divestments were, by far, mainly concentrated in computer, consumer goods and services.

The most popular divestment methods in 2007 were repayment of loans, sales to other private equity firms and sales to trade buyer, as in Exhibit 20.7. The high percentage of repayments of loans is probably due to the increase of leverage financing coming from banks and private equity firms that Europe has experienced, between 2002 and 2007. The high proportion of trade sales and sales to other private equity firms shows that most divested companies were healthy and promising.

Exhibit 20.6 Industrial Sectors

	2001	2002	2003	2004	2005	2006
Communications	0,14	0,09	0,17	0,13	0,15	0,14
Computer Related	0,12	0,06	0,07	0,09	0,10	0,22
Other Electronics	0,02	0,03	0,02	0,02	0,02	0,04
Biotechnology	0,03	0,04	0,02	0,02	0,02	0,01
Medical/Health	0,07	0,07	0,06	0,08	0,07	0,09
Energy	0,03	0,01	0,01	0,02	0,02	0,02
Consumer	0,15	0,21	0,19	0,23	0,27	0,15
Industrial Products/Services	0,08	0,17	0,07	0,05	0,09	0,10
Chemical	0,07	0,03	0,02	0,03	0,02	0,03
Industrial Automation	0,01	0,01	0,02	0,01	0,02	0,01
Other Manufacturing	0,06	0,06	0,08	0,07	0,06	0,05
Transport	0,02	0,03	0,05	0,02	0,02	0,03
Finance	0,02	0,04	0,02	0,04	0,03	0,03
Other Services	0,06	0,08	0,09	0,14	0,05	0,15
Agriculture	0,01	0,01	0,01	0,01	0,01	0,01
Construction	0,06	0,02	0,03	0,02	0,03	0,02
Other	0,04	0,04	0,07	0,06	0,05	0,06
High-Tech	0.28	0.12	0,24	0,20	0,17	0,18

Exhibit 20.7   European Divestment at Cost (%)

	2001	2002	2003	2004	2005	2006	2007
Other	9,5	11,0	14,1	17,5	18,0	18,2	11,8
Sale to Financial Institution	4,3	3,9	6,0	2,9	4,0	5,4	3,3
Repayment of Shares/Loans	14,5	8,4	15,9	21,3	23,3	17,1	19,0
Secondary	3,8	3,9	20,2	13,1	18,4	16,6	29,7
Write-Off	22,8	30,0	11,6	9,7	4,7	3,8	2,0
Sale of Quoted Equity	9,1	5,3	6,2	7,0	4,5	7,2	4,8
IPO	2,0	6,6	5,6	4,8	4,5	9,0	4,5
Trade Sale	34,0	30,9	20,4	23,7	22,6	22,7	24,9

Source: EVCA Yearbook 2008 at www.evca.com.

INTERNATIONALIZATION OF PRIVATE EQUITY

The private equity industry is still heavily concentrated in two economies, the United States and the United Kingdom. These two markets are by far the most mature and developed and accounts for approximately 55 percent of the PE funds raised in the period 2005 to 2007, as Exhibit 20.8 illustrates:

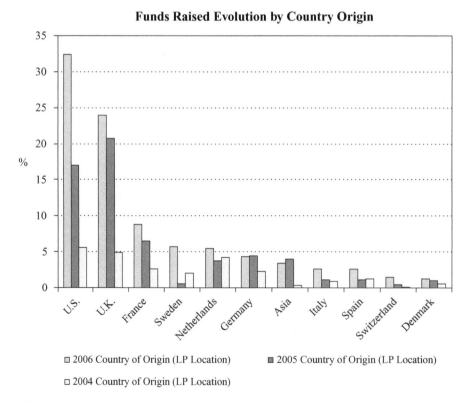

Funds Raised Evolution by Country Origin

□ 2006 Country of Origin (LP Location)   ■ 2005 Country of Origin (LP Location)

□ 2004 Country of Origin (LP Location)

Exhibit 20.8   Country of Origin of LPs in 2004, 2005, and 2006

Country of Origin and Country of Management of European Funds Raised (2006)

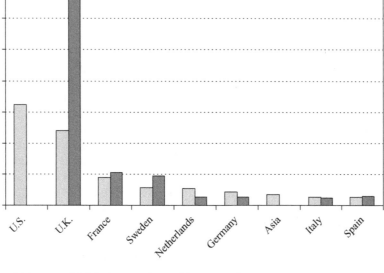

☐ Country of Origin (LPs location)   ■ Country of Management (GPs location)

Exhibit 20.9 Country of Origin of LPs and Location of Fund Management Team (assets under management, € billions), Top Seven EU Member States in 2006

Historically, funds raised in Europe were largely composed of local investors. Over the course of the last decade, however, there has been an increasing tendency for inflows from the European Union and other countries, especially the United States. Today, around 40 percent of the funds raised by European private equity and venture capital funds come from outside the EU member states. Exhibit 20.9 shows the significant differences between the domicile of the LPs and of the GPs.

On the investment side, this trend clearly reflects the increasingly transnational nature of the private marketplace. European cross-border private equity transactions have grown at high rates: the compounded annual growth rate of transnational private equity deal volumes between 1995 and 2006 reached 37 percent. Also, the ratio of cross-border to total deals has increased substantially. Whereas in 1996, cross-border deals accounted for only 16.3 percent of all European private equity transactions, this share reached 38 percent in 2006. In the exhibit, the dominance of the United Kingdom is apparent, because the larger pan-European funds are almost invariably headquartered in London. Exhibit 20.10 lists the four countries that have attracted the highest number of investments in 2007: United Kingdom, France, Germany, and Spain (see Exhibit 20.11).

The internationalization of PE investment have been driven by numerous factors—in particular, the increased supply of funds of institutional investors, such as pensions, mutual funds, and insurance companies, eager to invest in

Exhibit 20.10   Top Five Countries in Attracting Investments in 2007

	U.K.	France	Germany	Netherlands	Spain
Top five countries in attracting investments in 2007	26,7%	15,1%	13,5%	7,3%	5,4%

Source: PEREP_Analytics for 2007 figures.

high-return projects for an ageing population. At the same time, developing nations have undertaken radical institutional, legal, and regulatory reforms that have made it easier and safer to invest abroad for all investors, including PE investors.

This phenomenon is well documented by the IMF and pertains to all international capital flows and to the question of financial globalization. A considerable amount of research has been carried out into international capital flows (e.g., Gelos and Wei 2004; Brennan and Cao 1997). For several types of international capital flows, such as bank lending and foreign direct investments of banks, the recent literature shows that the economic growth in the deal country is an important factor for attracting foreign capital flows (Goldberg 2004; Goldberg 2007). The studies on international capital flows also put particular emphasis on transaction costs (Barron and Valev 2000; Portes et al. 2001; Portes and Rey 2005).

Countries with a limited domestic supply of funds have also tried to attract foreign capital by fostering entrepreneurship and innovation and developing the

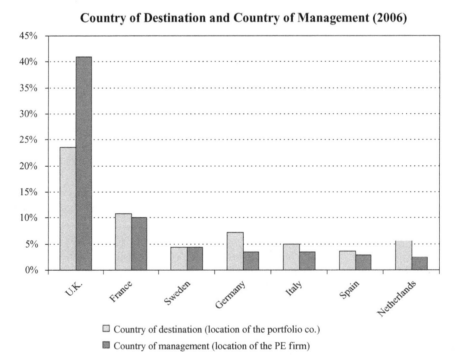

Country of Destination and Country of Management (2006)

☐ Country of destination (location of the portfolio co.)
■ Country of management (location of the PE firm)

Exhibit 20.11   Country of Destination of Investment (€ billions) and Location of Fund Management Team (assets under management, € billions), Top Seven EU Member States in 2006

financial markets to allow exit opportunities to investors. Other factors that have increased the internationalization of the PE market have been the creation of networks of contact, as there is evidence of path dependency and persistence in PE flows. The existence of cultural links as well as the availability of partners with PE experience and local country knowledge (Guiso, Sapienza, and Zingales et al. 2006; Bottazzi, Hellmann, and Da Rin (2008a,b)), are other significant factors in directing these flows. Additionally, the presence of high-end human capital, a better business environment, and deeper financial markets are important local factors that attract international private equity.

Research focusing on issues related to the internationalization of PE firms has increased lately. Macro studies have examined cross-country evidence and comparison among countries to investigate the determinants of the development of PE industries. For Europe the main results show that the opening of the "New" stock markets for entrepreneurial firms had a large positive impact on the supply of early-stage venture capital, providing support for the theory that relies on the importance of creating exit options for venture capital, as suggested by Black and Gilson (1998), Michelacci and Suarez (2004).

Cumming and Johan (2007) investigate institutional investors' allocation of funds to domestic and foreign private equity investors. They offer insights into the determinants of cross-border investments by U.S. private equity investors, such as the stock market capitalization and the number of patent applications in the deal country.

Micro studies have analyzed more deeply the determinants of cross-border investment and the behavior of PE investors internationally. Bottazzi, Hellmann, and Da Rin (2008a,b) have studied how trust, language, distance, information, legal standards, and different level of development of the financial market affect cross-border VC investment. Aizenman and Jake Kendall (2008) develop a similar study for private equity investments.

Lerner and Schoar (2005) find evidence that private equity investors use different kinds of securities when investing in countries with different legal systems. Kaplan, Martel, and Stromberg (2007) demonstrate that when investing abroad, deal contracts of private equity investors located in civil law countries differ significantly from those of private equity investors located in common law countries. Bottazzi, Hellmann, and Da Rin (2008a,b) study European VCs cross-investment and they also find that legal standards affect not only the geographical location of investment but also the financial instruments and the contracts between investors and VC.

One avenue through which PE investors invest abroad is by forming syndication networks (Sorensen and Stuart 2001; Lerner 1994b; Hochberg, Ljungqvist, and Lu 2007), in order to achieve portfolio diversification and larger deal flows. Through the syndicate, partners' complementary skills, knowledge, and contact networks (Lindsey 2008; Hsu 2004), are also able to generate additional value in their portfolio companies (Brander, Amit, and Antweiler 2002). Reputational mechanisms, repeated relationships, and reciprocity diminish potential agency conflicts among the syndicate partners. The investment patterns of private equity syndicates, involving partners from several countries, are likely to differ from those of single investors and domestic syndicates, since transnational private equity syndicates may invest in the most promising countries at a relatively low cost, relying on the information provided by the network's local partner. Complementary skills within transnational private equity syndicates, such as a syndicate's familiarity with capital and product markets in several countries, may be particularly valuable to portfolio companies planning an expansion into markets outside their home countries.

PRIVATE EQUITY PERFORMANCE

The last issue that we want to discuss is private equity performance. We start by briefly analyzing the literature that studies the return on PE. We then discuss the most important performance measures that have been developed in the literature and the European experience.

The Literature

There exists a growing literature that examines the return of private equity investments using detailed macro and micro data.

Kaplan and Schoar (KS) (2005) investigated individual fund returns and found that performance increases with experience and is persistent: General partners, whose funds outperform the industry in one fund, are likely to outperform the industry in the next and vice versa. Their analyses are based on fund level data of a sample of 746 private equity funds, which is obtained from Venture Economics. In their study they also show that better performing funds are more likely to increase follow-on funds and that average returns earned by PE investors, in funds started in 1995, exceed those of the S&P 500 gross of fees, in the same period.

Phalippou and Zollo (2005) use an updated version of KS dataset and, after adjusting for additional funds, and weighting by the present value of invested capital, they find that returns by private equity funds have been 3.3 percent below the return on public equity markets. Ljungqvist and Richardson (2003a,b) use a dataset that contains detailed information on cash flows of individual investments, to study the behavior of private equity fund managers. Following a cash flow–based approach, they focus on mature and liquidated funds. They report an average outperformance of the private equity investments of 6 to 8 percent relative to S&P 500, and of 3 to 6 percent relative to the NASDAQ composite Index. They also find that fund managers time their investment and exit decisions in response to competitive conditions in the market for private equity and that improvements in investment opportunities increase performance.

Kaserer and Diller (2005) analyze the determinants of European private equity returns using a comprehensive data set provided by Thomson Venture Economics. They document the typical time pattern of cash flows for European private equity funds. Specifically, it is recorded that the average European private equity fund draws down 23 percent of total committed capital on the vintage date; within the first three years 60 percent of the total commitment is drawn down. It turned out that limited partners on average get back the money invested in slightly more than seven years. They show that GPs' skills as well as the stand-alone investment risk of a fund have a significant impact on its returns. Moreover, they seem to be unrelated to stock market returns and negatively correlated with the growth rates of the economy as a whole. They also calculate various performance measures in the period from 1980 to June 2003. For that purpose they use only liquidated funds or funds with a small residual net asset value, and they analyze to what extent performance measures are associated with specific funds characteristics, such as size, payback period, and vintage year, respectively. While the payback period and the vintage year seem to have a statistically significant influence on a fund's performance, the results with respect to size are inconclusive.

Schmidt, Nowak, and Knigge (2006) study timing abilities of private equity fund managers using a unique set of cash-flow data. They show that investment timing has an effect on the performance of venture-capital funds.

Chen, Baierl, and Kaplan (2002) examine 148 venture capital funds using TVE-data. The authors explain the long-term risk-return characteristics of venture capital investment and its role in a long-term strategic asset allocation. While there are limited market performance data on venture capital, they find that from 1960 through 1999, venture capital has had an annual arithmetic average return of 45 percent with a standard deviation of 115.6 percent. The geometric average return (compounded average) is estimated to be about 13 percent. The correlation coefficient between venture capital and public stocks is estimated to be 0.04 percent. Because of its relatively low correlation with stocks, an allocation to venture capital of 2 to 9 percent is warranted for an aggressive portfolio (i.e., all-equity).

Performance Measures

It is usually believed that private equity performance is much higher than that attained through traditional public market investment. However, to assess the performance of private equity investment is rather difficult. In fact private equity funds have a typical finite life of 10 to 12 years: they invest the capital committed by investors in the first half while their proceeds primarily occur during the second half of their life.

As a result, valuation of ongoing private equity investments are inevitably imprecise since equities of private equity companies are not continuously traded and funds differ in the extent to which they attempt to "mark the market."[5] In addition, if performance is measured before the fund has exited all the investments, then the *residual value*, the net asset value, is measured by the fund itself, creating clearly a bias. Therefore, a private equity fund's return estimated on the basis of net asset values (NAV) is biased. As a consequence, PE funds performance should be realistically and accurately measured only at the end of their life, when viable investments are realized. However that would entail an evaluation on a very limited number of funds as more recent funds would be systematically left out.

One possible solution would be to rely on only very long-term returns. However, since the returns are realized only when the company in which the funds have invested is acquired or is introduced on the stock market, that is, when the value of the company is significant, we might incur a selection bias. The observed returns belongs only to the firms whose value has increased. This selection bias has been studied by Cochrane (2005) for U.S. venture capital and it can be particularly severe. When taken into account, Cochrane estimates of the average returns of venture capital drop from 108 to 15 percent per year. On the contrary, at the fund level, the measured performance includes both successful as well as failure investments, dampening the bias. The other possible solution would be to measure private equity returns at individual direct investment or at the fund level. The latter measure reduces a possible selection bias that might occur using the first measure. Therefore we will concentrate our analyses on fund performance data.

The most widely used measure of PE funds performance is the internal rate of return (IRR), net of management fees, and carried interest generated, which is the annualized rate of return of all corresponding cash flows. The calculation of the IRR takes into consideration the timing of cash contributions and distributions to and from the partnership and the length of time an investment has been held:

$$\sum\nolimits_{i=0}^{T} cf_i (1 + IRR)^{-1} = 0 \tag{20.1}$$

where T is the lifetime of the fund and cf_i is the cash flow accrued in period t (IRR[CF]). In the case of unrealized investments the residual values are treated as a terminal period cash flow to investors, allowing the researcher to consider the net asset value of existing assets (IRR[NAV]). The valuation bias caused by this approach becomes less important the smaller the impact of this last hypothetical cash flow is.

In general, the performance based on these two returns measures is not equal. Kaplan and Schoar (2005) compute the correlation between IRR(CF) and IRR(NAV) for funds of five years old or older, correlation which is about 0.9 in the United States, and conclude that the two returns should deliver a similar valuation. However, as pointed out by Groh and Gottschalg (2008), a high correlation means only that the changes of the two measures are correlated over the fund's life.

The use of IRR, as a measure of performance, has some other important drawbacks: First, it assumes that the cash flow generated by the investment is reinvested at an interest rate equal to the IRR. Second, the timing of the underlying cash flows have a high effect on it and in the case of PE, the pattern of cash flow is different from the "buy-and-hold" strategy of the public equities.

For these reasons, other measures of performance have been developed in the literature. A more suitable approach to compare the performance of private equity to public market investments is the profitability index (PI), the present value of the cash flows received by investors divided by the present value of the capital paid by investors. There are various measures of this index: the most widely reported are the total amount distributed to investors as a percentage of paid-in capital (DPI); and the total amount distributed plus the residual value attributable to investors as a percentage of paid-in capital (TVPI).

By using the rate of return of comparable public market investments as the discount rate in these present value calculations, it is possible to obtain a PI that directly indicates outperformance of the comparable public market investments and which is referred to as Public Market Equivalent (PME) return:

$$PME = \sum_{t=1}^{t=T} cf_t \prod_{i=t+1}^{T} (1 + R_{it}) \bigg/ \prod_{t=1}^{T} (1 + R_{it}) \tag{20.2}$$

where R_{it} is the net return on the public market index to which the investment is compared, in period t, and cf_t is the cash-flow distribution of the private equity fund in period t. PME assumes that intermediate cash flows are reinvested in the public bench mark, and hence it shows the amount of money necessary to invest in the public market index for every dollar invested in the private equity fund in order to yield an equivalent cash flow to the ones generated by the fund. Consequently, a PME higher than one indicates that the private equity investment outperforms the public market alternative, providing the LPs with a sensible and useful measure of relative return.

Evidence from Europe

We can now measure performance in Europe using the above indices. Over the years, the European Venture Capital Association (EVCA) has become the primary source for information about the private equity industry in Europe. In association with Thomson Venture Economics, EVCA has been collecting information, resulting in comprehensive data going back to 1984, while data on performance have been collected since 1996. As we have affirmed in a previous paragraph, the dataset is, however, biased. Data are collected from two primary sources, GPs and LPs, via questionnaires. Because the data are self-reported, there are clearly biases, because GPs tend not to disclose performance figures for funds when negative, that is, in the first few years of existence. This is the case of the period 2000 to 2003, in which the representativeness of the sample decreases. The data are also subject to other biases. First of all, as highlighted in the previous section, reported NAV are evaluated by the GPs. Hence they are subjective valuations. Second, their value might even be a function of the different accounting standards around the world.

TVE calculates three main types of IRRs: the cumulative return from the inception, horizon returns, and time-weighted returns. The first is an IRR calculation from the inception of the fund to a certain reporting time period, taking into account all the inflows and outflows. The horizon return is an IRR calculation between points in time, where the beginning point is variable and the end point is fixed. The time-weighted return is calculated by computing the rate of return between two or more periods and multiplying these returns together geometrically, then taking a geometric mean of the results. Finally they also compute the TVPI, which is the total amount distributed plus the residual value attributable to investors as a percentage of paid-in capital.

In this section, we present the results that have been obtained with respect to IRRs. Exhibit 20.15 attests to the performance obtained with respect to NAV-based IRRs (IRR [NAV]). This exhibit is directly taken from TVE. All the figures are net of management fees and carried interest, and represent the net return to limited partners.

As one can see, funds with vintage years after 2000 have performed unsatisfactory. Evidently, this is due to a decline in market prices since 2000 and the induced pressure to decrease the book values of portfolio companies. Additionally, the J-curve phenomenon may be responsible for the negative IRR (NAV) of the funds founded in the years 2000 till 2003.[6]

From the exhibit, it appears clear that funds with vintage years 1992 to 1997 performed rather well on the basis of the IRR (NAV). In Exhibits 20.12 and 20.13,

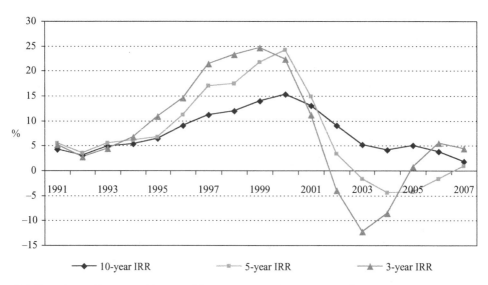

Exhibit 20.12   European Venture: Three-, Five-, and Ten-Year Rolling IRRs

the three-, five-, and ten-year rolling IRR illustrate the development of European private equity performances over time until the end of 2007. When looking at the performance of all funds in recent years, the convergence of the performance of all investment registered in 2000 is weakening with a gap between buyout funds and venture funds, with buyout having a consistently higher IRRs.

In Exhibit 20.14, the returns are broken down by stages of investment. In the past 27 years, if all such investments were considered as single European portfolio, the IRR would have been extremely low at any horizon. Returns are

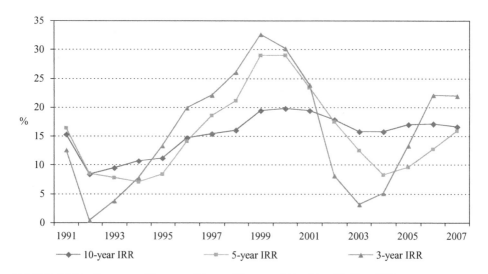

Exhibit 20.13   European Buyouts: Three-, Five-, and Ten-Year Rolling IRRs

Exhibit 20.14 Indicators Show Good Average Performance for Europe
European Private Equity Funds Formed 1980–2007
Investment Horizon IRR (%) for period ending 31-Dec-2007

	3-year	5-year	10-year	20-year
Early Stage	2.03	−4.70	−1.1	0.00
Development	6.09	1.02	7.01	8.05
Balanced	6.06	−1.80	7.09	8.01
All Venture	4.04	0.09	1.08	4.06
Buyouts	21.09	15.09	16.06	16.02
Generalist	15.02	9.00	8.00	9.05
All Private Equity	17.01	11.05	11.05	11.09

Source: Thomson Financial on behalf of EVCA.

instead higher in the case of later stage and buyout financing. Balanced venture capital funds exhibit higher average returns while buyouts reach an average IRR of 15 to 20 percent. However, returns on buyouts tend to overstate their returns relative to returns on VC investments, because they are highly leveraged (see also Exhibit 20.15).

Finally, Exhibit 20.16 shows the PME-based performance measure, which is calculated by investing the equivalent cash flows that were invested in private equity into the public market index. Then, an equivalent IRR is calculated for each index. It is calculated using a publicly available index, the MSCI Europe Index, a European government bond performance index, the J.P. Morgan European Government Bond index, the HSBC Small Company Index, and Morgan Stanley Euro Equity index. The exhibit shows that PEs outperform consistently public markets.

CONCLUSION

The European private equity market has been presented as a homogeneous pan-European market. Unfortunately, the PE markets are still highly fragmented, even though a risk capital market for all of Europe is a strategic objective of the European

Exhibit 20.15 European Performance by Vintage-Year Groups
Net IRRs to Investors Grouped by Vintage Years from Inception to 31-Dec-2007

Stage	1980–1984		1985–1989		1990–1994		1995–1999		2000–2004		2005–2007	
	IRR	DPI	IRR	DPI	IRR	DPI	IRR	DPI	IRR	DPI	IRR	DPI
All Venture	6.05	0.08	8.01	1.46	8.07	1.04	4.03	0.07	−2.00	0.16	0.04	0.03
All Buyouts	9.02	0.10	12.06	1.05	19.04	0.11	12.06	1.24	22.00	1.04	3.05	0.13
All Private Equity	9.05	1.32	8.09	1.18	15.06	0.09	9.08	1.08	16.20	0.06	3.01	0.12

Source: Thomson Financial on behalf of EVCA.

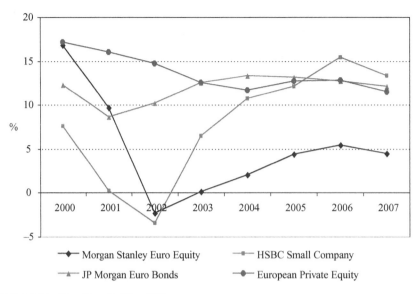

Exhibit 20.16 Ten-Year Rolling IRR

Union. The standing of the private equity market differs considerably from country to country in Europe. According to the European Private Equity Survey, the amount of funds has increased substantially over recent years, but still represents less than 5 percent of the European GDP. The percentage varies from country to country, as Exhibit 20.18 shows, and is valid both for the percentage of VC and of BO over each country GDP (see Exhibits 20.17 and 20.18).

This holds for both structural and cyclical aspects. The efficiency of the EU private equity industry suffers from an overly complex and ill-suited fund-structuring environment that limits and does not support cross-border investing. The additional costs and the additional risks for investors and funds associated with this serve to make the European industry less effective than it could be, particularly in comparison with the United States.

Exhibit 20.17 Venture Capital and Buyout, 2000–2006

Year	VC as % of GDP	BO as % of GDP
2000	0,22	0,17
2001	0,13	0,13
2002	0,10	0,18
2003	0,08	0,21
2004	0,10	0,26
2005	0,11	0,31
2006	0,15	0,45

Source: EVCA Yearbook 2007.

Exhibit 20.18 2007 Investment as Percent of GDP (%)

	Investments/GDP
United Kingdom	1,69
Sweden	1,25
Netherlands	0,70
France	0,66
Europe	0,58
Finland	0,56
Denmark	0,53
Norway	0,34
Germany	0,30
Switzerland	0,29
Spain	0,29
Belgium	0,28
Romania	0,24
Greece	0,19
Poland	0,18
Ireland	0,15
Czech Republic	0,10
Portugal	0,09
Italy	0,09
Austria	0,09
Hungary	0,03

Source: EVCA Yearbook 2007 & PEREP_Analytics for 2007 figures.

To overcome these difficulties, the member states have partly harmonized their legislation, but there are still major differences between their tax systems and legal arrangements, such as in insolvency law. The frictions that remain reduce liquidity and market capitalization. This weighs on the efficiency of European private equity financing and it is one of its most significant structural disadvantages compared with the United States.

The legal framework and the tax systems in the European states influence the national PE markets in two ways: first, on the supply side, the private equity companies are directly affected by taxes and regulations, and, second, on the demand side, entrepreneurs and company founders are either supported or hampered by the frameworks.

The EU institutions and Member States have been urged to take appropriate steps to codify the mutual recognition of each other's fiscally transparent private equity fund structures for capital gains. Guiding principle have been developed by major experts.

In particular, from the investor's point of view, the tax systems should be simple, transparent, and nondiscriminatory. This means that the tax office should not treat investments in PE funds any differently from those in direct company stakes and should prevent double taxation.

Company founders and entrepreneurs attach importance to a low level of regulation and red tape, as this means that they can concentrate on their actual business.
Low income-tax rates promote performance. Low corporate taxes, especially for
companies set up as partnerships, also encourage entrepreneurial activity.

The European Venture Capital Association has developed an indicator that
roughly reflects the quality of the tax and legal frameworks in the different countries of Europe. The index shows that the United Kingdom, Luxembourg, and
Ireland had the most favorable environments for the PE industry in 2004. Finland,
Germany, Austria, and Denmark were the worst environments according to this
ranking. Finland nevertheless has a relatively large PE market, while Germany
and Denmark occupy mid-table positions in the ranking of European PE markets
according to relative size. This suggests that the legal and tax systems are very
important, but do not have a dominant influence on the development of the PE
market.

United Kingdom, in particular, has a leadership role because it has a more established capital market than in continental Europe, a functioning market segment
for initial public offerings (IPOs), and strong economic growth.

The reason that functioning stock exchange access is so important for the
PE market is that the IPO is the most lucrative form of exit channel. Without a
few extremely profitable holdings, it is impossible to achieve the average returns
investors demand. Investors expect a premium for the higher risk of this asset class.
Write-off rates of 40 percent or more are not uncommon in the portfolios of the PE
companies. More generally, countries without a functioning market segment for
IPOs will not be able to raise the significance of their PE markets substantially in
the long run.

NOTES

1. See Bottazzi and Da Rin (2002) for an analysis of the VC experience in Europe.
2. See Cendrowski, H., J.P. Martin, and L.W. Petro (2008).
3. See Bottazzi and Da Rin (2001).
4. The leading example of such an entity is 3i, which is one of the largest private equity
   organizations in Europe (certainly by number of portfolio companies, if not capital under
   management).
5. Within Europe, there has been an initiative to agree valuation guidelines, and there now
   exists an agreed-upon approach to valuation that has been endorsed by all the main
   national industry associations in Europe, and many countries outside Europe.
6. The life-cycle of private equity funds requires at least six years to deliver significant
   returns. In the early years of a typical fund the returns are largely negative.

REFERENCES

Aizenman, Joshua, and Jake Kendall. 2008. The internationalization of venture capital
    and private equity. NBER Working Paper No. W14344. Available at SSRN: ssrn.com/
    Abstract=1271377.
Axelson, Ulf, Per Stromberg, and Michael Weisbach. 2007. Why are buyouts levered? The
    financial structure of private equity funds. *Journal of Finance*, forthcoming.

Baker, George, and Cynthia Montgomery. 1994. Conglomerates and LBO associations: A comparison of organizational forms. Harvard Business School Working Paper.

Balboa, Marina, and José Marti. 2001. The determinants of private equity fund-raising in western Europe. EFMA Lugano Meetings. Available at SSRN: ssrn.com/abstract= 269789.

Barron, John M., and Neven T. Valev. 2000. International lending by U.S. banks. *Journal of Money, Credit and Banking* 32 (3):357–381.

Black, Bernard, and Ronald Gilson. 1998. Venture capital and the structure of financial markets: Banks versus stock markets. *Journal of Financial Economics* 47 (1):243–277.

Bottazzi, Laura, and Marco Da Rin. 2002. European venture capital. *Economic Policy* 34 (April):231–269.

Bottazzi Laura, T. Hellmann, and Marco Da Rin. 2008a. What is the role of legal systems in financial intermediation? Theory and evidence. *Journal of Financial Intermediation*.

Bottazzi Laura, Thomas Hellmann, and Marco Da Rin. 2008b. Who are the active investors? Evidence from venture capital. *Journal of Financial Economics* 89 (3):488–512.

Brander, James A., Raphael Amit, and Werner Antweiler. 2002. Venture capital syndication: Improved venture selection versus the value-added hypotheses. *Journal of Economics and Management Strategy* 11 (3):423–451.

Brennan, Michael J., and H. Henry Cao. 1997. International portfolio investment flows. *Journal of Finance* 52 (5):1851–1880.

Cendrowski, Harry, James P. Martin, and Louis W. Petro. 2008. *Private equity: History, governance, and operations.* Hoboken, NJ: John Wiley & Sons.

Chen Peng, Gary T. Baierl, and Paul D. Kaplan. 2002. Venture capital and its role in strategic asset allocation. *Journal of Portfolio Management* (Winter):83–89.

Cochrane, John. 2005. The risk and return of venture capital. *Journal of Financial Economics* 75 (1):3–52.

Cumming, Douglas, and Sofia Johan. 2007. Regulatory harmonization and the development of private equity markets. *Journal of Banking & Finance* 31 (10):3218–3250.

EVCA. 2006. Preliminary activity figures, 2005.

EVCA. 2007. European benchmark performance statistics. EVCA Statistics & Performance Working Group Paper, March.

EVCA. 2007. Preliminary performance figures, 2005.

Gelos, R. Gaston, and Shang-Jin Wei. 2004. Transparency and international portfolio holdings. *Journal of Finance, American Finance Association* 60 (6):2987–3020.

Goldberg, Linda S. 2005. The international exposure of U.S. banks. NBER Working paper 11365.

Goldberg, Linda S. 2007. Financial sector FDI and host countries: New and old lessons. *Economic Policy Review* 13:1.

Gompers, Paul. 1994. The rise and fall of venture capital. *Business and Economic History* 23 (2):1–26.

Groh, Alexander P., and Oliver Gottschalg. 2008. Measuring the risk-adjusted performance of U.S. buyouts. NBER Working Paper No. W14148. Available at SSRN: ssrn.com/abstract=1152689.

Guiso Luigi, Paola Sapienza, and Luigi Zingales. 2006. Does culture affect economic outcomes? *Journal of Economic Perspectives* 20 (2):23–48.

Hochberg, Yael V., Alexander Ljungqvist, and Yang Lu. 2007. Whom you know matters: Venture capital networks and investment performance. *Journal of Finance* 62 (1):251–301.

Hsu, David H. 2004. What do entrepreneurs pay for venture capital affiliation? *Journal of Finance* 59 (4):1805–1844.

Jenkinson, Tim. 2008. The development and performance of European private equity. OFRC, Working Papers Series, No. 2008.

Jones, Charles M., and Matthew Rhodes-Kropf. 2003. The price of diversifiable risk in venture capital and private equity. AFA 2003 Washington, DC, Meetings. Available at SSRN: ssrn.com/abstract=342841.

Kandel, Eugene, Dima Leshchinskii, and Harry Yuklea. 2006. VC funds: Aging brings myopia. EFA 2006 Zurich Meetings Paper. Available at SSRN: ssrn.com/abstract=905963.

Kaplan, Steven N., and Jeremy C. Stein. 1993. The evolution of buyout pricing and financial structure in the 1980s. *Quarterly Journal of Economics* 108:313–357.

Kaplan, Steven N., Frederic Martel, and Per Stromberg. 2007. How does legal enforcement and experience affect financial contracts? *Journal of Financial Intermediation* 16:273–311.

Kaplan, Steven N., and Antoinette Schoar. 2005. Private equity performance: Returns, persistence, and capital flows. *Journal of Finance* 60 (4):1791–1823.

Kaserer, Christoph, and Christian Diller. 2005. Private equity funds: Return characteristics, return drivers, and consequences for investors. *Journal of Financial Transformation* (Wealth issue) 15:107–119.

Lerner, Josh. 1994a. Venture capitalists and the decision to go public. *Journal of Financial Economics* 35 (1):293–316.

Lerner, Josh. 1994b. The syndication of venture capital investments. *Financial Management* 23 (3):16–27.

Lerner, Josh, and Antoinette Schoar. 2004. The illiquidity puzzle: Theory and evidence from private equity. *The Journal of Financial Economics* 72 (1):3–40.

Lerner, Josh, and Antoinette Schoar. 2005. Does legal enforcement affect financial transactions? The contractual channel in prvivate equity. *Quarterly Journal of Economics* 120:223–246.

Lindsey, Laura. 2008. Blurring firm boundaries: The role of venture capital in strategic alliances. *Journal of Finance* 63 (3):1137–1168.

Ljungqvist, Alexander, and Matthew Richardson. 2003a. The investment behavior of private equity fund managers. Working Paper Series, RICAFE Working Paper No. 005, October.

Ljungqvist, Alexander, and Matthew Richardson. 2003b. The cash flow, return, and risk characteristics of private equity. NYU, Finance Working Paper No. 03-001, January.

Metrick, Andrew, and Yasuda, Ayako. 2008. The economics of private equity funds. *Review of Financial Studies*, forthcoming.

Michelacci, Claudio, and Javier Suarez. 2004. Business creation and the stock market. *Review of Economic Studies* 71 (2):459–481.

National Science Board. 2000. Science and engineering indicators, available at www.nsf.gov/statistics/seind00/pdfstart.htm.

Phalippou, Ludovic, and Maurizio Zollo. 2005. What drives private equity fund performance? Working paper, SSRN. http://fic.wharton.upenn.edu/fic/papers/05/p0541.html.

Portes, Richard, and Hélène Rey. 2005. The determinants of cross-border equity flows. *Journal of International Economics* 65 (2):269–296.

Sahlman, William. 1990. The structure and governance of venture-capital organizations. *Journal of Financial Economics* 27 (2):273–521.

Schmidt, Daniel, Eric Nowak, and Alexander Knigge. 2006. Private equity funds: Return characteristics, return drivers, and consequences for investors. *Journal of Financial Transformation* 16:123–134.

Sorenson, Olav, and Toby E. Stuart. 2001. Syndication networks and the spatial distribution of venture capital investments. *American Journal of Sociology* 106 (6):1546–1588.

Swensen, David. 2000. Pioneering portfolio management: An unconventional approach to institutional investment. New York: Free Press.

Wright, Mike, and Ken Robbie. 1998. Venture capital and private equity: A review and synthesis. *Journal of Business Finance and Accounting* 25 (5/6):521–570.

Wright, Mike, Steve Thompson, and Ken Robbie. 1992. Venture capital and management-led buyouts: A European perspective. *Journal of Business Venturing* 7 (1):47–71.

ABOUT THE AUTHOR

Laura Bottazzi received a Ph.D. in Economics from M.I.T. and is Professor of Economics at Bologna University. She is a Fellow of IGIER, of the Fondation Banque de France, and of RCEA. In 2006 she has won, together with Marco Da Rin and Thomas Hellmann, the NASDAQ Award for the best paper on capital formation. She specializes in international finance. She has published articles in academic journals such as *Journal of Financial Economics*, *Economic Journal*, *Journal of Financial Intermediation*, and the *Journal of Money Credit and Banking*.

CHAPTER 21

Private Equity and Leveraged Buyouts in Italy

To Prohibit or Not to Prohibit, That Is the Question

SIMONA ZAMBELLI
Professor, University of Bologna, Department of Management, Forlì School of Business

INTRODUCTION

The legal environment regulating mergers and acquisitions is essential for the development of the private equity (PE) industry and leveraged buyout (LBO) transactions.[1] Recent economic literature demonstrates how the legal environment affects the behavior of private equity investors in line with the La Porta, Lopez-De-Silanes, Shleifer, and Vishny (1997, 1998) studies (see, e.g., Cumming, Schmidt, and Walz 2008, Kaplan, Martel, and Stromberg 2006, Lerner and Schoar 2005, Cumming, Fleming, and Schwienbacher 2006, Kaplan and Stromberg 2004; Allen and Song 2003). Despite the existence of growing literature highlighting the positive impacts of PE and LBO transactions on the performance of acquired firms (see, among others, Davis, Haltiwanger, Jarmin, Lerner, and Miranda 2008; Achleitner, Nathusius, Herman, and Lerner 2008; Jelic 2008; Amess and Wright 2007; Cumming et al. 2006, 2007; Guo, Hotchkiss, and Song 2007; Nikoskelainen and Wright 2007; Renneboog 2007; Cao and Lerner 2009; Wright, Wilson, and Robbie 1996; Wright, Renneboog, Simons, and Scholes 2006[2]), a current international concern is whether PE transactions, and especially LBOs, should be allowed without restrictions or be heavily regulated instead (see, e.g., the Financial Services Authority 2006 discussion paper).[3] Regulatory restrictions may be introduced by legislators around the world in order to prevent potential opportunistic behaviors by management to the detriment of the target's stakeholders (Ferran 2007). In the economic literature relatively little attention is dedicated to the effects of regulation on the PE market. This chapter aims at contributing to filling in this gap, by focusing on the regulation of LBO transactions within the Italian PE market.

The recent evolution of the Italian PE market shows a puzzling trend that seems highly correlated with the latest changes in the domestic corporate governance law (Cumming and Zambelli 2009).[4] These regulatory changes may provide an innovative solution to the current international criticism against LBO transactions. In the United States, critics have even argued that LBOs should be prohibited outright, given the high default risk involved and the potential negative effects on the target's stakeholders (Stein 2006). As highlighted by Bongaerts and Charlier (2009) and Jelic (2008), private equity investors financing LBOs have even been qualified as "locusts"[5] who contribute to the weakening of the acquired firm and destroy jobs. In line with this view, Italian scholars (doctrine) and courts (jurisprudence) have strongly criticized LBOs over the last decade, emphasizing the need for more regulatory restrictions of this type of transaction in order to better protect the interests of the acquired companies (Zambelli 2008). In 2000, the Italian Supreme Court further reinforced this view by deeming the LBO scheme illegal and prohibited the adoption of such a financial technique within the domestic buyout market (Supreme Court Decision 5503/2000). This decision increased the legal uncertainty on the consequences of carrying out LBOs and probably prevented entrepreneurs and PE investors from undertaking these types of deals. In 2004, Italy introduced a new corporate governance reform that overruled the Supreme Court decision and legalized LBOs under certain disclosure conditions (Legislative Decree number 6/2003, applicable as of January 1, 2004, hereafter the 2004 reform). Notwithstanding the new corporate governance reform, several issues remain unresolved, and the legitimacy of certain types of LBOs is still debated.[6]

In line with the current international criticism surrounding the legitimacy of LBOs, in this chapter we intend to discuss the most critical issues raised against LBOs, as well as to analyze the economic impact of the 2004 corporate governance reform that legalized these types of transactions. In particular, the purpose of this chapter is threefold: (1) to discuss the evolution of the Italian PE market in association with the most relevant changes in the Italian regulatory environment; (2) to shed some light on unresolved issues associated with the Italian LBO regulation that may affect the validity of LBOs in the future, especially with reference to investors' liability; and (3) to analyze the economic impact of the new LBO reform on the Italian buyout market and investor's behavior. This analysis is based upon a new hand-collected dataset derived from a survey of private equity investors operating in Italy. The database consists of 103 target firms acquired during the 1999 to 2006 period and includes approximately 85 percent of the buyout funds actively involved in Italy over the same period. The Italian buyout market, whose transactions were previously prohibited and only recently legalized, offers a unique example that allows us to better evaluate the international debate on the legitimacy of LBOs, as well as the impact of the new LBO reform on investors' behavior.

The remainder of this chapter is organized as follows. The next section describes the evolution of the buyout market in association with the changes in its regulatory environment. The third section discusses the main critical aspects ("side effects") of LBOs. The fourth section focuses on the legal environment regulating LBOs. First, the fourth section sheds some lights on the reasons why LBOs were considered illegal and prohibited in Italy. Second, it describes the recent LBO reform introduced in Italy, with the aim of legalizing LBO transactions under certain disclosure conditions. The fifth section analyzes the economic impact of the new LBO reform on the buyout market and on investor behavior. The last section provides concluding remarks.

THE BUYOUT MARKET AND ITS PUZZLING TREND

For the purpose of this chapter, we define a buyout as an acquisition of the risk equity capital of a firm (called target) by another company (called newco). Buyouts exist in many different forms and can be classified according to the party that originates the acquisition process. This results in the following types of buyouts:

- The *institutional buyout* (IBO) refers to the acquisition of part of the equity capital of a company by an institutional investor.
- The *management buyout* (MBO) is the acquisition of a company by its own management.
- The *management buy-in* (MBI) is the acquisition of a company by an outside management team.
- The *buy-in management buyout* (BIMBO) refers to the acquisition of a company by both outside and inside managers.
- The *management-employees buyout* (MEBO) refers to the acquisition of a target company by its own employees.
- The *turnaround buyout* occurs when outside investors acquire a company that is experiencing a financial crisis.[7]

The term *leveraged buyout,* on the other hand, describes a particular technique used to accomplish the acquisition. An LBO is a method of financing the acquisition, and can occur in conjunction with any of the above buyout types. In a leveraged buyout the acquisition of the target company is financed with a large amount of debt relative to the asset base of the acquired company (see, e.g., Axelson, Stromberg, and Weisbach 2007b; Wright, Thompson, and Robbie 1992; Wright, Hoskisson, Busenitz, and Dial 2001; Kaplan 1997; Jensen 1989).

In Italy, approximately 60 to 65 percent of the target value is typically financed by debt (Ferrari 2007; Capizzi 2005a, 2005b).[8] Over the last decade, the debt/equity ratio has progressively increased in Italy, from 1.6 in 1993 to 2.2 in 1998, and subsequently slightly decreased over time, approaching an average level of approximately 1.9 in 2006.[9] An LBO is also characterized by the fact that the debt financing is initially arranged by the newco under the expectation that it will be repaid by the target whose assets often serve as collateral.

Leveraged buyouts have always played a crucial role within the Italian private equity market. According to the Italian Venture Capital Association (AIFI), the total amount invested in LBOs during 2007 was €3,295 million, representing 78 percent of the entire PE industry.[10] Exhibit 21.1 provides some information on the evolution of the Italian buyout market from 1988 to 2007 (in terms of frequency, average deal size, and number of investors actively involved in the buyout industry). Both the volume and the value of buyouts carried out in Italy increased sharply over the 1990s. Subsequently, the evolution of buyouts in Italy followed a puzzling trend, alternating periods characterized by strong decreases in the number of buyouts (e.g., from 2000 to 2001) with periods characterized by sharp increases in the buyout frequencies (as seen after 2004).

One possible explanation of this interesting puzzle could be associated with the recent changes in the legal environment experienced by the Italian buyout industry, as summarized in Exhibit 21.2 and discussed in the following sections. As shown in Exhibit 21.2, in 2000 the Supreme Court deemed LBOs illegal in Italy

Exhibit 21.1 Buyout Market over the 1988–2007 Period

	1988	1989	1990	1991	1992	1993	1994	1995	1996	1997
Number of Buyouts	20	38	19	44	35	17	30	12	24	27
Average Value (ml. Euro)	1,1	0	1,3	2,3	2,2	3,8	3,3	2,9	6,5	7,2

	1998	1999	2000	2001	2002	2003	2004	2005	2006	2007
Number of Buyouts	38	65	53	30	76	59	48	75	100	87
Average Value (ml. Euro)	6,4	13,5	25,7	33,8	20,4	38,3	19,1	32	15,1	na
Total Amount Invested (ml. Euro)	242	878	1363	1014	1550	2258	916	2401	2444	3295
Percentage of Buyouts, Relative to Other PE Transactions	15%	18%	8%	6%	25%	18%	19%	27%	34%	29%
Number of Active Investors within the Buyout Market	na	na	35	21	36	36	30	44	54	50

Source: AIFI Yearbook and statistics reports; EVCA Yearbook, various years.

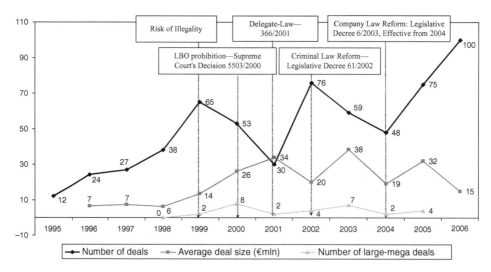

Exhibit 21.2 The Puzzling Evolution of the LBO Market in Comparison with Its Regulatory Changes over the Period 1995–2006

Source: AIFI Yearbook, various years; Zambelli (2008).

(Supreme Court's Decision 5503/2000) and prohibited investors from undertaking them.[11] The Supreme Court's decision increased the debate on the legitimacy of LBOs in Italy, rather than solving it. The legal uncertainty surrounding LBOs and the risk associated with these types of transactions raised concerns among private equity investors and probably diminished their incentive to undertake buyout deals. Despite the Court's prohibition, LBOs did not disappear from the market. Thereafter, by the end of 2001, the Italian Parliament announced its intention to overrule the Supreme Court Decision and to make LBOs legal (Delegated Law 366/2001). In 2002, a new criminal law came into force (Legislative Decree 61/2002) and new criminal prosecutions were introduced, with a potential applicability to LBOs. In 2004, a new corporate governance reform became effective (Legislative Decree number 6/2003, applicable as of January 1, 2004) and LBOs became legal under specific conditions, especially with reference to disclosure.

As demonstrated in Cumming and Zambelli (2009), the changes in the legal environment regulating LBOs have affected the evolution of the Italian buyout market (Exhibit 21.2). The puzzling trend of the Italian market appears more evident if compared with the evolution of the European buyout market (as illustrated in Exhibit 21.3). After 2001 (and especially after 2004), buyout investments increased more in Italy than in the United Kingdom and Europe in general (see the Annual PE Reports by: the Italian Venture Capital Association [AIFI], the British Venture Capital Association [BVCA], the European Venture Capital Association [EVCA]). As emphasized in Cumming and Zambelli (2009), the number of buyout transactions carried out in Italy over the 2001 to 2002 period increased from 6 percent to 25 percent, while pan-European buyout investments moved from 9 percent to 11 percent. On the contrary, the number of buyout deals completed in the United Kingdom over the same period decreased from 18 percent to 15 percent

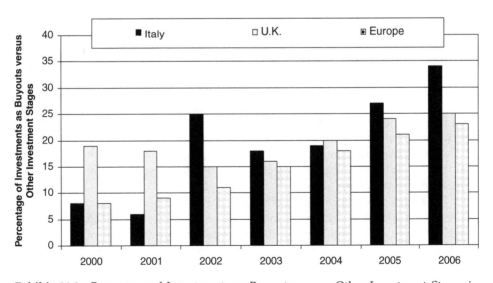

Exhibit 21.3 Percentage of Investments as Buyouts versus Other Investment Stages in Italy, Europe, and the United Kingdom, over the Period 2000–2006
Source: AIFI Yearbooks (for Italy), BVCA Annual Reports (for the United Kingdom), and EVCA Annual Reports (for pan-European averages).

(BVCA Annual Reports). After 2004, the number of buyout investments increased more in Italy than in both Europe and the United Kingdom. Over the period 2004 to 2006, pan-European averages gradually moved from 18 percent in 2004 to 23 percent in 2006 (EVCA Annual Reports). Similarly, buyouts in the United Kingdom increased from 20 percent in 2004 to 25 percent in 2006 (BVCA Annual Reports). In Italy, instead, the number of buyout investments increased with a greater speed, moving from 19 percent in 2004 to 27 percent in 2005, and 34 percent in 2006.[12]

As mentioned, over the last decade LBOs have been severely criticized and accused of contributing to the weakening of the target firms. Several LBO transactions have been invalidated by Italian courts (as discussed in the following section). In order to better understand the reasons underlying the criticism raised against LBOs, the purpose of the following section is to analyze the typical LBO scheme and to discuss the most critical issues associated with it.

THE LBO SCHEME AND RELATED CRITICISMS

Critical Features

Most of the criticisms against LBOs refer to the economic result underlying the LBO investment process. An LBO involves the acquisition of the equity capital of the target company with the adoption of a large portion of debt relative to the target's asset (Gilligan and Wright 2008; Amess and Wright 2007; Nikoskelainen and Wright 2007). A typical LBO transaction is accomplished via several steps.

The first step is represented by the establishment of a new company (newco), with the purpose of acquiring a specific firm (target). In order to accomplish the acquisition, the newco obtains debt financing (leverage) provided by lending institutions. The debt is used to acquire the majority of the target's shares.

Following the acquisition, the newco and the target are merged. The merger may take two forms: (1) forward merger and (2) reverse merger. In a forward merger the target is merged into the newco and the target legally disappears (the newco is the only surviving company). A reverse merger occurs when the newco is merged into the target, which is then the only remaining company. In both cases, the post-merger combined entity will enjoy all the rights and bear all the debts that the two prior companies had before. The term-leveraged buyout captures the fact that the merged firm has a higher leverage ratio (total debt/total assets) than the target firm had before the merger.

As a result of the merger, the debt originally arranged by the newco is merged into the target's liabilities, and any claims by preexisting newco creditors are then transferred to the target's assets.

The target company is expected to repay the debt obligation with its future cash flows and, as a consequence of the merger, the assets of the merged company secure the debt financing. In this manner, the target company bears most of the economic costs of its own acquisition. LBOs differ from other leveraged acquisitions because the debt is effectively secured by the acquired company and not by the buyer.

The typical LBO scheme summarized in the preceding discussion comprises several critical features.

First, the debt is arranged by the newco and is ultimately secured against the assets of the firm that is being acquired.

Second, the financing is obtained under the expectation that it will be repaid with the cash flows generated by the acquired company or by the sale of its nonstrategic assets. In this manner, the target has to pay the economic price of its own acquisition. PE investors who finance LBOs are even defined as "asset-strippers"[13] to reinforce the view that leveraged acquisitions increase the risk of depriving the target firm of the opportunity to use internally generated funds to undertake new investments.

Third, the archetypal LBO involves the merger between the newco and the target. As a result of the merger, the combined firm has a higher leverage ratio (total debt/total assets) than the target firm had before, and this may be detrimental for its financial equilibrium. The high degree of leverage that characterizes most post-LBO firms has at least two effects. On one hand, the presence of a high level of debt puts pressure on the management team and serves as a motivator and disciplinary device.[14] On the other hand, the increase in the leverage ratio increases the firm's default risk. The default risk tends to be especially high in cases of a turnaround leveraged buyout, where the target firm is already in a financial crisis before the LBO transaction.[15]

Furthermore, as emphasized in Cumming and Zambelli (2009), LBOs have also been accused of (1) increasing the probability of default of the target, (2) involving a lack of full disclosure against the interests of preexisting creditors and shareholders, (3) promoting a conflict of interest with managers against the target's shareholders, and (4) providing managers with greater incentive to violate their business duties against the interests of the company's stakeholders.

THE LBO LEGAL ENVIRONMENT: PAST, PRESENT, AND FUTURE TRENDS

The Past Debate

Prior to the 2004 Company Law Reform (hereafter the 2004 reform) the legitimacy of LBOs was uncertain and strongly debated in Italy, especially toward the end of the 1990s.[16] As emphasized in Zambelli (2008), several LBOs were invalidated by Italian courts as they were interpreted as instances of indirect financial assistance fraudulently provided by the target, with the intermediation of the newco, for the acquisition of the target's shares (a situation that was severely restricted by the Italian law).[17] Relevant criminal consequences were also applied to the managers and investors involved in the transaction, who ran the risk of receiving criminal prosecutions and sentences of up to a maximum of three years' imprisonment.

Divergent interpretations existed among legal scholars and courts. On one hand, the LBO scheme was perceived as a method of fraudulently allowing the target to provide a guarantee for the acquisition of its own shares, against Italian law ("substantial view"). On the other hand, some judges and legal scholars considered LBO transactions legal ("formal view").[18] The debate intensified in 2000 when the Supreme Court intervened and further reinforced the interpretation of considering the LBO scheme as illegal, and prohibited its adoption within the Italian context (Supreme Court Decision 5503/2000). This decision increased the debate on the legitimacy surrounding LBOs instead of solving it. The following section provides an overview of the relevant Italian case-law on LBOs.

The Inconsistent Case-Law and the Supreme Court Prohibition

Exhibit 21.4 summarizes the evolution of the legal environment regulating leveraged buyouts in Italy. The left-hand-side of the box shows the relevant jurisprudence against the validity of LBOs (Farmitalia case, Courgne' case, Pepperland case, D'Andria case) that contributed to increasing the uncertainty surrounding LBOs and the related transaction risk in the case of legal disputes.

As shown in Exhibit 21.4, the past case-law on LBOs was characterized by inconsistent and ambiguous decisions, which did not provide adequate interpretative guidance to legal scholars, entrepreneurs and investors.[19] For example, in 1992 the Civil Court of Milan decided in favor of the legitimacy of an LBO transaction (the Farmitalia case) accused of breaching the limits regulating the share-buyback (Civil Court of Milan, May 14, 1992). Surprisingly, a month later the criminal Court of Milan examined the same case and declared it illegal because it was considered to conflict with the limits regulating the acquisition by a company of its own shares (Criminal Court of Milan, June 30, 1992). In 1995, the Ivrea Court declared a leveraged buyout transaction (the Cuorgnè case) illegal because it contravened the financial assistance prohibition imposed by article 2358 of the Italian Civil Code (c.c.) (Court of Ivrea, August 12, 1995). A similar decision of illegality was made in May 1999 by the Court of Milan, with reference to the Pepperland case (Court of Milan, May 4, 1999). Considering the LBO scheme illegitimate was not the only feasible interpretation. Following a different line of reasoning, a decision by the Court of Milan (with reference to the Trenno case[20]) declared that LBO transactions should be considered legal if they are supported by "valid" business reasons aimed at promoting the development of the company with a proper project ("rule

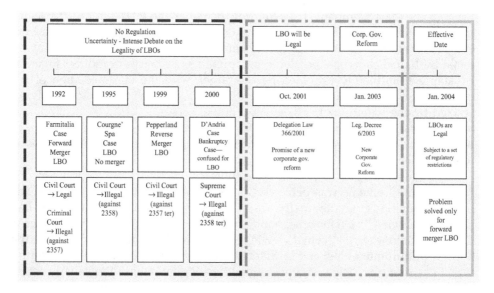

Exhibit 21.4   The Evolution of the LBO Reform in Italy

of reasons"). According to this principle, an LBO would be invalidated only in case of absence of a "valid" business reason underlying the LBO transaction. The decision on the Trenno case, however, did not provide investors with sufficient guidance, nor examples of business reasons that could have been considered relevant for the legitimacy of LBOs. Notwithstanding the uncertainty surrounding the applicability of the above principle ("rule of reasons"), the decision on the Trenno case represented an important change of perspective for the Italian doctrine and jurisprudence on LBOs.[21] In 2000, however, the Italian Supreme Court (Supreme Court's Decision 5503/2000, regarding the D'Andria case) declared the LBO scheme illegal by explicitly stating that the LBO scheme *cannot be imported into the Italian system because it is in contrast with article 2358 of the Civil Code*" (see Appendix 21.A for a critical discussion of the Supreme Court's Decision[22]).

The Investors' Reaction and the Subsequent Turning Point

The Supreme Court's decision mentioned above diminished the frequency of buyouts but did not exclude them altogether from the market. By looking at the AIFI statistics and at the Italian case-law over the last decade, it is puzzling to notice that LBOs were carried out anyway, despite their uncertain legitimacy, and especially in the form of mega deals (over €150 million) with a pyramidal structure (characterized by more than one newco, one of which was located abroad). Consequently, given the uncertainty surrounding the LBO-legitimacy and the related high transaction risk in case of a legal dispute, investors were willing to run this risk only for relevant deals, in terms of size and expected returns. Moreover, in order to minimize the risks of receiving an illegitimacy declaration by a court in case of a dispute, several buyout transactions were structured as multilayered deals, with more than one newco firm. Typically, a first holding company (newco 1) was established abroad with the only purpose of setting up a second firm (newco 2), usually located in Italy and fully capitalized by newco 1 (see Exhibit 21.5 for details). As discussed in Negri-Clementi and Montironi (2002) and Zambelli (2008), the acquisition of newco 2 was accomplished thanks to debt financing (D1)

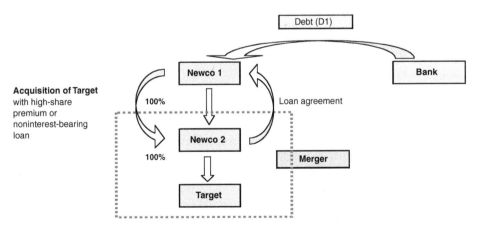

Exhibit 21.5 Multilayered Buyout Deal
Source: Zambelli (2008).

contracted by newco 1, and indirectly transferred to newco 2 (in the form of either high share premium or through a noninterest-bearing loan). Newco 2, in turn, was set up in Italy as a vehicle to purchase a majority equity stake in the target company (T). Following the acquisition of the target company, newco 2 and the target merged. Thereafter, once the merger procedure was completed, the share premium (or the noninterest-bearing loan) was paid back to newco 1 through a loan agreement between newco 2 and newco 1, and the latter could ultimately reimburse the original debt (D1). Silvestri (2005) also emphasizes the existence of another LBO structure adopted by investors to minimize the legal risk of receiving an illegality declaration. This structure implies the acquisition of the target company with short term bridge financing (D1), which is originally secured by newco shareholders only. Following the acquisition, newco, and target merge, the newly combined company receives a new medium-long–term loan (D2) secured against the assets of the merged firm. De facto, the new debt (D2) serves to payoff the original debt (D1) contracted by newco.[23]

Despite these complex buyout structures, the illegality risk was not eliminated and a reform was still necessary. By the end of 2001, the Italian Parliament assigned the government the task of reforming the corporate law, as well as issuing specific provisions in order to legalize LBOs (Bill of Law 366, October 2001, article 7, point d). This Bill of Law provided some hope for a new and more favorable legal treatment of LBOs. However, in 2002 the government issued a new criminal law (Legislative Decree 61/2002), adding a set of crimes potentially applicable to LBOs. A few years later, the Italian Government introduced a new Corporate Governance Law (the 2004 reform hereafter[24]), aimed at better qualifying LBOs, as well as legalizing the LBO technique under specific conditions (article 2501-bis civil code, introduced by: Legislative Decree 6/2003, applicable as of January 1, 2004[25]). The 2004 corporate law reform represents the most important turning point for the buyout industry in Italy. The 2004 reform diminished the incentive of adopting multilayered LBO structures. It also encouraged a more rapid growth of the buyout market, in terms of number of deals (which increased from 48 in 2004 to 100 in 2006) and number of investors actively involved in the industry (which rose from 30 in 2004, to 54 in 2006, as previously highlighted in Exhibit 21.1).

Notwithstanding the new LBO reform, a few issues remain unresolved and the legitimacy of certain types of LBOs is still under debate, especially with reference to some particular types of LBOs. In order to better evaluate potential unresolved issues and the legal risk that may affect the validity of LBOs in the future, the following section provides a closer examination of the reasons why LBOs were considered illegal over the last decade.

Regulatory Restrictions of LBOs prior to 2004: A Closer Look

The purpose of this section is to discuss in greater detail the regulatory restrictions applied by Italian courts to LBOs in order to invalidate this type of transaction.

As mentioned, prior to 2004 LBOs were severely criticized in Italy and their legitimacy was highly debated. At the core of the debate was the interpretation of the ultimate economic result of a leveraged buyout, often perceived as an indirect financial assistance fraudulently provided by the target for a share-buyback purpose ("substantial view" or "share-buyback view"[26]).

A closer examination of the Italian doctrine and jurisprudence reveals that the debate on the LBO legitimacy was focused around the interpretation of three provisions of the Civil Code: articles 2357, 2358, and 1344 of the Civil Code (see the Appendix 21.A for details[27]).

Article 2357 limits the possibility for a company to purchase its own shares (share buyback restrictions). The share-buyback is allowed only within the limits of the distributable net profits and shall not exceed 10 percent of the share capital. The above limits also apply to the purchases of shares implemented through the intermediation of a third party or fiduciary company. A famous case accused of eluding the provisions of article 2357 c.c. is represented by the Farmitalia case (the Decision of the Tribunal of Milan, May 14, 1992[28]).

Article 2358 prohibits a company from providing financial assistance for the purchase of its own shares (financial assistance ban). Famous cases accused of eluding the provisions of article 2358 c.c. are: The Manifattura di Cuorgnè case (Decision of Ivrea Tribunal, August 12, 1995), and the D'Andria case (Supreme Court Decision 5503/2000[29]).

Article 1344 invalidates any agreement performed with the intention of eluding imperative legal provisions.

According to the share buyback view, an LBO would represent merely a financial tool fraudulently adopted by the target with the sole purpose of eluding the law, providing financial assistance for the repurchase of its own shares. Therefore, the provision underlying Article 1344 would make the LBO transaction void. In line with the above interpretation, the economic result of an LBO transaction is to shift the debt obtained for the target's acquisition onto its assets, against the rights of preexisting unsecured creditors and minority shareholders. Following this reasoning, critics argued that after the completion of an LBO the target appears to acquire its own shares (share buyback) or to provide a guarantee for this purpose (financial assistance) through the intermediation of the newco, eluding the restrictions stated by Italian law in articles 2357-2358 of the Civil Code (c.c.).

A closely related argument against the validity of an LBO was associated with another provision of the Italian Civil Code (article 1344), according to which any agreement made with the intention of eluding imperative rules of the law should be invalidated and declared void. Applying article 1344 to LBOs, part of the doctrine supported the view ("substantial view") that the implicit purpose of the LBO scheme is to elude the financial assistance prohibition stated by article 2358, achieving exactly the result that the lawmaker intended to prohibit through article 2358.

This fraudulent result was considered particularly evident in the case of *non-merger LBOs*. In this case, the newco and the target do not merge and the target's assets often serve as a direct guarantee for the acquisition of its own share, contravening the application of the Italian law (article 2358). However, the legal validity of a *merger LBO* was also highly disputed. Critics argued that, as a consequence of the merger, the target's assets effectively become a guarantee for the payment of the debt previously contracted by the newco. The newco in turn was interpreted as an intermediary acting on behalf of the target company, and the merger was perceived only as an instrument to elude the law. The LBO scheme was then considered only an instrument to allow entrepreneurs to elude Italian law against the interests of the target's stakeholders. For these reasons, the LBO scheme was considered illegal and several LBO transactions were invalidated by courts (see Exhibit 21.4).[30] The transaction risk was particularly high in the case of *reverse merger LBOs* (where the newco is merged into the target, and the latter is the only surviving company). In this case, financial assistance for a share buyback purpose seemed more evident. As emphasized in Zambelli (2008), in a reverse merger LBO the newco is merged into the target and legally disappears. The target remains the only surviving company. As a consequence of the merger, the target's participation (originally acquired by the newco) will appear in the target's assets. This result is often interpreted as a share-buyback by judges. Moreover, once the merger is completed, the target's assets serve as a guarantee for the debt originally arranged by the newco for the acquisition of the target. This result is often interpreted as financial assistance provided by the target for the acquisition of its own shares.[31]

In case of a breach of the financial assistance ban, relevant criminal prosecutions were also applied to the directors involved in the transaction, who ran the risk of being punished with a sentence of up to three years of imprisonment (according to article 2630 c.c., 1st paragraph, point 2, now abolished by Legislative Decree 11/4/2002).

The European Context

The financial assistance prohibition for the acquisition of shares was originally introduced in the United Kingdom by the Companies Law Act 1928 (section 16), subsequently reframed in section 45 of the Companies Act 1929. A few exemptions existed though: for example, the financial assistance ban was not applied in the case of purchase of new shares (Wyatt 2004). The granting of financial assistance remained prohibited until the introduction of the Companies Law Act 1981 (subsequently reconfirmed by sections 151-158 of the Company Law Act 1985), which limited the financial assistance ban to public companies only and introduced a special procedure (known as the "whitewash procedure") to allow private companies to provide financial assistance for a share buyback purpose under certain conditions (for additional details on the evolution of the financial assistance ban within the United Kingdom context, see the Appendix 21.B[32]).

In Europe, the financial assistance prohibition was introduced on December 13, 1976, by article 23 of the Second European Commission Directive on Corporate Law (Directive 77/91/EC), according to which a company is not allowed to provide guarantees for the purchase of its own shares.[33] Thereafter, all European member states interpreted and implemented such financial assistance provision in different ways.[34] On one hand, some countries, such as the United Kingdom and Germany, introduced a set of exceptions to the financial assistance ban, restricting the prohibition to public companies only. Private companies are then allowed to provide guarantees for the acquisition of their own shares if certain requirements are satisfied (see, e.g., sections 151–158 of the U.K. Company Law Act 1985, now abolished, as summarized in Appendix 21.B). Instead, other countries, such as Italy, interpreted the Second Directive quite broadly, prohibiting any kind of financial assistance provided by public and private companies, and extending the prohibition to LBO transactions.[35]

In 2006, the European Union introduced a new Directive (European Directive 2006/68/EC) aimed at harmonizing the buyout legislations in Europe, as well as guaranteeing a more favorable legal treatment to the financial assistance event (see article 23). According to the new formulation of article 23, financial assistance shall now be permitted if certain conditions are fulfilled, such as shareholders' approval.[36] Each member state has two options:

1. to maintain the existing general prohibition on financial assistance;
2. to introduce new principles in order to apply the new formulation of article 23 and to legalize the financial assistance under certain conditions.

The Italian legislator has chosen the second option, and introduced an innovative reform of corporate governance law (Legislative Decree 6/2003, applicable as of January 1, 2004) aimed at legalizing LBO transactions under specific conditions (as discussed in the following section). This reform represented an important turning point for the Italian buyout market. It is worth noting that the 2004 corporate governance reform legalizes merger LBOs and clarifies that these types of deals should not be considered a breach of the financial assistance rule if a set of conditions are fulfilled. On September 15, 2008, Italy introduced a new law (Legislative Decree 142/2008), aimed at creating more exceptions to the financial assistance ban outlined by article 2358 c.c., in line with the principles included in the European Directive 2006/68.[37]

The following section highlights the requirements introduced by the 2004 reform for the legitimacy of LBOs.

The 2004 Reform: Conditions for the LBO Legitimacy and Unsolved Issues

Despite the international debate on whether or not to prohibit LBOs, Italy decided to legalize these types of transactions under the fulfillment of specific conditions (Legislative Decree 6/2003, applicable as of January 1, 2004).

This LBO reform is the result of several regulatory changes. In 2001 the Italian Parliament issued a bill of law (Law 366/2001) indicating a few guidelines for a reform of the entire corporate governance regulation. Among these, Parliament clearly stated that LBO transactions should never be considered illegal (article 7 point d).[38] However, this law was not directly applicable in Italy and had only formal efficacy. It was simply an enabling act through which Parliament assigned the Government the task of issuing one or more legislative decrees by 2002 in order to reform the Italian corporate law according to a set of principles and conditions. A few years later, the Government reformed the corporate governance law and introduced a new provision (article 2501-bis) in order to clarify the legal status of LBOs (Legislative Decree number 6/2003, applicable as of January 1, 2004). But, instead of declaring that LBOs should always be considered legal, the Government preferred to specify a set of requirements to be satisfied for the legitimacy of an LBO transaction (contingent legalization). In light of the new reform, LBOs are then presumed legal if certain conditions are fulfilled, especially with reference to information disclosure, fair deal certification, and business plan reasonableness.

Requirements for LBO Legitimacy

Article 2501-bis states that: "In case of merger between companies, one of which has assumed obligations to acquire control of the other, if by virtue of the merger the assets of the latter become the source of reimbursement of such obligations, the following rules apply." According to article 2051-bis, merger LBOs are no longer considered a breach of the financial assistance rule and are allowed under specific requirements as discussed below.[39]

1. First condition: *merger LBOs*. Under the new regulation, only certain types of buyouts are legalized. More specifically, Article 2501-bis applies only to those leveraged buyouts that:
   a. involve a merger between the newco and the target;
   b. are characterized by the absence of specific guarantees (such as a pledge) on the target's assets.[40] As a consequence, in the case of default of the target firm, the lender will not benefit from any particular priority claim over a specific target's asset. To the contrary, if the target plays an active role and provides a specific guarantee for the purchase of its own shares, the illegality risk remains and the transaction could be invalidated by a court because it is interpreted as a breach of the financial assistance rule (as seen over the last decade).

2. Second condition: *disclosure* on reasons, objectives, and sources of funds. Subsequent to the acquisition of the target's shares and its merger with the newco, the board of directors of each merging company must write an economic and financial report indicating:
   a. The business reasons justifying the entire LBO transaction (not only the merger);
   b. The objectives of the merger;
   c. A merger plan, containing information on the funding and a description of the expected cash flows to be used by the combined company to satisfy its obligations. Furthermore, the merger plan needs to show the share exchange ratio of each firm. The purpose of the merger plan is twofold:
      To show that the combined entity is able to meet all its financial obligations (including the debt originally contracted by the newco for the acquisition of the target's shares);
      To demonstrate that the target's stakeholders, especially minority shareholders and preexisting creditors, are not damaged by the LBO transaction.

3. Third condition: *experts' appraisal and auditors' report*. An independent financial expert must attest the fairness of the financial resources indicated in the business plan, especially with reference to their underlying assumptions, as well the reasonableness of the share exchange ratio (fairness report).[41] Ultimately, if one of the merging companies needs to certify its financial statements, an external auditors' report must be completed in order to validate the content of the merger plan.

Contrary to what has happened in the past, the burden of proof is now reversed: if the above requirements are satisfied, LBOs should then be considered legal, unless proven otherwise. The risk of illegality should be minimal if the LBO transaction is implemented by adhering to the requirements specified by the new law. Complex multilayered ownership structures (with more than one newco), typically adopted in the past to minimize the illegality risk of LBOs, are no longer necessary, at least from a legal point of view.

It is worth noting that the requirements outlined by article 2501-bis of the 2004 reform appear similar to those introduced in the United Kingdom through the "whitewash procedure," in order to allow private companies to provide financial assistance (see Appendix 21.B for details; see also the U.K. Companies Act 1985 sections 155–158). The Italian 2004 reform, however, took a step forward by allowing the financial assistance for an LBO purpose to all companies (both private and public firms). In the United Kingdom the whitewash procedure has been strongly criticized because it is considered excessively cumbersome and subsequently the U.K. Company Act 2006 abolished it. Therefore, private companies in the United Kingdom are now allowed to provide financial assistance without restrictions and the ban remains for public companies only.[42]

Considering the previous debate on the legitimacy of LBOs and the high transaction risk involved, the new Italian LBO reform represents a crucial step forward, which is in line with the recent European Union's intention of providing a more favorable legal environment to LBOs (see the European Directive 2006/68/EC). However, the debate on the legitimacy of LBOs is not over, especially with reference to the directors' liability in case of bankruptcy of the target. The following sections intend to discuss unresolved issues currently under debate.

Unresolved Issues

Within the European Union, the new Italian LBO reform provides an innovative approach to the regulation of merger LBOs. The corporate governance reform has definitely reduced the ambiguity surrounding the legal validity of LBOs in Italy and spurred the buyout market. However, the new LBO legislation has not completely resolved the debate on the legitimacy of LBOs: a few issues remain unresolved, especially with reference to the applicability of the requirements specified by the law.

First, according to the new LBO reform (article 2501-bis), the board of directors has to write a merger plan showing the entrepreneurial reasons justifying the transaction. But what type of "business reasons" should be considered valid for the legitimacy of an LBO deal? The law does not provide any interpretative guidelines in order to evaluate the reasons behind each LBO deal. This implies that, in the worst-case scenario in which a court must intervene to evaluate the transaction, the ultimate validity of an LBO deal is left to the discretion of the judge in charge of the case. As highlighted by La Torre and Rio (2002) *"It may prove difficult to ascertain a valid business reason for a merger in the case of a typical LBO carried out by professional investors such as private equity players, where a leveraged newco vehicle has been established solely for the purpose of the transaction."* We shall have to wait for new doctrine and jurisprudence in order to have clearer guidelines on the business reasons that might justify the merger and the transaction as a whole.

Second, article 2501-bis states that the business plan and the expected cash flows included in the merger plan should be validated by an independent financial expert (assessment on fairness). This is not an easy task to complete, given the high responsibility placed on the expert assessing the feasibility and reasonableness of the business plan.

Third, the reform only qualifies the legal status of certain types of LBO transactions. As noted, the new corporate governance regulation applies to merger LBOs only, excluding all the other types of LBO transactions. How should we consider the other types of LBOs that are not specifically disciplined by article 2501-bis? What are the consequences of undertaking them?

Over the past decade, criticisms on LBOs have been especially strong for reverse merger LBOs. The new reform does not even specify the type of merger (forward or reverse) that should be considered valid for the legitimacy of LBOs. The legal consequences of reverse LBO transactions (which occur when the newco is incorporated into the target company) remain uncertain for the same reasons emphasized in the preceding decade. In a reverse merger, the target is the only entity that remains after the merger. The economic result of the whole transaction may still be interpreted as a violation of the financial assistance prohibition and, in case of a dispute, it could be deemed illegal by a Court (according to the financial assistance rule set by article 2358 c.c.). The reverse merger LBO may also be perceived as an indirect instrument used by the target to acquire its own shares outside the restrictions imposed by article 2357 Civil Code.[43] Furthermore, LBOs may be implemented without a merger. Following a similar line of reasoning, the legitimacy of nonmerger LBOs also remains uncertain.

According to the main intention of the legislator, we expect that the risk of receiving an illegality declaration should be minimized if the requirements introduced by article 2501-bis are fulfilled (especially with reference to the disclosure requirements). The satisfaction of the legal conditions required by law could be interpreted as proof of "good faith."[44]

New Criminal Prosecutions in Case of Financial Assistance

In 2002, a criminal reform was introduced (Legislative Decree April 11, 2002, number 61) according to which a violation of the financial assistance ban is no longer automatically a crime, as it occurred in the past under the previous provision of article 2630 c.c.[45]

By combining the criminal reform (effective since April 2002)[46] with the 2004 corporate governance reform (article 2501-bis c.c.) aimed at clarifying the legal status of LBOs, the financial assistance rule should be applied more cautiously to LBOs and only on a case-by-case basis. In line with this view, Italy recently issued a new law (Legislative Decree 142/2008) aimed at introducing more exceptions to the financial assistance prohibition (outlined by article 2358 c.c.).[47] However, the 2002 criminal reform introduced new crimes that may be applicable to LBOs if:

- The acquisition of the target damages its equity value to the detriment of its stakeholders;
- The interests of preexisting creditors are negatively affected by the merger between the newco and the target.

We expect that the risk of receiving a criminal sentence should be minimal if the transaction is implemented by following the conditions introduced by article 2501-bis c.c. The debate on the criminal consequence is still open, especially with reference to the directors' liability.

Consequences in Case of Bankruptcy

A strong increase in the leverage ratio of a company may increase its default probability and could cause a bankruptcy declaration as a result of an irreversible insolvency status. What happens if the acquired firm files for bankruptcy after the LBO transaction is completed? At present, divergent opinions exist.

The recent criminal law reform (introduced by the legislative decree 61/2002[48]) modified the Italian bankruptcy law and introduced three legal prosecutions which may be applicable to leveraged buyouts if demonstrating a causal relationship between the LBO transaction and the bankruptcy of the target company. The contents of these provisions are summarized as follows.

Article 2628 c.c.: According to article 2628 c.c., the directors could be punished with a sentence of one-year imprisonment if they elude the limits regulating the acquisition by a company of its own shares outside the exceptions specified by the law and, as a result of this breach, cause a deterioration of the target's share capital. (*"Illegitimate transactions on shares or quotas of the company or of the controlling company."*)

Article 2629 c.c.: According to the new formulation of article 2629 of the civil code, the directors may be punishable with up to three years imprisonment if they damage the preexisting creditors by implementing an LBO or a merger against the Italian law ("transactions to the prejudice of creditors").[49] According to article 2629 c.c., *"The directors who, in breach of the provisions of law for the protection of creditors, arrange for the reduction of the capital or for mergers with other companies or for demergers, causing damage to the creditors are punished . . . with imprisonment from six months to three years,"* subject to the specific request by the damaged parties.

Article 2634 c.c.: The directors could also be liable with up to three years imprisonment if the merger is implemented against the interest of the target (conflict of interest case). If there is no interest for the target to be merged and the directors approve the merger anyway, they may be criminally liable according to the new wording of article 2634 c.c (*"unfaithfulness on assets"*). Article 2634 c.c. in fact states that *"the creditors, the general manager and the liquidators having a conflict of interest with those of the company, adopt resolutions or concur in the adoption of resolutions for the disposal of corporate assets for the purpose of procuring an unjust profit or other advantage to themselves or to others intentionally causing to the company a patrimonial damage are punished with imprisonment from six months up to three years. . . ."*[50] In the case of an LBO transaction, the merger plan that the board of directors must disclose (in accordance with article 2501-bis) would play a crucial role, especially with regards to the reasons that justify the whole LBO transaction. The directors of each merging company could also be liable, with a sentence of up to three years of prison, if they intentionally disclose false information in the merger plan and, as a result of this false communication, the creditors and the entire company are damaged (*"False corporate communications to the damage of members or creditors"*). Article 2622 c.c. in fact states that *"the directors, the general managers, the auditors and the liquidators who, with the intention to deceive the members of the public and for the* *purpose of obtaining an unjust profit, cause patrimonial damage to the members or to the creditors represented in the accounts, in the reports or in other corporate communications requested by law and directed to the members or to the public, material facts which do not correspond to the truth even if subject to evaluations, or omitting information the communication of which is imposed by law on the economic, asset or financial status of the company or of the group of belonging so to induce in error the destinees on such status, causing patrimonial damage to the members or to the creditors are punished, subject to the criminal action of the offended person, with imprisonment from six months to three years. . . ."[51]*

In the case of creditors' prejudice and bankruptcy of the merged company, the criminal prosecution of the directors involved is debated. According to the new bankruptcy law (article 223 c.c.), the directors of newco and target may be accused of fraudulent bankruptcy if the new combined entity resulting from the merger enters into irreversible financial distress, and it is demonstrated that the LBO transaction caused it. However, in case of bankruptcy of the target company, an LBO can be invalidated by a court only if: (1) the transaction occurred after the period in which the company entered into a financially distressed status, and (2) if management was aware of it.

By combining the criminal law reform (introduced in April 2002 by Legislative Decree 61/2002) with the new LBO reform (article 2501-bis, effective as of January 1, 2004), we expect that the directors should not be considered criminally liable if the LBO and the merger procedure are implemented by following the rules, especially with reference to the new requirements imposed by article 2501-bis c.c., even in case of bankruptcy. However, the risk of a bankruptcy accusation or a criminal sentence still exists. At present, opinions with respect to the issues highlighted above are not consistent. We shall have to wait for new jurisprudence.

THE ECONOMIC IMPACT OF THE 2004 REFORM

This section analyzes the economic impact of the LBO reform on the behavior of private equity investors, by considering a new detailed hand-collected dataset, whose characteristics are summarized below. In this section, we provide a descriptive analysis of the results obtained with our survey. First, we provide information on the methodology adopted to collect the data, the characteristics of our sample, in terms of geographical, sector and yearly distribution. Second, we provide a descriptive analysis of the impact of the LBO reform on the buyout market and investors' behavior. A multivariate analysis is implemented in a closely related study (see Cumming and Zambelli 2009).

Data and Methodology

In the absence of detailed public information on buyout deals, we carried out a survey of Italian private equity investors. In December 2005, we sent a semistructured questionnaire to all members of the Italian Venture Capital Association (AIFI) by following the steps highlighted in Dillman, Phelps, Tortora et al. (2004).[52] In order to maximize the response rate, we adopted a *Sequential Mixed Mode Survey Approach*, by using a different survey mode in a sequential way (e.g., nonrespondents to our mail survey [phase 1] were contacted by phone or by mail and asked to answer the questionnaire through a subsequent interview [phase 2]). Recent evidence shows that this approach improves the response rate (see, e.g., De Leeuw 2005; Dillman et al. 2004).

The questionnaire was addressed to the partners of each private equity firm active in the Italian market (further details on the specific methodology adopted to collect the database are included in Appendix 21.C). Despite the difficulties of implementing the survey (especially due to the confidential information requested in the questionnaire), we obtained a high response rate: considering the number of the investors actively involved in the entire PE industry, we obtained a response rate of 47 percent (27 of 57 active investors); while considering the buyout sector only, we achieved a response rate of 84 percent (21 of 25 active investors). Both response rates compare favorably with previous surveys in finance, ranging from approximately 9 percent (Graham and Harvey 2001) to 19 percent (Brau and Fawcett 2006).

Trust was the major constraint to the effectiveness of our survey, as it involved confidential information about the specific private equity deal. Several factors may have contributed to establish a trust relationship with the investors, allowing us to improve the response rate: personal visits aimed at providing detailed information on the objective and motivation of our survey, the university affiliation of the authors, the nonprofit goals of the project, and the confidentiality agreement included in the questionnaire package given to each investor in both phases.

Our dataset comprises detailed information on actual contractual provisions and control rights requested by the investors, as well as qualitative data on the relevance of different screening criteria for undertaking the investment. In particular, our dataset includes information on the entire private equity investment cycle, carried out by the investor:

- Transaction characteristics and deal structure;
- Screening criteria, due diligence and valuation of the target;
- Forms of finance used to accomplish the acquisition of the target;
- Board representation, governance, and other control rights required by investors;
- Exit expectations, as well as exit routes chosen by investors to divest their equity participation.

We further completed our database by collecting information from different sources (Datastream by Thomson Corporation, Borsa Italiana, Italian Venture Capital Association [AIFI], Private Equity Monitor [PEM®] database, managed by AIFI, and Private Equity Fund web sites) in order to consider relevant control variables, such as: market returns, industry market to book values, and characteristics of funds (i.e., starting date, age of activity, capital under management, portfolio size, legal structure, and independency).

Sample Characteristics and Representativeness

Our new hand-collected dataset is much more detailed than all currently existing public datasets on Italian private equity deals and consists of 162 firms acquired by 27 private equity funds during the 1999 to 2006 period.

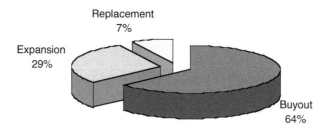

Exhibit 21.6   Type of Transaction Included in Our Database

Among the 27 private equity funds, 12 (44 percent) are Italian independent closed-end funds,[53] 4 (15 percent) are Italian bank subsidiaries, 8 (30 percent) are international independent limited partners, and 3 (11 percent) are subsidiaries of international banks. Among the 162 target firms, 103 were acquired through a leveraged buyout transaction by approximately 85 percent of the buyout funds actively involved in Italy over the same period.[54]

As highlighted in Exhibit 21.6, 103 transactions (64 percent) are leveraged buyouts; the remaining transactions are represented by other private equity deals (expansion and replacement).[55]

Exhibit 21.7 shows the distribution of the transactions by type of investors (independent and bank subsidiaries[56]). As shown in Exhibit 21.7, independent investors tend to be more concentrated on the buyout sector, while bank subsidiaries tend to focus on other types of private equity deals (expansion and replacement deals) characterized by a lower level of associated risk.

Exhibit 21.8 provides some information on the geographical and sector distribution of the transactions included in our sample. The private equity deals included in our sample are concentrated in the North of Italy (8 percent). Moreover, the majority of the target firms are active in the manufacturing and basic material sector (which covers 56 percent of the buyout deals). These findings are in line with the private equity data collected by the Italian Venture Capital Association (included in the Private Equity Monitor [PEM(R)] database).

Exhibit 21.9 shows the yearly distribution of the buyout transactions included in our database relative to other private equity transaction (PE). In line with the AIFI statistics, the number of buyouts increased dramatically after 2004, moving from 13 (in 2003) to 26 (in 2005). During the period in which the legitimacy of LBO

Exhibit 21.7   Types of Transactions by Types of Investors

		Buyout	Expansion	Replacement	Total
Independent	N.	63	9	9	81
	%	77,8%	11,1%	11,1%	100,0%
Bank Subsidiaries	N.	27	38	3	68
	%	39,7%	55,9%	4,4%	100,0%
Total	**N.**	**90**	**47**	**12**	**149**
	%	**60,4%**	**31,5%**	**8,1%**	**100,0%**

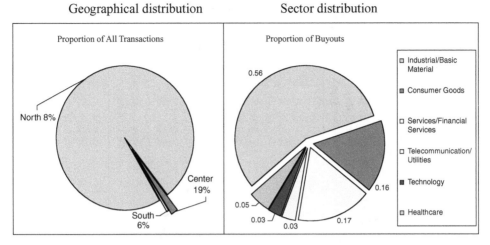

Exhibit 21.8 Geographical and Sector Distribution, 1999–2006

deals was uncertain and strongly disputed (1999 to 2001) the number of buyouts was instead relatively low.

The new LBO reform (effective as of January 1, 2004) seems to have positively affected the buyout market, despite the cumbersome procedure outlined by the new law for the legitimacy of LBOs (see article 2501-bis, as previously discussed).

In order to evaluate the representativeness of our database, in Exhibit 21.10 we compare our sample with the Private Equity Monitor (PEM®) database, which includes PE deals carried out in Italy, with some information on deal type and value of target firms. In Panel A of Exhibit 21.10 we compare the yearly distribution of our entire sample with that associated with the PEM database. Apart from a few exceptions (2000 to 2004), the comparison tests indicate no statistically significant differences between our sample and the PEM dataset. In Panel B we

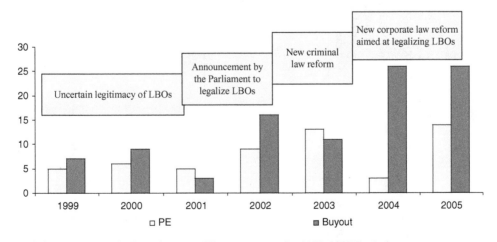

Exhibit 21.9 Yearly Distribution of Buyouts over the 1999–2005 Period

Exhibit 21.10 Comparison Tests between the PEM Database and Our Sample

Panel A

Yearly Distribution	PEM® SURVEY		OUR SURVEY		
	Total Number of Transactions Included in PEM Database (99–2005)	Proportion of Buyouts Included in PEM Database (99–2005)	Total Number of Transactions Included in Our Sample (99–06 1st Sem)	Proportion of Buyouts Included in Our *Dataset* (99–06 1st Sem)	Comparison of Proportion Tests
1999	56	0.45	12	0.58	−0.84
2000	69	0.33	15	0.60	−1.95*
2001	60	0.20	8	0.38	−1.12
2002	61	0.56	25	0.64	−0.68
2003	71	0.56	24	0.46	0.86
2004	55	0.71	29	0.90	−1.94*
2005	89	0.70	40	0.65	0.57
2006	NA	NA	9	0.56	NA

Panel B

Sector Distribution	PEM® SURVEY		OUR SURVEY		
	Number of Buyouts Included in PEM Database (99–2003)	Proportion of Buyouts Included in PEM Database 99–2003	Total Number of Buyouts Included in Our Sample (99–06 1st Sem)	Proportion of Buyouts Included in Our *Dataset* (99–06 1st Sem)	Comparison of Proportion Tests
Industrial/Basic Material	134	0.57	103	0.56	0.15
Consumer Goods	134	0.19	103	0.16	0.60
Services/Financial Services	134	0.15	103	0.17	−0.42
Telecommunication/Utilities	134	0.04	103	0.03	0.41
Technology/ICT	134	0.03	103	0.03	0.00
Healthcare	134	0.01	103	0.05	−1.87*

Panel C

PEM® SURVEY

OUR SURVEY

Geographical Distribution	Total Number of Transactions Included in PEM Database (99–2003)	Proportion of All PE Transactions Included in PEM Database (99–2003)	Total Number of Transactions Included in Our Sample (99–06 1° Sem) (Excluding 5 Deals Carried Out Abroad)	Proportion of All PE Transactions Included in Our *Dataset*	Comparison of Proportion Tests
North	317	0.81	157	0.75	1.51
Center	317	0.15	157	0.19	−1.11
South	317	0.04	157	0.06	−0.97

Exhibit 21.11   Transaction Profile

		Our Database
1. Type of transaction	→	Buyout + Expansion
2. Period	→	1999–2006
3. Area	→	North (mainly in Lombardia)
4. Sector	→	Industrial
5. Average N. of co-investor	→	2
6. Average N. of financing rounds completed by the fund	→	1
7. Average Enterprise Value	→	31 Mln. Euro
8. Multiple used to estimate the enterprise value	→	(EV/EBITDA) = 5.4
9. Average size of the investment	→	7 Mln. Euro
10. Average equity stake held by the *lead investor*	→	37%
11. Average equity stake held by all private equity investors	→	58%
12. Typical exit route	→	Trade sale
13. Average period of involvement in the target firm (averaged holding period)	→	2 years and a half

compare the sector distribution of the buyout transactions included in our sample with the sector distribution of the buyouts included in the PEM sample. The two distributions do not show significant differences. In Panel C we compare the geographical distribution of the PEM dataset with that related to our database. No relevant differences are shown in terms of area distribution.

As shown in Exhibit 21.10, our sample is comparable with the PEM database, in terms of geographical, sector, and yearly distribution. Exhibit 21.11 summarizes the typical profile of the transactions included in our database.

Impact on Investor Behavior: A Descriptive Analysis

In this section we analyze the impact of the new LBO regulation on investors' behavior, deal structure, governance of target firms, and due diligence.

In order to better evaluate the economic impact of the LBO reform on the buyout market and the investors' behavior, we divided the years covered by our data into three subperiods (defined as Dark, Hope, and Sun), in accordance with the main regulatory changes of the Italian legal environment (discussed in section 4). The three periods are summarized below in Exhibit 21.12 (see also Cumming-Zambelli 2009).

Impact on the Buyout Market

Exhibit 21.13 shows the evolution in the number and percentages of buyouts over the three subperiods, defined in Exhibit 21.12: Dark, Hope and Sun. As shown in Exhibit 21.13, the frequency of buyouts significantly increased after the 2004 corporate law reform, moving from 54 percent over the period in which the legitimacy of LBOs was uncertain (Dark period) to 73 percent in the Sun period. The differences in the frequencies, associated with the Dark and the Sun period, are statistically significant (Exhibit 21.13, Panel B).

Exhibit 21.12   The Three Subperiods of LBO Regulation: Dark, Hope, and Sun

Dark Period →	→ Hope Period →	→ Sun Period
Period in which the legitimacy of LBOs was uncertain or even prohibited.	Period in which the Italian Parliament announced the intention to legalize LBOs.	Period in which LBOs were legalized.
Timing: January 1999 –September 2001	Timing: October 2001 – December 2003	Timing: January 2004 – July 2006

It is worth noting that, according to AIFI statistics, the percentage invested in early stage and start up transactions remained almost stationary over the 2004 to 2006 period (both in terms of amount invested and number of deals realized). Furthermore, as shown in Exhibit 21.14, the change in regulation increased the number of buyout transactions carried out by independent PE funds relative to those undertaken by bank subsidiaries. In particular, the percentage of buyout transactions carried out by independent funds increased from 58 percent (over the Dark period) to 84 percent (over the Sun period). To the contrary, the percentage of buyout deals completed by bank subsidiaries decreased over time, moving from 42 percent (over the Dark period) to 16 percent (over the Sun period). Over time, bank subsidiaries have paid more attention to other PE deals, mainly expansion and replacement investments (see Exhibit 21.14).

Exhibit 21.13   Evolution of Buyouts Over the Dark-Hope-Sun Periods

Panel A

Periods			Buyout	Expansion	Replacement	Total
1	Dark					
	Before Oct. 2001	N.	19	14	2	35
		%	54%	40%	6%	100%
2	Hope					
	Oct. 2001–Dec. 2003	N.	27	14	8	49
		%	55%	29%	16%	100%
3	Sun					
	After Jan. 2004 (up to July 2006).	N.	57	19	2	78
		%	73%	24%	3%	100%
Total		N.	103	47	12	162

Panel B

	Dark	Sun	Difference of proportion test	
Average	0.54	0.73	−1,717*	Difference statistically significant at 10%

Note: *, **, and *** denote significance at the 10 percent, 5 percent, and 1 percent level, respectively.

Exhibit 21.14   PE Investors over Time

Panel A Buyout Deals		Dark Period	Hope Period	Sun Period	Total
Independent Funds	# of deals	11 (58%)	17 (63%)	48 (84%)	76 (74%)
Bank Subsidiaries	# of deals	8 (42%)	10 (37%)	9 (16%)	27 (26%)
	Total	19 (100%)	27 (100%)	57 (100%)	103 (100%)
Panel B Other PE deals		Dark Period	Hope Period	Sun Period	Total
Independent Funds	# of deals	4 (25%)	10 (46%)	4 (19%)	18 (31%)
Bank Subsidiaries	# of deals	12 (75%)	12 (56%)	17 (81%)	41 (69%)
	Total	16 (100%)	22 (100%)	21 (100%)	59 (100%)

Note: *, **, and *** denote significance at the 10 percent, 5 percent, and 1 percent level, respectively.

Impact on the Deal-Structure and Investors' Involvement

The new LBO reform had a positive impact not only on the frequency of buyouts, but also on the deal-structure, in terms of involvement of the PE investors and their control rights over the target firm. In particular, the new, safer legal environment increased the willingness of PE investors to be actively involved in the management of the target firm. The LBO reform increased the amount invested and the average equity stake acquired by the investors.

Exhibit 21.15 shows the evolution of the amount invested over the pre-money valuation of the target firm, while Exhibit 21.16 highlights the equity stake acquired by investors. Moving from the Dark to the Sun period, the amount invested over the premoney valuation of the target firm increased sharply from 17 percent to 27 percent (Exhibit 21.15). Investors also increased their equity stake in the target from an average of 26 percent, over the Dark period, to 51 percent in the Sun period (Exhibit 21.16). In both cases, the differences are statistically significant at the 1 percent level (Exhibits 21.15–21.16, Panel A).

Impact on the Governance of the Target Firm

We investigated the control rights detained by private equity investors, in terms of holding the right of board representation and the right to replace the target's CEO.

Exhibit 21.17 shows the impact of the buyout reform on the evolution of the investor right of taking a majority position on the target's board of directors, while Exhibit 21.18 highlights the effect of the buyout regulation on the investors' right to replace the CEO.

As indicated in Exhibits 21.17–21.18, the new LBO regulation did have a strong impact on the governance of the target firms. Private equity investors are more willing to hold higher control rights over the target firm, as well as to be more actively involved in the value-added creation of the target firm. Over the Dark period (in which the LBO legitimacy was doubted or even prohibited), investors tended to minimize their involvement, by holding fewer control rights, in order to minimize

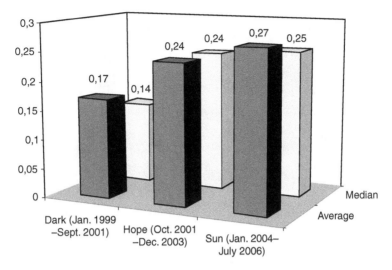

Panel A			Difference of	
	Dark	**Sun**	**Proportion Test**	
Median	0.14	0.25	p < = 0.000***	Difference statistically significant at 1% level

Exhibit 21.15   Evolution of the Invested Amount over the PreMoney Valuation
Note: *, **, and *** denote significance at the 10 percent, 5 percent, and 1 percent level, respectively.

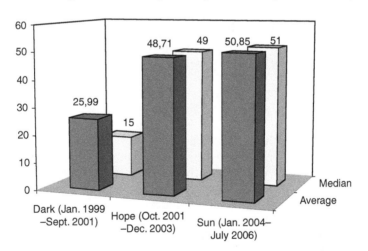

Panel A			Difference of	
	Dark	**Sun**	**Proportion Test**	
Average	0.25%	0.51%	Test = −3.811***	Difference statistically significant at 1% level
Median	0.15%	0.51%	p < = 0.009***	Difference statistically significant at 1% level

Exhibit 21.16   Equity Stake Detained by Investors
Note: *, **, and *** denote significance at the 10 percent, 5 percent, and 1 percent level, respectively.

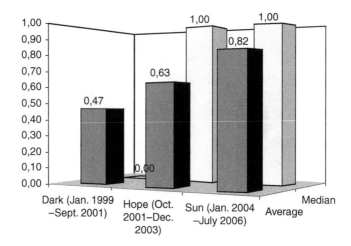

Panel A			Difference of	
	Dark	Sun	Proportion Test	
Average	0.47	0.82	Test = −2.737***	Difference statistically significant at 1% level
Median	00	1	p < = 0.007***	Difference statistically significant at 1% level

Exhibit 21.17   Investors' Right to Take a Majority Position in the Board of Directors of the Target Company
Note: *, **, and *** denote significance at the 10 percent, 5 percent, and 1 percent level, respectively.

the legal risk associated with the transaction in case of a dispute. As soon as LBOs were legalized (after 2004), investors enormously increased their involvement in the management of the target, by detaining a higher board representation and a majority position in the target's board of directors. As shown in Exhibit 21.17, the proportion of transactions in which investors held a majority position on the board of directors of the target firm increased from 47 percent (over the Dark period) to 82 percent (over the Sun period). This difference is statistically significant at the 1 percent level (see Exhibit 21.17, Panel A).

Furthermore, the LBO reform also increased the investors' willingness of holding the right to replace the CEO (which represents a strong control mechanism that is usually exercised in cases of poor performance of the target firm[57]). With the transition from the Dark to the Sun period, the percentage of deals including the investor's right of replacing the CEO rose from 37 percent (over the period of illegality) to 70 percent (after the new 2004 LBO reform). This difference is statistically significant at the 1 percent level (in terms of average, Exhibit 21.18, panel A).

Impact on the Adoption of Convertible Securities
The change in regulation had a positive effect on the financial instruments used to accomplish the acquisition of the target firm (straight equity, straight debt, or convertible securities). According to the recent economic literature (Cumming 2005a, b, 2006; Hellmann 2006; Repullo and Suarez 2004; Schmidt 2003; Cornelli and Yosha 2003; Casamatta 2003; Kaplan and Stromberg 2003) the adoption of

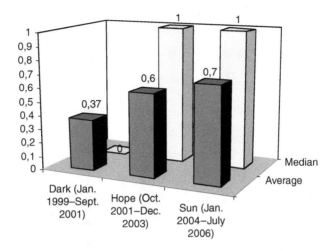

Panel A			Difference of	
	Dark	Sun	Proportion Test	
Average	0.37	0.68	Test = −2.437***	Difference statistically significant at 1% level
Median	0	1	p < = 0.031**	Difference statistically significant at 5% level

Exhibit 21.18 Investors' Right to Replace Target's CEO
Note: *, **, and *** denote significance at the 10 percent, 5 percent, and 1 percent level, respectively.

convertible securities is associated with a more effective risk management of the acquired firm, because convertible instruments appear to minimize the consequences derived from asymmetric information between the investor and the acquired firm (namely, adverse selection and moral hazard).

The LBO reform had a positive impact on the use of convertible securities. Exhibit 21.19 shows a relevant increase in the adoption of convertible debt to finance the purchase of the target company. Over the Dark period, none of the examined buyout transactions used convertible debt. Over the Sun period, approximately 12 percent of the buyout deals involved a financing with convertible debt in association with the "automatic conversion option" upon the occurrence of specific events (indicated in the contract). In the case of conversion, the investor becomes more involved in the management of the target firm. This reinforces the view that the LBO reform improved the governance of the target firm, by increasing the willingness of investors to be more actively involved in the governance of the acquired firm and, consequently, improving the value-added of the target (see, e.g., Cao and Lerner 2009, on the positive role of private equity funds in corporate governance).

Impact on the Due Diligence Process and Motivations
Underlying the LBO Transaction
In this section we concentrate on whether the legalization of buyouts had an impact on the selection of the target firms and the due diligence process implemented by PE funds.

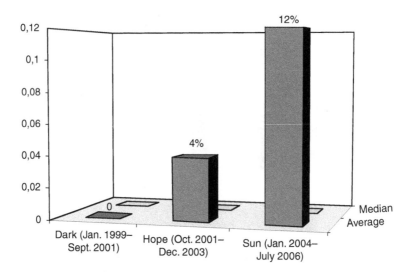

Exhibit 21.19   Convertible Debt Adoption

Note: *, **, and *** denote significance at the 10 percent, 5 percent, and 1 percent level, respectively.

During our survey, we asked the PE investors to rank the relevance of different selection criteria by using a Likert scale ranging from 1 to 5 (where 1 indicates the minimum relevance of a certain criterion and 5 the maximum importance).[58] In line with Sahlman (1999), we grouped the various criteria into the following categories:

1. "Firm," which includes selection criteria within the firm (firm objectives, development stage, business history, etc.);
2. "Management," which considers selection criteria within the management team (such as, management's objectives);
3. "Opportunity," which refers to selection criteria related to the business plan content (such as the growth potential underlying the cash flow and financial plan provided by the target firm);
4. "Context," which includes external selection criteria referring to the market context in which the firm is involved;
5. "Investments," which considers selection criteria referring to the quality of the investment (amount, equity stake, time to reach the break-even point, strategic fit with other portfolio firms, risk, and expected IRR).

The most important selection criteria used by investors are summarized in Exhibit 21.20. The results are in line with Zacharakis and Meyer (1998, 2000), Shepherd (1999a, 1999b).

Exhibit 21.20 Selecting Criteria by Type of Transaction

Buyout Transactions	Average Value	Other PE Transactions	Average Value
1. Management	3.93	1. Management	3.95
2. Market	3.87	2. Firm	3.5
3. Business plan	3.84	3. Market	3.46
4. Firm	3.68	4. Business Plan	3.44
5. Investment	3.1	5. Investment	1.9

Note: Investors were asked to rank the relevance of different selecting criteria by using a Likert scale ranging from 1 to 5 (where 1 indicates the minimum relevance of a certain criterion and 5 the maximum importance).

Exhibit 21.21 shows the evolution of the most important selection criteria (Firm; Business plan [BP], Market [Mkt], and Investiment [I]) over the 1999 to 2006 period, according to the three subperiods previously defined: Dark, Hope, and Sun. The 2004 reform also affected the due diligence process. The criterion associated with the quality of the business plan (BP), especially with reference to the growth potentiality of the target firm, significantly increased in importance after the introduction of the new LBO reform. Similarly, the criterion related to the quality of the investment (which refers to the amount of invested capital, equity stake in the target firm, expected IRR, and strategic fit of the investment within the fund's portfolio) became extremely important after the 2004 reform (rising from 2.26 in the Dark period to 3.54 in the Sun period). On the other hand, the criterion related to the compatibility with the firm's objectives was relatively

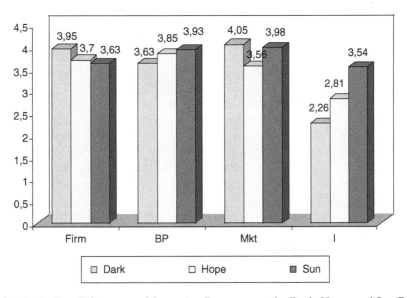

Exhibit 21.21 Due Diligence and Screening Process over the Dark, Hope, and Sun Periods
Note: Investors were asked to rank the relevance of different selecting criteria by using a Likert scale ranging from 1 to 5 (where 1 indicates the minimum relevance of a certain criterion and 5 the maximum importance).

more important over the Dark period (average value of 3.95), while its importance decreased significantly after the introduction of the new LBO reforms.

Overall, the buyout reform had a positive impact on the quality of due diligence, helping investors to select the very best firms. Over the Dark period, LBOs were more intensively screened for their fit with the target firm in terms of agreeableness with their management team. Investors seemed more focused on minimizing the transaction risk in case of a legal dispute, rather than on selecting the firms according to their growth potential. Over the Sun period, instead, LBOs seemed to be more intensively screened for more crucial criteria, such as: the quality of the investment structure, the quality of the business plan and the growth potential of the target firm.

Our findings provide evidence that prohibiting LBOs is not an effective way to better protect the interests of target firms and their stakeholders. Instead of prohibiting LBOs, it would seem better to legalize them and specify a set of conditions in order to prevent abusive opportunistic behaviors by the directors involved to the detriment of the target's stakeholders.

CONCLUSION

When evaluating the opportunity of investing in the buyout industry, especially in some European countries, one of the most critical issues for entrepreneurs, managers, and private equity investors is the legal risk associated with LBO transactions. In Italy, for example, LBOs have been strongly criticized by doctrine and jurisprudence because they are accused of increasing the default probability of the target firm to the detriment of its creditors and other stakeholders. For this reason, several LBO transactions were declared illegal and invalidated by Italian courts.

In this chapter we have described the evolution of the legal environment surrounding LBOs in Italy and evaluated the impact that a change in the LBO regulation may have on the buyout market and the behavior of investors.

First, we discussed the most critical aspects (side effects) associated with LBOs, highlighting the reasons why LBOs have been highly criticized in Italy over the past decade. The LBO financial scheme was considered an instrument fraudulently adopted by the target's management with the sole intention of eluding the financial assistance provisions (especially article 2358), because the target in the end appears to provide a guarantee for the purchase of its own shares. The debate intensified in 2000 when the Supreme Court prohibited the LBO scheme in Italy, as it was perceived to be in conflict with the financial assistance prohibition (Supreme Court's decision 5503/2000).

Second, we described the characteristics of the new LBO reform, effective from 2004. Among other things, it aimed at regulating the leveraged buyout process (Legislative Decree 6/2003, applicable as of January 1, 2004). The new regulation clarified the legal status of LBOs and legalized these types of transactions under specific conditions, especially with reference to disclosure. Thanks to the new regulation, the burden of proof has now been reversed: LBOs should be considered legal, unless otherwise proven. Complex buyout deals with a pyramidal ownership structure are no longer necessary, at least for legal purposes. Notwithstanding the new corporate governance rule, the legal debate on LBOs does not seem to be completely over, mainly with respect to:

1. The legitimacy of those LBO deals that are not specifically regulated by article 2501-bis;
2. The criminal law consequences for the directors involved in the transaction. These consequences are particularly evident for those types of buyouts that remain outside of the scope of application of the new corporate governance law (e.g., nonmerger LBOs). In any case, the risk of illegality should be minimal if the LBO transaction is implemented by following the requirements specified by the new law. This would represent potential proof of good faith. We shall have to wait for new jurisprudence. Despite these unsolved issues, the Italian experience of LBO legalization offers useful guidelines on how these transactions may be regulated in order to better protect the interests of the target's stakeholders.

Third, we evaluated the economic impact of the new LBO reform by describing the main results derived from a survey of private equity investors. Our sample includes 162 private equity transactions (among which 103 are leveraged buyouts) carried out in Italy over the period 1999 to 2006 (first semester). Overall, our data shows that the new reform marked an important turning point for the buyout industry, encouraging its development within the Italian private equity market. The change in regulation had a positive impact not only on the frequency of buyout transactions, but also on the deal structure and the governance of the firms involved. Following the 2004 regulatory change, private equity investors are in fact more willing to increase their involvement in the governance of the target firms, particularly in terms of invested capital, ownership percentage, board control, and other control rights.

With reference to the current international concern on whether LBOs should be prohibited or at least severely restricted, our results show that rendering LBOs illegal is not an efficient instrument to protect the interests of the target firms. First, LBOs were still carried out, despite the prohibition, especially in the form of multilayered mega deals. Over the period of uncertain legitimacy (Dark period), these types of transactions were structured in different ways, preventing private equity investors from being actively involved in the governance of the target firm (in terms of control rights, ownership percentage and invested amount). A prohibiting regulation seems capable only of preventing the efficient structure of the buyout investment, by distorting the governance of the target firms and the due diligence process to the detriment of the target firm and its stakeholders. Policy makers seem to obtain the exact opposite of what they wish to achieve since the stakeholders' interests would be better protected by a nonprohibiting regulation.

The new Italian LBO reform offers an alternative solution: to legalize the adoption of the LBO financial scheme, under a set of specified conditions in order to protect the interest of the target. The Italian experience provides legislators and policy makers around the world with an example of how a nonprohibiting regulation, aimed at legalizing LBOs under specific disclosure requirements, might spur buyout transactions, as well as protect the interests of target firms and their stakeholders. Despite the unsolved issues, the Italian experience of LBO legalization offers useful guidelines on how these transactions may be legitimized under a set of conditions aimed at protecting the interests of the target's stakeholders.

An LBO is merely a financial tool. Like other tools, it can be used properly or misused. When properly used, it allows a company to access an alternative source of finance and improves the performance of the acquired firms. Instead of prohibiting LBOs, legislators should legalize them, by specifying a set of conditions to be satisfied by companies in order to prevent abusive opportunistic behaviors by the directors involved, to the detriment of the target's stakeholders. The made-in-Italy LBO solution represents an innovative example towards this direction.

APPENDIX 21.A: THE PAST DEBATE ON THE LEGITIMACY OF LBOs IN ITALY

Over the past decade an intensive juridical debate about the legitimacy of LBOs in Italy has developed. Even though the jurisprudence did not show a clear and consistent interpretation, several LBOs were invalidated by Italian courts because they were considered examples of financial assistance fraudulently provided by the target for a share buyback purpose ("share buyback view" or "substantial view"; for a discussion of this interpretation, see Zambelli 2005, and Fava and Fuschino 2003).

The interpretation of considering the LBO scheme as illegal was not the only feasible one. In 1999, for example, following an opposing line of reasoning (known as "formal view"), the Court of Milan declared that an LBO cannot be considered illegal if the whole transaction is accompanied by a business project aimed at promoting the financial and economic development of the company (Milan Tribunal, May 13, 1999). However, a year later, the Supreme Court reinforced the view of interpreting the LBO scheme as illegal and prohibited its adoption in Italy (Supreme Court's Decision, February 4, 2000, n. 5503).

This appendix describes in greater detail the reasons why LBOs were considered illegal in Italy. In particular, it analyzes the content of the regulatory restrictions against the legitimacy of LBOs, and provides a critical discussion on their applicability to LBO transactions.

A CLOSER EXAMINATION OF WHY LBOs APPEARED TO BE ILLEGAL IN ITALY

Most of the criticism raised against LBOs was focused on the interpretation of two legal provisions (articles 2357 and 2358 of Civil Code) that limit the possibility for a company to repurchase its own shares or to provide a financial assistance for a share buyback purpose.

Article 2357: Share Buyback Restrictions

Article 2357 restricts the purchase of own shares *by a company*. According to this article, a company cannot purchase its own shares except within the limits of the available net profits remaining after the creation of the statutory reserves (article

2357, 1st paragraph). Article 2357 furthermore states the following limits: (1) the purchase must be authorized by the shareholders' meeting (II paragraph), and (2) the par value of the purchased shares shall not exceed 1/10 of the entire share capital (III paragraph). Furthermore, the law specifies that the above limits also apply to eventual purchases accomplished through an *intermediary or a fiduciary company* (V paragraph).

The rationale behind the above restrictions is to protect the target's paid-in share capital, avoiding a weakening of guarantees granted to the target's creditors. The acquisition of own shares by a company with funds other than current profits would result in a partial restitution of equity capital to shareholders. Consequently, by draining funds from the company and increasing the leverage ratio, preexisting loan obligations become more risky, to the obvious detriment of the firm's creditors. Another closely related argument is that the share repurchase may produce a hidden reduction of the firm's equity base, misleading investors and business partners. From a financial and economic perspective, however, it is important to distinguish two situations. On one hand, the repurchase of own shares is reported in the financial statements of the company. Hence, investors and other stakeholders interested in the company should have little difficulty assessing the firm's true equity base from publicly available information. On the other hand, only prior creditors and other parties with preexisting contracts with the firm may be vulnerable to opportunistic reductions in the firm's equity capital, because they are unable to change their contract terms in face of the share repurchase.

According to a particular interpretation of the law (also called "substance view"), the result of the entire operation was considered similar to a situation in which the target company acquires its own shares through the intermediation of the newco outside the limitation imposed by law (article 2357). This interpretation, however, does not seem justified from an economic viewpoint, given the rationale behind the article as outline above. First of all, in a simple share buy-back by the target company (even through the intermediation of a third party) the final ownership structure does not change. On the other hand, LBO transactions are fundamentally characterized by a change in ownership structure. The ultimate owners of the combined entity are the owners of the newco. Hence, the economic goal of an LBO is fundamentally different from the goal of a simple share buy-back. The empirical evidence shows that the main goal for investors who want to undertake an LBO is to create and add value to the target, exploiting unrealized growth opportunities (see, e.g., Jelic, 2008; Davis et al., 2008). Second, depending on the specifics of any deal, creditors may or may not be in favor of the buyout transaction. Does the protection of investors and other parties with preexisting contracts justify the application of article 2357 to LBO transactions? Under the current Italian Law, creditors have the ability to oppose any LBO transaction that appears to lower the value of their claims. This veto right of creditors opens up the possibility of mutually beneficial agreements among creditors, target company, and acquirer, which a restrictive interpretation of article 2357 would rule out.

Article 2358: Financial Assistance Prohibition

The most invoked provision against the validity of LBOs was represented by *article 2358,* which prohibits a company from making loans or providing guarantees for the purchase of its own shares, either directly or indirectly through the intermediation of a third party. The rationale underlying the above prohibition is twofold:

- To protect the equity of the target company in the interest of creditors, similarly to the rationale for article 2357. The legislator wants to avoid a deterioration of the target firm's capital structure;
- To avoid abusive behavior by the target's directors, for example, to prevent them from taking over the company fraudulently through a hidden acquisition of its own shares. If the actions described in article 1358 were permitted without restrictions, the directors could misuse the funds of the company by making loans or providing guarantees to an outside party (trustee). Then, through the intermediation of that party, the directors could indirectly take over the company and influence the shareholders' meeting.

Part of the doctrine and jurisprudence considered the LBO scheme as a tool to elude the financial assistance prohibition stated above (known as "substantial view"). As a consequence of the merger, in fact, the target's assets serve as a guarantee for the payment of the debt previously contracted by the newco. According to the above interpretation of the law, the result of an LBO transaction is to elude the provisions specified by article 2358, because the target company in the end provides a guarantee for the purchase of its own shares. The newco in turn is interpreted as an intermediary acting on behalf of the target company. This interpretation does not seem justified from an economic viewpoint. There is not an ex-ante equivalence between LBO transactions and the acquisition of own shares through an intermediary. First, in an LBO, the debt guarantee by the target company comes into effect only after the merger has been completed, that is, after the ownership of the target company has changed. Second, creditors will not be defrauded as long as they have the ability to object to any leveraged buyout that reduces the value of their claims. Furthermore, in the case of listed companies, LBOs are publicly announced and do not allow managers to take control of their own firms in a hidden manner.

APPENDIX 21.B: THE REGULATION OF FINANCIAL ASSISTANCE IN THE UNITED KINGDOM

Companies Act 1928/1929

The financial assistance ban for the acquisition of shares was originally introduced in the United Kingdom by section 16 of the Companies Act 1928, following the suggestions and recommendations highlighted by the "Company Law Amendment Committee," known as the "Greene Committee"(Command Paper number 2657/1926). The financial assistance prohibition outlined by section 16 was subsequently included in section 45 of the Companies Act 1929, according to which a company was not allowed to "*give, whether directly or indirectly, and whether by means of a loan, guarantee, the provision of security or otherwise, any financial assistance*" for a share buyback purpose. This section had only a limited purpose and did not apply to the financial assistance provided for the subscription of new shares (Fletcher 2006, Wyatt 2004).

Companies Act 1948

Despite the criticism raised against the financial assistance prohibition outlined by section 45 of the 1929 Act, the subsequent Companies Act 1948 reproduced the same ban within section 54.

The 1962 Jenkins Committee

In 1962, a new committee (the "Jenkins Committee") was established with the aim of reforming the U.K. company law. This committee severally criticized the financial assistance ban for the acquisition of shares and recommended its complete abrogation as considered *"an occasional embarrassment to the honest, without being a serious inconvenience to the unscrupulous."* (See the Command Paper 1749/1962, and Fletcher 2006). According to the Jenkins Committee, a company should be allowed to provide financial assistance for the acquisition of its own shares if certain requirements are met, especially with reference to solvency and disclosure (Fletcher 2006; Sterling and Wright 1990; Wright and Coyne 1985).

Companies Act 1981

In 1981, a new company law reform was issued in the United Kingdom and the financial assistance ban was imposed to public companies only (Companies Act 1981, sections 42–44). A special procedure (known as the whitewash procedure) was introduced to allow private companies to provide financial assistance under certain conditions. These conditions were further clarified in the subsequent Companies Act 1985, sections 151–158.

Companies Act 1985

The Companies Act 1985 (sections 151–158) maintained the financial assistance ban for public companies only. It also specified the conditions under which private companies were allowed to provide financial assistance for the acquisition of their shares (see sections 155–158; see also Roberts, 2005). According to the 1985 Act, a private company was allowed to provide financial assistance for a share buyback purpose only under the following conditions:

1. The net assets must not be reduced (section 155-2-). Alternatively, if the net assets are reduced, financial assistance should be provided out of the distributable profits;
2. A particular procedure must be followed to guarantee the solvency of the company. This procedure (known as the whitewash procedure) includes several steps, as summarized below:
   – *Statutory declaration* (or solvency declaration) by the directors of the target company aimed at guaranteeing the solvency of the firm within the following 12 months from the declaration date (sections 156);
   – *Report by the auditors* of the target company aimed at confirming the reasonableness of the solvency declaration provided by the directors of the company;
   – *Special resolution* by the shareholders of the target firm in order to approve the financial assistance (at least 75 percent of the shareholders must approve the transaction). Before providing any financial assistance, the company must wait four weeks from the special resolution date. Within 28 days from the date of the resolution, shareholders of at least 10 percent of the share capital have the right to oppose and, in case they do oppose, a court must intervene and the financial assistance procedure is suspended until the final judgment of the court.

Over the last decade, the whitewash procedure has been strongly criticized as it appeared rather complex and time-consuming (for additional information about the whitewash procedure see, among others, Roberts 2005).

Companies Act 2006 (effective from October 2008)

Recently, a new company law (Companies Act 2006) came into force and abrogated the "whitewash procedure" for private companies. In particular, the conditions imposed on private companies by sections 151–153 and 155–158 of the Companies Act 1985 have been repealed. Private companies are now allowed to provide financial assistance without having to follow the cumbersome whitewash procedure originally imposed by Companies Act 1981 (the changes related to private companies came into force last October 2008). New financial assistance provisions have been introduced for public companies (see the Companies Act 2006, sections 677–683 that will come into force in October 2009). According to these new provisions, the financial assistance prohibition continues to apply only to the acquisition of shares in public companies. Apart from a few exceptions, public companies are still prohibited from providing financial assistance for a share buyback purpose. The 2006 reform has at least two effects. On one hand, private firms have greater flexibility in taking financial decision related to the acquisition of their shares. On the other hand, the ultimate responsibility for any decision concerning the granting of the financial assistance is now placed on the directors of the company who need to authorize the transaction. If the company results insolvent after the completion of the transaction, the directors involved may be personally liable for any losses they caused to the creditors. For more detailed information, see The Companies Act 2006: A Guide to the Reforms, Linklaters, December 2006, Part III.

APPENDIX 21.C SURVEY DETAILS

Type of survey

Sequential mixed mode survey, characterized by two phases:

1. Phase 1: Structured mail questionnaire.
2. Phase 2: Structured interview.

Questionnaire characteristics

1. Objective of the questionnaire: Private Equity Investment Process
2. Unit of observation: Investee firm (Target firm)
3. Questionnaire parts:
   a. Transaction characteristics
   b. Screening criteria
   c. Due diligence and valuation
   d. Forms of finance and contractual provisions
   e. Board representation and venture corporate governance
   f. Exit expectations
4. Types of questions: multiple choices, numeric open-end questions; text open-end questions
5. Target respondent: Partner of PE firms operating in Italy
6. Length: 4 pages
7. Time to complete: 30–40 minutes (according to the pilot study)

| Mailing list | The final version of the questionnaire was sent to all members of the Italian Venture Capital and Private Equity Association (AIFI): 88 members (Source: AIFI statistics October 2005). According to AIFI statistics and the Private Equity Monitor Survey (AIFI-PEM survey), the number of investors active on the PE market was lower. In fact, the number of investors active in the buyout sector was 25 (according to AIFI statistics, 2005, 1st semester). The number of active investor in the private equity sector was 57 (according to the PEM Database, 2005). However, the identification of the investor active in the PE sector was not available. In order to minimize potential selection biases, we sent the questionnaire to all 88 AIFI members. According to our ex-post analysis the number of active investors in the PE sector was 56, in line with PEM database (57). |

Timing and data collection

1. September 2005 to November 2005: Pilot study. The first draft of the questionnaire was tested by a small sample of academics, PE investors and lawyers. We used the feedbacks to improve and revise the questionnaire.

   December 2005 to April 2006: Implementation of Survey: Phase 1 (Mail Questionnaire). By the end of this phase only five investors replied (response rate: 9%), for a total of 19 investee firms.

   We sent the following questionnaire package:

   a. Personalized and signed cover letter, indicating the university affiliation of both authors, with the aim of explaining the purpose of the research project and the questionnaire;
   b. Presentation by the authors;
   c. Questionnaire (6 parts, 4 pages long);
   d. Confidentiality Agreement;
   e. A reward promise, in terms of follow-on finding-reports and invitation to attend future potential related conferences organized by the authors (for those who declared an interest in being updated);
   f. A short booklet with the instructions for completing the questionnaire and the definitions of the key PE terms used in it.

2. May 2006: Follow-ups by e-mail and phone. This phase allowed us to better identify the active investors in the PE sector. Eight investors replied by fax (response rate: 14%), for a total of other 33 investee firms. For confidentiality reasons, 14 investors (24%) requested a personal visit (in their office), in order to evaluate in greater details the objective of the survey and the authors. After the personal visit, all investors decided to partake in the survey by filling out the questionnaire in a subsequent structured interview.

3. June 2006–August 2006: Implementation of Survey: Phase 2 (face-to-face Interview). We interviewed 14 investors (response rate: 24%), for a total of 110 PE investee firms. A few weeks before the interview, we sent to each investor the same questionnaire package sent in phase 1. To minimize potential response biases, during the interview each investor had a hard copy of the questionnaire and the possibility to read and to fill out the questionnaire in person.

Final sample   After eliminating nonusable questionnaires (not completed for at least 60% of the questions), our database consists of 162 investee firms acquired by PE investors during the period of 1999 to 2006 (first semester) by 27 PE investors. The PE deal can be divided into two parts:

1. Buyouts transactions in 103 target firms;
2. Other PE transactions (replacement and expansion) in 59 target firms.

Among the 27 PE investors, 21 declared to be active in the buyout sectors.

Response rate   Considering the number of the investor active in the PE sector, we obtained a response rate of 47% (27 over 57 investors).

Focusing only on the buyout sector, we obtained a response rate of 84% (21 over 25 investors).

Both the above response rates compare favorably with previous financial surveys. For example:

Brau and Fawcett (2006) obtained a response rate of 19%;

Graham and Harvey (2001) obtained a response rate of 9%. The authors emphasize that their response rate is in line with previous financial surveys.

NOTES

1. In line with the definition traditionally adopted by the Italian Venture Capital Association (AIFI), we use the term private equity to refer to the expansion financing of existing firms (Capizzi 2004, 2005). This definition excludes start-up financing (venture capital investments) and it includes leveraged buyouts (representing the acquisition of the equity capital of a firm with the adoption of a large portion of debt (Gilligan and Wright 2008; Amess and Wright 2007; Nikoskelainen and Wright 2007). See Stromberg (2008), Cumming, Siegel, and Wright (2007) and Axelson et al. (2007a); Jenkinson, Stromberg, and Weisbach (2007b) for an up-to-date literature review of buyouts. See Ljungqvist, Richardson, and Wolfenzon (2007) for a discussion on the determinants of buyout investments. See also Chou, Gombola, and Liu (2006) and Holmstrom and Kaplan (2001).

2. Other studies also study the performance of PE transactions. See, for example, Chou et al. (2006); Smith (1990); Kaplan (1989); and Opler (1992).

3. For a summary of the most debated issues underlying LBOs in Europe see, for example, the Report by the Financial Services Authority (2006); Ferran (2007); Silvestri (2005); Cleary Gottlieb Steen Hamilton European M&A Report (2003, 2004). For a general overview of the LBO-debate in the United States see *The Economist* (February 8, 2007), "Private Equity: The Uneasy Crown" available at: www.economist.com/finance/displaystory.cfm?story_id=8663441; Stein (2006).

4. Cumming and Zambelli (2009) empirically examine the effects of changes in the Italian legal environment on the buyout market, before and after the introduction of the corporate law reform (effective from January 2004). They show a strong relationship between the changes in the Italian legal environment and the buyout industry.

5. See the Financial Times (February 14, 2007), "German deputy still targets locusts," available at: www.ft.com/cms/s/0/55437712-bc4e-11db-9cbc-0000779e2340.html.

6. See Enriques and Volpin (2007) for a discussion of European corporate governance reforms.

7. The acquisition of Ducati Motor by the Texas Pacific Group (TPG) represents one of the most successful examples of such a turnaround LBO carried out in Italy. TPG bought

Ducati Motor in 1996 through a leveraged buyout alongside Deutsche Morgan Grenfell (now Deutsche Bank). Before the buyout transaction, Ducati was owned by the Cagiva Group, a private manufacturing conglomerate. In 1996, the Cagiva Group suffered a serious liquidity crisis, which also affected Ducati's business, reducing Ducati's motorcycle production, sales, and financial performance. Ducati came close to a bankruptcy declaration. TPG recognized the growth potential of Ducati and decided to acquire the company through a leveraged turnaround transaction. Subsequent to the acquisition, Ducati implemented a successful turnaround program that substantially increased the production of motorcycles and unit sales. Ducati went public in March 1999. For details, see Ducati's Initial Public Offering Prospect, published by CONSOB in "Archivio Prospetti," March 3, 1999, n. 4466. Other examples of Italian LBO acquisitions are Piaggio, Olivetti-Telecom, Galbani, Seat-Pagine Gialle, and Autostrade.

8. In the United States, the debt used to finance LBOs usually covers a greater percentage of the deal (Axelson et al. 2007a; Jensen 1989).

9. Usually, large-mega deals (over 150 million Euro) show a higher debt/equity ratio than smaller deals. In 2006, for example, large-mega deals on average applied a leverage ratio of 2.2 while the leverage ratio for small deals (less than 15 million Euro) was 1.6. See AIFI Yearbook (2006).

10. See AIFI statistics reports (2007), available at www.aifi.it.

11. The original wording of the decision is also reported online at www.diritto.it/osservatori/diritto_fallimentare/corte_cass2000.html#sent5503_2000. See Enriques (2002) for a discussion on the relevance of corporate law judges.

12. See also Cumming and Zambelli (2009) for a detailed discussion on the comparison between the Italian PE market and the European buyout market.

13. BBC News (June 20, 2007), available at news.bbc.co.uk/1/hi/business/6221466.stm.

14. There is extensive literature on the advantages and disadvantages of debt financing. See among others, Williamson, (1988); Bolton and Sharfstein (1990); Harris and Raviv (1990); Dessì (1999); Bonini and Zullo (2000), Cornelli and Yosha (2003); Repullo and Suarez (2004); and Cumming (2005a, b).

15. It is worth noting that a recent law (Law 244/2007) has diminished the tax shield associated with the debt (for details, see Article 96 of the Italian Fiscal Code, "Testo Unico delle Imposte sui Redditi").

16. See, e.g., Bernardi and Bernardi (2006), Silvestri (2005), Bruno (2002, 2006), Bernardi (2001), Varrenti (2000a, b), Mills and Seassaro (1990). General overviews of the Italian debate on LBOs are also available from several web sites:
www.altassets.com/casefor/countries/2005/nz6460.php;
www.altassets.com/casefor/countries/2004/nz4561.php;
www.altassets.com/casefor/sectors/2003/nz3097.php;
and www.altassets.com/casefor/countries/2002/nz3432.php.

17. Examples of court's decisions that are commonly considered part of the jurisprudence against the validity of LBOs are: Criminal Tribunal of Milan, June 30, 1992; Ivrea Tribunal, August 12, 1995; Tribunal of Milan, May 4, 1999; Supreme Court, February 4, 2000. Examples of Court decisions in favor of LBOs are Tribunal of Milan, May 14, 1992; Tribunal of Brescia, June 1, 1993; and Tribunal of Milan, May 13, 1999.

18. Authors in favor of the "substantial view" are, for example, Montalenti (1996). Authors in favor of the "formal view" are Accinni (2001) and Frignani (1996). See Ferrari (2007) and Fava and Fuschino (2003) for details.

19. For a critical discussion on the debate surrounding the LBO legitimacy see Appendix 21.A.

20. Court of Milan, May 13, 1999. This decision followed the line of reasoning underlying a previous decision by the Brescia Court (criminal Court of Brescia, June 1, 1993, with reference to the Marzoli case). See Zambelli (2005) for details.

21. This decision anticipated the future reform on the Italian corporate law that will be discussed in the next sections.

22. For an economic discussion of the Supreme Court's decision see Appendix 21.A and Zambelli (2008). For a legal review of this decision see: Bernardi (2001), Varrenti (2000a, b).

23. For more details see Silvestri (2005) and Negri-Clementi and Montironi (2002), available from: www.altassets.com/casefor/countries/2002/nz3432.php.

24. For a general outline of the 2004 corporate law reform see, e.g., Montalenti (2004).

25. This Decree was issued in January 2003, but came into force a year later.

26. In line with this view are the decisions of the Court of Milan, May 4, 1999 (with reference to the Pepperland case), the Court of Milan, June 30, 1992 (related to the Farmitalia case), the Court of Ivrea, August 12, 1995 (Manifattura di Cuorgnè case), and the Supreme Court (Decision 5503/2000 with reference to the "D'Andria case"). The Supreme Court even prohibited the adoption of the LBO scheme in Italy.

27. See also Zambelli (2008), Bernardi and Bernanrdi (2006), and Silvestri (2005).

28. For a review of the cases judged by Italian courts see, among others, Zambelli (2005), Fava and Fuschino (2003), and Bruno (2002).

29. See Zambelli (2005) for details.

30. Court decisions against LBOs are Criminal Tribunal of Milan, June 30, 1992; Ivrea Tribunal, August 12, 1995; Tribunal of Milan, May 4, 1999; Supreme Court, February 4, 2000. Examples of Court decisions in favor of LBOs are Tribunal of Milan, May 14, 1992; Tribunal of Brescia, June 1, 1993; Tribunal of Milan, May 13, 1999. See Zambelli (2005) for a discussion of the above decisions.

31. For a discussion on the reverse merger procedure in Italy, see Manzini (2000).

32. See also Roberts (2005), Wyatt (2004), Sterling and Wright (1990), and Wright and Coyne (1985).

33. *"A company cannot advance funds, nor make loans or provide security for the purchase of its own shares by a third party."*

34. For a legal overview of the different rules applied to the financial assistance in Europe, see Ferran (2007). For an overview on how the financial assistance is regulated outside Europe see, for example, Chow and Tjio (2006); Fletcher (2006).

35. In Italy, several LBO transactions were accused of breaching the financial assistance prohibition and declared void. For more information see Silvestri (2005), Zambelli (2005), and Bernardi and Bernardi (2006).

36. Another condition for the legitimacy of the transaction is represented by the fair price or fair market condition.

37. See Rusconi (2008) for more details.

38. Article 7 (d) states: *"The merger of two companies, one of which had received debt financing in order to acquire the control of the other, does not imply a violation of the prohibition to make loans or provide guarantees for the purchase or the subscription of own shares."*

39. For a legal overview of the LBO requirements highlighted in the new corporate governance reform see Silvestri (2005); Portolano (2003).

40. Article 2051-bis, in fact, clarifies that mergers between a leveraged vehicle (newco)

and the acquired company (target) where the target acts as general guarantee for the financing shall now be permitted subject to certain requirements.

41. Financial experts are chosen from a specific Register of Auditors.

42. See Appendix 21.B for details.

43. See Zambelli (2008) for a discussion of the effects associated with forward merger LBOs and reverse merger LBOs.

44. For further details see Portolano (2003).

45. Under the past provision of article 2630 c.c., a breach of the financial assistance prohibition (article 2358) was automatically punishable as a crime. The new corporate criminal reform (Legislative Decree 61/2002) has eliminated this risk. Consequently, the risk for the managers involved in an LBO transaction to be punished with a sentence of up to 3 years imprisonment does not exist anymore.

46. Legislative Decree April 11, 2002, number 61.

47. See also Rusconi (2008) and the Legislative Decree 142/2008 for details.

48. Legislative Decree, April 11, 2002, number 61.

49. See article 2629 c.c.

50. See article 2634 c.c. for more details.

51. See article 2621 c.c. for details.

52. See Appendix 21.C for details.

53. For more information on the organizational structure of Italian closed-end funds see Capizzi (2004); Caselli (2007).

54. According to the AIFI statistics reports, the number of buyout investors was 25 (with reference to the starting date of our survey).

55. In line with the definition provided by the Private Equity Monitor (PEM) database (available from www.privateequtiymonitor.it), our private equity dataset excludes start-up financing (venture capital investments) and includes leveraged buyout transactions, expansion, and replacement financing.

56. See, for example, Gervasoni and Bechi (2007) for a review of the characteristics of different types of private equity investors.

57. See, for example, Kaplan and Stromberg (2004); Sahlman (1990).

58. A Likert scale measures the extent to which a person agrees or disagrees with a particular question. The most commonly used scale ranges from 1 to 5, where: 1 = strongly disagree, 2 = disagree, 3 = not sure, 4 = agree, and 5 = strongly agree. In our survey we adopted the Likert scale to measure the relevance of the selection criteria indicated by investors.

REFERENCES

Accinni, G. P. 2001. Operazioni di leveraged buyout ed un preteso caso di illiceità penale. *Rivista delle Società* 193–210.

Achleitner, A., E. Nathusius, K. Herman, and J. Lerner. 2008. Impact of private equity on corporate governance, employment, and empowerment of a family in a divisional buyout: The case of Messer Griesheim. Globalization of Alternative Investments—The Global Economic Impact of Private Equity Report, 91–102.

Allen, F., and W. L. Song. 2003. Venture capital and corporate governance. In *Corporate governance and capital flows in a global economy*, eds. P. K. Cornelius and B. Kogut, pp. 133–156. New York: Oxford University Press.

Amess, K., and M. Wright. 2007. Barbarians at the gate? Leveraged buyouts, private equity and jobs. Available at SSRN: ssrn.com/abstract=1034178.

Axelson, U., T. Jenkinson, P. Stromberg, and M. S. Weisbach. 2007a. Leverage and pricing in buyouts: An empirical analysis. Working Paper available at SSRN: http://ssrn.com/abstract=1027127.

Axelson, U., P. Stromberg, and M. S. Weisbach. 2007b. Why are buyouts levered: The financial structure of private equity funds. NBER Working Paper No. W12826.

Bernardi, M. 2001. LBO: An economic tool or an economic crime? *International Financial Law Review*, Yearbook 2001, Special Supplement on Italy.

Bernardi, M., and A. Bernardi. 2006. Italy: Q&A. *International Financial Law Review*, Special Supplement: The 2006 Guide to Private Equity and Venture Capital.

Bolton, P., and D. Sharferstein. 1990. Theory of predation based on agency problems in financial contracting. *American Economic Review* 80:93–106.

Bongaerts, D., and E. Charlier. 2009. Private equity and regulatory capital. *Journal of Banking and Finance* 33 (7):1211–1220.

Bonini, S., and R. Zullo. 2000. Venture capital and debt financing with costly default. *The Journal of Multinational Financial Management*.

Brau, C., and S. Fawcett. 2006. Initial public offerings: An analysis of theory and practice. *Journal of Finance* 61:399–436.

Bruno, N., 2002. Il leveraged buyout nella casistica giurisprudenziale. Working Paper, LUISS Guido Carli, CERADI.

Bruno, N. 2006. Divieto di assistenza finanziaria e operazioni di "merger leveraged." *Diritto e pratica delle società* 17. Available from: www.professionisti24.ilsole24ore.com/art/AreaProfessionisti/Diritto/Dossier/CERADI/DIR_CER_17_06.shtml?uuid=b1915ab2-52ee-11db-8eb3-00000e25108c.

Cao, J., and L. Lerner. 2009. The performance of reverse leveraged buyouts. *Journal of Financial Economics* 91:139–157.

Capizzi, V. 2005. Leveraged acquisitions: Technical and financial issues. In *Structured finance: Techniques, products, and market*, eds. Gatti Caselli, chap. 5. Berlin: Springer-Verlag.

Capizzi, V. 2004. The constitution of a venture capital company: The case of Italian closed-end funds. In *Venture capital: A Euro-system approach*, eds. S. Caselli and S. Gatti. Berlin-Heidelberg, New York: Springer-Verlag.

Casamatta, C. 2003. Financing and advising: Optimal financial contracts with venture capitalists. *Journal of Finance* 58 (5):2059–2086.

Caselli, S., 2007. What role do closed-end funds play? In *Venture capital: A European perspective*, eds. G. N. Gregoriou, M. Kooli, and M. Kraussl. London: Elsevier.

Caselli, S., and S. Gatti. 2005. Structured finance: Techniques, products, and market. Berlin-Heidelberg, New York: Springer-Verlag.

Chow, M. E., and H. Tjio. 2006. Providing assistance for financial assistance. *Singapore Journal of Legal Studies*, 465–478.

Chou, D.-W., M. Gombola, and F.-Y. Liu. 2006. Earnings management and stock performance of reverse leveraged buyouts. *Journal of Financial and Quantitative* 41 (2):407–428.

Cleary Gottlieb Steen Hamilton European M&A Report. 2003, 2004. Available at: www.clearygottlieb.com/files/tbl_s47Details%5CFileUpload265%5C418%5CCCGSH_CGSH_European_MA_Report_October_2003.pdf; www.clearygottlieb.com/files/tbl_s47Details%5CFileUpload265%5C382%5CCGSH_CGSH_European_MA_Report_April_2004.pdf

Cornelli, F., and O. Yosha. 2003. Stage financing and the role of convertible securities. *Review of Economic Studies* 70:1–32.

Cumming, D., G. Fleming, and A. Schwienbacher. 2006. Legality and venture capital exits. *Journal of Corporate Finance* 12:214–245.

Cumming, D. 2006. The determinants of venture capital portfolio size: empirical evidence. *Journal of Business* 79:1083–1126.

Cumming, D. 2005a. Capital structure in venture finance. *Journal of Corporate Finance* 11:550–585.

Cumming, D. 2005b. Agency costs, institutions, learning and taxation in venture capital contracting. *Journal of Business Venturing* 20:573–622.

Cumming, D., D. Schmidt, and U. Walz. 2008. Legality and venture governance around the world. *Journal of Business Venturing*, forthcoming.

Cumming, D., D. Siegel, M. Wright. 2007. Private equity, leveraged buyouts and governance. *Journal of Corporate Finance* 13:439–460.

Cumming, D., and S. Zambelli, 2009. Illegal buyouts. *Journal of Banking and Finance*, forthcoming.

Davis, S., J. Haltiwanger, R. Jarmin, J. Lerner, and J. Miranda. 2008. Private equity and employment. Working Paper, Harvard Business School.

De Leeuw, E. D. 2005. To mix or not to mix data collection modes in surveys. *The Journal of Official Statistics*, 21 (2):233–255.

Dessi, R. 1999. Financing entrepreneurs: Optimal contracts and the role of intermediaries. Working Papers, Financial Market Group.

Dillman, D. 1978. Mail and telephone surveys: The total design method. New York: John Wiley & Sons.

Dillman, D., G. Phelps, R. Tortora, K. Swift, J. Kohrell, and J. Berck. 2004. Response rate and measurement differences in mixed mode surveys using mail, telephone, interactive voice response and the Internet. Working Paper, Washington State University.

Enriques, L. 2002. Do corporate law judges matter? Some evidence from Milan. *European Business Organization Law Review* 3:756–821.

Enriques, L., and P. F. Volpin. 2007. Corporate governance reforms in Continental Europe. *Journal of Economic Perspectives* 21:117–140.

Fava, P., P. Fuschino 2003. *Il leveraged buyout*. Piacenza: La Tribuna.

Ferran, E. 2007. Regulation of private equity-backed leveraged buyout activity in Europe. ECGI Working Paper 84/2007.

Ferrari, P. 2007. Gli intermediari finanziari e le operazioni di leveraged buyout. *Forestieri* 381–418.

Financial Services Authority. 2006. Private equity: A discussion of risk and regulatory engagement. FSA (November).

Fletcher, K. 2006. Financial assistance around the Pacific Rim: The persistence of dysfunctional provisions. Working paper, University of Queensland, available at www.law.uq.edu.au/clta/abstracts.html.

Forestieri, G. 2007. *Corporate e investment banking*. Milano: Egea.

Frignani, A. 1996. *Factoring, leasing, franchising, venture capital, leveraged buyout, hardship clause, countertrade, cash and carry, merchandising, know how, securitization*. Torino: Giappichelli.

Gervasoni, A., and A. Bechi. 2007. I fondi chiusi di private equity nell'esperienza italiana. Bologna: Il Mulino.

Gilligan, J., and M. Wright. 2008. Private equity demystified. London: ICAEW.

Graham, J. R., and C. R. Harvey. 2001. The theory and practice of corporate finance: Evidence from the field. *Journal of Financial Economics* 60:187–243.

Guo, S., E. S. Hotchkiss, and W. Song. 2007. Do buyouts (still) create value? Working Paper.

Harris, M., and A. Raviv. 1990. Capital structure and the informational role of debt. *Journal of Finance* 45:321–349.

Harris, M., and A. Raviv. 1991. The theory of capital structure. *Journal of Finance* 46 (1):297–355.

Hellmann, T. 2006. IPOs, acquisitions and the use of convertible securities in venture capital. *Journal of Financial Economics* 81, 649–679.

Holmstrom B., and S. N. Kaplan. 2001. Corporate governance and merger activity in the United States: Making sense of the 1980s and 1990s. *Journal of Economic Perspectives* 15:121–144.

Jelic, R. 2008. UK private equity market—Longevity, exit strategies, and performance of management buyouts. European Financial Management Association Annual Meeting, Athens.

Jensen, M. 1989. Active investors, LBOs, and the privatization of bankruptcy. *Journal of Applied Corporate Finance* 2:35–44.

Kaplan, S. N., and P. Strömberg. 2004. Characteristics, contracts, and actions: Evidence from venture capitalist analyses. *Journal of Finance* 59:2177–2210.

Kaplan, S. 1989. The effects of management buyouts on operating performance and value. *Journal of Financial Economics* 24:217–254.

Kaplan, S. 1997. The evolution of U.S. corporate governance: We are all Henry Kravis now. *Journal of Private Equity* 7–14.

Kaplan, S., F. Martel, and P. Stromberg. 2006. How do legal systems and experience affect financial contracts? Working Paper, University of Chicago.

La Porta, R., F. Lopez-De-Silanes, A. Shleifer, R. Vishny. 1997. Legal determinants of external finance. *Journal of Finance* 52:1131–1150.

La Porta, R., F. Lopez-De-Silanes, A. Shleifer, R. Vishny. 1998. Law and finance. *Journal of Political Economy* 106:1113–1155.

La Torre, M., and R. Rio. 2002. Italian government set to change LBO legislation. *Southern Europe Unquote* (October 22):10–11.

Lerner, J., and A. Schoar. 2005. Does legal enforcement affect financial transactions? The contractual channel in private equity. *Quarterly Journal of Economics* 120: 223–246.

Ljungqvist, A., M. Richardson, and D. Wolfenzon. 2007. The investment behavior of buyout funds. NBER Working Paper No. 14180.

Manzini, G. 2000. La fusione c.d. inversa, ossia l'incorporazione della controllante nella controllata. *Contratto e impresa* 850–873.

Mills, M., and F. Seassaro. 1990. Italy. *International Financial Law Review* (Special Supplement):47–51.

Montalenti, P. 1996. I giudici italiani e il leveraged buyout tra responsabilità della capogruppo e divieto di assistenza finanziaria. *Giur. It* (sez. II.):195.

Montalenti, P. 2004. The new Italian corporate law: An outline. *European Company and Financial Law Review* 3:368–378.

Musco, E. 2002. *I nuovi reati societari*. Torino: Giuffrè.

Negri-Clementi, A., and P. Montironi. 2002. Leveraged buyouts. Discussion paper available from: www.altassets.com/casefor/countries/2002/nz3432.php

Nikoskelainen, E., and M. Wright. 2007. The impact of corporate governance mechanisms on value increase in leveraged buyouts. *Journal of Corporate Finance* 13:511–537.

Opler, T. 1992. Operating performance in leveraged buyouts: Evidence from 1985–1989. *Financial Management* 21:34–41.

Portolano, F. 2003. Italian corporate law reform. Available at: www.pccp.it.

Renneboog, L. 2007. Leveraged and management buyouts in Europe. *MCA— Tijdschrift voor Organisaties Control* 11, forthcoming.

Repullo, R., and J. Suarez. 2004. Venture capital finance: A security design approach. *Review of Finance* 8 (1):75–108.

Roberts, C. 2005. Financial assistance for the acquisition of shares. Oxford: Oxford University Press.

Rusconi, L. 2008. Italy enacts new regulation on financial assistance. Available at: www.bakernet.com/NR/rdonlyres/117CF60F-D2EB-4463-B7AB-8F663B2F3610/0/italy_newfinancialassistance_ca_nov08.pdf.

Sahlman, W. A. 1999. Some thoughts on business plans. In *The entrepreneurial venture*, eds. William A. Sahlman, Howard H. Stevenson, Michael J. Roberts, and Amar Bhide, pp. 138–176. Boston: Harvard Business School Press.

Sahlman, W. A. 1990. The structure and governance of venture capital organizations. *Journal of Financial Economics* 27:421–473.

Schmidt, K. M., 2003. "Convertible Securities and Venture Capital Finance." *Journal of Finance* 58:3, 1139–1166.

Shepherd, D. A. 1999a. Venture capitalist's introspection: A comparison of in use and "espoused" decision policies. *Journal of Small Business Management* 27:76–87.

Shepherd, D. A. 1999b. Venture capitalists' assessment of new venture survival. *Management Science* 45 (5):621–632.

Silvestri, M. 2005. The new Italian law on merger leveraged buyouts: A law and economics perspective. *European Business Organization Law Review* 6:101–147.

Smith, A. J. 1990. Corporate ownership structure and performance. The case of MBOs. *Journal of Financial Economics* 27:143–164.

Stein, B. 2006. On buyouts, there ought to be a law. *New York Times*, September 3, available at: www.nytimes.com/2006/09/03/business/yourmoney/03every.html?ex=1314936000&en=6679077c5af5c4a6&ei=5088&partner=rssnyt&emc=rss

Sterling, M., and M. Wright. 1990. Management buyouts and the law. Oxford, UK: Blackwell Law.

Stromberg, P. 2008. The new demography of private equity. In *Globalization of Alternative Investments*, eds. G. Anuradha and J. Lerner. Working Papers, Volume 1: Global Economic Impact of Private Equity 2008, New York, World Economic Forum USA.

Varrenti, A. 2000a. A follow-up to the legal saga on leveraged buyouts: Italian Supreme Court holds LBOs transactions to be illegal. *Corporate Finance* (London, November):37–38.

Varrenti, A. 2000b. Leveraged buyouts in Italy: An update on a highly debated acquisition system. *Corporate Finance* (London):75–77.

Williamson, O. E. 1988. Corporate finance and corporate governance. *Journal of Finance* 43:567–591.

Wright, M., and J. Coyne. 1985. Management buyouts. London: Croom Helm, Beckenham.

Wright, M., R. E. Hoskisson, L. W. Busenitz, J. Dial, 2001. "Finance and management buyouts: agency versus entrepreneurship perspectives". *Venture Capital: An International Journal of Entrepreneurial Finance* 3:239–262.

Wright, M., L. Renneboog, T. Simons, and L. Scholes. 2006. Leveraged buyouts in the U.K. and Continental Europe: Retrospect and prospect. *Journal of Applied Corporate Finance* 18:38–55.

Wright, M., S. Thompson, and K. Robbie. 1992. Venture capital and management-led leveraged buyouts: A European perspective. *Journal of Business Venturing* 7:47–71.

Wright, M., N. Wilson, and K. Robbie. 1996. The longer term effects of management-led buyouts. *Journal of Entrepreneurial and Small Business Finance* 5:213–234.

Wyatt, M. 2004. Company acquisition of own shares. Bristol, U.K.: Jordan.

Zacharakis, A. L., and G. D. Meyer. 2000. The potential of actuarial decision models: Can they improve the venture capital investment decision? *Journal of Business Venturing* 15: 323–346.

Zacharakis, A. L., and G. D. Meyer. 1998. A lack of insight: Do venture capitalists really understand their own decision process? *Journal of Business Venturing* 13:57–76.

Zambelli S. 2008. The dark side of LBOs: Private equity investors be forewarned! *Corporate Ownership & Control* 5 (4):59–78.

Zambelli S. 2005. Il leveraged buyout in Italia: Controversie e casi aziendali. Rome: Aracne Editrice.

ABOUT THE AUTHOR

Simona Zambelli received a Ph.D. in Economics of Financial Intermediaries with a Law and Finance focus from the University of Siena (Italy). Subsequently, Dr. Zambelli specialized in Finance at Birkbeck College (London) and Harvard University. Afterward, she worked as a visiting professor at Rensselaer Polytechnic Institute (New York). Currently, she is assistant professor at the University of Bologna (Italy) where she teaches Venture Capital & Private Equity. Her main research interests are interdisciplinary with a law & finance perspective. She has written several publications on the topics of private equity financing and leveraged acquisitions, and corporate governance.

CHAPTER 22

Venture Capital and Private Equity in Germany

WOLFGANG BESSLER
Professor of Finance and Banking, Justus-Liebig-University Giessen

JULIAN HOLLER
Research Assistant, Center for Finance and Banking, Justus-Liebig-University Giessen

MARTIN SEIM
Research Assistant, Center for Finance and Banking, Justus-Liebig-University Giessen

INTRODUCTION

The importance of venture capital (VC) has been well documented in the academic literature in that an efficient venture capital market is important in providing risk capital to start-up firms, thereby reducing financing problems for risky ventures and stimulating economic growth (Gompers and Lerner 1999). Hence, supporting venture capital firms has been on the political agenda in many countries during the last decade. The main reason for this support is that, first of all, venture capitalists provide important functions during the start-up phase of a company such as screening, monitoring and consulting (Berlin 1998). In particular, they are able to deal efficiently with possible information asymmetries between the investor and the VC firm as well as between the VC firm and the entrepreneur (Gompers and Lerner 2001). They further increase the success rate by closely monitoring and enforcing incentive-compatible contracts (bonding) so that management is motivated to maximize the market value of the venture (Gompers and Lerner 1999). In addition, VC firms reduce the return volatility for the investor by increasing the portfolio size and through diversification, and they mitigate the information problems between the VC firm and the entrepreneur by taking control over supervisory board seats, voting rights as well as cash flow and liquidation rights. Moreover, funds for start-up firms are usually provided in smaller tranches and financing continues only when specific milestones or performance measures are achieved (Gompers and Lerner 1999; Tirole 2006). Finally, venture capital has a positive effect on economic growth and employment as well as on innovation (Guellec and van Pottelsberghe 2007). Consequently, venture capital is one of the most interesting and important financing sources for young and small start-up companies. It needs to be kept in mind, however, that investments in these companies—even after taking appropriate measures—are typically extremely risky because of the high uncertainty with respect to the viability and to the success of the ventures and the new business ideas.

Before we concentrate in the remainder of this article on venture capital in Germany, it seems important to distinguish between venture capital, on one hand, and private equity, on the other hand. In Germany, this distinction between venture capital and private equity is not as clear cut as it is in the United States. Hence, the facts and figures presented in this paper refer to both early and expansion stage as well as buyout financing.

The size of the venture capital industry in Germany is still relatively small, given the size and the importance of the German economy, although it has increased in relative terms during the past decade. Until the end of the 1990s, Germany was usually viewed as the archetype of a bank-dominated universal banking system in which bank loans were the primary source of financing. It was certainly not a too-well-advanced country with respect to financing start-up firms, growth opportunities, and technology firms, as well as employing venture capital as an important financing instrument (Bessler and Kurth 2004). However, with the beginning of the "new economy period" and the introduction of the new stock market segment, "Neuer Markt," for high-growth and technology companies at the German Stock Exchange (Deutsche Börse) in 1997, venture capital experienced a substantial increase in Germany in terms of invested funds and investment opportunities, especially into young and innovative firms. One possible explanation for this development is that VC firms most likely expected superior exit opportunities through initial public offerings (IPOs). Nevertheless, the still relatively minor importance of the German VC market is not only reflected in a comparatively low total portfolio volume, but also in a different behavior of VC firms with respect to the general development of the VC market (Bessler and Kurth 2003; Schertler 2006), exit behavior (Bessler and Kurth 2004 and 2005; Bienz and Walz 2006; Tykvová 2006), and stock price performance of venture-backed companies after going public (Franzke 2004; Bessler and Kurth 2007; Tykvová and Walz 2007).

The purpose of this article is to provide in the first part the basic information and a detailed analysis of the relevant figures for the German VC industry and its development over the past two decades. This includes first of all an international comparison of the German venture capital industry with respect to the volume of funds and its importance relative to the size of the German economy. We then analyze the sources of venture capital funds in Germany and differentiate venture capital investments by industry composition and geographic dispersion as well as by the importance of different investment stages. In addition, we investigate the specialization and ownership structure of German VC firms and the financing instruments they usually employ. Finally, we discuss the various routes that German venture capital firms use to exit from their portfolio companies. This sets the stage for the second part of this article where we concentrate on going public as the most interesting exit route for venture capital firms. After a review of the literature and the empirical findings, we provide our own empirical evidence on underpricing and long-run performance of venture-backed IPOs in Germany. This is followed by a discussion of the relevance of lock-up agreements and a differentiation between different VC types as well as a discussion of the impact of venture capital on innovation. The last section summarizes our findings and concludes.

THE DEVELOPMENT OF THE GERMAN VENTURE CAPITAL INDUSTRY

Concurrent with significant changes in the structure of the German economy and the continuous improvement of the capital market environment, especially the opening of new stock market segments for high-technology and growth companies ("Neuer Markt," 1997 to 2003, and "Entry Standard" since 2005), the attractiveness of the German venture capital industry has improved significantly during the last two decades. Most visibly, these changes are reflected in increasing inflows and higher total portfolio volumes (Exhibit 22.1), in the growing number of active venture capital firms (Exhibit 22.2) as well as in the amount of funds raised and in venture capital investments and exits (Exhibits 22.4 and 22.11, respectively) by members of the German Venture Capital Association (BVK), the umbrella organization for venture capitalists in Germany. These developments are best characterized by three distinct time periods, so that it seems appropriate to divide our analysis into the following periods: 1990 to 1996, 1997 to 2003, and 2004 to 2007. The last period includes the beginning of the financial crisis in 2007 and we use the latest data available up to the third quarter of 2008. We use these three periods to structure our analysis of the development of the German venture capital market in the remainder of this section.

The first period of our analysis covers the time before 1996. Due to the traditional focus on bank financing and the relatively low attractiveness of the German stock market during that period, the market for venture capital was not well established in Germany in comparison to markets in more capital market–oriented countries, such as the United States or the United Kingdom. In the early 1980s, the total VC volume invested by BVK members hardly exceeded €1 billion. In the

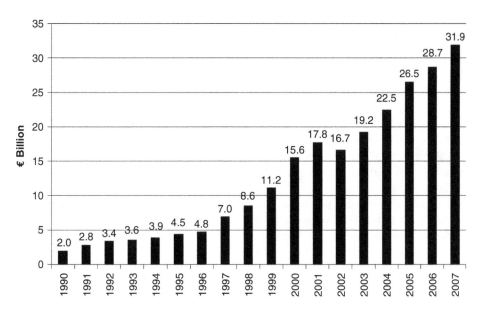

Exhibit 22.1 Development of Total Venture Capital Portfolios in Germany
Source: BVK (2008).

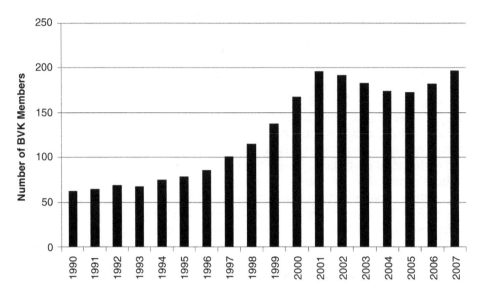

Exhibit 22.2   Number of BVK Members over Time
Source: BVK (2008).

1990s, however, the VC volume started to grow impressively. The portfolio volume increased at an annual growth rate of 15.7 percent from €2 billion in 1990 to €4.8 billion in 1996. Nevertheless, for a long period of time, the venture capital industry was not at a level necessary to provide sufficient funds for start-up firms, given the size of the German economy. The second period ranges from 1997 to 2003 and corresponds to the new economy or high-technology period. During this period, the largest increase in VC volume occurred, with the total portfolio volume growing at an annual rate of 22 percent between 1997 and 2003, reaching €17.8 billion in 2001 and €19.2 billion in 2003. Evidently, a large share of this extraordinary growth was driven by the new economy euphoria and the global boom in technology stocks in the late 1990s and the opening of the "Neuer Markt" in 1997 in Germany, creating profitable exit opportunities for venture capital firms. The third and last period extends from the recovery of equity markets in 2004 until 2007. During this period, there was a steady increase in total portfolio volume, up to €31.9 billion at the end of 2007.

Parallel to the development of the portfolio volume of venture capital financing, the number of market participants (members of the BVK) operating in Germany also increased rapidly from 63 venture capital firms in 1990 to 196 venture capital firms in 2001 (see Exhibit 22.2). It appears that the dramatic downturn of the stock market in 2000 and the closing of the "Neuer Markt" in 2003 had only minor effects on the commitment of venture capital firms to the German market, as evidenced by a small decline to 183 active venture capital firms in 2003, before eventually increasing again to 197 members in 2007. Overall, VC firms in Germany employ a staff of about 1,800 people of which roughly 1,600 are professionals (BVK 2007).

In order to provide more insights into the evolution of the German venture capital market and changes in the market environment, the rest of this chapter is divided into six sections. The next section compares the relative size of the German venture capital market to other countries and provides several explanations for the observed differences. The following section focuses on sources of funding for venture capital firms. The investment process of venture capital firms in Germany is analyzed in the subsequent section with a focus on the clustering of investments in specific industries, regions and financing stages. In the next section we address the specialization and the ownership structure of venture capital firms in Germany before providing insights into some institutional details of financial contracting by venture capital firms, such as the instruments used, and the propensity to syndicate their investments. This includes a discussion about why the German venture capital market is different from other markets. Finally, we explore the various routes that venture capital firms use to exit from their portfolio companies in Germany and highlight the importance of going public.

An International Comparison of the Relative Importance of Venture Capital

Despite the substantial growth of the German venture capital industry over the past 20 years, it is still relatively small by international standards given the size and importance of the German economy. In fact, due to the immense importance of venture capital for financing technology and innovation (Popov and Roosenboom 2008), it appears that this is a major competitive disadvantage for the German economy compared to countries with more vibrant venture capital markets such as the United States and the United Kingdom. In the next section we first analyze the relative importance of the venture capital industry in various countries by comparing the size of the invested VC funds relative to GDP (gross domestic product). In the second section we review the literature with respect to the impact of the institutional setting on VC financing and provide suggestions for creating a more venture capital–friendly environment in Germany.

Relative Importance of the Venture Capital Industry in Germany

At the end of the "new economy" period and during the down-market in 2002, when total venture capital investments declined in all countries, the total volume of new venture capital investments in Germany reached about $2.4 billion or only 0.21 percent of GDP. In contrast, in the more capital market–oriented countries, the total amount exceeded $62.7 billion, or 0.60 percent of GDP in the United States, and $9.6 billion, or 0.62 percent of GDP in the United Kingdom, even during that difficult market environment. Moreover, other countries with less capital market–oriented financial systems also have a higher level of venture capital investments. In France, for instance, the total volume of new venture capital investments reached 0.39 percent of GDP in 2002 (for detailed data see PwC/3i 2003). Overall, these figures support the view of a relatively small VC market in Germany.

This overall ranking did not change much during the subsequent market recovery, according to recent figures provided by the National Venture Capital Association (NVCA 2008) and PricewaterhouseCoopers (PwC 2008). While in 2007 venture capital investments reached again high levels with almost $30 billion of venture capital invested in the United States and approximately €58 billion in

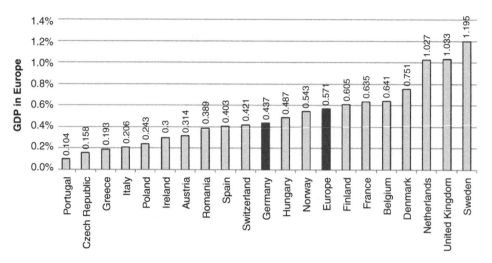

Exhibit 22.3 Venture Capital Investment as a Percentage of GDP in Europe in 2007
Source: EVCA (2008).

the Asia-Pacific region (33 percent annual growth rate), the amount of venture capital investments remained relatively small in Germany, with only €4 billion (BVK 2008). Consequently, the ratio of venture capital investments to GDP also remained small by international comparison in 2007 (EVCA 2008).

Exhibit 22.3 provides the relevant figures for venture capital investments relative to GDP for European countries in 2007. In Europe, on average 0.57 percent of GDP was invested in venture capital. German venture capital investments were below the European average with only 0.44 percent of GDP in 2007—up from 0.21 percent at the bottom of the market in 2002. Thus, the data reveals that much fewer funds were invested in Germany relative to other European countries. The ratios for most southern and eastern European countries are also below the European average. In contrast, countries such as France (0.63 percent), Belgium (0.64 percent), and the Netherlands (1.03 percent) exceed the mean. It is also well documented that the Nordic countries such as Norway (0.54 percent percent), Finland (0.61 percent), Denmark (0.75 percent), and in particular Sweden (1.12 percent), are characterized by a strong entrepreneurial spirit and have a relatively large venture capital industry. Similarly, in the United Kingdom, with its greater emphasis on capital market–based mechanisms, 1.03 percent of GDP was invested by VC firms in 2007. In Germany, the volume of invested venture capital funds will have to increase substantially in the future in order to provide sufficient risk capital for start-up firms with promising prospects and innovative business ideas.

The Financial System and the Venture Capital Industry in Germany
So far, the data analysis suggests that the size of the German venture capital industry is relatively small given the importance of technology and innovation, as well as the size of the German economy. One main problem appears to be related to the structure of the German financial system. In fact, Booth, Junttila, Kallunki, Rahiala, and Sahlström (2006) provide empirical evidence that capital market–based financial systems provide more funding to risky ventures, such as technology

and start-up firms, than bank-based financial systems. According to Rajan and Zingales (2003) the major impediments to the development of venture capital markets in bank-based financial systems such as Germany are the lack of transparency and high information asymmetries. One reason for the vibrant U.S. venture capital market appears to be the advanced development of the U.S. stock market (Black and Gilson 1998). In particular, reliable information and stringent disclosure rules are necessary in order to develop liquid capital markets that facilitate the ultimate exit of venture capital firms from their investments and allow them to generate high returns. Moreover, stringent investor protection rules are needed in order to force venture capital firms to exert sufficient monitoring efforts (Bottazzi, Da Rin, and Hellmann 2008). Given the size and the growth of the German venture capital market during the last couple of years, recent shifts towards a more capital market–oriented system apparently were not sufficient, although the opening of the "Neuer Markt" in 1997 helped to facilitate the going-public of venture-backed firms on the German stock market. However, this stock market segment was closed in 2003 after a disastrous performance of many firms as well as some legal and accounting scandals. Since 2005, companies planning to go public have the chance to get listed on the "Entry Standard" of the German stock exchange (Deutsche Börse). Thus, a lack of entrepreneurial spirit in Germany and an unfavorable institutional environment for the development of young firms might be two reasons for the relatively low development of the German venture capital industry (Becker and Hellmann 2005). Further reforms of the German capital market architecture as well as of the institutional infrastructure appear to be necessary in order to promote the development of a competitive venture capital industry providing sufficient risk capital to start-up and technology companies (Cumming, Schmidt, and Walz 2008).

Moreover, there is additional empirical evidence from various countries on the positive impact of other factors that should be considered in any reform efforts. For the United States, Gompers, Lerner, Blair, and Hellmann (1998) identify that decreases in capital gains tax rates stimulate the demand for VC as well as R&D expenditures. In addition, a fund's track record, as well as its reputation, is positively related to fund-raising. Felix, Gulamhussen, and Pires (2007) verify these findings for Europe. Hellmann, Lindsey, and Puri (2008) address the role of banks for providing capital to VCs. The probability of a lending relationship to a company increases significantly with a prior VC investment in that company. Winton and Yerramilli (2008) derive a theoretical framework to show under which conditions an entrepreneur should finance his venture with bank loans or VC. In a recent study Cumming, Fleming, and Suchard (2005) investigate for the Australian market the flows from pension funds to VC firms. Besides a positive track record, they conclude that VC funds attract higher commitments the more financial and strategic support is provided to entrepreneurial firms. In addition, a high performance fee, low management fees, and a high proportion of exits are associated with capital commitments. Surprisingly, pension funds are more reluctant to fund VC firms that exit via an IPO, while the opposite holds for exits through trade sales. This finding can be attributed to a two-year mandatory lock-up period in Australia that made IPO exits compared to trade sales relatively illiquid. This research offers additional insights and suggestions for actions due to the important role of banks and pension funds in Germany. Tax reforms are an important issue that the German government has avoided to address so far.

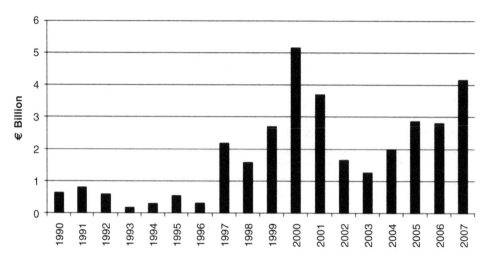

Exhibit 22.4   Development of Fund-Raising in Germany
Source: BVK (2008).

Sources of Venture Capital Funds in Germany

As in most other financial systems, venture capital in Germany is provided by different types of investors. Venture capital firms range from financial intermediaries such as banks and insurance companies to pension funds and government agencies. These providers of venture capital differ significantly with respect to their ability and willingness to take risks, their level of sophistication and knowledge of specific industries as well as their own or in some cases even externally determined objectives. Therefore, the shift in the relative importance of these different VC investors during the last two decades has important implications for the venture capital industry in Germany.

In Exhibit 22.4, we present the development of the total amounts of funds raised by venture capital firms in Germany for the period from 1990 to 2007. Overall, there is a substantial increase in fund inflows during that time period, although some weaker intervals are quite visible. Exhibit 22.5 provides an overview of the funds raised differentiated by the type of venture capital firms for the period from 1994 to 2007. The major institutions providing venture capital in Germany are banks, insurance companies, pension funds, and public or government agencies. Although these four groups were the most important sources for venture capital in Germany during the last decades, their level of activity and their relative importance has not only fluctuated widely over time but its basic structure has changed as well.

Until 1996, banks used to be the largest supplier of venture capital, with about €320 million of new funds raised in 1995, reflecting the traditional importance and the dominant role of commercial banks in the German financial system. More precisely, banks provided approximately 61 percent in 1994, 59 percent in 1995, and about 58 percent of funds in 1996 and 1997. Concurrent with the low attractiveness of the German stock market during that time period, the high level of bank activity might explain the relatively minor importance of the German venture capital

Exhibit 22.5   New Funds Raised by Venture Capitalists in Germany

Year	Banks	Insurance	Pension Funds	Public Sector	Rest	Volume
1994	61%	11%	0%	5%	23%	300.1
1995	59%	6%	9%	8%	18%	546.7
1996	58%	7%	11%	7%	17%	318.9
1997	58%	10%	12%	5%	15%	2,185.7
1998	50%	14%	14%	4%	18%	1,593.6
1999	29%	10%	30%	12%	19%	2,709.8
2000	29%	17%	12%	16%	26%	5,164.2
2001	18%	17%	38%	6%	21%	3,707.8
2002	22%	14%	45%	11%	9%	1,669.5
2003	11%	10%	25%	4%	49%	1,274.1
2004	20%	31%	6%	16%	28%	1,983.1
2005	12%	8%	52%	8%	21%	2,874.8
2006	30%	13%	24%	11%	22%	2,819.5
2007	20%	24%	20%	12%	24%	4,169.7
Year	**Banks**	**Insurance**	**Pension Funds**	**Public Sector**	**Rest**	**Volume**
Q1-Q3 2007	n.a.	n.a.	n.a.	n.a.	n.a.	3,145.8
Q1-Q3 2008	n.a.	n.a.	n.a.	n.a.	n.a.	1,286.3

Source: BVK (2008).

market and the lack of capital for the most risky and early-stage ventures. There may have been also a low demand for venture capital funds, given the relatively little entrepreneurial activity in Germany. In addition, banks usually have a limited ability to absorb risks and might often be more inclined to invest in relatively safe ventures in order to secure their future banking business (Hellmann, Lindsey, and Puri 2008).

Between 1997 and 2000, the period of the new economy euphoria, higher valuations of technology stocks were accompanied by a tremendous increase in fund inflows from €2,186 million to €5,164 million (see Exhibits 22.4 and 22.5). This sharp rise in overall fund flows was associated with a continuous decline in the relative share of funds raised from banks. Their overall importance started to decline during that time period when the German financial system evolved towards a more capital market–oriented system (Krahnen and Schmidt 2004). While the absolute amount of capital provided by banks remained constant, their relative share fell to 29 percent. Consequently, other investors entered the German venture capital market to provide additional funds. There was a large increase in institutional investments, such as from insurance companies and pension funds, which are traditionally also major providers of venture capital in more capital market–oriented financial systems, such as in the United States or in the United Kingdom. Insurance companies increased their relative share from 10 percent in 1997 to 17 percent in 2000, quadrupling the absolute volume of funds provided. Moreover, recognizing the importance of financing of start-ups and innovation for economic growth in Germany the relative share of government agencies increased from 5 percent to 16 percent. While these investments are ultimately driven by other public policy objectives, such as generating employment and regional development, these investments are nevertheless to some extent guided by market signals. In many programs, the government-owned Kreditanstalt für Wiederaufbau (KfW) syndicates their investments and acts as a co-investor who free-rides on the deal-screening abilities of more experienced venture capital firms. However, the supply of government funding distorts the market function by creating incentives for private market participants, for example, to select deals and structure transactions in a way that conforms to the government expectations and program designs. In effect, Bascha and Walz (2002) argue that this might be one reason for the low use of incentive-compatible financing arrangements in Germany.

During the stock market decline starting in 2000, however, fund inflows decreased sharply from their previous peaks. In 2001, the total amount of capital provided declined to €3,708 million and decreased even further to only €1,274 million in 2003. Interestingly, the shifts in the investor base for venture capital funding continued even during this difficult market environment. In particular, the relative share of banks continued to decline to 11 percent in 2003, while pension funds substantially increased their venture capital investments to 45 percent of new funds in 2002 and to 25 percent in 2003. For the years thereafter, fund-raising recovered steadily.

Over the period from 2004 to 2007 VCs' fund inflows grew from €1,983 million to €4,170 million. This is about 50 percent more than in 2006, but it is still €1 billion less than at the "new economy" peak in 2000. In 2007, most of the capital was provided by insurance companies with almost 24 percent of all funds raised, followed by banks and pension funds with 20 percent each, and public and government agencies with 12 percent, such as the programs provided by the state-owned KfW banking group. Overall, the data suggests that there is substantial volatility in the availability of funds for venture capital firms in Germany. This became even more apparent during the recent financial crisis when venture capital experienced a sharp drop in new funding, from €3,146 million in 2007 (Q1 to Q3) to only €1,286 million for the corresponding period in 2008.

Overall, the composition of venture capital funding in Germany underwent significant structural changes during the last decade. While banks contributed close to 60 percent of all new funds in the middle of the 1990s, banks account for only about 20 percent of new funds at the present time. Thus, banks have somewhat lost their supremacy as the main provider of venture capital in Germany. This drop has been compensated by an increase in funds provided by insurance companies, government agencies, and, most importantly, pension funds. Especially the importance of pension funds has increased in that they enlarged their relative share from 12 percent in 1997 to more than 50 percent in 2005. In recent years, however, they have lost again some of their importance by declining to 24 percent in 2006 and to 20 percent in 2007. VC commitments of insurance companies grew slightly over the last decade, on average, as is the case for funds provided by the public sector. The lower figures for 2008 reflect the negative impact of the current financial crisis. Overall it seems fair to conclude that with respect to the composition of funding sources for venture capital firms, the German venture capital industry has been moving closer to a more capital market–oriented system during the last decade.

Venture Capital Investments

After successfully raising sufficient venture capital funds in the first stage, the second stage in the venture capital process consists of screening promising projects and deciding whether or not to invest capital into specific projects or firms either alone or in cooperation with other VC firms or government entities. Depending on their skills, background, and experience, some VC firms specialize on specific industries, on certain geographical regions as well as on particular stages in the product or company life cycle.

In fact, in Germany as well as in many other countries, we observe that venture capital firms concentrate on certain industries, but also shift their focus and their investment strategies from time to time between different industries. Often this may depend on some current technology hype or herding behavior among venture capital firms. Moreover, venture capital firms and investments are often concentrated in certain regions of a country and they usually choose projects that are in their geographical proximity, especially in large countries such as the United States and Canada (Cumming 2007), so that regular consulting and close monitoring are possible. In addition, certain provinces or states within a country may create a better environment for venture capital investments and innovation so that specific technology and financing clusters emerge. Finally, venture capital firms may specialize on certain types or stages in the financing process depending on their own experience and skill, such as seed and start-up financing or buyouts and expansion financing. These issues are addressed in the rest of this section with a focus on Germany.

Industry Composition of Venture Capital Investments

Prior to the beginning of the "new economy" period, the consumer goods and the engineering industries accounted for the largest share of VC investments in Germany. Between 1992 and 1996, these two industries captured between 13 percent and 18 percent and between 10 percent and 21 percent of all investments, respectively. Investments into more risky industries such as chemicals, computers, or communications received at that time less than 10 percent of all funding in almost every year. In fact, this focus on relatively low risk and established industries is consistent with our earlier observation that banks used to be the largest providers of venture capital during that time period (Winton and Yerramilli 2008), staying away from the investments in more innovative and risky industries.

During the high-technology period and the opening and closing of the "Neuer Markt" between 1997 and 2003, the allocation of investments shifted strongly to riskier projects and firms in the newly emerging computer (software) industry, as was the case in most other countries. In 1998 this industry accounted for the highest share of investments from venture capital funds, with 15 percent or €249 million, followed by 11 percent in engineering, and 9 percent in the consumer goods industry. In 2000, the allocation of funds into the computer industry peaked with a relative share of about 26 percent or more than €1 billion of all VC funds. The other main areas of investments were in communications (12 percent) and in the consumer goods industry (10 percent). These three industries attracted almost 50 percent of all investments (Exhibit 22.6).

Exhibit 22.6   Investments by Industry in Germany

Year	Consumer Goods	Engineer- ing	Computer	Communi- cations	Medical Services	Chemicals	Rest*	Volume
1990	9%	16%	6%	1%	0%	7%	62%	481.1
1991	8%	10%	3%	3%	0%	4%	71%	509.2
1992	13%	14%	4%	1%	0%	10%	58%	527.6
1993	15%	21%	2%	1%	0%	7%	55%	516.9
1994	18%	15%	4%	1%	0%	7%	55%	536.9
1995	17%	12%	8%	4%	0%	6%	53%	541.5
1996	13%	10%	8%	3%	0%	4%	62%	611.5
1997	15%	16%	7%	7%	0%	3%	52%	1,210.7
1998	9%	11%	15%	5%	4%	4%	53%	1,700.0
1999	7%	10%	20%	12%	4%	2%	46%	2,816.2
2000	10%	6%	26%	12%	5%	1%	40%	4,450.8
2001	11%	11%	16%	8%	5%	15%	32%	4,434.9
2002	6%	17%	11%	7%	6%	17%	36%	2,506.2
2003	4%	8%	6%	12%	4%	7%	61%	2,415.4
2004	11%	9%	3%	3%	20%	2%	52%	3,765.8
2005	11%	9%	5%	12%	8%	3%	52%	3,039.6
2006	4%	19%	4%	3%	4%	2%	64%	3,637.9
2007	26%	14%	4%	13%	5%	8%	30%	4,124.4

Year	Consumer Goods	Engineer- ing	Computer	Communi- cations	Medical Services	Chemicals	Rest*	Volume
Q1-Q3 2007	30%	14%	3%	14%	3%	4%	31%	3,518.7
Q1-Q3 2008	11%	20%	3%	5%	6%	28%	27%	4,465.9

*BVK classifies investments into more than 20 different industries. Here the industries are presented which on average received the highest funds over our investigation period.
Source: BVK (2008).

Subsequent to the end of the stock market decline in 2003 and the end of the high-technology euphoria, medical services started to attract significant investments, capturing about 20 percent of all investments in 2004, while at the same time funding of the computer industry declined to just 3 percent, which did not recover until recently. In 2007, the largest VC investments in Germany were made in the consumer goods industry, engineering, and communications, with relative shares of 26 percent (€1.1 billion), 14 percent (€675 million), and 13 percent (€517 million), respectively. After the end of the technology bubble, German venture capital firms apparently started to shy away from riskier industries such as biotechnology, which are attracting significant venture capital investments in other countries. In addition, the computer hard- and software industries accounts for only 4 percent of all investments and not more than 5 percent were allocated into the medical services industry. This trend has continued during the recent financial crisis. In particular, during the first three quarters of 2008 28 percent of the investments were allocated to the more traditional chemicals industry up from only 4 percent during the first three quarters in 2007. This might indicate the lack of promising start-up ventures to invest in and the cautiousness in taking risky investment decisions during the financial crisis.

Overall, venture capital investments by German VC firms appear to be concentrated on a small number of promising industries. This is in line with the observation for Europe that VC investment mostly clusters in a few industries due to firm characteristics, potential returns, and exit opportunities in these industries. Moreover, there are significant shifts in venture capital investments across industries and over time, as firms in new industries mature, more collateral becomes available and pronounced information asymmetries decline, allowing them to have access to more conventional financing instruments. However, it appears that venture capital firms in Germany make only very limited investments in more risky industries, where financing constraints are most severe. Whether this is due to a lack of entrepreneurial spirit, to a limited supply of feasible projects in these industries, to a limited willingness and ability to take on risks by German venture capital firms or to limited exit opportunities on the German capital market remains an open question.

Geographic Distribution of Venture Capital Investments

Venture capital investments are often concentrated in certain regions of a country because new technologies are often developed in technology clusters. In the United States these are, for example, Silicon Valley, the Boston area and the North Carolina research triangle. Moreover, venture capital firms usually choose their location close to these clusters in order to facilitate their screening, monitoring, and consulting activities of portfolio companies (Cumming and Johan 2006). These basic patterns are also observable in Germany, where a small number of the 16 states are attracting a disproportionately high share of venture capital investments. Moreover, there exist several technology clusters in Germany (Audretsch and Lehmann 2005; Fromhold-Eisebith and Eisebith 2005; Sternberg and Litzenberger 2004). Some of them are related to university-based research. The regional concentration by states of venture capital investments is presented in Exhibit 22.7.

From 1990 to 1996 the largest share of venture capital investments was attracted by just four out of the 16 German states, namely Baden-Wuerttemberg, Bavaria, North Rhine-Westphalia, and Lower Saxony, each of which attracted about 15 percent of all funds. Moreover, Baden-Wuerttemberg and Bavaria have continuously attracted the largest shares of venture capital funding for the whole time period during which the BVK collected data. Other factors explaining the regional distribution of VC financed companies are regional governmental initiatives to promote new industries.

During the technology boom and the "Neuer Markt" period, especially North Rhine-Westphalia with its large Internet and media industry attracted the largest share of venture capital investments with 23 percent (€261 mio.) and 26 percent (€392 mio.) of all funds in 1997 and 1998, respectively. Subsequent to the end of the technology bubble in 2003, 37 percent or €726 million of all venture capital investments were made in North Rhine-Westphalia, while Baden-Wuerttemberg's and Bavaria's share reached 9 percent and 22 percent, respectively. In the following years, however, the highest shares of investments were in Bavaria (28 percent in 2004, 51 percent in 2006) and Baden-Wuerttemberg (21 percent in 2005, 53 percent

Exhibit 22.7   Investments by States in Germany

Year	Baden-Wuerttem-berg	Bavaria	Hesse	Lower Saxony	North Rhine Westphalia	Rest*	Volume
1990	n.a.	n.a.	n.a.	n.a.	n.a.	n.a.	481.1
1991	14%	17%	23%	7%	9%	30%	509.2
1992	16%	16%	8%	8%	16%	37%	527.6
1993	12%	15%	9%	14%	17%	34%	516.9
1994	14%	20%	7%	10%	14%	36%	536.9
1995	16%	20%	6%	10%	17%	32%	541.5
1996	17%	21%	7%	14%	16%	26%	611.5
1997	14%	16%	11%	6%	23%	28%	1,210.7
1998	14%	25%	8%	3%	26%	25%	1,700.0
1999	14%	20%	9%	6%	19%	32%	2,816.2
2000	13%	20%	9%	4%	20%	34%	4,450.8
2001	12%	22%	15%	4%	19%	28%	4,434.9
2002	19%	17%	7%	25%	11%	22%	2,506.2
2003	9%	22%	4%	2%	37%	27%	2,415.4
2004	16%	28%	5%	14%	28%	9%	3,765.8
2005	21%	14%	6%	6%	19%	34%	3,039.6
2006	14%	51%	13%	5%	8%	11%	3,637.9
2007	53%	10%	7%	13%	5%	13%	4,124.4

Year	Baden-Wuerttem-berg	Bavaria	Hesse	Lower Saxony	North Rhine Westphalia	Rest*	Volume
Q1-Q3 2007	60%	8%	3%	14%	4%	10%	3,518.7
Q1-Q3 2008	11%	16%	14%	5%	39%	15%	4,465.9

*In Germany, there are 16 federal states, so the share of "Rest" represents 11 federal states.
Source: BVK (2008).

in 2007). In 2007, more than 75 percent of all funds were invested either in Baden-Wuerttemberg (53 percent), Bavaria (10 percent), and Lower Saxony (13 percent). The share of investments in North Rhine–Westphalia experienced a strong rebound in the first three quarters of 2008, increasing from 4 percent in 2007 to 39 percent in 2008.

Apparently it seems that a limited number of innovation clusters attracts a disproportionate share of venture capital investments in Germany, most likely due to comparative advantages regarding innovation, research and development, and intellectual property. This view is supported by empirical evidence for the German market in that venture capital appears to be an important catalyst in the transformation of new ideas into successful products and firms. While the emergence of these clusters and this regional "knowledge capital" is often related to the existence of "university-based research"-cooperations, the federal and regional governments provide subsidies to foster the development of such clusters (Engel 2002). For instance, government support helped to create an emerging computer chip industry near Dresden in former East Germany.

Investigating a sample of firms listed on the "Neuer Markt" in Germany in 2001, Dohse and Schertler (2004) report a positive relationship between the number of listed firms in a particular region and the "knowledge capital" (proxied by the number of patents or other R&D related variables) of that region. Additionally, the regional supply of venture capital also has an impact on the regional distribution of listed firms. The rationale behind this relationship are lower transaction costs for screening, monitoring, and consulting, with a decreasing distance between VC firm and the entrepreneurial firm (Bessler and Kurth 2003). For European panel data, Schertler (2007) reports that the amount of VC investments is positively related to the number of patents and the number of R&D researchers in a specific country. Both variables have a positive and significant impact on the volume and the number of investments at all stages. Also, weak evidence is found that a large amount of government-financed knowledge capital increases the probability of VC investments in a specific country. Furthermore, the probability of board membership, and hence the opportunity to fulfill monitoring and consulting functions, increases significantly with the geographical proximity between the VC firm and the financed company (Lerner 1995).

Venture Capital Investments and Financing Stages

Over the life cycle of young technology and start-up firms, the risk-return tradeoffs and the nature and extent of agency problems and information asymmetries change significantly. Consequently, many venture capital firms concentrate on specific industries and types of investments, as well as on specific stages in a company's life cycle. Exhibit 22.8 provides a breakdown of venture capital investments by financing stages for the period from 1990 to 2007. In Exhibit 22.9 we illustrate the relative shares of the different investment stages in total financings during the same period.

In the early period between 1990 and 1996, the largest share of venture capital investments was provided to expansion stage firms, that is, firms with a sound business model requiring more capital to finance growth. The share in these relatively low risk firms fluctuated between 45 percent and 67 percent. Moreover, venture capital firms provided about 20 percent of their total investments to buyouts of rather mature firms, which are often characterized by low levels of innovative activities.

This focus on less risky ventures changed during the high-technology boom period from 1997 to 2001, when most funds were provided to risky start-up companies. Moreover, this time period witnessed also the largest share of seed financings, that is, supply of capital to firms that are in the product development stage. This is not surprising because during this boom phase of the high-technology mania, a large number of small businesses started with too optimistic business plans convincing venture capital funds to finance their ideas or dreams. While prior to 1996 less than 2 percent of investments were allocated to these very young ventures, they received 7 percent in 1998 and 1999 and 9 percent in 2000. Overall, the "Neuer Markt" phase with a wave of emerging young firms requiring financing was certainly the main reason for the shift from later stage financings to seed and start-up financings.

The end of the high-technology bubble triggered a significant change in the composition of venture capital investments away from risky start-up firms with

Exhibit 22.8 Investments According to Financing Stages in Germany

Year	Seed	Start-up	Expansion	Bridge/ Replacement/ Turnaround	LBO	MBO	MBI	Rest	Volume
1990	1%	5%	67%	5%		22%*		0%	481.1
1991	2%	4%	67%	2%		13%*		12%	509.2
1992	1%	6%	45%	13%		24%*		12%	527.6
1993	1%	8%	60%	3%		21%*		7%	516.9
1994	3%	10%	57%	3%		26%*		1%	536.9
1995	3%	11%	54%	11%		20%*		2%	541.5
1996	6%	9%	55%	8%		22%*		1%	611.5
1997	5%	11%	47%	19%		18%*		1%	1,210.7
1998	7%	18%	30%	19%	6%	19%	0%	1%	1,700.0
1999	7%	26%	35%	17%	4%	10%	1%	1%	2,816.2
2000	9%	27%	35%	13%	9%	6%	2%	0%	4,450.8
2001	4%	22%	31%	6%	22%	14%	2%	0%	4,434.9
2002	3%	19%	28%	4%	22%	22%	1%	0%	2,506.2
2003	1%	11%	16%	2%	51%	20%	0%	0%	2,415.4
2004	1%	9%	16%	3%	52%	18%	1%	0%	3,765.8
2005	0%	10%	31%	1%	48%	10%	1%	0%	3,039.6
2006	1%	6%	18%	3%	56%	15%	0%	0%	3,637.9
2007	1%	7%	10%	0%	59%	19%	2%	2%	4,124.4

Year	Seed	Start-up	Expansion	Bridge/ Replacement/ Turnaround	LBO	MBO	MBI	Rest	Volume
Q1–Q3 2007	1%	7%	7%	1%	68%	14%	2%	0%	3,518.7
Q1–Q3 2008	2%	6%	14%	3%		76%		0%	4,465.9

*Prior to 1998 there was no explicit differentiation between LBO, MBO, and MBI.
The report for Q1 to Q3 2008 does not explicitly differentiate between LBO, MBO, and MBI.
Source: BVK (2008).

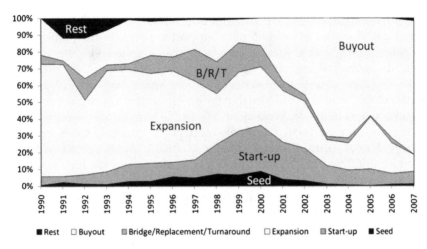

Exhibit 22.9   Investments According to Financing Stages in Germany, 1990–2007
Source: BVK (2008).

unproven business models towards more mature firms and buyout transactions. While these attracted less than 20 percent prior to and during the technology boom period, their share surged to one-third in 2001. In 2007 more than 80 percent or €3,285 million of all investments are attributable to buyout financings (Exhibit 22.8). The German umbrella organization for venture capitalists, BVK, reports that there were some very large buyout transactions combined with a high number of medium-sized transactions. This extraordinary high proportion of buyouts could be due to the financial crisis that fully hit the markets in 2008, forcing many companies to require financial support from venture capital or private equity firms. For the first three quarters of 2008 these figures indicate that 76 percent of all funds were employed for buyouts. However, expansion financings recovered from 7 percent to 14 percent for 2007 and 2008, respectively.

Overall, there is evidence that the distribution of German venture capital investments is skewed towards less risky ventures that are already in advanced stages of their life cycle. The new economy period was one exception that proved costly for venture capital firms. Again, whether this is due to a lack of entrepreneurial spirit and too little early-stage ventures, due to possibly missing skills, sophistication, and experience of German venture capital firms or due to the German capital market environment remains an open question.

Specialization and Ownership Structure of Venture Capital Firms in Germany

The essential venture capital functions of first screening promising new ventures and then later on monitoring portfolio firms requires up-to-date information and very industry-specific knowledge. In fact, successful venture capital firms need to have access to intimate knowledge of the portfolio firm's industry, products and technology. For that reason, venture capital firms in many countries specialize on specific industries in order to mitigate the high information asymmetries and the agency problems associated with inferior information in order to be able to provide strategic and financial advice and offer support to portfolio companies.

There is empirical evidence, however, that German venture capital firms usually do specialize less on certain industries. Comparing the portfolio strategies of German and French venture capital firms between 1991 and 2003, Schertler (2006) provides evidence that the specialization was significantly lower in Germany, where only 38 percent of VC firms focused on specific industries. This finding may be related to banks and government agencies being important providers of venture capital funds in Germany and their lack of knowledge needed for fulfilling the screening, monitoring, and consulting functions. This lack of industry-specific knowledge also explains why German bank-dependent and government-backed venture capital firms are less likely to invest in innovative ventures (Hirsch and Walz 2006). In contrast, it appears that independent venture capital firms have less significant conflicts of interest. This is reflected in empirical evidence that independent venture capital firms are more active in corporate governance and monitoring of portfolio companies in Germany (Tykvová 2006).

Overall, German venture capital firms appear to specialize less than their foreign counterparts. Most likely, they have less skill to invest in innovative ventures, which explains the low level of investments in early-stage financings in Germany. Moreover, while this problem appears to be related to the ownership structure of German venture capital firms, the high level of involvement by banks and government agencies creates additional problems that may have contributed to the small and relatively low development of the venture capital industry in Germany.

Financial Contract Design by Venture Capital Firms in Germany

Financial contract design is an important mechanism used by venture capital firms to reduce adverse selection and moral hazard problems and to be able to provide adequate financing. As the contracts in Germany differ to some extent from contracts used in other capital markets, we provide a brief review of financing contract designs employed by German venture capital firms. While we focus in the next section on the choice of financing instruments we briefly analyze in the following section to what extent German venture capital firms syndicate their investment with co-investors.

Financing Instruments Used in Venture Capital Investments

Venture capital firms carefully design financing contracts in order to address adverse selection and moral hazard problems associated with young technology and start-up firms (Cumming 2005). The contract design is essential from the venture capitalists' perspective, because it determines the risk-return profile of their investment. The ideal profile has an option-like payoff function where the loss is limited, but where the VC participates in profits if the venture is successful. It is also important to create a financial instrument that reduces adverse selection and moral hazard problems between the VC firm and the entrepreneur. Convertible securities are such a financing instrument that provides this flexibility in terms of the allocation of control rights and the appropriate profit and loss function, including the timing of an optimal exit. In fact, convertibles are a combination of a fixed claim on the firm's assets (comparable to debt) and a call option on the firm's equity. The debtlike part of the convertible instrument protects the venture capitalist against the downside risk in case of bankruptcy, and the equity part provides the upside potential. All these features make convertibles an ideal instrument in VC contracts.

Consequently, U.S. venture capital firms make extensive use of convertible preferred stocks (Kaplan and Strömberg 2003) that provide them with sufficient flexibility in the allocation of cash flow and control rights between the entrepreneur and the venture capital firm. Recently, Cumming (2008) reassessed the use of convertible instruments in VC financing for a sample of 11 European countries for the period from 1996 to 2005. He provides evidence that the use of convertible debt or convertible preferred equity offers more control rights at the time of the VC exit. In addition, a higher use of convertible instruments is positively related to the likelihood of an exit via acquisition, and negatively related to the probability of a write-off or an IPO. In other countries and especially in Germany, however, the use of these instruments is rather limited. While about 20 percent of venture capital financings in Europe employ convertible securities (Schwienbacher 2008), only 10 percent of all transactions in Germany use convertibles (Bascha and Walz 2002). These findings cannot only be explained by the lower sophistication and inexperience of venture capital firms. Rather, the institutional framework appears to affect the contract design (Cumming 2007). In Germany, venture capital firms are only allowed to use convertible securities if the portfolio firm is incorporated as an "Aktiengesellschaft" or AG (corporation), that entails higher legal and administrative costs than the "Gesellschaft mit beschränkter Haftung" or GmbH (limited liability company), which is favored by most small companies (Bascha 2001). Furthermore, independent VCs utilize convertibles more frequently than bank- and government-dependent VCs (Hirsch and Walz 2006).

Instead, German venture capital firms often use "Stille Beteiligungen" (silent partnerships) as shown in different studies. They account for 13 percent to 39 percent of all venture capital financings in Germany. The popularity of these contracts results from their flexibility in the allocation of cash flow and control rights. This effectively allows German venture capital firms to replicate the payoff function and allocations of corporate control rights of convertible preferred stocks used by their U.S. counterparts. A more detailed analysis of venture capital investments, however, provides evidence that German venture capital firms employ convertible securities often for the more risky ventures. In fact, the use of convertible securities is higher for smaller ventures, early-stage financings, and transactions involving R&D-intensive companies (Stein 2008). Moreover, over the past 10 years, financing structures used by German venture capital firms have become more similar to those in the United States with an increasing use of convertible securities. This finding can be attributed to the increased sophistication of German venture capital firms (Schwienbacher 2008) and may also be due to more cooperation or syndication with foreign venture capital firms (Stein 2008).

Venture Capital Financing and Syndication
Syndication is another important aspect in venture capital financing and investing. In this case, multiple venture capital firms provide concurrently funds for a VC investment. This cooperation can stimulate venture capital financings as it allows for risk sharing between venture capital firms and enables them to share information regarding the venture's prospects. Schwienbacher (2008), however, argues that this

indicates less active venture capital firms implying lower value creation. In fact, each venture capital firm's efforts to monitor may decline with a higher degree of diversification and a lower risk exposure, hoping for the other VC firm to do the required monitoring and consulting. For example, in Ireland and Sweden, less than 20 percent of all investments are syndicated. Countries with syndication rates of nearly 50 percent are Belgium, France, Switzerland, and Germany (Schertler 2006). Nevertheless, there seems to be a positive trend in international syndication indicating its growing importance.

From an international perspective, historic syndication rates are rather high in Germany with almost 50 percent of transactions involving more than one venture capital firm (Schertler 2006). Recent data of the BVK (2007, 2008), however, reveals that the fraction of syndications in Germany has substantially declined over the recent two years. While in 2006 more than 50 percent of all deals were syndicated, this figure decreased to only 15 percent in 2007. Moreover, while a high share of syndicated deals is consistent with financing larger investments in later stages, which is the case in the German venture capital market, a large proportion of the deals are cofinanced by government-sponsored programs. This might also indicate the low level of specialization of German venture capital firms that forces them to team up with more experienced investors.

Exit Alternatives and Exit Strategies of Venture Capital Firms in Germany

Venture capital firms usually will exit from their investments when the expected value added by another venture capital round is smaller than the associated costs (Cumming and MacIntosh 2003). Although venture capital investors and firms usually take a longer-term perspective in that VC investments have an average duration between seven to ten years, venture capital is by definition a financing source for a start-up firm either for a limited time period or for specific events and the VC will exit eventually from the investment either in part or fully (Cumming, Fleming, and Suchard 2005). This is in contrast to hedge funds that often take a shorter-term perspective or private equity that may stay invested for extended periods of time. The exit is the final stage in the venture capital process and it is as important as the other stages because it mainly determines the return that the investment generates for the VC. A venture capital firm's decision to exit and the timing of the exit usually depend on a number of factors, such as the profitability of the investment, the contractual arrangements, and the actual market environment as well as the VC's alternative investment opportunities. In the next section we analyze briefly the different types of exit channels and then provide empirical evidence on the importance of different exit channels for VC in Germany.

Analysis of the Exit Alternatives

The terms at which venture capital firms can exit from their portfolio firms are the ultimate driver of their performance and therefore have an important impact on the willingness of current and future investors to provide funds to venture capital firms (Black and Gilson 1998). Consequently, the quality of exit alternatives is a major determinant of the attractiveness and the development of the venture capital industry in a country. In principle, the VC has the following alternatives to exit: write-off, management buyback, secondary purchase, trade sale, or initial public offering. The investment is usually written off if the venture fails. Thus, the least desirable exit alternative for all participants is the liquidation of an unsuccessful venture. The second alternative is a management buyback in which the entrepreneur repurchases the shares from the venture capitalist. This exit alternative, however, is often a challenge for the venture-backed firm due to the immense capital requirement imposed on the entrepreneur. The third exit option is to sell the VC stake to another VC firm, which means that one VC is substituted by another VC. Although this secondary purchase is an exit route for the originating VC firm, the VC financing continues for the firm—maybe with different consulting and monitoring services from the new VC. The fourth exit route is a trade sale in which the VC stake is sold to a corporate investor either in another industry in order to gain diversification benefits or to an investor in the same industry with the proper expertise to integrate the venture into his company. Reasons for acquiring a start-up firm are, for example, to gain access to R&D, patents, and technology. If there are exploitable synergies or other benefits, then a trade sale could lead to a higher firm valuation compared to other exit routes such as an IPO. In addition, the proceeds from a trade sale may depend less on general market conditions, as is the case for IPOs. Finally, selling the VC stake in the stock market either at the time of the going public or later on in the secondary market is the fifth and most interesting exit route for the VC firm. An initial public offering usually results in both raising additional equity and creating a wider dispersion of the ownership structure. To mitigate agency problems between the venture capitalist and outside investors, the VC firm is often allowed to sell its stake only after a certain lock-up period that, on the one hand, offers the VC firm further profit opportunities for well-performing firms, but, on the other hand, also exposes the VC firm to additional risk if the company has an inadequate performance or if the stock market declines sharply.

Empirical Evidence on Exit Strategies of Venture Capital Firms in Germany

The various exit routes for German venture capital firms for the period between 1990 and 2008 are presented in Exhibit 22.10. Again, we divide our analysis into the three different periods (1990 to 1996; 1997 to 2003; 2004 to 2007). During the first period from 1990 to 1996, the total volume of exits by venture capital firms increased slowly but continuously from €142 million to €359 million, which was still a relatively small amount compared to other countries. During this period the main exit channels were trade sales and buybacks with relative shares well above 20 percent. Exits via the stock market played only a minor role, hardly exceeding 10 percent of total exit volume, and the percentage of unsuccessful ventures increased from 10 percent in 1992 to 19 percent in 1996.

The second time interval covers the period from 1997 to 2003, which coincides with the new economy boom and the creation of the "Neuer Markt." It was characterized by a sharp increase in total exit volumes, from €728 million in 1997 to €2.132 million in 2002. However, due to the dramatically declining stock prices, the total volume of VC exits eventually dropped to €820 million in 2003. Interestingly, these fluctuations in the exit volume closely follow the investment cycles of new funds. This is shown in Exhibit 22.11, in which total volumes of investments and

Exhibit 22.10   Exit Routes of Venture Capital in Germany

| | | | Stock Market | | | | | |
Year	Trade Sale	Buyback	IPO	Secondary Market	Secondary Purchase	Write-Off	Rest	Volume
1990	n.a.	n.a.	n.a.*		n.a.	n.a.	n.a.	141.6
1991	n.a.	n.a.	n.a.*		n.a.	n.a.	n.a.	172.3
1992	17%	22%	8%*		6%	10%	37%	195.8
1993	17%	24%	10%*		5%	15%	29%	331.8
1994	27%	25%	9%*		2%	23%	14%	352.3
1995	31%	19%	5%*		3%	13%	28%	403.9
1996	23%	41%	7%*		2%	19%	9%	358.9
1997	34%	22%	3%*		4%	15%	22%	728.1
1998	22%	30%	14%*		0%	17%	17%	537.4
1999	25%	20%	19%*		4%	21%	10%	772.1
2000	39%	17%	12%*		7%	18%	6%	1,261.9
2001	20%	18%	8%*		8%	36%	9%	1,855.0
2002	31%	4%	0%	6%	12%	44%	4%	2,131.8
2003	18%	10%	1%	7%	14%	40%	10%	820.4
2004	25%	11%	4%	2%	23%	27%	7%	1,481.4
2005	21%	19%	6%	17%	29%	10%	5%	1,863.5
2006	25%	13%	2%	19%	31%	5%	5%	2,066.3
2007	30%	5%	11%	20%	21%	8%	4%	2,161.2

| | | | Stock Market | | | | | |
Year	Trade Sale	Buyback	IPO	Secondary Market	Secondary Purchase	Write-Off	Rest	Volume
Q1-Q3 2007	30%	4%	13%	21%	23%	7%	3%	1,895.9
Q1-Q3 2008	53%	10%	0%	5%	27%	3%	1%	1,395.8

*Prior to 2002 there was no explicit differentiation between exits via the primary and the secondary market.
Source: BVK (2008).

exits between 1990 and 2007 are presented. Apparently, high-exit volumes coincide with high investment volumes and vice versa. One reason is the recycling of funds that happens when venture capital firms reinvest proceeds from the exit of their previous investments. Another reason why the financing increases is that VCs are able to attract new funds when the industry has performed well.

Another interesting aspect is that the sharply increasing investment volumes from 1997 to 2000 were followed by higher exits, but with an apparent time lag of one year. Most investments were arranged in 2000 and 2001, while the highest exits were realized in 2001 and 2002, respectively. One reason for this time lag is—at least for the IPOs exit route—that VCs preferred not to exit at the time of the IPO but at the end of the lock-up period, as will be discussed later on. Moreover, attractive exits and high realized returns may also have made it easier

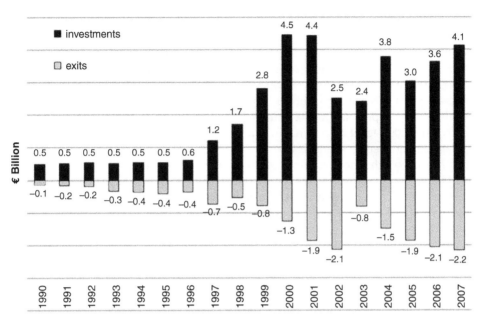

Exhibit 22.11 Investments and Exits in Portfolio Volumes in Germany
Source: BVK (2008).

to attract new investors. Breaking down the total volume further by exit routes, it becomes obvious that going public became a major exit route and source of returns for venture capital firms during that time period. In 1999 19 percent of total exit volume was originated from IPOs. One reason is the opening of the "Neuer Markt" as a special market segment designed to offer growth and technology firms the choice to go public. Trade sales continued to be an important exit route as well, with about 25 percent of proceeds while the importance of buybacks declined substantially, from 30 percent in 1998 to 4 percent in 2002. However, with the sharp stock market decline, the importance of IPOs as an exit route also suffered a major setback as no single IPO took place in 2002. Moreover, due to a lack of profitable exit opportunities and limited prospects of many portfolio firms, venture capital firms terminated many investments during the downturn and write-offs reached a level of about 40 percent between 2001 and 2003.

During the more recent time period from 2004 to 2007, capital markets again became the primary exit venue for venture capital investments. Exit in the primary market at the time of the IPO reached 11 percent in 2007 and was at its highest level since the new economy boom period and the hype for high-technology companies. Interestingly, sales of equity stakes in the secondary market after the firm first went public accounted for about 20 percent in 2007, which was also the highest level for the last years. This is quite interesting and suggests that VCs seemed to have expected a higher return from their investment when they first stayed invested in the portfolio firm for a certain period after the IPO, maybe first signaling quality and commitment, and then exiting later on by selling their stakes at higher prices in the stock market. The realized return from this strategy could have been higher for the VC firm compared to selling the shares at the time of the IPO first due to the usual high underpricing or first-day returns, and second due to stock price increases during the first months after going public. The underwriter also might have helped the VC firm to exit at favorable terms in order to generate future underwriting business. Moreover, trade sales continued to account for about 25 percent of all divestments. Secondary purchases were 21 percent in 2007, while management buybacks played only a minor role in terms of exit routes, with a share of only 5 percent in 2007. However, write-offs with 8 percent in 2007 were above the 2006 level of 5 percent, but still far below the 40 percent failure rate observed between 2001 and 2003.

Most recently, the beginning of the financial crisis had a huge impact on the exit behavior of venture capital firms in Germany. While until the third quarter of 2007 about 34 percent of all exit proceeds were generated via stock market exits, there was no single venture-backed initial public offering in 2008, and only a minor amount of proceeds was generated by secondary market exits. Consequently, the share of trade sales surged from 30 percent in 2007 to 53 percent in the first three quarters of 2008.

Overall, the currently most important exit alternative are trade sales, which account for 30 percent in 2007; secondary purchases are more than 20 percent and exits via IPOs in the primary and secondary market have a relative share of over 30 percent, at least until the beginning of the financial crisis in late 2007. From an academic perspective, initial public offerings appear to be the most interesting exit route because most information about exit prices and performance is publicly available. Thus, we concentrate on the exit behavior and performance of venture-backed IPOs in more detail in the next section.

GOING PUBLIC AS AN EXIT ROUTE FOR VENTURE CAPITAL AND THE PERFORMANCE OF VENTURE-BACKED IPOs IN GERMANY

From the perspective of the venture-backed firm going public means selling shares in the primary market that results immediately as well as over time in a change in the ownership structure and usually in a broader dispersion of ownership (free float). Moreover, it ensures the supply of additional equity at the time of the IPO and access to capital market financing in the future, if the firm performs well (seasoned equity offering). Analyzing the performance of venture-backed companies that went public is a challenging but rewarding endeavor that may offer new insights into the value that venture capital firms may provide, but also into the inherent agency problems that the two-staged venture capital financing relationship may create. The purpose of this section is to discuss first the issues related to the going public of venture capital backed companies, and then analyze the underpricing and long-run performance of these IPOs in Germany. In addition, we are interested in the valuation effects related to lock-up agreements and other venture capital–related issues, such as the behavior of different types of VC firms, hot and cold issue periods, as well as the impact of venture capital on innovation.

Going Public as an Exit Route for Venture Capital

If venture capitalists do have a significantly positive impact on the success, valuation, and long-run performance of start-up firms, then this should be observable initially at the time of the initial public offering, for example, in a different underpricing of venture-backed relative to non-venture-backed IPOs, and then later on in significant performance differences at the expiration of the lock-up period, and finally in the long-run operating and financial performance. Because some venture capitalist firms repeatedly use initial public offerings as an exit route for their portfolio firms, one would expect that these VC firms are sensitive to any negative reputational effect that may be caused by an underperforming IPO or by any inappropriate exit behavior. Consequently, reasonable offer prices and prudent exit behavior should be generally observable for well-established and reputable VC firms. These VC firms often choose an underwriter with a high reputation (Doukas and Gonenc 2005). If this is the case, then VC firms should be in a position to signal convincingly the quality and value of an IPO, thereby reducing adverse selection problems. Hence, venture-backed IPOs should have a lower underpricing and a superior long-run performance compared to non-venture-backed IPOs. In contrast, it seems also quite possible and realistic to assume that VC firms possess private information and will seek to achieve an optimal exit price, either in the primary or secondary market in order to maximize their own return. Thus, one may expect to observe that VC firms are tempted to exploit privileged information to the disadvantage of other uninformed outside investors, either in the primary or secondary market.

In addition, the underwriter may play an important role in supporting the performance of the IPOs in the primary or secondary market, thus helping the VC firm to exit at favorable terms, either at the time of the IPO or later on at the end of the lock-up period in order to generate future underwriting business. Price support or favorable outlooks are usually provided by the analysts of the underwriter in the form of positively biased earnings forecasts and repetitive and strong buy recommendations during the first year after going public (Bessler and Stanzel 2009). Moreover, the mutual funds associated with the underwriter may either get the best performing IPOs allocated in order to generate high abnormal returns or have to invest in poorly performing firms after the IPO for price support purposes (Stanzel 2007). In sum, there exists an array of agency problems between the various parties involved in an IPO that may have tremendous implications for the pricing and performance of IPOs in general and of venture-backed IPOs in particular. These conflicts of interest appear to be especially pronounced in the German universal banking system, where banks are providing a wide range of financial services (Bessler and Kurth 2007).

In contrast, there is some empirical evidence that VCs monitor the financial reporting of their portfolio firms around the IPO quite well and more accurately than underwriters, because these are more interested in exploiting revenue generating opportunities. However, the timing of a VC exit through an IPO depends not only on firm-specific characteristics but also on general market conditions, such as high firm valuations and "windows of opportunity" (Cumming and MacIntosh 2003). For the United States, Lerner (1994) and Gompers and Lerner (2003) document that exploiting these "windows of opportunity" can result in returns of more than

50 percent for VC firms, while the returns in a down market may be negative. For IPOs in Germany, Bessler and Kurth (2005) also find evidence that VC firms exploit these "windows of opportunity" in that they exit relatively quickly at the end of the lock-up period in hot issue markets, but stay invested when a firm goes public in a cold issue period and stock prices decline further before the lock-up period expires.

Moreover, during hot issue periods, VC firms usually generate above average returns and also exit from portfolio firms, which results in additional VC funds available for reinvestment. In addition, new venture capital inflows are attracted during this market phase. This availability of additional venture capital results in increasing valuations in subsequent periods. Consequently, higher inflows are chasing a relatively smaller number of investment opportunities, driving up valuations in the current period, which negatively affects fund returns in subsequent periods (Kaplan and Strömberg 2008.) This finding is similar to the well-known performance-flow relationship for hedge funds and mutual funds (Bessler, Blake, Lückoff, and Tonks 2009). Nevertheless, VC firms have to find adequate investments for these higher inflows, and consequently invest more in later-stage investments (Gompers 1998). This behavior can also be observed in Germany, as was already documented in our analysis of the development of the German venture capital market.

Performance of Venture-Backed Initial Public Offerings in Germany

After this more general discussion of the exit motives and behavior of venture capital firms through initial public offerings, we concentrate in the next section on the empirical evidence with respect to underpricing and long-run performance of venture-backed IPOs in Germany. In order to examine these issues for IPOs in Germany in detail, we address a number of different questions, with an emphasis on analyzing whether there are significant differences between venture-backed and non-venture-backed IPOs. We differentiate between these issues for the German capital market in the next sections:

- Are there substantial and significant differences in firm valuation, underpricing, and long-run performance between venture-backed and non-venture-backed IPOs, and does the exit strategy of the venture capital firm in the primary market influence underpricing and long-run performance?
- Are there substantial and significant differences in the return patterns regarding exit strategies and lock-up agreements between venture-backed and non-venture-backed IPOs?
- Are there substantial differences in behavior and performance of different types of venture capital firms?
- What is the impact of hot and cold issue periods on fund-raising, investments, and exit behavior of venture capital firms?
- What is the impact of venture capital on innovation such as R&D and patents?

Empirical Evidence on the Long-Run Performance and Exit Behavior of Venture-Backed IPOs in Germany

With respect to underpricing and long-run performance, the "certification hypothesis" (Megginson and Weiss 1991) predicts that venture-backed IPOs should have a lower underpricing and a better long-run performance compared to non-venture-backed IPOs. Consequently, VC involvement should signal higher firm quality and reduce the information asymmetry for outside investors. In contrast, it seems quite possible that venture-backed IPOs could be overpriced at the time of the IPO, because the return to the VC firm is mainly determined by the difference between the price the venture capital firm paid at the time of the investment and the price received at the time of the exit. In fact, VC firms often hold several board seats and significant equity stakes and therefore have the opportunity to influence the timing and the terms of the initial public offering. Obviously, such a behavior creates new agency problems between the entrepreneur and the VC firm, but also between the VC firm and potential outside investors. It seems fair to assume that the VC firm may have access to private or privileged (inside) information due to the special involvement in a firm's business plan, product development, marketing strategy, and research and development. Thus, a VC exit at the time of the IPO could signal an overvaluation and may suggest to the outside investor a poor performance in the future. Eventually such a strategy, when repeatedly implemented, may result in a loss of reputation for the VC firm. In contrast and as already mentioned, VC firms can fulfill a certification role as VC involvement should signal higher firm quality. This certification effect might be especially pronounced when they keep a substantial part of their equity stake at the time of the IPO and for some time after the IPO. In two related empirical studies, Brav and Gompers (1997) and Barry, Muscarella, Peavy, and Vetsuypens (1990) support the value enhancing function of venture capital for the United States by documenting the general long-run outperformance of venture-backed IPOs compared to non-venture-backed IPOs. In the next section we will discuss the empirical evidence for Germany.

Long-Run Performance of IPOs in Germany

The long-run performance of IPOs in Germany was investigated in a number of studies covering various time periods. For the period from 1970 to 1995, which is the time before the opening of the "Neuer Markt," Bessler and Thies (2007a) find the usual long-run underperformance over a 36-month period. Exceptions are those IPOs with subsequent seasoned equity offerings, which outperformed the market significantly (Bessler and Thies 2007b). Bessler, Kaen, and Sherman (1998) also examine the operating and financial performance for German IPOs covering the same period. They find some evidence that corporate governance issues, that is, the structure of the German universal banking system, may influence both the firms' decisions to go public and their performance in the secondary market.

There are also studies that concentrate on the long-run performance of venture-backed IPOs that went public on the "Neuer Markt" in Germany during the period from 1997 to 2003. The findings generally indicate a long-run underperformance of these IPOs. Moreover, Bessler and Kurth (2005, 2007) find strong evidence that VCs and especially bank-affiliated VCs time their exit quite well in the primary as well as in the secondary market. When bank-affiliated VCs sell a large fraction of

Exhibit 22.12a   Performance of Venture-Backed and Non-Venture-Backed IPOs

	N	Mean	Median	t (means)	z (U-Test)
Underpricing					
VB IPO	101	55.0%	19.0%	0.87	0.70
NVB IPO	206	47.1%	17.5%		
6 Months Performance					
VB IPO	101	36.0%	4.1%	0.87	1.16
NVB IPO	206	24.5%	−0.48%		
24 Months Performance					
VB IPO	101	6.5%	−6.9%	0.23	0.29
NVB IPO	206	3.0%	−8.3%		

***, **, and * denote significance at the 1 percent, 5 percent, and 10 percent level, respectively.
Source: Bessler and Kurth (2007).

their shares at the time of the IPO, these firms underperform significantly in the secondary market. The opposite is generally true if bank-affiliated VCs keep their shares. It is very interesting to observe that there is a strong superior performance in the first six months of trading, but a tremendous decline in abnormal returns thereafter. Obviously, for the early investors as well as for the investors that got shares allocated at the time of the IPO, the end of the lock-up period is a crucial event at which a dramatic decline in stock prices and firm value is often observed. Because it is important to take a closer look at the optimal timing of the going public decision and at the exit behavior of VCs over the stock market cycle, we will address these issues in the next section.

As already discussed, there is the testable hypothesis that venture capital firms, due to their special screening, monitoring, and consulting abilities, should have a positive impact on firm quality and IPO performance. Thus, Bessler and Kurth (2007) analyze the returns of 101 venture-backed and 206 non-venture-backed IPOs for the period from 1998 to 2001, with respect to initial returns (underpricing) and long-run performance (Exhibit 22.12a). Both subsamples reveal a significant underpricing of 55.0 percent for venture-backed and 47.1 percent for non-venture-backed IPOs. Moreover, the abnormal returns (BHAR) after six months of trading are positive with significant returns of 36.0 percent and 24.5 percent, respectively. Interestingly, after 24 months of trading (500 trading days), the performance of the IPOs in both subsample groups is nearly identical with 6.5 percent and 3.0 percent, respectively. These results suggest that, on average, the initial shareholders (owners) have much better exit opportunities after six months than at the time of the IPO or later on. It is important to note, however, that the differences in initial returns (underpricing) and returns after six and twenty-four months for the venture-backed and non-venture-backed IPOs are not statistically significant, meaning that our conclusions apply to both groups of IPOs. At a very general level and without much differentiating, we have to conclude from the empirical evidence that VC involvement does not appear to have a significant impact on IPO underpricing (initial returns) and IPO long-run performance in Germany.

These findings are to some extent in contrast to the empirical evidence from other countries. Reviews of empirical studies are provided in Bessler and Becker (2007) and Jenkinson and Ljungqvist (2001). One reason for these results that is often given is the inexperience of German venture capital firms (Rindermann 2004; Tykvová and Walz 2007). However, another possible explanation is that German VC firms, given the dramatic increase in venture capital funds during the late 1990s, did not have the time needed to have a significantly positive impact on portfolio firms in order to outperform non-venture-backed IPOs. Moreover, there is some international evidence that young and inexperienced VC firms take their portfolio firms public much earlier than the more experienced VC firms, in order to build up some reputation and to accelerate fund-raising. This is usually referred to as the grandstanding hypothesis (Gompers 1996). For Germany, Tykvová (2003) explains the differences in the exit behavior between German and foreign VCs partially with this grandstanding hypothesis. Accordingly, German VCs are typically younger and smaller compared to foreign VCs, which are considered to be more established and have more experience. It needs to be added, however, that many IPOs, at least the ones of the year 2000, had a very weak operating and financial performance, raising doubts that they were ready for a successful listing. However, the great opportunity offered by extremely high stock price levels convinced many CEOs to go public sooner rather than later, even when it was one, two, and sometimes three or even more years before they were realistically ready for an exchange listing. Thus, this very special market environment may not be the best setting to make a verdict on the quality and contribution of VCs in Germany.

However, when accounting for banks being a provider of venture capital financing, the conclusions change. In fact, 44 out of the 101 venture-backed IPO firms at the "Neuer Markt" are bank-financed, which means that banks held equity stakes of more than 4 percent before the IPO through subsidiary VC firms (Exhibit 22.12b). Bessler and Kurth (2007) report an underpricing or first-day return of 73.6 percent for bank-financed IPOs and a significantly lower 40.7 percent for other venture-backed IPOs. This difference can be attributed to the conflicts of interest in the German universal banking system. Accordingly, bank venture–backed IPOs required a higher underpricing, which was disadvantageous for venture-backed companies going public but favored investors to whom these IPOs were allocated. For the long-run performance, there does not seem to be a substantial difference in performance. Bank-financed IPOs exhibit a six-month BHAR of 26.4 percent, compared to 43.5 percent for other venture-backed IPOs. After two years (24 months) the BHAR are −11.1 percent and 20.1 percent, respectively, but their performance is not significantly different from each other.

These results suggest again that there are considerable conflicts of interest depending on the type of venture capital provider, especially when banks act as venture capitalist. When differentiating by additional factors, these differences become even more pronounced and significant. These additional factors are analyzed in the following sections.

Venture Capital and Exit Behavior in the Primary Market

For the "Neuer Markt" in Germany (1997 to 2003), a number of studies investigate the impact of venture capital firm's involvement on the exit behavior and the underpricing of IPOs. With respect to the underpricing, Bessler and Kurth (2007)

Exhibit 22.12b   Performance of Bank-Financed and Venture-Backed IPOs

	N	Mean	Median	t (means)	z (U-Test)
Underpricing					
Bank	44	73.6%	30.2%	2.07**	1.76*
VC	57	40.7%	18.3%		
6 Months Performance					
Bank	44	26.4%	−11.1%	−0.78	1.39
VC	57	43.5%	11.6%		
24 Months Performance					
Bank	44	−11.1%	−7.3%	−1.25	−0.60
VC	57	20.1%	−5.2%		

***, **, and * denote significance at the 1 percent, 5 percent, and 10 percent level, respectively.
Source: Bessler and Kurth (2007).

do not find a significant difference between venture-backed and non-venture-backed companies. Surprisingly, there seems to be a positive relationship between the reputation of the VC and underpricing, meaning that IPOs backed by reputable VCs are more underpriced (Franzke 2004; Tykvová and Walz 2007). Despite these findings, VCs in Germany appear to sell more shares at the time of the IPO than their U.S. counterparts (Bessler and Kurth 2004). Moreover, there is some empirical evidence that venture-backed IPOs are significantly more underpriced when the VC firm is either a member of the underwriting syndicate or a subsidiary of a bank (Bessler and Kurth 2007). Obviously, there seems to exist severe conflicts of interest between VC financing, IPO underwriting, and analyst behavior in the German universal banking system so that it appears interesting to analyze the VC exit behavior in more detail.

The VC firms usually have the choice between selling their equity stake either in the primary or secondary market. Given the information advantage of the VC firm, an immediate exit at the time of the IPO is usually perceived by the market as a signal of inferior future performance. In contrast, a commitment by the VC to keep an equity stake for some time after going public is usually viewed as positive information about expected long-run returns. In fact, it has to be assumed that the VC who stays invested in the stock is hoping for a superior exit opportunity later on. In order to analyze the exit behavior of VCs at the "Neuer Markt" in more detail, Bessler and Kurth (2007) separate the 57 venture-backed IPOs (banks excluded) into two subsamples. The first group includes 28 IPOs in which the VCs sold a relatively high percentage of their shares at the time of the IPO (High VC Exit). The other group includes the 29 IPOs in which the VCs sold a relatively low percentage of their equity stake in the primary market (Low VC Exit). The empirical results reveal that the group selling more shares has a higher underpricing of 54.5 percent compared to 27.4 percent for the other group (Exhibit 22.13a). Thus, the market seems to understand this signaling mechanism and is aware of potential agency problems. After the first six months of trading, the VC group with high initial exits has an inferior performance relative to the other group (39.4 percent and 47.4 percent, respectively). Thus, the second group with the higher VC commitment

Exhibit 22.13a Performance of Venture-Backed IPOs: Exit Behavior

	N	Mean	Median	t (means)	z (U-Test)
		Underpricing			
High VC Exit	28	54.5%	31.0%	1.79*	1.98**
Low VC Exit	29	27.4%	6.7%		
		6 Months Performance			
High VC Exit	28	39.4%	16.6%	−0.29	0.06
Low VC Exit	29	47.4%	9.0%		
		24 Months Performance			
High VC Exit	28	41.1%	−2.7%	0.95	0.22
Low VC Exit	29	−0.3%	−6.2%		

***, **, and * denote significance at the 1 percent, 5 percent, and 10 percent level, respectively.
Source: Bessler and Kurth (2007).

at the time of the IPO first has lower initial returns (underpricing) of 27.4 percent and then a higher outperformance of 47.4 percent over the first six months of trading. However, these differences are not significantly distinguishable from each other. On the contrary, after 24 months of trading the BHAR for venture-backed IPOs with a high exit remain at their high level (41.1 percent), while the performance of venture-backed IPOs, where a high number of shares is kept after going public (low exit), deteriorates to −0.3 percent. Hence, a high portion of retained shares of the VC at the IPO date leads to a strong decline in BHAR after six months, but the difference is statistically insignificant. Thus, if the VC does not exit immediately at the time of the IPO, this does not automatically serve as a positive signaling device for the long-run performance.

Again, Bessler and Kurth (2007) obtain remarkable differences when investigating bank-financed IPOs separately (Exhibit 22.13b). Mean IPO underpricing in case of a high exit of bank-financed IPOs is slightly higher compared to bank-financed IPOs with a low exit (87.8 percent versus 63.7 percent). Much more interesting is the performance of the two groups after six months of trading. When banks keep their shares, the BHAR are on average as high as 70.3 percent, whereas a high exit at the time of the IPO is associated with negative BHAR of −17.4 percent. The difference in performance of nearly 90 percent is statistically significant at the 1 percent level, but declines thereafter to insignificant 21 percent after 24 months. The difference in the relative performance of the two groups is obvious and it appears that the bank-financed IPOs in which VCs have sold their shares at the time of the IPO do not have a price increase at all. In contrast, the VC group that does not exit at the time of the IPO has an excellent relative performance for the first six months of trading. The highest abnormal returns are reached around the end of the lock-up period. Subsequently, returns start to decline sharply. A look at the performance clearly indicates that an exit immediately after the end of the lock-up period was an exceptional time to sell the shares. Thus, the bank-affiliated VCs had either a great ability to forecast return patterns very precisely or they or someone else had the opportunity to positively influence stock prices in the secondary market pointing to conflicts of interest in the German universal banking system.

Exhibit 22.13b   Performance of Bank-Financed IPOs: Exit Behavior

	N	Mean	Median	t (means)	z (U-Test)
			Underpricing		
High VC Exit	22	87.8%	61.2%	1.01	1.17
Low VC Exit	22	63.7%	9.1%		
			6 Months Performance		
High VC Exit	22	−17.4%	−26.2%	−2.84***	−3.10***
Low VC Exit	22	70.3%	22.1%		
			24 Months Performance		
High VC Exit	22	−22.0%	−6.0%	−0.77	0.09
Low VC Exit	22	−1.2%	−7.4%		

***, **, and * denote significance at the 1 percent, 5 percent, and 10 percent level, respectively.
Source: Bessler and Kurth (2007).

Lock-up Agreements and Venture Capital

Lock-up agreements have been widely used in initial public offerings. Usually, the company and the underwriter sign this lock-up agreement, which forces early investors, management, and venture capital firms to stay invested for a minimum period of time subsequent to the IPO. These agreements can be interpreted as a signaling or commitment device (Brav and Gompers 2003). Consequently, lock-up agreements and the expiration of lock-up periods may have a significant impact on the investor behavior and on the performance of IPOs. At the German "Neuer Markt," there was first the mandatory lock-up period of six months that applied to the founding shareholders and early investors of the IPO, and second the tax-lock-up period of twelve months that applied especially to the private—more wealthy—investors who got shares allocated at the time of the IPO. As documented in Bessler and Kurth (2005, 2006, 2007) these two options created some severe agency problems. In addition to these two lock-up periods that usually expired within the first two years, there was another two-year lock-up period for employees who received stock options as part of their compensation package. The empirical findings with respect to the impact of the different lock-up periods are analyzed in the following sections.

Exit Strategies and Lock-Up Agreements

The ownership structure, changes in the ownership structure, and consequently the exit behavior of the founders, early investors, and management of start-up companies around the time of the IPO, are important in that they signal the commitment of these groups to the firm and their expectations about the future performance. There are different means to signal quality, such as continuous VC investment and lock-up agreements. The interaction between both may also be of interest. Lock-up agreements are contracts between the underwriter and the firm restricting the investor to sell their shares before a defined expiration date. These periods are often six months, but periods of up to two years are common as well. In addition, staggered lock-up periods are also feasible (e.g., Google). In contrast to other countries, the German Stock Exchange imposed a mandatory lock-up period of at least six months in its rules and regulations of the "Neuer Markt." This was based on the belief that it would signal the quality of the IPO and would increase investor confidence in the companies listed at this newly created stock market segment for high-technology firms.

For the United States, Field and Hanka (2001) provide empirical evidence that there are significantly negative stock price reactions around the expiration of lock-up agreements and that VCs are heavily involved in trading. In fact, they report significant abnormal returns of –1.5% around the expiration date and provide evidence that the negative stock price effect is three times larger for venture-backed IPOs compared to non-venture-backed IPOs. Furthermore, they report a permanent increase in trading volume of about 40 percent during this period. This clearly suggests that some VCs are using the first opportunity to exit by selling their investment in the secondary market. From the perspective of the VC's returns, this makes perfect sense, because if stock prices at lock-up expiration are comparatively high relative to the offer price at the time of the IPO, then staying invested up to the end of the lock-up period is a rational choice. At least in hot issue periods, this offers an attractive opportunity for generating high returns for the investors with lock-up agreements and for investors who got shares allocated at the time of the IPO. In addition, the underwriter may have an incentive to offer good exit opportunities to early investors and especially for VCs by supporting the stock price for the duration of the lock-up period.

Venture Capital and Lock-Up Commitments: Empirical Evidence

The rules and regulation with respect to the lock-up period on the "Neuer Markt" in Germany were unique in that a minimum period of six months was mandatory and nonnegotiable, whereas in other countries it is usually based on a contract between the firm and the underwriter and can take various forms (Bessler, Kurth, and Thies 2003). Bessler and Kurth (2007) find for their sample that for 12 out of 57 venture-backed IPOs (banks excluded) and for 16 out of 44 bank venture–backed IPOs, the VCs made a commitment to extend the required lock-up period up to 12 months. Most likely, a voluntary extension should signal the confidence of the VC in the future performance of the IPO. Thus, we would expect a lower underpricing and a superior long-run performance for these firms due to the VC's higher commitment. Nevertheless, an extended lock-up period for the founders, management, and VC firms could also be demanded by the underwriter in order to place the shares successfully in the market, and therefore may signal adverse selection problems.

A comparison of the results for venture-backed IPOs where banks are excluded reveals that the initial return of 22.1 percent for the 12 IPOs with extended lock-up periods is smaller than the initial returns of 45.7 percent for the 45 IPOs with the standard six-month lock-up period (Exhibit 22.14a). However, after six months of trading, the stocks with the six-month lock-up period have a significant BHAR of 37.1 percent compared to 67.4 percent for the other group. After 24 months of trading the difference in returns increases substantially. The group with the extended lock-up period now has BHAR of 67.7 percent compared to 7.4 percent for IPOs with the standard six-month lock-up period. This return pattern seems to indicate that the VC firms that agree to longer lock-up periods signal the quality of the IPO. The group with the minimum lock-up period of six months was fortunate

Exhibit 22.14a   Performance of Venture-Backed IPOs: Lock-Up Agreements

	N	Mean	Median	t (means)	z (U-Test)
			Underpricing		
Lock-up = 6	45	45.7%	18.4%	1.89*	0.25
Lock-up > 6	12	22.1%	6.0%		
			6 Months Performance		
Lock-up = 6	45	37.1%	6.0%	−1.02	−1.76*
Lock-up > 6	12	67.4%	37.2%		
			24 Months Performance		
Lock-up = 6	45	7.4%	−8.0%	−1.08	−1.04
Lock-up > 6	12	67.7%	−1.9%		

***, **, and * denote significance at the 1 percent, 5 percent, and 10 percent level, respectively.
Source: Bessler and Kurth (2007).

to have the performance peak close to the end of this period, whereas the abnormal returns of the other group started to increase later on, reaching a peak some time later. There seems to be a parallel shift into the future of about three months.

For the 44 bank venture–backed IPOs, the empirical results are quite different from the ones for the non-bank venture–backed IPOs in the first part of this section (Exhibit 22.14b). Bessler and Kurth (2007) do not find any differences in mean underpricing for bank-financed IPOs related to the length of the lock-up commitment. The performance (BHAR) for bank-financed IPOs with extended lock-up periods is negative and reaches a level of −9.0 percent after six months. This figure is not only negative but significantly lower than the performance of other bank-financed IPOs, which generate a positive performance of 49.5 percent. However, the difference in the performance of both groups after 24 months is smaller. Now the mean BHAR are 6.6 percent and −38.6 percent. For the group with lock-up agreements of only six months we observe a strong positive performance for the first six months followed by a tremendous decline after lock-up expiration. It appears that a longer lock-up period of bank venture–backed IPOs is not a credible signal to convey the quality of the IPO to the market. In these cases the extended lock-up agreement is irrelevant and has little value, but may point to some conflicts of interest resulting from the different functions performed by the bank.

With respect to employee stock options, the "Neuer Markt" required a lock-up period of at least two years for German firms. Stock options plans (SOPs) were frequently employed as a compensation scheme at these new economy firms in that 91 percent of all IPOs granted stock options at the time they went public or later on. Interestingly, we observe a broad-based granting pattern, including rank-and-file employees, rather than only executives, as the primary beneficiary of the stock options in Germany. This observation for new economy firms is in sharp contrast to the usual practice and requires a different explanation. In line with some previous research Bessler, Becker, and Wagner (2009) provide empirical results for German IPOs, suggesting that employee's prediction of the up-side potential of the stock price and the options' value was too optimistic at the time the option plans were initiated. Because the "Neuer Markt" was characterized by an immense stock

Exhibit 22.14b Performance of Bank-Financed IPOs: Lock-Up Agreements

	N	Mean	Median	t (means)	z (U-Test)
		Underpricing			
Lock-up = 6	27	66.7%	29.4%	−0.26	0.50
Lock-up > 6	16	73.9%	48.3%		
		6 Months Performance			
Lock-up = 6	27	49.5%	−10.5%	2.16**	1.11
Lock-up > 6	16	−9.0%	−4.4%		
		24 Months Performance			
Lock-up = 6	27	6.6%	−6.9%	1.60	0.80
Lock-up > 6	16	−38.6%	−7.4%		

***, **, and * denote significance at the 1 percent, 5 percent, and 10 percent level, respectively.
Source: Bessler and Kurth (2007).

price increase during the period from 1998 to 2000 (hot issue market) followed by a sharp stock price decline that started in March 2000 (cold issue market), almost all of the options were out of the money at the time they could be exercised. One explanation for the poor performance is that the design of the SOPs suffered from a succession of lock-up periods, where the two other groups of option holders could exercise their options earlier on, making a profitable option exercise for employees very difficult. In fact, the option holder had to settle for the stock price after the downward pressure caused by the exit of other investors and after the burst of the new economy stock market bubble. Although stock option plans were common among new economy firms and initially appeared very attractive from an employee's point of view, the final outcome was that most stock options were out of the money when they could have been exercised.

Other Venture Capital–Related Issues

With respect to the valuation and performance of initial public offerings, there exist a number of other venture capital–related issues that we address in this section. First of all, we will analyze the influence that different types or groups of venture capital firms have on the behavior and performance. We then investigate the impact of hot and cold issue periods on the exit behavior and the returns of venture-backed IPOs. Finally, we examine the interaction between venture capital and innovation.

Venture Capital Types and Strategies

Venture capital firms are not all alike, and therefore different types or groups of venture capitalists may have different objectives that may be reflected in the performance of their portfolio company. For Germany, Tykvová and Walz (2007) analyze whether there are differences in the short- and long-run IPO performance depending on the VC type. They classify venture-backed IPOs—not only into bank-dependent and other VCs—but assign them to four categories: public VCs, independent VCs, bank-dependent VCs, and corporate VCs. Overall, the authors report for Germany notable differences between these VC types with respect to their structure and corporate governance, which is in line with the results of Bessler and Kurth (2007). From this follows the hypothesis that different VCs mitigate agency problems in different ways. However, there are no significant differences in underpricing between these different types of VCs for German IPOs at the "Neuer Markt." Nevertheless, Tykvová and Walz (2007) provide evidence that financing by independent, foreign, and reputable VCs leads to a significantly better performance for portfolio firms, compared to their non-venture-backed firms and firms backed by other VCs. Furthermore, price volatility of IPOs with an independent VC is much less pronounced than for all other firms. They conclude that independent VCs involvement results in a superior post-IPO performance, but with less risk.

Venture Capital and Hot and Cold Issue Periods

The equity issuing activities of firms are usually highly volatile and markets are therefore divided into hot and cold issue periods, where hot issue periods are characterized by relatively high and increasing stock prices and a large and increasing number of IPOs (Lerner 1994; Ritter 1984). In contrast, cold issue periods are characterized by declining stock prices and low valuations that are accompanied by few or no IPOs. Consequently, IPO volume fluctuates over time and creates windows of opportunities that are related to firms' demand for capital and investor sentiment (Lowry 2003; Lowry and Schwert 2002). Yung, Colak, and Wang (2008) provide evidence that a positive shock to the economy such as the new economy period raises overall growth projections and equity valuation and offers the opportunity for low-quality firms to go public along with a number of high-quality firms. This leads to higher uncertainty about the true firm quality for investors which in turn forces firms to accept higher levels of underpricing. Thus, hot issue periods can provide an ideal setting for an optimal venture capital exit from high-quality firms, but most importantly from low-quality firms, because they may be overvalued in an overly optimistic environment.

Gompers and Lerner (2003) find empirical evidence that realized VC returns are usually above average in hot issue periods and below average in cold issue periods. Because the underpricing or the initial first-day return of IPOs is particularly high in hot issue periods, it seems sensible for the VC not to exit at the time of the IPO but to sell the shares in the secondary market. However, if the VC has to adhere to a lock-up period and this lock-up period expires after the stock market has peaked, the VC may miss the opportunity for an optimal exit. For Germany the number and volume of IPOs over the period from 1980 to 2008 are presented in Exhibit 22.15. There is clear evidence of hot and cold issue periods. The market as measured by the NEMAX index peaked in March 2000 with a tremendous stock price decline thereafter. In an empirical study, Bessler and Kurth (2005) focus on the exit behavior in these two different market periods and find, on average, a change in VC ownership from 29.4 percent to 16.5 percent from before to after the initial public offering, respectively (Exhibit 22.16).

However, depending on the year of the IPO, there were lucrative exit strategies for VCs during the hot market phase on the "Neuer Markt." Due to the mandatory lock-up period of six months, VCs had the best opportunity to exit when they took their portfolio companies public before the third quarter of 1999. There were hardly any profitable exit strategies for IPOs after 2000 when the market turned into a cold issue period. VCs were too late to exit if they took their portfolio firms

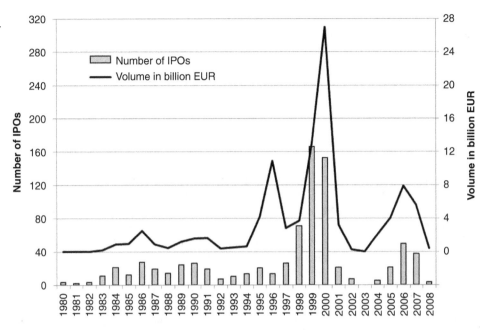

Exhibit 22.15 Number and Volume of IPOs in Germany
Source: Author's calculations.

Exhibit 22.16 Venture Capital Ownership around IPO

	N	Mean	Median	STD	Min.	Max.
Pre-IPO	86	29.4%	24.4%	20.3%	4.4%	89.8%
Post-IPO	86	16.5%	13.3%	12.9%	0.0%	71.3%
% Shares Sold	86	26.1%	22.4%	25.1%	−49.7%	100.0%
Lock-Up (Month)	84	7.5	6.0	2.6	6.0	12.0
Ownership after 3 Years	84	4.2%	0.0%	9.8%	0.0%	76.5%

Source: Bessler and Kurth (2005).

public in 2000 because they had to wait until the end of the mandatory lock-up period. In this environment, they would have been better off selling their shares in the primary market (Kurth 2005). In fact the time window for an exit at relatively high prices was very limited on the "Neuer Markt" and lasted only several months.

Venture Capital and Innovation

Another interesting and important issue is whether VCs in general and in particular venture-backed IPOs relative to non-venture-backed IPOs are more involved in the development of new technologies and whether a possible outperformance of VC is related to innovation. Technology is usually measured with R&D expenses, the firm's patent stock or patent filings. Thus, we are interested in the importance that innovations play in the success and survival of young firms and how this is further supported and enhanced by venture capital financing.

Evidence for a positive relationship between VC investments and patented innovations in the United States is provided by Kortum and Lerner (2000) for the period between 1965 and 1992. Hellmann and Puri (2000) examine venture-backed and non-venture-backed Silicon Valley companies and report that "innovators," that is, companies that are the first in their market, are more likely to be financed with VC and obtain VC at an earlier point in time than "imitators," that is, relatively new firms with new products following the first movers. Additionally, venture-backed firms bring their products faster to the market than non-venture-backed firms, which holds true in particular for innovators. Hence, an early product launch seems valuable for VCs.

In a similar study for IPOs in Italy covering the period from 1995 to 2004, Caselli, Gatti, and Perrini (2009) find more innovation in venture-backed firms relative to non-venture-backed firms. They not only find that venture-backed IPOs outperform a control sample of non-venture-backed IPOs as measured by operating performance, but also provide evidence that innovation is an important factor for VC investment decisions and deal screening. Venture-backed firms register more patents than non-venture-backed firms in the five years before receiving VC funding. However, once the VC firm decides to provide capital to an entrepreneur, VCs seem to block the innovation process as venture-backed firms register, on average, a smaller number of patents in the years after the initial VC investment. One possible conclusion is that these firms used innovations before receiving financing to signal growth potential and success. It is also possible that innovation are not patented any longer but kept secret.

For venture capital and IPOs at the "Neuer Markt" in Germany, Bessler and Bittelmeyer (2008) provide empirical evidence that patents reduce the pricing uncertainty and are value enhancing in that they find a significant impact of patents on underpricing and long-run performance of IPOs. However, the magnitude of these findings depends on the market phase. The different lock-up periods also play an important role. IPOs with innovation are less underpriced in hot issue periods but more underpriced in cold issue periods, suggesting that innovation may signal quality and therefore reduces pricing uncertainty. With respect to the long-run performance, innovative IPOs outperform IPOs without technology during the first year after the IPO, supporting the relevance of the growth potential stemming from innovation. In a related study, Bessler and Bittelmeyer (2007) provide further evidence that the survival probability of IPOs is positively related to the patent stock and the number and quality of patent applications. Interestingly, venture capital does not seem to be a relevant factor (Bittelmeyer 2007). Thus, in contrast to the empirical evidence for other countries, there appears to be no clear and significant contribution of venture capital to innovation in Germany.

CONCLUSION

The purpose of this review was first to provide some basic information on the venture capital industry in Germany relative to other, often more mature, markets for venture capital. Our results indicate that there still exist some differences between the German venture capital industry and the markets in the United States and the United Kingdom. The differences are quite pronounced with respect to the absolute volume of fund-raising, invested capital, and portfolio volumes. In addition, significant differences in the contracting behavior between U.S. and German VC firms are revealed. Convertible instruments are rarely used by VCs in Germany. Because these instruments offer important features to mitigate agency problems between the VC firm and the entrepreneur, their pay-off profile and control structures are duplicated with other contract designs. However, at least some studies indicate a convergence to the international standard in the use of convertible securities in VC financing in Germany.

Our research also reveals that the impact of venture capital on underpricing and long-run performance of IPOs in Germany is by far not as obvious as proposed by research on venture-backed and non-venture-backed firms in the United States and other countries. Empirical evidence for IPOs in the United States indicates that underpricing is lower and the long-run performance is higher for venture-backed compared to non-venture-backed IPOs. For Germany, however, we find considerable differences in the performance of venture-backed IPOs. The different roles that banks play in the German universal banking system seem to create conflicts of interest between the various parties involved. For example, there are obvious agency problems when the bank acts simultaneously as venture capitalist and underwriter, provides investment research and advice as well as manages mutual funds, and finally acts as the major commercial bank for the company before and after the IPO. Hence, there are evidently considerable differences in the institutional settings between the United States, other European countries, and Germany that strongly influence the development of the venture capital industry in these countries and may explain the observed differences. Others claim, however, that there is a lack of entrepreneurial spirit and activity in Germany, as well as a low tolerance for risky investments resulting in a relatively low development of the German venture capital market. In any case, the new economy period and the opening of the "Neuer Markt" created a major increase in VC fund-raising and investments, and, after a subsequent downturn in VC activity, we were recently back to that level, although the current financial crisis poses a challenge to all financial markets participants, including venture capital firms.

REFERENCES

Audretsch, David, and Erik Lehmann. 2005. Does the knowledge spillover theory of entrepreneurship hold for regions? *Research Policy* 34 (8):1191–1202.

Barry, Christopher, Chris Muscarella, John Peavy, and Michael Vetsuypens. 1990. The role of venture capital in the creation of public companies: Evidence from the going public process. *Journal of Financial Economics* 27 (2):447–471.

Bascha, Andreas. 2001. *Hybride Beteiligungsformen bei Venture-Capital: Finanzierung und Corporate Governance in jungen Unternehmen.* Wiesbaden: DUV.

Bascha, Andreas, and Uwe Walz. 2002. Financing practices in the German venture capital industry—An empirical assessment. Working Paper, Center for Financial Studies, Frankfurt. publikationen.ub.uni-frankfurt.de/volltexte/2005/998/pdf/02_08.pdf.

Becker, Ralf, and Thomas Hellmann. 2005. The genesis of venture capital——Lessons from the German experience. In *Venture capital, entrepreneurship, and public policy*, eds. Christian Keuschnigg and Vesa Kanniainen, pp. 33–67. Cambridge: MIT Press.

Berlin, Mitchell. 1998. That thing venture capitalists do. *Business Review Federal Reserve Bank of Philadelphia* (January/February):15–26.

Bessler, Wolfgang, and Christoph Becker. 2007. Underpricing und Performance von IPOs. In *Enzyklopädisches Lexikon für das Geld, Bank und Börsenwesen*, ed. Friedrich Thießen, Frankfurt: Fritz Knapp Verlag.

Bessler, Wolfgang, Christoph Becker, and Daniil Wagner. 2009. " The Design and Success of Stock Option Plans for New Economy Firms." Journal of Entrepreneurial Finance and Business Ventures 12 (4):1–34.

Bessler, Wolfgang, and Claudia Bittelmeyer. 2007. Performance and survival of technology firms: The impact of intellectual property. In *Empirical entrepreneurship in Europe—New perspectives*, eds. Michael Dowling and Jürgen Schmude, pp. 155–176. Cheltenham, UK: Edward Elgar.

Bessler, Wolfgang, and Claudia Bittelmeyer. 2008. Patents and the performance of technology firms: Evidence from initial public offerings in Germany. *Financial Markets and Portfolio Management* 22 (4):323–356.

Bessler, Wolfgang, David Blake, Peter Lückoff, and Ian Tonks. 2009. Why is persistent mutual fund performance so difficult to achieve? The impact of fund flows and manager turnover. Working Paper, University of Giessen. www.cfr-cologne.de/download/kolloquium/2009/bessler_et_al.pdf.

Bessler, Wolfgang, Fred Kaen, and Heidemarie Sherman. 1998. Going public: A corporate governance perspective. In *Comparative corporate governance—The state of the art and emerging research*, eds. Klaus J. Hopt, Hideki Kanda, Mark J. Roe, Eddy Wymeersch, and Stefan Prigge, pp. 569–605. Oxford: Clarendon Press.

Bessler, Wolfgang, and Andreas Kurth. 2003. Zur Bedeutung von Venture Capital für die Finanzierung von kleinen und mittleren Unternehmen. In *Unternehmensbewertung und Basel II in kleinen und mittleren Unternehmen*, ed. Jörn-Axel Meyer, pp. 267–287. Lohmar: Eul Verlag.

Bessler, Wolfgang, and Andreas Kurth. 2004. Finanzierungsstrukturen von Neuemissionen. *FinanzBetrieb* 6 (1):59–69.

Bessler, Wolfgang, and Andreas Kurth. 2005. Exit strategies of venture capitalists in hot issue markets: Evidence from Germany. *Journal of Entrepreneurial Finance and Business Ventures* 10 (1):17–51.

Bessler, Wolfgang, and Andreas Kurth. 2006. Die Auswirkungen der Spekulationssteuer auf die Verkaufsentscheidungen der Anleger in Deutschland. *Zeitschrift für Bankrecht und Bankwirtschaft* 18:1–15.

Bessler, Wolfgang, and Andreas Kurth. 2007. Agency problems and the performance of venture-backed IPOs in Germany: Exit strategies, lock-up periods, and bank ownership. *European Journal of Finance* 13 (1):29–63.

Bessler, Wolfgang, Andreas Kurth, and Stefan Thies. 2003. Grundsätzliche Überlegungen zur Kapital- und Aktionärsstruktur beim Börsengang von jungen Wachstumsunternehmen. *FinanzBetrieb* 5 (10):651–665.

Bessler, Wolfgang, and Matthias Stanzel. 2009. Conflicts of interest and research quality of affiliated analysts: Evidence from IPO underwriting. *European Financial Management* 15 (4):757–786.

Bessler, Wolfgang, and Stefan Thies. 2007a. The long-run performance of initial public offerings in Germany. *Managerial Finance* 33 (6):420–441.

Bessler, Wolfgang, and Stefan Thies. 2007b. Initial public offerings, subsequent seasoned equity offerings, and long run performance: Evidence from IPOs in Germany. *Journal of Entrepreneurial Finance and Business Ventures* 12 (1):1–37.

Bienz, Carsten, and Uwe Walz. 2006. Evolution decision and control rights in venture capital contracts: An empirical analysis. Working Paper Center for Financial Studies, Frankfurt. ssrn.com/abstract=966155.

Bittelmeyer, Claudia. 2007. *Patente und Finanzierung am Kapitalmarkt*. Wiesbaden: DUV.

Black, Bernard, and Ronald Gilson. 1998. Venture capital and the structure of capital markets: Banks versus stock markets. *Journal of Financial Economics* 47 (3):243–277.

Booth, Geoffrey, Juha Junttila, Juha-Pekka Kallunki, Markku Rahiala, and Petri Sahlström. 2006. How does the financial environment affect the stock market valuation of R&D spending? *Journal of Financial Intermediation* 15 (2):197–214.

Bottazzi, Laura, Macro Da Rin, and Thomas Hellmann. 2008. Who are the active investors? Evidence from venture capital. *Journal of Financial Economics* 89 (3):488–512.

Brav, Alon, and Paul Gompers. 1997. Myth or reality? The long-run underperformance of initial public offerings: Evidence from venture and nonventure capital-backed companies. *Journal of Finance* 52 (5):1791–1821.

Brav, Alon, and Paul Gompers. 2003. The role of lockups in initial public offerings. *Review of Financial Studies* 16 (1):1–29.

BVK. Bundesverband deutscher Kapitalbeteiligungsgesellschaften (ed.), *Yearbook* (different volumes).

Caselli, Stefano, Stefano Gatti, and Francesco Perrini. 2009. Are venture capitalists a catalyst for innovation? *European Financial Management* 15 (1):92–111.

Cumming, Douglas. 2005. Capital structure in venture finance. *Journal of Corporate Finance,* 11 (3):550–585.

Cumming, Douglas. 2007. United States venture capital contracting: Foreign securities. *Advances in Financial Economics* 12 (1):405–444.

Cumming, Douglas. 2008. Contracts and exits in venture capital finance. *Review of Financial Studies* 21 (5):1947–1982.

Cumming, Douglas, Grant Fleming, and Jo-Ann Suchard. 2005. Venture capitalist value-added activities, fundraising, and drawdowns. *Journal of Banking and Finance* 29 (2):295–331.

Cumming, Douglas, and Sofia Johan. 2006. Provincial preferences in private equity. *Financial Markets and Portfolio Management* 20 (4):369–398.

Cumming, Douglas, and Jeffrey MacIntosh. 2003. A cross-country comparison of full and partial venture capital exits. *Journal of Banking and Finance* 27 (3):511–548.

Cumming, Douglas, Daniel Schmidt, and Uwe Walz. 2008. Legality and venture capital governance around the world. *Journal of Business Venturing,* forthcoming.

Doukas, John, and Halit Gonenc. 2005. Long-term performance of new equity issuers, venture capital, and reputation of investment bankers. *Economic Notes* 34 (1):1–34.

Dohse, Dirk, and Andrea Schertler. 2004. Explaining the regional distribution of new economy firms—A count data analysis. Working Paper Kiel Institute for World Economics. ideas.repec.org/p/kie/kieliw/1193.html.

Engel, Dirk. 2002. Welche Regionen profitieren von Venture Capital-Aktivitäten? Working Paper Centre for European Economic Research (ZEW), Mannheim. opus.zbw-kiel.de/volltexte/2003/861/pdf/dp0237.pdf.

EVCA. 2008. European Venture Capital Association (ed.), *Yearbook.* 2008.

Felix, Elisabete, Mohamed Gulamhussen, and Cesaltina Pires. 2007. The determinants of venture capital in Europe—Evidence across countries. CEFAGE Working Paper. ideas.repec.org/p/cfe/wpcefa/2007_01.html.

Field, Laura, and Gordon Hanka. 2001. The expiration of IPO share lockups. *Journal of Finance* 56 (2):471–500.

Franzke, Stefanie. 2004. Underpricing of venture-backed and non-venture-backed IPOs: Germany's Neuer Markt. In *The Rise and Fall of Europe's New Stock Markets,* eds. Giancarlo Giudici and Peter Roosenboom, pp. 201–230. Amsterdam: Elsevier.

Fromhold-Eisebith, Martina, and Günter Eisebith. 2005. How to institutionalize innovative clusters? Comparing explicit top-down and implicit bottom-up approaches. *Research Policy* 34 (8):1250–1268.

Gompers, Paul. 1996. Grandstanding in the venture capital industry. *Journal of Financial Economics* 42 (1):133–156.

Gompers, Paul. 1998. Venture capital growing pains: Should the market diet? *Journal of Banking and Finance* 22:6–8, 1089–1104.

Gompers, Paul, Josh Lerner, Margaret M. Blair, and Thomas Hellmann. 1998. What drives venture capital fundraising? Brookings Papers on Economic Activity: Microeconomics, 149–204.

Gompers, Paul, and Josh Lerner. 1999. *The venture capital cycle*. Cambridge: MIT Press.

Gompers, Paul, and Josh Lerner. 2001. The venture capital revolution. *Journal of Economic Perspectives* 15 (2):145–168.

Gompers, Paul, and Josh Lerner. 2003. Short-term America revisited? Boom and bust in the venture capital industry and the impact on innovation. *Innovation Policy and the Economy* 3 (1):1–27.

Guellec, Dominique, and Bruno van Pottelsberghe. 2007. *The economics of the European patent system*. Oxford: Oxford University Press.

Hellmann, Thomas, Laura Lindsey, and Manju Puri. 2008. Building relationships early: Banks in venture capital. *Review of Financial Studies* 21 (2):513–541.

Hellmann, Thomas, and Manju Puri. 2000. The interaction between product market and financing strategy: The role of venture capital. *Review of Financial Studies* 13 (4):959–984.

Hirsch, Julia, and Uwe Walz. 2006. Why do contracts differ between VC types? Market segmentation versus corporate governance varieties. Working Paper, Center for Financial Studies, Frankfurt. ssrn.com/abstract=907002

Jenkinson, Tim, and Alexander Ljungqvist. 2001. *Going public: The theory and evidence on how companies raise equity finance*. 2nd ed. Oxford: Oxford University Press.

Kaplan, Steven, and Per Strömberg. 2003. Financial contracting theory meets the real world: An empirical analysis of venture capital contracts. *Review of Economic Studies* 70 (2):281–315.

Kaplan, Steven, and Per Strömberg. 2008. Leveraged buyouts and private equity. Working Paper University of Chicago. ssrn.com/abstract=1194962.

Kortum, Samuel, and Josh Lerner. 2000. Assessing the contribution of venture capital to innovation. *RAND Journal of Economics* 31 (4):674–692.

Kurth, Andreas. 2005. *Agency-Probleme und Performance von Initial Public Offerings*. Wiesbaden: DUV.

Krahnen, Jan Pieter, and Reinhard Schmidt. 2004. *The German financial system*. Oxford: Oxford University Press.

Lerner, Josh. 1994. Venture capitalists and the decision to go public. *Journal of Financial Economics* 35 (3):293–316.

Lerner, Josh. 1995. Venture capital and the oversight of private firms. *Journal of Finance* 50 (1):301–318.

Lowry, Michelle. 2003. Why does IPO volume fluctuate so much? *Journal of Financial Economics* 67 (1):3–40.

Lowry, Michelle, and William Schwert. 2002. IPO market cycles: Bubbles or sequential learning? *Journal of Finance* 57 (3):1171–1200.

Megginson, William, and Kathleen Weiss. 1991. Venture capitalist certification in initial public offerings. *Journal of Finance* 46 (3):879–903.

Popov, Alexander, and Peter Roosenboom. 2008. On the real effects of private equity investment: Evidence from firm entry. Working Paper European Central Bank. ssrn.com/abstract=1091094.

PwC. 2008. PricewaterhouseCoopers (ed.), *Private equity trend report 2008: Germany—Still the golden opportunity for international investors?*

PwC/3i. 2003. *Global private equity 2003*.

Rajan, Raghuram, and Luigi Zingales. 2003. Banks and markets: The changing character of European Finance. CRSP Working Paper. ssrn.com/abstract=389100.

Rindermann, Georg. 2004. *Venture capitalist participation and the performance of IPO firms: Empirical evidence from France, Germany, and the UK.* Frankfurt: Peter Lang.

Ritter, Jay. 1984. The "hot issue" market of 1980. *Journal of Business* 57 (2):215–240.

Schertler, Andrea. 2006. *The venture capital industry in Europe.* Houndmills, UK: Palgrave Macmillan.

Schertler, Andrea. 2007. Knowledge capital and venture capital investments: New evidence from European panel data. *German Economic Review* 8 (1):64–88.

Schwienbacher, Armin. 2008. Venture capital investment practices in Europe and the United States. *Financial Markets and Portfolio Management* 22 (3):195–217.

Stanzel, Matthias. 2007. *Qualität des Aktienresearchs von Finanzanalysten.* Wiesbaden: DUV.

Stein, Ingrid. 2008. Kapitalstruktur erfolgreicher Venture-Capital-Investitionen: Empirische Evidenz für Deutschland. *Kredit und Kapital* 41 (2):261–298.

Sternberg, Rolf, and Timo Litzenberger. 2004. Regional clusters in Germany—Their geography and their relevance for entrepreneurial activities. *European Planning Studies* 12 (6):767–791.

Tirole, Jean. 2006. *The theory of corporate finance.* Princeton: Princeton University Press.

Tykvová, Tereza. 2003. Is the behavior of German venture capitalists different? Evidence from the Neuer Markt. Working Paper Centre for European Economic Research (ZEW), Mannheim. www.ifk-cfs.de/papers/03_24.pdf.

Tykvová, Tereza. 2006. How do investment patterns of independent and captive private equity funds differ? Evidence from Germany. *Financial Markets and Portfolio Management* 20 (4):399–418.

Tykvová, Tereza, and Uwe Walz. 2007. How important is participation of different venture capitalists in German IPOs? *Global Finance Journal* 17 (3):350–378.

Winton, Andrew, and Vijay Yerramilli. 2008. Entrepreneurial finance: Banks versus venture capital. *Journal of Financial Economics* 88 (1):51–79.

Yung, Chris, Gönül Colak, and Wei Wang. 2008. Cycles in the IPO market. *Journal of Financial Economics* 89 (1):192–208.

ABOUT THE AUTHORS

Wolfgang Bessler is Professor of Finance and Banking at Justus-Liebig-University in Giessen. Previously, he was a faculty member at Syracuse University, at Rensselaer Polytechnic Institute, and at the Hamburg School of Economics. He has published widely in the leading academic journals. His main research interests are corporate finance with an emphasis on financing new ventures and initial public offerings, financial markets and institutions as well as asset management. He serves on the editorial board of various international journals.

Julian Holler is a research assistant at the Center for Finance and Banking, Justus-Liebig-University in Giessen. He holds a degree in business administration and focuses in his research on alternative investments and hedge funds.

Martin Seim is a research assistant at the Center for Finance and Banking, Justus-Liebig-University in Giessen. He holds a degree in business administration and focuses in his research on corporate finance and security offerings.

CHAPTER 23

Private Equity in Denmark

Capital Structure and Taxes

MORTEN BENNEDSEN
Professor, Department of Economics, Copenhagen Business School

KASPER MEISNER NIELSEN
Assistant Professor, Department of Finance, Chinese University of Hong Kong

SØREN BO NIELSEN
Professor, Department of Economics, Copenhagen Business School

STEEN THOMSEN
Professor, Ph.D., Managing Director, Center for Corporate Governance,
Copenhagen Business School

INTRODUCTION

This chapter analyzes private equity takeovers in Denmark, focusing on the consequences for capital structure on the part of portfolio companies and the associated implications for general tax revenues. The focus on Denmark allows us to analyze the capital structure using firm level data after the acquisition by the private equity funds. Moreover, the Danish case also provides insights to the discussion of recent regulative initiatives in European countries to limit the dilution of the corporate tax base.

To frame the analysis we begin the chapter with a brief overview of the private equity industry in Denmark. The overview highlights that the development of the Danish private equity industry has been similar to other continental European countries. From a slow start in the late 1980s, activities have peaked recently, culminating with the takeover of the telecommunication company TDC in 2006—a deal that at the time was the second largest in the history of LBOs. The surge in activities initiated a public debate on the social welfare implications of such transactions, centered mainly on the heavy use of leverage and its implication for taxation.

After the general introduction to the Danish buyout industry, we first look at the consequences of private equity takeovers for capital structure of target companies. We attempt to gauge the extent to which leverage has increased following buyouts in Denmark, and deliberate reasons to worry about the trends. To measure the changes in the capital structure we exploit a requirement in Danish law that obliges firms to make their annual report publicly available. Our analysis shows that although leverage increases at the firm level, the incremental increase is relatively modest. On average the debt to equity ratio increases from 1.4 to 2.5 in the year around the acquisition, but decreases to 1.8 three years after the acquisition. Similarly, the debt ratio increases from 53 to 67 percent one year around the transactions and decreases to 61 percent three years after. We find consistent evidence using alternative samples of firms for which we have more observations, but a shorter window of data. As such, our analysis shows that the heavy debate on the leverage policies of private equity funds tends to focus on a few cases in which debt was used aggressively. However, the relatively modest use of debt financing might be due to the relatively small size of some of the private equity investments, as debt financing in our sample tends to be increasing with firm size.

Next, and related to the changes in capital structure, we look at the implications of private equity takeovers for overall tax revenues. To understand the tax issues involved in a private equity takeover we provide a simple illustrative example that we utilize in both a numerical example and in a more conceptual discussion. Based on this discussion we argue that the view that private equity investments are harmful to overall tax revenue is too simplistic. On one hand, it is true that the higher leverage will increase the interest deduction on the income statement and thereby lower revenues from corporate taxes. On the other hand, private equity provides a vast range of investors with financial gains that are taxable, from the previous owners to institutional investors as the ultimate owners of the private equity funds. In the end private equity is much more neutral to tax revenues that one might think.

The rest of this chapter is organized as follows: The following subsection provides a historic overview of buyouts in Denmark. Section 2 analyses consequences for corporate leverage, whereas Section 3 discusses the implications for tax revenue. Finally, Section 4 offers concluding remarks.

History of Buyouts in Denmark

The history of private equity buyouts in Denmark begins in the late 1980s. The first LBO in Denmark was the 1987 takeover of the now-defunct Danish airline company Sterling Airways. The buyers were a group of investors headed by SDS, one of the bigger banks in Denmark. In 1990, the first Danish buyout fund was born. The equity fund in question, Nordic Private Equity Partners (NPEP), still exists and is by today's standards merely a tiny equity fund with investor commitments of less than DKK 165 or EUR 22 million. Still, the fund managed to take over the company Broen Armatur, originally a significant supplier of water-efficient shower systems.

Since these initial days, the Danish private equity industry has witnessed tremendous growth in activity. To the best of our knowledge, there have been at least 192 buyouts by private equity funds in Denmark. Exhibit 23.1 shows the number of buyout deals for every year since 1991. We notice that the activity has indeed accelerated after 2000; in the three years from 2005 through 2007 we have witnessed more than half of the total deals for the whole period.

This development is somewhat similar to other Nordic countries and continental Europe in general. In 2007 the Nordic market accounted for 11 percent of the

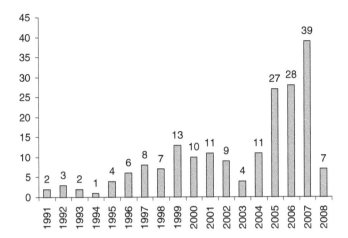

Exhibit 23.1 Number of Takeovers by Private Equity Funds in Denmark, 1991–2008
Source: Danish Venture Capital Association.

total buyout activities in Europe (EVCA 2008). Within the Nordic region Sweden accounts for around 50 percent of the activities, whereas the rest is shared almost equally among Denmark, Finland, and Norway.

We estimate that there are (in mid-2008) at least 17 active buyout funds with headquarters in Denmark, which have more than DKK 39 (EUR 5.2) billion under management. Exhibit 23.2 lists the 10 most active funds in Denmark based on the number of transactions they have been involved in. We see that many of the funds are anchored in Denmark (Axcel, LD Equity, Polaris, Odin Equity Partners) or Scandinavia (Capman, EQT, Nordic Capital, and Industri Kapital). As these funds are mainly focusing on domestic and intra-Nordic investments, the Nordic funds account for the majority of the buyout deals in Denmark.[1] However, we also notice that many of the truly large global private equity funds are operating in Denmark, including CVS, Apax, Blackstone, KKR, Permira, and Providence. In 2006, the latter five private equity funds formed a consortium that bought the former national telephone company TDC in a deal that at the time was the largest private equity deal in Europe, and second globally only to the infamous RJR Nabisco deal. This deal alone was responsible for bringing Denmark to the top of the country tables of buyout activities in 2006, relative to the size of the local economy.

The buyout funds have to a certain extent differentiated their strategies in the Danish market. There are a number of smaller funds that target small and medium-sized firms with an enterprise value below DKK 200 (EUR 27) million. These funds try to position themselves as an alternative exit model for traditional family-owned companies. The bigger funds target firms with enterprise values above DKK 150 (EUR 20) million, and the biggest Nordic and international funds have targeted the largest Danish companies. The differentiation reflects, among other things, that Denmark is mainly populated by small and medium-size family firms.

The investors in the private equity funds that operate in Denmark are typically institutional investors. In 2007, 38 percent of the DKK 39 (EUR 5.2) billion committed to private equity funds in Denmark came from pension funds. Another 28 percent came from insurance companies and banks. Generally speaking, the

Exhibit 23.2   Number of Deals among the Most Active Buyout Funds in
Denmark, 1991–2008

Private Equity Company	Established	Country	Number of Deals
Axcel	1994	Danmark	31
LD Equity	2005	Danmark	23
Polaris	1998	Danmark	17
Capman	1989	Finland	13
EQT	1994	Sverige	10
Odin Equity Partners	2005	Danmark	8
Nordic Capital	1990	Sverige	8
CVC	1981	Storbritannien	6
3i	1983	Storbritannien	6
Industri Kapital	1989	Sverige	6

Source: Danish Venture Capital Association.

composition of investors in Danish private equity funds is similar to the composition of investors in private equity funds in other Nordic and European countries. Compared to the domestic equity market where (domestic) institutional investors in total hold around 30 percent, they are somewhat overrepresented as a funding source for private equity funds.

CONSEQUENCES FOR CAPITAL STRUCTURE OF PORTFOLIO COMPANIES

Leverage and Takeovers

A general characteristic of private equity fund operations, in Denmark as well as other countries, seems to be that they to a large extent finance company takeovers and follow-up investments in acquired companies by debt. This characteristic has drawn criticism and reservations from several fronts. First, it is claimed that heavy indebtedness is the cause of a fall in the revenue from corporate taxation of the acquired companies and hence overall tax revenue (e.g., PES 2007). Second, worries have been voiced that the PE funds, by heavily debt-financing their operations, endanger the competitiveness of their portfolio firms (PES 2007, Ferran 2007, Thomsen and Vinten 2008, Thomsen 2008). Being financially strained, the companies will not, the argument goes, be able to pursue all available business opportunities; they will not be able to carry out necessary long-term investment; and they will therefore lose out relative to their less constrained rivals.

Third, heavy indebtedness increases the companies' vulnerability to bankruptcy which may have broader consequences for the financial system. In the first instance, the firm's creditors will, of course, be directly affected by closure of the firm, but the argument implies that entire networks of financial institutions may be hit in the process, resulting in externalities that should be taken into account when considering the capital structure of portfolio firms. Systemic risk of high leverage has been analyzed by, for example, Allen and Gale (2000) or Kyle and Wei (2001).

It should be noted that moves toward more intensive debt financing and higher gearing have been taken by a series of publicly traded companies as well, either directly by taking loans for ongoing investments, or indirectly via stock repurchases or large dividends to shareholders. And of course, in other parts of Danish society extensive debt finance is well known. This is almost the order of the day in owner-occupied housing (conceivably more so in Denmark than in most other countries), as purchases of homes to a very high degree rely on loans from specialized mortgage institutions. Almost every buyer in the housing market during the past decade has indeed undertaken a highly leveraged investment, whereby a relatively small down payment has eventually translated into sizeable equity in a rising market. It follows that challenges for the financial system materialize when house prices start to fall. Anyway, the upshot is that extensive debt financing of investments is neither unusual elsewhere nor necessarily suspect in private equity fund operations.

The tax-based critique of private equity takeovers is taken up in detail in the next section, although we forego further discussion of the other points of criticism against private equity funds' investment leveraging. Here, instead, our main concern is whether we can actually identify, in Danish data, a substantial move toward debt in the capital structure of private equity target companies.

Capital Structure of Private Equity Funds

The simple mechanics of the working of private equity funds are important for understanding capital structure issues.

The resources in a private equity fund are brought about by pension funds, insurance companies, and other "passive" investors committing specified amounts to the private equity fund. Management in the fund, employed by the associated management company, has, in a specified period, the right to call in funds from investors in order to invest in target companies. These funds they then supplement with borrowed funds, enabling them to purchase a portfolio company. All funds are placed in an investment company (holding company). From here, the fund pays off previous owners and—to the extent necessary—pays back creditors of the company. In major transactions it is not unusual to see a series of holding companies on top of each other; partly for tax reasons and partly because this enables differential treatment of different creditors. Debt in the portfolio company itself or in the "first" holding company can be made more secure than debt in holding companies "further up." Moreover, capital gains tax may in some jurisdictions be avoided if the shares in the holding company can be held for more than a certain period, beyond which capital gains are tax exempt, even though the target company is divested.

A thorough understanding of the capital structure in a private equity-owned company requires an overall understanding of this structure. For example, there may be a strong pressure on the target company to generate sufficient profits to enable the holding company to service its debt via dividends from the target. On the other hand, it is possible for the management company in the PE to call in further funds from the passive investors, if so required.

One crucial question is to what extent debts at higher levels of ownership interfere with the health of the underlying business company, that is, to what extent the "veil" of corporation can be pierced from above. Is it reasonable to take the financial structure of the owners into account (i.e., to consolidate)? If so, this should apply both to debt and equity including investment commitments, which could provide a cushion in times of financial distress. Ideally, rational owners would maximize the net present value of their investments regardless of their own capital structure, but in practice capital rationing and distress costs might very well influence decisions in the subsidiary. For example, owners could become impatient and respond with short-term thinking if pressured by high debt costs, or they could become more intent on good performance. Both descriptions fit into the "sense of urgency," which some believe to be a characteristic of private equity funds. Our case studies of private equity funds indicate that they do not keep an arm's length distance from their portfolio companies, which we interpret as evidence that it is indeed important to take both levels into account.

An Empirical Investigation

In this subsection we analyze the available data on a series of private equity-owned companies before and after the acquisition by the relevant private equity funds. Data for this analysis has been combined from previous work of Vinten (2008), the magazine *A4*, and Spliid (2007), all analyzing Danish companies that have been taken over by one or more PE funds. This data is combined with data from the Danish statistical bureau Experian, which collects financial data from companies as these data are reported to the Ministry of Economic and Business Affairs. Because of data availability and comparability, we apply data for the target companies rather than the financial holding companies that take on some of the debt.

The figures in our sample naturally are sensitive to structural differences in capital structure over time (such as the repealing of shareholder loans due to a change in the tax law). In addition, the figures are sensitive to differences across firms in regard to holding companies and the placement of debt. Thus, the figures should be taken merely as an indication of the extent of leverage of the companies.

Some of the recent private equity takeovers of Danish companies, not least the huge takeover of the Danish telecommunications company TDC and the facility service company ISS, are large enough to significantly affect averages. Due to this and to the fact (which we brought forth in section 1.1) that so many takeovers are rather recent, we distinguish between three different data sets:

A. Twenty-seven companies taken over by private equity funds, where we have data from three years before to three years after the takeover. Here we can see a longer period, although one can still inquire whether the period is long enough to catch the reduction of debt that may occur if the strategies of the funds are successful. This group includes neither TDC nor ISS.

B. Thirty-four companies, where we have data from two years before to two years after the takeover. This group includes all companies in group A. ISS is in, but not TDC.

C. Forty-eight companies, where we have data from one year before to one year after the takeover. The group spans all companies in groups B and A, and also both ISS and TDC.

Exhibit 23.3 Capital Structure in 27 Firms before and after Takeover by Private
Equity Funds

	Year						
	$t-3$	$t-2$	$t-1$	t	$t+1$	$t+2$	$t+3$
Balance Sheet							
Assets	503	541	537	693	679	668	719
Equity	223	242	206	193	184	219	250
Debt	244	256	286	455	452	411	438
Gearing Ratios							
Debt/Assets	0.49	0.47	0.53	0.66	0.67	0.61	0.61
Debt/Equity	1.10	1.06	1.39	2.36	2.45	1.88	1.76

This table shows weighted averages of debt and leverage for 27 firms for which we have access to data
three year before and after the deal. Debt is defined as the sum of short and long term interest carrying
debt. t is the acquisition year. $t-1, t-2, t-3$ is 1, 2, and 3 years before takeover, while $t+1, t+2$ and
$t+3$ is 1, 2, and 3 years after takeover, respectively.
Source: Experian and the authors' calculations.

In Exhibit 23.2 we present the development in balance sheet items and leverage
of the companies in group A. Similarly, we display in Exhibits 23.4 and 23.5 the
data for the companies in groups B and C. All reported results are averages for
the group. Because there are large differences between companies, there is much
variation in the data, and that can influence the extent to which the averages
represents a typical private equity-owned firm. If we alternatively use medians in
lieu of averages, we get similar results, though.

As explained, Exhibit 23.3 follows 27 companies from three years before to
three years after private equity-ownership. The average (asset weighted) acquired
company in this group has assets of around DKK 500 (EUR 70) million at the
time of takeover, and assets typically exhibit strong growth following the takeover,
leveling off afterwards. Capital structure is also markedly affected by the takeover.
Equity decreases slightly and rises again thereafter. Debt, however, increases by
around 50 percent. Leverage, measured by debt to assets, almost doubles in the
years after the takeover, but an average of 2.5 times equity in the year after the
takeover does not appear alarming, and leverage does decrease again 2 and 3 years
after the takeover.

In Exhibit 23.4 we follow the somewhat larger group B, albeit over a shorter
period. Again, we see an increase in debt and a lowering of equity in the period
after the takeover, but within this shorter time horizon there is no sign of leverage
decreasing again.

In Exhibit 23.5, covering the 48 companies in group C, we see a pattern similar to
that in Exhibit 23.3 and Exhibit 23.4. Equity is brought down, while debt increases,
so that leverage almost doubles. A fortiori, leverage expressed as debt relative to
equity of the order of 1.4 cannot be termed alarming.

In sum, we do not find these numbers worrying. Debt does rise following
the typical private equity takeover, but not to more than what companies seemingly could bear a couple of years prior to the takeover. Debt is even reduced in

Exhibit 23.4 Capital Structure in 34 Firms before and after Takeover by Private
Equity Funds

	Year				
	$t-2$	$t-1$	t	$t+1$	$t+2$
Balance Sheet					
Assets	760	789	988	876	911
Equity	357	334	318	288	283
Debt	364	413	626	550	597
Gearing Ratios					
Debt/Assets	0.48	0.52	0.63	0.63	0.66
Debt/Equity	1.02	1.24	1.97	1.91	2.11

The table shows weighted averages of debt and leverage for 34 firms for which we have access to data two years before and after the deal. Debt is defined as the sum of short and long term interest carrying debt. t is the acquisition year. $t-1$ and $t-2$ is 1 and 2 years before takeover, while $t+1$ and $t+2$ is 1 and 2 years after takeover, respectively. All items in the balance sheet are in million DKR. The exchange rate from EUR to DKR is 7.45.
Source: Experian and the authors' calculations.

absolute numbers shortly after the takeover, and measured relative to turnover and income—regarded as the most relevant measures by both lenders and the funds themselves—there probably is a significant fall after the initial increase in debt.

We must, however, draw attention to the uncertainty in the figures. Debt that is raised by the holding companies is not included in the numbers, and we know that a considerable share of debt of private equity funds is raised by exactly those holding companies. Further research on the influence of private equity funds on capital structure will thus require additional data and a more thorough study.

Exhibit 23.5 Capital Structure in 48 Firms before and after Takeover by Private
Equity Funds

	Year		
	$t-1$	t	$t+1$
Balance Sheet			
Assets	1092	1063	990
Equity	589	433	394
Debt	453	586	554
Gearing Ratios			
Debt/Assets	0.41	0.55	0.56
Debt/Equity	0.77	1.35	1.41

The table shows weighted averages of debt and leverage for 48 firms for which we have access to data one year before and after the deal. Debt is defined as the sum of short and long term interest carrying debt. t is the acquisition year. $t-1$, 1 year before takeover, while $t+1$, 1 year after takeover respectively. All items in the balance sheet are in million DKR. The exchange rate from EUR to DKR is 7.45.
Source: Experian and our own calculations.

Add to this that the period that is reflected by the figures is in the midst of a beneficial economic environment, in which leverage has not been challenged by low economic growth, credit constraints, increasing interest rates, falling share prices, or other adversities.

However, there are solid reasons to assume that the future will not reflect the past. In Denmark, as other countries across the world, the financial crisis has been accompanied by value losses, credit rationing, increases in credit spreads, and a worsened business outlook. Thus, the private equity business model will be severely stress-tested. So far only one company (Biva—a furniture retailer) has gone bankrupt, but other companies also appear to have economic problems (e.g., Idemøbler—another retailer). A highly spectacular and highly leveraged buyout, ISS (owned by EQT), has announced that it is scaling back its acquisition-led growth because of the crisis. Debt positions in ISS and EQT are being traded at huge discounts. Moreover, it will be well near impossible for the equity funds to exit with value increases, given the 50 percent drop in share prices during 2008 and the expected economy-wide decline in earnings. In fact, as leveraged investors they stand to lose large amounts of equity. However, give the capital committed to the funds they may also play a role by reinvesting in distressed portfolio companies, and lower value may imply bargains for those who have the savvy to buy at the right moment.

Some Case Studies

In connection with our study of private equity in Denmark, we had the opportunity to obtain information on many aspects of the takeovers of ten companies. In particular, we conducted interviews with management in the portfolio companies, with chairmen of the boards, and with representatives of the acquiring private equity funds. Also, for seven of the ten companies we received more quantitative information on the companies and their takeover processes.

This sample of seven companies is, of course, not large, and the numbers are obviously affected by a couple of large companies, viz. the above-mentioned TDC and ISS. (But they are also the very companies that spurred much of the debate on private equity–ownership in Denmark.) We look at the period of only from one year before to one year after the takeover. Exhibit 23.6 reports the development of items on the balance sheets of these companies plus their leverage.

It emerges that the reduction in equity and the decrease in indebtedness is much more significant in these seven case companies than in the official figures reported in Exhibits 23.3 to 23.5. As regards leverage, both the share of debt and financial leverage before the takeover is markedly smaller than in the bigger sample. This could mean that in these sample companies there was an extraordinary solidity and debt capacity pre-takeover—which the PE funds wanted to exploit as an integral part of the takeover.

The size of debt relative to company assets almost triples in the year of the takeover, and in parallel leverage increases by more than a factor 10, to six times the equity of the company. To some extent, this is due to the injection of shareholder loans. However, we see that debt is reduced already during the first year after the takeover, while equity grows, implying a decrease in leverage.

Exhibit 23.6   Leverage in Seven Case Companies before and after Takeover by Private Equity Funds

	Year		
	$t-1$	t	$t+1$
Balance Sheet			
Assets	17831	17086	19272
Equity	7379	1751	2549
Debt	3788	11046	9834
Gearing Ratios			
Debt/Assets	0.21	0.65	0.51
Debt/Equity	0.51	6.31	3.86

The table shows weighted averages of debt and leverage for 7 firms. Debt is defined as the sum of short and long term interest carrying debt. t is the acquisition year. $t-1$, 1 year before takeover, while $t+1$, 1 year after takeover respectively. All items in the balance sheet are in million DKR. The exchange rate from EUR to DKR is 7.45.
Source: Experian and the authors' calculations.

Financial Performance of Investments

Our current data does not allow us to assess the financial performance of private equity investments in Denmark. For example, we lack systematic data on purchase and exit prices. However, a couple of related studies provide some circumstantial evidence. Vinten (2008) studies the accounting performance of 73 Danish buyouts and finds that private equity–owned firms underperform in terms of profitability and other measures, compared to a control group of firms that also change ownership structure. Nielsen (2008) finds that direct private equity investments by Danish pension funds tend to underperform relative to investments in public stock markets. The Danish Ministry of Economics and Business Affairs (2006) finds that private equity fund ownership is associated with higher growth rates in employment and sales. However, this study includes venture capital investments that may have higher growth in employment and sales than buyout funds.

Altogether, the financial performance of Danish private equity does not appear to be impressive. However, there have also—to our knowledge—been relatively few bankruptcies (e.g., Partner Electric in 2001 and Biva in 2008).

Summing Up

Debt finance may well be the most important characteristic of private equity funds and their chief source of value creation. Debt finance of a company's or a PE fund's activities is not necessarily a problem, but rather a natural part of economic activity in modern society. The raising of debt in acquired companies has, however, spurred much public debate, and this debate is to some extent justified, because overly aggressive borrowing can render the companies and the economy at large more vulnerable in a downturn.

The borrowing of private equity funds constitutes only a limited part of total borrowing in the economy and in particular has only a peripheral connection to the ongoing credit crisis, which instead can be related to the pattern of financing of owner-occupied housing, housing construction, and ordinary bank lending to firms. Like other borrowers, private equity funds have benefited from ample credit and favorable borrowing conditions. However, there are reasons to believe that banks in the future will be more cautious in their lending—including making loans to private equity funds.

Whether the gearing of private equity funds' portfolio companies is sustainable may become evident when the previous boom period is replaced by a period of falling stock prices, credit squeezes, or low economic growth, which will in any case challenge the private equity model.

Our empirical analysis has demonstrated that in the typical company taken over by private equity, debt goes up, in some cases dramatically. However, increased indebtedness is mirrored in the risk faced by professional lenders who presumably act in their own interest. In Danish portfolio companies, the main portion of this debt is held by well-known and well-regarded Danish and Nordic banks, such as Danske Bank, Nordea, and others. The raising of debt also intensifies the pressure on the acquired companies, and indeed this constitutes part of the philosophy on the part of the private equity funds involved. The model may not, however, be suitable to all companies. But it probably is a good match for mature firms with a stable cash flow.

Compared to previous studies (e.g., Nikoskelainen and Wright 2007) the leverage observed in Denmark does not appear to be excessive. Even for the highly leveraged case studies, we observe a debt to equity ratio of 3.8 one year after takeover, which is comparable to the average ratio of 3.5 observed in the United Kingdom by Nikoskelainen and Wright (2007).

In sum, we have not found reasons to express reservations concerning the capital structure in private equity-owned companies in Denmark, because gearing at the target company level is well within reasonable limits. Moreover, while debt ratios increase substantially at the time of takeover, they tend to drop again after a few years. However, in the case studies we have found indications that consolidated leverage is much higher and that it may be necessary to take this into consideration to obtain the complete picture. Moreover, debt covenants and other complex aspects of private equity takeovers have not been analyzed.

IMPLICATIONS FOR TAX PAYMENTS

Taxes and Takeovers

In recent years, private equity funds and their target companies have taken central stage in the tax debate in Denmark. There are good reasons for this.

First, private equity funds are in several respects distinct from other financial institutions. They are in some ways similar to mutual funds, but they receive funds only from a limited number of investors; they strive to become sole owners of companies; and the partners of the associated management company perform the role of active investors in their portfolio companies.

Second, the takeovers of the target companies in themselves contain elements that focus attention on various problem areas in the tax system. When the private equity funds take over a company they establish holding companies and other intermediaries between the target company and the ultimate investors; the primary objective of this is to control the timing (and extent) of payments of taxes.

Third, there are important tax issues related to the remuneration of the active partners in the management company; these partly commit their own funds, but equally importantly, they supply their time and effort and thereby their commercial expertise to the target companies. To some extent they can control the form and composition of their remuneration, and thus the way it will be taxed.

Finally, private equity funds are known to increase the debt share in their portfolio companies (including the associated holding companies). This leveraging of the capital base is intended to increase earnings and exploit access to relatively cheap debt finance. But the immediate consequence is lower tax payments from the target companies, ceteris paribus.

It is this final tax aspect that has been debated the most in Denmark. The tax payments from some portfolio companies of PE funds have been altered so dramatically, that this fact in itself is responsible for a major change in the Danish corporate tax law in 2007. New rules were installed that aim to limit the amount of tax deduction for interest expenses. (At the same time, the general corporate tax rate was lowered two percentage points.)

The most well-known private equity takeover is the acquisition, by a consortium of five foreign private equity funds, of the biggest Danish telecommunications company, TDC, which was followed by a huge fall in its taxable income. But there are also other cases, and in early 2007 an internal committee in the tax administration was set down by the Danish tax authorities to closely investigate the tax issues in selected takeover cases. The relevant committee has yet to report its findings, but at an early stage the committee reported that the seven takeover cases that it investigates most closely, together stood for a drop in annual corporate tax payments on the order of DKK 2 billion (EUR 270 million), corresponding to some 3 to 4 percent of the total revenue from corporate income taxes.

A Simple Example of a Private Equity Takeover

To understand some of the tax issues involved in a private equity takeover of a target company, we begin by looking at a very simple and standardized example. The example contains the following series of events:

1. At the outset, the private equity fund in question (hereafter PE) is established. The group of investors consists of three groupings—institutional investors (pension funds, etc.), individual (wealthy) investors, and the partners in the associated management company that we henceforth call MAN. The former two groups of investors are referred to (and thought of as) passive investors, while the MAN partners are active investors; they select PE's portfolio companies and they monitor and support the acquired companies. PE's investments are regulated by a Limited Partnership Agreement that, among many other things, specifies the remuneration of the active investors in MAN.
2. PE spots the target company TC. (TC can be publicly traded or privately held, e.g., a family firm.) PE sends an offer to buy TC to its current owners.

3. Having obtained an acceptance, PE establishes a holding company, HOLD, and injects part of PE's funds into it. HOLD also arranges loans from banks in order to conduct the takeover of TC. Management in TC is invited to inject funds into HOLD, too.

4. The previous owners of TC are bought out, and (a portion of) current debt in TC is paid back.

5. The first immediate tax implications of the takeover have to do with the capital gains accruing to the previous owners of TC. To what extent they are held liable for capital gains tax may depend on the holding period, that is, how many years they have held their shares in TC.

6. TC continues operations, now with the support from the active partners in MAN. TC and HOLD, considered a unit for tax purposes, are taxed jointly. Taxable income will reflect, at least, (a) altered operations, (b) altered capital structure, in particular altered leverage. (a) may reflect the active ownership on the part of PE/MAN, while (b) reflects the debt and equity changes associated with the takeover. The second immediate tax implication of the acquisition thus may well be a drop in taxable income and thus tax payments from the company, if the takeover has implied an increase in the level of debt and accordingly larger, tax-deductible interest payments.

7. Often PE ownership is interpreted as more active ownership as compared to the situation where a diffuse number of small shareholders are the owners of the company. The close relationship between management in the acquired company and PE/MAN's representatives may boost the size of the company and eventually its earnings. If this is the case, a third consequence may be that taxable income of the TC/HOLD group increases relative to what would have been the case in the absence of the takeover.

8. After a certain period, PE decides to exit. Several exit routes may be relevant—an IPO, a trade sale, or a sale to another private equity fund, presuming that the company is not dissolved. When sold, all investors in HOLD—the passive and active investors in PE itself, plus management in TC—are paid and can register a capital gain. The third immediate tax implication then revolves around the taxation of these capital gains.

9. Having exited all its target companies in one way or another, PE closes.

The nine steps in the example will be utilized below, both in some numerical examples and in a more conceptual discussion of tax implications of private equity fund acquisitions. We start with a simple numerical example.

The Example with Numbers: Implications for Corporate Tax Payments

Assume that the price PE has to pay for TC is 2 billion. Further, let current debt of TC amount to 1 billion, meaning that previous owners harvest 1 billion from the deal.[2] To finance the acquisition, PE secures 370 million from passive investors, 10 from MAN partners, and furthermore management of TC puts 20 million into HOLD. New equity in HOLD is thus altogether 400 million, and the remainder of the acquisition price, 1.6 billion, is financed via new loans. New loans comprise standard loans of 1.25 million at 8 percent and mezzanine loans of 350 million at an interest rate of 12 percent.

Imagine that the takeover takes place at the end of an accounting year. At the beginning of that year, debt amounted to 1.078 billion, and the earnings of the firm before interest and taxes are 190 million in the year. With an interest rate on old loans of 8 percent, taxable income becomes 104 million. With a corporate income tax rate of 25 percent, after-tax income is 78 million, and this amount is used to bring debt down to 1 billion, which is the sum paid back to lenders following the takeover.

In the first and subsequent three years (years 1, 2, 3, and 4) following the takeover, preinterest earnings (EBIT) are taken to rise to, respectively, 200, 210, 220, and 230 million. After four years of ownership, PE sells TC at a price of 2.4 billion. In the meantime, earnings after interest and taxes are used to pay back debt (here, for the sake of simplicity, mezzanine debt, although it might more realistically be standard debt as a result of a debt clause).

The computation of tax payments from TC/HOLD in the four-year holding period are reported in Exhibit 23.7.

While TC paid 26 million in tax the year before the takeover, under PE-ownership TC/HOLD pays, respectively, 14.5, 18.3, 22.5, and 27 million in tax. Hence, PE-ownership seems to lead to a drastic cut in tax revenue to be had from the TC company—close to a halving of tax payments.

Now, the acquisition and subsequent sale of TC also leads to taxes on the capital gains from the two groups of owners, first the original ones and later on the investors in PE and HOLD, which may perhaps compensate for the loss in corporate tax revenue. However, to determine whether this will occur, it is necessary to make clear what the alternative to PE ownership would be.

Exhibit 23.7   Example: Earnings and Taxes under PE Ownership

	Year				
	0	1	2	3	4
Income Statement					
EBIT	190.0	200.0	210.0	220.0	230.0
Interest	86.0	142.0	136.8	130.2	122.1
Earnings after interest	104.0	58.0	73.2	89.8	107.9
Tax	26.0	14.5	18.3	22.5	27.0
Net income	78.0	43.5	54.9	67.3	80.9
Balance Sheet					
Debt, primo	1078.0	1600.0	1556.5	1501.6	1434.3
Net income	78.0	43.5	54.9	67.3	80.9
Debt, ultimo	1000.0	1556.5	1501.6	1434.3	1353.4

The table shows the computation of earnings and tax payments in the base case, where the target company TC is taken over by the private equity fund PE. The price is 2 billion ultimo year 0, and the company is held until ultimo year 4. Earnings grow by 10 million per year, and the corporate tax rate is 25 percent. Retired debt amounts to 1 billion and new debt to 1.6 billion (1.25 billion standard loan at 8 percent, 0.35 billion mezzanine loan at 12 percent). All net income is used to pay down debt.
Source: Experian and the authors' calculations.

A suitable alternative for the comparison would be a scenario in which

- TC is not sold ultimo period 0
- TC is subsequently, ultimo period 4, sold to the same group of investors who would take over TC from PE in the scenario with PE ownership.

To shed light on this alternative, Exhibit 23.8 reports computed earnings before and after interest and taxes, when TC continues in the hands of the original owners. The same assumptions pertaining to the development in earnings and in the use of net profits (to pay back debt) are employed. The resulting tax payments in the four years are 30, 34.3, 38.8, and 43.7 million, respectively. The sum of these figures are 146.8 million, as compared to the sum 82.3 million under PE ownership. The increased leverage of the firm—debt initially increased from 1 billion to 1.6 billion leading to a similar increase in interest deductions—indeed brings down tax payments to almost a half as a result of the PE takeover.

With the Danish experience in regard to private equity funds, and with the recent changes in the Danish corporate tax law, two reservations to the tables above can be put forward.

First, the very idea of the establishment of private equity funds, namely the practicing of active ownership and ensuing stronger development of acquired companies, is not adequately reflected in the comparison above. One way to illustrate this aspect is to assume a larger rate of growth of EBIT in the example. If the increase in EBIT is 15 million rather than 10 million per year as a result of PE ownership, the series of tax payments can be computed (on otherwise unchanged assumptions) at 15.8, 20.9, 26.6, and 32.7 million, totaling 96 million. Of course, accelerated growth as a possible consequence of PE ownership enhances corporate tax payments (although in this particular example a much stronger growth will be required to make up for the immediate corporate tax losses related to the PE takeover).

Second, the new Danish tax regime, which passed legislation in 2007, puts limits on the amount of deduction for interest payment when firms calculate their taxable income. The rules are in several respects similar to the rules applying in

Exhibit 23.8 Example: Earnings and Taxes in the Alternative Scenario

	Year				
	0	1	2	3	4
Income Statement					
EBIT	190.0	200.0	210.0	220.0	230.0
Interest	86.0	80.0	72.8	64.6	55.2
Earnings after interest	104.0	120.0	137.4	155.4	174.8
Tax	26.0	30.0	34.3	38.8	43.7
Net income	78.0	90.0	102.9	116.6	131.1
Balance Sheet					
Debt, primo	1078.0	1000.0	910.0	807.1	690.5
Net income	78.0	90.0	102.9	116.6	131.1
Debt, ultimo	1000.0	910.0	807.1	690.5	559.4

Source: Experian and the authors' calculations.

Germany, the United Kingdom, and other places. These regulatory initiatives aim at attempting to avoid that leverage dilutes the corporate tax base.

In Denmark, there are three steps in the process in which taxable income can be adjusted as a result of the interest deduction limitations. (1) A first set of rules is designed to limit deduction for group-internal interest payments; these rules are part of the set of rules aimed at avoiding "thin capitalization." (2) A second set of rules allows Danish companies to only deduct "net financial expenditures" to the extent that these do not exceed the tax-related value of the company's assets multiplied by a standard rate (of interest). (3) Finally, a third set of rules test for the so-called EBIT rule. The rule implies that taxable income before net financial expenditures can maximally be reduced by 80 percent as a result of deducting net financial expenditures.

The way we have constructed the example, (1) is not relevant, because debt in question is external to the group. Numbers are not so drastic as to render (3) relevant either. However, (2) may well have some bite in the example. To see this, assume that the group's assets throughout the whole period amount to 500 million. With a standard rate of 8 percent, rule (3) would merely allow a deduction for interest payments of 40 million per year. Taking this into account leads to Exhibit 23.9 below, a modified version of Exhibit 23.7.

The limitation to interest deduction "bites" in all four periods. Deductions for interest payments are way below the actual interest payments, implying that taxable income is adjusted upwards, and more taxes must be paid in every period. Profits are similarly reduced, entailing a slower reduction in the company's debt level. At an unchanged sales price at the end of period 4, the capital gain of PE will be significantly lower than if the interest deductibility limitation had not been enforced.

Exhibit 23.9   Example: The Effects of Interest Deductibility Limitation

	Year				
	0	1	2	3	4
Computation of Corporate Tax					
EBIT	190.0	200.0	210.0	220.0	230.0
Tax-related interest	86.0	40.0	40.0	40.0	40.0
Taxable income	104.0	160.0	170.0	180.0	190.0
Tax	26.0	40.0	42.5	45.0	47.5
Computation of Earnings after Tax					
EBIT	190.0	200.0	210.0	220.0	230.0
Actual interest	86.0	142.0	139.8	136.5	131.9
Tax	26.0	40.0	42.5	45.0	47.5
Net income	78.0	18.0	27.7	38.5	50.6
Balance Sheet					
Debt, primo	1000.0	1600.0	1582.0	1554.3	1515.8
Net income	78.0	18.0	27.7	38.5	50.6
Debt, ultimo	1000.0	1582.0	1554.3	1515.8	1465.2

Source: Experian and the authors' calculations.

The latter conclusion might be strengthened, if the limitation were directly reflected in the price at both the date of acquisition and the date of sale. Conceivably, the original owners of TC might not be able to obtain the price of 2 million for the company, if the acquiring private equity fund would be subject to the interest deductibility limitation. And likewise, PE might not be able to sell TC for the price of 2.4 million, if the buyer in question anticipates paying more in corporate income tax on account of the interest deductibility limitation. From a public finance perspective, an interesting question emerges as to the incidence of such limitations on interest deductibility. It is to be expected that the impact of rules such as (2) and (3) end up being partly borne by all parties involved—previous owners, temporary PE owners, and subsequent owners—and possibly workers in the target companies, too.

A heavy critique has been launched in Denmark against this type of interest deductibility limitations. First, it is argued that companies can have fully legitimate reasons for raising the share of debt in the capital base, reasons that have nothing or at least little to do with tax considerations. In particular, PE funds can with good reason claim that they do not need as large an equity share of the capital base, because they can always call in extra funds from the investors in the PE fund. Second, and at least as important, it is alleged that many companies other than those acquired by PE funds will be hit by the interest deductibility limitations. In our example—see Exhibit 23.8—in the scenario where TC is not acquired by PE, the limit on interest deductions would also be 40 (with the same value of assets). This figure is lower than the actual interest payments in all four years also in the non-PE scenario, whence TC would be liable to the interest deductibility limitation.

Likewise, nontarget companies may also be hit by the rules in (3) above.

Wider Tax Implications of PE Takeovers

The previous subsection focused on possible reductions in corporate tax payments following a private equity takeover of a target company. Prior to the numerical example we also acknowledged that the takeover in itself will lead to other immediate tax consequences:

- Previous owners may pay capital gains taxes on proceeds from selling to PE.
- Investors in PE (in the holding company) will pay capital gains taxes (or perhaps corporate income taxes) on the proceeds once the target company is sold off to a new owner.

As noted above, these tax payments might seem to offset the possible reductions in the corporate tax payments from the target company. We also observed, however, that one needs to carefully specify the alternative to the PE takeover and include the possible tax implications of this alternative. Among such tax implications would be at least

- Possible capital gains tax payments from previous owners, once they sell to the new group of owners (to whom PE sells in the base case).

These extra tax payments of course make it less likely that the overall tax consequences of a PE company takeover will be favorable. But a number of questions remain unanswered, and they have to be confronted as part of estimating the overall tax consequences of PE takeovers. These are

- If institutional and other investors did not invest in HOLD via PE, where would they then have invested, and with what tax consequences?
- If PE/MAN's partners had not invested in HOLD, where would they alternatively have invested their funds, and what would be the resulting tax payments? The same question applies to management of TC. (If these borrow in order to buy shares in HOLD, the tax consequences of this borrowing also has to be taken into account.)
- Where will the payments received by the previous owners of TC be invested, and what taxes will they pay on the returns?
- How will banks which have their loans paid back by PE use these funds?
- Where will banks that supply funding for PE's takeover of TC get those funds from, and with what tax consequences?

Merely asking these questions makes clear that the computations of the overall tax consequences of a PE takeover are destined to become complicated.

A Hypothetical Case

A specially designed hypothetical case (based on the numerical example above) illustrates how under certain "ideal" circumstances the computation can turn out somewhat easier. Assume

- Passive investors in PE, MAN's partners and TC's management would alternatively have placed their funds (400 million) in the local stock market.
- Previous owners of TC who receive 1 billion place 400 million of this in the local stock market and the remainder in local banks.
- These local banks are paid back 1 billion and at the same time receive 600 million from the previous owners of TC. This altogether will enable the banks to place debt in HOLD in the order of 1.6 billion.

This hypothetical situation is illustrated in Exhibit 23.10. It is easily seen that if the assumptions are fulfilled, neither stock nor credit markets need to be (noticeably) affected by the PE takeover. In stock markets, 400 million of shares are sold, but a similar amount is bought. And in credit markets there is a new demand for 1.6 billion, but a similar new supply. Provided that portfolio patterns of parties involved are not noticeably different, price implications can be very modest, so that tax analysis only need to focus on the payment streams in the figure. In fact, the tax analysis of the difference between the base scenario with PE ownership of TC, and the alternative scenario without, needs *only* to

- answer the questions above
- register the difference in corporate tax payments from TC/HOLD, and
- register the capital gains tax payments of previous owners and PE investors.

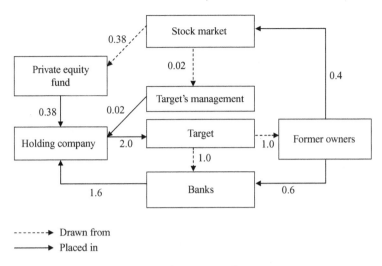

Exhibit 23.10 Example: A Hypothetical Financing Pattern

Looking a bit more closely at the hypothetical example, one sees that the main tax consequences of the PE takeover will be (1) the drop in corporate tax payments due to increased leverage, (2) different timing of capital gains taxes, plus (3) extra tax payments from the previous owners on their return to deposits (interest from the 600 million placement in banks). The latter would be found as 600 million times the relevant interest rate times the personal tax rate on interest. Summing negative and positive differences in tax payments between the two scenarios may lead to a negative or positive net value, depending on the tax treatment of the various parties involves. There is at least no guarantee that a PE takeover will hurt overall tax revenue in the country in question.

More Complications

The simple example above is, of course, at best a highly stylized picture of a private equity takeover of a company. In reality, a host of factors complicate the picture. Instead of a single company, the fund could be taking over a large multinational concern with a series of affiliates in other countries. There could be extraordinary dividend payments to the investors in PE; there could be "debt push-down" (operations whereby debt is effectively pushed down from the holding company to the target company itself), and so on. Some of these complications are merely technicalities when it comes to the tax implications of private equity takeovers. An acquisition of a multinational concern implies that the fund will face the intricacies of tax planning in an international context. But the concern already had to deal with these prior to the takeover, so in this sense the takeover is not essential.

One aspect of private equity takeovers that we should discuss here, however, is the involvement of international financial institutions. Recognizing that private equity takeovers are likely to involve increased leverage, participants in the debate on private equity in Denmark have expressed fears that the loss of revenue from corporate taxation will be for good, if lenders to the holding companies of PE funds are foreign-based. In this way, recipients of interest payments from Danish target companies (the associated holding companies) on their scaled-up debt will not lead to any tax payments at all to the Danish fiscs. Accordingly, it is seen as a special problem, if private equity funds use international banks to finance their takeovers, relative to the situation where Danish banks are involved (and the earnings of the bank as well as the interest payments to deposit holders would be taxable by Danish tax authorities).

While intriguing at first sight, this fear of involvement of foreign financial institutions is unfounded. Let us consider two otherwise identical takeover situations in which a Danish private equity fund acquires a Danish company. The first uses Danish banks exclusively, while the second uses foreign banks. Should we, other things being equal, expect a larger loss in domestic tax revenues from the latter takeover?

No. The former takeover situation is simpler, and it could be as simple as the hypothetical situation in subsection 3.3 where only the previous owners, investors in PE, and banks are involved, so that tax revenue effects can be relatively easily considered. The fact that foreign financial institutions are involved adds an extra layer of complexity, but not necessarily a tax revenue loss.

The argument is as follows: The fact that a company is traded and turned over from previous owners to a private equity fund has no immediate effect on a country's balance of trade, and thereby its net foreign asset position. When only domestic agents are involved, this is evident. But the same effect also occurs, even if foreign banks finance the private equity takeover. If they do so, the rest of the world immediately receives an additional IOU on the domestic economy, thereby seemingly weakening the country's net foreign asset position vis-à-vis the rest of the world. However, exactly because the private equity takeover is but an asset transaction, the country's NFA position cannot be altered. As a result, there must be at least one other transaction of the same size and opposite sign for the NFA position to remain unchanged. Going back to the hypothetical example, suppose that PE uses foreign banks to supply (the 1.6 billion) funds for the takeover. This supply needs to be financed, and the simplest way to accomplish this is to have the local banks (who receive 1 billion) and the previous owners (who wish to deposit 0.6 billion) lend to the foreign banks in question. If they do so, they will earn interest on altogether 1.6 billion of deposits, and this interest income is liable to domestic tax, so would counteract the immediate loss of corporate tax revenue on account of increased leverage in the PE takeover. (Of course, the matching of the need for funds on the part of the foreign banks and the supply of funds on the part of previous owners and domestic banks might not be this direct, but financial intermediaries could still make ends meet.)

Similar arguments can be put forth, if there are other foreign agents involved, be it foreign owners of the target company or the private equity fund itself.

Finally, we have not addressed the taxation of carried interest (performance-related fees to fund managers; see Thomsen 2008; Thomsen and Vinten 2008). Carry is currently taxed as capital gains which are usually lightly taxed, in Denmark and elsewhere. But some argue that carry accounts for a substantial fraction of fund manager compensation and therefore ought to be taxed harder, as labor income (i.e., a "Schwarzman tax"). In the United States, several congressional hearings have been held on this question. In the beginning of September 2007, the House

Committee on Ways and Means held hearings on this issue. During these hearings, it was proposed that the tax rate on carried interest should be raised from 15 to as much as 35 percent. Another suggestion has been to differentiate between investor-type and manager-type partners in private equity funds, where solely the investor-type partners should be entitled to capital gains treatment.

Summing Up

The aim of this section has been to consider likely tax revenue consequences of private equity fund takeovers of Danish firms. A few highlighted cases of such acquisitions have reportedly led to a large loss of corporate tax revenue, and the public at large has probably taken this to mean that private equity activities are bound to hurt overall tax revenue.

Hopefully, we have been able to argue above that this is too simplistic a view. Increased leverage related to enhanced use of debt in the capital base of target companies (including holding companies) unquestionably will lower corporate tax payments. Deductions for interest soar and bring down taxable income. But this is only part of the story. A full-fledged analysis must include at least the tax consequences of all relevant transactions of investors in the PE fund, the previous owners of the target company, and financial institutions. Accomplishing this, one discovers that the presence of private equity funds and their acquisitions of local companies will be much more neutral to the tax intake than one might think to begin with.

CONCLUSION

Increases in debt are a defining feature of private equity, as evident in the term *leveraged buyouts*.

As expected we observe increasing leverage in a study of Danish firms. The average leverage at the portfolio company level was not found to be alarming, and we also observed that gearing ratios tend to drop after a few years. The consolidated leverage including the financial holding companies established as vehicles for acquisition appears to be much higher, but also tends to decrease over time.

The overall tax consequences of private equity takeovers are fairly hard to ascertain, and even their sign is not unambiguous. On account of increased leverage, the typical direct tax effect is lower corporate tax payments from a target company; however, this is only part of the story, and a serious investigation will reveal indirect and long-term tax effects that may well counteract the direct effects.

Aside from tax consequences there is no doubt that the risk of financial distress and bankruptcy increases as a consequence of private equity takeovers. Whether this increase is so large as to be problematic is much less certain. Theoretically, there is reason to believe that leverage will influence the allocation of risk rather than overall risk and capital costs, particularly if we assume that business risk is constant. We can think of situations in which leveraged companies will be limited in their choice of strategy and investments, but whether the resulting welfare losses exceed the gains from reduced agency problems is difficult, perhaps impossible, to say.

NOTES

1. According to EVCA (2008) around 75 percent of the Nordic buyout funds' investments in 2006 and 2007 were domestic or intra-Nordic, whereas the remaining 25 percent mainly involved deals with targets headquartered in other European countries.

2. All numbers in this section are in Danish Kroner (DKK). The exchange rate from Euro to DKK is 7.45.

REFERENCES

Allen, Franklin, and Douglas Gale. 2000. Financial contagion. *Journal of Political Economy* 108 (1):1–33.

Bradley, Michael, Gregg A. Jarrell, and E. H. Kim. 1984. On the existence of an optimal capital structure. *Journal of Finance* 39 (3):857–878.

Cheffins, Brian R., and John Armour. 2007. The eclipse of private equity. Working Paper European Corporate Governance Institute. Available at SSRN: ssrn.com/abstract= 982114.

Andrade, Gregor, and Steven N. Kaplan. 1998. "How costly is financial (not economic) distress?" Evidence from highly leveraged transactions that became distressed. *Journal of Finance* 53 (5):1443–1493.

Cotter, James F., and Sarah W. Peck. 2001. The structure of debt and active equity investors: The case of the buyout specialist. *Journal of Financial Economics* 59 (1):101–147.

Cuny, Charlge J., and Eli Talmor. 2007. A theory of private equity turnarounds. *Journal of Corporate Finance* 13:629–646.

EVCA. 2008. *EVCA 2008 Nordic report.* European Venture Capital Association. Brussels.

Ferran, Eilis. 2007. Regulation of private equity-backed leveraged buyout activity in Europe. Working Paper European Corporate Governance Institute. Available at SSRN: ssrn.com/abstract=989748.

Jensen, Michael C. 1989. Active investors, LBOs, and the privatization of bankruptcy. *Journal of Applied Corporate Finance* 2 (1):35–44.

Jensen, Michael C. 2007. The economic case for private equity. Working Paper, Harvard University. Available at SSRN: ssrn.com/abstract=963530.

Jensen, Michael C., and William H. Meckling. 1976. Theory of the firm: Managerial behaviour, agency costs, and ownership structure. *Journal of Financial Economics* 3 (4):303–360.

Jones, Charles M., and Matthew Rhodes-Kropf. 2004. The price of diversifiable risk in venture capital and private equity. Working Paper, Columbia University. Available at SSRN: ssrn.com/abstract=342841.

Kaplan, Steven N. 1989. Management buyouts: Evidence on taxes as a source of value. *Journal of Finance* 44 (3):611–632.

Kyle, Albert S., and Wei Xiong. 2001. Contagion as a wealth effect. *Journal of Finance* 56 (4):1401–1440.

Lerner, Josh, and Anuradha Gurung. 2008. Globalization of alternative investments. The Global Economic Impact of Private Equity Report 2008. World Economic Forum Report, Geneva.

Nielsen, Kasper, M. 2008. The return to pension funds' direct private equity investments: New evidence on the private equity premium puzzle. Working Paper, Chinese University of Hong Kong. Available at SSRN: ssrn.com/abstract=1095289.

Nikoskelainen, Erkki, and Mike Wright. 2007. The impact of corporate governance mechanisms on value increase in leveraged buyouts. *Journal of Corporate Finance* 13 (4): 511–537.

OECD. 2007a. *The implications of alternative investment vehicles for corporate governance: A synthesis of research about private equity firms and activist hedge funds*. Report. Paris.

OECD. 2007b. *The implications of alternative investment vehicles for corporate governance: A survey of empirical research*. A report prepared for the Steering Group on Corporate Governance by Mike Wright, Andrew Burrows, Rod Ball, Louise Scholes, Miguel Meuleman, and Kevin Amess. Centre for Management Buyout Research, Nottingham University Business School.

PES—Socialist Group in the European Parliament. 2007. *Hedge funds and private equity—A critical analysis*. Report. Brussels.

Spliid, Robert. 2007. *Kapitalfonde—Rå Pengemagt Eller Aktivt Ejerskab*. Copenhagen: Børsens Forlag.

Stromberg, Per J. 2008. The new demography of private equity. Working Paper, Stockholm Institute for Financial Research.

The Danish Ministry of Economic and Business Affairs. 2006. *Private equity funds in Denmark* (in Danish). Report. Copenhagen.

Thomsen, Steen. 2008. Should private equity be regulated? Working Paper, Copenhagen Business School.

Thomsen, Steen, and Frederik Vinten. 2008. A review of private equity. Working Paper, Copenhagen Business School.

Vinten, Frederik. 2008. The performance of private equity buyout fund owned firms. Working Paper Copenhagen Business School. Available at SSRN: ssrn.com/abstract=1114603.

ABOUT THE AUTHORS

Morten Bennedsen obtained a Ph.D. in Economics from Harvard University in 1998. He has done research on closely held corporations, capital structures, venture capital, investor protection, ownership structures, family firms, and privatization. His work has been published in top finance and economics journals, such as *Journal of Financial Economics, Journal of Political Economy*, and *The Quarterly Journals of Economics*. Professor Bennedsen has won a number of research and teaching prices including the Danish National Research Award (2008). He is also the current editor of Scandinavian Journal of Economics, has served as an advisor on Corporate Financial Policy for the Danish Ministry of Economics and Business Affairs, and has done consultancy work for A.O. the Danish Ministry of Foreign Affairs, the World Bank, and Novo Nordic Foundation.

Kasper Meisner Nielsen received his Ph.D. in Economics from the University of Copenhagen. His research interests are applied microeconometrics, corporate governance, family firms, and private equity. He has published in academic journals including *The Quarterly Journal of Economics, Review of Finance*, and *Journal of Banking and Finance*. His research has also been awarded with external financing from competitive research grants on several occasions. On his area of expertise Professor Nielsen has served as an external advisor, consultant, and lecturer to several agencies and companies in Denmark and Hong Kong.

Søren Bo Nielsen received his Ph.D. in Economics from the University of Copenhagen. After a period as economist for the Economic Council of Denmark he became Associate Professor of Economics at the University of Copenhagen and later moved to Copenhagen Business School. There he has been Director of the

Economic Policy Research Unit (EPRU) 1993 to 1998 and Professor since 1998. His main interest areas are public finance, in particular taxation, plus intertemporal macroeconomics and corporate finance. He has been a member of the chairmanship of the Economic Council of Denmark and vice-chairman of the Danish Social Science Research Council. He has published widely in international journals in economics, and he is affiliated with the Centre for Economic Policy Research (CEPR), London; CESifo, Munich; and Oxford University Centre for Business Taxation.

Steen Thomsen specializes in corporate governance as a teacher, researcher, consultant, commentator, and practitioner. His publications include more than 26 international articles in management, law, and economics journals, as well as four books. Steen has served as a board member in several business companies and is currently a nonexecutive chairman of two consulting firms. He writes columns for the leading Danish business newspaper, *Børsen,* and has served as a consultant and lecturer to several large companies and government organizations, including the EU, the UN, Copenhagen Stock Exchange, and the Danish Central Bank. He has also contributed to the Danish corporate governance codes on listed companies and small and medium-sized companies.

CHAPTER 24

Venture Capital and Private Equity in Canada

Phasing Out an Inefficient Tax Credit[1]

DOUGLAS CUMMING
Associate Professor and Ontario Research Chair, York University, Schulich School of Business

SOFIA JOHAN
University of Tilburg, AFM Senior Research Fellow, Tilburg Law and Economics Centre (TILEC)

INTRODUCTION

Government bodies around the world provide much support to entrepreneurs and innovators in their capital-raising efforts (see, e.g., World Bank 1994, 2002, 2004). This support comes in the form of tax subsidies and other entrepreneur-friendly regulation (e.g., lenient bankruptcy laws and lax securities laws, etc.), as well as direct government programs to provide capital for entrepreneurs. One rationale for this support is that there is a perception of the existence of a capital gap for entrepreneurs,[2] because the risks to financing early-stage high-tech companies are very pronounced and the rewards are not sufficient to entice enough investors. Another rationale is that there are returns to society for having entrepreneurship and innovation. Because the private returns do not account for the social returns, there is an insufficient supply of capital for entrepreneurship and innovation.

In Canada, the primary mechanism for supporting entrepreneurial finance has been through Labour Sponsored Venture Capital Corporations (LSVCCs, also known as Labour Sponsored Investment Funds, or LSIFs). LSVCCs have existed in the Province of Ontario since Ontario adopted LSVCC legislation in 1992. The first LSVCC in Canada was introduced in Quebec in 1983. LSVCCs are tax-subsidized mutual funds that invest in privately held firms. The after-tax cost of a CAN\$5,000 LSVCC investment made as a Registered Retirement Savings Plan (RRSP) eligible investment in Ontario ranges from CAN\$1,180 to CAN\$2,390, or roughly 27 to 48 percent of the nominal dollar cost of the investment (the after-tax cost is lower the higher the income of the investor). In exchange for the tax subsidy, LSVCC fund managers agree to be subject to a number of covenants that govern their permissible investment activities. LSVCCs have multiple objectives, including regional development, enhancing financing for small firms, creating jobs, and creating returns for their investors.

On August 29, 2005, the Government of Ontario announced the phasing out of the tax credit towards LSVCCs.[3] Initially, the phase-out was scheduled for 2010, but with lobbying it has been pushed back to 2011. It is understandable why the Government of Ontario sought to phase-out the tax credit, and understandable why interested parties would lobby to get back the tax credit. As empirically shown in earlier work (e.g., Carpentier and Suret 2005, 2006; Carpentier, L'Her, and Suret 2006), LSVCCs are expensive programs that do not generate rates of return to investors. The economic rate of return (not accounting for tax subsidies) to investors since 1992 has been approximately zero. The LSVCC performance index (see www.globefund.com) generally fared worse than the 30-day risk-free T-bill index, which is the lowest possible performance benchmark. The only time the LSVCC index crept above the 30-day T-bill index was in late 1999 and early 2000 at the peak of the Internet bubble. Even at that time, LSVCCs barely achieved better performance than 30-day T-bills, and lagged other metrics, including the U.S. venture-capital performance index and the TSX large- and small-cap indices (see Exhibit 24.1).[4] Despite this poor performance, LSVCCs charge very high management expense ratios (on average, over 5 percent) (Sandler 2001; Anderson and Tian 2003; Cumming and MacIntosh 2006 2007; Cumming and Johan 2009). In short, without the tax subsidies to LSVCCs, it seems likely that LSVCCs would not continue to exist in Ontario, at least in their present form.

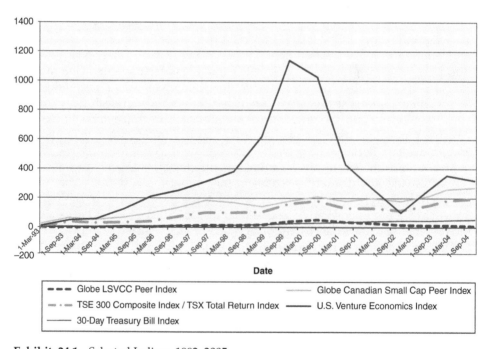

Exhibit 24.1   Selected Indices, 1992–2005

In response to the phase-out of the Ontario LSVCC tax credit, many commentators have suggested that entrepreneurs and emerging companies raising capital in Ontario will face difficulties. For instance, a headline released by the Canadian Retail Venture Capital Association (CRVCA) on April 26, 2007, indicated that "Innovative companies will leave Ontario."[5] Further, the CRVCA argued that "Ontario taxpayers have reaped impressive returns from federal and provincial government policies to encourage investment in labour-sponsored investment funds."[6] Other media reports have indicated entrepreneurs and emerging companies are facing increasing difficulty in obtaining funding since the announcement of the phase-out of the Ontario LSVCC tax credit,[7] albeit there is mixed anecdotal evidence as to the causes. It has been noted, for instance, that ". . . companies funded between 2001 and 2004 are having trouble raising more money.". . . Further, it has been noted that "the lack of venture capital (is) driving some companies, particularly in the biotechnology sector, to seek capital by going public on the Toronto Stock Exchange (TSX) and the London Stock Exchange (AIM)."[8]

In short, the phase-out of the tax subsidy in Ontario raises some important policy questions. Most importantly, are entrepreneurs and emerging companies concerned about this phasing out, and if so, which ones in particular, and why? These questions are the focus of this chapter. Other related issues will be discussed, as detailed herein.

To address these questions, we refer to survey data collected by YORKbiotech Inc. (yorkbiotech.ca). The surveys were distributed to innovative healthcare companies (e.g., biotechnology, medical diagnostics, medical devices, healthcare information technologies, etc.) in the Province of Ontario in 2008. These surveys were designed to solicit feedback on a variety of issues associated with capital-raising efforts. None of the survey questions were mandatory and respondents were free to answer only the questions that they felt appropriate. The survey was targeted only to firms in Toronto, York Region, London, and Ottawa. As such, while the data are not completely representative of all innovative healthcare companies in the Province of Ontario, the data nevertheless provide some important and timely insights associated with the changing institutional environment for entrepreneurial finance in the Province of Ontario. We are explicit about the limitations and extent of inferences that can be drawn from the data presented herein.

In a nutshell, the data indicate the following. Innovative healthcare companies in Ontario typically do not rank very highly a concern regarding the removal of the tax credit in regard to their capital-raising efforts. The median ranking to the issue of concern over the removal of the LSVCC tax credit on a scale of 1 (lowest) to 5 (highest) is 1. Those companies that are concerned about the removal of the LSVCC tax credit are ones that are currently financed by LSVCCs. In regression analyses controlling for other things being equal (such as age of company, other sources of capital, and R&D expenses, etc.), the only significant variable in explaining concern over removal of the tax credit is the prior percentage of capital obtained from LSVCCs. We explain this finding in view of terms in shareholder agreements written between emerging companies and VCs. We show with actual examples of these terms used by LSVCCs in Canada (as well as by private VC funds) that the investors have significant control rights, including rights of sale (redemption, co-sale, drag-along, and tag-along rights), voting rights, and preemptive rights (known as pro rata participation rights, where the fund can participate pro rata in future financing). This means that all else being equal, once a company obtains capital from a particular investor, the company is disadvantaged if that particular investor cannot raise future funds to finance subsequent rounds.

The data further indicate information about the number of months companies will be able to continue operating if unable to obtain new external capital. Firms at greatest risk are ones whose equity is held to a greater degree by private equity firms and universities. We see some suggestive evidence, albeit marginally significant, that companies financed by LSVCCs are more likely to fail quicker if they are unable to obtain additional external capital. By contrast, companies with greater research and development (R&D) expenditures are much more likely to fail quicker if they are unable to obtain new external capital, as would be expected.

Finally, the data indicate that companies financed by private equity are more likely to hold more patents and have greater R&D expenses than those financed by LSVCCs. Companies financed by private equity are more likely than those financed by LSVCCs to move to another jurisdiction if unable to obtain additional financing. Firms financed by angels (wealthy private individuals) are least likely to move to another jurisdiction if they fail to obtain additional financing.

It is particularly noteworthy that companies are most concerned about the cost of taking a product to market and access to risk capital. At the same time, companies are generally not concerned with the removal of the LSVCC tax credit, unless they already have received capital from LSVCCs, for reasons indicated above.

Overall, the results in the data reported herein are broadly consistent with academic work on public policy towards venture capital and entrepreneurship. Tax policy can facilitate entrepreneurship and entrepreneurial finance, but theory[9] and evidence[10] indicate that tax policy and government programs have the potential to be distortionary.[11]

This chapter is organized as follows. We describe the data in the next section. Thereafter, we present multivariate regression analyses of capital-raising hurdles, time to failure if a company is unable to raise additional capital, and the extent of value-add associated with different types of investors. Concluding remarks follow in the last section.

DESCRIPTION OF 2008 YORKBIOTECH SURVEY DATA

YORKbiotech is a nonprofit organization based in the Greater Toronto Area with a mission to:[12]

- serve as a gateway to relevant companies and resources;
- advance entrepreneurship, enhance commercialization, and increase investment; and
- become the preferred business development partner for regional entrepreneurs and organizations.

Since the announcement of the removal of the LSVCC tax credit in the Province of Ontario in August 2005, some YORKbiotech members indicated concern to YORKbiotech's executive director, Robert Foldes, about current and future capital-raising efforts. This concern inspired data collection by YORKbiotech to assess the severity of capital-raising concerns for innovative healthcare firms and entrepreneurs in the Province of Ontario.

An online survey was distributed to innovative healthcare firms in Ontario in early 2008. The survey addressed questions about the firm's size (employees), revenues, industry subsector, sources of capital, and terms in shareholder agreements with investors. A total of 58 questions were asked, each comprising responses that requested yes/no or ranked responses. All ranked responses were on the scale of 1 (lowest) to 5 (highest). A copy of the survey is available upon request.

The survey was distributed to 231 firms in Toronto, York Region, London, and Ottawa. There were a total of 43 replies, or an 18.6 percent response ratio. We do not report in detail on many characteristics of the nonrespondents in our sample, except for their date of incorporation and whether or not they are privately held or publicly traded. Among the respondents, 32 of 43 (74.4 percent) are currently privately held, while 118 of 188 (62.8 percent) nonrespondents are currently privately held; this difference is significant at the 5 percent level. Among the respondents, the average (median) incorporation date was 1993 (1999), while the average (median) incorporation date for nonrespondents was 1987 (1993). The difference in the median incorporation date is significant at the 5 percent level across respondents versus nonrespondents, but the difference in the average incorporation date is not statistically significant. Overall, relative to the population of innovative healthcare companies in Ontario, our sample comprises a greater proportion of earlier stage private companies that were more recently incorporated. If our sample is distorted, therefore, it is distorted towards firms that have a greater interest in receiving capital from venture capitalists and other private equity providers.

It is noteworthy that our response rate of 18.6 percent compares favorably with previous financial surveys. For example, Brau and Fawcett (2006) obtained a response rate of 19 percent, and Graham and Harvey (2001) obtained a response rate of 9 percent. Likewise, these authors emphasize that their response rate is in line with previous financial surveys.

Of the 43 firms that replied, 33 were actively seeking new capital from external sources. The range of external sources of capital sought included friends and family, angel investors (wealthy individuals), banks, private equity, labor-sponsored venture capital, universities, government programs, initial public offerings, and subsequent equity offerings.

It is worthwhile to point out that 17 firms in the sample obtained financing from LSVCCs, and 17 obtained other private (non-LSVCC) venture capital/private equity finance. Fifteen (of these 17) firms had both LSVCC and private venture capital. In other words, LSVCCs and private venture capitalists had syndicated with 15 of the 17 firms; there are two private venture capital-backed firms and two LSVCC-backed firms that did not syndicate with different types of venture capitalists. Further, among all firms in the sample, including those that were syndicated with different types of venture capitalists, the data reveal the extent of capital provided by the different investor types.

A key item in the survey was a question targeted at capital-raising efforts. Specifically, Question 19 of the survey asked for ranked responses for capital-raising concerns associated with a variety of potential hurdles. This question appeared to respondents in the following manner:

19. What in your opinion are the main hurdles to your impending capital-raising exercise? (Please rank lowest to highest of the following 5 issues)

Degree of importance	Lowest			Highest	
	1	2	3	4	5
Repeal of tax credits for LSIF [LSVCC] investments....	☐	☐	☐	☐	☐
Repeal of Foreign Property Limits for institutional investors..	☐	☐	☐	☐	☐
Lack of knowledgeable investors......................	☐	☐	☐	☐	☐
Access to risk capital is limited........................	☐	☐	☐	☐	☐
Cost of taking product to market prohibitive..........	☐	☐	☐	☐	☐
Other? Please name:	☐	☐	☐	☐	☐

Prior to May 19, 2005, registered Canadian pension plans were limited to investing no more than 30 percent of their assets in foreign property.[13] The removal of these limits has the potential effect of, among other things, lowering institutional investment in Canadian private equity funds. As this change might pose a concern to Canadian companies raising capital, and because this change occurred in the same year as the removal of the LSVCC tax credit, this survey question asked for replies to both legislative changes to assess comparative importance to companies raising capital.

The additional parts to Question 19 reflected entrepreneurs oft-repeated comments that investors have a lack of knowledge of the healthcare industry, and that taking product to market is particularly long for the healthcare sector and thereby costly. Further, Question 19 asks about general concerns over access to risk capital.

The responses are summarized in Exhibits 24.2 and 24.3. Exhibit 24.3 shows that the average ranking for concern over removal of the LSVCC tax credit was 1.879, and the median ranking was 1, on a scale of 1 (lowest) to 5 (highest). Similarly, the rank of concern over the change in foreign property ownership limits received an average ranking of 1.727 and a median ranking of 1. By contrast, the average (median) rank for lack of knowledgeable investors was 3.303 (3). The average (median) rank for access to risk capital was 4.000 (4). The average (median) rank for cost of taking product to market was 2.485 (2). Overall, therefore, we may infer that an average innovative healthcare company in London, Ottawa, and the Greater Toronto Area is not very concerned with the removal of the LSVCC tax credit in regard to their capital-raising efforts as of January 2008.

Exhibit 24.2 presents a histogram of the survey replies to Question 19. Exhibit 24.2 indicates a very similar pattern of concern among innovative healthcare companies in regard to the repeal of the foreign property limits for institutional investors and the repeal of the tax credit for LSVCC investments. By contrast, companies express greater concern over the lack of knowledgeable investors and access

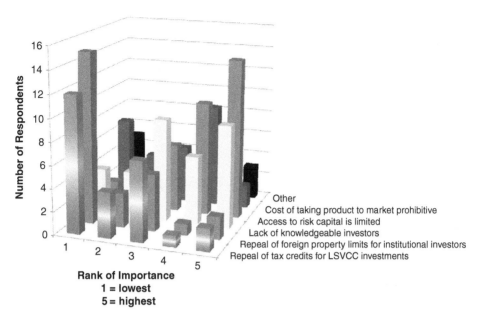

Exhibit 24.2 Barriers to Capital-Raising for Ontario Innovative Healthcare Firms

to risk capital. We may infer from Exhibit 24.2 that, consistent with Exhibit 24.1, LSVCCs are not viewed as sufficient risk capital for most Ontario innovative healthcare companies. In Exhibit 24.2 it is further noteworthy that a significant number of these companies have expressed concern with regard to the cost of taking their product to market. Empirical studies of investment duration have shown longer horizons with the healthcare industry (Giot and Schwienbacher 2007).

Exhibit 24.3 presents summary statistics for a variety of other variables in the YORKbiotech dataset. As well, a correlation matrix is provided to indicate univariate relations across the variables. Note that the ranking of the concern over the repeal of the LSVCC tax and the extent of capital previously obtained from LSVCCs is 0.59 and statistically significant at the 1 percent level, while none of the correlations between concerns over LSVCCs with other sources of capital are significant. Firms more concerned about the repeal of the foreign property limits are more likely to have previously obtained a greater proportion of their capital from private equity (correlation is 0.43 and significant at the 1 percent level). Firms more concerned about the lack of knowledgeable investors are less likely to have obtained their capital from management (correlation is –0.34 and significant at the 5 percent level). Firms more concerned about access to risk capital are more likely to have previously raised capital from private placements (correlation is +0.29 and significant at the 5 percent level). Firms more concerned about the cost of taking product to market are more likely to have obtained a greater proportion of their capital from angel investors.

Other correlation statistics in Exhibit 24.3 provide further insights into the role of different sources of capital. For instance, firms that previously obtained a greater proportion of their capital from private equity are much more likely to have greater R&D expenses relative to revenues (correlation is 0.65 and significant at the 1 percent level). By contrast, the correlation between R&D/revenues and LSVCC

Exhibit 24.3 Summary Statistics

Variable	# Firms	Mean	Median	Correlations											
				[1]	[2]	[3]	[4]	[5]	[6]	[7]	[8]	[9]	[10]	[11]	[12]
[1] Ranking of Repeal of Labor Fund Tax Credit	33	1.879	1	1.00											
[2] Ranking of Repeal of Foreign Property Limits for Institutional Investors	33	1.727	1	0.66	1.00										
[3] Ranking of Lack of Knowledgeable Investors	33	3.303	3	-0.14	-0.06	1.00									
[4] Ranking of Access to Risk Capital Is Limited	33	4.000	4	0.18	0.25	0.27	1.00								
[5] Ranking of Cost of Taking Product to Market Is Prohibitive	33	2.485	2	0.18	0.06	0.03	0.13	1.00							
[6] Founders	43	56.556	50	-0.23	-0.33	0.22	-0.35	0.04	1.00						
[7] Friends, Family	43	3.756	0	-0.31	-0.25	0.10	0.27	-0.03	-0.29	1.00					
[8] Management	43	10.077	0	-0.09	0.02	-0.34	0.20	-0.08	-0.37	0.15	1.00				
[9] Angels	43	7.756	0	0.06	0.05	-0.04	0.18	0.41	-0.35	0.08	-0.19	1.00			
[10] Private Equity	43	5.826	0	0.13	0.43	0.18	-0.14	-0.03	-0.36	0.01	-0.15	0.01	1.00		
[11] Labor Sponsored Venture Capital	43	4.012	0	0.59	0.36	-0.26	0.10	-0.16	-0.31	-0.12	-0.09	-0.13	0.01	1.00	
[12] Private Placement	43	1.419	0	-0.07	-0.09	0.16	0.29	-0.02	-0.26	0.01	-0.03	0.02	0.00	0.01	1.00

586

Variable	N	Mean	Median	[1]	[2]	[3]	[4]	[5]	[6]	[7]	[8]	[9]	[10]	[11]	[12]	[13]	[14]	[15]	[16]	[17]	[18]	[19]	[20]	[21]
[13] University	43	2.495	0	0.08	0.11	-0.13	-0.25	0.04	-0.08	-0.14	0.02	-0.13	-0.05	-0.08	-0.10	1.00								
[14] Government	43	1.826	0	-0.12	-0.10	-0.07	0.01	-0.20	-0.05	-0.11	-0.08	-0.09	-0.02	-0.07	-0.04	-0.06	1.00							
[15] Initial Public Offering	43	1.942	0	-0.08	-0.13	0.09	0.21	-0.08	-0.34	0.08	-0.05	0.07	0.13	-0.08	0.33	-0.06	-0.01	1.00						
[16] Subsequent Equity Offering	43	2.023	0	-0.20	-0.16	0.17	0.29	-0.31	-0.33	0.07	0.06	-0.12	0.00	-0.01	0.53	-0.06	-0.02	0.76	1.00					
[17] Year of Incorporation	43	1991.3	2000	0.06	0.17	-0.24	0.23	-0.22	-0.28	0.02	0.04	0.12	0.08	0.08	0.07	0.10	0.09	0.14	0.11	1.00				
[18] Research and Development Expenses/Revenues (2006)	43	0.813	0.667	0.33	0.19	0.13	-0.01	0.04	-0.41	-0.11	-0.09	-0.10	0.65	0.38	0.26	-0.01	0.05	0.17	0.11	0.12	1.00			
[19] Research and Development Expenses ($ millions 2006)	43	9.384	1	0.26	0.07	0.07	-0.17	0.06	0.01	-0.18	-0.18	-0.15	0.54	0.03	0.01	-0.06	-0.04	0.04	0.00	0.03	0.58	1.00		
[20] Revenues ($ millions 2006)	43	12.244	0.5	0.11	0.04	0.06	0.05	-0.14	0.17	-0.07	-0.08	-0.07	-0.02	0.05	-0.22	-0.14	-0.13	-0.09	0.06	-0.04	-0.24	0.40	1.00	
[21] Move to Another Jurisdiction if Fail to Obtain Desired External Capital	33	0.364	0	0.18	0.23	0.24	0.22	-0.08	-0.33	0.08	0.46	-0.26	0.26	0.02	0.22	0.03	-0.14	0.03	0.16	0.15	0.28	0.09	0.00	

This table presents summary statistics for the respondents in the sample (means, medians and correlations). The sample comprises 43 firms, but 10 were not seeking capital and hence the correlations are presented for the 33 firms seeking external capital. Correlations greater than 0.33 (0.28) [0.42] in absolute value are significant at the 5% (10%) [1%] level.

capital is 0.38 and significant at the 5 percent level. R&D expenses/revenues is uncorrelated with other sources of capital.

There are a variety of other variables in the YORKbiotech dataset, but not reported for reasons of conciseness. Additional details are available upon request. In the next section below we consider multivariate regressions to control for other things being equal when assessing relations between variables of interest.

MULTIVARIATE REGRESSION EVIDENCE

In this section we explore the YORKbiotech dataset further by first considering multivariate regressions for factors that influence capital-raising hurdles. Thereafter, we consider the amount of time firms will be able to continue operating before failure if they are unable to raise capital. Finally, we consider the relation between sources of capital and firm innovative activity, as well as firm mobility.

Capital-Raising Hurdles

Exhibit 24.4 presents multivariate regression evidence for capital-raising hurdles. The dependent variables are the ranking of capital-raising hurdles as in question 19 discussed above. There are five regression models for the five different ranked variables in question 19. Rankings are on an ordinal one to five scale. As such, we employ ordered logit regressions, and not ordinary least squares, to account for the ordinal and finite range of values of the dependent variable. Explanatory variables include different sources of capital (angels, private equity, LSVCC, private placement, universities, government programs, IPO; variables for other sources of capital are suppressed to avoid estimation problems as a result of collinearity), R&D expenses/revenues[14] to control for asset intangibility (firms with higher R&D expenses that are not funded by revenues are typically subject to greater capital-raising hurdles, at least from traditional lenders), and the year of incorporation to control for age.

Model 1 indicates that the only significant variable influencing the ranking for concern over the repeal of the LSVCC tax credit is the extent to which firms have previously obtained capital from LSVCCs. All other variables are statistically insignificant. The LSVCC effect is statistically significant at the 5 percent level. The economic significance is such that a 10 percent increase in capital from LSVCCs is associated with a 49.1 percent reduction in the probability that the firm indicates a rank of one out of five for a concern with the removal in the LSVCC tax credit, a 34.4 percent increase in the probability of a rank of three out of five, and a 2.2 percent increase in the probability of a rank of five out of five. In other words, the effect of prior capital from LSVCCs is both statistically and economically significant, and the only statistically and economically significant factor.

In order to understand why the effect of LSVCCs is statistically significant, it is helpful to take a look a look at the terms of shareholder agreements with venture capital (VC) firms. The YORKbiotech data do not comprise details on such agreements used in all VC–company relationships, but there are nevertheless complete details for two LSVCC agreements and five private VC agreements (and two of the five private VC agreements were investments that were syndicated with the same two LSVCCs for which contractual details are known). These details are summarized in Exhibit 24.5. We present these details not for the purpose of

Exhibit 24.4 Regression Evidence for Rankings of Capital-Raising Hurdles

| | Model 1 | | Model 2 | | Model 3 | | Model 4 | | Model 5 | |
| | Ranking of Repeal of Labor Fund Tax Credit | | Ranking of Repeal of Foreign Property Limits for Institutional Investors | | Ranking of Lack of Knowledgeable Investors | | Ranking of Access to Risk Capital Is Limited | | Ranking of Cost of Taking Product to Market Is Prohibitive | |
	Coefficient	t-statistic	Coefficient	t-statistic	Coefficient	t-statistic	Coefficient	t-statistic	Coefficient	t-statistic
Constant	6.341	0.354	−150.603	−1.200	38.280	1.383	−18.783	−1.070	28.554	1.476
Angels	0.017	1.528	0.006	0.424	−0.005	−0.546	0.003	0.287	0.036	2.989***
Private Equity	−0.029	−0.988	0.078	2.882***	0.010	0.447	−0.016	−0.838	−0.030	−1.475
Labor Sponsored Venture Capital	0.125	2.526**	0.042	2.474**	−0.034	−1.927*	0.007	0.497	−0.022	−1.414
Private Placement	−0.134	−1.555	0.102	1.037	0.044	0.597	0.132	1.449	−0.042	−0.604
University	0.018	0.877	0.024	1.177	−0.016	−0.819	−0.023	−1.162	0.008	0.400
Government	−0.029	−0.652	−0.014	−0.324	−0.015	−0.667	−0.003	−0.122	−0.055	−0.814
Initial Public Offering	−0.017	−0.290	−0.120	−0.962	−0.003	−0.079	0.070	0.873	−0.041	−0.738
Research and Development Expenses/Revenues	0.638	1.571	−0.664	−1.722*	0.406	1.040	−0.079	−0.271	0.585	1.906*
Year of Incorporation	−0.004	−0.396	0.075	1.197	−0.019	−1.343	0.010	1.162	−0.014	−1.471
Ordered Logit Cut-Off Parameters										
Mu(1)	0.418	2.216**	0.410	1.930*	0.448	2.459**	0.252	1.180	0.412	2.334**
Mu(2)	1.768	3.705***	1.428	3.403***	1.273	5.534***	1.143	4.709***	0.929	3.927***
Mu(3)	2.677	2.527***	1.897	3.235***	1.907	6.733***	2.113	7.485***	2.500	4.980***
Model Diagnostics										
Number of Observations	33		33		33		33		33	
Loglikelihood	−29.215		−25.231		−46.183		−38.047		−39.421	
Chi-squared	19.346***		18.843***		10.618		10.456		15.731***	
Pseudo R²	0.249		0.272		0.103		0.121		0.166	

This table presents ordered logit estimates of factors that influenced rankings of company views associated with capital raising hurdles in 2008 Q1. The dependent variables in the five models are ranks of different factors based on a 1–5 scale. The sample comprises 43 firms, but 10 were not seeking capital and hence the models use 33 firms that provided rankings. The explanatory variables include variables for the percent of capital obtained from different sources (variables for founders, friends, family, management, and secondary equity offerings were suppressed to avoid problems of collinearity), the extent of R&D expenses/revenues (2006 financial year end), and age (based on incorporation year). White's (1980) HCCME is used in all regressions.

*, **, and *** denote significance at the 10 percent, 5 percent, and 1 percent level, respectively.

Exhibit 24.5   Contracts Used by Private Independent Limited Partnership Funds versus Labor-Sponsored Funds

	% of Private VC Funds	% of Private VC Funds (same investments as Labor Sponsored VC Funds)	% of Labor Sponsored VC Funds
Shares Held by Fund			
Common shares	20%	0%	50%
Debt	0%	0%	50%
Convertible preferred shares	80%	100%	100%
Convertible debt	20%	50%	100%
Other	20%	0%	0%
Voting Rights			
Special voting or class rights designated exclusively for the type of shares held by the Private Equity fund	20%	50%	50%
An override to certain matters that shareholders of a class other than held by the Private Equity fund would otherwise be entitled to vote on	60%	50%	50%
Redemption Rights			
Redemption right of company will expire after a certain period	40%	100%	100%
Fewer than all of the shares may be redeemed	20%	50%	50%
Full redemption is paid in full	20%	50%	50%
Redemption carried out as per an agreed payment schedule, with a security requirement	40%	50%	50%
Dividend Rights			
Fund's shares receive dividends pro rata with common shares	0%	0%	0%
Fund's shares receive dividends in preference to common shares	40%	100%	100%
Cumulative	40%	100%	100%
Noncumulative	0%	0%	0%
Payable annually	0%	0%	0%
Payable upon liquidation/exit	60%	100%	100%
Fund shares pro rata entitlement to dividends with other common shares after the payment of its preferential return	20%	50%	100%
Liquidation Rights			
Preferential liquidation rights	80%	100%	100%
Fund is fully participating (i.e., it will get its preferred amount out first, then participate pro-rata with the other shareholders)	20%	50%	100%

Exhibit 24.5 *(Continued)*

	% of Private VC Funds	% of Private VC Funds (same investments as Labor Sponsored VC Funds)	% of Labor Sponsored VC Funds
Fund's shares are capped participating (i.e., a rate is for pro rata participation up to a specified level and then it will participate with other shareholders up to a particular return	40%	50%	50%
Fund's shares are nonparticipating	0%	0%	0%
Sale of substantial/all assets designated as liquidation event	80%	100%	100%
Change of control designated as liquidation event	60%	100%	100%
A change of control that results from a future financing designated as a liquidation event	20%	50%	100%
Antidilution			
Full ratchets	0%	0%	0%
Weighted average antidilution provision	60%	100%	100%
Shareholder Rights Held by Fund			
Board participation	100%	100%	100%
Information rights (i.e., requirement to provide Private Equity fund with periodic financial statements and any other management reports)	80%	100%	100%
Veto rights (i.e., right to participate in management decisions that would otherwise not require shareholder input, including hiring/firing of senior/executive officers, business decisions, etc.)	60%	100%	100%
Registration and corresponding rights	80%	100%	100%
Right to appoint/remove CEO	40%	100%	100%
Co-Sale/Drag Along/Tag Along Rights	80%	100%	100%
Preemptive Rights also known as Pro Rata Participation Rights where the Private Equity fund can participate pro rata in future financing. Also right to purchase any shares not taken up by pro rata right exercise of other investors.	80%	100%	100%
Right of first refusal	60%	100%	100%

This table summarizes terms used by private independent limited partnership venture capital (VC) funds and labor sponsored VC funds. The full sample comprises firms that obtained financing from 13 LSVCC backed firms and 12 private independent VC backed firms (and of these, 10 had both private and labor sponsored backing). The respondents offering such details included 5 private VC agreements and 2 labor sponsored agreements. For the 2 labor sponsored VC agreements, details on the syndicated private VC agreements are also indicated. Values indicate % of total agreements using particular terms. Values indicate % of total agreements using particular terms.

statistical analyses, but rather, we show these details in order to highlight the effect of shareholder agreement terms on capital-raising concerns.

Shareholder agreements between VCs and companies separately allocate cash flow and control rights.[15] Cash flow rights pertain to the form of finance (common equity, preferred equity, convertible preferred equity, debt, convertible debt, warrants) and if applicable the ownership percentage, dividends, and antidilution protection. Control rights reflect voting rights, redemption rights, liquidation rights, and various shareholder control and veto rights. A detailed list of different rights found in private VC and LSVCC contracts is found in Exhibit 24.5. The allocation of cash flow and control rights need not be correlated. Generally, however, the greater the bargaining power of the investor (i.e., through more capital provided by the investor, reputation, and other things), the stronger the cash flow and control rights held by the investor (Cumming and Johan 2009). We see in Exhibit 24.5 that VCs in Canada use extensive and detailed cash flow and control rights.

The detailed control rights held by VCs influence the capital-raising efforts of emerging companies. VCs typically have at least one board seat, and may hold a majority of the board seats. Regardless, even when VCs do not have a majority of the board, they may nevertheless hold special rights that enable effective control over the entrepreneurial firm. For instance, VCs typically have a special right to appoint and remove the founding entrepreneur as the CEO of the firm. VCs have control over capital-raising efforts through co-sale/tag-along and drag-along rights.[16] VCs hold rights of first refusal such that they can buy from the company any offer that is presented by the company to another investor, pre-empting any possible new owner. Further, VCs hold antidilution rights that protect their ownership share in the company, which can act as a deterrent to new sources of capital. In short, once a company has funding from one VC or a group of syndicated VCs, those VCs typically hold substantial equity rights and control rights that make decisions to raise capital from other investors particularly challenging if the current VCs do not agree with the terms of the proposed capital-raising efforts.

The reason why this is of public policy concern in regard to the removal of the LSVCC tax credit is as follows. LSVCCs in Ontario have experienced difficulty in raising new capital since the announcement of the phase-out of the tax credit in 2005. VC investments in entrepreneurial firms typically span two to seven years prior to an exit event, such as an IPO, acquisition, secondary sale, buyback, or write-off (Giot and Schwienbacher 2007; Cumming and Johan 2009). Companies that were financed by LSVCCs, particularly those financed before August 2005, face an unexpected challenge associated with being bound to their LSVCC investor(s). As their investor becomes increasingly cash poor due to the phase-out of the tax credit, those entrepreneurial firms seeking additional rounds of financing become increasingly disadvantaged.

In short, there is a role for the Government of Ontario to examine the financing conditions of companies backed by LSVCCs, particularly those that first received LSVCC capital prior to August 2005 when the phase-out of the tax credit was first announced. Our dataset does not enable an empirical answer to the particular role for policy, but does identify the need for a policy response. A first step would be for the Government of Ontario to obtain and examine additional financial information from companies currently backed by LSVCCs.

We believe policymakers arguably should be much less concerned about those companies financed by LSVCCs after August 2005, because those firms should have been savvy enough to recognize the possibility that capital-raising hurdles would be more pronounced in the future.

Turning back to Exhibit 24.4, it is instructive to examine comparable evidence from multivariate regressions giving rise to other types of concerns with capital-raising efforts. Model 2 considers the ranking of the repeal of the foreign property limits for institutional investors. The data indicate that entrepreneurial firms with a greater extent of capital from private equity are most likely to be concerned with the repeal of foreign property limits for institutional investors. This effect is statistically significant at the 1 percent level of significance. The economic significance is such that a 10 percent increase in capital from private equity gives rise to a 21.9 percent reduction in the probability of a ranking of one of five, a 0.8 percent increase in the probability of a ranking of two of five, a 1.2 percent increase in the probability of a ranking of three of five, a 1.6 percent increase in the probability of a ranking of four of five, and a 0.1 percent increase in the probability of a ranking of five of five. This effect is intuitive: private equity funds in Canada obtain capital from institutional investors. Private equity funds are typically very geographically proximate to their investee firms and a majority of investments are intraprovincial, so that investors provide more value to their investee firms (Cumming and Johan 2009). Institutional investors, by contrast, can invest worldwide. Instituting more flexible terms for Canadian institutional investors has the potential effect of dampening capital-raising efforts of Canadian private equity investors.

In Model 2, we note that the effect of LSVCC capital is significant as well at the 5 percent level. The economic significance is smaller than the effect of private equity, but nevertheless material in that a 10 percent increase in capital from LSVCCs gives rise to a 1.2 percent reduction in the probability of a ranking of one of five, a 0.4 percent increase in the probability of a ranking of two of five, a 0.6 percent increase in the probability of a ranking of three of five, a 0.1 percent increase in the probability of a ranking of four of five, and a 0.04 percent increase in the probability of a ranking of five of five. It is more difficult to reconcile this effect with the change in institutional investor rules, as LSVCCs do not get capital from institutional investors. One likely explanation, however, is that LSVCCs may syndicate with private funds, and concerns by companies with LSVCC capital are reflected in the fact that the same companies have also raised private capital. Finally, we note that the R&D/revenues variable is negative and significant at the 10 percent level in Model 2, but that variable is not robust to the exclusion of other variables (other specifications are not reported for reasons of conciseness, but are available upon request).

Model 3 considers the ranking of the lack of knowledgeable investors. The only significant factor in Model 3 is the extent of capital from LSVCCs, which is negative and statistically significant at the 10 percent level. This result indicates that companies financed by LSVCCs are less concerned about a knowledge gap among investors, which is a positive sign for LSVCCs in the healthcare industry. However, we acknowledge that this effect is only marginally significant at the 10 percent level, and sensitive to the inclusion of other variables (i.e., not robust to other specifications).

Model 4 considers the ranking of access to risk capital. We do not find any statistically significant variables that explain the ranking of risk capital. Nevertheless, referring back to Exhibits 24.2 and Exhibit 24.3, we note that access to risk capital was the highest-ranked concern among the firms in the data. We may infer from Model 4 that all firms have an equally pronounced concern over the extent of risk capital in Canada.

Finally, Model 5 considers the ranking of the cost of taking the product to market. The most significant factor is the presence of angel investors, which is significant at the 1 percent level. The economic significance is such that a 10 percent increase in capital from angel investors gives rise to a 15.5 percent reduction in the probability of a ranking of one of five, a 0.9 percent reduction in the probability of a ranking of two of five, a 2.1 percent increase in the probability of a ranking of three of five, a 1.1 percent increase in the probability of a ranking of four of five, and a 1.5 percent increase in the probability of a ranking of five of five. It is natural to expect angel-backed firms to have a greater concern about time to market because these firms tend to be in the most nascent stages of development at the time of investment. Further, Model 5 indicates firms with higher R&D expenses/revenues rank cost to market higher, and this effect is significant at the 10 percent level. The economic significance is such that a 10 percent increase in R&D/revenues gives rise to a 21.9 percent reduction in the probability of a ranking of 1 of 5, a 1.5 percent reduction in the probability of a ranking of two of five, a 3.4 percent increase in the probability of a ranking of three of five, a 17.5 percent increase in the probability of a ranking of three of five, and a 2.4 percent increase in the probability of a ranking of five of five. It is natural that more R&D-intensive firms are more concerned about cost to market.

The statistical and economic significance observed in the models is intuitive. Overall, the models show moderate fit to the data for the sample size. Pseudo R^2 values are 24.9 percent in our central model of interest (Model 1), and range from 10.3 percent to 27.2 percent in the other models in Exhibit 24.4. In the next subsections, we examine complementary issues associated with capital-raising efforts, including the time to failure in the event of unsuccessful capital-raising efforts and the extent of value added with different investor types.

Time to Failure

In this section we model factors that influence expected time until failure for firms in the event that they are unable to raise additional external capital. In other words, we assess the immediacy of a severe concern associated with inability to raise capital.

Fourteen of the firms in the dataset indicated that they did not think that they would fail if they could not raise additional capital. Excluding these firms, the average (median) expected time to failure in the event of being unable to raise additional capital is 10.8 (12) months. For firms that indicated they did not expect to fail if they could not raise additional capital, we proxy time to failure by using 99 months. That is, instead of assuming they could last an infinite number of years, we assumed a more finite horizon of 8.25 years. Our empirical estimates discussed below are robust to a wide range of different horizons used for firms that thought they could last forever. Including these firms, the average (median) expected time to failure was 48.2 (14) months.

Exhibit 24.6 presents three different regression models (Models 6, 7, and 8) of expected time to failure (in months) with different sets of explanatory variables.

Exhibit 24.6 Regression Evidence for the Number of Months until Failure if Unable to Obtain External Capital

	Model 6		Model 7		Model 8	
	Months until insufficient funds to continue operating		Months until insufficient funds to continue operating		Months until insufficient funds to continue operating	
	Coefficient	t-statistic	Coefficient	t-statistic	Coefficient	t-statistic
Angels	0.006	0.728			0.004	0.301
Private Equity	−0.018	−0.803			−0.013	−0.609
Labor Sponsored Venture Capital	0.017	1.611			−0.002	−0.141
Private Placement	0.139	2.150**			0.152	2.140**
University	0.034	1.771*			0.026	1.314
Government	0.031	1.460			0.038	1.677*
Initial Public Offering	0.020	0.551			0.032	0.869
Year of Incorporation	0.008	0.670	0.008	0.893	0.006	0.554
Research and Development Expenses	0.141	2.031**			0.117	1.653*
Revenues	0.008	0.427			0.018	0.876
Ranking of Repeal of Labor Fund Tax Credit			0.317	2.080**	0.415	1.728*
Ranking of Lack of Knowledgeable Investors			−0.090	−0.723	−0.190	−1.293
Ranking of Cost of Taking Product to Market is Prohibitive			0.025	0.191	−0.006	−0.035
Model Diagnostics						
Number of Observations	33		33		33	
Loglikelihood	−90.199		−94.744		−87.986	
Chi-squared	19.840**		7.314		24.838**	
Pseudo R²	0.078		0.031		0.101	

This table presents Cox proportional hazard duration model estimates of factors that influence the number of months that the firm will be able to continue operating (i.e., by paying staff and overhead costs) in the event that it is unable to obtain external financing. The sample comprises 43 firms, but 10 were not seeking capital and hence the models use 33 firms that are seeking external finance. The explanatory variables include variables for the percent of capital obtained from different sources (variables for founders, friends, family, management, and secondary equity offerings were suppressed to avoid problems of collinearity), R&D expenses and revenues (2006 financial year end), and age (based on incorporation year), as well as the firms' rankings of the importance of hurdles to obtaining external capital for the repeal of the LSVCC tax credit, the lack of knowledgeable investors, and the cost of taking the product to market (other rankings are excluded to avoid collinearity). Three different models are presented to show robustness to the inclusion/exclusion of different explanatory variables. White's (1980) HCCME is used in all regressions.

*, **, and *** denote significance at the 10 percent, 5 percent, and 1 percent level, respectively.

595

Different models are presented to show robustness to alternative specifications. In Model 6 we present variables similar to those used in Models 1 to 5 in Exhibit 24.5, including prior sources of capital, R&D expenses, and revenues. Model 7 uses variables for the ranking of the concern with the repeal of the LSVCC tax credit, the lack of knowledgeable investors, and the time to take the product to market.[17] Model 8 combines all variables.

Model 6 indicates firms with a greater proportion of ownership held by private placements and universities are more likely to expect to fail earlier than firms with other sources of investment, and these effects are statistically significant at the 5 percent and 10 percent levels, respectively. The economic significance is such that a firm with 10 percent more capital raised in private placements is expected to fail 1.4 percent faster,[18] and a firm with 10 percent more university ownership is 0.3 percent faster. These results indicate firms with private placements and university shareholders are less likely to have surplus cash reserves to enable them to continue operating in the absence of additional capital.

Model 6 further indicates that a firm that spends an extra $1 million in R&D expenses is likely to fail 1.4 percent faster. The significance of R&D expenses is expected as the scale of research activities in a firm indicates the necessity to continue to do R&D to bring development efforts to fruition. Without extra capital, a greater scale of R&D is more likely to lead to failure.

Model 7 shows that companies that are more concerned about the repeal of the LSVCC tax credit are more likely to fail quicker if they do not receive extra capital. For reasons discussed above in relation to the terms in related shareholder agreements, this result is expected. Firms locked into LSVCCs are likely facing pronounced capital-raising hurdles. The economic significance is such that an increase in the ranking by one gives rise to a faster rate of failure by 3.2 percent.

Finally, Model 8 shows results that are similar to those with Models 6 and 7, with one exception. Unlike Model 6, the university variable is insignificant and the government variable is significant in Model 8. The government variable indicates that failure to obtain capital from government programs increases the rate of failure by 0.4 percent. In other words, firms with government support are more dependent on receipt of additional government funds.

In sum, the results for factors that influence expected time to failure in the event of inability to raise additional capital show firms with private placements, university-held equity, and government funding are more dependent on new sources of funds. Firms with a greater scale of R&D expenses are similarly more reliant on new capital. Finally, firms more concerned with the repeal of the LSVCC tax credit have a shorter expected time until failure.

The Extent of Value-Added

In this section we consider evidence of investor value-added in terms of investee firm R&D expenses and patents. We also consider the probability that the investee firm will move to another jurisdiction if it fails to obtain additional capital.

Exhibit 24.7 presents four alternative models. The dependent variable in Model 9 is R&D expenses/revenues. The dependent variable is Model 10 is similar with R&D expenses, except revenues are not in the denominator (revenues are instead used as an explanatory variable). In Model 11, the dependent variable is the

Exhibit 24.7 Regression Evidence for Value Added

	Model 9 (Tobit) Research and Development Expenses (2006) / Revenues (2006)		Model 10 (Tobit) Research and Development Expenses (2006)		Model 11 (Tobit) Patents (as at 2006)		Model 12 (Logit) Move to Another Jurisdiction if Fail to Obtain Desired External Capital	
	Coefficient	t-statistic	Coefficient	t-statistic	Coefficient	t-statistic	Coefficient	t-statistic
Constant	6.719	0.828	118.810	0.995	2.449	0.226	−20.440	−1.103
Angels	0.0004	0.078	0.020	0.295	0.003	0.564	−0.020	−2.124**
Private Equity	0.029	4.733***	0.149	2.175**	0.028	4.567***	0.018	1.817*
Labor Sponsored Venture Capital	0.025	3.591***	0.007	0.091	0.025	3.502***	−0.004	−0.617
Private Placement	0.074	2.028**	0.517	1.231	0.029	0.771	0.078	1.413
University	0.010	0.862	0.130	0.999	−0.001	−0.062	0.000	−0.043
Government	0.015	1.142	0.155	1.024	0.008	0.598	−0.019	−0.509
Initial Public Offering	0.019	0.802	0.030	0.113	−0.026	−1.094	−0.024	−1.138
Year of Incorporation	−0.003	−0.799	−0.062	−1.034	0.0004	−0.079	0.010	1.100
Research and Development Expenses (2005)			0.790	12.539***	0.027	6.299***	0.036	−1.153
Revenues (2006)							0.011	1.117
Model Diagnostics								
Number of Observations	33		33		33		33	
Loglikelihood	−48.360		−147.916		−44.587		−14.526	
Chi-squared	25.064***		140.163***		9.468		14.211	
ANOVA based fit Measure (Models 9-11) or Pseudo R² (Model 12)	0.380		0.783		0.706		0.328	

This table presents tobit estimates of factors that influenced research and development expenses and patents, as well as logit estimates of the probability that a firm will move to another jurisdiction if it does not obtain its desired form of financing. The sample comprises 43 firms, but 10 were not seeking capital and hence the models use 33 firms that provided rankings. The explanatory variables include variables for the percent of capital obtained from different sources (variables for founders, friends, family, management, and secondary equity offerings were suppressed to avoid problems of collinearity), the extent of R&D expenses (2005), revenues (2006), and age (based on incorporation year). White's (1980) HCCME is used in all regressions.

*, **, and *** denote significance at the 10 percent, 5 percent, and 1 percent level, respectively.

total number of patents held by the firm. Models 9 to 11 use Tobit regressions. We use Tobit regressions because the dependent variable is bounded below by zero, and the dependent variable is equal to zero for many firms in the sample (e.g., see Graham, Lang, and Stratford 2004, Table V, for a similar justification for the use of Tobit for debt-to-value regressions); regardless, OLS estimates are quite similar. Finally, Model 12 is a logit regression of the likelihood that the firm will move to another jurisdiction (other than Ontario) if it fails to obtain the external capital that it seeks.

Models 9 and 10 for R&D expenses/revenues and R&D expenses, respectively, show a pronounced and robust role for private equity in stimulating research and development. This finding is consistent with U.S. evidence.[19] The effect of private equity is statistically significant at the 1 percent level in Model 9 and the 5 percent level in Model 10. An increase in private equity by 10 percent increases R&D/revenues by approximately 0.3, or 37 percent of the median level of R&D/revenues. The effect is slightly larger than that for LSVCCs in Model 9,[20] but smaller than that for other private placements. But note that for the alternative specification in Model 10, the effect of private equity is statistically significant, unlike the impact of LSVCCs and other private placements. In Model 10, a 10 percent increase in private equity gives rise to an additional $1.5 million in R&D expenses. Similarly, Model 11 shows an increase in private equity by 10 percent gives rise to an extra 0.3 patents. This is a nontrivial effect, as the average (median) firm in the data has 2.1 (2) patents. The effect of private equity on patents is larger than that for LSVCCs, consistent with Models 9 and 10.

Model 12 shows logit analyses of the probability of moving to another jurisdiction in the event of failure to obtain additional capital. Recall from Exhibit 24.3 that 36 percent of the firms in the data indicated they would move if they failed to obtain additional capital. Model 12 indicates firms backed by angel investors are least likely to move, which is understandable, as those firms are in the most nascent stages of development and likely unable to relocate for financial reasons and the relationships developed with local angel investors. A 10 percent increase in angel investment is associated with an approximately 2 percent reduction in the probability of moving to obtain additional capital. By contrast, later-stage private equity firms are more likely to back companies that are able to relocate, if necessary. A 10 percent increase in private equity is associated with a 2 percent increase in the probability of moving if unable to obtain capital. By contrast, firms backed by LSVCCs are neither more nor less likely to move if they fail to obtain additional capital.

CONCLUSION

This chapter presented 2008 survey data evidence from Ontario innovative healthcare companies regarding capital-raising efforts and concerns with potential capital-raising hurdles. The data were derived from a small but representative sample. The conclusions drawn are derived only from the firms surveyed.

The data indicate the following:

1. The average innovative healthcare company indicates little concern over the phasing-out of the LSVCC tax credit (announced in 2005) in regard to their capital-raising efforts. The average (median) ranking was 1.879 (1) on a

scale of one (lowest) to five (highest), which was roughly the same average and median for concern over the repeal of the foreign property limits for institutional investors. Innovative healthcare companies rank access to risk capital as of much greater concern: the average and median ranking was four out of five.

2. The lack of concern with the removal of the LSVCC tax credit is consistent with the low economic value-added provided by LSVCCs to the Ontario economy, as documented in Exhibit 24.1 and prior research (Carpentier and Suret 2005, 2006; Cumming and MacIntosh 2006, 2007; Cumming and Johan, 2009).

3. Innovative healthcare companies are more concerned about the removal of the LSVCC tax are those that had previously received a greater proportion of capital from LSVCCs. This finding is statistically and economically significant, and robust to controls in a multivariate regression setting. This finding is consistent with evidence on the terms of shareholder agreements and strong rights of control held by LSVCCs in regard to capital-raising decisions, among other things. A public policy response is warranted, particularly for companies that obtained LSVCC capital prior to the 2005 announcement of the phasing-out of the tax credit.

4. There is no statistically significant link between the extent of LSVCC capital obtained and the expected time to failure if the firm is unable to raise additional capital. Nevertheless, there is a positive correlation between the expected number of months to failure and the ranking of concern over the removal of the LSVCC tax credit.

5. Private equity capital has a more robust statistically significant and economically larger effect on R&D expenditures and patents obtained by innovative healthcare firms in Ontario than does LSVCC capital.

6. Firms with a greater extent of angel capital are less likely to move to another jurisdiction if they fail to obtain their desired external capital. By contrast, firms with a greater extent of backing by private equity funds are more likely to move to another jurisdiction if they are unable to raise their desired amount of capital. There is no statistical relation between LSVCC backing and the probability of a firm moving jurisdiction if it fails to obtain external capital.

NOTES

1. We owe thanks to the seminar participants at the CD Howe Institute, September 2008. We have benefited from helpful comments from comments and assistance from YORKbiotech, particularly Robert Foldes, Adrienne Ng, and Lyudmila Kurochkina. YORKbiotech collaborated in the design of the survey and collected the data reported herein.

2. Cosh, Cumming, and Hughes (2009) show entrepreneurs typically are able to raise the capital they want, but not necessarily in the form that they desire.

3. www.fin.gov.on.ca/english/media/2005/nr08-lsif.html.

4. It is worth noting that it is generally difficult to successfully structure government VC programs to add value (Armour and Cumming 2006). However, Australia's IIF program, the U.S. SBIR program, the Israeli Bilateral Industrial Research and Development Foundation (BIRD), and the Canada Israel Industrial Research and Development

Foundation (CIIRDF) (http://www.ciirdf.ca/) are all examples of relatively more successful government programs to stimulate entrepreneurial finance (Lerner 1999; Cumming and Johan 2009).

5. www.crvca.com/press/index.html.

6. Ibid.

7. Susan Hickman, "Show me the money: The hunt for fresh funding." Ottawa Citizen (March 27 2008). www.canadait.com/cfm/index.cfm?It=106&Id=26196&Se=0.

8. Ibid.

9. For theoretical work on topic, see Keuschnigg and Nielsen (2001; 2003a, b; 2004a, b, c) and Cressy (2002). For policy discussions, see Osborne and Sandler (1998) and Sandler (2001).

10. Armour and Cumming (2006, 2008), Kooli, L'Her, and Suret (2006), Carpentier and Suret (2005, 2006), Cumming (2007), Cumming and MacIntosh (2006, 2007), and Cumming and Johan (2009).

11. More generally, see also World Bank (1994, 2002, 2004).

12. yorkbiotech.ca/

13. See, for example, www.cansofunds.com/current2_may05.htm; library.findlaw.com/2005/Jun/15/246359.html.

14. R&D/revenues is scaled by 1 in the denominator since some firms did not have revenues.

15. Cumming and Johan (2009) review analysis of theory and evidence on venture capital contracts from a number of countries around the world.

16. A co-sale/tag-along right means that if the company wants to sell its shares, the VC can also sell at the same terms. A drag-along right means that if the VC wants to sell, then the VC can force other shareholders to sell as well at the same terms.

17. One concern with the ranking variables is that they may be endogenous. There does not appear to exist suitable instruments; therefore, we present the specifications with and without the ranking variables.

18. The calculation is exp(0.1 * 0.139) − 1.

19. For example, while venture capital-backed companies averaged less than 3 percent of corporate R&D in the period 1983 to 1992, it was nevertheless responsible for more than 8 percent of United States' industrial innovations in that decade. See Kortum and Lerner (2000).

20. As discussed above, many of the LSVCC investments in the sample were syndicated with private equity investments; hence we would not expect large differences between the real effects from LSVCCs and private equity.

REFERENCES

Anderson, Scott, and Yisong S. Tian. 2003. Incentive fees, valuation, and performance of labour sponsored investment funds. *Canadian Investment Review* 16 (3):20–27.

Armour, John, and Douglas J. Cumming. 2006. The legislative road to Silicon Valley. *Oxford Economic Papers* 58:596–635.

Armour, John, and Douglas J. Cumming. 2008. Bankruptcy law and entrepreneurship. *American Law and Economics Review* 10 (2):303–350.

Brau, James C., and Stanley F. Fawcett. 2006. Initial public offerings: An analysis of theory and practice. *Journal of Finance* 61:399–436.

Carpentier, Cecile, and Jean-Marc Suret. 2005. The indirect costs of venture capital in Canada. CIRANO Research Centre. www.cirano.qc.ca/pdf/publication/2005s-25.pdf.

Carpentier, Cecile, and Jean-Marc Suret. 2006. Some evidence of the external financing costs of new technology-based firms in Canada. *Venture Capital* 8:227–252.

Carpentier, Cecile, Jean-Francois L'Her, and Jean-Marc Suret. 2006. Canadian private equity: Nature and evolution. *The Journal of Private Equity* 9:48–58.

Cosh, Andy, Douglas J. Cumming, and Alan Hughes. 2009. Outside entrepreneurial capital, *Economic Journal* 119:1494–1533.

Cressy, Robert. 2002. Funding gaps: A symposium. *Economic Journal* 112:F1–F16.

Cumming, Douglas J. 2007. Financing entrepreneurs: Better Canadian policy for venture capital. *CD Howe Institute Commentary* No 247.

Cumming, Douglas J., and Sofia A. Johan. 2009. *Venture capital and private equity contracting: An international perspective*. Elsevier Science Academic Press.

Cumming, Douglas J., and Jeffrey G. MacIntosh. 2006. Crowding out private equity: Canadian evidence. *Journal of Business Venturing*. 21:569–609.

Cumming, Douglas J., and Jeffrey G. MacIntosh. 2007. Mutual funds that invest in private equity? An analysis of labour sponsored investment funds. *Cambridge Journal of Economics* 31:445–487.

Giot, Pierre, and Armin Schwienbacher. 2007. IPOs, trade sales, and liquidations: Modeling venture capital exits using survival analysis. *Journal of Banking & Finance* 31:679–702.

Graham, John R., and Campbell R. Harvey. 2001. The theory and practice of corporate finance: Evidence from the field. *Journal of Financial Economics* 60:187–243.

Graham, John R., Mark H. Lang, and Douglas A. Shakelford. 2004. Employee stock options, corporate taxes and debt policy. *Journal of Finance* 59, 1585–1618.

Keuschnigg, Christian, and Søren Bo Nielsen. 2001. Public policy for venture capital. *International Tax and Public Finance* 8:557–572.

Keuschnigg, Christian, and Søren Bo Nielsen. 2003a. Tax policy, venture capital, and entrepreneurship. *Journal of Public Economics* 87:175–203.

Keuschnigg, Christian, and Søren Bo Nielsen. 2003b. Taxes and venture capital support. *Review of Finance* 7:515–539.

Keuschnigg, Christian, and Søren Bo Nielsen. 2004a. Progressive taxation, moral hazard, and entrepreneurship. *Journal of Public Economic Theory* 6:471–490.

Keuschnigg, Christian, and Søren Bo Nielsen. 2004b. Start-ups, venture capitalists and the capital gains tax. *Journal of Public Economics* 88:1011–1042.

Keuschnigg, Christian, and Søren Bo Nielsen. 2004c. Public policy for start-up entrepreneurship with venture capital and bank finance. Working Paper, University of St. Gallen and Copenhagen Business School.

Kooli Marc, Jean-Francois L'Her, and Jean Marc Suret. 2006. Do IPOs really underperform in the long-run? New evidence from Canadian market. *The Journal of Private Equity* 9:48–58.

Kortum, Samuel, and Josh Lerner. 2000. Assessing the contribution of venture capital to innovation. *Rand Journal of Economics*, 31:674–692.

Lerner, Josh. 1999. The government as venture capitalist: The long-run effects of the SBIR program. *Journal of Business* 72:285–318.

Osborne, Duncan, and Daniel Sandler. 1998. A tax expenditure analysis of labour-sponsored venture capital corporations. *Canadian Tax Journal* 46:499–574.

Sandler, Daniel. 2001. The tax treatment of employee stock options: Generous to a fault. *Canadian Tax Journal* 49:259–302.

World Bank. 2004. *World Bank group support for small business*. Washington, DC: World Bank.

World Bank. 2002. *World Bank group review of small business activities*. Washington, DC: World Bank.

World Bank. 1994. *Can intervention work? The role of government in SME success*. Washington, DC: World Bank.

ABOUT THE AUTHORS

Douglas Cumming, B.Com. (Hons.) (McGill), M.A. (Queen's), J.D. (University of Toronto Faculty of Law), Ph.D. (Toronto), CFA, is an Associate Professor of Finance and Entrepreneurship and the Ontario Research Chair at the Schulich School of Business, York University. His research is primarily focused on law and finance, market surveillance, hedge funds, venture capital, private equity, and IPOs. His work has been presented at the American Finance Association, the Western Finance Association, the European Finance Association, the American Law and Economics Association, the European Law and Economics Association, and other leading international conferences. His recent publications have appeared in numerous journals, including the *American Law and Economics Review, Cambridge Journal of Economics, Economic Journal, European Economic Review, Financial Management, Journal of Business, Journal of Business Venturing, Journal of Corporate Finance, Journal of International Business Studies, Oxford Economic Papers*, and *Review of Financial Studies*. He is the coauthor (along with his wife, Sofia Johan) of the new book *Venture Capital and Private Equity Contracting: An International Perspective* (Elsevier Science Academic Press 2009, 770 pp.). His work has been reviewed in numerous media outlets, including *Canadian Business*, the *Financial Post*, and *The New Yorker*. He was the recipient of the 2004 Ido Sarnat Award for the best paper published in the *Journal of Banking and Finance* for a paper on full and partial venture capital exits in Canada and the United States. As well, he received the 2008 AIMA Canada-Hillsdale Research Award for his paper on hedge fund regulation and performance, and the 2009 Best Paper Award from the Canadian Institute of Chartered Business Valuators for his paper on private equity valuation and disclosure. He is a research associate with the Paolo Baffi Center for Central Banking and Financial Regulation (Bocconi University), Groupe d'Economie Mondiale at Sciences Po (Paris), Capital Markets CRC (Sydney), Venture Capital Experts (New York), Cambridge University ESRC Center for Business Research, Center for Financial Studies (Frankfurt), Amsterdam Center for Research in International Finance, and the University of Calgary Van Horne Institute. He has also consulted for a variety of governmental and private organizations in Australasia, Europe and North America, and most recently is working with Wilshire Associates.

Sofia Johan, LL.B (Liverpool), LL.M. in International Economic Law (Warwick), Ph.D. in Law (Tilburg), is the AFM Senior Research Fellow at the Tilburg Law and Economics Centre (TILEC) in The Netherlands. Her research is primarily focused on law and finance, market surveillance, hedge funds, venture capital, private equity, and IPOs. Her work has been presented at the American Law and Economics Association, the European Law and Economics Association, the European Financial Management Association, and other leading international conferences. Her recent publications have appeared in numerous journals including the *American Law and Economics Review, Journal of Banking and Finance, European Financial Management, European Economic Review*, and *Entrepreneurship Theory and Practice*, among numerous other journals. Prior to her Ph.D., she was the head legal counsel at the largest government-owned venture capital fund in Malaysia. She has also consulted for a variety of governmental and private organizations in Australasia and Europe.

Index

CPSIA information can be obtained
at www.ICGtesting.com
Printed in the USA
BVHW01*0935161018
529718BV00020B/34/P